To Chuck & Katy —

May you be encouraged by the Oregon Christians!

Jerry Rushford
July 11, 1999
Heb. 12:1–3

CHRISTIANS ON THE OREGON TRAIL

Churches of Christ and Christian Churches in Early Oregon 1842-1882

Jerry Rushford

COLLEGE PRESS PUBLISHING COMPANY • JOPLIN, MISSOURI

Printed and Bound in the
United States of America

Library of Congress Cataloging-in-Publication Data

Rushford, Jerry, 1942–
Christians on the Oregon Trail: Churches of Christ and Christian Churches in early Oregon, 1842-1882 / Jerry Rushford.
p. cm.
Includes bibliographical references and index.
ISBN 0-89900-777-5 (hardcover)
1. Disciples of Christ—Oregon—History—19th century.
2. Restoration Movement (Christianity) - Oregon—History—19th century. 3. Oregon Trail. 4. Oregon—Church history—19th century.
I. Title.
BX7317.07R87 1997
286.6'795—dc21 97-12265
CIP

To

Lori, Hilary and Ashley,

my three sojourners

on the trail of life

Acknowledgments

My interest in Oregon was late in developing. I began with a desire to write a history of Churches of Christ in California, but in the opening chapters I kept running into Oregonians who were responding to the California gold rush. Many of these Oregon Christians had already been on the West Coast for several years, preaching in meetings, establishing congregations, and preparing to open Christian schools. The more I learned about their experiences, the more I wanted to know.

The sheer priority of the Oregon Christians was the ultimate attraction. They were among the first to carve out a trail, and among the first to die on that trail. They were in the vanguard of those who preached Christ in the western territories, and they were ahead of California Christians in establishing churches and schools. The heroic dimensions of their epic 2000-mile journey across the continent captured my imagination, and I longed to know more about them. So, California was put on hold temporarily, while I made numerous trips to Oregon and became overly familiar with Interstate 5 from Portland to Medford and back.

My main source in the beginning was C. F. Swander's *Making Disciples in Oregon.* When the author published his book in 1928, he closed with this appeal: "I sincerely hope that future historians will keep the work up-to-date, and may be able to correct the inaccuracies in this, so that in the far future generations yet unborn may be better informed as to our progress . . ." Then with a note of professional generosity, Swander concluded:

> I shall have no jealousy in my soul should some future historian excel this work to a degree that it shall be overshadowed. Hoping that this work may inspire some one to make the attempt I gladly write the closing word.

Swander's work did inspire me to want to know more about our spiritual ancestors, and I completely agree with his sentiments. I too look forward to the day when future historians will build on my research and "correct the inaccuracies." It is a story worth telling, and we can never have too many storytellers.

Many debts have been incurred along the way as I have badgered people for information on early Oregon. One of my former students in church history, Bonnie Miller, has been invaluable to this project. Her work as church secretary for the Andresen Road Church of Christ in Vancouver, Washington was often delayed while she responded to my frequent pleas for help. Bonnie was my pipeline to the wonderful resources in the Oregon History Center in Portland, the Clark County Genealogical Society in Vancouver, and numerous other libraries and historical societies. She pursued every lead with tenacity, and much information would have been left undiscovered without her enthusiastic commitment to locating primary source materials. She read the text with a passion for accuracy and assisted in culling out numerous errors.

I am grateful to Doug Dornhecker, who was minister of First Christian Church in Lebanon, Oregon at the time, for making it possible for me to obtain a copy of his excellent thesis entitled *A History of Annual Meetings of Disciples of Christ in Oregon to 1877*. Doug never wearied of showing me cemeteries and old churches and answering endless questions. He generously shared his research on the annual State Meetings in Oregon, and then assisted me in tracking down elusive information on obscure delegates to those meetings.

Charles Dailey of Northwest College of the Bible in Portland, and John McKeel, the former minister of the Eastside Church of Christ in Portland, are two of the most knowledgeable sources on the history of the Restoration Movement in Oregon. They have devoted years of study to this field, and they willingly shared their insights with me.

Sue Rhee, librarian at Northwest Christian College in Eugene, Melanie Bailey, librarian at Cascade College in Portland, and Lotte Larsen, librarian and archivist at Western Oregon University in Monmouth were helpful in locating rare items. It was Lotte who first introduced me to the three priceless reels of microfilm that contained scattered issues of the *Christian Messenger, Pacific Christian Messenger* and *Christian Herald.*

One of my most helpful proofreaders on this project has been Jim Cook, a doctoral candidate at the University of Alaska. Jim is especially knowledgeable about the growth and development of the Restoration Movement in the American West, and his careful and thorough reading of this book greatly improved its accuracy.

The various county historical societies in Oregon are a gold mine for anyone interested in the nineteenth century. I want to express my special thanks to the following: Olive Johnson, Lila Jackson, Bob Kuykendall and Jim and Reita Lockett of Yamhill County Historical Society; Katherine Johnson, Robert Marsh, Scott McArthur and C. F. Stevens of Polk County Historical Society; Sandy McGuire and Marian Charriere of Clackamas County Historical Society; Stephenie Flora, Addie Rickey and Sharon Frey of Marion County Historical Society; Dick Milligan and Laurel Malosh of Linn County Historical Society; Donald T. Smith of Lane County Historical Society; Ed Stelfox of Lane County Historical Museum; Marge Ingebretsen, Norma McBee and Pauline Camerer with the Oregon Genealogical Society in Springfield; and Fred Reenstjerna, a fine research librarian with the Douglas County Museum of History.

In Jackson County, my pursuit of Martin Peterson led me to two of his descendents, Verna Tucker and Linda Morehouse Genaw. Linda is a local historian who has already edited and published one volume of Peterson's diary, and Verna supplied me with a photograph of Peterson and gave me some books from his library. And to think, when I drove into the Medford area I doubted that I would be able to uncover any trace of the pioneer preacher or even locate his grave. That trip was serendipitous indeed.

I want to express a special thanks to Nancy Kitchen, Herb Gore, Bill Deese, David Pope and Melissa Nicholls of the Payson Library at Pepperdine University in Malibu for service over and beyond the call of duty. From the purchasing of rare papers on microfilm to the ordering of books on interlibrary loan from libraries all over Oregon, the staff of this fine library could not have been more helpful or more encouraging. In addition, David McWhirter, May Reed and the staff of the Disciples of Christ Historical Society in Nashville, Tennessee, and Erma Jean Loveland and Craig Churchill with the Brown Library at Abilene Christian University in Abilene, Texas, were helpful at several crucial moments in the course of this project. I also want to thank Don Meredith, librarian at the Harding Graduate School of Religion in Memphis, Tennessee.

Among the joys of teaching at Pepperdine University has been my involvement in the occasional meetings of a Restoration history faculty colloquium. The enviable experience of sharing ideas and research with Restoration historians such as Tom Olbricht, Richard Hughes and Mike Casey has been intellectually stimulating. Some of the concerns and directions of this research on Oregon Christians were first explored in those wonderful gatherings in the faculty dining room.

Some of my graduate students in Pepperdine's extension programs in Portland and Seattle worked on projects that were related to my Oregon research. I want to thank especially Don Henry from the Prineville Church of Christ; Clare Buhler of Tigard Christian Church; Jerry Wolfe with the Church of Christ in Federal Way, Washington; Jim Susee from Highline Christian Church in Seattle; and Robert Morris, Jr., from the Northwest Church of Christ in Seattle. In addition, many of my Pepperdine students in Malibu have assisted me in the painstaking task of finding obscure Oregon references in the microfilmed copies of nineteenth century Restoration periodicals. In particular, I want to express appreciation to

Andre Resner, Kevin Kragenbrink, Eric Gumm, Desiree Kinney, Marco Martinez, Tracie Sawyer, Willie Sanchez, Greg Daum, Jon Jones, Bridget Smith and Michelle Shumate.

Several direct descendents of Oregon Christians aided this project. I want to especially thank the following: Betty Gordon of Ocean Hills, California, a relative of John Foster; Vere McCarty of Salem, a relative of A. V. McCarty; Justine Jones of Salem, a relative of David R. Lewis; Lowell Dart of Boise, Idaho, a relative of Charles Bisbee Dart; Philip Mulkey Hunt of Portland, a relative of Philip Mulkey; Betty Kodad of Castle Rock, Washington, a relative of Keathley Bailes; Marilee Cash of Vancouver, Washington, a relative of the Parvin and Callison families; Don Rivara of Salem, a relative of Isaac Matheny and Daniel Boone Matheny; Helen Glodt and Ray and Miriam Helseth of Salem, relatives of John Ecles Murphy; and Jean Hunsaker of Salem, whose late husband was a relative of George William Burnett.

Many other interested friends contributed to this project as it slowly took shape, including: Kathryn Notson, a local church historian in Portland; Ray Renzema of the Oregon Christian Convention Center in Turner; Doug Foster with the Center for Restoration Studies at Abilene Christian University; Bill G. Fendall of Newport, who is an expert on "The Great Migration" of 1843; Randy Brown of Douglas, Wyoming, who provided photographs of the Joel Hembree gravesite; Donna Montgomery Wojcik of Portland, the author of *The Brazen Overlanders of 1845*; Pamela Brown with the Christian Board of Publication; Joyce White with the Oregon Trail Coordinating Council; and Darlene Ellis, a local historian in Springfield who assisted me with several pioneer families in Lane County.

Many church members in Oregon were generous in offering help. I would like to thank the following: Larry and Joan Hake with the Amity Church of Christ in Yamhill County; Bill Compton, Jr., and Katie Miller from the Pleasant Hill Church of Christ; Ron Murphy and Forrest Anderson from the Church of Christ in Oregon City; Judith Dyer, director of worship and music at First Christian Church in Salem; Jim Petty and Norm Schoenborn of the Church of Christ in Molalla; Don Henderson and Richard Carter from the Church of Christ in Oakland; Ray Lindley and Vicki McClanahan with First Christian Church in Albany; Dale Moore from First Christian Church in Silverton; John Schmidt with Alvadore Christian Church; Roger Pedersen with the Stayton Church of Christ; Ronald Osborn and Dorothy Blood from First Christian Church in Eugene; Dan and Wendi Jocoy with the Tri-City Church of Christ in Myrtle Creek; Sharon Baimbridge, secretary of First Christian Church in Monmouth; Rick Nease from the Roseburg Church of Christ; Tom Burgess with the Crossroads Church of Christ in Portland; and Bill Richardson, a retired professor of church history from Emmanuel School of Religion who now lives in Turner. Others who assisted me in locating source materials and burial sites were: Clarence E. Dugan, Elden Toll, Dale Toll, Marguariete Overholser, Thelma Goodnough, Lucille Lusk, Percy Langdon, Brian Monroe and Glover Shipp.

Several people collaborated to produce the dramatic image that adorns the dust jacket on this book, and I want to thank each of them. The artist who crafted "The Promised Land" was David Manuel. I am grateful to David and Lee Manuel and to the Manuel Gallery in Joseph, Oregon, for permission to use this image. The person who provided a slide of the statue was Jim Lockett of McMinnville, Oregon, and the one who developed the basic idea for the cover layout based on the slide was Bill Henegar from Pepperdine University. One of my former students, Sonserae Leese of Morningstar Design, was the skillful digital artist who created the final production art that was used on the cover.

I want to express my appreciation to five administrators at Pepperdine University, Andy Benton, Steve Lemley, John Wilson, Dwayne VanRheenen and Tom Olbricht, whose willingness to grant me a sabbatical from my teaching responsibilities in the fall of 1996 enabled me to complete this project on schedule. I also want to thank Craig Bowman, the manager of word processing, and Ron Hall, the university photographer, for devoting long hours of unique skill in helping to bring this book to completion.

I owe a great debt of gratitude to Bill Henegar, the assistant vice-president for creative services at Pepperdine University. We have officed next to each other for most of my 19 years at Pepperdine, and I have come to rely on his wise counsel in almost every project I have undertaken. Bill not only surrendered most of his Christmas holiday to editing the entire manuscript of this book, but he willingly designed the dust jacket and the 24 pages of photographs. His enthusiasm for "the glorious cause" that motivated our forefathers kept me going when my own enthusiasm waned.

I shall always be grateful for the good fortune of having a wonderful historian, R. L. Roberts, as my mentor. Our friendship spans more than three decades, and we have traveled to many restoration sites together. On one occasion he showed me the Kentucky house where Barton Warren Stone and Alexander Campbell met for the first time in 1824, and on another foray he led me up a thickly-overgrown hill to show me John Mulkey's grave. His encyclopedic knowledge of the Restoration Movement gave shape to this project from beginning to end, and his willingness to review each chapter was immensely helpful.

I want to thank five special friends at College Press, Chris DeWelt, John Hunter, Steve Cable, Dan Rees and Steve Jennings, who enthusiastically embraced this project from the beginning and offered many excellent suggestions. They not only failed to become discouraged when the project doubled in size and some deadlines were missed, but they actually increased the level of their encouragement and support. I am very grateful for their help in guiding me through every unfamiliar step of the publication process.

A word of appreciation is also due to my church relations "team" at Pepperdine. Tara Morrow, Patty Atkisson, Randy Gill and Emily Lemley each carried a heavier load than usual during the nine months that I worked on this book. They willingly relieved me of many routine tasks, so that I could devote large blocks of time to sustained research and writing. I am grateful for their constant encouragement and loyal friendship.

It would have been impossible to complete this task without the loving support of my family. Lori, in particular, was a co-worker in every phase of the book's development. She proofed and critiqued every chapter, offered many helpful suggestions, and spurred me on when I showed signs of growing weary. She patiently arranged our home around the exasperating schedule of a manuscript in process, and she kept me focused on the looming deadline. In that respect, our arduous project was a shared endeavor. Without Lori's constant encouragement, *Christians on the Oregon Trail* would never have made it to the land of promise.

TABLE OF CONTENTS

Prologue

The Restoration Movement

The growth of this body of Christians, sometimes called Campbellites, is unparalleled in the annals of religious history. . . . However much in error their doctrinal tenets may be regarded by their religious friends, the facts cannot be disguised, that during the past thirty or forty years, they have made more rapid progress than any other denomination in the United States.

— 1865 Editorial in the Baltimore American

The Restoration Movement originated on the American frontier in a period of religious enthusiasm and ferment at the beginning of the nineteenth century. The first leaders of the movement deplored the numerous divisions in the church and urged the unity of all Christians through a restoration of New Testament Christianity. The Protestant Reformation had gone astray, they felt, and the various denominations must be directed back to primitive Christianity. They believed that this would be possible if everyone would wear the name "Christian" and return to the Biblical pattern of the New Testament church in doctrine, worship, and practice.

Those two ideas—the restoration of New Testament Christianity and the reunion of all Christians—became a distinctive plea and unceasingly, "in season and out of season," the Christians penetrated the frontier with their appeal. They called their efforts the "Restoration Movement" or the "Current Reformation," and they saw themselves as participants in a movement within the existing churches aimed at eliminating all sectarian divisions.

The Christians accepted the Bible as the absolute and final authority in religion, and they believed that an intelligent investigation of the scriptures would result in the discovery of truth. An early motto was: "We speak where the Bible speaks, and we are silent where the Bible is silent."[1] With unabashed zeal they waged war on all human religious creeds and pleaded with all men and women to take "the Bible as the only sure guide to heaven."[2]

Of the two main streams of the movement, one was led by Kentucky preachers Barton Warren Stone and John Mulkey, and the other by Thomas and Alexander Campbell, a father and son team in Bethany, Virginia.[3] In the summer of 1804 at the Cane Ridge Meetinghouse outside Lexington, Kentucky, Barton Warren Stone and four colleagues left the Presbyterian Church to become part of an independent movement of "Christian" churches. Having renounced the name "Presbyterian" as sectarian, these churches agreed henceforth to call themselves "Christians" only. Beginning in the summer of 1807, they rejected the practice of sprinkling infants and restored the Biblical practice of the immersion of believers. In a short time, Stone had become the acknowledged leader, and the Cane Ridge Meetinghouse had become the center of a vibrant movement that was enjoying rapid growth in the states of Kentucky, Ohio, Indiana, and Tennessee.

Meanwhile, two preachers in the Stone movement, Benjamin Lynn and Lewis Byram, were having a powerful impact on the thinking of a Baptist preacher named John Mulkey.[4] In 1809, John Mulkey led his Mill Creek Baptist Church out of the Stockton Valley Baptist Association in southern Kentucky. Over the next two years more than half of the preachers in the Association followed his lead, including Thomas Crawford McBride, whose family later had such a strong impact on the growth of the church in Oregon.[5] These preachers reorganized their churches on the basis of "the Bible alone," and they adopted the name "Christian" to the exclusion of all others. One preacher said admiringly of John Mulkey that he "took the Word of God as his guide, the name Christian as the inspired name, and so lived and died."[6] The Mulkey movement was strong in southern Kentucky and throughout middle Tennessee and northern Alabama, and by 1811 it had joined forces with the Stone movement.

The Campbells, unaware of the Stone and Mulkey movements, severed their ties with the Presbyterian Church in 1809 and formed their own independent movement. They called themselves "Reformers" or "Disciples" and established their first congregation at Brush Run, Virginia, in 1811. Like the Stone movement before them, the Campbells rejected sprinkling and adopted immersion in 1812. For nearly 18 years (1813-1830), the Campbell movement had a tenuous relationship with Regular Baptists. In 1823 Alexander Campbell founded his first monthly, the *Christian Baptist,* and for seven years he used it to gain followers among the Baptists of western Pennsylvania, Ohio, Virginia, and Kentucky. Through the pages of this paper, Campbell exposed sectarianism and pleaded for the "restoration of the ancient order of things."[7]

Despite difficulties of travel and communication, the two streams crisscrossed on the frontier and gradually became aware of one another. When Barton Warren Stone and Alexander Campbell met for the first time in 1824, they recognized that the principles of the "Christians" and the "Disciples" were strikingly similar. In addition to similar restoration and unity themes, both groups were born as a reaction to Calvinism and its doctrines of total depravity, unconditional election, and limited atonement. These similarities paved the way for a future merger of the two restoration movements.

At the same time, the Campbell movement had experienced a positive reception among the Mahoning Baptist Association churches on the Western Reserve (northeastern Ohio). Through the evangelistic efforts of Walter Scott in 1827-1830, the Western Reserve became "the principal theater" of the "Disciples" movement.[8] Scott's preaching contained a sharply defined gospel plan of salvation. If believers would confess their faith in Christ, repent of their sins, and be baptized into Christ, God would respond by remitting their sins and granting them the gift of the Holy Spirit and eternal life. This message resulted in a great revival that so transformed the Association that it dissolved itself out of existence and was absorbed by the "Disciples" movement. That ended the 18-year marriage with the Baptists and freed Campbell's "Disciples" to come together with the "Christians" of the Stone-Mulkey movement.

When Stone saw the effectiveness of Campbell's *Christian Baptist,* he began publishing the *Christian Messenger* in 1826. In 1830 Campbell changed the name of his paper to the *Millennial Harbinger,* which reflected his optimistic faith that a golden age for Christianity was dawning. A number of consultation meetings between the leaders of "Christians" and "Disciples" in 1830 and 1831 led to a larger unity meeting at Lexington, Kentucky, over the weekend of January 1, 1832, in which both groups agreed that they should unite. Since neither group recognized any ecclesiastical authority above the local church, actual union could only be accomplished by going to the congregations and urging them to unite. This was accomplished on a broad scale, and it was estimated that the unified movement of Stone-Mulkey and Campbell probably had more than 25,000 members in 1832.[9]

The American religious movement that resulted from this merger never agreed on an exclusive name. Alexander Campbell preferred "Disciples of Christ," whereas his own father and Walter Scott both had a strong attachment to the name "Christian." Stone and Mulkey also insisted on the name "Christian" and their churches were usually designated "Church of Christ" or "Christian Church."[10] Stone's congregation at Cane Ridge was referred to as the "Church of Christ at Cane Ridge." Many of the churches in the Campbell orbit, including the Bethany church, also preferred the simplicity of "Church of Christ." Throughout most of the nineteenth century all of these names were accepted and used interchangeably.

Although Barton Warren Stone had a major role in bringing "Christians" and "Disciples" together and regarded the union as the "noblest act" of his life, Alexander Campbell soon became the dominant figure in the movement. "A scholar of the first rank, a proud and aggressive leader, and a forceful spokesman,"[11] Campbell gave direction to the youthful movement for another 30 years. His Bethany College, chartered in 1840 and opened in 1841, became the principal training school for a new generation of Christian preachers, and his *Millennial Harbinger* commanded the patronage of the entire brotherhood. In 1849 he was named president of the American Christian Missionary Society,[12] a national missionary organization established in Cincinnati by several prominent leaders of the Restoration Movement.

By the time the first members of the Restoration Movement migrated to Oregon Territory in 1842, the movement was in the process of becoming a religious body of significant size. The numerical strength was most noticeable in a band of seven contiguous states comprising Tennessee, Kentucky, Ohio, Indiana, Illinois, Missouri, and Iowa. Since these were the very states that supplied the largest number of immigrants to Oregon, it is not surprising to find the Restoration Movement well represented in the new land.

Introduction

Holding Fast the Name

The disciples were first called Christians at Antioch.

— Acts 11:26

Surely no name can possibly combine in it so many interesting considerations to excite us to every thing that is good, honorable, and praise-worthy, as the name CHRISTIAN. It is, without exception, the most exalting, the most honorable, and distinguishing title under heaven. Excited, therefore, by these considerations, let us hold it fast, and endeavor to walk worthy of it.

— Thomas Campbell, 1840

The members of the Restoration Movement insisted on calling themselves "Christians," without any denominational appendage, but they did not imply by this preference that they were the only Christians. On the contrary, they were motivated by an intense desire to unify all professing believers in one church family. It was their aversion to all denominational distinctions that drove them to insist on a pure speech in Biblical matters. With an obvious depth of passion, Thomas Campbell admonished members of the movement to never relinquish the precious right of wearing the name "Christian" for the very reason that it was consistent with what they had been about from the beginning, namely "the restoration of pure, primitive, apostolic Christianity in letter and spirit, in principle and practice."[1]

It is understandable that Acts 11:26 would become a favorite text for preachers in the Restoration Movement and that their audiences would be inundated with the repetitious reminder that "the disciples were first called Christians at Antioch." Thomas Campbell challenged all leaders of the movement, including his own son (who preferred the name "Disciple"), when he asked: "Can any name . . . be more appropriate, more distinguishing, more comprehensive, more glorious, or more scriptural that that of CHRISTIAN?" Pressing further, he asked: "Or can any name suit better with the ultimate intention of the proposed reformation: viz.—the scriptural unity and unanimity of the professors of Christianity, without which they can never convert the world? Surely no." The elder Campbell spoke for the entire movement in his soaring conclusion:

> Surely no name can possibly combine in it so many interesting considerations to excite us to every thing that is good, honorable, and praise-worthy, as the name CHRISTIAN. It is, without exception, the most exalting, the most honorable, and distinguishing title under heaven. Excited, therefore, by these considerations, let us hold it fast, and endeavor to walk worthy of it.[2]

A Most Reproachful Epithet

One name that was not accepted by anyone in the movement was the derisive term "Campbellite," which was first adopted by the opponents of Alexander Campbell in the 1820s. Campbell responded immediately to this slur by calling it "a most reproachful epithet."[3] Later, he wrote, "It is a nickname of reproach invented and adopted by those whose views, feelings, and desires are all sectarian: who cannot conceive of Christianity in any other light than an ism."[4] From Campbell's perspective, the nickname was not only obnoxious but a violation of the law of Christ. "If Christians were wholly cast into the mold of the apostles' doctrine," he argued, "they would feel themselves as much aggrieved and slandered in being called by any man's name as they would in being called a thief, a fornicator, or a drunkard."[5]

On another occasion Campbell wrote pointedly, "We do protest against christening the gospel of Jesus and the Christian religion, by the name of any mortal man."[6] This view was shared by Stone, Mulkey, Scott, and other church leaders, but as the Restoration Movement continued to embrace large numbers of believers from various backgrounds, the use of the slur not only continued but accelerated. Campbell lamented this development and called it "both unmanly, and unchristian,"[7] but he was powerless to overturn it. "Men fond of nicknaming," he wrote, "are generally weak in reason, argument, and proof."[8]

The Restoration Movement was noted for urging all believers everywhere to "come out of Babylon." The Babylonian bondage they referred to was denominationalism and the divisive practice of expending loyalty on party names and creedal statements. In the early days of the Restoration Movement, its proponents were overly optimistic in believing that most of church-going America would be willing to forego denominational language and return to "calling Bible things by Bible names." When it became apparent that many Methodists, Baptists, and Presbyterians preferred their denominational affiliation and had no intention of calling themselves "Christian" or governing themselves by "the Bible alone," they were dismissed as "sectarian." In this way, the battle lines were drawn between those in the Restoration Movement and those remaining in "the sects." Prior to the migration to Oregon, the Restoration Movement in the midwestern states had to contend often with "opposition from the sects." In particular, their opponents took delight in both denying them the use of "Christian" and in labeling them "Campbellites." To God-fearing people who despised the use of party names and longed for nothing more than to just be Christians, this was the ultimate insult.

A Stigma Transplanted

When the Christians began their long trek to Oregon Territory, they carried with them the fervent hope that they would be free to plant the principles of the Restoration Movement in that western Eden without the divisive prejudices that had plagued them back in the states. In this, they were sadly mistaken. From the very beginning, their every attempt to plead for the restoration of New Testament Christianity and the unity of all believers was met with "opposition from the sects." The unwanted term "Campbellite" surfaced repeatedly, and yet they not only persevered, they prospered. The relentless opposition seemed to strengthen their resolve to hold fast the name of "Christian" and to walk worthily of it.

Oregon Christians often sent progress reports back to the church papers in the states. A typical report from Dr. James McBride to the *Christian Evangelist* in Iowa read: "I can say, with much assurance, that the 'Christians' number not less than 800 in Oregon."[9] McBride had no hesitancy in calling the members of the Restoration Movement "Christians," but his use of quotation marks around the term implied that he was not suggesting they were the only Christians in the territory. His readers would have understood clearly what he meant. When a "Brother Disen from Australia" migrated to Oregon he was surprised and disappointed by the use of the term "Campbellite." G. W. Richardson reported to the *Christian Record*: "He stated to me that during his stay in Australia he never heard the nick-name 'Campbellite' applied to our brotherhood, but they are called *Christians* by all."[10]

Such was not the case in Oregon, where the Christians were stigmatized as "Campbellites" even by objective historians who should have known better. When Hubert Howe Bancroft published his monumental two-volume *History of Oregon* in 1888, he included a very informative section on "Churches and Church Schools." Bancroft began with a thorough discussion of the Methodists, Catholics, Congregationalists, Presbyterians, Episcopalians, and Baptists, none of which are offensive or unwanted terms, but then he added condescendingly: "Among the other religious denominations of Oregon were the Campbellites."[11] Why permit every religious group to be called by the name it preferred except the Christians? Bancroft did not mean to diminish the significance of the "Christian" movement, but he had carelessly fallen victim to the common prejudice of his day.

When Joseph Gaston published a four-volume series entitled *The Centennial History of Oregon* in 1912, it was praised for its thorough research and objective writing. Especially helpful to church historians was his alphabetically arranged treatment of denominational histories in Oregon, but once again the stigma appeared. Sandwiched between the Baptists and the Episcopalians was an excellent discussion of, not "The Christians," but "The Campbellites." It did not help that the author opened with the disclaimer that "No member of the Christian or 'Disciples of Christ' church need take umbrage at being called a 'Campbellite.'"[12] The point, simply put, was that they did take umbrage.

Joseph Schafer submitted a fine article on William Lysander Adams for the prestigious *Dictionary of American Biography,* but he inadvertently belittled Adams by writing: "Under Alexander Campbell's instruction he became a Campbellite."[13] It was true that Adams was a student at Bethany College and that he boarded in the Campbell home. It was also true that when he left Bethany he was a strong Christian, a fine preacher, and a person committed to the principles inherent in the Restoration Movement. But Campbell and Adams would both have been grieved by the use of the slur "Campbellite." It is unlikely that Schafer meant to demean Adams by the use of such an objectionable term. Like Bancroft before him, he simply fell victim to a common prejudice.

Oregon Christians had to constantly endure the term "Campbellite" in newspaper coverage. When State Senator Sebastian Adams, brother to William Lysander Adams, visited Washington Territory in May 1869, the *Vancouver Register* reported: "Honorable Sebastian C. Adams, Senator from Yamhill County, Oregon, is in the city . . . . He is a Campbellite preacher of fine abilities and bears the reputation before the public of a worthy Christian gentleman." Adams' father-in-law, Dr. James McBride, responded to the *Register* and objected strongly to the use of "the invidious epithet, *Campbellite.*" McBride pleaded: "We only ask, and we do ask it as a courtesy due us, to be known and called by the name which we have chosen, and that is 'Christian.'"[14]

When the Josephine County Historical Society erected a historical marker in front of an abandoned church to mark the site of the ghost town of Golden, it engraved these words on the marker:

> Established in 1890, this mining town was unique in Western annals in that it had two churches and no saloons. The Miners went to Placer or Grave Creek for "refreshments." Rev. William Ruble, leader of the group commonly known as "Campbellites" built the church in 1892. He was ordained and the church simultaneously dedicated by County Judge Stephen Jewell. Shortly afterward it became the Free Methodist Church. Another group led by Rev. Mark Davis used the schoolhouse for their services. Both ministers worked local mining claims.

There are two discrepancies in this wording. Not only would William Ruble and his congregation have objected to being called "Campbellites" instead of "Christians," they would have been equally opposed to the term "Reverend." They would have contended that the Bible used "reverend" only as an address for God, and that its usage as a designation for church leaders originated with Roman Catholicism. The Christians would have called William Ruble "Elder" or "Brother" or not used any designation beyond the assertion that he was their preacher. The irony here is that the Free Methodists were not opposed to being called Free Methodists, and Mark Davis was probably not opposed to being called "Reverend." It was only the Christians and their preacher who were improperly identified. As with many other cases, there was no intention to be deliberately demeaning by using the term "Campbellites." Once again, the Josephine County Historical Society was simply parroting the common prejudicial language used to describe this religious group.

Reclaiming the Name

There were some exceptions to this trend. An article on life in Linn County in the 1850s commented: "Dr. J. N. Perkins preached for the Christians and Rev. H. H. Spalding for the Presbyterians."[15] In *Oregon, Her History, Her Great Men, Her Literature*, published in 1921, John B. Horner wrote, "Bethel

College, near McCoy, Oregon, was built by the religious denomination known as The Christians."[16] A Baptist historian, chronicling the beginnings of Linfield College in McMinnville, noted that the school was first begun by the Christians.[17] Dr. James McBride, who was one of the Christians who established the school in McMinnville, would have appreciated this acknowledgment. He spoke for the entire movement when he pleaded, "We only ask . . . to be known and called by the name which we have chosen, and that is 'Christian.'" Thomas Campbell himself could not have expressed the case more eloquently.

It is historically accurate to call these people "Christians,"[18] and therefore the title of this volume is both deliberate and appropriate. This is the story of a courageous generation of Christians who migrated to Oregon Territory on the torturous Oregon Trail. Not all of them survived the journey, but those who did arrived with well-thumbed Bibles and a stubborn determination to hold fast the name Christian and to plant what they called "Bible Christianity" in "the wilds of Oregon."[19] To a great extent they were successful. "We now outnumber in the American population any of the sects," claimed Amos Harvey in 1848, "and if we only live up to our high profession, Oregon will soon become as noted for the religion of Jesus Christ, as it already is for its ever-verdant pastures, its grand and varied scenery, and its mild and healthy climate."[20]

Foreword

Alexander Campbell in Oregon

We . . . were obliged to hasten on to the residence of Mr. R. S. Jenkins, twelve miles south of St. Joseph, whose hospitalities we enjoyed that night . . . we departed, after surveying, with our eye, the Missouri and the Indian Territory, on the other side. Indeed, we had many opportunities of becoming better acquainted with this turbid and eccentric river, but at no two points more favorable for surveying the territory beyond the United States than at this place and Camden Point, to which we were directing our way.

– Alexander Campbell, November 26, 1852

On the last day of September 1845, 57-year-old Alexander Campbell left his home in Bethany, Virginia, on his first trip to the "Far West" of Missouri. From October 17 to 20 he was one of the featured speakers at the annual State Meeting in Columbia, Missouri[1], and no doubt heard stories about Christians who had migrated to Oregon Territory. It is altogether likely that Campbell visited with two Missouri preachers, Dr. James McBride and Glen Owen Burnett, who were already making plans to leave for Oregon with their large families in the spring of 1846.

Continuing on his journey to the very edge of the frontier, Campbell preached for the Christians in Independence on October 26.[2] This city served as the main supply depot and point of departure for travelers heading for the Oregon Trail, and once again Campbell probably heard several stories about Christian families who had already left for Oregon or were planning to leave in the spring. Even as the "Sage of Bethany" was preaching in Independence, two talented church leaders named Amos Harvey and John Foster had already arrived in Oregon. The following spring these men would be responsible for organizing the first two congregations of Christians in the Territory.

It was seven years before Alexander Campbell's travels brought him to the "Far West" again. In the intervening years, the constant migration of Christian families had swelled the ranks of the Restoration Movement in Oregon Territory. The fall and winter of 1852 saw Campbell involved in another lengthy preaching tour, this one centering in Illinois and Missouri and covering 76 days and 2,800 miles. At the farthest stop on this journey, he came to St. Joseph, Missouri, a city made famous as one of the most favorable departure points for the five-month, 2,000-mile overland trip across the rugged Oregon Trail to the Pacific Coast. The oft-traveled Campbell was clearly excited to reach this destination, and he wrote that he was standing on the shore "where the last wave of American population and civilization breaks upon the wild forest."[3]

Composing a report on his journey to the "Far West" for the readers of the *Millennial Harbinger*, Campbell wrote:

> We . . . were obliged to hasten to the residence of Mr. R. S. Jenkins, twelve miles south of St. Joseph, whose hospitalities we enjoyed that night . . . we departed, after surveying, with our eye, the Missouri and the Indian Territory, on the other side. Indeed, we had many opportunities of becoming better acquainted with this turbid and eccentric river, but at no two points more favorable for surveying the territory beyond the United States than at this place and Camden Point, to which we were directing our way.[4]

Standing on the banks of the mighty Missouri River, Campbell surveyed "the territory beyond the United States" and, no doubt, dreamed of preaching Christ in those far flung territories. It was reminiscent of the Apostle Paul standing on the shore at Troas and preparing to answer the "Macedonian call" to plant the faith on European soil. But unlike Paul and his companions, Campbell would not be crossing this body of water and setting forth on a great adventure. The 64-year-old reformer knew that this was the closest he would ever come to experiencing life on the Oregon Trail.

And yet, in a very real sense, Alexander Campbell was already in Oregon Territory in the persons of more than 1,200 Christians who looked to him for example and leadership.[5] They accounted for nearly ten percent of the non-Indian population in the territory, and they were demonstrating a remarkable zeal for evangelism. In fact, even as Campbell stood on the banks of the Missouri River and gazed westward, a derisive observation was making the rounds in Oregon Territory: "The Campbellites and the fern are taking the Willamette Valley."[6] Nor was it just in the Willamette Valley. One Baptist missionary observed from his post on the Clatsop Plains near Astoria: "the Campbellites are industriously engaged in making proselytes."[7] However, this missionary had just returned to the Clatsop Plains from an extended visit to the Willamette Valley, and he may have been referring to the zealous activity of the Christians in that region.

From his vantage point high above the Missouri River, Campbell took one last longing look at the beginnings of the trail in the hazy distance and then turned his back and began the long journey home to Bethany, Virginia. Bethany College needed his attention, and so did the *Millennial Harbinger,* the American Bible Union,[8] the American Christian Missionary Society, and a thousand other concerns. Oregon Territory would have to be entrusted to others—perhaps even to some Campbell-trained graduates of Bethany College.[9]

Chapter 1

The Land of Promise 1842

One Saturday morning . . . Mr. Burnett hauled a box out into the sidewalk, took his stand upon it, and began to tell us about the land flowing with milk and honey on the shores of the Pacific.

— Edward Henry Lenox, 1842

President Thomas Jefferson's negotiations with Napoleon's French government led to an American acquisition of the vast Louisiana Territory in 1803. This transaction nearly doubled the size of the United States overnight and made many Americans aware of the territory beyond the Rocky Mountains for the first time. A dangerous transcontinental expedition followed in 1804–06 led by Jefferson's personal secretary, Meriwether Lewis, and Lewis's lifelong friend, William Clark. They successfully followed the Missouri River to its Rocky Mountain headwaters, made their way through treacherous mountain passes and thick forests, and arrived safely at the Columbia, the great "River of the West." Fashioning canoes, they descended the wild and tumbling river all the way to the Pacific Ocean. Lewis and Clark and their courageous men had become the first Americans of European descent to ever travel overland to Oregon Territory, and with amazing swiftness America had joined Britain in the Pacific Northwest.

The Pacific Northwest

Friction between the British and Americans over ownership of Oregon Territory was just beginning during the War of 1812, and the issue was not seriously negotiated during the post-war peace talks. In 1817, the publication of William Cullen Bryant's poem, *Thanatopsis,* greatly popularized the name "Oregon" in American life, and by 1819, both Britain and America were laying claim to the territory. While the two nations vied for control of the coveted land, two British fur trading companies, Hudson's Bay and the North West Company, made plans to develop a base in the disputed region. The two companies merged in 1821, retaining the name of Hudson's Bay, and by 1824 they had established northwestern headquarters at Fort Vancouver. This was a strategic location at the confluence of the Columbia and Willamette rivers, and it gave the British an edge in the territorial dispute.

The arrival of Dr. John McLoughlin, chief agent for the Hudson's Bay Company, further solidified the British claim. Hubert Howe Bancroft wrote of Dr. McLoughlin at Fort Vancouver: "Here he held sway for many years, absolute monarch of the district of Columbia, comprising all the Hudson's Bay trapping-grounds west of the Rocky Mountains . . . ."[1]

A turning point occurred in 1831 when four Native Americans (three Nez Perce and one Flathead) from west of the Rockies appeared at General William Clark's office in St. Louis, Missouri, inquiring about the "white man's book of heaven." Christians everywhere were profoundly moved by this scene, and mission plans were set in motion overnight. Without the intervention of Protestant missionaries from America, the British might have been able to retain their monopoly in the Pacific Northwest indefinitely. But the call of the Lord was compelling, and Dr. McLoughlin's domain was an attractive target. A Methodist missionary named Jason Lee hastened overland in 1834 and began building a mission near present-day Salem in the Willamette Valley. His multinational congregation not only included American, British, Scotch-Irish, French, and Indian worshipers, but people from Hawaiian and Japanese ancestry as well.[2] Favorable reports sent back to the eastern states described Oregon Territory in glowing terms.[3]

Dr. Marcus Whitman, his wife, Narcissa, and Henry and Eliza Spalding were the first persons to reach the Pacific Northwest by covered wagon. When these Presbyterian missionaries came overland in 1835, the entire country was aware of their epic journey, because Narcissa Whitman and Eliza Spalding were the first white women to cross the American continent. Rather than remain together for strength, the Whitmans and Spaldings established separate missions in an effort to reach more Indians. The Whitmans built a mission near present-day Walla Walla, Washington, and the Spaldings began to minister near present-day Lewiston, Idaho.[4] Meanwhile, Jason Lee crossed the continent again in 1838 and appealed to President Martin Van Buren to support a plan that would encourage more American immigration to Oregon Territory. When he returned to his mission in the Willamette Valley in 1840, he brought a company of immigrants with him.[5] The tide was slowly turning in the direction of American occupation.

The United States Congress had been debating the "Oregon Question" since 1819, but in the early 1840s the debate assumed a new level of urgency. Senator Lewis Fields Linn from Missouri sponsored a bill in December 1841, that would donate 640 acres of Oregon land to every adult male settler, and an additional 160 acres for each child. In this way, Senator Linn argued, the American government could populate Oregon Territory with American families and validate its claim to the entire Pacific Northwest. News of the pending bill was electrifying to settlers living at the edge of the American frontier in Western Missouri, because they were the ones best positioned to take immediate advantage of it.

The year 1842 was a crucial year for American migration to Oregon Territory. Prior to that year the white population in Oregon was estimated at between 700 and 800, and most of those were Canadian fur trappers and traders. There were only about 150 Americans in the entire territory.[6] There was not even an established Oregon Trail yet, although some fur traders had been traveling over sections that would later be included in the trail. Then in 1842, 112 immigrants banded together in the "first typical wagon train" bound for Oregon.[7] There were 60 women and children in this train and 52 men 18 years or older. By this time Dr. McLoughlin had moved from Fort Vancouver to a small village at Willamette Falls near present-day Oregon City, and most of the immigrants in this first train settled near him. At the end of the winter of 1842–43, the budding village could boast of 30 houses.[8]

Reuben Lewis

Although it is possible, perhaps even probable, that some members of the Restoration Movement were represented in the 1842 migration, the only person who can positively be identified is 28-year-old Reuben Lewis. He traveled with the family of Gabriel Brown, and he walked most of the way across the trail. It is very likely that the Browns were Christians, as their daughter Cynthia was later a member of the Aumsville Church. For the privilege of traveling with the Brown family, Lewis agreed to keep the family supplied with meat during the journey. One record describes his prowess as a hunter and noted that he "succeeded so well that he just about supplied the whole train of sixteen wagons, killing as many as eleven buffalo in one day."[9]

Another traveler with possible church ties was Allan Davie, who later married Cynthia Brown. Upon arriving in Oregon Territory, Reuben Lewis and Allan Davie worked together, and they were both present at the historic mass meeting that assembled at Champoeg on May 2, 1843. This meeting of settlers was called to consider the advisability of forming a territorial government that would be loyal to the United States. In the hotly contested election that day, 52 votes were registered in favor of the proposition and 50 votes were opposed. One record commented on Lewis and Davie:

> Mr. Lewis was present at the famous conference at Champoeg, Marion County, at the time the vote was taken in favor of the Oregon country being held by the United States and of course voted with the majority. He always believed it was his vote and that of Mr. Allan Davie that turned the tide in favor of the United States, as they both arrived at the conference together and very late. Without their votes the destiny of Oregon would have been written as another story.[10]

Meanwhile, all was not well with the Whitmans and Spaldings. Their sponsoring missionary boards, bothered by what they considered a lack of tangible results, had ordered the missions closed. Dr. Marcus Whitman undertook a dangerous winter crossing of the continent in 1842–43 and appealed successfully to his boards to stand behind him.[11] This would be a fortunate break for the immigrants of 1843, as Dr. Whitman would catch up with them in western Nebraska territory and serve as an important resource from there to the Whitman mission near Fort Walla Walla.

Peter Hardeman Burnett

The story of "The Great Migration" of 1843 begins on the westernmost edge of the westernmost state with a debt-laden frontier lawyer named Peter Hardeman Burnett.[12] With debts totaling $15,000 and a wife seriously ill with consumption, Burnett was trying to eke out a living by running a small general store in Weston, Missouri. This little town nestled near a bend in the Missouri River in Platte County, equidistant from Independence and St. Joseph, was located in the very heart of "Oregon fever" contagion. To someone hopelessly mired in debt like Burnett, the prospect of free land in Oregon was almost too good to be true. Since he had a wife and six children, he would be entitled to 1,600 acres. Consulting with his creditors, he received their permission to seek his fortune in the Eden of the West.

Now nearing his 35th birthday, and with no prospects for economic prosperity in Missouri, Burnett seized the moment. In his own words, he "set to work most vigorously to organize a wagon company. I visited the surrounding counties, making speeches wherever I could find a sufficient audience, and succeeded even beyond my expectations."[13]

Edward Henry Lenox, a teen-age boy whose family lived five miles east of Burnett, later wrote about the tumultuous events of 1842–43. "The excitement in connection with the settlement of Oregon," he recalled, "was stirring the hearts of the pioneers on the Mississippi frontier."[14] After his father, David Lenox, and other neighbors heard about the bill proposed by Senator Linn, "Oregon became a sort of pioneer's paradise, and great were the stories told about it to induce emigrants to go." And one of the most persuasive of "wayside orators" beating the drums for Oregon was a merchant standing in front of his store. Lenox remembered:

> One Saturday morning father said that he was going . . . to hear Mr. Burnett talk about Oregon. I said, "Father, I want to go too," to which he replied, "all right son, come on," and together we went. When the hour for the address came, Mr. Burnett hauled a box out into the sidewalk, took his stand upon it, and began to tell us about the land flowing with milk and honey on the shores of the Pacific. Of his address that day I remember this much, that he told of the great crops of wheat which it was possible to raise in Oregon, and pictured in glowing terms the richness of the soil and the attraction of the climate, and then with a little twinkle of humor in his eye, he said, "and they do say, gentlemen, they do say, that out in Oregon the pigs are running about under the great acorn trees, round and fat, and already cooked, with knives and forks sticking in them so that you can cut off a slice whenever you are hungry." Of course at this everybody laughed.[15]

David Lenox was sold. His son remembered that he was the first to respond by walking into the store and signing the book that Burnett had prepared for potential recruits. Others soon followed, and the first steps were taken in what would become "The Great Migration" of 1843. It was the opinion of one pioneer who migrated to Oregon in 1844 that "no other individual exerted as large an influence in swelling the number of home-building emigrants to Oregon in the years 1843 and 1844 as Peter H. Burnett."[16] It is probably not surprising that Burnett was later elected by the immigrants to be captain of the wagon train. He had a natural gift for leadership.

Peter Hardeman Burnett was born in Nashville, Tennessee, in 1807. Although raised in a church-going culture, religion was not an important component in Burnett's life until he moved to Missouri and became aware of the Restoration Movement. It was there in his early 30s that he was converted to Christianity. He was immersed into Christ and became an active member of the Christian Church in his hometown of Weston. Burnett later wrote of this conversion: "I became thoroughly convinced of the entire truth of Christianity."[17] He was described by his contemporaries as one who "was very ready of speech" and "a popular stump speaker."[18] His younger brother, Glen Owen Burnett,[19] was already becoming widely recognized as a powerful spokesman for the Christians in Missouri, and it is possible that Peter himself may have preached on occasion between 1840 and 1843.

In the winter of 1842–43, several members of the Church of Christ in Missouri finalized their plans to accompany Peter Hardeman Burnett to Oregon. Included in this number were: William and Sarah Newby; Catherine Blevins Baker (wife of John Gordon Baker who was not a member of the church); Chesley B. Gray; Samuel and Martha Gilmore and their two small children; William H. Wilson; Daniel Holman (who would marry Martha Burnett, a daughter of Glen Owen Burnett, in 1846); John and Temperance Howell, Elizabeth Howell McCorkle (wife of George F. McCorkle who was not a member of the church) and three separate families from the Hembree clan, led by Joel Jordan Hembree, Absalom J. Hembree, and Andy T. Hembree.

Ahead of them lay an arduous five-month journey across an uncertain trail, but they were buttressed by a strong faith in the providential care of a loving God, and they were buoyed by an unshakable vision of "the land flowing with milk and honey on the shores of the Pacific"—a veritable land of promise.

Chapter 2

The Great Migration
1843

Thursday, July 20 – I came on ahead with Captain Gantt and an advance guard, passed over some very rough road, and at noon came upon a fresh grave with stones piled over it, and a note tied on a stick, informing us that it was the grave of Joel Hembree, child of Joel J. Hembree, aged 6 years, and was killed by a wagon running over the body. At the head of the grave stood a stone containing the name of the child. This is the first death that has occurred on the expedition. The grave is on the left hand side of the trail, close to Squaw Butte Creek.

– Colonel James W. Nesmith

A daughter had been born to Joel Jordan Hembree and wife, and christened Nancy Jane. Thus a death and birth had occurred in this family within nine days.

– Jesse Applegate

In New England, the end of the world was at hand! William Miller, the founder of Adventism, had prophesied that a cosmic cataclysm would take place between March 21, 1843, and March 21, 1844. Thousands of his followers had disposed of their property, settled their accounts, and were preparing for Doomsday.

In Western Missouri, another kind of madness was riveting the attention of the populace. "The Oregon fever is raging in almost every part of the Union," thundered one western paper. "Companies are forming in the east, and in several parts of Ohio, which, added to those of Illinois, Iowa, and

Missouri, will make a pretty formidable army."[1] Covered wagons by the dozens began converging on the frontier town of Independence. These crowds were not driven by the fear of Doomsday, but by the promise of a new beginning in the great American West.

Pushing Westward

Americans had been pushing westward for generations. It seemed to be in their blood. Previous generations had come from Europe to the New World, from Plymouth Plantation to the Alleghenies, and across the mountains to the wild west of Missouri. It mattered little that Great Britain and the United States were still debating the rightful ownership of Oregon Territory. What mattered was the lure of free land, boundless opportunity, and a new start in life. Meanwhile, in the nation's capitol, the United States Senate passed Senator Linn's Oregon Bill by a narrow vote of twenty-four to twenty-two. The historic date was February 3, 1843.[2] Within a few days, the good news was shouted from wagon to wagon on the roads leading west to Independence. This was all the encouragement they needed. Americans were pushing westward again.

The journey could not begin until the grass along the trail had grown high enough to feed the livestock that would be making the trip. Word spread that the migration would leave in May. Peter and Harriet Burnett and their six children left their home in Weston on May 8, 1843, and headed for Elm Grove, Kansas, a rendezvous point about 30 miles west of Independence where the wagons were assembling. On Monday, May 22, the migration officially began with nearly 900 people, 120 wagons, and about 5,000 head of livestock—horses, mules, oxen, and cattle.[3] It has rightly been called "The Great Migration," even though later ones were larger, because it was a landmark in the history of western migration. Nothing comparable had ever been attempted on the Oregon Trail. In recalling this historic occasion, Burnett wrote later:

> The place where we encamped was very beautiful; and no scene appeared to our enthusiastic visions more exquisite than

> the sight of so many wagons, tents, fires, cattle, and people, as were here collected. At night the sound of joyous music was heard in the tents. Our long journey thus began in sunshine and song, in anecdote and laughter; but these all vanished before we reached its termination.[4]

Pioneer Christians

Of the nearly 900 travelers in the historic migration of 1843 there must have been many families connected with the Restoration Movement, but only twelve families can be identified with certainty. Young unmarried men represented three of these families: Chesley B. Gray, Daniel Holman, and William H. Wilson. Two young women, 20-year-old Catherine Blevins Baker, and 21-year-old Elizabeth Howell McCorkle were married to non-Christians. The seven extended Christian families included the Burnetts, Newbys, Gilmores, Howells and the three separate Hembree families.[5] William and Milley Arthur were also part of the 1843 migration, and they would be among the first converts to the Restoration Movement in Oregon Territory. In addition, two teenagers in the Methodist family of Daniel and Mary Matheny, Isaiah Cooper and Daniel Boone, would become prominent Christians in the 1850s. It is possible that Alexander and Lavina Blevins, parents of Catherine Blevins Baker, were also Christians.

Twenty-three-year-old William Newby and his 20-year-old bride, Sarah McGary Newby, were in one wagon. William was originally from McMinnville, Tennessee, where he had known some members of the Hembree clan when they lived in that county. He met his future wife after moving to southwestern Missouri in 1840, and they were married on October 14, 1841, in Dade County by Dr. James McBride, a well-known preacher in the Church of Christ. It was Dr. McBride who led the Newbys to become Christians, and he is probably the one who baptized them into Christ in 1842. As they began the difficult journey, the Newbys did not have any children yet, nor was Sarah pregnant. All eight Newby children would be born in McMinnville in Oregon Territory, a town founded by their father, William, and named for his ancestral home-town in

Tennessee. Traveling with the Newbys was their good friend and brother in Christ, Chesley B. Gray.

The Hembree families were traveling close to the Newbys and Gray in the wagon train. Andrew and Martha Hembree and their children were in one wagon. Andrew was an uncle to the two Hembree brothers, Joel Jordan and Absalom. The Hembrees were all originally from McMinnville, Tennessee, but they had moved on to Missouri in the 1830s. The Hembrees had been affiliated with the Restoration Movement since Tennessee days.

Joel Jordan Hembree had married Sally Paine in McMinnville, Tennessee, on October 20, 1825. Their two oldest sons, James Thomas (age 16) and Wayman Clark (age 14), were old enough to drive wagons on the Oregon Trail. Wayman, who would later serve as an elder in the Christian Church in McMinnville, Oregon, for many years, always boasted that he was the youngest driver of a wagon in the 1843 migration. There were several other children in this family, including Lafayette, Albert, Isham, Joel, Houston, and Sarah. To make traveling in a bumpy wagon even more uncomfortable, Sally was nearly seven months pregnant when the train left Elm Grove, Kansas, on May 22.

Absalom J. Hembree was nine years younger than his brother Joel. He had married Nancy Dodson on January 22, 1835, in Tennessee, and they had moved to Missouri in 1836. Absalom and Nancy were traveling with their four small children, and four more would be born to them in Oregon Territory.

Samuel M. Gilmore was born in Bedford County, Tennessee, in 1814. He moved first to Clay County, Missouri, and later to Buchanan County in the same state. It was in Buchanan County that he met and married Martha, who was also a native of Tennessee and a devout Christian. The Gilmores were traveling in a wagon with their two small children. Seven more children would be born to them in Oregon Territory. The Bakers were traveling in a wagon with two small sons under the age of four. Five more children would be added to their family in Oregon.

John and Temperance Howell were born in Tennessee, but they had lived in Indiana for most of their married life and in Missouri for the past six years. They were traveling with several sons and a married daughter named Elizabeth McCorkle. George and Elizabeth McCorkle were in a separate wagon with their new-born daughter who had been named for her maternal grandmother. When John Howell died in 1869, Thomas C. Shaw said of him: "He had been an exemplary Christian for more than forty years, and was perfectly willing to meet death."[6] Of his daughter, Elizabeth McCorkle, one record said: "She became a member of the church in her early youth and remained a Christian until her death."[7]

The epic five-month trip on which they were embarking had been planned for months. It could take up to $1,000 to outfit a wagon with the necessary homesteading equipment and food supplies. A good wagon would cost from $70 to $100. A team of eight oxen would run $200, but some preferred a team of six mules which cost $600. In addition to arranging for their wagon and livestock, the pioneers had to carry enough supplies to last for the duration of the 2,000-mile journey. It was estimated that a typical family of four would have to carry the following: 824 pounds of flour, 725 pounds of bacon, 75 pounds of coffee, 160 pounds of sugar, 200 pounds of lard and suet, 200 pounds of beans, 135 pounds of peaches and apples, and a quantity of salt, pepper, and bicarbonate of soda.[8]

With the wagons loaded with provisions, almost everyone chose to walk along the trail in the early days. Since the train left in late May, the wildflowers were in full bloom, but most of the day was spent walking in the dust kicked up by wagons, cattle, and oxen. Each day began before dawn and closed near dusk. Except for a mid-day break, they traveled all day long and usually covered 15 to 20 hard miles a day. Two days into the journey they had to negotiate their first river crossing. Every wagon made it safely across this time, but fording rain-swollen rivers would become one of the most hazardous parts of the trip.

The Lord's Day

On Sunday, May 28, a minor crisis developed when most of the church-going population in the train made it clear that they were not going to travel on the Lord's Day. They needed a day of rest and so did their livestock. There was much grumbling and some threatened to break ranks and go on without the others. The Christians in the Restoration Movement had plenty of support from other Christians on this issue. David Lenox, who was chosen captain of one section of the train, was a devout Baptist who would not travel on the Lord's Day. According to his son:

> On that first Sunday morning father was resting in his tent, and mother and the four girls were taking it easy after an arduous week, when several from the families around us broke in impatiently upon us and wanted to know at what hour we were going to get off. "How is this, Captain Lenox," said one of them, "that you are not up and off this fine morning?" "We are not going to travel today," replied my father. "This is the Lord's day. The cattle need rest, and we need rest, and your families need rest." "Oh, you can't cram that down our throats," was the vigorous and irreverent reply; "We are going on." "Well," said Captain Lenox, "I have no authority to stop you, but you will find it to your interest to travel with a well-guarded company, rather than go it alone."[9]

Dr. Marcus Whitman caught up with the train on June 18. He agreed with the practice of resting on the Lord's Day, but he warned the immigrants that they were behind schedule and needed to travel faster and farther each day. The immigrants responded positively to his constant admonition—"travel, travel, travel."[10] The arrival of Dr. Whitman was a welcome sight. Here was a man who not only possessed valuable medical knowledge, but he had been across this trail on two previous occasions. His experience also proved helpful during the five-day fording of the South Platte River in the first week of July. The train passed Chimney Rock on July 7, reached Scott's Bluff on July 9, and rolled into Fort Laramie on July 12.

Fuel for cooking purposes was not always readily available to the travelers, and before long they had to rely on the bountiful supply of buffalo chips scattered along the trail. At first some were offended by this practice, including Harriet Burnett, the wife of Peter Burnett. One of the young daughters in the Matheny family remembered an incident that occurred soon after the fording of the South Platte River. She wrote later:

> We crossed on the fourth day of July, and Peter H. Burnett crossed a few minutes later. I remember that, because Aunt Rachel—who had gone over some days before—had a big dinner all cooked and ready for us. Someone had killed a buffalo, and Aunt had a great pan of juicy steaks all broiled and piping hot. We were all terribly hungry, and it was not till after the steaks were eaten that we found they had been broiled over buffalo chips. Mrs. Burnett was not altogether happy about it. She even said she would have starved before eating anything cooked on them if she had known it.[11]

But dry fuel of any kind was very scarce on the Oregon Trail, and Harriet Burnett soon got over her squeamishness about eating meat broiled over buffalo chips. A few mornings later, it was reported that her husband was seen at dawn gathering "a good supply" of buffalo chips "in a big white tablecloth."[12]

Daniel Boone Matheny was only 14 years old when he drove one of his father's wagons across the trail that summer. In later years he would become an effective evangelist in the Restoration Movement, but in the summer of '43 he was a very young teenager who was often bored by the slow and laborious pace of the wagon train. His sister remembered:

> One day my brother Daniel, a great easygoing dreamy-eyed boy, was driving one of our teams. He was well toward the rear of the long line of wagons when he fell asleep. His oxen, going slower and slower, finally stopped altogether, and the following drivers thought it a fine joke, when they pulled out and around, to leave the boy and the wagon standing there in the lonely road. It was not till camp was made several hours later that Father missed Daniel and his oxen, and hastily organized a party to go back for him . . . . Everyone was frightened, for we were in Indian country, but they found Daniel quite safe, still asleep in the middle of the dusty road. Father was very angry at the men who had left him behind—

> everyone was provoked about it. I suppose that something was said, there usually was when Father felt justified, but anyway it never happened to Daniel again—or to anyone else for that matter. And it was not laughed about or spoken of as a joke, either.[13]

The future preacher was fortunate that he was not the victim of a serious accident. Up to that time "The Great Migration" of 1843 had proceeded without any fatalities, but one Christian family was about to be engulfed in the horrible agony and suffering that attended death on the trail.

Life and Death on the Oregon Trail

The great tragedy of the trip for the Hembree family occurred without warning on July 18, just a few days beyond Fort Laramie. On that quiet and uneventful Tuesday, the train was slowly struggling over a stretch of very bad road. Six-year-old Joel Hembree[14] was riding on the tongue of his father's ox-pulled wagon when the violent jolting suddenly threw him to the ground, and before anyone realized what happened, both the front and back iron rimmed wheels ran over his little body. The train ground to a halt while despairing family members did everything possible to make him comfortable and relieve his suffering. He survived that day and night and died at two o'clock the next afternoon in the arms of his distraught parents, Joel and Sally. This was the first fatality in the 1843 wagon train.

Christian friends comforted the family and many prayers were offered, including one by the missionary, Dr. Marcus Whitman. William Newby prepared a headstone with "J. Hembree 1843" engraved on it. Newby, who had little formal education, engraved the 4 backwards. A grave was dug to the depth of four and one half feet at a site less than a hundred yards from Squaw Butte Creek.[15] The family pulled an oak dresser drawer from the wagon and placed it over the child's upper body, and then gathered short branches from nearby trees and laid them over the lower body. Earth and rocks were placed over the grave, and then Newby's headstone was reverently placed on top. A note was tied to a stick providing details on the one buried in the grave.

The next day Colonel James W. Nesmith, the future United States senator from Oregon, was in a group of soldiers that passed by this grave. His diary entry that night recorded the moment:

> Thursday, July 20—I came on ahead with Captain Gantt and an advance guard, passed over some very rough road, and at noon came upon a fresh grave with stones piled over it, and a note tied on a stick, informing us that it was the grave of Joel Hembree, child of Joel J. Hembree, aged six years, and was killed by a wagon running over its body. At the head of the grave stood a stone containing the name of the child. This is the first death that has occurred on the expedition. The grave is on the left hand side of the trail, close to Squaw Butte Creek.[16]

The grieving family could not afford to linger very long at the grave. As one account pointed out: "It was late July. The Blue Mountains of Oregon were 900 miles westward, early winter snows awaited them. Tragedy and sorrow could but momentarily impede a wagon train."[17] Nearly a thousand miles from their Missouri home and more than a thousand miles from their ultimate destination in Yamhill County, the Hembree families and their friends trudged on with heavy hearts. As far as we know, no one in the family was ever able to return to the site and care for the grave.

The passing of the years completely obscured any visibility of the headstone and other rocks over the grave. Interestingly, there is a sequel to the story. In 1961, 118 years after the death of young Joel, a Wyoming rancher stumbled across the headstone while clearing his land and asked Oregon Trail historians for help in identifying the marker. Their research confirmed that a young boy named Hembree had been buried beside the trail in that vicinity in 1843. Today, Joel's grave is in a secure location on private property and protected by a fence.[18] Visitors are welcome to visit the site where the Hembrees buried their son in the Christian hope of the resurrection.[19]

Three days after the death of Joel, the train almost suffered another fatality when they attempted to cross the north fork of the Platte River. William Newby's wagon overturned in the rapid current and floated away. He and two companions swam after the wagon and caught hold of it about a mile downstream, but the current was so strong they could not maneuver it to the shore. With darkness coming on they were compelled to let go and swim for their lives, and all three reached shore safely but at different points. They were too exhausted to call out to each other for a long time, but finally they revived and were reunited. Stumbling through the darkness, they returned to the camp "where they were received as men returned from the grave."[20] The next morning the wagon was found about three miles downstream and brought ashore. Although the Newbys had lost some possessions, they were back in the train again, and their friends had been spared the agony of a second funeral in less than a week.

Samuel Gilmore wrote a series of letters to friends back in Missouri encouraging immigration. Remembering the difficulties encountered in river crossings, he offered this suggestion: "Have your wagon beds made in such a manner that they can be used for boats; you will find them of great service in crossing streams." He also advised: "Have your wagons well covered, so that they will not leak, or your provisions and clothes will spoil." For those prospective immigrants who thought they could supply their own food by hunting and fishing along the trail, Gilmore had some blunt advice. "Make no calculations on getting buffalo or other wild meat," he warned, "for you are only wasting your time and killing horses and mules to get it."[21]

The grief-stricken Sally Hembree was due to give birth any day, and Dr. Marcus Whitman was staying close to her side. On the morning of July 26, she was "taken with violent illness," and the doctor ordered her wagon driven out of line and a fire kindled while the train continued on without her. Jesse Applegate's entry for that day reads:

> The train drove on and had already made its circular barricade for the night. There were anxious watchers for the absent wagon, they fear strange and startling practices of the Oregon doctor will be dangerous. But as the sun goes down the absent wagon rolls into camp, the bright, speaking face and cheery look of the doctor, who rides in advance, declare without words that all is well, and the mother and child are comfortable. A daughter had been born to Joel Jordan Hembree and wife, and christened Nancy Jane. Thus a death and birth had occurred in this family within nine days.[22]

The End of the Trail

For the next two and a half months, the train moved resolutely forward along the trail, arriving at Fort Walla Walla on the Columbia River in mid-October. Up to this point, the train had remained largely intact, but now with the end in sight the cohesiveness of the immigrants deteriorated. One modern account of the 1843 migration offers this analysis:

> A historian once compared the route of the Oregon Trail to a rope frayed on both ends; that is, emigrants began the odyssey from all points of the compass, followed a defined road from Missouri until they neared the beginning of settlement in Oregon, and then dispersed in the same manner as they had begun. In 1843 the final fraying began as the trains left the Umatilla River and approached Fort Walla Walla and the Whitman Mission.[23]

Some families sold their cattle at Whitman Mission and traveled downriver by boat. Others continued on in their wagons, but the trail ended abruptly at The Dalles. It was too late in the season to attempt a crossing of the Cascade Mountains, and there were not enough boats to assist all of the immigrants down the river. So everyone went to work cutting hundreds of trees and constructing rafts for the trip to Fort Vancouver. Beginning at The Dalles, the travelers floated on their rafts through 50 miles of quiet water until they reached the treacherous falls of the Columbia. This section of river, called the Cascades, witnessed a tragic accident. Alexander McClellan and two young Applegate boys drowned, and their bodies were never recovered.[24] Around the same time, William and Sarah Newby and their good friend, Chesley

Gray, almost perished in a similar boating mishap. One account of this incident reported:

> Mr. Newby, with a party of seven families, came down to the Cascades in canoes. And here they were not without their dangers. Just at sunset one evening, while they were all gliding smoothly down the river, the canoe that contained Mr. and Mrs. Newby and one young man, struck a hidden rock, throwing them out while the canoe floated on. Fortunately, they found just enough room for them to stand on the rock and wait for others of the party to go to the shore and unload and come out to their assistance. For hours Mrs. Newby, who was in delicate health, stood there knee deep and afraid to stir, as darkness had come on and they might slip off the rock. At last they were rescued and their canoe found. They were taken to the shore, where a good fire awaited them, and the next day they proceeded on their journey.[25]

The Hembree families floated down the Columbia River to Fort Vancouver. For them the end of the trail was in Yamhill County where they all took donation land claims northeast of present-day McMinnville. This area became known to other inhabitants in the county as "the Hembree settlement."[26] The Bakers settled on the site of present-day McMinnville. The Gilmores followed the Hembrees and Bakers but traveled a little farther south in Yamhill County and settled on a donation land claim three miles east of present-day Amity.

The Daniel Matheny family spent the first winter on the Tualatin Plains, but within a year they had moved to a claim adjacent to the Willamette River in Yamhill County. The Newbys and Chesley Gray pushed on from Fort Vancouver to Oregon City, arriving on November 6. By the spring of 1844, they had joined their church friends in Yamhill County, taking up donation land claims near the Bakers. The Arthur family settled along the Clackamas River in Clackamas County, where they would soon become converts to the Restoration Movement. The Burnetts remained at Fort Vancouver longer than the others. By April of 1844 they had taken a donation land claim in the Tualatin Plains in Washington County.

John and Temperance Howell gave their last name to a prairie northeast of Salem in Marion County. They settled on Howell Prairie in the fall of 1843. They were soon joined on this prairie by their married daughter and her husband. George and Elizabeth McCorkle moved to Howell Prairie in 1844, and Elizabeth gave birth to the first white child born in this settlement.[27]

The Restoration Movement had been transported to Oregon Territory. There were no preachers or churches or Christian schools to be sure—that was all in the future. For now, they were just glad to be alive. As one record of their achievement noted: "The great experiment had been far more difficult than anyone had expected. They had left Elm Grove in the spring in sunshine and song and arrived at Fort Vancouver in the late fall in darkness and lament, but the passage of time would reveal that in the process they had turned the tide of history."[28] The Oregon Trail was beaten hard by the footsteps of "The Great Migration" of 1843, and even as they staked out their donation land claims, hundreds more were ready to follow in their tracks.

Chapter 3

Confrontation with Rome
1844

In the fall of 1844 a Baptist preacher settled in my immediate neighborhood who had the published debate between Campbell and Purcell; and, as the Catholic question was often mentioned, and as I knew so little about it, I borrowed and read the book. I had the utmost confidence in the capacity of Mr. Campbell as a debater; but, while the attentive reading of the debate did not convince me of the entire truth of the Catholic theory, I was greatly astonished to find that so much could be said in its support. On many points, and those of great importance, it was clear to my mind, that Mr. Campbell had been overthrown.

— Peter Hardeman Burnett

Dr. John McLoughlin

Early in November 1843, Peter Hardeman Burnett reached Fort Vancouver and met Dr. John McLoughlin[1] for the first time. For more than two months the Burnett family availed themselves of McLoughlin's generosity while their cabin was being built at Linnton, a short distance away.[2] Here they were not without religious privileges, as Dr. McLoughlin was a very religious man and there was a church at the fort. Since Hudson's Bay was an English company, the Sunday services were those of the established Church of England. Bancroft commented on the religion at Fort Vancouver:

> The sabbath was observed with the decorum of settled society. The service of the established church was read with impressiveness by Doctor McLoughlin himself, and listened to with reverence by the gentlemen and servants of the company.

Respect for religion was inculcated both by precept and example.[3]

One factor that accounts for McLoughlin's unquestioned sovereignty over every aspect of life at this western outpost of civilization was his sheer size and his flowing white locks. Many visitors to the fort were struck by his personal appearance. One American settler in Oregon wrote:

> McLoughlin was one of nature's noblemen. He was six feet six or seven inches in height, and his locks were long and white. He used to wear a large blue cloak thrown around him. You can imagine a man of that sort—a most beautiful picture. See him walking down to his church Sunday morning—it was really a sight.[4]

Peter Hardeman Burnett was also taken with this gregarious giant of a man. "Dr. John McLoughlin was one of the greatest and most noble philanthropists I ever knew," he wrote many years later. "He was a man of superior ability, just in all his dealings, and a faithful Christian."[5] Upon further reflection, Burnett said: "I never knew a man of the world who was more admirable. I never heard him utter a vicious sentiment, or applaud a wrongful act. His views and acts were formed upon the model of the Christian gentleman."[6]

Although the Church of England was outwardly the official religion in this remote English settlement, there was another religious expression very much in evidence at Fort Vancouver, and that was Roman Catholicism. As Peter Burnett's brother, Glen Owen Burnett, would later confirm, Dr. McLoughlin was "a Roman Catholic of the truest stripe of that religion."[7] His parents were both Catholic and he had been baptized as a Catholic. But McLoughlin's "liberality of sentiment and freedom from sectarian prejudices"[8] were so natural that visitors were unaware of his religious orientation. Bancroft concluded that McLoughlin was "broad in his views" and that "he was above proselyting."[9]

Two Roman Catholic priests, Francis Norbert Blanchet and Modeste Demers, had reached Fort Vancouver five years earlier on November 24, 1838. A census taken upon their arrival had revealed 26 Catholics living at the fort and an additional 20 Catholic families living in the Willamette Valley.[10] The priests wasted no time in making their presence known. They visited the scattered settlements in the Willamette Valley, "baptized a considerable number of both whites and natives"[11] and performed several marriages. The third priest to arrive at Fort Vancouver, Pierre-Jean DeSmet,[12] came overland from St. Louis in 1842.

The first Catholic service at Fort Vancouver that Burnett attended (and possibly the only one) was a midnight High Mass on Christmas Eve of 1843. Presumably, Dr. McLoughlin was also in attendance. It is even possible that McLoughlin may have prevailed upon the Missouri lawyer to be his guest at this service. The impact of this event on Burnett's later conversion to Roman Catholicism was so crucial that it needs to be described in his own words. In 1859, Burnett published a 740-page book entitled *The Path which led A Protestant Lawyer to the Catholic Church,* and in his opening preface he wrote:

> My parents were Baptists; but until the age of thirty two, I was not a believer in the truth of Christianity. My own observation of men and things, as well as the arguments of others, at length satisfied me that the system was divine; and I at once acted upon my convictions, and joined myself to the Disciples, in 1840. In 1843 I removed with my family to Oregon. After my arrival, and while I was temporarily located at Fort Vancouver, I attended High Mass as a mere spectator, on Christmas, at midnight. I had never witnessed any thing like it before, and the profound solemnity of the services—the intense, yet calm fervor of the worshippers—the great and marked differences between the two forms of worship—and the instantaneous reflection, that this was the Church *claiming* to be the *only* true Church, did make the deepest impression upon my mind for the moment. In all my religious experience, I had never felt an impulse so profound, so touching. I had witnessed very exciting scenes in Protestant worship, and had myself often participated, and was happy. But I had never felt any impulse so powerful—an impulse that thrilled my inmost soul. I gazed into the faces of the worshippers, and they appeared as if they were actually looking at the Lord Jesus, and were hushed into perfect stillness, in His awful presence.[13]

Within two weeks, the Burnetts had departed Fort Vancouver and were on their way to their new home at

Linnton. Any fascination Peter Burnett had with Roman Catholicism was temporarily deferred as he threw himself into the rigors of developing a townsite. In less than four months, Burnett realized the Linnton venture was a losing proposition, and he moved to the Tualatin Plains in Washington County and began farming.[14] Later that fall, the subject of Roman Catholicism was again brought front and center in his life.

The Campbell-Purcell Debate

"In the fall of 1844 a Baptist preacher settled in my immediate neighborhood, who had the published debate between Campbell and Purcell," recalled Burnett, "and, as the Catholic question was often mentioned, and as I knew so little about it, I borrowed and read the book."[15] The Baptist preacher was most certainly Vincent Snelling,[16] who arrived with the migration of 1844. Snelling was the first Baptist preacher to reach Oregon Territory, and he settled a few miles north of Hillsboro in Washington County.[17] This was very close to Burnett's property.

Two of Burnett's trail companions in 1843, David Lenox and William Beagle, had been instrumental in establishing the West Union Baptist Church on the Tualatin Plains in May of 1844. This was the first Baptist church ever organized west of the Rocky Mountains, and upon his arrival on the Tualatin Plains, Vincent Snelling became the preacher for this church.[18] One history of the Baptists in Oregon commented on the Snelling-Burnett friendship: "In the middle 1840s Peter H. Burnett, a member of the Disciples of Christ . . . joined Vincent Snelling, the first Baptist minister on the Pacific Coast, in a protracted meeting to counteract Roman Catholic penetration of the territory."[19] The mental picture of Peter Burnett joining the local Baptist preacher to oppose Roman Catholic influence in Oregon seems a little out of focus, but there are several references to this protracted meeting.[20]

One can easily imagine the delight on Burnett's face when he saw a copy of the famous Campbell-Purcell debate in the sparsely settled neighborhood of Tualatin Plains. Even though the book was only seven years old, the odds of finding a copy in Oregon must have been considerable. Burnett admitted that he was predisposed to favor Campbell in this conflict, but he was eager to hear the arguments on both sides of the controversy. "All the prejudices I had, if any, were in his favor," Burnett said of Campbell, "but I knew that it was worse than idle to indulge prejudices when investigating any subject whatever . . . . I was determined to be true to myself, and this could only be in finding the exact truth, and following it when known."[21]

In January 1837, the eyes of the nation were focused on Cincinnati, Ohio, as Alexander Campbell and Bishop John B. Purcell debated the Roman Catholic religion for five hours a day over a period of nine days to overflowing crowds. Every seat was taken for every session, with more than 500 standing in the aisles and at the back, and with hundreds turned away. By any standard of judgment, it was one of the most significant debates in the annals of American Christianity. The 48-year-old Campbell was looked upon as a worthy spokesman for American Protestants in regard to this particular issue, and the 37-year-old Purcell was widely considered to be, next to Bishop John Hughes, the most influential figure in American Catholicism.[22] It was truly a monumental clash of Titans, and the published version of the debate was anxiously awaited and enjoyed a wide circulation.

Campbell came to this debate as one whose entire adult life had been devoted to "the restoration of pure, primitive, apostolic Christianity in letter and spirit, in principle and practice,"[23] and as one who was the avowed opponent of the disunity and chaos created by "the sects." And yet, Campbell seemed to clearly enjoy his role in the Purcell debate as the champion of American Protestants. He may have unwittingly set himself up for a fall when he declared in his opening remarks:

> I appear before you at this time, by the good providence of our Heavenly Father, in defense of the truth, and in

> explanation of the great redeeming, regenerating and ennobling principles of Protestantism, as opposed to the claims and pretensions of the Roman Catholic church. I come not here to advocate the particular tenets of any sect, but to defend the great cardinal principles of Protestantism.[24]

Purcell, for his part, was not impressed with "the great cardinal principles of Protestantism." He reasoned that the words "I believe in the holy catholic church" could only be used by Roman Catholics. "Applied to any other church they are a misnomer," he argued. "Protestants cannot employ such language. They are cut up into a thousand discordant and chaotic sects."[25] He must have wounded Campbell with this charge, for no one in American Christianity was more distraught over "discordant and chaotic sects" than Purcell's opponent. Campbell would have been a tougher adversary for Purcell if he had come to advocate "pure, primitive, apostolic Christianity" instead of the "principles of Protestantism."

Peter Burnett's Departure

"I had the utmost confidence in the capacity of Mr. Campbell as an able debater," Burnett acknowledged, "but, while the attentive reading of the debate did not convince me of the entire truth of the Catholic theory, I was greatly astonished to find that so much could be said in its support. On many points, and those of great importance, it was clear to my mind that Mr. Campbell had been overthrown."[26] The reading of the debate was a catalyst for further study, and he devoted the next 18 months to "an impartial and calm investigation" of the subject. On June 7, 1846, Burnett traveled to Oregon City where he was received into the Roman Catholic Church by a priest named Peter DeVos. To Burnett, he was "the heroic and saintly Father DeVos."[27]

Among the Christians in Oregon, there were, no doubt, some who assumed that Peter Hardeman Burnett would become the most visible and vocal leader of the Restoration Movement in the territory. His defection to Rome left a void that was filled by, among others, his own brothers. As it turned out, Peter Burnett did not remain in Oregon very long. He responded quickly to the California gold rush in 1848, and by 1850 he had been elected the first governor of that new state. He lived in California for the rest of his life. When he published his 740-page defense of Catholicism in 1859, he dedicated it to Archbishop John B. Purcell, "whose arguments laid the foundation of my conversion to the Old Church."[28]

Gunfight at Willamette Falls

In the spring of 1844 two Christian friends, Reuben Lewis and William H. Wilson, were working together at a sawmill in Oregon City. A number of settlers around the Willamette Falls area were complaining of bad relationships with a Molalla Indian named Cockstock and several of his fellow warriors. Cockstock was "an aggressive, impudent fellow," recalled Wilson, and "a kind of desperado, belonging to the Molalla tribe, not a chief of that or any other tribe, but the leader of a few young, reckless, hot-headed Indians."[29] The situation escalated out of control on March 4, 1844, when Cockstock and "seven or eight saucy young fellows, fully armed, came riding into Oregon City."[30] Bancroft noted they had put on war paint and were alarming the settlers with "many hostile demonstrations."[31]

An attempt was made to apprehend Cockstock, but he resisted and fired his pistol into the crowd. In an instant the air was full of bullets and arrows. Cockstock was killed in the melee, and two settlers, George W. Le Breton and Sterling Rodgers, died later from their wounds. One arrow buried itself in the hip of William Wilson. "Before I thought, I caught hold of it and tried to jerk it out," he wrote many years later, "but only partially succeeded, as it came out broken, leaving the head imbedded in the flesh, where I have carried it these fifty-six years." Wilson was convinced that it was his own bullet that had knocked Cockstock to his knees before he was killed with a rifle-barrel blow to the head. He explained:

> When Cockstock's body was examined there was found the mark of a bullet across the back of his head and neck, which

> no doubt was what knocked him down. I believe that was my bullet, for I was a good shot in those days, and from where I stood could have hit him in that way as he turned to run after firing his pistol. Colonel Nesmith thought that shot was his and I never disputed the honor, if honor it was, with him. However, ours were the only shots fired at that time. It was one of us, and it was a good job, whichever did it.[32]

One account confirms that Reuben Lewis and William Wilson were working together at the sawmill when the shooting started.[33] Wilson was standing in the middle of a wooden bridge when he fired his gun and was hit with the arrow. After the Indians fled the scene, he was urged to go to the hospital at Fort Vancouver, but he "was more afraid of the doctors" than he was of his wound. He admitted later that the wound was very painful for awhile, and that it remained tender and sore for many years.

The Pioneers of '44

A historian for the Restoration Movement in Oregon Territory might be tempted to surmise that 1844 was not a good year for the movement, since that was the year that Peter Burnett began to drift away. When C. F. Swander published *Making Disciples in Oregon* in 1928, he concluded: "The year 1844 yields no records that are of historical interest to disciples."[34] But this judgment fails to take into consideration the influx of Christians arriving in the 1844 migration. Following on the heels of the nearly 900 who came overland in "The Great Migration" of 1843, the 1844 migration attracted 1,500 people.[35] With the majority coming from the midwestern states, the Christians were undoubtedly well represented again. But once again, as with the 1843 migration, not many of the Christian families can be identified. However, five families that would have a significant impact on the growth of the church in Oregon, the Rowlands, Fords, Goffs, Hawleys, and Shaws, can be identified as coming overland in 1844.[36]

Judge Jeremiah Rowland was already a two-time widower when he came to Oregon with his three talented sons in 1844. John (age 20), Green (age 17), and Levi (age 13) were all strong Christians. John and Green would become leaders of the church in Yamhill County, and Levi, following his graduation from Bethany College, would return to Oregon to become president of Bethel College in Polk County and later of Christian College in Monmouth in the same county.

Colonel Nathaniel Ford married Lucinda Embree in Howard County, Missouri, in 1822, and one record confirmed: "He and his wife became members of the Disciples or Christian church at an early period of their married life."[37] Prior to the migration of '44, Ford worked as a surveyor, school teacher, flatboatman, clerk and later sheriff of Howard County. One account noted: "His title 'Colonel' reportedly came from his participation in a fight against Mormons at New Madrid."[38] The Fords were justifiably proud of their accomplished family. Twenty-one-year-old Marcus Ford was a graduate of Bacon College in Harrodsburg, Kentucky, the first college established by the Restoration Movement in America. Their two older daughters had attended another prominent church-related institution—the Female Seminary at Columbia, Missouri. Not surprisingly, one fellow traveler described "Ford and his entire family as being educated well beyond most others of the train."[39]

Settling next to the Fords in Polk County were their relatives and fellow Christians, David and Kezziah Goff and their children. Kezziah Goff was a younger sister to Nat Ford. Another important church family for northern Polk County was Cyrus and Eliza Hawley from Detroit, Michigan. Their nine-year-old son, John Henry Hawley, would one day become an elder in the Bethel Church and president of the board of trustees for Bethel College. The Christian cause in the Silver Creek district of Marion County was also strengthened by the 1844 migration with the arrival of 21-year-old Thomas C. Shaw. He would one day become well known in Marion County as Judge Thomas C. Shaw, and he would serve as an elder in the Bethany Church for many years.

It would be easy to overstate the significance of Peter Burnett's defection. Even if he had remained in the

Restoration Movement, the majority of his energy would have been devoted to politics and the law. Far more significant in 1844 for the future of the Restoration Movement in the Willamette Valley was the arrival of young men like Green Rowland, Levi Lindsay Rowland, John Henry Hawley, and Thomas C. Shaw.

Chapter 4

A Preacher Named Foster
1845

An unoccupied spectator, who could have beheld our camp today, would think it a singular spectacle. The hunters returning with the spoil; some erecting scaffolds, and others drying the meat. Of the women, some were washing, some ironing, some baking. At two of the tents the fiddle was employed in uttering its unaccustomed voice among the solitudes of the Platte; at one tent I heard singing; at others the occupants were engaged in reading, some the Bible, others poring over novels. While all this was going on, that nothing might be wanting to complete the harmony of the scene, a Campbellite preacher, named Foster, was reading a hymn, preparatory to religious worship.

— Joel Palmer on the Oregon Trail, Sunday, June 15, 1845

At the beginning of 1845, there were approximately 2,100 white people living in the territory that would one day become the State of Oregon. Nearly half of these settlers were less than 18 years of age, and only seven percent were 45 years old or older.[1] There were most likely about 100 Christians affiliated with the Restoration Movement in this number, but no preachers had arrived and no churches had been organized.

Oregon Christians

The best-known leaders among the Christians were 50-year-old Nat Ford on Rickreall Creek and the two brothers, 41-year-old Joel Jordan Hembree and 32-year-old Absalom Hembree in the Lafayette district. However, they were busy clearing land, planting and harvesting crops, and establishing homes. In the territorial government established by the settlers, Joel Jordan Hembree was appointed a judge in Yamhill County and his brother, Absalom, was made sheriff of the same county.[2] In the summer of 1845, Marcus Ford, the only son of Nat Ford, was elected prosecuting attorney with an almost unanimous vote of the people.[3] His father was the legislature's first choice for judge of the Supreme Court, the highest judicial office in the territory, but when he declined, Peter Hardeman Burnett was elected in his place.[4]

Apart from mealtime prayers and Bible reading in the evenings, there was not much time for organizing the religious life of the community. The Christians were too few and too scattered. But this began to change with the large migration of 1845. It is estimated that about 3,000 people came overland to Oregon that year, more than doubling the population. The Restoration Movement was immediately strengthened with the arrival of several Christian families. The historian has difficulty tracing all of them, but among those that can be identified were: Amos and Jane Harvey, James and Sarah Ramage, Stephen and Elizabeth Beauchamp, Truman and Peleuea Bonney, William and Rosanna Cole, William and Caroline Buffum, Andrew and Ann Hood, David R. and Mary Lewis, John and Nancy Foster, James B. and Nancy Riggs, Jacob and Elizabeth Hampton, William and Mary Dawson, Hardin and Eveline Martin, Isaac and Tabitha Butler, Absalom H. and Elizabeth Frier, Felix and Ellen Scott, and Samuel and Mahala Simmons. Among the Christian men arriving without families were: Elijah Bristow, Wesley Shannon, Davis Shannon, Johnson Mulkey, Enos Williams, Stanley Umphlet, David Stump, Thomas C. Davis, Francis Dillard Holman and William J. Herren.[5]

For the first time, California began to offer serious competition to Oregon. About 250 immigrants chose to leave the larger trains heading for Oregon and to take the California Trail and make their way in a southwesterly direction to Sutter's Fort. Included in this number were Elijah Bristow and Captain Felix Scott and his family. But this was just a temporary diversion, and by the following spring, Bristow, Scott, and others were on their way to Oregon to build permanent homes.

Amos and Jane Harvey

Amos Harvey was born into a Quaker family in Washington County, Pennsylvania, on March 24, 1799. Ten years later the Thomas and Alexander Campbell family arrived in the same county, and, while still a young man, Amos Harvey had an opportunity to hear Alexander Campbell preach. He was so taken with Campbell's mastery of language that he "went far and often" to hear him speak. Harvey became a "constant reader of the *Christian Baptist* and all the writings published by the great reformer," but he remained with the Quakers until his marriage to Jane Ramage.[6] According to one record: "He was expelled from the Quaker church because he was married out of harmony with the usual procedure of courtship and marriage in that church."[7]

Prior to their wedding, Amos and Jane agreed that they would read the Bible together and be completely obedient to its teachings. Many years later, at the funeral of Amos Harvey, one of their closest friends shared the story of how this agreement shaped the direction of their lives. He said:

> Shortly after this happy union, Brother Harvey took up their New Testament and began to read select passages that he thought faithfully sustained the doctrine of the Quaker people. Sister Harvey listened quite a while to his reading and remarked pleasantly "But, Amos, that is not the contract—we were to commence with the first chapter in Matthew and read the New Testament through and be governed by its teaching." "Well," said Brother Harvey, "we can soon read it through." Accordingly, they began the fourth chapter when a doubt arose in his mind in regard to the truth of the peculiar doctrine of the Friends and by the time they had finished reading the New Testament he was fully convinced of the truth of the doctrine as taught by Elder A. Campbell. It is hardly necessary to say that a great struggle then began in his mind in regard to the course to be pursued. Both promised unconditional obedience to the New Testament, without ever suspecting that they would be

> called upon to be buried in Baptism, but true to their promise and conviction they sought an opportunity to put on the Lord Jesus after the apostolic order; they were immersed by Dr. A. W. Campbell, uncle of Elder A. Campbell.[8]

In 1845, the Harveys left their home in Magnolia, Putnam County, Illinois, and began the long migration to Oregon. They were traveling with their relatives, James and Sarah Ramage. James was a brother to Jane Harvey, and his wife was a sister to Amos Harvey. The Ramages had arranged for a 24-year-old Christian named Caleb Payne, the son of a gospel preacher named Aaron Payne, to drive one of their ox-teams. The Harveys hired a teen-age girl to travel with them and take care of their small daughter, but the girl absconded with all their cash before they had traveled very far.

Despite this setback, the Harveys pushed ahead traveling in two wagons. Amos drove the lead wagon and he invited a 26-year-old bachelor named John Eakin Lyle to drive their second wagon. Interestingly, a parting friend gave Lyle a letter of introduction to a Miss Ellen Scott, whose prominent Missouri family would be crossing the trail that summer.[9] The Ramages, Harveys, Payne and Lyle attached themselves to a larger wagon train in Missouri, and it is likely that over the next few weeks they were introduced to several Christians who would become their close friends in Oregon Territory.

John and Nancy Foster

John and Nancy Foster[10] were married in Scott County, Kentucky, on August 15, 1814. They moved to the western edge of Illinois and settled in Adams County sometime in the late 1820s. John was a faithful preacher of the gospel for many years, and he preached often in Kentucky and Illinois prior to his overland journey in 1845. Although 53-year-old John Foster was probably not aware of it, he was the first preacher from the Restoration Movement to migrate to Oregon Territory. But he did not wait until his arrival in Oregon to begin preaching. According to the diary of General Joel Palmer, one of the leaders of the wagon train, John Foster was finding opportunities to preach to the immigrants early in the journey.

On Sunday, June 15, 1845, the large train consisting of 100 wagons halted on the Lord's Day and rested beside the north fork of the Platte River in western Nebraska territory. But this day of rest was far from quiet. Joel Palmer's oft-quoted diary entry for this day describes the full range of camp activities on the Oregon Trail. That evening, perhaps while sitting around the campfire, General Palmer reflected on the day and wrote:

> An unoccupied spectator, who could have beheld our camp today, would think it a singular spectacle. The hunters returning with the spoil; some erecting scaffolds, and others drying the meat. Of the women, some were washing, some ironing, some baking. At two of the tents the fiddle was employed in uttering its unaccustomed voice among the solitudes of the Platte; at one tent I heard singing; at others the occupants were engaged in reading, some the Bible, others poring over novels. While all this was going on, that nothing might be wanting to complete the harmony of the scene, a Campbellite preacher, named Foster, was reading a hymn, preparatory to religious worship. The fiddles were silenced, and those who had been occupied with that amusement, betook themselves to cards. Such is but a miniature of the great world we had left behind us, when we crossed the line that separates civilized man from the wilderness. But even here the variety of occupation, the active exercise of body and mind, either in labor or pleasure, the commingling of evil and good, show that the likeness is a true one.[11]

There is a remote possibility that Amos Harvey, who was 46, and John Foster may have met somewhere along the trail. The news that a "Campbellite" preacher was in the train would have attracted Harvey. If they did meet, they would have discovered that they had much in common. Perhaps they had an opportunity to become acquainted in conversations around the evening campfires. Although they were senior citizens in this predominantly youthful migration to Oregon, they were men with a keen vision for the future advance of the Restoration Movement. In less than a year, these two men would establish the first two congregations of Christians in Oregon Territory.

Elijah Bristow

Another train crossing the trail that summer, originating in the Illinois counties of McDonough and Hancock, contained two brothers, Davis and Wesley Shannon, and an elder in the church named Elijah Bristow. Joining this train in Missouri was Captain Felix Scott, his wife, Ellen, and their six children, including a 19-year-old daughter also named Ellen. This train could also have included another strong Christian family, Samuel and Mahala Simmons and their five sons and one daughter. Their daughter Elizabeth would marry Wesley Shannon two years later, and the young couple might have met for the first time on the trail west. We do know that this train caught up with the Joel Palmer party and camped with them somewhere along the Platte River. It was here that John Eakin Lyle and Ellen Scott met for the first time. One account speculated about this meeting:

> Hearts were young and eyes were bright and there were merry hours around the campfires at night within the barricade of covered wagons, beneath the starry, open skies. There was dawn, and noon, and twilight in which to talk of adventure and dangers braved and of the high sweet hopes that were winging toward the land of the setting sun. Love came then as now with roseate promise.[12]

The parties separated on the trail, but John and Ellen would meet again the following year in Oregon where their wedding would be performed by Glen Owen Burnett. Later in this journey, Elijah Bristow and the Scotts would divert to Sutter's Fort in California, but not before Elder Bristow had made an indelible impression on young Wesley Shannon. Many years later, at a gathering of pioneers, Shannon reminisced about the overland journey:

> In the spring of 1845 we left Knox county for Oregon. On our third day's travel we met Elijah Bristow, who was leaving home for the sunset west. Our acquaintance began at that time and soon ripened into an intimacy which ended only with his life. Almost from the first moment of our acquaintanceship he was the recognized leader of the party, and so continued until he left the Oregon road and took the trail leading to California. To lose "Uncle Bristow," as we affectionately called him, was a

> source of deep regret to the entire company, for we all entertained towards him a warm filial affection. He was a natural leader of men, and had his ascendant over all who approached him, not from any advantage in early life, for he was not a man of culture, but from natural qualities, cordial and graceful manners, elevated mind, fearless spirit, generosity and unassailable integrity. He was a grand specimen of the old Roman style . . . I have a sincere pleasure in recalling . . . this old pioneer friend and Christian gentleman.[13]

A letter has survived from Elijah Bristow to his wife and children, dated June 18, 1845, and written from somewhere along the trail. In a touching admonition, the 57-year-old elder in the church pleaded: "Stand firm in the Brotherhood and let your Polar Star be Truth. O Remember this again, I say, Remember this -- tell the Brethren I have not forgotten them." He signed off by sending best wishes from the Shannon brothers and closed with "Yours in all that pertains to Immortality, E. Bristow."[14]

The Barlow Toll Road

After Bristow and the Scotts diverted to California, most of the others continued on to The Dalles, where they faced a difficult choice. This was still the end of the trail for wagons, because the Barlow Toll Road around the south side of Mount Hood to the Willamette Valley was one year in the future. Shooting the rapids of the Columbia River was as treacherous as ever, but a majority of the immigrants chose this option. David and Mary Lewis (and their five children under the age of 12) were able to navigate the Columbia River, and they spent the winter in Oregon City. Amos and Jane Harvey (and their six children under the age of 12) were also successful in getting down the river. They made it to Oregon City where Amos found employment with Dr. John McLoughlin.

William and Caroline Buffum chose to remain with their leader, General Joel Palmer. "When we got to The Dalles we found we would be delayed for some time, for the want of boats," he remembered, "as none had yet come up the river from Fort Vancouver or the other settlements."[15] At this moment of indecision, Samuel K. Barlow arrived "with the news that we could make a road over the mountains, on the south of Mt. Hood; that a party of them could cut the road nearly as fast as the teams would travel. So we made up a party we thought sufficient, and started."[16]

Signing on to actually help create the famous Barlow Road with Barlow himself was more than the Buffums had bargained for. They nearly perished in the ordeal, but they were ultimately successful in reaching the Willamette Valley.[17] After Palmer had sent the Buffums on ahead to safety, he encountered Andrew and Ann Hood on a rainy hillside. He praised them (in his diary) for sharing "their scanty supply" of food and supplies with two families who had lost everything. The Hoods were former Irish Roman Catholics who had migrated to Canada and then on to United States where they lived in Ohio and Missouri. Sometime during their residence in Ohio and Missouri they had become affiliated with the Restoration Movement, and in 1847 they would invite Glen Owen Burnett to preach the gospel of Christ to a large audience in their Oregon City home.[18]

The John Lewis Clan

One wagon train coming across the trail in 1845 included the extended family of John and Elizabeth Lewis who were originally from Kentucky, but who had lived briefly in Missouri. They had intended to be part of the 1844 migration, but when the time came to start overland they decided that they were not adequately prepared for such a rigorous journey. They temporarily camped on the Missouri prairie for a year and raised a crop. They left Missouri on May 1, 1845, traveling with the party of Captain Levin English, and arrived in Oregon on November 1, having spent six months on the trail. The Lewises were traveling with their six children, four of whom were married, and a large number of grandchildren. Several members of this clan were Christians.

The captain of the Lewis part of the train was the oldest son, 31-year-old David R. Lewis. He was migrating to Oregon with his wife, Mary Redden, and their five children. Five more children would be added to their family in Oregon. A wagon overturned during the difficult Platte River crossing, but for the most part the Lewises had a safe journey. To discourage some Indians who were harassing the train, one of the Lewis children was painted with spots to simulate measles and then displayed prominently in the back opening of the wagon. When the Indians saw the child with the dreaded disease, for which they had no defense, they immediately fled to safety.[19]

Less than two months into their journey, the Lewis clan stopped along the banks of the Little Blue River in Nebraska Territory to celebrate a wedding. Margaret May Lewis, the fifth child of John and Elizabeth and just two weeks shy of her 19th birthday, was married to Charles Brown on Saturday, June 21. This was just six days after John Foster was recorded as preaching along the Platte River, and about the same time that John Eakin Lyle and Ellen Scott were meeting for the first time. It is not known who performed the wedding, but it is quite possible that it was her older brother, David R. Lewis. As an early justice of the peace in Oregon Territory he performed several marriages, and he may have been a justice of the peace prior to his migration to Oregon.

Toward the end of the journey some of the younger men in the train, tired of the monotony of travel, wanted to leave the security of the trail and explore the countryside and hunt buffalo. David R. Lewis, who was in a position of responsibility, refused to grant approval for such a risky venture. "There is danger from the Indians," he warned. "If you go it must be at your own risk. I won't endanger the lives of the women and children by stopping to hunt for you if you fail to return." But the young men persisted, and they were never heard from again either on the trail or after the train reached Oregon. In later years, Lewis told his grandchildren that the hardest thing he ever had to do was resist the pleadings of the men's families to stop the train and send out a rescue party.[20]

When the Lewis clan reached Oregon they settled in Polk County and established the village of Lewisville. The patriarch and his wife, John and Elizabeth, died within the first decade. But "Uncle Davy" and "Aunt Polly," as David and Mary were called, were prominent leaders in the Restoration Movement in Oregon for nearly half a century. When Mary died in 1897, an obituary account included this tribute: "Grandma Lewis had been an earnest Christian for 77 long years, and when the time came, she was willing and ready to go. Her last days were devoted to her Bible, and as her spirit departed, a pleasant smile wreathed her face."[21]

The Meek Cutoff

Not everyone remained with Joel Palmer, Levin English, David R. Lewis and the other captains in the main wagon train when they departed Fort Boise on the last leg of the journey. At Fort Boise, an experienced mountain man named Stephen Meek entered the picture. He promised the immigrants that he could guide them through a short cut to the Willamette Valley, in exchange for a fee. This would enable them to avoid the weary trek through the Blue Mountains and the treacherous journey down the Columbia River.

Meek's confident proposal had the ring of authenticity, and a large number of wagon drivers made the ill-conceived decision and veered off the main trail to follow this guide who appeared to be so knowledgeable. It is estimated that about 200 families, involving between 1,000 and 1,500 people, left the old emigrant trail at the hot springs in Vale and turned west up the Malheur River. They soon became lost and wandered for weeks through the high desert of Central Oregon.[22]

Several Christian families were in the trains that made this fateful decision. The ones that can be identified were: James and Nancy Riggs (with eight children), Jacob and Elizabeth Hampton (with eight children), David and Jeanette Pugh (with a married son, William Porter Pugh, and seven other children), Hardin and Eveline Martin, William and Mary Dawson (with two small daughters under 3), Absalom and Elizabeth Frier (with three small children and a new-born baby), John and Nancy Foster (with seven children), Isaac and

Tabitha Butler (married six months earlier on March 14) and John and Theodosha Herren (with eleven children).[23] One account reflected on their decision to follow Stephen Meek:

> It was a big mistake. The route along the Malheur River offered little grass for the livestock, and it was murder on the animals' feet. The emigrants sometimes went days without water. Fever struck the party and some children died. To top it all off, the travelers were lost, and Meek finally had to go ahead to find a rescue party.[24]

Actually, there were more than children who died. There were several letters reporting that as many as 50 people had died, but only 24 deaths have been documented by historians. The known dead included both young and old, but the majority were children. The exhausted survivors, who had been tortured by hunger, thirst, and disease, straggled into The Dalles on the Columbia River during the second week of October. From the time they left the main trail on August 25, they had been wandering aimlessly for more than six weeks. Most of them, like John and Nancy Foster and their family, spent the winter at The Dalles.

The migration of 1845 probably doubled (if not tripled) the number of Christians in the territory. More importantly, in the persons of John Foster and Amos Harvey, it brought two men who were ready to organize churches. Over the next three years, until the debilitating drain caused by the California gold rush, the Restoration Movement would dominate the Christian landscape in this rapidly developing land of promise.

Chapter 5

The Ancient Gospel in Oregon 1846

I am happy to be able to say that the "ancient gospel" has been planted in Oregon, and numbers are enlisting under the banner of King Immanuel . . . . In March we organized a congregation upon the Book alone – and this was the first congregation built upon this foundation in the Territory. We numbered at first but thirteen members . . . . Brother John Foster who wintered at the Dalles, came in, in the spring, and settled on the Clackamas, east of the Willamette, and organized a small congregation, consisting of his own family and two or three other members.

– Amos Harvey to Alexander Campbell

Amos and Jane Harvey arrived in Oregon City in the fall of 1845 and began making inquiries about the location of various families of Christians they knew were in the territory. When they learned that a few families had settled on the Yamhill River west of the Willamette River, they determined to join them and establish a church. They left Oregon City by canoe in January 1846 and landed near present-day Dayton in Yamhill County.[1] They settled first on a donation land claim near Lafayette but eventually moved south and settled five miles below Amity in a region called the Bethel Hills.[2]

Yesterday's News

Within two months, in March of 1846, the Harveys had succeeded in calling together a congregation of thirteen members. They were absolutely convinced that this was the first congregation established by the Restoration Movement in Oregon. However, at the very moment of their success, Alexander Campbell was preparing to publish an article in his *Millennial Harbinger* that would tell a much different story. This was the first time Oregon was ever mentioned in Campbell's paper, and unfortunately the story was littered with misinformation. The Harveys were stunned by the report, and Amos pronounced it "entirely untrue."[3]

The story ran in the April 1846 issue of the *Millennial Harbinger*. A large and dramatic headline proclaimed "THE GOSPEL IN OREGON" in all capital letters. It was followed by a page and a half article in the form of a letter dated March 6, 1846, and written by a Bethany College student from Missouri named Moses E. Lard.[4] The story he told about the beginnings of the Restoration Movement in Oregon was a fascinating blend of truth and error.

In summary, Lard told the story of "a most exemplary Christian" named Peter Hardeman Burnett who migrated to Oregon and found himself confronting "the arrival of ten Catholic Priests from the soil of Italy." How could he and others "oppose the wily tricks, or expose the pious frauds of this knavish pack" without help? According to Lard:

> In the midst of their dilemma a Baptist brother, whose name is Snelling, visited our brother B. to consult as to the best measure to be adopted. A union of effort was at last proposed by the latter, when it was answered upon the part of the former, that any thing like a creed would be an effectual bar to a union. To this our noble Baptist brother promptly responded, "Upon the Bible, and that alone, am I willing to unite in the cause of truth." Then all party distinctions ceased, and these two noblemen plighted their faith in the cause of eternal truth—brother B. to proclaim the word, and brother S. to set "things in order."[5]

In Lard's happy ending to this story, Burnett and Snelling immediately called a large meeting of the settlers and Burnett proclaimed "the original, unvarnished gospel" of Christ with astonishing results. The entire audience, with only five exceptions, made the good confession and "gave their allegiance to Prince Messiah." This moved Lard to close with a rhetorical flourish:

> Thus does the Lord ultimately bring good out of the base designs of men. And now where, but a short time since, naught was heard but the panther's shriek, or the red man's whoop, is heard to ascend, morning and evening, the voice of prayer and thanksgiving from many a joyous cottage. Thus in a land remote is planted the standard of the ancient apostolic faith—the Star of Bethlehem has risen to light up forever this region of deepest gloom, and another link in that great moral chain with which God will finally belt the world, is established.[6]

The story was not completely groundless. Burnett and Snelling were both neighbors and friends, and as mentioned in chapter 3, they evidently participated together in at least one well-publicized protracted meeting in their district. But the main thrust of the story, that Burnett and Snelling had not only joined forces to combat the menace of Roman Catholicism, but were now working together to promote "the original unvarnished gospel," was sadly misinformed. When the story hit Oregon a year later, it was greeted with dismay by the Christians.

The First Churches

In a spirit of gentleness, and without a note of rancor, Amos Harvey related to Alexander Campbell the true facts of what had transpired in Oregon. He began:

> Brother Campbell—In the Millennial Harbinger of April, A.D. 1846, brought into this country by one of last year's immigrants, I saw an article headed "The Gospel in Oregon," which, I am sorry to say, so far as relates to the labor and co-operation of Judge Burnett and Elder Snelling in building up the ancient gospel, is entirely untrue. P. H. Burnett, Esq., has himself joined the Roman Catholics, and been married in

> Oregon by a Catholic Priest to the wife of his youth. And Elder Snelling has been, and still is, engaged in assisting to build up the "Missionary Baptist Church," not "upon the Bible alone," but upon the Bible and a little summary of doctrine solemnly adopted.[7]

This must have been a difficult letter for Campbell to publish. His journal had been responsible for creating a false euphoria about the advance of "the gospel in Oregon," and now he was faced with the disappointing facts about both Burnett and Snelling. But Harvey was not writing this letter to moan about Burnett and Snelling. He wanted to trumpet some good news. "But I am happy to be able to say that the 'ancient gospel' has been planted in Oregon," he thundered, "and numbers are enlisting under the banners of King Immanuel." This really was good news, and Campbell's readers had their first accurate picture of "the gospel in Oregon" as Harvey explained:

> I came to this country late in the fall of 1845, and learned that a few families of Disciples lived on Yam Hill, west of the Willamette river. I settled there in January, and in March we organized a congregation upon the Book alone—and this was the first congregation built upon this foundation in the Territory. We numbered at first but thirteen members. We met, as the disciples anciently did, upon the first day of the week, to break the loaf, to implore the assistance of the heavenly Father, to seek instruction from his word, and to encourage each other in the heavenly way. Brother John Foster, who wintered at the Dalles, came in, in the spring, and settled on the Clackamas, east of the Willamette, and organized a small congregation, consisting of his own family and two or three other members. During the summer five persons in our neighborhood made the good confession, and were immersed for the remission of sins; and about the same number in the neighborhood of brother Foster.[8]

Harvey's narrative provided accurate information on the first two churches established in Oregon Territory. The first congregation began on the Yamhill River in Yamhill County in March, and the second congregation began on the Clackamas River in Clackamas County just a few days or weeks later, but still in the spring. And most encouraging of all, both congregations had experienced numerical growth with the baptism of converts in the summer of 1846. The "ancient gospel" had truly been planted in Oregon soil.

There is also some slight evidence that a third congregation was established that summer in a schoolhouse south of present-day Carlton. The source for the origin of this congregation is Green L. Rowland, a son of Judge Jeremiah Rowland and an older brother to Levi Lindsay Rowland. He claimed that he was present at the beginning of this congregation on Saturday, August 1, 1846, and that the congregation met in a schoolhouse on the Ruel Olds property and that baptisms took place in the Yamhill River just below the Andy Hembree place. He told this story to F. M. York, who in turn passed it on to C. F. Swander for inclusion in his 1928 book, *Making Disciples in Oregon*. Swander accepted it as factual. Green Rowland was 19 years old in the summer of 1846, and his testimony should be given credibility.[9] There certainly were enough Christian families in Yamhill County to have two congregations in 1846—one meeting around Whiteson and Amity, and the other around the Hembree and Rowland settlements ten miles to the north.

The McBride-Burnett Train

The migration of 1846 was considerably smaller than the 3,000 of the previous year. It was probably no more than 1,500, as more immigrants were choosing the option of settling in California.[10] With three congregations already functioning, the Oregon Christians were looking forward to an increase in their preaching ranks from the influx of new residents, and they were not disappointed. Among the large extended families that arrived that fall were the McBrides and Burnetts, and with them came 44-year-old Dr. James McBride and 37-year-old Glen Owen Burnett. McBride and Burnett had preached powerfully in Missouri for a number of years, and they were the best of friends. Their families had traveled together in the overland journey, and the two men had preached together along the trail. Upon arrival in the new land, they would quickly earn a reputation as worthy proclaimers for the Christians of Oregon Territory.

The McBrides and Burnetts left Missouri together in a party that consisted of 12 families and about 22 wagons. Another Christian family in this party was Zebedee and Sophronia Shelton. Sophronia was a sister to Mahala McBride. The party crossed the Missouri River at St. Joseph on April 16, and when they reached the rendezvous point in Indian Territory on April 20, they merged with several groups to form a train of about 100 wagons. Within a short time the train had swelled to 130 wagons.

Fortunately, John Rogers McBride, the 14-year-old son of Dr. James McBride, kept a book of reminiscences on the journey that has been preserved.[11] According to John McBride, the train of 130 wagons was a cumbersome caravan and difficult to organize properly. This led the McBride-Burnett party to pull off and move on in advance of the larger column. "Thenceforth our camp or train embraced twenty-eight teams with about sixteen families," wrote McBride. "We remained together until we reached the Willamette Valley in the last days of September."[12]

McBride's journal is full of fascinating stories. On one occasion a terrible storm arrived suddenly at midnight. The party was drenched with rain and buffeted by hurricane-like winds, and in the confusion that followed, many oxen and horses escaped. All were recovered the next day except two horses and a mule belonging to Dr. McBride. Ordering the train to continue on to the next campsite, McBride and two others went in search of the lost animals. After traveling 15 miles the search party accidentally stumbled into a grove where 150 Indians were encamped. As Dr. McBride later recounted to his son, in a matter of seconds "the Indians sprang for their horses, each grabbing a handful of earth and clapping it on his head, and yelling like demons they mounted and darted toward the white party."

The three frightened men retreated on the same route they had just traveled. They rode furiously for 15 miles and narrowly beat the Indians to the rear of the wagon train.

When word reverberated through the slow-moving wagons that McBride and the others could be seen in the distance "pursued by more than one hundred savages," pandemonium broke out. As John Rogers McBride remembered it:

> The consternation that prevailed on this announcement can hardly be described. Women shrieked and children ran in fright to bury themselves in hiding in the wagons. Men blanched with fear, and then began to look for their arms to meet the foe. Glen O. Burnett . . . took command of the movements of the train, and ordered it "corralled."

The teen-aged McBride was especially impressed with the leadership demonstrated by his mother. "My mother was a brave little woman about thirty-six years old, had passed through the early Indian disturbance in the state of Missouri when a child," he wrote, "and now that she realized that my father was safe and by her side, was as self-possessed as if she had marched over a hundred battle fields. She was excited but not unnerved, and the calm way she went to assisting in the preparations for defense at once quieted all our fears." Seeing the fortified train corralled and ready to fight, the Indians halted their pursuit and refrained from attacking. Within half an hour the crisis had passed.[13]

Later in the journey a woman in the party named Mrs. Cromwell became desperately ill one night, and Dr. McBride was called as a physician to her side. With her husband and three young children watching anxiously, McBride tried valiantly to save her life. His efforts were unsuccessful, and she died as the first streaks of dawn were coming over the horizon. John Rogers McBride was deeply affected by this death, and he wrote:

> My first knowledge of her illness was on waking at daylight and hearing the sounds of weeping in the tent near by, occupied by the Cromwell family. I shall never forget the grief of that motherless boy. Nothing could comfort him. His moans and sobs were heartrending; and the wild grief of the young girls, with the more quiet but deep anguish of the husband and father, left an impression on me that time cannot efface. She was buried that day on the lonely banks of the turbid river. Death on the plains in those days was a terrible

> thought. Hundreds of miles in the deep wilderness, nothing but the rushing of the waters, the tread of the Buffalo or of the savage around the spot; wolves sneaking over the plains ready the moment the grave was abandoned to commence the work of digging for the remains. It was thoughts of these things that made death so awful on the plains. Placed in a neat coffin made from portions of a wagon box used for the purpose, in a grave dug by loving hands, the lady was laid to rest forever.[14]

Glen Owen Burnett led a prayer at the grave, and the train moved on. "I have witnessed many funerals," John Rogers McBride wrote later, "but not one since in a long life so solemn, so gloomy and terrible as this." The Cromwells continued on for another 250 miles, but a life in Oregon without their mother and wife had no appeal for them. At Fort Laramie they decided to turn around and return to their Missouri home.

Another member of the party who was keeping a journal was Barnet Simpson, and he provided a glimpse of the religious character of the group when they arrived on the Sweetwater River in Wyoming Territory. Simpson wrote:

> When we came to the Sweetwater, Ben decided to have the train lay over Friday, Saturday and Sunday for washing clothes, repairing wagons and drying out supplies that had got wet. We had three preachers in our train. My father was a Primitive Baptist, Elder McBride was a Campbellite, and I have forgotten what the other preacher was, but each of them preached while we laid over on the Sweetwater.[15]

Simpson could not remember the name of the third preacher, but it was obviously Glen Owen Burnett. McBride and Burnett had preached together on occasion during their years in Missouri, and they were looking forward to preaching together upon their arrival in Oregon Territory. It was only natural that they would look for an opportunity to preach together on the Oregon Trail.

Christian Friends in Yamhill County

As the McBride-Burnett train rolled past the Boise River, they were overtaken by two men on horseback who were on their way to the settlements along the Yamhill River in the

Willamette Valley. They agreed to deliver a letter from Dr. James McBride to the Hembree families in that area. McBride was concerned that his teams were showing signs of exhaustion, and he asked the Hembrees to meet his party at The Dalles with fresh teams. John McBride recorded the results of the letter:

> Our teams had shown such signs of exhaustion even then that my father had written to some old friends of his, who had preceded us some years and resided there, to meet us, if possible, at The Dalles with fresh teams. They had received the letter, and with a promptness which none but pioneers could emulate, and a generosity that makes gratitude a pleasing burden, they had answered the call, and three yoke of fresh oxen and two horses laden with provisions and supplies came to our assistance.[16]

It was a dramatic moment when help arrived. "We saw two men descending a long, steep hill in front of us, driving oxen before them," recalled John McBride. "The camp wondered at such a sight; but my father had been for several days hopefully looking for what now occurred." The two Christians who had quickly responded to the news that the McBrides and Burnetts were nearing Oregon and needed help were Joel Jordan Hembree and Chesley B. Gray. "That was a joyful meeting of old friends," wrote John. "J. J. Hembree and C. B. Gray were the messengers, and the contributions were from a settlement that joined to aid their brother immigrants."[17]

The remainder of the journey was comparatively easy. With Hembree and Gray leading the way, the McBride-Burnett party made it to Oregon City in eight days. From there, the Burnett families[18] went to the Tualatin Plains to find their brother, Peter Hardeman Burnett, and to hear for the first time the stunning news of his conversion to Roman Catholicism three months earlier. The McBrides pushed on to Yamhill County which, according to John, "was forty miles over a new road through a heavy forest." With a note of triumph, John wrote: "A few more hours, and we were under the roof of an old friend of other days, A. J. Hembree, and the long journey was at an end."[19] This was a reference to

Absalom J. Hembree, younger brother of Joel Jordan Hembree, who was now serving as the sheriff of Yamhill County.

The Pioneers of '46

The impact of the McBride and Burnett families on the growth of the Restoration Movement in Oregon Territory was so enormous that it is easy to overlook the fact that many other strong Christian families came overland in 1846. Special mention should be given to the Cox families who settled west of Silverton in Marion County and gave the name of "Bethany" to their new community. They were devout Christians, and they arrived with a dream of establishing their own "Bethany College" in their new home. One historical record noted:

> There was a time when all the beautiful country westward from Silverton, through Bethany and across Silver Creek and Pudding River to the Prairie, was owned by members of the Cox family, who came in 1846. Peter Cox acquired land just west of Silverton. John T. Cox was a little further west. Gideon S. Cox was on Pudding River. Samuel S. Cox was south of Silver Creek. Elias Cox had a claim nearby.[20]

The first settler to stake a claim in what would become Lane County, was Elijah Bristow. In the spring of 1846, Bristow and the Felix Scott family left Sutter's Fort near Sacramento, California, and moved north to Oregon Country. During the month of June, four men on horseback, including Bristow and Scott, rode through the Willamette Valley in search of prime farmland. When they reached a point between the Coast and Middle Forks of the Willamette River where the panorama of mountain and vale is breathtaking, Elijah Bristow is reported to have declared, "This is my claim! Here I will live, and when I die, here shall I be buried." Bristow named the spot Pleasant Hill.[21]

Along with Wesley Shannon, Bristow returned to his claim in July and began constructing a log cabin and making other improvements on the land. The Bristow cabin, completed later that fall, was the first permanent dwelling erected in Lane

County. Meanwhile, Ellen Scott had been reunited with John Eakin Lyle and a wedding date set for November. Lyle was boarding with the Nat Ford family on Rickreall Creek, and he had opened a school called "Jefferson Institute." The school was housed in a log cabin erected for that purpose about one mile west of the Ford place.[22] One account reported, "A pulpit was placed in Jefferson Institute" making it useful "for church and for all general gatherings."[23]

One Missouri preacher who wanted to come overland in 1846 was 59-year-old Thomas Riggs. A family history confirms that although he was once a Baptist minister, he had "adopted the theological views of Alexander Campbell."[24] He started with his family for Oregon, but he became ill and died on the west bank of the Missouri River. He was buried at Iowa Point in the northeast corner of Kansas Territory.[25]

Several members of the Graves family, most of whom were Christians, came overland in 1846. The most significant to this story was 22-year-old Charles B. Graves, who married the daughter of Glen Owen Burnett in 1850. Another important addition to the Restoration Movement in Oregon was the family of Truman and Peleuea Bonney, who settled in Marion County. Their 21-year-old son, Bradford Sherwood Bonney, later became an elder in the church. As all of these Christians journeyed across the trail in the late summer of 1846, somewhere behind them was the ill-fated Donner party that was moving slowly toward their destiny in the snow-capped Sierra Nevada Mountains of California.

The Applegate Trail

Beginning in 1846, there were two new options for travelers bound for the Willamette Valley—the Barlow Toll Road and the Applegate Trail. The Barlow Road gave travelers the opportunity to keep their wagons and avoid the Columbia River. This road ran between The Dalles and Oregon City and curved around the southern side of Mt. Hood and crossed the Cascades. The toll was five dollars per wagon and the trip could be made in a week if the weather cooperated. The majority of travelers arriving at The Dalles, like the McBride-Burnett train, took advantage of this new road.

The Applegate Trail was named for its founders, Jesse and Lindsay Applegate. The Applegate brothers had each lost a 10-year-old son in the same tragic rafting accident in the cataracts of the Columbia River in 1843, and they were determined to create a safer route for future immigrants. It was an ambitious attempt to give travelers the option of a southern approach to the Willamette Valley. Although this route was a little farther in actual mileage, it had the advantage of avoiding the Blue Mountains and the treacherous Columbia River. One account describes the route of the Applegate Trail:

> The southern route left the main emigrant trail in Idaho, passed over a tip of Utah, then followed the Humboldt River in Nevada to a point southwest of Winnamucca, then northwest through the Black Rock Desert, over a tip of California, then into Oregon. The final 300 mile segment extended north for the breadth of Oregon into the Willamette Valley.[26]

Several Christians were in the very first wagon train to take the Applegate Trail, and the leaders of this train were Christians. This was the train led by brothers-in-law Harrison Linville and Medders Vanderpool. Vanderpool was married to Margaret Linville, a younger sister to Harrison. Among the other Christians in this train were John Bird Bounds and his wife, Elizabeth Lovelady Bounds. Their oldest daughter, Nancy Bounds Linville, was married to Harrison Linville. Except for one 77-year-old man, the oldest travelers in the train were Richard and Mary Linville, both in their 70s. They were the parents of Harrison Linville, Margaret Vanderpool and Catherine Crowley.

Thomas and Mary ("Aunt Polly") Lovelady were also in this train. He was a brother to Elizabeth Bounds. Three other Christian families in this train were Absalom and Mary Ann Faulconer, Robert and Sarah Lancefield, and John Burris and Emily Smith. John Burris Smith was a gospel preacher, and his arrival brought the number of Christian preachers in Oregon to four.

On August 9, a few miles west of American Falls, the members of this train met Jesse and Lindsay Applegate traveling east. The Applegates not only persuaded them to take the new route that had just been scouted out and marked, but they arranged for two guides, Levi Scott and David Goff, to travel with them part of the way. David Goff was the brother-in-law of Nat Ford and a Christian. He lived on Rickreall Creek in Polk County. Bancroft comments on the first wagon train to traverse the Applegate Trail:

> The first companies to take the road after the explorers were those led by Harrison Linville, and a Mr. Vanderpool; and although upon them fell the severer toil of breaking the track, and reopening the road over the Cascade Mountains made by Applegate's company, which a fire had filled in places with fallen timber, they arrived in the Rogue River Valley on the 9th of October.[27]

Another account of this pioneering train on the Applegate Trail commented: "The travelers found a shortage of food for their livestock, a scarcity of game for their own food and backbreaking toil in building a track for their wagons."[28] Unfortunately, they also had to confront the horrors of death on the trail. In a period of just ten days, Harrison and Nancy Linville each lost a parent.

Elizabeth Bounds, Nancy's mother, died from the privations of the trail on November 13 and was buried the next day. She died near present-day Roseburg in Douglas County. After burying her on the trail, the wagons passed over the road several times to obliterate any sign of the grave. This was done to eliminate any possibility of Indians robbing her grave or of wild animals digging up her grave. On November 22, during the dangerous fording of the Calapooia River, one of the Linville wagons overturned and Mary Linville, Harrison's 72-year-old mother, was drowned. She was buried that same night.

But no individual in this party suffered more than 44-year-old Catherine Linville Crowley, an older sister of Harrison Linville. Her daughter, Matilda, and son, Calvin, along with his wife and child, all died on the plains before the train ever detoured to the Applegate Trail. They probably died from typhoid or mountain fever. Calvin died on July 26 and his body was wrapped in a sheet and buried without a coffin. After detouring to the Applegate Trail, Catherine's 16-year-old daughter, Martha Leland Crowley, died of typhoid on October 18 in present-day Josephine County. Two more daughters, Melissa and a nameless baby, died on the same day, October 27. Finally, her husband, Thomas Leland Crowley, died of pneumonia on December 4 in the vicinity of Creswell, a little south of present-day Eugene in Lane County. With her remaining five children, all 12 years old and younger, Catherine Linville Crowley continued resolutely on to a new home and a new beginning in Polk County.[29]

At Home in Polk County

Two wagons slowly pulled by exhausted oxen came to rest in front of "a small log hut" in the Bethel Hills at dusk on October 9, 1846. Glen and Sarah Burnett had finally reached their Oregon home. Years later, Glen remembered the moment:

> As the wagons neared the lonely spot, the wife and mother of the seven children belonging to the family, gazed with intense interest upon all the surroundings visible at that hour of the evening. Many long months of patient toil, and hardships had marked her journey across the wide plains, in quest of a little spot on earth she could call a home. We stopped in front of the opening, in the side of the rude hut; and for the first time, began to take what little of this earth's goods we had, from the wagons, and place those tattered fragments in our little house. This finished, and our frugal supper partaken of, we layed our weary bodies upon the floor to rest. Sweet was that night of sleep to us all. The morning came, and with it new responsibilities. I will never forget the sensations of that eventful period of my ministerial life.[30]

Despite the burdens of carving out a living in a sparsely settled land, Burnett was eager to begin preaching. He and Dr. McBride had already met Nat Ford and agreed to preach at the "Jefferson Institute" near his home on Rickreall Creek. Accompanied by "Brother Andrew Hembree," McBride and Burnett fulfilled this appointment one Saturday in October.

While there they met John Eakin Lyle, who was preparing to wed Miss Scott. Burnett joined them in marriage on November 3, 1846.[31] Around the same time they received an invitation from John Foster to come over and preach in a protracted meeting for his small flock that was meeting on the Clackamas River about seven miles from Oregon City, and a date was agreed on for later in November.

Some of the wagons in the Linville-Vanderpool train reached their destination in Polk County in late November, and others were delayed until late December. The Linvilles spent their first winter in Polk County at Jesse Applegate's place on Salt Creek. Harrison Linville soon selected a donation land claim on the Luckiamute River not far from where John and David Lewis and their wives had settled the year before. The Lewis families had taken possession of rectangular claims of 640 acres for each couple on land formed by the forks of the Luckiamute River. John and Elizabeth settled on the west bank and David and Mary on the east bank. The north-south road that formed the border between the two claims became the main street of Lewisville.

The Lovelady s were thrilled to see the Glen Owen Burnett family again. They had left Missouri together and had traveled together on the trail for many miles before the Loveladys and others had decided to detour on the Applegate Trail. The Loveladys settled temporarily on land adjacent to the Glen Owen Burnett family, and on occasion the two Christian families ate dinner together. Burnett reported that "the daily bill of fare" for the two families consisted of "wheat bread without shortening, sometimes meat if a deer had been killed, Irish potatoes roasted in the ashes or boiled in clear water, and boiled wheat with salt, and for a beverage coffee made of parched peas."[32]

However, the Loveladys soon moved to a more desirable claim two miles east of present-day Dallas along the banks of Rickreall Creek. This made them neighbors to the Fords, Goffs, and Lyles. The support of the Loveladys greatly strengthened the little congregation that was meeting on Sundays in the Jefferson Institute log cabin, and Glen Owen

Burnett kept up a regular appointment of preaching for this congregation. Thomas Lovelady became active in civic affairs. In fact, the first three judges appointed in Polk County were Thomas Lovelady, Harrison Linville, and David R. Lewis.[33] The Christians had arrived in Polk County in significant numbers, and they were making their presence known.

Dr. Zedekiah Davis and his wife, Virginia, sold their Kentucky farm and many of their possessions and started overland in the 1846 migration. They had been married in Kentucky in 1824, were personal converts of "Raccoon" John Smith, a legendary preacher in the Restoration Movement, and were full of zeal for planting the cause of primitive Christianity in Oregon Territory. But tragically, Virginia died en route somewhere along the Oregon Trail in Utah Territory. Bereft of his companion of 22 years, Dr. Davis continued on alone and settled near Buena Vista in Polk County where he assisted Harrison Linville in establishing a congregation in 1848.[34]

Oregon's First Gospel Meeting

Dr. James McBride and Glen Owen Burnett agreed to meet at Absalom Hembree's place in late November and then travel together to John Foster's neighborhood to conduct their first gospel meeting in Oregon. About noon on the day before they were to meet, Burnett began walking the twenty-five miles to the Hembree settlement. "As I walked alone along the winding pathway leading to a crossing on Yamhill River, called Edson's Ford, I thought of many things," he wrote later. "My family I had left in the care of God, who would take care of them, with the record of his will in my pocket. I passed along, being cheered with the happy thought, that it was a blessed privilege to preach Christ; a thing I have regarded as a great favor."

Burnett became thoroughly soaked fording the deep waters of the swollen Yamhill, but he pressed on. "About sundown, I got to Jordan Hembree's, as true a man as I ever met, and . . . with Brother Jordan I remained all night," he recalled. The next morning he met Dr. McBride right on schedule. McBride came riding up on a horse, and Burnett accepted the loan of a horse from Absalom Hembree.[35] Buoyed by the encouragement of Christian friends and neighbors, McBride and Burnett rode off to meet John Foster.

The picture of Dr. James McBride and Glen Owen Burnett riding horseback through the Willamette Valley to preach Christ in November 1846 is an exciting one. Since Amos Harvey was not a preacher, John Foster did not travel much, and John Burris Smith had not settled in yet, these two preachers from Missouri carried the hopes of Oregon Christians with them as they rode confidently toward a rendezvous at the Clackamas River. Fortunately for the cause of Christ, their friendship was deep and unshakable. Their individual gifts complemented one another, and they thoroughly enjoyed being in the arena together. Burnett summed it up later: "I take pleasure in saying, that never in my long intercourse with preachers, has it been my lot to be cast in company with a brother whose breast contained a nobler heart than palpitated in the bosom of Dr. James McBride."[36]

They spent that evening "safely sheltered at old brother Arthur's on the Clackamas," and the meeting began in the same house the next day. William and Milley Arthur, pioneers of "The Great Migration" of 1843, were recent converts of John Foster. "Many brethren came to the meeting from the surrounding country," reported Burnett. In addition to the Fosters and Arthurs, Burnett was personally encouraged to see 67-year-old Stephen Beauchamp[37] from Missouri in the audience. "I knew him well," explained Burnett, "having some years before baptized him, and his household, near Barry, in Clay County, Missouri." More than 30 years later, Burnett reflected on that first great Oregon meeting with McBride and wrote:

> Our meeting I think resulted in much good to the cause of Christ. In looking over in memory, the names of the dear ones present, I find all have passed over the river, save three or four. I am almost left alone to tell of the joys of that meeting. When the meeting closed, we all with cheerful hearts started home, and on our arrival, found all well. Long time have I

> been permitted to live for Christ since this, and many have been the pleasant refreshments from the presence of the Lord.[38]

All things considered, 1846 had been a very encouraging year for the Christians in Oregon. They had survived the potentially devastating loss of Peter Hardeman Burnett, and witnessed the organization of their first three churches. More importantly for the long term, they had welcomed the arrival of three powerful proclaimers in Dr. James McBride, Glen Owen Burnett, and John Burris Smith. The ancient gospel had been planted in Oregon Territory and the multitudes were beginning to assemble. The best years were just around the corner.

Chapter 6

The Multitudes Are with Them

1847

This brother took occasion in his sermon to say some pretty hard things about Alexander Campbell, and those who sympathized with him in his great work of reformation . . . . It may be as Dr. McBride and my humble self had just arrived in the Territory, he thought it best to warn his brethren as one said of old, "these that have turned the world upside down have come hither also, and Jason has received them."

– Glen Owen Burnett

Sunday, June 13, 1847. There is a great meeting today, judging from appearances, at the city hotel, as it is called. The Campbellites are holding their first great meeting in this place. They have the multitude with them.

– Reverend George Gary

When the Glen Owen Burnett family arrived in Oregon in the fall of 1846, they went immediately to Tualatin Plains to see the Peter Hardeman Burnett family. Glen and Peter had married sisters, and the two families had not seen each other for more than three years. This long-anticipated joyful reunion was strained for everyone from the start, however, when Peter and Harriet announced that they had just become Roman Catholics.

Encounter with the Baptists

During this difficult visit, Glen attended his first church service in the new land. A Baptist preacher from Oregon City, whose name was Hezekiah Johnson, was scheduled to preach at a schoolhouse in the neighborhood and Glen went out to hear the gospel of Christ. What followed was a surprisingly rude welcome to Oregon Territory. As Glen remembered it:

> This brother took occasion in his sermon to say some pretty hard things about Alexander Campbell, and those who sympathized with him in his great work of reformation. Why Mr. Johnson took this occasion to forecall public opinion against us is just what I never learned. It may be as Dr. McBride and my humble self had just arrived in the territory, he thought it best to warn his brethren as one said of old, "these that have turned the world upside down have come hither also, and Jason has received them."[1]

Burnett's reference to the story in Acts 17 is enlightening. He and McBride are likened to Paul and Silas, preaching gospel truth with encouraging results in a strange land. Johnson is likened to the Judaizers in Thessalonica, using unfair tactics to prevent the people from hearing the truth. "It has always seemed to me to be a little unmanly to take advantage of the situation when no reply could be heard," thought Burnett, "to say hard things about others calculated to lessen them in the estimation of the people."

Burnett had expected fairer treatment from the Baptists, and he was surprised at the animosity exhibited toward the Christian movement. "At that time I think our Baptist brethren were as strong in that vicinity as any of the surrounding denominations," he wrote later. "But as touching the Disciples, they were everywhere spoken against."[2] This experience in Washington County, where the Christians had fewer members, may have caused Burnett to overstate the level of opposition. The Christians were numerically strong in Yamhill and Polk counties, and they may not have been "everywhere spoken against" in those districts.

The result of this experience was that McBride and Burnett were invited to speak at the schoolhouse in the spring of

1847—to defend themselves as it were. "To benefit the few, and to correct improper impressions superinduced by the untimely expose of what was supposed to be a terrible heresy" was the reason Burnett gave for the journey. The congregation was waiting for them when they arrived, "expecting doubtless to hear some strange thing." What they got was a strong dose of what McBride would have called "Bible Christianity." "The doctor, ever ready for any emergency, discoursed to the audience upon the simple Gospel of Christ," Burnett wrote approvingly. "His manner was so simple and plain, and so full of the New Testament." This theme was continued a second day, "and some believed and were baptized."[3]

Two of the most respected Baptists in Oregon, John Holman and William Beagle, were in the audience for both lessons. Burnett called them "substantial Baptists" and said they "doubtless had heard what Brother Johnson had said about us the previous fall in the same house." These veterans of "The Great Migration" of 1843 "were both smitten by the sword of the Spirit" when McBride preached. "As we rode away from the meeting one day in company with Brothers Holman and Beagle," recalled Burnett, "the last one named raised his hands up towards heaven and exclaimed, 'I never saw anything so plain.'" The Christians felt vindicated. "Our prime object was to present Christ in the Gospel as the only Savior of sinners, and to accept his teachings as found in the New Testament Scriptures as the only safe guide to salvation," said Burnett.[4]

The positive reception at Tualatin Plains led McBride and Burnett to return to that neighborhood "several times during the summer and fall months" of 1847. "Amongst the goodly number that threw off all human appendages, and gave adherence to Christ alone and to the word of his grace, was Dr. Evans," reported Burnett. Evans had been a Baptist minister for several years, but upon hearing McBride and Burnett, he chose to cast his lot with the Christians. But the partnership was short-lived: "He in a short time went into the ministry with us, and preached with great acceptance, and bid fair to become very useful to the cause of Christ; but alas! soon fell a victim to death in the infancy of his usefulness to the cause."[5]

During the winter of 1846–47 the labors of McBride and Burnett were concentrated in Polk County at the Jefferson Institute. A beautiful stream called La Creole flowed through that neighborhood where the Nat Ford and David Goff families lived. "Our preaching soon began to make an impression upon the hearts of the people, and they came from ten to fifteen miles around to hear," enthused Burnett. "The La Creole afforded a most convenient stream in which to perform the action called baptism, its waters were remarkably clear and pure."[6] When Reverend George H. Atkinson, the first Congregational Minister sent to Oregon, visited this area on Saturday, May 15, 1848, he wrote in his diary: "We came to the farm of Col. Ford and Mr. Goff. These are on the North side of the La Creole. These gentlemen are Campbellites. They have meetings at their house. Mr. Burnett, Mr. McBride & others preach there."[7]

Encounter with the Methodists

The Christian movement took such a hold in Polk County in 1847 that the Methodists began to despair about making an effort. One of their ministers, a man named Parish, attempted to make inroads in the county, and Burnett invited him to preach one Sunday to the Christian congregation assembled at Jefferson Institute. It evidently was a modest effort. "If my memory is not at fault," Burnett wrote, "he never came back there to preach again. It seemed that from that day they gave up that side of the Willamette, at least in Polk County, to us."[8] This was not the case in Salem, on the east side of the Willamette, where the Methodists had the largest church in town. However, Burnett was given a small window of opportunity in Salem, and he made the most of it. Years later he described what happened:

> Tidings soon reached the ears of a Mr. Shaw that had come out to Oregon the same year that I had, that our Methodist brethren had said we could do nothing in Salem.

> Mr. Shaw wrote to me, inviting me to Salem, and offering to seat off his large cabinet shop for me to preach in. Accordingly I sent him the time when I would be there. The day came at last for me to start. I had some misgivings in going to the very headquarters of the Methodistic temple, but I went, and when I arrived, his shop was all seated in good style, and a fine congregation in attendance. I spoke twice that day, dwelling largely upon the sixth chapter of the Roman letter, and in harmony with the teaching of the chapter, I led I think six into the water, and planted them in the likeness of the Saviour's death, by burying them in baptism unto his death. Thus a small beginning was formed for the church of Christ, that stands to this day in the city of Salem.[9]

The Methodist minister in Oregon City was the Reverend George Gary, and his diary provides accurate information on when McBride and Burnett decided to make an effort in that community. For Sunday, June 13, 1847, Reverend Gary wrote: "There is a great meeting today, judging from appearances, at the city hotel, as it is called. The Campbellites are holding their first great meeting in this place. They have the multitude with them." McBride and Burnett were drawing such large crowds on that Sunday that Reverend Gary added, "Our congregation is, of course, considerably smaller than usual."[10]

The Pioneers of '47

Meanwhile, the very large migration of 1847 was on its way to Oregon Territory. It is estimated that about 5,000 people reached the Pacific Northwest that year, with the majority settling in Oregon. Bancroft attributes this high number to the fact that Great Britain and America had recently settled the boundary dispute,[11] and there were favorable prospects that a donation land claim law would soon be passed by the United States Congress.[12] Bancroft adds, "Of the 5,000 persons added to the population of the country at this juncture few names have been preserved."[13] This unfortunately is also true of the Christian population. From subsequent references to the strength of the Restoration Movement in Oregon Territory, we know that a large number of Christian families were included in the migration of 1847, but only a small number can be identified.

John Downing was just 20 years old when he came overland in 1847. During part of the journey his wagon train traveled with one led by John Shotwell Hunt, and one night "a little frolic" was staged around the evening campfires. John Downing danced a jig on that occasion much to the delight of the weary travelers. One member of his appreciative audience was 13-year-old Temperance Hunt, and two years later they were married on April 12, 1849.

The donation land claim selected by John Downing was located about two miles north of Sublimity in Marion County. He lived on this property for 40 years until his death in 1887. Downing was described by one of his descendants as "a devout member of the Christian Church," and he served as a deacon in the church for many years.

One caravan on the overland trail that summer, comprising about 40 wagons, was made up mainly of residents from Oskaloosa, Iowa, and several members of this party were Christians. Among the Christians were William and Betsy Matlock and Isaac and Eliza Baker. Wiley Chapman and his wife, Ruhamah Stockton, were Christians from Pike County, Illinois, but they attached themselves to this train of Iowans, and the 37-year-old Wiley was chosen captain.

While traveling through Wyoming Territory, little 4-year-old Elizabeth Baker was afflicted with camp fever and died. She was buried at Fort Bridger. At the Grand Ronde Valley in eastern Oregon, Ruhamah Chapman also contracted camp fever and died suddenly. Her husband was left with four little children. Eliza Baker took care of these four children during the remainder of the journey. A few years later, Wiley Chapman married Ellen Matlock, the daughter of William and Betsy Matlock.

A father and son from Iowa, Isaac and Elias Briggs, migrated with their families to Lane County in 1847. They were devoted to the Restoration Movement and eager to see it gain a footing in this new land. They settled temporarily near Elijah Bristow at Pleasant Hill, but within three years they had founded the community of Springfield, across the Willamette River from Eugene.

The Briggs family had been prominent Christians in Iowa for a decade, and one history of the Restoration Movement in that state noted:

> In the year 1836, a time when Iowa, Wisconsin and Minnesota were part of the territory of Michigan, when the population of this vast empire consisted of a few settlements of rugged pioneers scattered along the shore of the Mississippi, David R. Chance, preached at the cabin of Isaac Briggs, near Lost Creek, in Lee County. In July of that year eight members were enrolled, and Lost Creek church was organized, and I believe the fire on its altar has never gone out. This was the start of "Our Plea" in Iowa.[14]

Three Mulkey brothers, Thomas, Johnson, and Luke, brought their families overland from Missouri in 1847. They were nephews to the John Mulkey who had joined forces with Barton Warren Stone in 1810. All three of the Mulkey brothers were leaders in the church, and Thomas was a fine preacher. But tragedy struck at the end of the journey when Thomas contracted mountain fever while crossing the Blue Mountains in eastern Oregon. His son wrote later, "My father died near the foot of Laurel Hill, in the Cascade Mountains. They buried him there by the side of the road." Thomas Mulkey had just passed his 40th birthday. His shaken family continued on to Clackamas County and spent the winter in the vicinity of John Foster's congregation. Johnson and Luke went to Benton County and took donation land claims near present-day Corvallis.[15]

As mentioned in chapter 4, Johnson Mulkey first came to Oregon alone in 1845. He returned to Missouri in the fall of 1846 with glowing accounts of what he had seen. He was not only responsible for leading his two brothers back to Oregon, but he persuaded his good friends and neighbors, Isaac and Margarette Headrick, to also move west. One record noted of Isaac, "He was a member of the Christian church and a man of deep piety, tender hearted and kind. It was said of him that the story of Christ's crucifixion always brought tears to his eyes and his Bible was his daily solace." The same record called Margarette "a woman of deep religious convictions."[16] Nine of their children came with them, including 20-year-old Josephine, who would marry Thomas C. Shaw (see chapter 3) in 1850. The Headricks settled on Howell's Prairie where they continued to live until their deaths in the early 1880s. They were stalwart members of the historic Bethany Church, where their son-in-law, Judge Thomas C. Shaw, was an elder for many years.

Alfred and Phoebe Stanton were married in Indiana in 1831, and they had lived in that state for 16 years when they started overland with their five children in 1847. After reaching Oregon they filed on 640 acres just east of Salem. Alfred was an experienced farmer and nurseryman, and he ran a nursery in Salem for the rest of his life. The Stantons were among the charter members of the Salem Church, and Alfred was a member of the board of trustees for Christian College in Monmouth for several years.

Joseph Warren Downer was just 22 years old and single when he came overland in 1847. He settled in Polk County, married Eleanor Ann Pigg, and became a leader in the Bethel Church. He served on the board of trustees of Bethel College for a number of years. He was a saddler by trade and conducted a business in Salem for several years. During those years, he was one of the leaders of the Salem Church. "He spent the best energies of his manhood in the service of the Master," wrote a friend. "He had so imbibed the Master's Spirit that his old age was kindly and beautiful."[17]

Samuel and Elizabeth Markham had been married in Michigan and lived for awhile in the town of White Pigeon near the Indiana state line. Elizabeth was a devout member of the Church of Christ in that community, but Samuel was never a member of any church. Inspired by the vision of a new beginning in the great American West, the Markhams joined a caravan of wagons that were heading west that spring. One account reported: "The Markhams moved from Michigan to Oregon in 1847 with a company of Campbellites."[18] Unfortunately, it is not possible to identify the other Michigan Christians traveling in this party.

The Markhams settled in Oregon City and built a log cabin with a store attached on the front. Their son, Charles Edward Markham, (he later took the name Edwin) was born in this log cabin on April 23, 1852. Although he did some preaching as a young man when he was a student at Santa Rosa Christian College in California, Edwin Markham was destined to become better known for his literary achievements. He was once called "the most talked-of literary man in America" by *The Saturday Evening Post*, and "America's greatest poet" by *The New York Globe*.[19]

Among the new Christian families who settled in Yamhill County that fall were Robert and Eliza Kinney, James and Betsy Toney, and Owen and Melissa Turner. Jesse Dutton Walling and his wife, Eliza Ann, settled in Polk County. A number of young unmarried men who later became church leaders were also in the '47 migration. Isaiah Johns settled in Yamhill County and became a leader in the McMinnville Church, and Orlando Alderman, who was just a teenager, settled in Marion County. Alderman developed into a capable preacher for the Christians in the 1860s when he moved to the northeast corner of Polk County.

Alexander Vance McCarty

One party of Christians traveling west that summer included the McCarty families from Missouri. John and Rosanna McCarty had been married in Boone County, Missouri, in 1824 and were migrating to Oregon with their nine children. Their oldest son, 22-year-old Alexander Vance McCarty, had married Jane Bounds the year before, and they were traveling with an infant daughter named Elizabeth Ann. Jane's parents, John and Elizabeth Bounds, had traveled to Oregon the year before, but Elizabeth had died in the Umpqua Valley before they reached their destination.[20]

River crossings were always dangerous, and the McCarty wagon train experienced this first hand when they attempted to cross the Platte River. A. V. McCarty's wagon floated away during the crossing, taking his wife and infant daughter with it. Disaster was averted when "friendly Indians" swam to catch the wagon and tore a hole in the wagon-top. They rescued Jane and "resuscitated the drowning baby girl."[21] This precious little girl, the first grandchild in both the McCarty and Bounds families, undoubtedly received special care that evening around the campfire.[22]

A document has been preserved in the Hembree family papers in the Oregon History Center that contains a list of Christian families that contributed money to enable the A. V. McCarty family to migrate to Oregon. Despite his youth, the evangelistic potential of A. V. McCarty was well known to many Missouri Christians who had gone to Oregon, and they were eager to secure his talents for the cause of Oregon evangelism. Of the 19 contributions, the largest were $50 from Joel Jordan Hembree and $20 from William T. Newby. Those who contributed $10 each to the McCarty fund were Robert Crouch Kinney, Jacob Hampton, Jeremiah Rowland, Owen P. Turner and Milton Lacy. The other contributors were John Carlin, John Gordon Baker, James Thomas Hembree, Wayman Clark Hembree, Melinda Paine, Samuel F. Staggs, Dr. A. B. Westerfield, Jacob Wisecarver, Absalom B. Faulconer, William Toney, James A. Campbell and Thomas Faulconer.[23]

Within a few short years, Alexander Vance McCarty would emerge as one of the most effective evangelists in the Christian movement in Oregon and California. His contemporaries called him the "silver tongued" orator. One historian said he "had a wonderful memory, a musical voice, and could preach for two hours without tiring his hearers."[24]

Hugh McNary Waller

Another large party of Christians, traveling in 23 wagons, originated in Pittsfield, Illinois. One record confirmed, "Nearly all in this train were members of the Church of Christ."[25] Among the family names connected to this train were: Waller, Landess, Scholl, Whitley, Johnson, Richardson, Ritchey, Humphrey, and Barrow. The Lewelling brothers from Iowa were also members of the Church of Christ, and their families merged with this train somewhere along the trail. By far, the most significant person in this train for the future of the church in Oregon was a gospel preacher named Hugh McNary Waller. He had begun preaching at the age of 13 and had preached for nearly 17 years in Illinois and Missouri when he started overland to Oregon. He arrived in Oregon City on his 30th birthday, September 9, 1847. In a ministry that would span nearly a half century in Oregon, H. M. "Mac" Waller would baptize thousands of converts.

The news that Mac Waller was moving to Oregon Country was received with excitement by the preachers who were already at work in the Willamette Valley. One account reveals their glad anticipation:

> Before he arrived in Willamette Valley he received messages from Brethren James McBride, of Yamhill county, Glen O. Burnett, of Polk county, and Foster, living up on the Clackamas, asking him to come to their places and aid them in meetings. Not having any shelter for the winter, he could not accept their courtesy till he had cast about for a home. He left his mother and brother at Oregon City while he and others took a journey up the river as far as Salem and Corvallis. On returning to Oregon City, he preached a few times for the brethren there.[26]

Aaron Payne

Mac Waller and A. V. McCarty were not the only preachers in the 1847 migration. Aaron Payne, a 58-year-old veteran preacher from Putnam County, Illinois, came overland that summer. Like Elijah Bristow, Aaron Payne had fought with General Andrew Jackson at New Orleans in the War of 1812. He also fought in the Blackhawk War of 1832 and was a member of the Light Horse Dragoons. He was wounded at the battle of Bad Axe, near the place where Blackhawk was taken prisoner. Aaron Payne married May Murphy in 1815 and they raised a family of 11 children. His wife's death in 1846 prompted him to follow many of his friends and family who had moved on to Oregon.

Caleb Payne, the son of Aaron Payne, had migrated to Oregon as a 24-year-old bachelor in 1845. As he was a Christian, he looked for an opportunity to travel with members of the church. He was fortunate in being able to travel with two fine Christian families, Amos and Jane Harvey and James and Sarah Ramage, and he worked with John Eakin Lyle in driving two of their wagons. Caleb Payne settled in Yamhill County on a donation land claim three and a half miles east of Sheridan, and in 1850 he married a Christian named Malinda Toney. Her parents, James and Betsy Toney, were members of the McMinnville Church.[27]

When Aaron Payne arrived in the fall of 1847, he considered living with his son near Sheridan, but he decided instead to settle near the McBrides on Panther Creek. He did not waste any time in making his presence known. In the fall of that year, he was the catalyst in organizing a congregation of 15 members at Blackhawk Schoolhouse. Later he represented Yamhill County in the legislature. Although he was considered elderly by the standards of the time, Aaron Payne served the church in Oregon for 36 years until his death in 1883.

Thomas Crawford McBride

One of the most unexpected arrivals in the migration of 1847 was the elderly father of Dr. James McBride. Thomas Crawford McBride was one of the patriarchs of the Restoration Movement—a man who had preached side by side with Barton Warren Stone and John Mulkey in the early years of the movement. He had been the first Christian preacher to migrate to Missouri, and he had devoted more than 30 years of his life to building up the cause in that state. The death of his wife and the removal of most of his family to Oregon had left a vacuum in his life, and in the spring of 1847, he packed his meager belongings and made the difficult overland journey to rejoin his family. He traveled with his son-in-law and daughter, Caleb and Margaret Woods. Others in the party included a son, Dr. Thomas McBride, two grandsons, Thomas and Isaac Davis, and their 28-year-old brother-in-law, Elisha Bedwell. McBride celebrated his 70th birthday on July 25, 1847, while traveling on the Oregon Trail.

The McBride family was stunned when their aged father and grandfather and four others arrived at the log cabin on

Panther Creek on September 13. They had no advance word that he was coming. John Rogers McBride wrote in his journal:

> My grandfather was then seventy years of age, and his hair was white as winter's snow. He looked wearied from his long travel of two thousand miles, and he had ridden for forty-one days continuously on horseback, sleeping in his blankets on the ground at night without shelter, to find us.

His traveling companion, Elisha Bedwell, became one of the first converts to the Restoration Movement in Oregon and married into a devout Christian family.[28] Although plagued with failing eyesight, Thomas Crawford McBride was not ready to be put out to pasture. The veteran proclaimer of the gospel was eager to be of service to the cause, and he preached in Oregon Territory for a decade before his death in 1857.

Blackhawk Schoolhouse

When Dr. James McBride and Glen Owen Burnett arrived in Oregon Territory in the fall of 1846, three small congregations were already meeting. Two of these were near the Yamhill River in Yamhill County about ten miles apart, and the third was John Foster's group in Clackamas County. The fourth and fifth congregations in 1847, although not formally organized and probably not meeting every week, were the ones at the Jefferson Institute in Polk County and at the schoolhouse at Tualatin Plains in Washington County.

A sixth congregation, meeting at Blackhawk Schoolhouse six miles northwest of present-day McMinnville in Yamhill County, was the one called together by Aaron Payne in the fall of 1847. The 15 charter members included Payne, six couples, and two women. The six couples were: James and Mahala McBride, William and Mary Dawson, William and Sidney Burnett (a brother to Glen Owen Burnett), Andrew and Mary Shuck, Franklin and Ann Martin, and John and Martha Carlin. The two women were Catherine Blevins Baker, the wife of John Gordon Baker, and Rebecca Calhoun.

A seventh congregation was probably meeting occasionally around the Bethany and Howell's Prairie district. It would have included the various Cox families, the Simmons, the

Headricks, and Thomas C. Shaw. Wesley Shannon married Elizabeth Simmons on July 15, 1847, and they would have been a part of any church gatherings.

Clatsop Plains

A possible eighth congregation is shrouded in mystery. Ezra Fisher, a Baptist missionary sent out to Oregon by the American Baptist Home Missionary Society and serving on the Clatsop Plains (Astoria area) in Clatsop County, wrote in his diary for October 20, 1847, "The Campbellites are industriously engaged in making proselytes."[29] Perhaps several families of Christians had migrated to this district, but if so, none of them can be identified now. If they truly were as "industrious" as Fisher claimed, they probably established a church. However, Fisher had just returned to the Clatsop Plains from an extended visit to the Willamette Valley, and he was most likely referring to the Christians in that region. There is no record of a Christian Church being established in Clatsop County during this period.

Oregon City

It was Jesse Applegate who suggested to Glen Owen Burnett that the Christians ought to hold a meeting in Oregon City in December 1847, when the legislature would be in session. He thought "it would be a favorable time to hold a meeting there," remembered Burnett, "for in this way our plea would be made known to the leading men of the new territory."[30] In addition to the governor and other elected officials, there were 18 elected members of the legislature. At least two of those legislators, Marcus Ford from Polk County and Absalom Hembree from Yamhill County, were fellow-Christians whom Burnett knew very well.

On Burnett's first night in town, he was welcomed by Wilson Blaine, the Presbyterian minister, and invited to preach in the Presbyterian building. "The next evening we had the satisfaction to meet a large audience in Mr. Blaine's own church," reported Burnett. "Among the audience we saw

Mr. Blaine and Dr. McLoughlin, a man of excellent standing, a fine scholar, and deservedly popular with the people, and, with all, a Roman Catholic of the truest stripe of that religion." For the remainder of the week, Burnett was offered the use of Legislative Hall where the government sessions were being held during the day. On Sunday morning he preached from Matthew chapter 16 and elaborated the fact that Christ was the foundation upon which his church would be built.

Following this service, Burnett received an invitation to attend the Catholic service at two in the afternoon and he consented to attend. To his surprise, the priest preached from the same text in Matthew 16. "His effort was directed in trying to make Peter the foundation, instead of Christ," Burnett commented. "One can see the importance with Catholics in trying to make Peter the foundation, because if he is not the foundation, their claim to be the church of Christ is vain."

When the Catholic service was over, Burnett "went to a brother's house whose name was Hood; he and his wife had left Catholicism and had given their adhesion to the church of Christ." This was a reference to Andrew and Ann Hood, who had been born in Ireland and reared as Catholics. They had become Christians while living in Missouri prior to their migration to Oregon in 1845 (see chapter 4). Burnett was surprised again when Dr. John McLoughlin and the Roman Catholic priest suddenly dropped by for a visit. He anticipated a confrontation, but none occurred. That evening Burnett preached to a full house, and one woman confessed her faith that Jesus was the Christ and made known her desire to be immersed into Christ. The decision was made to baptize her that very evening at the Willamette Falls. In Burnett's description:

> About the hour of 10 o'clock that dark and cloudy night, could be seen a long and silent procession, with torches in the hands of those who went before, winding their way to the landing below the falls on the river. This strange spectacle excited some of the people on the opposite side of the river, who came over in boats and lanterns. What does all this mean? And how is it we hear this beautiful singing? . . . The place was below the falls of the river, and as the water rushed

> in fury with one long leap to the bottom below, and the mountains returning the confused echo, we led the lady down into the water, and gently laid her beneath its yielding waves.[31]

This faithful group in Oregon City, including Andrew and Ann Hood and Elizabeth Markham and others, brought to eight the number of congregations meeting by the end of the year.[32] Fueled by the large influx of Christian families in the migration of 1847, several other districts were capable of supporting a congregation if someone would organize it. The fields were white and ready to harvest, but would there be enough laborers?

The Cayuse Indian War

Before the territorial legislature completed its deliberations in December 1847, the news of the Whitman massacre reached Oregon City. The Cayuse Indians had been overwhelmed by the large companies of white settlers traveling through their lands, and their numbers had been decimated by the ravages of disease carried by the whites. The measles epidemic, brought by the immigrants of 1847, was the final outrage. Many Indians were convinced that the whites had deliberately introduced the diseases to kill off the Indians and take their land, and they blamed the missionaries, Marcus and Narcissa Whitman, for creating this situation.

On November 29, 1847, the Whitmans and 12 other persons were atrociously murdered at the Whitman mission. When the horrible news reached the Willamette Valley, volunteers began mobilizing for war with the Cayuse Indians and a force of several hundred soldiers was recruited and supplied with arms. The main result of the Cayuse Indian War of 1848 was to make the Oregon Trail safer for the long line of immigrant trains passing through north-central Oregon.

Several Christians volunteered for service in the Cayuse Indian War, including George William Burnett, John T. Cox, Isaiah Matheny, Caleb Payne, Thomas C. Shaw, John Downing, and William and Silas Pugh. According to one record, the log cabin that housed the Jefferson Institute in Polk County was used as a recruiting station for the war effort.[33]

A Harvest without Workers

As 1847 turned into 1848, the sheer number of Christians in the territory was encouraging, but the workmen were few. The Christians could only count on three outstanding proclaimers—McBride, Burnett, and Waller—who would travel tirelessly throughout the Willamette Valley preaching Christ. A fourth, young A. V. McCarty, would be ready to join them soon. John Burris Smith would preach much more in later years, but he was not traveling much at the present. There were three other wonderful preachers in John Foster, Aaron Payne, and the elderly Thomas Crawford McBride, but they rarely traveled outside their own neighborhoods. Amos Harvey and Elias Cox did not preach often, but they possessed fine organizational skills. Young men like Marcus Ford and Thomas C. Shaw would have made fine preachers if they had not chosen to devote themselves to the law and a life of public service. In addition, the unfortunate deaths of Dr. Evans and Thomas Mulkey had robbed the Christians of two talented workers for the harvest.

When Amos Harvey wrote to Alexander Campbell in April 1848, to report on the progress of the cause in Oregon Territory, he said:

> The immigration of 1846 brought two proclaimers (brothers Dr. James McBride and Glen O. Burnett) who, though encumbered with the care of providing for large families, in a new and uncultivated country, have spent much of their time in proclaiming the word. Their labors have been particularly blessed, and their success beyond anything that could have been anticipated in a new and thinly settled country. The immigration of last year brought three other proclaimers. Our meetings are well attended, and generally more or less make the good confession at every meeting where the gospel is proclaimed. There are many calls from various neighborhoods which the teaching brethren are entirely unable to fill. Would to Heaven that we had a number more brethren of teaching talent and Christian character, to teach the way of life and salvation to an inquiring population![34]

Chapter 7

At Home in the Willamette Valley 1848

As I look upon that trio who began the work in Oregon, I can not do less than to thank God that in the very incipiency of this movement three such lovely men gave it form and character, Waller, McBride, Burnett – Oregon thanks God for them.

– G. M. Weimer

The Campbellites and the fern are taking the Willamette Valley.

– An Anonymous Preacher

When Americans talked about "Oregon" in the late 1830s and early 1840s, they were referring to the vaguely defined, expansive country that today encompasses the entire states of Washington, Oregon, and Idaho. As the territory became better known, however, most of the interest began to center on the Willamette Valley, and by the time nearly 900 people came overland in "The Great Migration" of 1843, "Oregon" and the Willamette Valley were practically synonymous. There were minor exceptions. Some chose the Clatsop Plains near Astoria, and others settled in the Umpqua Valley south of Eugene, but the overwhelming majority of immigrants in the 1840s and 1850s felt right at home in the lush meadows and forests of the Willamette Valley.

Meandering across 110 miles, from Portland in the north to Eugene in the south, the fertile Willamette Valley lies nestled between the Coast Range and the Cascades. Salem's central location in the valley led to its selection as Oregon's capital city. This valley is a region of mild climate and abundant rain, with enough sunshine to offset the gray winters. The majestic snowy peaks of Mt. Hood and Mt. Jefferson are dramatic landmarks, and they are visible most days of the year. A. V. McCarty spoke for the Christians living in this western Eden when he wrote:

> If ever there was a place in the wide creations of God, where his glories are displayed on the most magnificent scale, this lovely valley seems to me to be the place. Here you contemplate its variegated vales, jubilant hills, lofty mountains, and deep, shady forests of hoary pines, and lofty aspiring firs. Situated on some convenient stand point in the elysian valley, clothed with a spirit-like calmness, one can behold everything to incite to the discharge of duty.[1]

Large numbers of Christians settled in this idyllic garden between 1843 and 1848. "We now outnumber in the American population any of the sects," boasted Amos Harvey in April 1848, "and if we only live up to our high profession, Oregon will soon become as noted for the religion of Jesus Christ, as it already is for its ever-verdant pastures, its grand and varied scenery, and its mild and healthy climate."[2] The Christians had the numbers on their side, but who would organize them in Willamette Valley for what McCarty called "the discharge of duty"?

A Triumvirate of Preachers

One of the most strategic meetings of the Restoration Movement in Oregon took place on Sunday, May 7, 1848. The three proclaimers, McBride, Burnett, and Waller, agreed to meet at the log schoolhouse that housed Jefferson Institute and officially organize the believers there by appointing elders and deacons and charging the church to meet every week to celebrate the Lord's Supper. One account commented on Waller's role at Jefferson Institute: "Here he soon organized a Church of Christ, the first organized church west of the Rocky Mountains. This was on the first Lord's Day in May 1848.

Here elders and deacons were chosen and scripturally ordained."[3] There may have been eight or more different congregations of Christians meeting by this date, but the article might be correct that this was the first congregation organized with its own elders and deacons. In that early day when the Christians were mostly in a disorganized condition, this would have been seen as a major accomplishment.

While all of these Christians were together at one place and perhaps experiencing some euphoria over seeing the first church scripturally organized, a question arose as to the proper strategy for organizing the work in the Willamette Valley. Specifically, the issue of "who should take the lead in the work in the Valley" was addressed, and there was a vigorous discussion of options available. The most attractive option was to involve Mac Waller more fully in the work. He was only 30 years of age and still single. According to one report: "At last, Brother McBride said: 'I now proclaim Brother H. M. Waller as pope of the Church of Christ in Oregon.'"[4] The meeting broke up, no doubt, with gales of laughter. The future looked bright for Oregon Christians. Forty-five years later, one observer looked back on that historic meeting at Jefferson Institute on May 7, 1848, and offered a belated tribute:

> As I look upon that trio who began the work in Oregon, I can not do less than to thank God that in the very incipiency of this movement three such lovely men gave it form and character, Waller, McBride, Burnett—Oregon thanks God for them.[5]

The Christians living in the southern part of Polk County, led by Harrison and Nancy Linville, invited Mac Waller to visit their area in 1848 and organize a church. The McCartys and Bounds were living in this district, as were David and Mary Lewis, David Stump, and Dr. Zedekiah Davis. The Linvilles offered the use of their fine residence situated on the Luckiamute River for a meetingplace. Harrison Linville operated a ferry across the Luckiamute, and as a result, the main county road running from Nat Ford's place south into Benton County led past the Linville house. Waller accepted the invitation, and a congregation was set in order on the Luckiamute.

Constant Preachers on the Circuit

Very early in the settlement of Oregon Territory a persistent saying began to make the rounds: "The Campbellites and the fern are taking the Willamette Valley."[6] It may have been coined by the Reverend George H. Atkinson, a Presbyterian minister who frequently traveled throughout the length and breadth of the Willamette Valley.

In the summer of 1848, Reverend Atkinson rode on a horse through Yamhill County in search of Presbyterians. His diary entry reflected his frustration: "I cannot learn of any Presbyterians or Congregationalists in Yamhill County. It is surprising." Further reflection prompted him to add, "The Campbellites are numerous in the Territory and especially in this county."[7] One month earlier he had observed, "The Campbellites occupy large portions of the southern counties."[8] On July 20, 1848, Atkinson wrote, "The Campbellites are numerous, and they have constant preachers on the circuit."[9] But the "constant preachers on the circuit" could only have been the triumvirate of McBride, Burnett, and Waller. John Foster, Aaron Payne, and the elderly Thomas Crawford McBride were largely limited to their own neighborhoods, and A. V. McCarty and John Burris Smith were not traveling as widely in their preaching tours as they would later.

Dr. James McBride would have been pleased with Reverend Atkinson's perception that the Christian preachers were "constant" in their circuit-riding. McBride gave his own favorable assessment of 1847–48 in a letter to friends back home in Missouri:

> Brother Glen O. Burnett and myself commenced operations in the spring of 1847, and the good results far exceeded our most sanguine anticipations. The incentive was sufficient to induce us to spend all the time which our domestic avocations would allow, in the proclamation of the glad tidings among our new neighbors. Many turned to the Lord, and became obedient to the faith once delivered to the

> nations. Some of the richest and most refreshing seasons from the presence of the Lord, ever witnessed by me, have been in the wilds of Oregon. It possessed a charm which, under the circumstances, no pen can describe.[10]

Nevertheless, McBride did use his pen in an attempt to describe the emotional response of Christians being reunited with Christians in a far distant land. He wrote:

> At our public meetings, perhaps a dozen familiar faces would be added to the number of the congregation while preaching, who had not seen us, nor we them, for years before; but who, having heard of us and the appointment, came a distance, not to see one who had risen from the dead, but an old friend and brother, who, like themselves, had come to the distant shores of the Pacific. When the sermon and exhortations were over, and, as usual, the songs of praise would commence, then, with eyes sparkling for heaven, through tears of joy, we would greet each other in the transport of Christian love; and to witness brothers and sisters, and not unfrequently parents and children, embracing each other in tears of love and joy, while singing, gave to the scene a zest, a richness and a charm, which no tongue can tell, nor heart conceive, who has not been one of the number.[11]

The joyful reunion of Christians on "the distant shores of the Pacific" must have been repeated time and again during gospel meetings of McBride, Burnett, and Waller. This triumvirate of gospel preachers was both "constant" and effective in mobilizing Oregon Christians throughout the first half of 1848. The younger Waller felt honored to be joined in partnership with the two veteran proclaimers who had preceded him in the work. "They both were excellent men, strong in the faith, and unusually lovely in life," he said later. "They were most efficient in their ministry. They preached and lived as those who had been with Jesus, and learned of him."[12]

Another observer who commented on the affectionate fellowship of Christians in early Oregon was Inez Adams. She was just a young girl at the time, but she remembered clearly how the church meetings provided an opportunity for bonding between fellow Christians. More than 70 years later she wrote:

> The poorest people of today would consider our pioneer life one of unbearable hardship, yet no people were ever happier or healthier than were we. We had our meetings, church, with good, old-fashioned preaching, which were also social re-unions of warm-hearted Christian brethren, (this includes the women), who, after "meeting", as we always called it, those, living near the church or schoolhouse, would invite those farther away, home to dinner, and sometimes over night. You would have thought the whole congregation were blood-related to each other by the affection shown by one and all, to each other.[13]

A Mad Rush for California Gold

The Christians in Oregon were confident and unified in the late summer of 1848 and anxiously awaiting the arrival of many reinforcements in the fall migration when news of another kind jolted them and arrested their momentum. The news of the California gold rush reached Oregon in August, and within an incredibly brief span of time, a major exodus to the mines was in full stride. One record noted that in the first flush of excitement "about two-thirds of the able-bodied men of the territory left hurriedly for the new El Dorado."[14] Entire communities were almost completely deserted, and farms were abandoned to women and boys. The ripening harvest was neglected for lack of manpower. Bancroft noted, "Even their beloved land-claims were deserted; if a man did not go to California it was because he could not leave his family or business."[15]

A wagon company was hastily organized with Peter Hardeman Burnett as captain. He commanded 150 men and rode at the head of a train of 50 wagons loaded with mining implements and provisions for the winter. One account reported that "only five men were left at Salem" and Oregon City was reduced to "only a few women and children and some Indians."[16] As a result, the religious advancement of the Christians in Oregon Territory was temporarily halted. Even some of the preachers, notably Dr. James McBride and Aaron Payne, joined the trek to the gold diggings. Glen Owen

Burnett did not personally go, but he permitted his oldest son to go with the others.

Meanwhile, back in the nation's capital, President James Polk signed the historic legislation on August 14 that finally made Oregon an official territory of the United States. However, it postponed addressing the long-promised resolution of donation land claims. But at that precise moment, most Oregonians were preoccupied with the California gold rush. In the midst of this feverish excitement, the immigrants of 1848 began arriving in the newest American territory. Some immigrants, upon hearing of the discovery of gold, immediately diverted to the California mines.

The Pioneers of '48

Despite all the tumult surrounding the gold rush and the unfortunate interruption in the organization of churches, the Christians in Oregon were strengthened significantly by the immigration of 1848. To begin with, Elijah Bristow had sent word back to Illinois that everything was now in readiness, and his large extended family came overland that summer and settled around him at Pleasant Hill in Lane County. Included in this caravan were his wife, Susannah, and several children and their spouses. Abel King Bristow and his wife, Almira, were strong Christians. Two other sons, 22-year-old William Wilshire and 15-year-old Elijah Lafayette, were yet unmarried.

Three Bristow daughters had married church leaders, and two of these families were part of the 1848 migration. Those families were James and Elizabeth Hendricks and Robert and Polly Callison. The third family, John and Delilah Gilfrey, came to Oregon in 1852. Two single daughters, Catherine and Zilphia, would soon marry Christians in Oregon. The impact of the Bristow family on the growth of the Restoration Movement in Oregon Territory would be hard to overestimate.[17]

It is also known that the William Lysander Adams family was part of the Bristow caravan. Although 27-year-old Will

Adams was five years older than W. W. Bristow, the two young Illinois Christians had been close friends for a few years and had talked of migrating to Oregon. The young daughter of Will Adams remembered that her family traveled in a train of 40 wagons and that most of the immigrants in this train were Christians.[18]

Four other Christian families—Harrison and Jane Shelley, Michael and Sena Shelley, William and Polly Bowman, and Abel and Elizabeth Russell—were also in the Bristow caravan. Along with the Bristow clan, these four families chose to settle in Pleasant Hill. When added to Isaac and Elias Briggs who were already there, this became the nucleus of one of the strongest churches in Oregon. Unfortunately, the seeds of sectional strife that precipitated the Civil War were also in evidence in the Pleasant Hill Church from the very beginning. For the first 15 years of its existence, this historic church was plagued periodically by partisan strife. Despite these temporary setbacks, the Pleasant Hill Church of Christ became one of the most influential of Oregon churches.

The Christian movement in Marion County also fared well in the 1848 migration. At least five families, and probably more, settled in the district between Silverton and Aumsville. No one among these families was more significant for the long-term growth of the church in Oregon than the Indiana preacher, Caleb P. Chapman. When he and his wife, Elizabeth, settled near Bethany in the fall of 1848, it was the beginning of a 44-year ministry in Oregon that would yield wonderful fruit.[19]

Nebuzaradan and Elizabeth Coffey were both nearing the age of 60 when they began the difficult overland journey to Oregon. They were traveling with two married daughters and two unmarried daughters. The Coffeys were all dedicated Christians, and their sons-in-law, William Porter and Dr. Joseph Blackerby, became prominent leaders in the Restoration Movement in Oregon. Through their youngest daughter, Elizabeth, they became connected to the Elijah Bristow clan in Pleasant Hill. Elizabeth Coffey married William Wilshire Bristow in 1850.

William and Sarah Coffey Porter settled near Aumsville. Unfortunately, Sarah contracted mountain fever on the trail and died soon after arriving at her new home. She became the first person buried in Aumsville Cemetery. William married her sister, Martha, and the two of them donated the land for the Mill Creek church building. William was a leader in the church in this community for more than a half century until his death in 1899. Dr. Joseph Blackerby and his wife, Cassandra Coffey, settled near Silverton. In later years they were active members of the Bethany Church.

This was also the year that John Foster received preaching help in Clackamas County when Daniel Trullinger arrived from Iowa. Daniel and Elizabeth and their large extended family settled near Rock Creek southwest of Molalla. Daniel Trullinger had preached in Fountain County, Indiana, in the 1820s and 1830s, and in Henry and Davis counties in Iowa from 1838 to 1848. For the next 20 years, Foster and Trullinger would be co-laborers in Clackamas County, and they would die within ten months of each other in 1868–69.[20]

William Lysander Adams

Beyond any shadow of a doubt, the most colorful addition to the Christians in Oregon in 1848 was 27-year-old William Lysander Adams. A gifted preacher and outstanding teacher, Adams would be satirized by his political opponents in the Oregon *Statesman* as "Parson Billy"[21] for his constant moralizing, but he would make a vital contribution to the fledgling Restoration Movement in his new home. He was the first of Campbell's Bethany College students to migrate to the Pacific Northwest.

Will Adams had boarded with the Alexander Campbell family during his student days at Bethany College, and he had been chosen to deliver one of the commencement day orations on July 4, 1844. Campbell tried to discourage him from migrating to Oregon. "Is there not land enough, and are there not people enough in Illinois for your talent and enterprise," Campbell asked, "without burying yourself and family in the Oregon wilderness among the savages?" Will assured him, "No. Illinois is not big enough or good enough for me. My soul hungers for something that Illinois cannot give. In Oregon I expect to find what I desire." [22]

Traveling with his wife, Frances, and their two small daughters, Inez and Helen, Adams joined the Bristow train of 40 wagons and crossed the Missouri River on May 2. One record noted:

> While crossing the Cascades they lost the third of their four oxen and had to yoke the 14-year-old milk cow, Rose, with the remaining ox. The family credited the old cow with having saved their lives as she not only helped haul the wagon but provided milk as well. She lived another 10 years as a family pet after reaching Oregon.[23]

In traversing the Barlow Toll Road, the Adams wagon came to the foot of treacherous Laurel Hill. This was the very spot where a fellow-preacher named Thomas Mulkey had died and been buried exactly one year earlier. After cresting the peak, Frances carried Helen down to the bottom of the hill and returned to get Inez. One narrative described the event:

> Helen was extremely fair and had been greatly admired by the Indians whenever they saw her. Often they had tried to buy the little blonde baby with ponies and other riches they possessed. When Frances looked back she saw about a dozen Indians on horseback surrounding the baby. Terrified, she grabbed Inez and raced back to the bottom of the hill where she could see the Indian ponies jumping about crazily. She began to cry, for she thought the horses were trampling the baby, but when she rushed frantically through them she found the little tot sitting unharmed and gleeful in the center of a circle which the Indians had made on their prancing ponies. Her fear was for naught, for the Indians motioned that they were only attempting to protect the infant. She conveyed her gratefulness and they smiled and went on their way.[24]

Will and Frances decided to join the Christians living in Yamhill County, settling adjacent to the McBrides on Panther Creek. Although James and Mahala McBride had ten children living at home, they took the Adams family in until another cabin could be completed. Will always remembered their limited menu: "They boiled peas for breakfast, dinner and supper, and browned them for coffee."[25]

In addition to the McBrides, the other Christian families in this settlement were the Woods and the Sheltons. Inez Adams always remembered how impressed she was with the children in these families, and many years later she wrote:

> My sister, brother Will and I were associated closely at school or in play with the McBrides, Woods and Sheltons as children and youths, and I can truly say I never heard an indecent word, much less saw a vulgar act from one of them. They were thoroughly, inherently clean-minded, honorable and reliable. Perfectly frank and out-spoken, they thought originally and independently — no youth of the present day more so — never hesitating to say so, when they differed from their elders; but always with the deference and respect due their elders. They honored their parents, not only because the Bible said they should, but because they were fortunate in having parents worthy to be honored; and they were unrebelliously subject to them until their majority was reached.[26]

That winter Will was persuaded by the women in the neighborhood to open a school in a lean-to that was built as an addition to a log cabin. Over the door leading into this unpretentious room, Adams placed a sign, written in charcoal, that announced the existence of "Yamhill University."[27] Later, this school occupied one of the three rooms in the James McBride log cabin.

Will Adams taught about 20 students that winter, using a blackboard, crude benches, and a few books. In later years, he was especially proud of four of his students: John Rogers McBride, who served as a United States Congressman; Thomas A. McBride, who was appointed chief justice of the Oregon Supreme Court; George Lemuel Woods, who was elected governor of Oregon; and Levi Lindsay Rowland, who became president of Christian College in Monmouth. These four young men, all devout Christians who grew up to be leaders in both the community and the church, credited Will Adams for much of their early training and progress.

"Adams proved a treasure to me," John Rogers McBride wrote later. "He had a library of about one hundred and fifty volumes of choice books containing much of the best literature of the day." McBride was forever grateful that the Bethany College graduate had instilled in him proper study habits during the long winter evenings of 1848–49. "He corrected my mathematical methods, criticized my efforts at literary composition, and instructed me how to study and think for myself," recalled McBride.[28]

A Pause in the Action

The upheaval caused by the California gold rush had a desultory effect on the advance of the Restoration Movement in Oregon Territory for the next two or three years, but 1848 would still be remembered as a banner year for Christian immigration. Will Adams, Caleb Chapman, and Daniel Trullinger were gifted preachers. The prominent Christians moving into Lane County made that area a stronghold of the church for the next 150 years. Devout churchmen like Robert Callison, James Hendricks and William Porter, provided much-needed leadership in Oregon churches for the next half century. The saying could still be heard in frequent conversations: "The Campbellites and the fern are taking the Willamette Valley." But, for the moment, the church was distracted by the swirling events in the neighboring state of California, and everything was "on hold."

Chapter 8

The Gold Mines of California 1849

We have now six respectable churches in Oregon; some are small, as a matter of course, while others are large and flourishing; and though we are doing as well as our neighbors, yet I must confess, that the gold of California has, to some extent, shaded our prospects.

— Dr. James McBride, March 24, 1850

In the late afternoon of January 24, 1848, while supervising the construction of a sawmill at Coloma, California, on the American River, James Marshall discovered gold in the tailrace of the mill. This incident has been called "the most remarkable event in California's remarkable history." The sheer magnitude of this discovery was not comprehended at first. When San Francisco's early newspaper, the *Californian,* broke the story in its March 15, 1848, issue, the news was relegated to the bottom of the second page. Nevertheless, though somewhat hidden and limited to eight lines, the announcement was stunning:

> GOLD MINE FOUND—In the newly made raceway of the Saw Mill recently erected by Captain Sutter, on the American Fork, gold has been found in considerable quantities. One person brought thirty dollars worth to New Helvetia, gathered there in a short time. California, no doubt, is rich in mineral wealth, great chances here for scientific capitalists. Gold has been found in almost every part of the country.[1]

A few adventurous individuals responded, but there were no great crowds on the road to Coloma. The real "rush" began in earnest on May 12, 1848, when Sam Brannan paraded through San Francisco waving a quinine bottle filled with gold dust and shouting "Gold! Gold! Gold from the American River." Brannan's news was like a sudden explosion, and within days San Francisco was almost deserted. In the midst of this hysteria, the *Californian* suspended publication on May 29, 1848, announcing:

> The majority of our subscribers and many of our advertisers have closed their doors and places of business and left town . . . . The whole country, from San Francisco to Los Angeles and from the seashore to the base of the Sierra Nevada, resounds with the sordid cry of "gold! Gold!! GOLD!!!!"—while the field is left half planted, the house half built, and everything neglected but the manufacture of shovels and pick-axes, and the means of transportation to the spot where one man obtained one hundred and twenty-eight dollars' worth of the *real stuff* in one day's washing, and the average for all concerned is twenty dollars per diem![2]

Oregon Prospectors

By the end of May, gold had been discovered at distances up to 30 miles from Sutter's Mill. Two thousand men were already on site digging for the precious metal in early June, and by the 1st of July that figure had doubled. The news reached Oregon's Willamette Valley near the end of July, and by the close of August a massive exodus had already begun. "No one doubted longer," wrote one observer, "covetous desire quickly increased to a delirium of hope."[3] The exodus continued "as long as weather permitted, and until several thousand had left Oregon by land and sea."[4]

Among the Oregon Christians who went to California to mine for gold were: Dr. James McBride, William Lysander Adams, Caleb Woods, George William Burnett, Jeremiah Rowland, Levi Lindsay Rowland, Robert Crouch Kinney, Cyrus Hawley, William Buffum, Horace Burnett, Harrison Linville, Medders Vanderpool, David R. Lewis, John A.

Bounds, Wiley Chapman, Hiram Alva Johnson, and William Wilshire Bristow.

There were not many women who accompanied the men to California, but 34-year-old Caroline Buffum chose to make the journey with her husband. The Buffums traveled to the mines with their friends and neighbors, James and Dorcas McDonald.[5] William Buffum wrote: "Our wives were great friends; had no children; both fine and easy riders, could manage a horse as well as the most of men, insisted on going with us." The presence of these women at the diggings did not go unnoticed. "Our wives being the only women in the mines," recalled Buffum, "the miners would come from all around to see the Oregon white women." The Buffums and McDonalds worked the mines for five months and enjoyed "a fair return" for their labors.[6]

John Rogers McBride, the 16-year-old son of Dr. James McBride, chronicled the excitement in his little book of reminiscences. "It will be no exaggeration of the facts to state that between the months of July and November, 1848, two thirds of the male inhabitants of the country north of the California line, had dropped their home pursuits, and joined in this crusade for gold," he declared. "In the Yamhill settlement the percentage was even more."[7] Although McBride saw most of the men in his neighborhood leave home to join the diggings, including his own father, he commented, "A. J. Hembree and William Dawson never visited the mines." The very fact that this was worthy of a mention in his journal is an indication that Hembree and Dawson were among the very few men in Yamhill County who did not go to California.

Those who were able to get to the California gold fields in 1848 found gold in seemingly inexhaustible quantities. According to one record, "The year's operations marked the beginning of the greatest bonanza the world has ever known."[8] The digging was soon expanded beyond the American River to the Feather River and its tributaries. On the Yuba River, the findings were even more abundant, and one account reported, "The first five prospectors there made

$75,000 in three months, and other miners are said to have averaged $60 to $100 a day."[9] One of the most successful strikes on the American River was at a spot called Dry Diggings. This later became Hangtown, and still later Placerville. During the summer of 1848, the daily yield was sometimes as high as five pounds to the man, which led the historian Bancroft to wryly observe, "The 300 Hangtown men were the happiest in the universe."[10]

Among the Christians from Oregon, four of the most successful prospectors were William Lysander Adams, Levi Lindsay Rowland, Wiley Chapman, and Hiram Alva Johnson. In the early summer of 1849, Adams turned over the running of "Yamhill University" to his wife Frances while he went to California to dig for gold. When he returned to Panther Creek, he had mined enough gold dust to pay off all his considerable debts and buy a farm. His daughter recalled:

> He brought enough gold dust ($900) to purchase the "Carey Place," just one mile south of, and adjoining Dr. McBride's 640-acre farm. There was a comparatively comfortable house on it, built of logs . . . . This Carey house consisted of two fair-sized rooms, a small bedroom, and a front porch. Father later added another bedroom, and a large "lean-to" used as a store-room and woodshed. There was a well in one corner of the kitchen which was twenty-six feet deep . . . Father never would live long anywhere without a fireplace, and one of his first jobs after we were settled was to build a generous-sized one into our "fore-room."[11]

In 1851 Will Adams made a second trip to the California mines, this time fighting his way through the Rogue River Valley in southern Oregon which was infested with hostile Indians. Once again he returned "with a large quantity of gold dust."[12]

Jeremiah Rowland permitted his teen-aged son, Levi, to accompany him to California and try his skills at mining. Levi earned enough money to finance a four-year education at Alexander Campbell's Bethany College in Virginia, where his training equipped him to return to Oregon and become president of Christian College in Monmouth.[13] Wiley Chapman may have been the most successful of the Oregon

Christians. One record noted he brought back $5,000 in gold dust contained in "a beautiful camphor wood chest bound in brass" that remained a treasured heirloom kept by his children and grandchildren.[14]

Another successful prospector was Marion County's Hiram Alva Johnson. He and his wife had come west in 1847 with Mac Waller and several other Illinois Christians. "In the fall of 1848, he went to the California gold fields," noted one account, "and in 38 days he cleaned up over $2,000. He came home from San Francisco on a sailing vessel and brought with him such luxuries as coffee, sugar and a few dishes."[15]

Tragedies in the Ford Family

Not all of the mining stories had such happy endings. Marcus Ford, Nat Ford's only son and one of the most promising young leaders among the Christians in Oregon, died tragically while returning from the mines. He was just 26 years old. He had been elected prosecuting attorney by an almost unanimous vote of the people and had served in the provisional legislature as a member from Polk County. More importantly for the church, this graduate of Bacon College was positioned to render valuable spiritual leadership in the years ahead.

Marcus Ford had married Amanda Thorp on January 14, 1847, and their son was born in November. When Amanda's health began to decline the next year, her physician recommended that a sea voyage and a change of climate might prove helpful. Leaving their young son with his grandparents, Nat and Lucinda Ford, Marcus and Amanda departed for San Francisco where they had booked passage to the Sandwich Islands. But three days after arriving in San Francisco, Amanda died on December 19, 1848. Following her funeral, a despondent Marcus decided to remain in California for a time and see the mining country for himself. He devoted nine profitable months to digging out gold, and then boarded a leaky old lumber schooner in San Francisco on November 15, 1849, for the journey home to Oregon.

It was a dreadful voyage of nearly 50 days. The ship was buffeted by numerous storms and drifted off course. Provisions ran low, scurvy broke out, and one man died. By the time they reached the mouth of the Columbia River, the situation had become desperate and intolerable. It was assumed that a pilot from Astoria would come out and guide the vessel safely across a dangerous river bar. When the pilot was delayed, Marcus Ford and three other men attempted to reach shore in an open boat. A heavy gale drove them into Shoalwater Bay where they were smashed into the rocks and drowned. The sad date of this disaster was January 1, 1850. Three of the bodies were recovered, but the body of Marcus Ford was never found.

Later, a story circulated that an exhausted Marcus Ford had actually survived the crash and been murdered on the shore by Indians who saw how much money he was carrying.[16] The following tribute ran in the *Oregon Spectator* on January 26, 1850:

> Mark Ford, Esqr., was a gentleman of much promise to the country. He enjoyed a good education and legal learning; and bid fair to stand high among the active and influential men of the Territory. He was during one session of the Provisional Legislature, an active member . . . His loss is not only a great bereavement to his friends, but also to the Territory.[17]

Christians in Territorial Government

Another casualty of the 1848 exodus to California was Oregon's provisional government. There were not enough members left in the state, and the meeting scheduled for December 1848, was suspended. Among the Christians elected to the 1848 legislature were William Porter from Champoeg (later Marion) County, Harrison Linville and Thomas J. Lovelady from Polk County, and Absalom J. Hembree from Yamhill County. However, now that Oregon was an official territory of the United States, there would be a new government in place some time in 1849. President James Polk appointed General Joseph Lane of Indiana to be

Oregon's first territorial governor, and he arrived in Oregon City on March 2, 1849. The next day he issued a proclamation extending the laws of the United States over the Territory of Oregon.

The first elected Territorial Legislative Assembly met at Oregon City on July 16, 1849. In addition to Governor Lane, the legislature was organized with 9 councilmen and 18 members of the house of representatives. At least three Christians, Wesley Shannon (Champoeg), Nat Ford (Polk), and James Graves (Yamhill) were included among the nine councilmen. Christians elected to the house of representatives included Absalom J. Hembree and Robert Crouch Kinney from Yamhill County and Johnson Mulkey from Benton County. Another representative, Jerome B. Walling from Yamhill County, would be baptized into Christ by Dr. James McBride in 1855. The chief clerk of the legislature was a devout Christian from Champoeg (later Marion) County named William Porter.

The legislature appointed Dr. James McBride to be superintendent of schools. In the next legislature, elected in 1850, Dr. McBride was added to the nine councilmen, and Aaron Payne and Samuel M. Gilmore from Yamhill County were added to the house of representatives.[18] Bancroft supplies an undated observation from an anonymous member of the first Territorial Legislative Assembly:

> I have heard some people say that the first legislature was better than any one we have had since. I think it was as good. It was composed of more substantial men than they have had since; men who represented the people better. The second one was probably as good . . . . I know there were no such men in it as go to the legislature now.[19]

With the organization of churches on temporary hold, and with very little preaching activity in 1849–50, it is interesting to find several Christians seeking an avenue of community service that included involvement in the highest levels of territorial government. It is particularly interesting to see the political activism of preachers like McBride and Payne. But as the anonymous legislator pointed out, the day would soon come in Oregon when the legislature was an arena for professional politicians and not for farmers and preachers.

The Pioneers of '49

President James Polk's message to Congress on December 5, 1848, in which he presented the real facts concerning California gold, triggered a migration of unprecedented proportions. Even before the discovery of gold in 1848, westward migration was rapidly gaining momentum. In the spring of 1849 it became a stampede. It is estimated that about 23,000 people traveling in 6,200 wagons came overland that summer. Some diarists wrote of continuous wagon trains that were six miles long. Another 15,000 chose to come by boat via Panama or Cape Horn. Not surprisingly, the overwhelming majority were bent on joining the great army of gold-seekers in northern California. Only about 130 wagons carrying 400 to 500 people turned their backs on the great wealth that beckoned southward and proceeded to Oregon.[20]

Among the comparatively few who came to Oregon in 1849 were five families of Christians who would play important roles in strengthening the Restoration Movement in the territory. Included in this group was an outstanding 43-year-old preacher named Alfred R. Elder. Alfred and Martha Elder and Alfred's sister and brother-in-law, Sanford and Maria Elder Watson, traveled together in a party of 25 from Illinois. The Elders settled in Yamhill County near the Hembrees and McBrides, and the Watsons settled in the Bethel Hills of northern Polk County near the Burnetts and Harveys. Sanford Watson was a member of the board of trustees for Bethel College for 15 years.

The other three families of Oregon "49ers" were the Brunks, Boothbys, and Butlers. Harrison and Emily Brunk and their five children migrated from Troy, Missouri. They settled first near Rickreall but moved to Eola in 1856. Emily was a sister to Mac Waller, and they settled near him in 1856 and became members of the church he established at Eola.[21] Reason Rounds Boothby had married Mary Ann Waller, sister to Mac Waller and Emily Brunk, in 1834 in Morgan County,

Illinois. They moved to Texas in 1845 where Reason joined the Texas Rangers and fought the Indians. They returned to Illinois in 1848 and finalized plans to accompany the Brunks to Oregon Territory in the migration of 1849.

Joseph Bradley Varnum Butler and his wife, Elizabeth, were Illinois Christians. They came west with their three little boys and lived in Portland for two years. They moved to Eola in 1851 and opened a large country store, then moved on to Monmouth in 1857. The Butlers were vital supporters of Christian College in Monmouth.[22]

There were many other outstanding leaders in the Restoration Movement who came across the trail in 1849, but they were bound for California instead of Oregon. Three talented preachers were among the historic "49ers" who changed the California landscape overnight. Thomas Thompson from Missouri, William Wilson Stevenson from Arkansas, and John G. Parrish from Virginia would preach the first sermons, baptize the first converts, and organize the first churches in the Golden State. Their vigorous efforts would be limited to California, however, and none would ever travel north to assist in organizing the Christians of Oregon Territory.[23]

Approximately 80 families of Christians can be positively identified as being among the historic "49ers" who migrated to California that year. The majority were either single men or men who came without their families, but about 30 wives came with their husbands. These figures do not include Oregon Christians, most of whom stayed for a year or two before returning to their homes in Oregon.

William and Mary Dawson

One Oregon congregation that continued to meet regularly in 1849, despite the turmoil of the exodus of most men to California, was the one at Blackhawk Schoolhouse in Yamhill County. With the occasional availability of three preachers, Dr. James McBride, Aaron Payne, and William Lysander Adams, and the constant presence of a corps of dedicated women and teen-agers, this congregation persevered through a disruptive time. One of the greatest strengths of this church was the faithful shepherding of a quiet and learned Christian named William Dawson, who was never dazzled by the lure of California gold. He and his wife, Mary, had migrated from Missouri with their two little girls in 1845, and a third daughter had been born in Oregon. John Rogers McBride worked as a cowboy on their ranch in the spring of 1849, and many years later he penned this remembrance:

> While thus engaged I made my home with the other employees at the house of Mr. William Dawson, an educated and accomplished Scotchman, who had an interesting and amiable wife. Dawson was a fine reader of poetry, and the works of Burns, Scott, Byron and Bulwer were in his collection. An intimacy between myself and these two people, who were of mature years whilst I was a mere boy [16], began then, for which I cannot account. Both took a great interest in my reading and welfare, such as would only have been expected of an elder brother and sister. Both are long since among the immortals, but the memory of their kindness and service to me can only perish with life. For years after, I was a frequent visitor at their delightful home, where love, peace, and happiness were constant as the sun, and where I was as welcome as if I had been one of its inmates. Dawson often occupied positions of importance in the county, but his ambitions were centered about his home, and he lived and died loved and honored most by those who knew him best.[24]

The Case for Optimism

After three great years of advancement, from the fall of 1845 to the fall of 1848, the Restoration Movement in Oregon experienced a sudden disruption in the closing months of 1848 that seriously impeded the growth of the movement for the next two or three years. In addition to the Christians who took their chances in the California gold diggings, others became involved in territorial government. The organizational labors of Burnett and Waller were limited in 1849–50, and yet Dr. James McBride could write optimistically to his friends back home in Missouri on March 24, 1850:

> We have now six respectable churches in Oregon; some are small, as a matter of course, while others are large and

> flourishing; and though we are doing as well as our neighbors, yet I must confess, that the gold of California has, to some extent, shaded our prospects. We have seven or eight preachers, yet three or four do all the labor, without pecuniary assistance. We have talented and influential opponents, who enjoy "sanctuary" ease and opportunities, while we are poor, (and wealth, you know, has its charms) and are, therefore, deprived of doing what otherwise would be easy to accomplish. Our opponents have earthly advantages on their side; but we have God our Father, the Lord Jesus Christ and the Bible on our side—hence, we thank God and take courage. Our numbers, at present, are greater than any other denomination. May God smile upon us, and save us in heaven at last![25]

When the exodus to California began in the fall of 1848, the Christians in Oregon had as many as 10 or more congregations that met at least occasionally for preaching and worship. The "six respectable churches" in March 1850 were probably Jefferson Institute and Luckiamute in Polk County; Amity; the Hembree settlement; and Blackhawk Schoolhouse in Yamhill County; and Brother John Foster's congregation in Clackamas County. Other possible congregations included Tualatin Plains in Washington County; Oregon City in Clackamas County; and Howell's Prairie, Bethany, Mill Creek and Salem in Marion County. In addition, Johnson Mulkey may have established a small congregation near his home in Benton County.

It was a small base of operation, and there were not enough preachers. But McBride was probably correct in his assessment that the number of Christians in Oregon Territory was greater than those of any other group. More important for the future, the Christians in Lane and Linn counties were preparing to organize their first churches.

Chapter 9

The Church on a Pleasant Hill

1850

We organized on the 4th of August, 1850. We copied, as a heading to our Church Book, a preamble and agreement from the Millennial Harbinger . . . at the time of organizing.

— Elijah Bristow, Lane County

By 1850 the population of Oregon Territory had reached 12,093. It was distributed among the eight counties as follows: Marion, 2,749; Washington, 2,652; Clackamas, 1,859; Yamhill, 1,512; Polk, 1,051; Linn, 994; Benton, 814; and Clatsop, 462. Four new counties were formed soon after: Lane and Umpqua in 1851 and Douglas and Jackson in 1852. After the diversion of the gold rush, immigration began to accelerate again with 2,000 arriving in 1850 and 1,500 in 1851.

Numbering the Christians

The Christians were distributed in all eight counties in 1850, but they were especially well represented in Yamhill, Polk, Clackamas, and Marion counties. Of the new counties, the Christians would organize quickest in Lane County, thanks to the large extended family of Elijah Bristow. During this time period, Glen Owen Burnett was the evangelist who traveled the farthest and visited the most Christians in the Willamette Valley, and as a result, he had the best grasp of the numerical strength of the Restoration Movement in Oregon.

Corresponding with Jesse Ferguson, the editor of the *Christian Magazine* in Nashville, Tennessee, on May 15, 1851, Burnett gave an update on the numerical situation in Oregon from the perspective of a traveling evangelist. "We have in this far-off country about 500 brethren professing one Lord, one faith and one baptism," he informed the Nashville editor, "surrounded by a strong band of well-disciplined Methodist preachers, all intent on pulling us down, but thanks to God our way is onward and upward."[1] However, in a letter to Alexander Campbell intended for publication in the *Millennial Harbinger*, and dated October 23, 1851, Burnett offered this revised assessment: "From the best information I have been able to get, we have in Oregon about 1200 disciples, but mostly in a disorganized condition."[2]

This was a remarkable increase of 700 members in Burnett's estimate in less than six months time. It is unlikely that 700 Christians arrived in the 1851 migration. Evidently Burnett was traveling wider in his preaching circuit and compiling more comprehensive information on the Christian population, but his dramatic increase in numbers may not be accurate. If Burnett's revised estimate was correct, the Christians accounted for about eight percent of the population. However, at this distance it appears that Burnett's estimate of 1,200 members was too high.

The only other traveling evangelist who attempted to gather statistics was Dr. James McBride, and his figures were significantly lower than Burnett's. In his letter of March 24, 1850, McBride wrote "our numbers, at present, are greater than any other denomination,"[3] but he did not offer an estimate. In a letter to Elias Briggs in early 1852, McBride estimated the number of Christians at from 400 to 600. Writing to Daniel Bates in Iowa on July 24, 1854, McBride reported: "I can say, with much assurance, that the 'Christians' number not less than 800 in Oregon."

The statistic of 800 baptized believers may seem small for a group claiming to be the largest of the various church groups represented in Oregon. However, in George H. Himes' study of the beginnings of Christianity in Oregon, he presented statistics that may inadvertently validate this claim. After pointing out that the Roman Catholics in Oregon Territory numbered only 303 at the end of 1854, he analyzed thoroughly the growth patterns of five leading Protestant denominations in early Oregon. "It is impossible to state with any degree of certainty the number of professed Christians connected with Protestant churches in Oregon at the close of the year 1852," he acknowledged, "but it will be seen from the foregoing that the Methodist, Congregational, Baptist, Presbyterian and Episcopalian denominations were represented in an organized form – the aggregate of all probably not exceeding 1,000 persons."[4]

Himes was aware that there was another vibrant Christian group in early Oregon, but with their lack of official denominational machinery and the resulting absence of reliable data, he did not know how to get a handle on them. "To my knowledge there was a goodly number of Disciples of Christ—sometimes known as 'Campbellites'—in this field," he wrote, "but I do not think there was any regular organization."[5] If the five leading Protestant denominations combined numbered only 1,000 at the end of 1852, then the 800 Christians were clearly the largest group. As was pointed out in chapter 8, the view that they did not have any regular organizations was not accurate. Dr. McBride was aware of "six respectable churches" in the spring of 1850, and that would expand to 16 churches by 1853. But although the Christians accounted for a "goodly number," Himes was correct in pointing out that they were slow in organizing churches.

Preaching to the Indians

The Klikitat Indians from north of the Columbia River had migrated southward into the Willamette Valley in the 1820s, but gradually most of them were forced back to their old home. They finally ceded their lands to the United States in 1855 and settled on the Yakima Indian Reservation in Washington Territory. When the Will Adams family arrived in Yamhill County in the fall of 1848, some of the migratory

Klikitats were still spending their winters in that neighborhood. Inez Adams remembered how her father communicated with them: "He had already learned the Chinook, a simple language created by the Hudson's Bay Company as a means of communication between themselves and all the tribes of Oregon savages."

Through their chief, Wy-an-a-shut, the Klikitats sought and obtained permission from Will Adams to camp on his land near a spot where Panther Creek flowed through the property. Wy-an-a-shut would often visit with the Adams family at their house, but he did not understand the courtesy of knocking first. "Indians never knock," Inez wrote later, "but glide in soundlessly as shadows." Since their white neighbors were not within easy walking distance, the Adams girls spent much of their winter months playing with the Indian children.

Inez Adams also remembered that her father shared his religious faith with the Indians who were temporary guests on his land. "On pleasant evenings father would take me down to their camp," she recalled, "and sitting on an upturned keg, as they had no seats, would stand me between his knees, holding the big family Bible before me, and have me read a verse from it." Will Adams would then translate and explain the verse in Chinook. On some occasions, the Indians were invited to attend church services. "The chief and his principal men attended church with us sometimes at Dr. McBride's house," Inez wrote later. She remembered that "they learned and sang our hymns, and the chief sometimes prayed aloud with fervor."

On some occasions, Will Adams would convene a little church service for the Indians in his own front yard. Inez recalled:

> On other pleasant clear evenings, the tribe would gather in our large front yard, and squat around on the grass, while father stood on the steps, the family sitting on the porch, and gave them a talk in Chinook, pointing to and naming the planets and constellations, and telling all about the sun, moon and earth, and in short, telling in simple terms, all we know of their sizes and stupendous distances from us, how they

> swing in their orbits, never missing a second or a cog in their movements in a thousand years.[6]

It is apparent from these stories that Will Adams was just as much at home when he was explaining the providence of God to Indians, as he was in preaching the unsearchable riches of Christ to the white settlers in the territory. Soon he would be summoned to Lane County in the southern extremities of the Willamette Valley to be the featured preacher at the organization of the Pleasant Hill Church of Christ.

The Elijah Bristow Clan

In Oregon's 1850 census it was apparent that a majority of people lived in the northern half of the Willamette Valley, and this same pattern held true for the distribution of Christians in the valley. However, beginning with the establishment of the Pleasant Hill Church of Christ in 1850, the Christians in the southern half of the Willamette Valley began to demonstrate numerical strength in the area that would become Lane County. The story of the founding of Pleasant Hill and the Pleasant Hill Church of Christ is so intertwined with the life and family of the remarkable Elijah Bristow, that some background is necessary.

Elijah Bristow was actually six months older than Alexander Campbell whom he greatly admired. He was born in Virginia in April 1788, and married Susannah Gabbert in 1812. Bristow fought in both the War of 1812 and the Creek Indian War, where his marksmanship brought him to the attention of General Andrew Jackson who frequently assigned him to special duty. He was cited for bravery at the battle of Taledega. He immigrated to western Illinois and lived in McDonough and Hancock counties close to the Iowa-Missouri line for about 23 years. His capacity for leadership can be seen in the following incident:

> During the Black Hawk War, his neighbors becoming alarmed, commenced to build a fort in which to place their families for safety. In order to quiet their fears, Mr. Bristow volunteered to go to the front and ascertain if any immediate

> danger was pending; in doing which, he went alone from his home to Rock Island and back, a distance of over a hundred miles, through a country which was then uninhabited except by Indians. Finding the territory clear of hostiles, he returned to his neighbors, quieted their fears and caused the little settlement to again resume its round of peaceful occupations.[7]

In 1837, the year of the Campbell-Purcell debate and five years after the Campbell and Stone-Mulkey merger, Elijah Bristow became a Christian. He was 49 years old. He was immersed into Christ that winter in an icy stream near his home. The ice was two feet thick and a hole had to be cut for the purpose of the baptism. He became a faithful proponent of the principles of the Restoration Movement, and one of his first contributions to the movement was to use his carpentry skills to erect a meetinghouse for the Liberty congregation near his home. This was the first congregation organized by the Christians in McDonough County.[8]

At the age of 57, Bristow migrated from Illinois to California in 1845. He spent the winter of 1845–46 at Sutter's Fort, where he sustained a broken arm when he was thrown from a horse. He moved north to Oregon Territory the next spring and became the first settler to stake a claim in what would become Lane County. As mentioned in chapter 5, he called his claim Pleasant Hill and he built the first permanent dwelling in Lane County. Once his family had arrived safely in the fall of 1848 and the first year of building homes and planting and harvesting crops had been completed, Bristow set aside "five acres of land for Church, school, and cemetery purposes." In 1850, assisted by his son-in-law, James Hendricks, he built a log cabin to serve the needs of Pleasant Hill Church and Pleasant Hill School. It was situated in the southwest quarter of present-day Pleasant Hill Cemetery. This log cabin had the distinction of housing the first church and the first school established in Lane County.[9]

Twenty-four-year-old William Wilshire Bristow, Elijah's son, served as the first teacher in Pleasant Hill School in 1850. In that same year he married into a strong Christian family when he wed Elizabeth Coffey at Aumsville in Marion

County. Her sisters were married to William Porter and Dr. Joseph Blackerby, two well-known church leaders in that district. W. W. Bristow became an outstanding church leader in his own right, and he later rose to prominence as a Republican state senator in Oregon.[10]

The Pleasant Hill Church was organized on Sunday, August 4, 1850, "taking the Bible alone as their only rule of faith and practice." The charter members were: Elijah and Susannah Bristow, James and Elizabeth Bristow Hendricks, Abel K. and Almira Bristow, Robert and Polly Bristow Callison, William Wilshire and Elizabeth Bristow, Sarah Bristow, Katie Bristow, Zilphia Bristow, Isaac Briggs, Elias and Mary Briggs, William and Polly Bowman, Michael and Sena Shelley, Abel and Elizabeth Russell, John Russell, and Harrison and Jane Shelley.[11]

William Lysander Adams was the guest preacher on that historic Sunday of August 4, 1850. He had come to Pleasant Hill to perform the wedding ceremony for Katie Bristow and George Johnston Baskett.[12] Adams had known the Bristow family back in Illinois, and he was a good friend of W. W. Bristow. In fact, the Adams family had traveled in the same train with the various Bristow families in the overland journey from Illinois in 1848.

In a letter to the editors of the *Christian Evangelist* in Iowa, Elijah Bristow wrote, "We organized on the 4th of August, 1850. We copied, as a heading to our Church Book, a preamble and agreement from the *Millennial Harbinger* . . . at the time of organizing."[13] The heading they copied into their church book began with these words:

> The congregation of Jesus Christ at Pleasant Hill, was organized on the 4th day of August, 1850. It was composed of the following persons: [charter members listed] . . . In coming together as a congregation, having already been immersed upon a confession of their faith in the Messiah, as the only begotten Son of God: they declared it to be their full purpose and determination to acknowledge no leader but Christ; no infallible teachers but the apostles and prophets; and no articles of belief but the Old and New Testaments: and the latter, as containing their faith, and the rules of their behaviour as Christians.[14]

The Pleasant Hill Church continued to meet in the little log building until 1854. At that time Elijah Bristow donated a forty-acre site for the construction of a larger schoolhouse that also became a meetinghouse for the church. Church discipline was an unfortunate necessity from time to time. If the worldly lifestyle of a member brought reproach on the church, his name was stricken from the record book. When members drifted away from the church of their own accord, it was recorded in the church book that they had "returned to the beggardly elements."[15]

The Butler-Davidson-Murphy Orbit

At the same time the Pleasant Hill Church was being organized, a group of families from the city of Monmouth in Warren County, Illinois, was arriving in the territory. These immigrants were almost all related to the Butler, Davidson and Murphy families, and they were sent as an advance party to prepare the way for a larger migration of settlers that would come overland in 1852 and 1853.

In the early 1830s, several of these families, all strong Christians committed to the Restoration Movement, had migrated from Barren and Warren counties in southern Kentucky to establish Warren County in northwestern Illinois. They had roots in the Mulkey and Stone movements, but they had recently become aware of Alexander Campbell. They settled about 15 miles from the Mississippi River which served as the boundary between Illinois and Iowa Territory.

The first congregation established by these families was called Coldbrook, because a cold water spring in the area formed a brook near the meetinghouse. In the church record book, the Coldbrook congregation called itself "the Church of Christ on Cedar Fork of Henderson River," and the opening entry read, "On the 30th day of April, 1831, this church was constituted upon the belief that the Scriptures of the Old and New Testaments are the only rule of faith and practice and sufficient for the government of the church."[16] Included among the 17 charter members were Elijah and Margaret Davidson and John Ecles and Frances Murphy. A quarter-century later, Elijah Davidson and John Ecles Murphy would be two of the best-known preachers in Oregon Territory.

Another outstanding Christian leader among these new residents of Illinois was Major Peter Butler, a veteran of the War of 1812. He surveyed a town in Warren County and named it after his family's ancestral home in Monmouth, Wales. On the last Lord's Day in March 1839, 22 members from the Coldbrook Church joined the Butler family and others in planting the Monmouth Church.[17] Peter Butler's son, Ira F. M. Butler, was one of the bright young leaders in this church. Four years earlier he had married Mary Davidson, a daughter of Elijah Davidson.

In the late 1840s, several families in the Butler-Davidson-Murphy orbit developed an exceptionally severe case of "Oregon Fever." Between 1846 and 1850 many meetings were held in the home of Ira F. M. Butler to discuss plans for a large migration to the Willamette Valley. It took a great deal of persuasion to get the women to see the advantages of such a difficult move, and when they finally consented, it was with the understanding that certain specific conditions would be met.

"The women exacted from their men a promise that a school and a church would be established before they consented to going," noted one account. "The school would be patterned after Bethany College in Virginia which was founded by Alexander Campbell, and would be a school 'where men and women alike might be schooled in the science of living and in the fundamental principles of religion.'"[18]

Finally, in the spring of 1850, the advance party left Warren County, Illinois, and began the long trek to Oregon. Even the news of the California gold rush failed to derail the carefully laid plans to settle in the Willamette Valley. Among those traveling in this train were Elijah Davidson, his sons-in-law Squire S. Whitman and Thomas H. Lucas, his sons, Elijah B. and Alexander, and a number of single men.[19] Both Elijah and Elijah B. were gospel preachers as well as farmers, and between them they would devote more than a half century to preaching in Oregon.[20]

This advance party was given the responsibility of locating the best area for a future settlement, and "in due course they sent back a map of the country-side and a full description of the country and its climate and vegetation." This map was the centerpiece of more meetings in 1851 at the Ira F. M. Butler home in Monmouth, Illinois, and on this map the proposed site for a town and college campus were agreed upon. As a result of all this visionary planning, the town of Monmouth, Oregon, and the campus of Christian College would eventually take root in Polk County.[21]

The Pioneers of '50

On May 1, 1850, a 55-year-old ardent Christian named John Udell said good-bye to his wife and friends in Davis County, Iowa and began the difficult overland journey. Although he knew several Christians who were bound for Oregon, he was drawn to the riches of the California gold fields. He recorded his motives for undertaking such a hazardous trip in a diary that was later published, and he wrote:

> There are three very important reasons why I undertake so long a journey at my advanced age: first, the improvement of my health in journeying and change of climate; second, I hope to be more beneficial to my fellow beings there than I can be here, in correcting their morals by precept and example, and perhaps influencing some to obey the Lord and become Christians, which will abundantly recompense me for all the hardships and deprivations I may have to endure; the third reason is, by misfortunes I am reduced to low circumstances in the things of this life, and it would render me very unhappy for my wife and myself to be dependent on a cold-hearted world for support, which must be the case soon unless some change takes place in our circumstances; and as the gold and the whole earth is the Lord's, and I believe he is as willing to lend me some of it as another man. I will go and labor to dig it out of the earth and make a good use of it. I believe he will uphold and protect me there as well as here, if I serve and honor him . . . .[22]

Udell was bothered by the practice of traveling on the Lord's day. "This day we should have rested out of respect to the laws of God," he wrote on June 2, "but the great majority voted against stopping and we were compelled to go on." However, a week later it was a different story, and Udell wrote:

> Today our company consented to rest. By permission I preached to them, and there being some skeptics with us, I presented to their minds some of the evidences of the authenticity of the holy scriptures, and of a future state of existence, and closed with a few remarks upon the necessity of preparing for a future state.[23]

But for a Christian like Udell, traveling with non-believers led to a series of never-ending confrontations. He was "so harassed by the wicked company" because of his Christian principles, that he left the train and traveled alone for a time. Eventually he returned and remained with "the wicked company" all the way to California.[24]

Thomas and Anna Rigdon and their three small children were ahead of Udell on the trail that summer. They left Iowa in March, bound for Oregon instead of California. They hired a 16-year-old boy named Silas Higgins[25] to drive their ox team, and Thomas, who was seriously ill, spent most of the journey on a bed in the back of the wagon. One record noted of the Rigdons: "This family were Baptist as to their faith until Alexander Campbell personally visited them and then they joined the new church organized by him at that time called the Campbellites, later known as the Christian church."[26]

At the dangerous crossing of the Platte River, the Rigdon's wagon and oxen began to drift down stream. One account noted that Silas "became quite frightened"[27] and another account recorded that he "lost his nerve and became very much frightened, thinking all was lost."[28] Both accounts agree that 25-year-old Anna saved the day. She quickly tossed her 2-year-old baby boy, Townsend, into the back of the wagon where her husband and two little daughters were lying, and she took command of the situation. Anna "climbed to the back of the lead oxen. By much wielding of the lash she had snatched from Silas' hands, and shouting lustily at the oxen, she gave the needed impetus that turned their heads to the opposite bank and thus the family, as well as their worldly possessions, were saved."

As if this harrowing experience was not enough, Anna had to confront a knife-wielding Indian along the trail who was demanding food that she did not have. He held a knife to the throat of Anna's little daughter, Artilissa, but the mother remained calm. She bartered with him until she saw the dust of approaching wagons, and then she warned him that he had better leave while he had the chance. He released the little girl and fled to the hills.

Anna Rigdon was a strong woman, and she would need all of that strength after arriving in Oregon. She and Thomas were the first Christians to settle in the mining town of Jacksonville in southern Oregon, and Anna was one of only three women in the town. She gave birth to a son in the winter of 1851–52, and he was the only baby in the town. When her husband died early that spring, Anna was left with small children and virtually no resources. She sold her wagon for $100 and then bought one hundred pounds of flour. She made this into bread and sold it to the miners for $200, doubling her money. She sent word to Silas Higgins to come and get her and the children, and she moved to Marion County to be near her parents. Later, she remarried and bore four more children.

Among the numerous Christian families who chose Oregon over California in 1850 were the ones headed by Christian Deardorff, Jesse Dutton Walling, Melchi Johnson, Horace Lindsay, C. F. Mascher, and George Woolen. Christian and Matilda Deardorff migrated from Burlington, Iowa, and settled near Milwaukie in Clackamas County and became members of the congregation for which John Foster was preaching. The Wallings, Jesse Dutton and Eliza Ann, and the Johnsons, Melchi and Delilah, settled in Polk County. Horace Lindsay and Mary Ritchey married in Morgan County, Illinois in 1847. They settled in Washington County and became members of the Tualatin congregation.

Two families in the 1850 migration were related to each other and became charter members of the Bethany Church near Silverton in Marion County when it was established in

1851. C. Frederick Mascher had married Sarah Eisenhardt, and George Woolen had married her sister, Juliann Eisenhardt. Both couples were married in Baltimore, Maryland, and both had lived in that city for several years before migrating westward together.

A young Christian named Andrew Jefferson Nelson was also in the 1850 migration, but he chose to mine for gold in California before deciding where to settle. He earned nearly $5,000 in two years of digging and then moved north to Oregon Territory, settling in Yamhill County. He married Lucretia Burnett, daughter of George William Burnett and niece of Glen Owen Burnett. Andrew later became an elder in the McMinnville Church.

Sebastian Adams

There was one other person in the 1850 migration who was destined to have a powerful impact on the church in Oregon. Twenty-five-year-old Sebastian Adams, the younger brother of William Lysander Adams, also came overland from Illinois that summer. He lost almost everything during the course of the journey, suffered from starvation, and nearly died. A man named Joel E. Ferris remembered his father and a friend "finding a man named Sebastian Adams wandering in the desert and sagebrush nearly naked and badly wounded by the Indians." They placed him in their wagon and took him on to California. Adams was "practically just a skeleton" and he lost consciousness during the last stage of the trip.[29]

Sebastian Adams remained in California for 40 days, recuperating from his ordeal. Sufficiently recovered to travel, he sailed to Oregon and arrived in Portland on September 13, 1850. Soon he was reunited with his brother in Yamhill County, and before long he had settled on a donation land claim in the same area. Sebastian was a skilled carpenter, and he brought a chest of tools with him from Illinois. He spent part of his first winter in making furniture for families in the Adams-McBride settlement.

Inez Adams remembered her uncle Sebastian as being "of a jovial, social nature, full of quips and jokes."[30] When Sebastian met the family of James and Mahala McBride and was introduced to their oldest daughter, 19-year-old Martha, it must have been love at first sight. They were married on February 6, 1851. Sebastian taught school for the next four years and began to speak publicly for the church. Later, he would serve as a state senator and would preach for the Christian Church in Salem for 20 years.[31]

The Christians in Oregon Territory were still suffering from the effects of the California exodus in 1850, but there was much for which to be thankful. The organization of the Pleasant Hill Church in Lane County, the coming of an advance party of families determined to plant a "Bethany College" in Oregon, the addition of faithful preachers like the Davidsons, and the safe arrival of the gifted Sebastian Adams were all of vital importance to the growth of the church in the decades just ahead.

Chapter 10

Three Brothers for Oregon 1851

We left Illinois in April, 1851, and after a tedious journey of five months, we arrived in this Valley . . . . One of my brothers and myself commenced preaching in the neighborhood and got up a little church of 38 members.

— John Alkire Powell, Linn County

Caleb P. Chapman was born on the frontier in Illinois Territory about 12 miles from St. Louis on October 3, 1810. When he was three years old, his large extended family of parents, grandparents, aunts, uncles, and cousins moved to the southwestern corner of Indiana and settled north of Evansville. His entire family were members of the Methodist Church, and his early religious training was confined to that church. One of his closest friends in his adolescent years was his first cousin, Elijah Goodwin. Goodwin was just three years older, but Caleb always looked up to him. The boys were both reared on Methodist sermons, which contained a strong dose of "hell-fire and damnation" terror.

Around 1820, Elijah Goodwin became attracted to a new religious movement that was advancing through southern Indiana. One account noted:

> When he was about thirteen years old some newcomers who called themselves Christians, but whom the people called New Lights, settled in the community. He then heard a different style of preaching. The former preachers dealt largely with hell-fire and damnation but these new ministers talked about the love of God and the death of Christ for sinful

> men. They taught that Christ died to reconcile men to God and not to reconcile God to man. That kind of preaching pleased the boy very much.[1]

Elijah Goodwin was baptized into Christ in October 1822, and he began preaching in the mid-1820s. But the watershed year in his life occurred in 1835 when he made the conscious decision to become more bold and fearless in his proclamation of the ancient gospel. It was during that summer "that he resolved to declare the apostles' doctrine at all hazards, and exhort the people to obey the gospel as believers did on the day of Pentecost." He reasoned: "If I preach the same facts to be believed and the same commands to be obeyed; and if the people believe and obey, surely all will be well, for the Lord is faithful that promised: but if they are contentious, and will not obey the truth, but persist in unrighteousness, then the consequence shall be upon their own heads—I shall have delivered my soul."[2]

Caleb P. Chapman

Three summers later Elijah Goodwin welcomed one of his most enthusiastic converts when Caleb Chapman was immersed into Christ. "I was a proselyte from the Methodist Church," Chapman wrote later, and "I went trying to preach as soon as I could get on dry clothes, such as it was." One year later it was Elijah Goodwin who again played a decisive role when he assisted his first cousin in being set apart for the ministry of the Word. "I was ordained for a preacher by the imposition of his hands by order of the church at Cynthiana, Posey County, Indiana, in the summer of 1839," Chapman remembered.[3] Nearly a half-century later, Chapman identified himself to a church leader by saying: "I am a cousin to the noted Elijah Goodwin."[4]

For nearly a decade, Caleb Chapman preached in Indiana and Arkansas. He married Elizabeth Smith in Arkansas in 1842. With nine years of preaching experience behind him, Chapman migrated to Oregon Territory with his family in the summer of 1848. They arrived in September and chose to settle near several families of Christians who were living west of

Silverton in Marion County. These families were scattered along Silver Creek and Pudding River, but no congregation had been organized yet. Nor did Chapman find time for this work during his first two busy years of farming and home-building.

By October of 1850, Chapman was ready to make "an attempt to preach the glad tidings to the new settlers around him."[5] The times were still unsettled with the upheaval of the California gold rush continuing to lure vast numbers of his neighbors to the diggings. For the next year and a half, Chapman devoted his energy to preaching the gospel and organizing churches, and his efforts met with considerable success. In a letter back home to the *Christian Record* in Indiana, Chapman wrote:

> I send you fifteen names for the *Record*. I have been proclaiming the glad tidings to the best of my ability, for some 18 months, in this new country, and during that time we have organized several congregations, numbering some thirty members, some more and some less, and besides these I have had the pleasure of baptizing many penitent believers throughout the country, and have obtained quite a number of proselytes from the sects. In short, the cause of our divine Master is advancing in this part of Oregon, and would advance much more rapidly if we only had more preachers.[6]

From the beginning of October 1850 to the close of March 1852, Chapman had demonstrated remarkable effectiveness. Dr. McBride had been aware of "six respectable churches" in October 1850, and now Chapman had supplemented this by organizing "several congregations." This probably meant four to six more churches in just 18 months. In addition to "baptizing many penitent believers throughout the country," Chapman had appealed to his denominational neighbors to relinquish their sectarian names and creedal formulations and just be Bible-believing Christians. This is what he meant by the assertion that he had "obtained quite a number of proselytes from the sects."

The Bethany Church in Marion County

The California gold rush was showing no signs of abatement in 1851, and large numbers of Oregonians were either still in California or making plans to go. Accurate statistics on how much gold was actually being mined in these years are not available, but the California State Mining Bureau estimated the yield at approximately $10 million for 1848; $10 million for 1849; $41 million for 1850; $76 million for 1851; and $81 million for the peak year of 1852. Production numbers declined rapidly between 1853 and 1855.[7]

Despite the distractions, some influential congregations were being established in Oregon during these years. As important as the founding of the Pleasant Hill Church in Lane County in August of 1850, was the founding of the Bethany Church in Marion County in April of 1851. Several Cox families were included among the pioneers who settled in the Silverton area in the fall of 1846, and one account recorded:

> There was a time when all the beautiful country westward from Silverton, through Bethany and across Silver Creek and Pudding River to the Prairie, was owned by members of the Cox family, who came in 1846. Peter Cox acquired land just west of Silverton. John T. Cox was a little further west. Gideon S. Cox was on Pudding River. Samuel S. Cox was south of Silver Creek. Elias Cox had a claim nearby.[8]

Twenty-four-year-old Wilburn King was also in the 1846 migration. In November 1846, he married Marcilia Cox, the daughter of Gideon Cox. The only Christian living in this district when the Cox families arrived was Thomas C. Shaw, but several other Christian families settled around the Cox families in subsequent years. Isaac and Margarette Headrick arrived with the 1847 migration, and their daughter, Josephine, married Thomas C. Shaw in 1850. The first physician in the area, Dr. Joseph Monroe Blackerby, and his wife, Cassandra Coffey, were important additions to the Christian community. Through his wife's family, Dr. Blackerby was a brother-in-law to William Porter at Aumsville and later to William Wilshire Bristow at Pleasant Hill. Samuel and Sarah Tucker came overland with the Chapmans in the

1848 migration, and their daughter, Lucia, married Elias Cox in 1851. The C. Frederick Mascher family arrived in 1850.

With the beginning of Caleb Chapman's ministerial efforts in the fall of 1850, it was only a matter of time before the families along Pudding River and Silver Creek were organized for church work. The name of this congregation was never completely finalized. It was called "The Church of Christ at Bethany" and "The Bethany Christian Church." It was also called "The Church of Christ on Silver Creek" and "The Silver Creek Christian Church." The organizational statement read as follows:

> We whose names that are first subscribed having under consideration the necessity of uniting ourselves into church order, did therefore organize ourselves into such church order on the fourth Lord's day in April A.D. 1851, on the waters of Pudding River, under the superintendence and Eldership of C. P. Chapman (presiding) and by the consent of each other did covenant together to first give ourselves to the Lord, and then to each other, to enable ourselves thereby to keep all the ordinances of the House of the Lord, and to know more perfectly that we are built together upon the foundation of the Apostles and prophets, Jesus Christ himself being the chief corner stone.[9]

There were 27 charter members listed in the document beginning with Isaac and Margarette Headrick. Prominent leaders included Peter Cox and his younger brother, Gideon Cox, and Thomas C. Shaw and C. F. Mascher. But the acknowledged spiritual leader of the Bethany Church from the very beginning was Elias Cox, the oldest son of Peter Cox. Elias was born in Indiana in 1823. His wife, Jemima Griffin Cox, died on the Oregon Trail during the overland journey in 1846. The church at Bethany might have been organized sooner, but Elias succumbed to "gold fever excitement" and rushed to the California diggings in 1849. Seven months after the Bethany Church was established, he married Lucia Tucker, daughter of Samuel and Sarah Tucker, on November 27, 1851. One tradition claimed the Bethany Church met for a time in the Elias Cox home. When the Bethany meetinghouse was erected in 1858, it was on his land. He did some preaching through the years, and one obituary account said, "For fifty years Mr. Cox preached the gospel of the Christian Religion."[10]

The Powell Clan

The largest group of Christians migrating to Oregon in 1851 came from Menard County in central Illinois. This was the Powell wagon train led by three brothers who were all preachers of the gospel. John Alkire Powell, Noah Powell, and Alfred Powell had moved with their parents from Ohio to Illinois in 1825.[11] The three brothers eventually settled on adjoining farms on Salt Creek, about 20 miles north of Springfield, and each of them soon married. John and Noah married sisters.[12] When Abraham Lincoln moved into the area in 1831, he settled about 12 miles from the Powell farms at a village called New Salem. The Powell brothers were each converted to the Restoration Movement in the early 1830s, and all three became preachers for small churches in Menard County.

Along with Abraham Lincoln, John was a volunteer in the Blackhawk Indian War in 1832. John was 25 and married, and Lincoln was 23 and unmarried. They were acquainted, but to what extent they were friends is unknown. In that same year, John became attracted to the principles of the Restoration Movement and was baptized into Christ in the Sangamon River. One record noted of John: "He was a great student of the Bible, theology, and historical literature. The Powells in Ohio were United Brethren, but he was attracted to the movement, then in its infancy, which had for its object the discarding of human creeds and the restoration of New Testament Christianity."[13]

John began preaching soon after his baptism, and for many years he was the regular preacher for the Sugar Grove (also called Sweet Water) congregation in Menard County. One historical memoir noted, "On one or several occasions, Lincoln was in the audience when John Powell preached."[14] Somewhere around 1838, John Powell was instrumental in establishing another congregation in the Menard County town of Athens. One account reported: "About that time a large, well-formed man, with a powerful voice and dressed in homespun, began to preach there; he spoke just as the Disciples preached on Pentecost and afterward. That was John A. Powell of Sugar Grove."[15]

John Powell was not only the oldest of the three brothers, he was the strongest leader in the family and the acknowledged captain in the western migration to Oregon Territory. "John had a powerful physique; he was six feet in height and weighed two hundred twenty-five pounds," wrote one biographer. "A man of indomitable will, he knew no task insurmountable. He was a man of force and influence, highly esteemed by all who knew him."[16] Led by John's commanding appearance and strong voice, the Powell families departed Menard County on April 3, 1851, and began the long trek to Oregon.

The Death of Theresa Powell McFadden

In addition to the three Powell brothers, there were two young married men and their families traveling in the train. These were the children of John and Savilla. Theresa, their oldest daughter, had married William McFadden in 1847. They were traveling with a small daughter and Theresa was pregnant with their second child. Franklin Powell, the oldest son of John and Savilla, had married Jane Peeler just two weeks before the wagon train left Menard County. She was the daughter of Abner Peeler, a well-known preacher in the Restoration Movement in Illinois.

The wagons reached Council Bluffs, Iowa, on the first day of May. It was here that a family of Christians, the William Churchill family, joined themselves to the train and accompanied the Powells all the way to Oregon. The caravan proceeded without incident until June 27, when Theresa McFadden went into labor and delivered the first grandson in the John Powell family. He was large and healthy and was named after his proud grandfather. Theresa recovered quickly from her pregnancy and "was soon able to get out of the wagon and help at camp." But her good health was short-lived.

Several years later, Jane Peeler Powell provided an account of the sudden tragedy that afflicted the Powell family in the final month of their trip. She wrote:

> About August 1st we camped on Snake river. One very hot day Theresa lay down in her wagon and went to sleep; about 4 p.m. the wind came up very cold and blew on her for some time before she awoke. From this she took a very bad cold and gradually went down, and died August 10 in the Blue Mountains. We were then a long way from civilization. Grandpa took the side boards from the wagons and made a coffin and used the boards we had for a table for head and foot of the grave, cutting her name and age on them with his knife. Meacham Station is now near that place.[17]

With heavy hearts the Powells completed the last three weeks of their journey. They chose to travel the Barlow Toll Road around Mount Hood, and like so many others before them they struggled mightily to get their wagons up and down Laurel Hill. At noon on September 3, 1851, they arrived at Oregon City—five months to the day from when they had left their home in central Illinois. They pushed on to Linn County to file land claims, but their grief was compounded when Theresa's little baby boy died just as the wagons were reaching their final destination.

Central Church in Linn County

Most of the Powells settled along the Santiam River about seven miles east of Albany in Linn County. The exception was Noah, who chose to build a home on Howell's Prairie in Marion County. "We all liked the country and soon forgot the difficulties of the journey," recalled Jane Peeler Powell. "Grandpa expressed himself as well pleased with the change with only one regret, that of losing Theresa and baby." Jane also remembered the log house they built on the prairie:

> Our house was sixteen feet square. It was built of hewn logs . . . . There were two doors; one in the south, and the other in the north opening onto a porch without a floor. The house had a rough floor made of boards split out of fir

> timber. There was no window, but we could usually keep one door open for light. In the east side were the fireplace and hearth, made of rock. The chimney was built of sticks and mud, and was run up on the outside of the wall. Our fire shovel was a board until Pa made one from a piece of iron from an old wagon. Our furniture consisted of trestle benches for a bedstead, home-made stools, tables and one chair which we brought with us.[18]

It did not take John Powell long to evaluate the numerical strength of the Christians in his new home territory. Somehow he knew in advance that the best informed person would probably be Glen Owen Burnett. Powell mounted a horse and rode about 20 miles to meet with Burnett. It seems unlikely that Powell and Burnett would have ever known each other back in the states, since one lived in Illinois and the other in Missouri. But now they gave one another the right hand of fellowship and forged a bond of friendship. The 44-year-old Powell was only two years older than Burnett, and they were cut from the same cloth. "From him I learned that there were several churches in the Willamette Valley," Powell wrote excitedly, "with a great many brethren scattered over the country; in the aggregate, supposed to be a thousand or twelve hundred."[19]

After receiving this encouraging report from Burnett, John returned home determined to establish a congregation in his own district. He and his younger brother, Alfred, canvassed their immediate community and rallied the Christians to join them. In a report to the *Christian Record,* John wrote, "One of my brothers and myself commenced preaching in the neighborhood and got up a little church of 38 members."[20] This congregation would always be known as the Central Church in Linn County. They scheduled a protracted meeting for June of 1852, and they were thrilled when four other preachers showed up to share the labor. The meeting lasted four days and resulted in seven additions to the church. In addition to John and Alfred, the preachers included Dr. James McBride, A. V. McCarty, Alfred Elder, and Caleb Chapman.[21] The Powells had been in Oregon for only nine months, but they were already providing much-needed organization and leadership.

The Children of John A. Powell

One young man who married a daughter of John Alkire Powell was Robert Earl. Although he did not have formal schooling, he kept a journal of daily life. Despite his poor grammar and misspelled words, he portrayed the impact that his father-in-law had on the community. "When John A. Powell come in that neighborhood we dident do nothing in winter time but dance," Earl recalled. "He wasent there over 2 years and we couldent git up a dance. He converted about the hol neighborhood. He was a number one man and good Preacher. He preached in that neighborhood once a month for over 30 years and he always had a house full."[22]

The children of John A. Powell made a strong contribution to the Restoration Movement in Oregon. Franklin and Jane Powell were active members of the Central Church for 19 years. In 1870 they moved to Monmouth in order to give their children the benefit of an education at Christian College in that town. Franklin served on the board of trustees for Christian College for many years. "He was a devout member of the Church of Christ, and a most liberal financial supporter," noted one account. "He was an officer in the church for more than sixty years, and served as elder in the Monmouth Christian Church for thirty-five years."[23]

Augustus Steuben Powell, the second son of John A. Powell, married a 20-year-old Christian named Ruhama Marshall in 1853 and settled near Albany. Six years after Franklin and Jane relocated, they also moved to Monmouth in order to give their children the opportunity of an education at Christian College. "Steuben was a devoted member of the Christian Church," wrote one of his descendants. "He was always cheerful and manifested a sweet, Christlike spirit. In his last sickness he never complained, and just before the end came, he said, 'I'm crossing the river, and it looks bright on the other side. I'll soon see my loved ones.'" Of his wife it was said: "She united with the Christian Church at the age of sixteen, and was faithful to the end. When she was passing away she called the family to her bedside, and as she bade them good-bye she asked each one to live so that all might meet her in heaven."[24]

Stephen Dodridge Powell, the third son of John A. Powell, married Margaret Umphlet on May 23, 1858. Her parents, Stanley and Jane Umphlet, were Iowa Christians who migrated to Oregon in 1845 and were active church members in Linn County. Stephen and Margaret were the first Christians to homestead in Tillamook County, where he taught school, served as justice of the peace, and operated a saw-mill. There was no organized congregation in the county when they moved there, and they probably held services in their home.

When Thomas Franklin Campbell established the monthly *Christian Messenger* in Monmouth in 1870, Stephen Powell served as one of the "agents" for the periodical. Stephen and Margaret moved to Hillsboro in Washington County in 1885, and he devoted the last 25 years of his life to the cause of Christ in that community. One historical record confirms that Stephen "was a devout member of the Christian Church for fifty-five years."[25]

Another young man who became a member of the John A. Powell family was a nephew named John Wesley Propst. His mother was a sister to John A. Powell. When both of Propst's parents died on the overland journey in 1852, the 15-year-old continued on to Oregon and was taken in by his uncle. He was baptized into Christ in 1853 and married Margaret Jane Cole in 1860. John Wesley Propst remained in the Powell neighborhood east of Albany, and he later served as an elder in the Central Church for many years. He lived to be 102.[26]

More Preachers for Oregon

Altogether there were six gospel preachers who migrated to Oregon Territory in 1851, making that the most productive year to date for attracting evangelists to this new and developing country. The Willamette Valley gained three talented preachers when the Powell brothers arrived, and that achievement alone would have made 1851 an exceptional year in Oregon church history. But this was also the year in which G. W. Richardson, Samuel Bates Briggs, and Dr. John Nelson Perkins arrived in the territory.

The migration that year brought a young and talented gospel preacher to Oregon in the person of George Washington Richardson. He was born in Greene County, Illinois, on September 26, 1824, and he was just turning 27 when he arrived in Oregon. His parents, John and Orpha Richardson, and several other family members were strong supporters of the Restoration Movement back in Illinois, and they all migrated to Oregon together in 1851. They settled on donation land claims near present-day Scio in Linn County, about ten miles northeast of the Powells. Because they all settled on land adjacent to each other, the area became known as "Richardson's Gap."[27]

G. W. Richardson was ordained to the ministry and began preaching when he was just 18 years old. By the time he moved to Oregon from Adams County in western Illinois, he had already been preaching for nine years. He was not able to organize a church as quickly as the Powells had in their neighborhood, but it did not take him long. By 1852 he had organized a church consisting of his parents and other relatives and neighbors. This congregation met regularly at Hester Schoolhouse near Scio in Linn County.[28] In April 1857, Richardson described the growth of this congregation in a letter to James Mathes for publication in the *Christian Record*:

> I immigrated to Oregon in 1851, and located in the forks of the Santiam River, Linn County. The white inhabitants were few in number, and as a general thing, far from being religious. I often thought of the expression of Abraham, "Surely the fear of God is not in this place." Shortly after my settlement there, we organized a church containing six members; it now numbers about fifty-five members.[29]

Samuel and Susannah Briggs arrived in Oregon via the Applegate Trail. Like many of the travelers who came before them on that famous trail that entered Oregon from the south, this family never made it to the Willamette Valley. They fell in love with the rugged beauty of the Umpqua Valley in what is now Douglas County, and they chose to live in the small settlement of Canyonville. The 46-year-old Samuel Bates Briggs was a mechanic by vocation, but he was also a talented gospel preacher. He became the first member of the Restoration Movement to preach in Douglas County. He was also one of the prime movers in the organization of Douglas County on January 7, 1852, and he served as County Commissioner for a number of years.

Like Dr. James McBride before him, 35-year-old Dr. John Nelson Perkins was a physician-preacher. He settled with his family in Linn County not far from the Powells and Richardsons. He preached in Oregon throughout the 1850s and early 1860s. He was still living in Lebanon in Linn County in the fall of 1862, but some time after that he moved to Washington Territory. One historical record commented on Perkins: "Finally business and politics drew him away from the gospel ministry and he went to Eastern Washington where he engaged in stock-raising and became noted as a cancer doctor."[30]

The Pioneers of '51

A Christian named Zadok Riggs was captain of a wagon train that left Knox County, Illinois, on April 2 and crossed the Missouri River at Council Bluffs, Iowa. By the time the company reached the Oregon Trail it had swelled to include 27 wagons and 100 people. Zadok was traveling with his wife, Jane Leib Riggs, and several children.

The parents of Zadok Riggs, Scott and Hannah Berry Riggs, were dedicated Christians who had made a great contribution to the Restoration Movement in Illinois in both Lawrence and Scott counties. One family record noted of Scott Riggs, "He had been reared in the Baptist faith, but in early life he espoused the views of Alexander Campbell, and devoted much time and thought to the dissemination of those views, both by example and public preaching."[31] Scott and Hannah Riggs had been instrumental in uniting the Stone and Campbell forces in their part of Illinois.[32]

The brother of Zadok Riggs, James Berry Riggs, had already migrated to Oregon in 1845 and was farming in Polk County. He was one of the leaders in the Salt Creek congregation in that county. Zadok and Jane were planning to settle near their relatives in Polk County. Unfortunately, Zadok was ill when they left home, and rather than improving on the journey he became steadily worse. On July 4, at the last crossing of the Sweetwater River at Independence Rock, Zadok Riggs died.

One member of the company, John O. Fry, was keeping a journal of the trip. Concerning the death of their captain, he wrote:

> Several times during the trip we had seen places where people had been buried, and, for lack of a shovel, the graves had been made so shallow that wild animals had dug up the remains and the bones were lying scattered around. We made up our minds that wild animals should not have the remains of our dead captain, so we dug a grave about six feet deep. I had put partitions in my wagon box, with lids over the apartments, and I took them out and made a box. Placing the body in this box, we lowered it into the grave, put enough dirt over it to cover it, and then filled up the grave with large rocks. With our teams we went to the side of a mountain, about two miles distant, and secured small logs, with which we built a pen around the grave; covered the pen with logs, and heaped a lot of large rocks on top of it. When this had been done, his wife and children felt more satisfied to come away and leave him. This was the 4th of July, and it was very warm.[33]

Zadok Riggs had died eight days before his 40th birthday. His determined 37-year-old wife gathered her children together and continued on to Oregon and took up residence in Polk County as planned. She never remarried in Oregon. She raised her children and remained faithful to Christ.

A future Oregon preacher, 12-year-old Jasper V. Crawford, was in the 1851 migration. His parents, Philemon and Lelitia Crawford, were Christians and were desirous of locating in a settlement where there were other Christians. They decided to settle in Yamhill County, and in later years Jasper Crawford commented on their decision:

> My parents, who were then in the prime of their lives, being on the sunny side of forty, were very earnest and devout disciples . . . . One of the first things they did after reaching their destination was to take a kind of religious census of the community to discover if there were any of their own faith and order. The results were highly gratifying. They were upon all sides of us.[34]

The Future Looks Bright

It was on October 23, 1851, that Glen Owen Burnett wrote the letter to Alexander Campbell in which he estimated the numerical strength of the Restoration Movement in Oregon Territory at 1,200 members. In his conversation with John Alkire Powell that same fall, he gave the impression that the membership was somewhere between 1,000 and 1,200. If Burnett's statistics were anywhere close to accurate, the Christians were still the largest religious group in the territory at the close of 1851. They had been in that position for at least four years, and they were showing no signs of numerical decline. Their weakness was still a lack of organization, but they had made significant progress in just one year.

The zealous labors of Caleb Chapman and the emergence of the young A. V. McCarty were high points in the year. The organization of the Bethany Church in Marion County and the Central Church in Linn County would have a long-term impact for good. The addition of the three Powell brothers and G. W. Richardson, Samuel Bates Briggs, and Dr. John Nelson Perkins greatly strengthened the preaching force in the territory.

For the first time, there was talk of organizing an annual state meeting like the ones back home in Missouri, Iowa, Illinois, and Indiana. Such a meeting would bring all the preachers together at one time, and a strategy for evangelizing the territory and organizing churches could be implemented. At least a dozen churches had been organized, but there was so much more work that needed to be done in that regard. There were now 21 gospel preachers living in the territory, and that did not include church leaders like Amos Harvey and Elias Cox who preached on occasion. The future looked bright for Oregon Christians as the calendar moved from 1851 to 1852.

Chapter 11

The Glorious Cause of Truth 1852

I would just observe that the glorious cause of truth is gaining ground in this far off country, very fast . . . .

We have many good brethren here, who love the cause, and are devoted to its advancement.

— A. V. McCarty, November 9, 1852

On a cold, rainy Lord's Day morning in the winter of 1852–53, Glen Owen Burnett left his "humble log cabin to walk a distance of three miles to a school house where a few disciples were wont to meet to worship God according to his word." He was wearing his "Oregon overcoat" to protect himself from the elements. This was "a blanket with a slit in the middle just large enough to run our head in." As he walked along his "thoughts looked forward to a time when brighter days would span our Oregon sky, and men true, able and faithful would be raised up to help us in the grand and glorious work of preaching Christ."

The schoolhouse stood on a small ridge and could be seen a long way off. From a distance, it appeared that no one had arrived yet. "Oregon, on that day, seemed to have put on her most gloomy appearance," Burnett remembered years later, "but as we approached the door, we discovered some one had entered before us." The young man inside who was bending over the stove and trying to kindle a fire was 21-year-old Levi Lindsay Rowland.

Levi Lindsay Rowland

In 1844, at the age of 13, Levi Lindsay Rowland had migrated to Yamhill County with his father, Jeremiah Rowland, and several brothers. In 1848–49 he had studied under William Lysander Adams, a graduate of Bethany College, at his log cabin schoolroom called "Yamhill University." With his father's permission, Levi had worked in the California gold mines in 1849–51 and had invested his considerable earnings in cattle that were grazing on his father's farm. He was now a boarding student living at the home of Dr. Nathaniel Hudson in the Bethel Hills of northeastern Polk County, where he was studying Greek and Latin.

Twenty-six years later, Glen Owen Burnett could still clearly remember the moment when he walked into the cold schoolhouse and greeted Levi. He wrote:

> Upon our entrance he arose to speak to us. The lineaments of his youthful countenance are fresh still in my memory. I see how he looked then. I can still trace in that youthful face, on the page of memory, a strong desire for knowledge, and over against that desire a settled determination to acquire it. He was a stranger to duplicity of every type, a child of honest parentage, and loved the truth, whose generous heart had yielded to the claims of the dear Savior, and was a child of God. As we looked at him we loved him, and as the years rolled round we love him still.[1]

Burnett seized the moment to encourage a future leader in the church. "Whilst we spent a part of that rainy Sunday in that lonely house with open cracks on all sides," recalled Burnett, "we proposed to him to go to Bethany College, and promised to give him a letter of introduction to Brother Campbell, if he would consent to go." The challenge fell on a willing heart. Rowland "seemed almost enraptured with the idea of going to college," but he was fearful that his father would not approve. Burnett promised to loan him a horse if he would ride to his father's house and ask his permission.

Levi Lindsay Rowland rode off on the borrowed horse the next morning, and when he returned a few days later, there was radiance on his face. He reported to Burnett that "to his great delight his father was very willing and anxious for him to go, and had agreed to take his cattle and sell them and forward the means to pay his way." Rowland left his Yamhill County home for Bethany College on February 8, 1853, and did not return for six years. He completed the B.A. and M.A. degrees at Bethany College and then taught school for a time in Tennessee and Alabama. He married Emma Sanders, a graduate of Tolbert Fanning's Franklin College in Nashville, Tennessee, on November 18, 1858.

By the fall of 1859, Levi Lindsay Rowland had returned to Oregon to join the faculty of Bethel College, and within a year he had become its president. Glen Owen Burnett concluded his "Reminiscence of a Rainy Sunday" by observing:

> He went, and well did he improve the time. Years rolled round; meanwhile a college was built close by the school house, and Levi returned from his long stay, a ripe scholar and a polished teacher, and it was the pleasure of the writer of these reminiscences to install him as president of the college. Levi, do you remember that rainy Sunday? Many years, my honored brother, have passed since that little episode in your history took place. Your life has been given to God and humanity: I am satisfied.[2]

Glen Owen Burnett recognized in 1852 that the greatest need confronting the church in Oregon was the need for more leaders. Every letter sent from Oregon to the church papers back in the states during those years emphasized this need. Christians had migrated to the territory in large numbers, but the cause was understaffed when it came to talented proclaimers who could both evangelize and organize churches.

The Rise of Annual Meetings

The practice of Christians gathering together in "annual meetings" for the purpose of edification and evangelism had roots in the early years of the Stone and Mulkey movements. Most of the Christians migrating to Oregon had participated in such meetings on a county, district, or state level back home, and the wisdom of creating such opportunities in the sparsely settled Willamette Valley seemed obvious. In particular, the preachers wanted to get better acquainted and to devise some kind of strategy for evangelizing and organizing churches. It is not surprising, therefore, that the practice of holding "annual meetings" for the Christians in the Willamette Valley began as early as the fall of 1852.

Alexander Campbell had endorsed the concept of annual meetings from the beginning of his relationship with the Baptists in 1813, but he was aware of the charge that such meetings could become ecclesiastical or synodical conventions that would attempt to govern local churches. The autonomy of each local church was a precious principle in the Restoration Movement, and Campbell was not eager to lend credence to an emerging ecclesiasticism. Therefore, his article entitled "Conventions," published in the November 1851 *Millennial Harbinger* less than a year before Oregon's first annual meeting, is enlightening. Campbell wrote:

> Our Lord's days are weekly convocations around the table of the Lord, in the house of prayer, the pillar and stay of the gospel in the world. But these are not all that is necessary to the wants, the duties, and the enjoyments of the Christian age. We as much need annual festivals, conventions, or big meetings, in the Christian Kingdom of God, as they did in the Jewish Kingdom of God . . . . But the conventions for which we now plead are very unlike ecclesiastic, synodical, or hierarchical conventions of church judicature. Ours are meetings of Christians "in the fullness of the blessing of the gospel of Christ," when they assemble to congratulate one another as members of the great family of God, and of the household of faith, and to "exhort one another in psalms, and hymns, and spiritual songs, singing with gratitude in their hearts to the Lord." . . . There are fields of labor to be selected, evangelists or missionaries to be sent abroad, and the ways and means of accomplishing these objects are to be considered and provided for. Brethren, as individuals, nor churches as individual communities, cannot, in their individual capacities, accomplish these objects. There must be church, as well as individual co-operation, in order to the accomplishment of our obligations to the Lord and his cause in the world.[3]

With Campbell's strong endorsement before them, the leaders of the Restoration Movement in Oregon began to discuss the logistics of such a meeting taking place in the Willamette Valley. When C. F. Swander published *Making Disciples in Oregon* in 1928, he alluded to this discussion and wrote: "In 1852 Glen O. Burnett called the disciples of the Valley to assemble together for fellowship and worship. This was hailed as an inspiration. This first meeting was held in an oak grove near the present town of McCoy."[4] Subsequent historians accepted Swander's assertion for the next half century, until Douglas Dornhecker questioned it in 1979. "Swander fails to document his account of that gathering," noted Dornhecker. "Although contemporary newspapers reported other conventions and religious gatherings during the summer of 1852, no mention appears to have been made of the Disciples' meeting."[5]

Although no evidence has survived to document the meeting that Swander alluded to, there is evidence for a "co-operation meeting" in the fall of 1852 that was called by John Alkire Powell and hosted by the Central Church in Linn County. In a letter dated September 21, 1852, Powell wrote to James Mathes, editor of the *Christian Record* in Indiana, and informed him that the idea for this meeting had originated during a protracted meeting at the Central Church in June of that year. As mentioned in chapter 10, this earlier four-day meeting was conducted by six preachers: John A. Powell, Alfred Powell, Dr. James McBride, A. V. McCarty, Alfred Elder, and Caleb Chapman. At the close of this successful meeting, Powell said: "We then appointed a co-operation meeting commencing on Friday before the first Lord's day in this month (September)."[6]

The Annual Meeting Begins in Oregon

On Friday, September 3, 1852, the first annual meeting of Oregon Christians began at a site about seven miles east of Albany in Linn County. John and Alfred Powell and the members of the Central Church were the hosts for this ambitious effort, and since there was no available church building in the area, it presumably took place in a schoolhouse or outdoors in a brush arbor. The duration of the meeting is not given, but the prototypical annual meeting in those days was ten days long and included two Lord's Days. This meeting probably adjourned on Sunday evening, September 12.

Eight preachers shared in the public proclamation of the gospel of Christ. Glen Owen Burnett and Mac Waller were added to the six who had planned the event. "Ten congregations were heard from," enthused Powell, "numbering in all some 300 members who were liberal in their offers to support the cause." One of the main purposes of this "co-operation meeting" was to encourage the churches to cooperate in supporting an evangelist for the Willamette Valley. Powell announced the results:

> Your humble brother was selected as an Evangelist for a year, with a recess of four months, during the rainy season, for which they agree to pay me $700.00. I consented to ride, and have commenced my labors. I held a three day's meeting in the forks of the Santiam, embracing the 3rd Lord's day in this month, and had seven additions. Very few of the Churches here are properly organized. Since the above date, I have met with brother J. Rigdon from Iowa.[7]

Eight preachers and representatives from ten different congregations together at one time was certainly an unprecedented event for Oregon Christians. On the other hand, only 300 of the 1,000 Christians in the territory were represented at this historic first meeting, underscoring the lack of organization that was still limiting the impact of the movement. In addition, 13 of the 21 preachers in the territory were not present.

It is perhaps not surprising that John Foster and Daniel Trullinger from Clackamas County and Thomas Crawford McBride and Aaron Payne from Yamhill County were absent. These men were older and they rarely traveled great distances to preach. The father and son team of Elijah Davidson and Elijah B. Davidson was also missing, but the father was elderly and the son was living in Portland. The brothers, William Lysander Adams and Sebastian Adams, did not preach very often during this chapter of their lives, and they were involved in journalistic and educational pursuits. In addition, their mother and other family members were just arriving in the fall migration. Polk County's John Burris Smith was not devoting much of his time to traveling and preaching at this time, and the distance was probably too great for Samuel Bates Briggs in Douglas County.

The greatest surprise was that Noah Powell, G. W. Richardson and Dr. John Nelson Perkins were not present. All three lived a short distance from the place of meeting and could easily have attended. In subsequent years they were strong supporters of the annual meeting. Perhaps they were in attendance but did not preach that first year. Ten additional preachers arrived in the fall migration just after the close of the first annual meeting. They were: Abbott Levi Todd from Arkansas; Henry W. Taylor from Missouri, John Rigdon, Harrison H. Hendrix, and Lewis Casteel from Iowa; and John Ecles Murphy, Gilmore Callison, Edmund Green Browning, Charles Bradshaw, and George R. Caton from Illinois.[8]

The World's Longest Graveyard

The migration of 1852 was the largest since 1847, with an estimated 2,500 persons coming overland. "They have been coming in since the last of July," John Powell wrote in September, "and thousands are yet behind. They have been very sickly, and hundreds have died on the road."[9] Unfortunately, he was speaking from personal experience. The news of the deaths of his sister and brother-in-law had just reached him.

Lucinda Powell, a younger sister to the three preachers, had married Anthony Propst in 1836. They were both faithful members of the Church of Christ in Menard County, Illinois. With five children of their own and one nephew, they left Illinois and started across the Oregon Trail in the spring of 1852. "All went well until they reached the Blue Mountains," recalled one of their descendants. "While crossing the mountains Lucinda became ill and died. She was buried on Butler Creek in Umatilla County August 19, 1852. In a few days Anthony was taken ill but lived until after crossing the Cascade Mountains. He was buried at a place called Foster."[10] The six grieving children, now suddenly orphaned, continued on their journey and found homes with their Powell uncles.[11]

One family of Christians named Watkins left Clarksburg in Wayne County, Indiana, and joined the 1852 migration to Oregon. William Lynch Watkins and his wife, Sarah Smith Watkins, were traveling with four young sons and a 17-year-old daughter named Mary. It soon became evident that a young man in the train named Calvin Walker was very much interested in Mary Watkins.

Like many other trains that summer, this train was racked by cholera. Upon reaching the Platte River, William Lynch Watkins died and was buried along the trail. His wife contracted the same dreaded disease and survived only to the crossing of the Sweetwater River. Now suddenly orphaned, Mary wed Calvin Walker on July 4 at Independence Rock, and the ceremony was performed by a Christian preacher named Begley.[12] Once again, Mary faced catastrophe. Calvin died before they reached Oregon City.[13]

Mary was not yet 18, but she had buried her father, mother, and husband in the course of one overland journey, and she had four young brothers to raise. She married a young widower named George Riches on December 22, and they settled between Silverton and Sublimity in Marion County. Mary remained a faithful Christian for the rest of her life. One account confirms that she "was a member of the Christian church and died at a ripe old age."[14]

John Udell was on the trail again in 1852 for his second overland crossing. Early in the trip, while still at the Missouri River, he ran into some Christian friends. "Here we met with brother H. L. Woodford, and brother C. C. Padgett, and family, from Ray County, Missouri, and bound for Oregon," he wrote in his diary. "They are old acquaintances, and brethren in the Lord. How it rejoices our hearts to meet with such in a strange country!"[15] No doubt Woodford and Padgett rejoiced to see Udell, too, but before long their journey would be shrouded in sorrow.

Harry L. Woodford and Christopher C. Padgett were brothers-in-law. Woodford was married to Padgett's sister. Like so many others, their trek across the plains began with great anticipation and optimism, but somewhere along the route Mrs. Woodford died. Surrounded by his three small sons, Harry Woodford buried his wife at the side of the Oregon Trail and then continued on to Oregon. They settled in Douglas County.[16]

Shelby County, Indiana, was the former home of William and Eliza Jane Huntington. With five children in tow, these ardent Christians joined the throngs who were heading west. Sadly, they lost two of their children to cholera before they reached Oregon. Eliza Jane cut up her wedding gown and used the material to wrap the bodies of her children. They were buried along the Oregon Trail. The Huntingtons spent one winter in Oregon and then pressed on to Washington Territory. They settled at Castle Rock in Cowlitz County, and William Huntington became a dedicated preacher of the gospel in southwestern Washington and northwestern Oregon.[17]

It was said of Henry W. Taylor, that "he early espoused the cause of the Christian church, and almost up to the end of his life devoted a large share of his time to preaching in local pulpits."[18] Henry and Charlotte Taylor had lived in Highland County, Ohio, for eight years before moving to Missouri. In the spring of 1852 they decided to push west and settle in Oregon Territory. Their journey began under the most favorable circumstances, but before long, cholera invaded their little train, and they buried two of their children along the trail. Although disheartened and distressed, they continued on their sorrowful way without further loss. They settled in Lane County four miles south of Cottage Grove, and Henry looked for opportunities to preach. One record confirms: "For many years he was known as one of the most zealous of early day preachers."[19]

Michael and Sena Shelley and their ten children migrated to Oregon from Jefferson County, Iowa, in 1848. They settled in Pleasant Hill and became charter members of the Pleasant

Hill Church of Christ in 1850. Their reports back to Iowa were so favorable that Michael's elderly Christian parents decided to undertake the rigorous overland trip and join their Oregon relatives in 1852. Once again, as with so many others, the presence of cholera shattered their hopes. George Shelley died at the crossing of the Snake River. His widow continued on to Oregon and joined her family, but she died soon after arriving at Pleasant Hill.[20]

Another tragedy in the 1852 crossing was that experienced by the family of Gilmore and Elizabeth Callison. They had married in Kentucky in 1829 and moved to Hancock County in western Illinois in 1833. In that western outpost they had been successful in establishing the Mt. Pleasant Church of Christ in their home. One historical record noted:

> Into this locality, in 1833, there came, from near Columbia, Adair County, Ky., Gilmore Callison and his wife Elizabeth . . . and others. These five persons met, on the first Lord's Day after their arrival, at the home of Mr. Callison, to "break bread," and then formed a church of Christ. This was the first Christian Church in Hancock County and became the mother of congregations.[21]

Gilmore's younger brother, Robert Callison, had lived for a time in the adjoining county of McDonough. He married one of Elijah Bristow's daughters and was part of the large party of Bristows that migrated to Pleasant Hill in Lane County in 1848. His glowing reports back to Illinois prompted Gilmore and Elizabeth to make the difficult decision to sell their home and come overland in 1852. Traveling with them were their six sons and two daughters. Their oldest son, John Joseph, kept a diary of the journey that was published a century later by the Lane County Historical Society. His journal is a chronicle of tragedy and impending doom.

Other Christians traveling in the Callison train included Dr. John Kennedy Bristow, oldest son of Elijah Bristow, and his wife and children. Before arriving in Oregon Territory, Dr. Bristow watched helplessly as his wife, Emeline Match Bristow, and his daughter, Josephine Bristow, succumbed to cholera.[22]

The Oregon Trail has been described in some books as "the world's longest graveyard." One record commented "Cholera killed thousands. Others died by accidental gunshot or rattlesnake bite. Indian attacks claimed a few lives. In all, about one in seventeen adults died along the trail. For children, the toll was even higher. Of every five children who started the trip, one would fail to finish."[23] This was certainly true in the 1852 migration. The diary of John Joseph Callison paints a stark picture of life on the trail as cholera swept through the Callison wagon train. He wrote:

> May 31st. Lay by on account of sickness. Absalom Newingham very bad with cholera, nearly half the company down with diarrhea, some very bad. Very poor water to drink and exceedingly warm weather.
>
> June 1st. Absalom Newingham still getting worse, died half past two o'clock and we traveled 4 miles this evening to a spring of very good water and encamped.
>
> June 2nd. Traveled 6 miles and stopped at eleven o'clock on account of Josephine Bristow's being very sick, she still continues to grow worse, died at half past four o'clock. The rest of the company but very little better.[24]

The last entry in the diary is dated June 25 on the Sweetwater River near Independence Rock. The author had himself become a victim of the dreaded cholera, and he was evidently too weak to continue the daily entries. On August 13, 1852, John Joseph Callison celebrated his twenty-second birthday, but he was grievously ill and would live only ten more days. Slightly ahead of him on the trail, 35-year-old Lucinda Powell Propst died at Butler Creek on August 19. She was buried near the place where her niece, 22-year-old Theresa Powell McFadden, had died one year earlier. John Joseph Callison died on August 23 and was buried along the trail near the site of present-day LaGrande, Oregon.[25] His father fashioned a coffin from the side boards of John's wagon.[26]

Gilmore and Elizabeth grieved over the death of their firstborn, but their sufferings were far from over. Elizabeth had not been well for the last part of the journey, and now as they neared their new home in Lane County she worsened. Less than two months after arriving at Pleasant Hill, Elizabeth died on November 4, 1852, one day before her forty-fifth birthday. She was buried in the little cemetery at Pleasant Hill, close to the schoolhouse where the church met for worship on the Lord's Day. Gilmore and his remaining children settled in the valley about a mile from the cemetery.[27]

Gilmore Callison lost more than just his oldest son and his wife. His 40-year-old sister, Nancy Callison Browning, also died of cholera in the course of the grief-stricken journey. She died in childbirth near the Great Salt Lake in Utah Territory, and her baby died at the same time. She was survived by her husband and four children. Her husband, a gospel preacher named Edmund Green Browning, moved his motherless children down to Myrtle Creek in Douglas County where he lived and preached for the last 35 years of his life.

In the midst of the trail of sorrows, there were some genuine moments of rejoicing for anxious families when the mother safely delivered a child. Abbott Levi Todd and his wife, Angeline, welcomed their second child during the long trek to Oregon. Elijah Todd was born in a covered wagon near the Umatilla River. The Todds reached Howell's Prairie in Marion County in October, and the following year they moved south to Lookingglass Valley in Douglas County. For the next 30 years, E. G. Browning and A. L. Todd were co-laborers in the gospel in Douglas and surrounding counties. They died within two years of each other in the 1880s.

The Pioneers of '52

The migration of 1852 swelled the number of Christians living in the Willamette Valley. The second wave of families from Monmouth, Illinois, settled in Polk County near the future site of Monmouth, Oregon. Included in this number were the families of a gospel preacher, John Ecles Murphy, and his son-in-law, Albert Whitfield Lucas. Traveling in their train was William Mason, a professor from Bethany College. His wife, Margaret Davidson Mason, was the daughter of an Oregon preacher named Elijah Davidson. This was also the year when the families of Hezekiah Burford, John H. Robb, Frederick X. Shoemaker and William Menifee settled in Polk County.

Lane County Christians rejoiced that three preachers, John Rigdon, Gilmore Callison, and Charles Bradshaw, settled with their families in the Pleasant Hill district, and that two others, Lewis Casteel and George Caton, located in the Eugene area and that Henry W. Taylor chose to live south of Cottage Grove. A future preacher, 18-year-old Joseph H. Sharp, was another promising addition to Lane County's growing corps of preachers. Equally significant for the cause of Christ in Lane County was the arrival of William and Matilda McCall, Samuel and Elizabeth Baughman and John and Delilah Bristow Gilfrey. These families were thoroughly committed to the principles of the Restoration Movement, and all three men served as elders in the church for many years.

Clackamas County was another area that benefited greatly from the 1852 influx of new Christian families. Charles Bisbee Dart and his wife, Isabelle, settled with their large family near the Daniel Trullingers on Rock Creek south of Molalla. The Rock Creek Church of Christ was formed when several other Christian families, including Joseph and Polly Quinn, moved into the district that fall. The large extended family of Edward and Lettice Pedigo settled on the Clackamas River in the Damascus area. This was a great encouragement to John Foster and the little congregation he had been nurturing for more than six years. One of the Pedigo daughters was married to a fine gospel preacher, Harrison H. Hendrix, who had been preaching powerfully in Iowa for several years. Hendrix began preaching in Clackamas County but he saw an even greater opportunity in neighboring Washington County.[28]

The church in Washington County was strengthened when Zephaniah and Sarah Ann Bryant arrived from Van Buren County, Iowa. They were soon joined in that county by fellow Iowans Harrison and Zerelda Hendrix. In a short time, there were two congregations of 60 members each meeting in Washington County, and Hendrix was preaching for both congregations. One young couple from Clark County, Illinois, Perren and Mary Eleanor Steeples, came overland that fall and settled near Hillsboro. They would provide leadership for the cause of Christ in Washington County for the rest of the century.

Two families in the '52 migration that provided immediate leadership in Marion County were W. H. and Lucy Brayton and Calvin and Margaret Murphy. They would be instrumental in the organization of the Mill Creek and Salem churches respectively. Two young men who were the sons of gospel preachers arrived in 1852 and became influential Christians in the Salem area. Nathan T. Caton, the 19-year-old son of George Caton, and William P. Murphy, the 21-year-old son of John Ecles Murphy, complemented the efforts of the Stantons, Herrens and Murphys in organizing a church in the capital city.

The Progress of the Cause

In November 1852, two Oregon preachers sent off reports to editor James Mathes of the *Christian Record* in Indiana. Their contagious enthusiasm was an accurate barometer of how the Christians defined their position at the end of 1852. Writing on November 1 from his home in Marion County, Caleb Chapman was looking back on two solid years of ministerial labors. "I wish to say to you and the brethren that the cause of our blessed Lord is rapidly advancing in these ends of the earth," he reported. "The spirit of investigation is abroad among the people. They are searching the Scriptures to learn its teachings on the subject of baptism and the Lord's Supper."[29]

Alexander Vance McCarty, now 27 years old and preaching with both power and eloquence throughout the Willamette Valley, echoed those sentiments in his letter mailed from his home in Polk County on November 9. He wrote:

> I would just observe that the glorious cause of truth is gaining ground in this far off country, very fast. Religious society here has felt the chilling influence of the gold hunting mania. Still, I have the pleasure to inform you, that our cause is progressing. Fresh auxiliaries are brought into requisition. The tide of interest seems high in many bosoms, gathering new strength, as it sweeps on Heavenward. Many are

> enlisting in the good cause, with strong emotions of love, and hearts beating high for the glory set before them in the gospel of Christ. I hope that the cause may continue to spread its heavenly influence on these Pacific shores, until every obstacle has been removed, and the cross of Christ be venerated and loved by all. We have many good brethren here, who love the cause, and are devoted to its advancement. They regard Christianity, not as a cold formula, or heartless ceremony, but as a living, life-conducting principle, reared up in the temple of the heart. Numbers have been immersed here within the last few months. We have an evangelist in the field who is doing good service. May the Lord prosper him.[30]

When the outstanding scholar of Oregon history, George H. Himes, published his findings on the "Beginnings of Christianity in Oregon" in the *Oregon Historical Quarterly*, he concluded by describing the situation in the territory at the close of 1852. His research indicated that the five leading Protestant denominations—Methodist, Baptist, Congregational, Presbyterian and Episcopalian—had 1,000 members between them. The Roman Catholic population was less than 300. Then Himes reported: "To my knowledge there was a goodly number of the Disciples of Christ—sometimes known as 'Campbellites'—in this field, but I do not think there was any regular organization."[31] He was correct about the "goodly number," but he was in error about the lack of "any regular organization."

By the end of 1852, the Christians in Oregon Territory probably numbered about 1,000 members and they could identify more than 30 preachers in their midst. There were at least a dozen organized congregations, but it is possible that there were actually 14 or 15. The first annual meeting had been successful, and the churches were now supporting John Alkire Powell for eight months of evangelistic travels and labor in the gospel. A second annual meeting had been announced for the fall of 1853. From the perspective of those who were actually in the heat of the battle, "the glorious cause of truth" was gaining ground very rapidly in the "far off country" of Oregon.

Chapter 12

The Upheaval of Family Life
1853

> *. . . he told me that my wife and child, mother, sister and brothers had gone and were now over three months on their way across the plains to Oregon. . . . After traveling over fifteen thousand miles to meet my loved ones expecting to clasp them to my heart only to learn that they were far away journeying toward the setting sun to meet me was almost more than I could bear and I was for awhile completely stunned, but there was nothing to do but to return the way I had come.*
>
> — James Addison Bushnell, August, 1853

Given the number of Christians traveling the Oregon Trail, it was inevitable that some would meet who had not known each other before. Friendships forged in the midst of danger and privation were not soon forgotten once the parties landed in the promised land. Such was the case when the party from Indiana consisting of the McClure, Bond and Bruce families chanced to meet Benjamin Franklin Owen and his traveling companions from Missouri during the final week of July 1853.

The Nicest Looking Folk on the Plains

The wagon train that left Shaker Prairie in Knox County, Indiana, on March 21, 1853, consisted of 23 related members of the McClure, Bond, and Bruce families. Most of the adult members of this train were Christians. The acknowledged leader and the man chosen by the others to be the "captain" of the train was 37-year-old Vincent Scott McClure. He had been a prominent leader in the church in Indiana, and he would be instrumental in organizing a congregation in his new neighborhood in Lane County, Oregon.

Traveling with Vincent was his wife, Sarah "Sallie" Bruce, and their children. Their oldest daughter, Hetty, was traveling with her husband of two years, Isaac William Bond. Vincent's brothers, Harrison and James, were in the group. James had married Mary Ann "Nancy" Bruce, a sister to Vincent's wife. They were traveling with four children, the oldest of which was 10-year-old Jane. Another relative in the party was Andrew S. McClure. He was only 23 years old, but he was actually an uncle to the three McClure brothers. From a historian's point of view, Andrew's presence was crucial. He maintained a daily diary on the journey that was published over a century later by the Lane County Historical Society.[1]

Three young men who were Christian friends, Benjamin Franklin Owen, Joel Kistner, and Christian H. Norman left their home in Bloomfield, Stoddard County, Missouri, on March 31, 1853, and began their trek to Oregon. For the first few days they were accompanied by a Christian preacher, Elder W. W. Norman, who was the father of one of the boys. Once again the historian is assisted, as B. F. Owen kept a diary of his journey that was also published more than a century later by the Lane County Historical Society.

On Saturday evening, April 16, they "camped at Mr. Smith's." Smith was most likely a church contact that had been arranged ahead of time by Elder Norman. The three young men were still in Missouri and could take advantage of contact with fellow Christians on the Lord's Day. Ben Owen's diary entry for the next day reads:

> Sunday April 17th—From Mr. Smith's we went to Mr. Hooker's, who was a Christian preacher. He, his wife, & three grown daughters, showed a good interest in trying to make us feel at home, they were all interesting talkers, and good singers, much of their time was devoted to sacred music.[2]

There were no more references to "sacred music" and associations with Christians until the three friends met up with the McClure train somewhere in Idaho Territory on Saturday afternoon, July 23. That night Owen wrote in his diary (without great attention to correct spelling and punctuation):

> The McClure Train stoped for their Noon Lunch, & turned their stock loose to graze. We drove about 50 yds passt them, & stoped also. Kistner, & I were alike impressed with the Genteel bearing of the whole Train, he said, By George! Boys those are the nicest looking Folk Ive seen on the plains, & when I agreed with him, he said before they leave, I think one of us better go, & talk some with them, & if they prove to be as nice as they look I think we better try, & get to travel in their company. I agreed to the proposition . . . So Kistner went & talked to them, & came back, more pleased than ever.[3]

That night they camped near the McClure train. Nearby was a train that included five preachers from the United Brethren Church, and on the next day Owen wrote: "Three of those preachers preached the first public divine service that we had attended since we left our homes in Missouri." The next evening, Monday, July 25, the boys camped about 100 yards from the McClures. It was a dark night with heavy timber all around them, but across the way they could hear the sounds of singing. The McClures were engaged in their evening devotions, and Ben Owen wrote that the music "completely captivated us, we were very naturally drawn to it, & were received kindly, & invited to take part in their devotions."

The boys returned to their camp site spiritually refreshed, having participated in what Ben called in his diary "the most beautiful, & thrilling vocal music in the world." Spending an evening with the McClures in their family devotions around the campfire moved him to write: "One can almost realize heaven is in our midst."[4] From that time on, the boys traveled in the McClure train. When Ben became ill a month later, Jim and Nancy McClure took him into their tent and nursed him back to health. The entire train refused to travel until he was well enough to make the journey. Six years later, Ben married young Jane McClure and became a member of the family that had adopted him on the trail.

The Lost Wagon Train of 1853

At the Malheur River, the McClure train, along with groups totaling more than 1,000 persons, left the Oregon Trail and turned west over a new route that was said to be many miles shorter than the old route. Their guide was Elijah Elliott. Among the Christians who chose this cut-off were several members of the Bushnell-Adkins party and two families named Preston.[5] The exact number of people who followed Elliott is not known, but one account provides this information:

> W. W. Bristow, one of the men who helped to rescue the immigrants that fall, counted 615 men with 412 women and children as they came out of the mountains at Pleasant Hill. Also counted were 3,970 cattle, 1,700 sheep, 222 horses and 64 mules.[6]

Unfortunately, these groups became confused in the great Central Oregon desert and wandered off course. They became known to trail historians as "The Lost Wagon Train of 1853." Three extra weeks were spent in traveling through the desert which exhausted their oxen and depleted their store of provisions. The situation had become very grave on September 14, when Ben Owen, Andrew McClure, and six other young men were sent ahead to find help.

This advance team also became lost and almost perished. They reached the "high banks" of the McKenzie River (near the present town of Springfield) about the same time the main group of wagons in their train were being rescued by settlers already in the Willamette Valley. Owen and McClure were starving when they were rescued by Isaac Briggs and Charles Hardesty, Christians from Springfield, on October 20. Ben Owen's diary entry for that day, written sometime later (and with several misspellings), described his feelings:

> Before reparing, to our rest for the Night, Uncle Briggs, & Mr. Hardesty Sang a Number of good Sacred Songs,—The Angels, that watched Round the Tomb being one. After which ferveant Prayer, & Thanksgiving, was Offered up to the God of Love, & Mercy on account of our Preservation, & deliverance, which devotion filled my heart with gratitude,

> for through all my penegranations I have attributed all my deliverancies, to the Sustaining Care of the Father of lights.[7]

Eventually, Ben Owen and the McClure, Bond, and Bruce families would all be reunited in the Grand Prairie district eight miles northwest of Eugene. These veterans of "The Lost Wagon Train of 1853" would establish a congregation of Christians in their neighborhood and add their considerable strength and talents to "the glorious cause of truth" in Oregon Territory.

The Good Cause Is Greatly Strengthened

On December 28, 1852, A. V. McCarty corresponded with editor James Mathes in Indiana. He was eager to report the safe arrival of John Rigdon, John Ecles Murphy, "and others through whose exemplary piety, and labors of love, the good cause is greatly strengthened." As he reflected on his five years in Oregon, McCarty regretted that more had not been accomplished. "The cause has rather languished here in time past," he lamented, "for want of an efficient organization. We are too much scattered to act in concert and have therefore had rather to fight single-handed," he admitted. However, the 27-year-old evangelist had not sat down to write a disparaging letter—he was far too optimistic for that. With mounting determination he announced, "But we expect to make the coming year more interesting and fruitful for the cause of God."[8]

McCarty's epistle proved to be prophetic. For the scattered Christians in the Willamette Valley, 1853 was both "interesting" and "fruitful" for the cause they held dear. The evangelistic labors of John A. Powell were certainly a centerpiece of that fruitfulness, but there was good news from several fronts. With the annual meeting now in place and at least 23 preachers in the territory, the Christians were positioned to be more effective than they had been previously. Even more encouraging, the advance word from back home in "the states" pointed to a large migration of Christians coming west in 1853.

There was still "opposition from the sects," to be sure, but the Christians seemed to rise above this kind of intramural skirmishing. "Some of the sects have already said that a 'Campbellite' ought not to be allowed his vote," Elias Briggs wrote impatiently to a friend in Iowa. "There is no place in America that needs a good set of preachers worse than Oregon," he opined, "and if you can influence some good brethren . . . to come and preach for us, I think they would be well supported." His friend was horrified that religious people could be so intolerant, and he responded: "What fine servants such would make to the officers of an inquisition."[9]

The Labors of John Rigdon

Prior to his migration from Iowa to Oregon, John Rigdon had heard heart-warming stories about the progress of the Restoration Movement in the far west. However, when he arrived in the territory he was surprised at the extent to which the California gold rush had stunted the growth of the movement. In a letter back home to Daniel Bates, the editor of the *Christian Evangelist* in Fort Madison, Iowa, Rigdon wrote:

> Our good cause has prospered here gloriously in former years, but it is at present somewhat obscured and impeded. But you must not think for a moment that I am disposed to yield to despair. No, never! We have the power of God (the Gospel) here as well as elsewhere; and we can sing with the poet—
>
> "Some few like good Elijah stand,
> While thousands have revolted—
> In earnest for the Heavenly land,
> They never yet have halted."
>
> An effort is being made to bring the means at the disposal of the disciples, to bear more effectually on the work of evangelizing. Brother Powell is laboring by direction of the brotherhood, to set the congregations in order, and from his talents and weight of character we hope for the speedy dawning of a brighter day in the religious career of Oregon.[10]

Rigdon did not elaborate on what caused the movement to be "somewhat obscured and impeded," but Bates knew what he meant. "The check the cause has sustained in Oregon is, I suppose, the result of the unexpected discoveries of such immense earthly treasures on the shores of the Pacific," he answered back. "It is to be hoped, however, that the excitement consequent upon this discovery will speedily subside; and that all Christians will again remember that they are called to a higher destiny than mere worldly possessions and enjoyments."[11]

In a letter to a friend back home, dated April 25, 1853, Rigdon gave an encouraging update on the situation in Oregon. "The Christian cause has suffered a severe wintry season here for more than a year past," he reported, "produced by a sad devotion of the mass of the population to the mammon of unrighteousness; but thanks be to God, the unmistakable signs of a better and brighter season are being seen in our midst." To document this change of fortune, Rigdon colorfully wrote:

> Zion begins to travail, and sons and daughters are being born to God. I have witnessed, within a few weeks, the submission of some eight or ten noble souls to the Lord. The brethren are awaking to a sense of their duty, and I confidently expect to see the cohorts of the conquering king, doing such battle for their great leader as shall strike terror to the hearts of the king's enemies. I trust the day has gone by forever, in which the cause of truth will be expected to prevail without the zealous, united, and well directed efforts of the disciples. We have a very fair proportion of talents on the side of the reformation in Oregon, and the benevolence and liberty of the brethren here leaves, far in the distance, anything of the kind I have seen elsewhere.[12]

Rigdon admitted that his failing eyesight was troublesome, but he refused to allow this affliction to dampen his spirits. "My health is good, my heart is bold, my hope is firm, my purpose is fixed to blow the Gospel trumpet till I die," he thundered. "I beg all the brethren to pray for me, that I may hold the beginning of my confidence firm to the end." He was aware that time was not on his side. "We have much to do and but a brief space in which to work," he admonished his friend. "Let us therefore lay aside every weight, and run the appointed race, that we may reach the goal and wear the crown."[13]

The Labors of A. V. McCarty

This sense of urgency was shared by A. V. McCarty, and June of 1853 found him evangelizing in Marion County. Among the fastest-growing congregations in Marion County in 1853 were the ones at Howell's Prairie and Bethany. Their meeting places were within five miles of each other, and they leaned on each other for mutual edification and strength. C. F. Swander said that the Howell's Prairie Church, located in a farming community about eight to ten miles east of Salem, was organized in 1847.[14] Samuel and Mahala Simmons and their large family had settled on Howell's Prairie in November 1846, and they were undoubtedly involved in the establishment of this congregation. Also in 1846, the various Cox families arrived in the Bethany area, but the Bethany Church was not organized until April 1851.

McCarty began a one-week meeting at Howell's Prairie on Friday, June 10, 1853. His efforts resulted in "about thirty additions, mostly by confession and immersion." This brought the membership to "about 85" and prompted McCarty to observe, "The brethren appear to be disposed to fight the good fight of faith." Returning to his own congregation on the Luckiamute River in Polk County, McCarty joined John A. Powell, Glen Owen Burnett, and John Ecles Murphy in a brief meeting in which four persons were baptized into Christ. "We now number 64," he wrote proudly, "and meet every Lord's day."

In the month of July, McCarty headed south to assist a little congregation meeting on Long Tom River north of Eugene in Lane County. They had organized in the spring with 12 members and had experienced some growth. As a result of McCarty's labors, "five additions were obtained to the good cause" bringing the size of the congregation to "about 25." There was some opposition to contend with, but the young preacher had refused to shy away. He wrote:

> The last emigration brought a few members to that place. Sectarian feeling and prejudice run very high here. When I was at this point last, I strove hard to impress upon the minds of all, the erroneousness of many of their statements concerning us. At the close of my effort, a young man who was a Methodist exhorter and class leader, came forward, made the good confession, and was immediately buried with the Lord in baptism. The cause of the Bible is rapidly advancing in this Territory. It is already more influential than any other religious cause. May the Lord grant it abundant success in time to come![15]

In Defense of "Oregon Fever"

While Christians were continuing to migrate to Oregon and California in large numbers, not everyone back home was pleased with this development. Many churches in the midwestern states were decimated when a strong case of "Oregon fever" attacked their communities. One historian of the Restoration Movement in Iowa wrote, "Just as Iowa began to develop as a state, her people became afflicted with the Oregon and California fever. The church did not escape its ravages, and many times nearly whole congregations moved to the West. Often the preacher went, too. In the church records, notation is often made after a great many names, 'moved to Oregon.'"[16]

An editorial comment appeared in Iowa's *Christian Evangelist* in March 1853, which ruffled feathers among some Oregonians. It read:

> The California and Oregon emigration has, it appears, unsettled the state of society in many places. The latest accounts from both places are of the most discouraging character; but nothing seems to deter people from going, as yet; but we sincerely desire to see the time come when our people will be content with the privileges and blessings they enjoy here, and be satisfied to remain where they are doing well. From all accounts, there are thousands in California and Oregon, too, whose only desire is to be back in the "States."[17]

Although their frustration at losing so many fine Christians was understandable, the editors ought to have exercised more restraint. The first to respond in the pages of the *Christian*

Evangelist was John Rigdon. He was not surprised that some in Iowa would believe these discouraging reports, "as the sufferings of the last emigrants were great indeed, and thousands were stripped of all their property and left to struggle with poverty and privations in a land of strangers." But as far as his own situation was concerned, he wanted to set the record straight. "I wish to assure all my friends that I am well pleased with Oregon, and only regret that I could not have made it my home at a much earlier day," he wrote defiantly, "and I can not conceive why any one should wish to return to the States, unless they are anxious to shake with the ague, or burn with the fever, so common in the father land."

This was an unfortunate parallel, although perhaps again understandable, given the one-sidedness of the editorial comment.[18] The editors were not eager to allow such language from a popular preacher like Rigdon to influence the people in their region, so they held the letter for six months before finally publishing it.

In fact, the letter Rigdon wrote a month later was published earlier in the *Evangelist*. No doubt the editors preferred its sweeter spirit. "The hope expressed in my last of the dawning of a better day in Oregon, is, I am happy to inform you, being realized," he wrote. "Some of the ground lost by reason of the gold fever is regained, and I trust the day is near in which the Gospel of favor shall be fully preached in Oregon." Looking back over the previous two and a half months, Rigdon said he had witnessed 28 people confess their faith and be immersed into Christ, and "a few united from other denominations." He estimated the increase, just within his district, to be "about 35."[19]

Many Christians back in the States were convinced that no one really migrated to Oregon or California for spiritual reasons, let alone to expand the borders of the Restoration Movement, but rather that every single immigrant was motivated entirely by the materialistic prospects of economic gain. John Ecles Murphy, who like Rigdon had come across with the large 1852 migration, felt obligated to defend himself. "As it respects your humble servant," he wrote, "I did not come to Oregon as Jonah attempted to do—to run away from the Lord or shun the responsibility of 'faithfully warning every man,' but came in search of a healthier country and milder climate, in neither of which have I been disappointed."[20] Murphy assured his former neighbors that he intended to "labor more extensively" for the cause in the coming years.

John Ecles Murphy never tired of lifting up the name of Jesus. Little Inez Adams, daughter of William Lysander Adams, always looked forward to his visits to their log cabin on Panther Creek in Yamhill County. She remembered Murphy as a "benevolent old lame preacher" who used to put his hand gently on her head and say, "I hope this little girl loves the Lord Jesus."[21] This gesture made an impact that was never forgotten.

The Second Annual Meeting

The reports from Oregon in the summer and fall of 1853 sounded like excerpts from the Book of Acts. In addition to Rigdon's 35 additions in Polk County and McCarty's 30 in Marion County, W. W. Bristow wrote from Pleasant Hill in Lane County to say, "The Church of Christ here is now in a flourishing condition. We number some 70 members."[22] One correspondent from Washington County wrote that a congregation had just been established at Hillsboro.[23] Dr. James McBride surveyed the Willamette Valley and wrote, "In some portions of Oregon, our cause (I mean Bible Christianity) is at a low ebb. In others, it is in its 'silver slippers.'" He reported on a meeting with Powell and McCarty that had resulted in 30 additions, and on another meeting that gained 12 more. He observed that "a few are being added in a number of places."[24]

The second annual meeting took place as scheduled during the second week in September. John A. Powell described the progress of organizing churches and reported on more than 100 additions in his meetings. Perhaps most significant was Powell's definite assertion: "There are some 16 congregations of Disciples in the Willamette Valley." The annual meeting chose to divide the Valley into two districts and support two evangelists for the coming year. A. V. McCarty agreed to evangelize on the eastern side of the Willamette River, and John Rigdon was assigned the western side. There was considerable discussion about building an educational institution to be known as "Oregon Christian University," and about the practicality of launching "a periodical devoted to primitive Christianity" in Oregon Territory. Both of these ventures were probably premature, but the very fact that the Christians were aggressively thinking about how to accomplish such tasks was an indicator of the growing vitality of the "glorious cause" in the fall of 1853.[25]

John A. Powell, for one, was willing to defend these bold plans. "The different sects are bringing all their influence and power . . . to build up their party institutions and churches," he explained. "But Bible Christianity appears generally to have the public ear."[26] More than six years earlier, a Methodist preacher had said of the Christians, "The multitude is with them," and Powell was persuaded that the Christians still had a corner on "the public ear." Rigdon and McCarty felt the same way, and they were eager to begin. "We have commenced our labors in our respective fields," McCarty wrote, "but the weather has been so unfavorable that we cannot effect a great deal for the cause till spring. A few additions however have been obtained since we entered upon our work."[27] What pleased McCarty the most was the strong support of Oregon Christians. "The brethren seem to be deeply interested in everything that pertains to the good cause," he declared. "It is true, we are not so well organized as we should be. But our utmost exertion will be needed. May the Lord enable us all to do our duty! The faithful in Christ every where pray for us!"[28]

The Pioneers of '53

The migration of 1853 was large—more than 6,000 settled in Oregon Territory that fall. The numbers were so great that it becomes difficult for the historian to identify a significant percentage of the Christian families entering the territory.[29] By far the most influential preacher arriving that fall was 51-year-old Philip Mulkey, a son of Kentucky's John Mulkey. A large family migrated with him including a 23-year-old nephew, John F. Mulkey, who became a gospel preacher in Oregon. Two other Christian families, the Crabtrees and Bargers, were related to the Mulkeys and traveled in their train. Despite his age, Philip's preaching career in Oregon would span 40 years.

The third and final wave of families migrating from Monmouth, Illinois, to establish a church and college in Monmouth, Oregon, occurred in 1853. The senior citizens in this company of 47 people[30] were Peter and Rachel Butler, but the elected leader of the train was their oldest son, Ira F. M. Butler. His wife, Mary Ann Davidson, and their five children accompanied him on the journey. The extended Butler family would be active in the founding of the town of Monmouth, Oregon, and in the establishment of both the Christian Church and Christian College in that community.

Traveling with the Butler train were Ira's three sisters and their husbands. These couples, all Christians, were: Edward and Eliza Butler Ground and their five children, Isaac and Margaret Butler Smith and their five children, and Thomas and Elizabeth Butler Hutchinson and their one small son. Elizabeth was pregnant during the journey, and she delivered a son on the Barlow Road near Laurel Hill. She named him Robert Cascade in honor of the location of his birth in the Cascade Mountains.[31]

Although Ira was the captain of the wagon train, his father was also very influential. Affectionately called the "old man," Peter Butler had been a powerful leader in the Restoration Movement in Illinois. One member of the Butler train remembered:

> Not a wheel turned in the morning until all hands had gathered while the old man offered prayer. On Sunday they camped. But, on the unlucky day when the Butler cow was swept away by the North Platte River, to the loss of the Butler breakfast coffee cream, the old man was human enough to "cuss out" both cow and river . . . .[32]

The Patrick Rivers Haley family also migrated to the Monmouth area with the Butler party. Patrick and his youngest son, 20-year-old William Thompson, were both gospel preachers. After assisting his family in the overland crossing, William Thompson Haley immediately returned east and enrolled at Alexander Campbell's Bethany College. Upon his graduation he returned to Oregon to serve both Bethel College and Monmouth University. He married Lucinda Ford, a daughter of Nat Ford, on June 11, 1858, and the wedding was performed by Glen Owen Burnett. Patrick Haley never did as much preaching as his son, but he served as an elder in the Monmouth Church for many years.[33]

The 48-member Butler train (counting Robert Cascade) had a relatively easy and safe crossing and no deaths were recorded. They arrived in Polk County on schedule that fall. However, as the Christmas season approached, Peter Butler experienced pangs of loneliness for those who had remained in Illinois. Writing to family and friends "back home" in Monmouth, Illinois, on December 11, 1853, the old man bared his heart. "You have no idea how bad we want to see you all," he confessed. "I would be glad to even see your old dog. I don't know how to reconcile it to myself never to see you agin in this wourld."[34]

The Bowen brothers—18-year-old Joshua and 16-year-old Peter—migrated from Missouri in the spring of 1853 even though their mother died just before the family was to start overland. Their father insisted that the family should keep to its plans, but he died somewhere along the Oregon Trail. The Bowen brothers and their younger siblings continued on to Oregon and settled in the Bethany area in Marion County. The brothers married sisters—the daughters of Gideon Cox—and became leaders in the Bethany Church for many years.[35]

Amos Harvey and Glen Owen Burnett welcomed a valuable Christian physician who settled near them in the Bethel Hills in the fall of 1853. Dr. William C. Warriner and his wife, Emily, and their three children came overland from Missouri. A Christian blacksmith from Independence, Missouri, William Cornett, also crossed the plains that summer. After a year in Oregon City, he came to Bethel where he married a sister of A. V. McCarty. Warriner and Cornett both played important roles in the organizing and building of Bethel Institute and Bethel College beginning in 1855. A young 20-year-old Christian named Lucien Frazer also came with the 1853 migration. A few years later he became a leader in the Bethany Church and remained so for many years until his death in 1900.

William and Ruth Ruble and their family arrived in the fall of 1853 and settled in the Eola Hills about four miles west of Salem. While living in Barry County, Missouri, William had built and operated a saw and grist mill, but upon arriving in Oregon he engaged in the nursery business, along with his farming. The Rubles were devout Christians, and William preached on occasion. One historical record noted of William:

> Before he left Missouri, he was ordained a minister of the gospel in the Christian church. This was not exactly his choice but his brethren thought he might be going to a country where there were but few preachers and that his services might be in demand, but upon arriving in Oregon he soon found out that preachers were equal to the demand and not being gifted with oratory he did but little in the ministry but he contributed much to the religious papers and also to the secular press.[36]

Included with the Christian pioneers of 1853 were Benjamin and Matilda Stanton from Tennessee. Like Elizabeth Butler Hutchinson, Matilda was pregnant for most of the overland trip. She too gave birth to a son after entering Oregon Territory, but her child soon died. Benjamin and Matilda buried their son at Laurel Hill on the slopes of Mt. Hood, not far from the spot where Elizabeth Hutchinson welcomed Robert Cascade into the world. With sorrowful hearts, the Stantons settled on Butte Creek about three miles north of Sublimity in Marion County. They were faithful Christians all their lives.

Benjamin Stanton was remembered as "a powerfully built man, tall, broad shouldered with a smooth-shaven face and crowned by heavy black hair." He was also remembered for being "jolly and fully of jokes." A story has also survived about "Grandma Stanton," as Matilda was lovingly called in later years, that provides a window on the pioneer life that Benjamin and Matilda lived in Oregon. This source wrote:

> We children of pioneer neighbors kindly remember her as a little old lady, smoking her brown clay pipe before the open fireplace and of seeing her dip her pipe into the ashes for a live coal to light her tobacco. She was kind to all and lovingly gave of her time to those in need, doing her best to relieve suffering and poverty wherever she found it. In pioneer days many elderly women smoked a pipe and little was thought about it . . . . The evenings were necessarily long. There were not many books to read and newspapers at best only issued once a week. It was just as impossible to sew by the dim lights, so in order to put in those long evenings, both husband and wife would smoke their pipes by the fireside. In those days there was no place even for the husband to spend his evenings loafing; so together they sat by the light of the fire and smoked contentedly.[37]

The Death of Slavery in Oregon

When Benjamin and Matilda Stanton migrated to Oregon Territory from Tennessee, they brought with them "an old negro slave named Ed."[38] Later, when the slaves were freed, Ed refused to leave the Stantons. Although it is difficult to trace the names and family connections of black slaves in Oregon Territory, before the Stantons there were at least two other families of Christians who arrived in Oregon with slaves. When James and Nancy Cook came overland from Kentucky in 1845, they brought with them a 45-year-old black slave named Abram Cuffy. He remained with them for at least five years, as he was listed as a member of their household in the 1850 census.[39]

However, the most highly publicized case of slavery in Oregon Territory was connected with Nat Ford at Rickreall in Polk County.[40] When Ford came to Oregon from Missouri in 1844, he brought with him three slaves. One was a single man named Scott, and the other two were a married couple named Robin and Polly Holmes. The Holmes family included three small daughters—Harriet, aged 7, Celi Ann, aged 4, and Mary

Jane, aged 2. They had three more children after arriving in Oregon.

Commenting on the number of black slaves transported to Oregon Territory, one record noted: "By the close of 1844 there were both slaves and free Negroes in Oregon, but their combined number was few. Although the 1850 census listed 207 Negroes, Jesse Douglas, a careful researcher, estimated there were only about 55."[41] This discrepancy is attributed to census-takers who indiscriminately listed many Indians and part-Indians as Negroes. It is not known how many of the 55 blacks were actually slaves, but the number would have been small. In the midst of a white population of 12,000, the few black slaves in Oregon in 1850 were the subject of intense scrutiny and passionate debate. A large majority of the Oregon populace was fiercely opposed to the introduction of slavery in their territory. This accounts for the spotlight on the Nat Ford situation.

The element of truth in the story of how and why three slaves accompanied Nat Ford to Oregon is elusive. The view that Ford was a passionate proslavery man who favored the extension of slavery to Oregon Territory is vigorously disputed by his descendants, who claim that the slaves approached Ford and urged him to take them with him to the new territory. It is known that when Ford arrived at Rickreall Creek, he built three cabins—a large one with two fireplaces for his own family, a smaller one with one fireplace for Robin and Polly and their children, and a third one for Scott. One historian for Polk County concluded, "There is no indication that Ford was anything akin to a 'Simon Legree' slave-owner pictured in the abolitionist literature of the period."[42]

By 1851, the situation had changed. The young black slave named Scott was dead. He had died in the same shipping accident that killed Mark Ford, Nat Ford's only son. The two oldest daughters in the Holmes family had died and were buried on the Ford farm. Robin and Polly and their youngest child had been released from their connection to Ford and had found employment in another district. Ford had retained the other three children, but he was holding them as wards and not as slaves. They would be free when they came of age according to the laws of Oregon.

The volatile issue of whether slaveholders could carry their slaves into Oregon Territory and hold them there as property came to a head in the spring of 1852. On April 16, Robin Holmes appeared before the Territorial Supreme Court at the Polk County Courthouse and applied for a writ of habeas corpus, declaring that Nat Ford was holding his three children unlawfully as slaves. It was more than a year before the case was decided, and by that time it had been heard by four different judges. On July 13, 1853, Chief Justice George H. Williams ruled in favor of Robin Holmes. Although the judge did not once speak of slavery, his decision had the powerful effect of declaring that slavery was now illegal in Oregon Territory.

A century later, Pauline Burch, a descendant of Nat Ford, wrote a document called "Pioneer Nathaniel Ford and the Negro Family" and deposited it in the Oregon Historical Society manuscript collections. In this document she stated that Robin Holmes brought the suit at Ford's behest as a test suit to not only determine the legal status of slavery in Oregon, but also to define Ford's legal responsibilities to his former servant. According to Burch, Ford and Holmes remained on good terms following the trial. Family tradition claimed that Ford and a son-in-law bought a lot in Salem and built, at their own expense, a four-room house for the Holmes family. Robin and Polly Holmes ran a successful nursery business in Salem for the rest of their lives.[43]

Later in the decade, the Democratic Party in Oregon suffered a schism between proslavery Democrats and antislavery "Independents" who formed a separate party of "National Democrats." Nat Ford was one of the leaders in the antislavery faction, and he was involved in the separate convention that met in Eugene in April 1858. The proslavery Democrats lashed out at Ford and all others who would join "this Eugene Negro equality movement." Ford and his friends were referred to as "certain malcontents" and "traitors" who were moving in the direction of "the black Republican Camp."

The *Oregon Statesman,* the voice of the Democratic Party, defined an "independent" as a "nigger-worshipping apostate from the Democratic Party."[44]

Nat Ford's reputation in his own district did not suffer from the years of publicity involving the Holmes family. During the years of territorial government, he served in the Senate in the 1849, 1850, 1856, and 1858 sessions, and in the House of Representatives in the 1851, 1852, and 1854 sessions. After Oregon achieved statehood, he was elected to the State Senate in 1866 and 1868. But despite all of his years of public service, Nat Ford is most remembered for being at the center of Oregon's swirling debate over slavery.

In commenting on the impact of the lawsuit, historian Scott McArthur has written:

> The litigation did make one thing certain—Oregon was a free state. The Dred Scott decision and Fugitive Slave Act notwithstanding, slavery had no place in Oregon, and all men were free.[45]

Odyssey in the American West

James Addison Bushnell left his wife and baby son in Missouri in the spring of 1852 and traveled to the California gold mines to seek his fortune. He was moderately successful and he wrote to his wife and mother to join him in Oregon Territory. Given the uncertainty of the mail service, he was never convinced that they had received his message. Not hearing from them, he took the $400 he had saved and returned home on a boat via the Isthmus of Panama. Fortunately, he kept a journal that was later published. In the first week of August 1853, he finally arrived back at his Missouri home, only to discover that his family had left for Oregon three months earlier. His journal entry described in stark language the upheaval of family life for families attempting to relocate on the American West Coast. Bushnell wrote:

> The next day I took a steamboat on the mighty Mississippi up to La Grange, from there to Adair county by stage, and afoot home reaching the neighborhood only after dark,

> meeting one of my brother-in-laws, Frank Adkins, he told me that my wife and child, mother, sister and brothers had gone and were now over three months on their way across the plains to Oregon, all gone except one brother George and far on their way across the plains. My feelings can be better imagined than described when I heard this fact. After traveling over fifteen thousand miles to meet my loved ones expecting to clasp them to my heart only to learn that they were far away journeying toward the setting sun to meet me was almost more than I could bear and I was for a while completely stunned, but there was nothing to do but to return the way I had come and try to get there as soon as they did.[46]

Returning by boat from New York via the Isthmus of Panama, Bushnell arrived in Portland after dark a little more than two months later, on October 18, 1853. He estimated that he had traveled 23,000 miles since July 1. Unbeknownst to him, the party that included his precious family had been persuaded to join the ill-fated "Lost Wagon Train" and had come close to perishing in the Central Oregon desert. His wife and child had been rescued and were staying temporarily with Elias and Mary Briggs in Springfield. Bushnell pressed on to Oregon City and then Salem in search of his family.

With his funds virtually depleted, Bushnell was reduced to walking from Salem. "I had paid my last dime for lodgings the night before," he wrote later in his journal, "and now struck out afoot and alone and penniless for Springfield where I hoped to find or hear from my family as being the nearest point where the emigrants from the middle fork would reach the valley." Late one night he found lodging at the home of Mahlon Harlow a mile and a half from Springfield. From Harlow he heard the good news that "there was a young woman and child at Mr. Briggs." It was too late to go on but he had difficulty restraining himself. "I did not sleep much that night," Bushnell recalled, "neither did I stay for breakfast next morning after a separation of twenty months and crossing the continent three times."

After nearly two years of disruption and upheaval in their lives, the young family was reunited in "the wilds of Oregon." At the Briggs residence, Bushnell learned that his mother and his brothers and sisters were temporarily located in the Grand

Prairie district in the neighborhood of the McClures. With his wife and small son he hastened to that area, took out a land claim, and erected a "cheap and primitive" house on the property. Their daughter was born in this house on November 1, 1854. But money was scarce and they retreated to Springfield to find employment. "We left our claim and went to work for Elias Briggs," Bushnell explained, "I to run the sawmill and she (my wife) to help cook. We stayed there six months and came home with two cows, some lumber and other things which we badly needed to fix up our house and farm."[47]

Ambitious Plans for the Future

At this point, the future of the Restoration Movement looked brighter in Oregon Territory than it did in the new state of California. In 1853, there were only three preachers actively engaged in evangelistic labors in California. When Thomas Thompson, a Christian preacher in Santa Clara, California, wrote to Alexander Campbell, editor of the *Millennial Harbinger,* on Christmas Day 1853, he included a report on the progress of the church in the Golden State. Campbell summarized this report for the readers of the *Harbinger* in the following words:

> Our brethren have been doing, as yet, but little in California for the Redeemer's Kingdom. Our brethren there have organized but three congregations—one at Stockton, one at Santa Clara, each having now about 60 members, and another in Napa County, of some 20 or 30 members. If other congregations there be in the State, our brother knows them not.[48]

By way of contrast, Oregon was in a much stronger position at the close of 1853. There were 16 organized congregations in the Willamette Valley and several others that were about to begin. At least 35 gospel preachers could be identified as living in Oregon at that time. It is difficult to estimate the total number of Christians living in the territory at the end of 1853, but an educated guess would place the numbers between 1,000 to 1,500. Plans were being drawn for the establishment of Christian schools, and there was even talk of a monthly periodical for Oregon Christians. John Rigdon and A. V. McCarty were crisscrossing the Willamette Valley, baptizing converts and organizing churches. It was true that a majority of Christians were still not functioning in organized congregations, and there was much work yet to be done. But by any standard of judgment, the Restoration Movement in Oregon Territory moved into 1854 with a full head of steam.

Chapter 13

The Progress of Primitive Christianity in Oregon 1854

Brother Campbell – Agreeably to request, I will endeavor to compile some statements of the progress of the cause of primitive Christianity in Oregon, as reported to me through private letters recently received.

— Levi Lindsay Rowland to Alexander Campbell, November 24, 1854

The first Christians to visit the Umpqua Valley were those who traveled across the newly-opened Applegate Trail in 1846. Some of them died and were buried in this valley. As far as can be determined now, the first Christian to settle in this part of the territory was William H. Wilson, a veteran of "The Great Migration" of 1843. He came to the Yoncalla district in the early summer of 1847, but rushed to the California gold fields in 1848.

Following his marriage to Hannah Gillan in 1850, Wilson settled on a 640-acre donation land claim two and a half miles southeast of present-day Yoncalla. During their 52 years of marriage, the Wilsons were committed Christians. One record said of Hannah, "She has ever been a believer in the religion of cheerfulness and has led a consistent Christian life." The same record commented on William, "He was a consistent member of the Christian church and his religion constituted a vital force in his career."[1]

Planting the Cause in the Umpqua Valley

When Samuel and Susanna Briggs came overland in 1851 they did not follow the masses to the California gold fields nor did they settle in the popular Willamette Valley. They were drawn to the thinly populated Umpqua Valley south of present-day Roseburg, and they chose to live in the small settlement of Canyonville. They arrived in their new home on September 18, 1851. The Briggs were Christians, and they longed for the day when they would be able to establish a congregation in their district.

William P. and Mary Preston and their two small sons settled near the Briggs in Douglas County in December 1853. They were devout Christians from Iowa, and like the Briggs, they were eager to reestablish church privileges in their new home. Although he was 20 years younger than Samuel Bates Briggs, William P. Preston was also a capable gospel preacher. Within three months of the Prestons' arrival, Samuel and William were laboring together in a gospel meeting, and by the summer of 1854 a small congregation was meeting regularly in their valley. On July 17, 1854, Mary Preston corresponded with her friend Daniel Bates, the editor of the *Christian Evangelist* back home in Iowa, and she informed Bates and his readers of this exciting new development. She wrote:

> Brother Bates—Being now over 2000 miles from you, I will, by the request of my husband, address you in a few lines.
>
> When we came here, Dec., 1853, we found Brother S. Briggs alone, as it were. No Christian brethren ever held a meeting here until the first of March. At that time Brother Briggs and my husband appointed a meeting, for the first, in this little valley. The people were very attentive, and requested them to continue their meetings. They did so, and the result has been truly encouraging. The news of this spread abroad; and the Disciples in the different valleys have got together. On the 2nd Lord's day in June, Brother Smith from Willamette Valley preached, and immersed 1 lady. Brother Briggs then gave a warm exhortation on Christian Union, and 13 came out and united on the Bible alone. On the 3rd Lord's day "the disciples met together to break bread." Since

> that time, they have kept up meetings regularly, and we have learned that there are some 6 or 8 more who intend uniting with us. May the Lord be praised, "for His mercy endureth forever."
>
> Let me not weary your patience, my brother, but let me crave an interest in the prayers of the good brethren there, that we may lead lives worthy of imitation, and that sinners, by seeing our good works, may "take knowledge of us that we have been with Jesus."
>
> I have just finished reading the "Editor's Sanctum," visited some of the sisters, and we concluded to send you $5.00 for the *Evangelist.* We have been doing all we could for it, and think by next year we will be able to get many more subscribers for it. We have been taking it ever since it had an existence, until we started across the "Plains," and now, that we are settled again, I wish to take it while we live, and will do all I can to extend its circulation.
>
> I have now written you quite a long letter; and if you think the news concerning our little congregation is worthy of a place in your publication, you can use it for that purpose. Prove faithful, my brother; reprove, rebuke and exhort with all long suffering, knowing that you shall reap if you faint not.
>
> Your friend and sister in the gospel. Mary Preston.[2]

The mention of "Brother Smith from Willamette Valley" probably refers to John Burris Smith of Polk County. Smith was a veteran of the 1846 migration and the fourth gospel preacher to arrive in Oregon. Until this preaching tour in Douglas County, there is no evidence of his having preached outside his own district. The most significant item in Mary Preston's letter was the revelation that there were Christians scattered in several "different valleys" along the winding route of the Umpqua River. This confirms Glen Owen Burnett's findings that there were hundreds of Christians living in Oregon Territory who were not yet enjoying church privileges.

Edmund Green Browning

A gospel preacher named Edmund Green Browning was among the new arrivals in the Umpqua Valley in the fall of

1852. With his brother-in-law, Gilmore Callison, he had preached powerfully in Illinois for many years. Writing from his home in Augusta, Illinois, on September 8, 1843, Browning had submitted a report to Barton Warren Stone's *Christian Messenger* in which he noted:

> The good cause here is on the advance—prejudice is giving way, and the congregations larger and more attentive. Brethren Stark and Callison preached in Round Prairie, where 4 made the good confession last Lord's day. Much good might be done through the country in every direction, if we had competent laborers to take hold and devote their time to the work.[3]

Browning lost his wife, Nancy Callison Browning, to the dreaded cholera epidemic that ravaged the immigrant trains of 1852. He also lost the baby she was carrying. She died in childbirth somewhere near the Great Salt Lake in Utah Territory. Nancy was a sister to Gilmore and Robert Callison, church leaders at Pleasant Hill. Gilmore Callison lost his wife and oldest son to the same epidemic that swept the trail that summer. Rather than remain with his relatives in Lane County, Browning moved south with his four small children (the oldest was 10) and established a home at Myrtle Creek in the Umpqua Valley. His children were not motherless for long. Browning married 18-year-old Nancy Allen in Oregon City on January 24, 1853.[4]

The news that a congregation had been established in the Umpqua Valley prompted two Christian preachers from the Willamette Valley, John Rigdon and Charles Bradshaw, to visit the area in the fall of 1854.[5] Seeing the potential for the organization of churches, Rigdon and Bradshaw urged Edmund Green Browning to ride through the county and become acquainted with the brethren. Browning's travels through the Umpqua Valley in the spring and summer of 1855 led him to conclude, "there are some Disciples in almost every neighborhood."[6]

After Briggs and Preston were successful in establishing the congregation near Canyonville, at least three additional congregations were organized in the Umpqua Valley during the course of the next year. These were located at

Lookingglass Prairie (west of present-day Roseburg), Myrtle Creek, and Cole's Valley. Mary Preston informed the *Christian Evangelist* that she and William were present at the organization of the church in Lookingglass Prairie. She wrote: "Brother Chapman from Willamette preached to a large and attentive congregation. 2 ladies and one gentleman made the good confession, and were buried with Christ by baptism. They organized a Church with 7 members, and 1 being added by baptism since, makes 8. The prospect is good, if they can get a Preacher. I introduced the *Evangelist* there, and think they will make up a club."[7]

A brother named Alpheus Ireland[8] wrote to James Mathes, editor of the *Christian Record* in Indiana, to tell him about the organization of the church at Myrtle Creek. "A few of us have associated ourselves together here as a congregation, upon the Bible alone, but have not chosen our officers," he explained. "We generally meet every Lord's day, and worship God the best we can. At first we numbered only about ten; but we now number some twenty. We were much edified and encouraged recently by a visit by some of our brethren from the North."[9]

On July 9, 1855, E. G. Browning wrote from Myrtle Creek to say, "On last Lord's day I heard the confession of 3 persons."[10] Two months later, while still based in Myrtle Creek, he wrote to the *Christian Evangelist* and reported: "I have just returned from Cole's Valley, where there are a few Disciples, who seem more in the spirit than usual. We immersed 1 lady while there. We think an efficient laborer might do much good in that region."[11] It is not certain from this brief reference that an organized congregation was meeting regularly in Cole's Valley, but that appears to be the case.

Abbott Levi James Todd

Abbott Levi James Todd was born in Davis County, Indiana, on October 12, 1820. At the age of 19 he was baptized into Christ by his cousin, Elijah Goodwin, who was one of the prominent leaders of the Restoration Movement in that state. One of his other cousins, Caleb P. Chapman, had been baptized into Christ the year before and began preaching in 1839. He would precede Todd to Oregon in 1848. Todd's first two wives died young, leaving him with two small children.[12] He married Angeline Tate in 1849, and they moved to the Arkansas frontier in 1850. Not satisfied with the situation in Arkansas, the Todds decided to press on across the plains to Oregon in 1852, even though Angeline was pregnant. In the back of their covered wagon, somewhere near the Umatilla River in northeastern Oregon, she gave birth to a son they named Elijah.[13]

The weary family reached Howell's Prairie in Marion County on October 18, 1852, and were reunited with Todd's cousin, Caleb P. Chapman, who was preaching often and with encouraging results in the Willamette Valley. In the summer of 1853, Chapman and A. V. McCarty held a protracted meeting at Howell's Prairie and immersed a number of converts, including Angeline Tate Todd. She had been reared in a Methodist home, but in the words of her son, she "became convinced of her duty of obedience to the command of Christ and was immersed and united with the Christian church."[14]

The Todds remained in Howell's Prairie through one harvest. In September 1853, they settled on a donation land claim near Lookingglass Creek at the lower end of Lookingglass Valley. This beautiful farm, situated in the picturesque Umpqua Valley of Douglas County, was located about eight miles southwest of present-day Roseburg. It would be their home for the next 27 years. A. L. Todd did not begin preaching regularly until the fall of 1856, but once he started he became an indefatigable circuit-riding preacher traveling throughout Douglas and surrounding counties for more than a quarter century.

The Rogue River Indian War

The constant stream of miners traveling between Oregon and California led to numerous clashes with the Indians living in the Rogue River Valley. Hostilities continued to escalate along the trail from 1851 to 1853, and by August of 1853 the

Indians were beginning to attack some isolated settlements. The Table Rock treaty, signed on September 10, 1853, led to a brief period of peace. However, sporadic attacks from roving Indians increased in the summer and fall of 1854.

A. L. Todd and his neighbor, J. M. Arrington, Sr., were appointed guardians of all the Indians in their region who favored peace over war. These Indians were counseled to give up their weapons, and they agreed to do so. There were constant rumors about the potential treachery of these Indians, but Todd and Arrington were convinced of their integrity. For their own protection, the Indians were collected together in one camp near the border of the Todd and Arrington farms. The two owners stood guard at night to protect these defenseless Indians from any possible raids by angry white men bent on revenge for atrocities committed by other Indians.

Several years later, A. L. Todd's son, Aurelius Todd, provided an account of what happened next. He wrote:

> One morning, in the first part of December, 1854, after father and Mr. Arrington had stood guard all night until about half past three in the morning, thinking there was no further danger for the night, they went to their homes which they had hardly reached when they heard firing and the shouts of the men and the screams of the Indians who were being attacked by the white men at early dawn of day while they were yet asleep in their tents.

A. L. Todd rushed into the middle of the massacre. "He lost sight of everything except that the Indians were his charge to succor and protect," declared his son. "Perfectly regardless of personal dangers, he placed himself on the side of the defenseless Indians and demanded that hostilities cease." Todd could have easily been killed, but his determined presence prevented any further bloodshed. "Abuses, curses and threats rained upon him for his interference," his son recalled, "but he stood his ground, ready to succor the Indians by action if he failed to do so by command and entreaty. The firing ceased at once, and the men (there were about fifty of them) reluctantly retired." Todd and Arrington spent the rest of the day burying the dead and caring for the wounded.

Aurelius Todd remembered that his father continued to work hard to create peaceful relations between Indians and whites and that he was successful in crafting a workable peace treaty with the Indians in his district. The son wrote admiringly of his father: "In this work he received the sobriquet of 'Peacemaker' and was long known among the Indians as well as the whites by that appellation."[15]

Christian Preachers in Oregon Territory

In the early months of 1847 the Restoration Movement in Oregon had only four preachers, and two of those rarely, if ever, traveled outside their local neighborhoods.[16] Seven years later the Christians in Oregon could point to at least 34 preachers in their midst, and probably more. Several of these evangelists traveled frequently among the churches in the Willamette Valley and the Umpqua Valley. Some may even have traveled to the Clatsop Plains south of Astoria, but there is no historical evidence to confirm this.

By Oregon standards, the age span of these laborers who were active at the beginning of 1854 was remarkably wide. The patriarchs of this preaching force included ten men who were over 50 years of age: the venerable Thomas Crawford McBride was 76; Elijah Davidson, 70; Aaron Payne, 64; Israel L. Clark, 63; John Foster, 61; John Rigdon, 57; Daniel Trullinger, 52; and Philip Mulkey, Dr. James McBride, and Patrick Rivers Haley, each 51. Added to their number were eleven other proclaimers who were in their 40s: Samuel Bates Briggs was 48; Alfred R. Elder and John Ecles Murphy, 47; John Alkire Powell, 46; Gilmore Callison, Henry W. Taylor and Noah Powell, 45; Glen Owen Burnett, 44; Caleb P. Chapman and Alfred Powell, 43; and Lewis Casteel, 40.

In contrast to these 21 veteran preachers among the Christians, the Methodists in Oregon were served by four preachers in their 40s, two in their 50s, and no one over the age of 57.[17] The Christians and the Methodists were the two largest religious groups in the territory going into 1854, but for the moment the Christians had a more experienced group of proclaimers pleading their cause.

Supporting the 21 veteran preachers in January 1854 were 14 talented preachers in their 30s and late 20s: John Burris Smith, Edmund Green Browning, and Dr. John Nelson Perkins were 37; H. M. Mac Waller, 36; Elijah B. Davidson, 34; William Lysander Adams, 32; Charles Bradshaw, 31; Harrison H. Hendrix and William Ruble 30; G. W. Richardson and Levi Burch, both 29; Sebastian Adams; Alexander Vance McCarty, 28; and George R. Caton, 26. The fall migration brought an additional preacher from Iowa named James R. Fisher, who was 35 years old.

There were several others, like Amos Harvey, Elias Cox, Thomas C. Shaw, William Wilshire Bristow, William Murphy, S. D. Evans, and William P. Preston, who were capable of preaching when called upon, but who did not consider themselves to be gospel preachers. In addition, there were several other preachers who may have been preaching in Oregon by 1854, but there are no historical records to confirm that they were in the field that early. Included in this group were: A. W. Flint, Samuel Y. Bailey, and Ephraim Nott.[18]

Waiting in the wings were nine young men in their early 20s who would one day preach for Oregon churches. Daniel Boone Matheny, 24, was a pioneer from "The Great Migration" of 1843 and living in Yamhill County. John F. Mulkey, 23, was a nephew of Philip Mulkey and living in the Eugene area. George M. Whitney, 23, was living near Mill Creek in Marion County. Francis Dillard Holman, 22, a future son-in-law of Dr. James McBride was living in Yamhill County. Levi Lindsay Rowland, 22, and William Thompson Haley, 20, were students at Alexander Campbell's Bethany College in Virginia. George L. Woods, 21, the future governor of the state, was in school at Bethel. Orlando Alderman, 20, was living in Marion County, and Joseph H. Sharp, 19, was living in Lane County. All nine of these young men would preach in Oregon between the late-1850s and the late-1860s.

Opposition from the Sects

The Christians in Oregon Territory entered 1854 on the crest of a wave of optimism. The disruption caused by the

California gold rush was over, and the number of organized churches was growing as more preachers from "the states" moved into the territory. But the optimism was muted somewhat by the continuing tactics of denominational preachers who were opposed to the principles of the Restoration Movement. "Sectarian feeling and prejudice run very high here," A. V. McCarty had commented on a preaching tour in Lane County in the summer of 1853. "When I was at this point last," he recalled, "I strove hard to impress upon the minds of all the erroneousness of many of their statements concerning us."[19]

Glen Owen Burnett, writing to Daniel Bates in Iowa on November 19, 1853, summed up the situation in Oregon:

> I think we are happily emerging, though slowly, from the gloom superinduced by the gold mines of California; and the day is not distant when we can see the cause of our common Master riding triumphantly and beautifully above all opposition . . . . But in Oregon we have strong opposition; every inch of ground is contested by well disciplined ranks of sectarian preachers, whose object it seems is to misrepresent those who have renounced all human appendages, and taken the Living Oracles alone.[20]

Writing to his father-in-law back in Missouri in August 1854, Burnett put "opposition from the sects" in a new light. "We have to contend with scores of well-disciplined opposers in this country," he admitted, "but I think, so far as we are concerned that is an advantage to us."[21] The primary detractors of the Restoration Movement were Methodists and Presbyterians. "But notwithstanding the Judaizing zeal of some of the Pedo-clergy," observed James McBride, "there are some highminded, honorable exceptions. And I am proud to say that our Baptist friends do not make a business of persecuting us . . . their preachers, with whom I have had the good fortune to form an acquaintance, are men of too much magnanimity and Christian prudence to become snarlers, railers or revilers."[22]

Baptizing More or Less Constantly

Despite the persistent opposition, 1854 was a good year for the cause in Oregon. "Times are improving in the bounds of my labors," A. V. McCarty excitedly announced on May 2. "My field on the east side of the Willamette was at first rather unpromising, but it now bids fair for an abundant harvest." Responding to the inevitable obstacles placed in the way by denominational opposition, McCarty wrote optimistically:

> Prejudice and sectarian bigotry are giving way to the pure gospel of Christ, as the flimsy mist of night fades away before the opening glories of the morning Sun. We have a series of protracted meetings ahead, the result of which I will forward to you. I hope they will prove a blessing to our glorious cause.[23]

Eight days later McCarty wrote, "I listened to the good confession of three last Lord's day, and the future is full of promise of prayed-for blessings."[24]

Perhaps no one line better describes the progress of the cause in 1854 than James McBride's declaration: "From reports, several of our preachers up Willamette Valley are baptizing more or less constantly."[25] When Alexander Campbell examined the reports coming in from Oregon, he wrote: "Upon the whole, we may regard the good cause as steadily advancing in that great Territory."[26] Amos Harvey reported a meeting in his neighborhood, conducted by McBride, Burnett, and Murphy, that resulted in 47 additions. McBride reported several successful meetings: Lafayette, 12 additions; South Fork, 17 additions; Pleasant Hill, 18 additions; Bethel, 30 additions; Hillsboro, 30 additions; and Gehalem, 2 additions.[27]

Every attempt to gather accurate statistics on the number of Christians living in the territory was difficult. Glen Owen Burnett's estimate of 1,200 Oregon Christians in 1851 was most likely too high, but there were probably between 1,000 and 1,500 by 1854. But Burnett refused to speculate on the numbers after 1851. In the summer of 1854 he wrote to his father-in-law in Missouri and commented: "Doubtless you would like to hear how the cause of Christianity is prospering in this far-off portion of the world. We have many Churches in Oregon, and quite an army of Disciples, with a score or more of preachers."[28] In this case, "many churches" was about 20, and the "army of Disciples" was probably 1,000 to 1,500. McBride also mentioned the 1,000 figure on occasion, but when pressed he wrote, "I can say, with much assurance, that the 'Christians' number not less than 800 in Oregon. All the Churches were not represented at our Annual Meeting; and besides the regularly organized congregations, there are quite a number of brethren scattered promiscuously here and there over the Territory."[29]

Alexander Campbell had asked his student, Levi Lindsay Rowland, to compile a report on "the progress of the cause of primitive Christianity in Oregon," and the results were published in the *Millennial Harbinger*. With several private letters from Oregon church leaders to assist him in gaining a consensus, Rowland concluded: "I feel authorized in saying that there are, in Oregon, about 1,000 Disciples; besides whom, it is presumable, there are many scattered promiscuously over the thinly settled portions of the territory, who are not known."[30]

The Burnett-Cornwall Debate on Baptism

As the Christian preachers were "baptizing more or less constantly," it was to be expected that pedo-baptist churches like the Methodists and Presbyterians would complain when their members were taught that sprinkling was not proper Biblical baptism. Whenever someone became dissatisfied with their sprinkling, they usually turned to the Christians for immersion. Several historical accounts have pointed out that the phrase, "Gone to the Campbellites," appears in many denominational record books for Oregon churches in the 1850s and 1860s.[31]

Given this tension, it was inevitable that one of the Christian preachers would one day be challenged to meet an opponent in a public debate on the subject of baptism. This became necessary during the course of a gospel meeting in Yamhill County, when Glen Owen Burnett was challenged to a debate. While Burnett was preaching, the Reverend J. A. Cornwall[32] of the Cumberland Presbyterians stood up and disrupted the meeting and demanded "proof" that the baptism referred to in Romans 6:4 and Colossians 2:12 was water baptism. Burnett responded politely with some "conciliatory remarks" and proceeded with his sermon. When Burnett was challenged a second time, and then again at the close of the sermon, it was agreed that the two men "should meet the next day and debate it out, which they did."[33]

Burnett and Cornwall had both been in Oregon for eight years and were popular leaders in their respective groups. Burnett was 45 years old and Cornwall was 56. In describing the debate for readers back in Iowa, Dr. James McBride wrote:

> As evidence that we are exciting some interest in the religious world, we had a handsome debate about two weeks since, between Brother Burnett, on the part of the Reformation, and Reverend Mr. Cornwall, on the part of the Cumberland Presbyterians. It was conducted in a prudent and dignified manner; and the best of feeling prevailed throughout . . . . Reverend Mr. Cornwall affirmed that Romans vi:4 and Colossians ii:12, had for their object Holy Ghost baptism. Brother Burnett denied. And notwithstanding the gravity and good deportment of the disputants, and the politeness and good decorum of the audience, yet there was something in the superinduction and phases of the controversy, which gave it the air of a *Theological Jollification.* I believe, however, it has effected much good. It is doubtless a good thing to "contend earnestly for the faith once delivered to the Saints."[34]

Immediately at the close of the debate, John Ecles Murphy addressed the audience for half an hour and called for believers to come and confess their faith in the Son of God and to be baptized into Christ. Three responded that evening and two others the next day. McBride informed the readers of the *Christian Evangelist* that he had the honor of immersing all five in the Yamhill River on the second evening. Gospel meetings usually ended at the river with the immersion of converts, and now the first debate in Oregon Territory had concluded with the same triumphal experience. One can picture the scene as the crowds followed the flickering torches from the river bank to their horse-drawn buggies, while the joyful singing of praises to God filled the starry night. For laborers like McBride, Murphy, and Burnett, trudging along in their wet clothing, it was a reaffirmation that the attraction of "primitive Christianity" would one day sweep the territory and unite all Bible-believing Christians in one church.

The Pioneers of '54

The migration of 1854 brought many Christians to Oregon Territory, but once again our knowledge of how many and of specific family names is slight. One family that would have a strong impact on the Pleasant Hill Church of Christ was that of James and Sarah Fisher. James R. Fisher had preached faithfully for several churches in Iowa, and his influence for good would be felt immediately in Lane County. Somewhere along the Oregon Trail, in the vicinity of Fort Laramie, he wrote back to Daniel Bates to say:

> We are traveling in a company of eleven wagons . . . and nearly all Christian brethren . . . . We try to keep the Lord's day as often as we can, but it is poorly done amidst the bustle and confusion of camp scenes. But the Lord has been merciful to us . . . .
>
> Oh! how I long to meet once more with the children of the Lord in His own house, where the songs of Zion arise as sweet incense. My dear Brother, be diligent, be faithful, and may the love, mercy, and peace of our Heavenly Father be with you and all the faithful in Christ Jesus.[35]

This incident underscores the difficulty facing any historian who attempts to tell the story of the Restoration Movement in Oregon Territory. The Fishers were traveling with a large number of Christians, but none of the other families can be identified with certainty. Did the entire train settle in Lane County? Were there any other preachers in the group? Were some of these families related to families already living in the territory? Were there any educators in this company who would be interested in establishing Christian schools in Oregon? Did anyone die along the Oregon Trail?

Upon arriving at Pleasant Hill, James R. Fisher wrote back to Iowa to say that he had been "introduced to the society of about one hundred brethren, a number of whom we had been acquainted with in years past." Fisher was eager to inform the readers of the *Christian Evangelist* that he was now living within a few miles of John Rigdon, Elijah Bristow, Charles Bradshaw, and Gilmore Callison. Fisher was persuaded that the only thing needed in Pleasant Hill was "a second Brother Bates who would in the face of the most adverse circumstances undertake the publication of a religious periodical, by which we could have more direct communication one with another."[36]

Christians in Washington Territory

While the church in Oregon Territory was growing steadily, the church in Washington Territory was completely devoid of organization. On October 6, 1851, Stephen and Winaford Ruddell and their five children arrived in Thurston County and settled in the area near present-day Olympia. They were probably the first Christian family to locate in Washington Territory. Four families of Christians who settled north of the Columbia River in 1853 were the Roundtrees, Murphys, Huntingtons, and Jacksons.[37] All four of these families came overland in 1852 and spent their first winter in Oregon Territory before continuing on north of the river in the spring of 1853.

When Tyrus and Emeline Himes and their four small children came overland in 1853, they were bound for Polk County, Oregon, and a reunion with their Christian friends from Monmouth, Illinois. All of that changed when they came upon a caravan of 32 wagons encamped on the side of the trail and they received a warm invitation to join the train. One historical record noted:

> Three of the families in that camp had lived in Pennsylvania near the birthplace of Tyrus and Emeline, and were also members of the Campbellite Church. The newcomers were cordially invited to stay with the train, and friendships were formed that lasted a lifetime.[38]

The caravan that the Himes family attached themselves to was bound for Washington Territory. A few weeks into the journey, Tyrus and Emeline revised their plans. Preferring to remain with their new Christian friends, they stayed with this train and decided to locate in Washington. This was the first wagon train to ever travel through the rugged Naches Pass in Washington's Cascade Mountains. The Himes family settled five miles east of Olympia in Thurston County.

Stephen Ruddell wrote from Olympia on May 7, 1854, and informed the readers of the *Christian Evangelist* of the plight of Washington Christians:

> We are like lost sheep wandering in the desert. A few members of the Christian Church have found their way here, and settled in various portions of this Territory. In Oregon, there is quite a respectable number. They have established Churches, in some places, and are in a prosperous condition. But in this Territory, we have not as yet any organized Church, nor any one to proclaim the Gospel to us regularly."[39]

When Levi Lindsay Rowland submitted his encouraging report to Alexander Campbell on the progress of "the cause of primitive Christianity in Oregon," he added this realistic note about Oregon's neighbor: "Washington Territory is almost entirely destitute of preaching of any kind. There are a few brethren there, but no minister."[40] One of the first Christian preachers to locate in Washington was Stephen Guthrie in the mid-1850s, and the first Oregon preachers to come to the assistance of their brethren to the north were John Rigdon and Lewis Casteel in the mid-1850s.

A Rich Repast for the People of God

The Restoration Movement in 1854 was very weak in northern California, virtually destitute in Washington Territory, and non-existent in Southern California. But in the words of Dr. James McBride, "the onward progress of Bible Christianity in Oregon" was indicative of "life in the body." "There is now a living, breathing, acting Christianity . . . which reminds me of better days East of the great dividing Ridge," he wrote in November 1854, "and which affords a rich repast to many of the people of God in these Western wilds."[41]

One encouraging example of the progress of the cause was the labors of McBride's own father. On his 77th birthday, July 25, 1854, Thomas Crawford McBride was preaching in a gospel meeting in Hillsboro with his son and Harrison H. Hendrix. There were four additions to the church. The sight of his venerable father in the pulpit led McBride to observe: "My father has been preaching fifty-nine years (this is the sixtieth). He abandoned all human creeds in 1810 . . . and has been pleading *the Bible alone* doctrine ever since; and though too blind to read, he still preaches."[42]

With veteran soldiers of the cross like Thomas Crawford McBride yoked together with young preachers like Harrison H. Hendrix for the restoration of primitive Christianity in Oregon Territory, the "glorious cause" appeared stronger than ever. Oregon Christians approached 1855 with eager anticipation, and there was optimistic talk emanating from many corners of the Willamette Valley about bold plans to launch Christian colleges and Christian academies in several different communities.

Chapter 14

The Bethanys of the West
1855

Colleges are, in every point of view, the most important and useful institutions on earth, second only to the Church of Christ in their inherent claims upon Christian liberality and Christian patronage.

– Alexander Campbell

. . . the Legislature of Oregon has granted a charter for the Rickreall Academy, which is under the patronage of the Brotherhood in that Territory. The Oregon brethren have taken early steps to promote Education within their borders.

– Daniel Bates, Christian Evangelist, April 1854

Nineteen educational institutions are known to have been founded by the Restoration Movement prior to November of 1841, but none of them survived beyond the Civil War. Only three were colleges, and the others were equivalents of our modern primary, middle, and high schools. It remained for the twentieth institution to become the "mother" of all subsequent colleges to which the movement gave birth.[1]

Alma Mater to a Movement

On November 1, 1841, Alexander Campbell welcomed the first students to his long-anticipated college constructed on a site adjacent to the Campbell mansion in the panhandle of Virginia. It would be difficult to overestimate the impact of Bethany College on the growth and development of the Restoration Movement in the next quarter century. Although there were educational institutions founded earlier, in a very real sense Bethany became the model for all colleges founded by the members of this religious tradition in the years after 1841.

According to one record, Campbell was the "chief architect" of the philosophy of higher education that became prevalent in the movement. Among other things, the Campbellian educational philosophy was characterized by its strong emphasis on: (1) the wholeness of the person; (2) the moral formation of character; and (3) the centrality of the Bible in the college curriculum. One of his successors at Bethany said admiringly of the former president, "He considered the Bible the great moral engine of civilization, the noblest of all classics, a book that spoke to the conscience, heart, and soul of humanity."[2] Campbell himself said, "A school without the Bible, is like a universe without a center and without a sun."[3]

Campbell repeatedly defended the use of the Bible as a textbook at Bethany College, and he called upon other colleges to follow his lead. In a morning lecture to the students at Bethany, later published in the January 1855 edition of the *Millennial Harbinger*, Campbell defined the role of the Bible as textbook:

> But while speaking of the Bible in the schools and colleges of our country, I do not mean the Bible on the shelf, in the college library, or locked up, like an amulet, in a trunk, to ward off specters, or diseases, or hobgoblins; but to be read, lectured upon, taught in all its facts, events, precepts, laws, ordinances, promises, threatenings.
>
> We do not mean that the Bible is to be taught or read theologically, as in schools of divinity, . . . It is to be read and studied historically, and with religious reference. Its whole moral power, and its whole spiritual power, are concentrated in its facts, precepts and promises; and not in those speculative theories called orthodoxy . . . these belong to denominations, and not to Christians.
>
> Theories and theologues make sectaries; but facts, precepts, promises, believed, obeyed and cherished, make Christians.[4]

Bethany College as Role Model

Between 1846 and 1853 many meetings involving Christians were held in the home of Ira F. M. Butler in Monmouth, Illinois. The people who attended these gatherings were afflicted with "Oregon Fever," and the purpose of the meetings was to lay the groundwork for a large exodus of Christians from Illinois to Oregon. As a direct result of these animated planning sessions, complete with maps of the Willamette Valley, three waves of immigrants traversed the Oregon Trail in 1850, 1852, and 1853. The large majority of these pioneers settled in Polk County and combined their energies to lay out and construct the town of Monmouth, Oregon.

Prior to leaving Illinois, the Christians in Monmouth agreed that upon arrival in Oregon Territory they would work together to achieve some important goals that were of mutual interest to everyone. As one historical record reported:

> The women exacted from their men a promise that a school and a church would be established before they consented to going. The school would be patterned after Bethany College in Virginia . . . founded by Alexander Campbell and would be a school "where men and women alike might be schooled in the science of living and in the fundamental principles of religion."[5]

Bethany College was a model, not only for the Monmouth Christians, but for several other Oregon-bound church leaders who aspired to establish Christian schools in the far west. Within the space of one decade (1846–1856), there were at least nine educational ventures in the Willamette Valley that involved families from the Restoration Movement. In the approximate order of their founding, these schools were: Jefferson Institute, Yamhill University, Oregon Academy, Pleasant Hill Academy, Bethany College, Rickreall Academy, McMinnville College, Bethel College, and Monmouth University.

Jefferson Institute

Jefferson Institute was mentioned in earlier chapters. It was an elementary school, taught by John Lyle, which began in the Nat Ford cabin in the winter of 1845–46. A separate log cabin was constructed to house the school in 1846, and a pulpit was placed at one end for church services. The school featured daily instruction in the Bible, but it was not consciously modeled after Bethany. Several Christians were connected with the school, including the Fords, Goffs, Loveladys, and Ellen Scott Lyle, and the Christians often used the building for Sunday services. McBride, Burnett, and Waller preached frequently in this log building. Swander noted that the Restoration Movement's second Annual Meeting in the fall of 1853 "appears" to have gone to Rickreall, and Dornhecker theorized that it may have been held at Jefferson Institute.[6]

Yamhill University

Yamhill University began in the winter of 1848–49. It had a briefer existence than Jefferson Institute, but it may have been more consciously modeled after Alexander Campbell's Bethany College. William Lysander Adams, the teacher of the school, had been a student at Bethany College, and he had boarded with the Alexander Campbell family. Most of the students and families connected with Yamhill University were Christians, including the McBrides, Woods, Adams, and Rowlands, and the school met for a time in the James McBride log cabin. Among the students who studied under Will Adams were George Lemuel Woods (a future governor of Oregon), John Rogers McBride (a future congressman from Oregon), Thomas A. McBride (a future chief justice of the Oregon Supreme Court), and Levi Lindsay Rowland (a future president of Christian College). The disruption of the California gold rush dashed any hopes for the long-term survival of Yamhill University.

Oregon Academy

The town of Lafayette, founded in 1846–47, is the oldest in Yamhill County. By the fall of 1849, John and Ellen Lyle had moved from their post at Jefferson Institute in Polk County and were conducting "a good sized school" in Lafayette. The Lyles apparently did not like their situation in Yamhill County, and they soon returned to Polk County. In the meantime, another couple moved to Lafayette and filled the void left by the departure of the Lyles. "When Edward R. Geary arrived in Lafayette in 1851," noted one account, "he and his wife started a school which was incorporated in January of 1852 as the Oregon Academy." Geary was a Presbyterian minister, and it is likely that his school included Bible study in its curriculum.[7]

At least three Christians, Absalom J. Hembree, Dr. James McBride, and Robert Crouch Kinney were included among the nine members of the board of trustees of Oregon Academy. Two other board members, Ahio S. Watt and James W. Nesmith, married into Christian families. Watt married Mary Elder in 1850. She was the daughter of Alfred R. Elder, a Christian preacher living in Yamhill County. Nesmith married Pauline Goff in 1846. She was the daughter of David and Kezziah Goff. Like Jefferson Institute, this school was not consciously modeled after Bethany College, but like Bethany, it almost certainly would have included daily instruction in the Bible. A school building may have been constructed for Oregon Academy, but it is not known how long the school remained in existence.

Pleasant Hill Academy

The Pleasant Hill School had its beginning in 1850. With the help of his son-in-law, James Hendricks, Elijah Bristow erected a small log cabin on the southwest corner of what is now the Pleasant Hill Cemetery. For the next four years this building was used as a schoolhouse during the week and as a meetinghouse for the Pleasant Hill Church of Christ on Sundays. William Wilshire Bristow, Elijah's son, was the first teacher at Pleasant Hill School. When the school and church both experienced growth, it became necessary to build a larger facility in 1854.

By 1855 the Pleasant Hill School had become Pleasant Hill Academy and was in need of a new teacher. A committee of five Christians was appointed to draw up an advertisement for publication in various church periodicals, including the *Christian Evangelist* in Iowa. The five men, all leaders in the Pleasant Hill Church of Christ were: Elijah Bristow, Gilmore Callison, John Rigdon, James R. Fisher, and James G. Mitchel. In describing the kind of person they were looking for, the ad stated, "He must be a moral man, and a Christian would suit better than a moralist." In describing the current status of Pleasant Hill Academy, the committee wrote:

> We wish to say to the friends of education, through your excellent periodical, that through the energy of the brethren of Pleasant Hill, there has arisen an Institution of Learning, bearing the above name. Our present building will accommodate 80 to 100 students. We thought best to commence upon a limited scale, and let the institute grow with our new and flourishing country. We made an effort in its behalf last spring, and, in the immediate vicinity, obtained a donation of more than one section of land, besides most of the materials necessary for the erection of a College edifice.[8]

It is interesting to see that the Pleasant Hill brethren had visions of their academy becoming a college. The model of Bethany College was clearly in the back of their minds, and they made a point to send the advertisement to Alexander Campbell for publication in the *Millennial Harbinger*. A rumor had spread that Moses E. Lard, a well-known Missouri preacher and an honor graduate of Bethany College, had decided to move to Oregon Territory, and the committee made a bid to attract him. "As we have been informed that Brother Moses E. Lard wishes to take up his residence in Oregon," the ad read, "we would be pleased to hear from him in relation to his disposition to comply with our wants."[9] As it turned out, Moses E. Lard never moved to Oregon, and the Pleasant Hill Academy never became a college. The academy, however, continued to serve the children of the Pleasant Hill community for the remainder of the century.

Bethany School

The fifth educational venture was the one attempted by the Christians living west of Silverton in Marion County (see chapter ten). They named their community Bethany, and they organized the Bethany Christian Church in April 1851. According to two historians, these Christian families developed plans to charter a college in their community to be known as Bethany College. Of course, Alexander Campbell's Bethany College was the inspiration for this plan.

No date is given for this attempt, but it must have been around the same time the church was established. "The settlers had big plans for Bethany," noted one account. "It was to be a college city . . . the school was to be known as Bethany College and to be managed under the Christian Church."[10] Another record gives the following information:

> It is thought that the first attempt to organize an institution of higher learning in the Silverton Country was that made by Thomas C. Shaw . . . Glen O. Burnett, a Mr. Gherkin and others, who promoted the plan for a school at Bethany, to be known as Bethany College, under the auspices of the Christian Church. Fones Wilbur, one of the promoters, had some of the brick for the building burned. The town of Bethany was platted by Elias Cox, with lots north and south of the main road leading from Silverton to Bethany. The spot chosen was across the road from the present Bethany School and church . . . .[11]

Both historical accounts mention that Peter Cox and his son, Elias Cox, were among the principal backers of the project, but in the end it failed because of the lack of funds. It is claimed that Glen Owen Burnett was sorely disappointed in the failure of this venture and that he later transferred his energy into the establishment of Bethel Institute near his farm in northern Polk County.

Although Bethany College proved to be too ambitious a project for its supporters, the effort did lead to the establishment of the Bethany School. It must have been in existence by the mid-1850s, but there are no clear records of where it met in the early years. A history of the school recorded, "Some say the first school at Bethany was held in the Christian Church next to the cemetery and was taught by Fones Wilbur. Others say school was held in the home of Elias Cox." This same history also reported, "One of the early locations of the school was in a building said to have been built to be a store by Thomas C. Shaw."[12]

Rickreall Academy

Not much is known about Rickreall Academy. It evidently was the successor to Jefferson Institute. According to an item in the *Oregon Statesman* for January 3, 1854, 16 men had been chosen as "the Trustees of the Rickreall Academy, for the purpose of establishing and maintaining an institution of learning, upon lands donated by Lovelady and others, situated in Polk County." This was a reference to Thomas Lovelady, who was an elder in the Christian Church that had been meeting in the same log building that housed the Jefferson Institute. The Fords and Goffs were members of this church, and so was Ellen Scott Lyle.

Among the 16 men chosen to serve on the board of trustees were 14 well-known Christians, including William Lysander Adams, Harrison Linville, David R. Lewis, Amos Harvey, Samuel M. Gilmore, Hardin Martin, Caleb P. Chapman, Gilmore Callison, Samuel Simmons, Hiram Alva Johnson, Truman Bonney, William Frazer, Richard Miller and John T. Gilfrey. The only two that were not affiliated with the Christians were Milton Tuttle, and John Eakin Lyle.

Milton Tuttle, who lived in Washington County, may have been a Presbyterian. He was good friends with Harvey Clark, the Presbyterian missionary, and he assisted Clark in the construction of Tualatin Academy at Forest Grove in 1851. Tuttle was an architect, carpenter and builder, and that may have led to his inclusion on this board. Lyle was a Presbyterian before he was joined in marriage to Ellen Scott by Glen Owen Burnett in 1846. Lyle may have occasionally attended the Christian Church with his wife.

The surprisingly large number of Christians included among the trustees of Rickreall Academy was explained in a brief item that appeared three months later in the April 1854 issue of the *Christian Evangelist*. Daniel Bates published the following note in his "Editor's Table" briefs:

> Brother J. T. Gilfrey, Lane County, Oregon, informs us that the Legislature of Oregon has granted a Charter for the Rickreall Academy, which is under the patronage of the Brotherhood in that Territory. The Oregon brethren have taken early steps to promote Education within their borders.[13]

Unlike its ecumenical predecessor, Jefferson Institute, Rickreall Academy was specifically designed to be a church-related institution from the very beginning. It was understood that it was "under the patronage of the Brotherhood." What is most impressive about the list of trustees is the geographical diversity inherent in the group. The trustees were not only from Polk County where the school was to be located. Church leaders were selected from four different counties in the Willamette Valley.

Polk County Christians were represented on this board by Linville, Lewis, and Harvey. Lyle was also from Polk County. The three Christians from Yamhill County were Adams, Martin, and Gilmore. Surprisingly, Marion County Christians had the largest representation on this board with Chapman, Johnson, Simmons, Bonney, Miller and Frazer. The Christians from the greatest distance were the Lane County duo of Callison and Gilfrey. Despite this promising beginning, Rickreall Academy was short-lived. It must have been a casualty of the two other schools begun by Christians in Polk County during the next two years.

McMinnville College

It was in 1854 at Newby's grist mill in Yamhill County that two Christians, William T. Newby and Sebastian Adams, had the chance conversation that led to the founding of a new Oregon town. By 1855 Adams had platted a town adjoining Newby's grist mill and named it McMinnville in honor of Newby's birthplace in Tennessee. Newby donated six acres for a school, and he persuaded Adams to move to the new townsite and run the school. Two other Christians, Dr. James McBride and William Dawson, were involved in the project from the beginning. This was the germ from which McMinnville College grew.[14]

Hubert Howe Bancroft noted of Sebastian Adams and his new school, ". . . as he and most of the leading men in Yamhill were of the Christian church, it naturally became a Christian school. James McBride, William Dawson, W. T. Newby, and Adams worked up the matter, bearing the larger part of the expense."[15] The school began in an unfinished building in 1855, but the project was beset with difficulty. The Christians living in the adjoining counties of Yamhill and Polk were being asked to support too many schools at once, and sufficient funding was not available. One Baptist historian wrote:

> An apparently good start for a denominational school had been made but there were serious discouragements ahead. During the winter of 1855–56 the unfinished building was very nearly demolished by a severe storm. The Christians, moreover, like the Baptists, were finding that a struggling frontier group may have too many infant institutions under its supervision. Their school at Bethel, only about 15 miles from McMinnville, was just getting established and their work at Monmouth was demanding attention. Little wonder, then, that they were not enthusiastic about accepting and sponsoring the uncertain McMinnville venture. [16]

Within a year, McMinnville College was offered to the Baptists, and on January 19, 1858, William and Sarah Newby deeded the property to a group of Baptist leaders who agreed to maintain a school on the site. McMinnville College became Linfield College in 1922. Today, Linfield College has more than 1,200 students, and it remains a church-related institution affiliated with the Baptist Church.

Bethel College

When Glen Owen Burnett settled in northern Polk County in 1846, he named the heights to the east the "Bethel Hills" after a church he had preached for in Missouri. Amos and Jane Harvey settled on the adjoining property some time later, and in the early 1850s the Bethel Christian Church was established. The failure of Bethany College in Marion County prompted Burnett and Harvey to make an attempt to organize a school in their own district. A preliminary board met for the first time on January 3, 1855, and on Burnett's motion they chose John Ecles Murphy as chairman and William Lysander Adams as secretary. On the motion of Amos Harvey, the name of Bethel Institute was adopted as the permanent name of the institution.[17]

John Ecles Murphy must have decided that it was a wiser use of his time to transfer his energy and resources to Monmouth University, which was closer to his home, because he was not included among the original nine board members chosen to guide the development of Bethel Institute. The nine board members, all church leaders affiliated with the Christians, were: Glen Owen Burnett, Amos Harvey, Joseph Warren Downer, William Lysander Adams, Samuel M. Gilmore, John H. Robb, A. V. McCarty, Absalom H. Frier, and Sanford Watson.[18]

On land donated by Burnett and Harvey, it was decided to erect a two-story frame building, 36-feet by 44-feet. A building committee began to acquire the necessary materials, and an announcement was published that the frame would be erected on July 4 in the midst of a patriotic celebration at Bethel. A history of Bethel offers this description:

> Wednesday, July 4, 1855, was one of the most momentous days in the history of Bethel. Early in the morning of that day men, many of them with their families, began to arrive at Bethel from all directions—some from long distances away—to volunteer their services in promoting the prospective educational institution . . . . By the close of the afternoon the framework of the building together with its covering structure were well advanced toward completion, and the happy people turned homeward with a deep feeling of thankfulness for the great accomplishment of the historic occasion . . . .[19]

The work was interrupted twice during the day for patriotic addresses on education. The speakers were two prominent Christian preachers who were also members of the Bethel board of trustees, William Lysander Adams and Alexander Vance McCarty. In the middle of the day a bountiful "basket dinner" was enjoyed by everyone. To finance the school, Amos Harvey gave 160 acres of land and Glen Owen Burnett gave 80 acres. This land was adjacent to the new school building and it was sold as residence lots to create the town of Bethel. When the school was completed and dedicated on October 22, 1855, it was the largest building in Polk County.

This was a proud achievement for the Christians of Polk County. A. V. McCarty corresponded with the *Christian Record* to share the good news. "We are trying to get up an institution of learning for the youth of Oregon Territory, to be under the supervision and control of our brotherhood," he announced to the Christians in the Midwest. "Our beloved brother G. O. Burnett and others have made many personal sacrifices, and have persevered in a series of uncompromising and zealous efforts worthy of the noble cause of education."[20]

There were several teachers and assistant teachers in the early years. The decision to introduce college work as soon as possible led to the hiring of William Thompson Haley in 1858. He was a recent graduate of Bethany College, and he took charge of the school from May 1858 to July 1859. When the school year began in 1859, Levi Lindsay Rowland, another graduate of Bethany College, was added to the faculty. He became the first president of Bethel College in 1860. Bancroft noted, "At this time the Bethel school was prosperous. It had a well-selected library, and choice apparatus in the scientific departments."[21]

Monmouth University

Meanwhile, the large migration of Christian families from Monmouth, Illinois, to Polk County was completed in the fall of 1853. By 1854 they had chosen the site for their new town and for the school that would be modeled after Bethany College. Five of these church leaders, Squire S. Whitman, Elijah Davidson, Albert Whitfield Lucas, John Burris Smith, and Thomas H. Lucas, donated a total of 640 acres between them to be sold as lots in the new town. Proceeds from the sale would go to finance the college they had promised their wives would be established in Oregon. It was decided to name the town Monmouth and to name the school Monmouth University. The first meeting of the board of trustees was held in the home of Thomas H. Lucas on March 10, 1855.[22]

One month earlier, the Methodists had established LaCreole Academy at nearby Dallas. According to one historian:

> There was an influential community of Disciples south of the Rickreall who did not relish the establishment of the Methodist academy at Dallas; and set their wits to work to hold their church people and rising generation together by establishing a College of the first class among themselves.[23]

The eleven original board members at Monmouth University included ten well-known church leaders among the Christians: Ira F. M. Butler, John Ecles Murphy, David R. Lewis, Squire S. Whitman, John Burris Smith, William Mason, Thomas H. Lucas, Samuel Simmons, Thomas H. Hutchinson and Hezekiah Burford. The other board member, Reuben P. Boise, was a prominent citizen of Polk County. He had previously served on the board of Oregon Academy and he was also on the board of LaCreole Academy. Boise was a graduate of Williams College in Massachusetts, and he had been admitted to the bar before migrating to Oregon in 1850. He was the prosecuting attorney for Polk County.

The summer of 1855 turned out to be a busy one for the Christians of the Willamette Valley. Four fine schools were competing for the loyalty of the brotherhood at the same time. In the southern part of the valley, Pleasant Hill Academy was placing ads in leading church periodicals and hoping to attract Moses E. Lard. In the northern part of the valley, three new towns, McMinnville, Bethel, and Monmouth, were in the process of selling lots and building colleges. Unfortunately, the three new towns were located within 30 miles of each other. It is not surprising that Rickreall Academy, with its fine board of 16 members scattered throughout the Willamette Valley, was not heard from again.

The Cause of Truth Prospers

Despite all the interruptions associated with the gold rush, Indian wars, and political issues, the Restoration Movement continued to make progress in Oregon. "The cause of Truth prospers here full better than might be calculated on by its friends," wrote John Rigdon, "when we take into account the obstacles to be overcome, and the very loose and inefficient manner in which the war is carried on." He continued:

> It is with the soldiers of the Cross in Oregon as it was with the people of Israel, in the days when there was no king. Every one does what is right in the sight of his own eyes, still quite a number of additions are being made to the company of the disciples; and if the skeptic would honestly mark the progress of the Truth amongst us, I think that he would be forced to admit that the cause must be under the special guardianship of its Almighty author.[24]

Dr. James McBride immersed three converts at Amity in Yamhill County in April. He and A. V. McCarty held a meeting at Stephen and Louisa McKinney's home in northern Polk County in May that resulted in seven additions, including six immersions. The following week McCarty immersed five when he preached at Amity. When McBride and Harrison Hendrix preached "at Brother Hill's near Wapatoo Lake," (on the border of Yamhill and Washington counties) a "fine young man announced his Christian faith and was baptized." At Shaddon Schoolhouse (near McMinnville) "a noble young man made the good confession" and was baptized. A month later, McCarty and Hendrix preached at Amity and "3 more confessed that Jesus was the Christ." Mac Waller preached in a meeting on Mary's River in Benton County (west of present-day Corvallis) and "obtained 10 accessions to the cause."[25]

"We have some talented men among us, and churches are being established in many parts of the Territory," reported Thomas M. Ward from Thurston in Lane County. "We organized one the 4th Lord's day of May, six miles East of where I reside, with 14 members," he wrote. "Brother Alfred Powell was with us. Brother J. A. Powell will probably be our evangelist this summer."[26] As mentioned in chapter 13, three additional congregations were established in Douglas County in the summer of 1855.

Eliza Ann Smith informed James Mathes that she traveled 20 miles to attend a gospel meeting "on the Willamette coast" in Lane County in September where "nine persons confessed the blessed Saviour." She attended another meeting 16 miles from her home in Lane County in October in which "ten were added to the number of the faithful." She heard Philip Mulkey preach to "a large audience" at her home church on Muddy Creek in October, "and at the conclusion he gave an invitation to such as were disposed to own their Savior, and two young persons responded favorably, and were immersed the same day about sundown. Thus, you see, my good brother Mathes," she concluded, "there are some faithful souls even in this extreme point. May the Lord multiply his faithful children in Oregon a hundred fold!"[27]

One area the Restoration Movement had yet to penetrate by 1855 was Portland and the surrounding Multnomah County. A brother named S. C. Ritchey corresponded with Daniel Bates about the need. "The cause of our Master is progressing slowly in this part of Oregon," he declared. "We greatly need a preacher who would wield an influence on the community around, and whose example would be worthy of imitation. This we have not. If we had some of our Illinois brethren I could name here, I think great good would be the result."[28]

William and Martha Ann Barlow

Occasionally the Oregon evangelists would give the names of those they baptized. When Dr. McBride preached in Amity he immersed "Judge Walling and his amiable lady."[29] This was a reference to Jerome B. Walling and his wife, Sarah. Glen Owen Burnett and John Ecles Murphy had baptized William and Martha Ann Barlow in 1855. Barlow's father had constructed the famous Barlow Toll Road around Mount Hood in 1845, and William and Martha were prominent citizens of Clackamas County who lived in a large residence near present-day Canby. The Barlows invited A. V. McCarty to preach in their spacious residence in the summer of 1855. McCarty wrote:

> On the third Lord's day in July, 1855, I held a meeting at brother William Barlow's in Clackamas County, and had 6 additions by confession and immersion, and 1 from the Baptists. Brethren Burnett and Murphy had previously been there on a funeral occasion, and prepared the minds of the people for the reception of the truth, by preaching the word and receiving some 5 or 6 into the kingdom of Christ, among whom were brother William Barlow and wife. One month after my visit I went back again. The audience increased in numbers and interest, though we had strong opposition from some other denominations who manifested some derision and ill-will toward us on the occasion. Nevertheless, our meeting was full of the love of God, and 6 more were added to the good cause. Everything bids fair for a blessed ingathering to the Lord, if the preaching brethren could only attend them. It is a wealthy and pleasure-loving country; but the Lord is turning their hearts to the promotion of his glorious cause.[30]

The Expiration of the Oregon Land Act

The United States government originally announced that the Donation Land Claim Act would expire on December 1, 1853, but in February 1853 the time was extended to December 1, 1855. By the terms of this act, passed in 1850, each white male over 18 years of age was entitled to 320 acres of land. If married, his wife could hold an additional 320 acres. Eventually, 7,437 patents were granted for donation land claims in Oregon Territory before the expiration date of December 1, 1855.

Chapter 15

The Unholy Fury of Political Partyism

1856

The cause is often made to bleed by cruel, raving, political partyism. Professed friends of the meek and lowly Saviour have been known to lay aside the lovely robes of religion, pure and undefiled, for the unholy and impure habiliments of political fury! . . . the want of union and brotherly love among the churches has greatly retarded the progress of truth.

— A. V. McCarty, January 28, 1856

Although a great majority of Christians felt that the energy and money devoted to the establishment of Christian schools was well worth the effort, there were some detractors. "The brotherhood have become so much engrossed in building up academies and high schools," observed John Alkire Powell, "that we seem almost to have forgotten to send the gospel to the destitute."[1] Powell issued an urgent call for "more proclaimers" who would "be able and willing to face the sectarian and infidel in the defense of the gospel."

The Absence of Spiritual Maturity

There were others, however, who were convinced that the biggest obstacle facing the movement was not a lack of schools or proclaimers, but a lack of spiritual maturity. They pointed out that there was too great an emphasis on gaining numbers and too little on modeling Christian behavior. Glen Owen Burnett himself, never shy about touting numbers, was bothered by what he perceived to be a lack of maturity in the churches. In a personal letter intended for publication in the *Christian Evangelist,* Burnett worried that "the zeal to proselyte," particularly among younger preachers, was often greater than the "anxiety to cultivate a Heaven-born piety among the discipled." "In many places," he wrote sadly, "weekly meetings are hardly thought of, and the house of prayer seldom visited."[2]

Less than six months later, a brother in Washington County named Zephaniah Bryant was even more blunt in his assessment of the Achilles' heel of the movement. Writing to James Mathes in Indiana, editor of the *Christian Record,* Bryant was pleased to report that there were two congregations of 60 members each meeting in his county, but he was troubled by their lack of spiritual maturity. "I am sorry to see so little growth in grace or in the knowledge of the Scriptures, and the practice of religion in the Christian church," he wrote candidly. It was the same problem he had witnessed back in "the states." He continued:

> I thought all the time, that if the reformation stopped here, in other congregations, as it did in ours, at being baptized in the name of Christ, there was a fault. I still think so. Having come to Oregon, and here finding brethren from many of the different states, all seem to have been instructed about the same way. Or, is this enough? being baptized for the remission of sins, may they expect that God will save them? Now it does seem to me, that the preachers think too much about gaining numbers, and pay too little attention, after they have obtained them, in properly instructing them, that they may grow in grace and in the knowledge of the truth. If this were done in proper time, I think we would not see so many, that after they are old enough to be teachers, they need some one to teach them again the first principles of the doctrine of Christ. There are many in all parts of the world that are mere drones, and like drones they must soon die; for the child that is born into the kingdom of Christ, cannot live without spiritual food, any more than the physical man can without his food . . . there are many that read but little, and pray none at all . . . . How can such live? Are they not dead while they yet live?[3]

Bryant also objected to members of the church becoming involved in Masonry and other secret fraternal organizations. The argument was that such organizations destroyed the doctrine of the all-sufficiency of the church. "I see many claiming to be Christians, stepping aside from the light, and joining secret societies; they say, for the good of the world," complained Bryant. "If the world is ever saved, it will be by the truth," he declared, "and that in open day light." Bryant laid the problem at the feet of the preachers and elders. He held them accountable for feeding the church a limited diet of "first principles" only. From his perspective, many Christians "have had no spiritual food since they have been in the kingdom."[4]

The Advancing Political Storm

John Alkire Powell agreed that there was a lack of maturity in the movement, but he identified a potentially more serious foe than secret societies. "The state of affairs in this part of Oregon is rather unfavorable to the cause of religion," he argued, "induced by the electioneering campaign, in which many of our brethren engaged too freely."[5] Polarizing political issues were buffeting the populace in the mid-1850s, and the political atmosphere was threatening to derail the progress of the church. Several church leaders occupied positions of leadership in the Democratic Party, and many others were integrally involved in the formation of the new Republican Party. Powell thought Christians in both parties were "engaged too freely" in these hotly-contested political issues.

A. V. McCarty was also of the opinion that strong political feelings were retarding the progress of truth. "The cause is often made to bleed by cruel, raving political partyism," he wrote accusingly. "Professed friends of the meek and lowly Saviour have been known to lay aside the lovely robes of religion, pure and undefiled, for the unholy and impure habiliments of political fury!" In McCarty's judgment, "the want of union and brotherly love among the churches has greatly retarded the progress of truth."[6] These were harsh words, spoken only five years before the smoldering situation erupted into a full-scale civil war, but they were unfortunately true.

Another political party, officially called the American Party, but more popularly called the Know-Nothing Party, appeared on the scene at this time. The engine that drove this party was the fear of the flow of immigrants into the United States from foreign countries, particularly those immigrants who were Roman Catholics. David R. Lewis, an active member of the Democratic Party, was bothered by the intolerance that was inherent in the platform of the Know-Nothing Party. In a letter written June 30, 1855, and published in the *Oregon Statesman,* Lewis offered a critique of this party and then concluded:

> To cut what I have to say short, no man can be a Christian and belong to the knownothings, or advocate their principles. We are commanded to do good to all men. They proscribe foreigners and Catholics. Thousands of them are pining in despotism and destitution in the old country, yet they must continue to be slaves there, or their inferiors here. If, to do this, is to have the spirit of Christ dwelling in them, I know nothing about it. My copy of the good book tells me to entertain strangers, and in so doing I might entertain an angel.[7]

The Pleasant Hill Church in Lane County was a mirror of the times. From the very beginning its membership had been a melting pot of political opinion. There were some leading families in the church who had deep roots in the slave-holding southern states, but there were many in the congregation who did not favor the extension of slavery to Oregon Territory. Feelings were so strong by 1853 that three veteran preachers, Glen Owen Burnett, Elijah Davidson, and John Ecles Murphy, were called in to resolve the conflict. In giving a summary of his labors for that year, Murphy revealed that he had intervened to help several churches. He wrote:

> I have, also, at the solicitation of the brethren, assisted in settling serious difficulties which existed in several congregations. My co-workers in this were Brethren J. Rigdon, G. O. Burnett and E. Davidson. The Lord has blessed

> our labors beyond our most sanguine expectations—especially was this the case in reference to the labors of Bros. Burnett, Davidson and myself, at Pleasant Hill, Lane County. Serious difficulties that had long existed were entirely removed. After peace and Christian union and fellowship were restored, we preached there for three days, during which time some 17 were gained.[8]

"The Church of Christ here is now in a flourishing condition," reported W. W. Bristow proudly after the unifying meeting. "We number some 70 members."[9] Seven months later, Gilmore Callison recorded more progress: "The Church at Pleasant Hill, which numbered 27 members in '52, now numbers about 100."[10] The church had outgrown the little log schoolhouse it had been meeting in and moved into a larger schoolhouse, built by Robert Callison on a 40-acre site donated by Elijah Bristow in the summer of 1854. Unfortunately, the political tensions were never completely eradicated or overcome. The Pleasant Hill Church struggled heroically to maintain its fragile unity in the years leading up to and including the Civil War.

The Republican Party in Oregon

The tumultuous years of 1855–56 witnessed some fine advances for the Christians in Oregon Territory, particularly in the area of Christian education. But there was cause for alarm as political tensions escalated and spilled over into church life. In March 1855, one of the best-known Christians in the territory, William Lysander Adams, bought a printing press and established the *Oregon Argus* at Oregon City. This 4-page weekly paper became the mouthpiece of the emerging Republican Party in Oregon, and it gained for its colorful editor the proud title of "Father of the Republican Party in Oregon."

At the same time, the *Oregon Argus* became the principal medium for presenting information to the public about Bethel Institute. This was a surprising combination, and it must have been met with mixed feelings by Democrats who were also strong Christians and supporters of Bethel Institute. One historian writing about Adams reported, "Early Oregon journalism was distinguished not for its restraint but for its vehemence; there were no libel laws to bring possible embarrassment to plain-speaking editors, and abuse and epithets flew thick and fast."[11] Another record noted of Adams, "As a Republican editor he was more feared and more hated than any man in his day in Oregon."[12]

The daughter of Will Adams remembered the volatile discussions between church leaders on the pros and cons of slavery. As a little girl, she was a witness to these historic deliberations in their log cabin on Panther Creek. Years later she wrote:

> . . . and to me, who always sympathized passionately with the "under dog" and who already at seven years had read "Uncle Tom's Cabin" with many tears, it was a joy to hear my father "walk all over" them and fairly demolish their "scriptural" grounds for slavery, by hosts of unanswerable Bible quotations against any such slavery as existed in our times. I do not recall any quarrels resulting from these discussions. In fact, he seemed usually to convince his opponents that they might be in the wrong.[13]

Will Adams published his first issue of the *Oregon Argus* on April 21, 1855. Amos Harvey and Dr. James McBride were just two of the prominent Christians who stood shoulder to shoulder with Adams in the founding of the Republican Party in Oregon. Others included his brother, Sebastian Adams, and John Rogers McBride, George Lemuel Woods, Samuel M. Gilmore, G. W. Burnett (brother of Glen Owen Burnett), A. W. Lucas, and Thomas C. Shaw. Among the leading Republicans in Lane County was William Wilshire Bristow from the Pleasant Hill Church who was elected a state senator in 1858. One of the most active Republicans in the Umpqua Valley was Samuel Bates Briggs, a gospel preacher and county commissioner for Douglas County.

In the same month that Will Adams launched the *Oregon Argus,* the Polk County Democratic Convention, led by a three-man Democratic County Committee, met at the court house to nominate candidates for the next June election. The three-man committee consisted of Mac Waller, Thomas J. Lovelady, and David R. Lewis—one preacher and two elders.[14] Among other Christians who were actively involved in the Democratic Party were William T. Newby and Andrew Shuck in Yamhill County, Nat Ford and Ira F. M. Butler in Polk County, and Nathan T. Caton and William J. Herren in Marion County. Most of the Hembree and Mulkey families were also affiliated with the Democratic Party. With so many multi-gifted church leaders so thoroughly involved on both sides of the polarizing political process, it is not surprising that John A. Powell and A. V. McCarty were worried about the "cruel, raving, political partyism." There was good reason for concern.

One Christian in Marion County, Benjamin Stanton, was a slave-owner who was described in one account as "an ardent Democrat." Another Christian who lived in the same district, Wiley Chapman, was described in the same account as "an ardent abolitionist."[15] Two brothers who were both Christians, Isaiah Cooper Matheny and Daniel Boone Matheny, were on opposite sides of the most vexing political issue of the day. Isaiah, having married into a Southern family, adopted a proslavery position and supported the Confederate cause. His brother, who was a Christian preacher, was adamantly in favor of the Union cause.[16] Two sons of Elijah Bristow were divided on this question as well. Elijah Lafayette Bristow was a proslavery Democrat, and William Wilshire Bristow was an antislavery advocate who became a supporter of the new Republican Party.[17]

The most vocal proslavery advocates in Oregon Territory were all members of the Democratic Party, but not all Democrats favored the extension of slavery into Oregon. Actually, a majority of Oregon Democrats were opposed to the extension of slavery in their territory. There were a large number of "independent" Democrats who were prepared to revolt against their proslavery colleagues in the party. Among the Christians who were leaders in the ranks of the "independent" Democrats were Nat Ford and Andrew Shuck.[18] The *Oregon Statesman,* the leading Democratic newspaper in the territory, defined an "independent" Democrat as "one who votes for the meanest kind of a Know

Nothing, nigger-worshipping apostate from the Democratic party."[19]

To underscore the involvement of Christians in the founding of the Republican Party in Oregon, a history of the party opens with this paragraph:

> The first nominee of any Republican convention in Oregon was S. C. Adams, nominated at a convention of Republicans in Yamhill county, November 22, 1856, to fill a vacancy in the lower house of the Legislature, and the first Republican elected in the state was John R. McBride, also nominated in Yamhill county, in the spring of 1856, as a member of the Constitutional Convention. He was the only member of the body that framed the constitution of Oregon who was elected on a straight Republican ticket.[20]

Oregon finally achieved statehood in 1859, but for several years prior to this the citizens of the territory struggled mightily over the issues of slavery and freedom. To Will Adams and his fellow-Republicans, the one paramount issue of the day was whether the new state would be listed in the proslavery column or characterized by its freedom for all inhabitants. One account noted that Will Adams "stumped the state, writing his editorials on his knee, armed with two revolvers and a bowie knife, as the 'slavocrats' were everywhere threatening his life."[21] Another historian wrote admiringly of Adams, "Through the *Argus* . . . he overthrew all opposition, dismantled their guns, licked the Republican party into shape, and laid the foundation for free Oregon."[22]

On November 9, 1857, the voters of Oregon approved the proposed state constitution by a vote of 7,195 to 3,215. At the same time, slavery was excluded from Oregon by a vote of 7,727 to 2,645. It was a moment of grand triumph for the Adams brothers, the McBride family, and their fellow-Christians in the Republican Party. However, in the same election, free Negroes were prohibited from settling in Oregon by a vote of 8,640 to 1,081. This was a reflection of the strong anti-Negro bias in the Pacific Northwest, and one historical record concluded by saying of Oregon in 1857, "The electorate wanted none of the Negro race; free Negroes were barred from Oregon by an even greater majority than slavery."[23]

Indian Troubles

The rancorous passion of political debate was not the only distraction affecting the progress of the Restoration Movement in Oregon Territory. One of the most disturbing realities facing the new residents of the territory was the constant danger of an attack by hostile Indians. The massacre at Whitman Mission in November 1847 led to the Cayuse War of 1848. That war was followed by other wars and by constant skirmishes between Indians and settlers throughout the territory. The danger of attack was very real, and it was inevitable that Christians would be drawn into the conflict.

Numerous efforts were made to achieve a peaceful settlement in the 1850s, but the conflict continued. "The whole story is a sort of merry-go-round, draped in black," one study concluded. "The Indians were angered by encroachments on their lands and later by their mistreatment on and off reservations. They reacted in the only way they knew, by killing."[24] One of those killed in the many conflicts with Indians was A. J. Hembree, a respected Christian and one of the most popular citizens of Yamhill County. He died in April 1856 while fighting in the Yakima Indian War in Washington Territory.

Absalom Jefferson Hembree

Absalom Jefferson Hembree was in the vanguard of the first Christians who crossed the Oregon Trail in "The Great Migration" of 1843. The 30-year-old farmer made the journey with his wife, Nancy Dodson, and three small daughters. Traveling with his older brother Joel Jordan and his uncle Andrew, and accompanied by good friends like William T. Newby and Chesley B. Gray, A. J. Hembree helped to blaze a 2,000-mile trail across the continent that would be followed by hundreds of fellow-Christians in the years ahead.

Nancy Dodson was the daughter of McMinn Dodson, a former Governor of Tennessee. She married her husband near McMinnville, Tennessee, in 1834 and then joined him in pushing west and building a new home on the edge of the Missouri frontier. When the United States Senate passed

Senator Linn's "Oregon Bill" on February 28, 1843, the Hembrees were perfectly positioned to pull up stakes and join the migration. The prospect of free land in the beautiful Willamette Valley was irresistible.

The five-month trek across the rugged Oregon Trail was not without its trauma. They buried their six-year-old nephew, Joel Hembree, along the trail, and their own lives were threatened when they attempted to cross a rain-swollen river. The journey down the mighty Columbia River on crude rafts was harrowing, but they survived. After spending the winter in Oregon City, they set out in the spring of 1844 to find their new home. They settled on a donation land claim in Yamhill County about five miles northeast of present-day McMinnville. One historical account noted, "It was said that Absalom made a splendid selection—the very 'Eden of Oregon.' Here he built his log cabin and began the life of a pioneer."[25]

After arriving in Oregon Territory, Absalom and Nancy welcomed five sons and another daughter to their growing family of nine children. Absalom would have been content to devote all of his time to farming, but he yielded to the pleas of his neighbors to represent them in governmental affairs. He served as a legislator in the Provisional Government (1846–1848) and then in the Territorial Government (1849–1851). He was a director of the Portland & Valley Plank Road Company, and he was president and organizer of the first telegraph project in Oregon—the Pacific Telegraph Company, which was incorporated in 1855 to connect with California. A natural leader of men, A. J. Hembree was also elected to be the sheriff of Yamhill County.

When Christians first arrived in the Territory they often contacted A. J. Hembree for guidance. One record noted, "In fact, he built a fairly large cabin so that new emigrants to the valley would have a place to stay until they were settled."[26] After the McBrides arrived in Oregon they went straight to Yamhill County in search of A. J. Hembree. John Rogers McBride, the 14-year-old son of Dr. James McBride, wrote in his diary, "A few more hours, and we were under the roof of an old friend of other days, A. J. Hembree, and the long journey was at an end."[27] When Dr. James McBride and Glen Owen Burnett planned their first Oregon preaching tour for November 1846, they agreed to meet at the A. J. Hembree cabin. Burnett rode off to preach the gospel with McBride on a horse loaned by Absalom Hembree.[28]

The Yakima Indian War

When the Yakima Indian War broke out in 1855, volunteers in every county began to mobilize for the seemingly unavoidable confrontation. Several years later, Absalom Hembree's young son, Joel Jordan, explained how his father became involved. "I remember very distinctly being out in the field one day helping father build a fence," he recalled. "George Olds and several other settlers rode up and told him that the company of volunteers had decided to ask him to be their captain."[29]

Once again Absalom agreed to the pleas of his neighbors, and everyone concerned with the war effort assembled in Lafayette on October 16, 1855, to organize and elect officers. One history declares, "Yamhill County sent about sixty-five of its bravest men to fight the Indians under the command of Captain Absalom Hembree."[30] Absalom's older brother, Joel Jordan, did not accompany the volunteers but he did send two of his sons, Wayman and Lafayette, to serve under their uncle.

Meanwhile, the preaching of the gospel was struggling to gain a hearing in communities distracted by Indian hostilities. In a letter dated February 5, 1856, John A. Powell wrote to James Mathes and described the dilemma facing the preachers. He commented:

> The Indian war in this country, and the frequent calls for troops has kept up such an excitement throughout the country, that we have been able to accomplish but little for the good cause.
>
> Since my last, at the meeting I attended there were 43 additions, with numerous additions at other points, through the labors of other brethren. And the prospects were very

good until the Indian war commenced. May God in his providence bring it to a speedy close.[31]

The Luckiamute Valley in Polk County was less affected by the war than some districts. "The cause of Christ is slowly advancing in this part of Oregon," David R. Lewis reported to Mathes in February. "On last Lord's day we had two additions by confession and baptism, and I think the prospect good for many more. May the Lord enable us all to honor our profession!"[32]

John A. Powell's prayer for a quick conclusion to the widespread war was partially answered. The conflict known as the Yakima Indian War came to a speedy close in two months, but with tragic consequences for the Hembree family. In a letter written in early April 1856, Absalom Hembree corresponded with his older brother, Joel Jordan, who was back home in Yamhill County. Attempting to accurately describe the difficulties under which they were laboring to accomplish their mission, Hembree wrote:

Dear Brother: I take this opportunity to let you know what we are doing in this God-forsaken country. We have been living for the past 15 days on horse beef. Our horses are all very weak, many of them giving out and left. We are laying by at present to recruit [more] horses and get provisions. [The commissary Department at The Dalles was so poorly administrated that the volunteers were without regular rations and supplies while the commissary staff was well fed and comfortable]. We have been across the Snake River and all through the Palouse country. The Indians fled. We have run them all out of their country . . . . We came down the Columbia to the mouth of the Yakima River. Five companies swam their horses across the Columbia River in order to get down to the Yakima country . . . Wayman and Lafayette are both well and are with me."[33]

Absalom Hembree died just days after writing this letter. "Father was killed April 10, 1856," his son remembered. "My father was riding B. F. Star's mule. In going down the steep hillside it fell and my father was thrown. Before he could get up the Indians were on him. He killed three of them, but he was shot under the eye and killed. They scalped him and rode away."[34] The Indians were driven from their fortified stronghold later that day, and the hostilities in that region came to an end. The next day the entire company began the return journey to Yamhill County bearing the slain body of their gallant leader. The funeral in Lafayette was one of the largest ever held in the Willamette Valley to that time, and the fallen commander was buried on the Hembree farm.

Fighting for the Prince of Peace

In the month following the Hembree funeral in Yamhill County, Levi Burch wrote to James Mathes from neighboring Polk County and provided an update on how the church was faring in such tumultuous times. "I am to start to a protracted meeting on tomorrow, some 50 miles distant, in hopes of enjoying a happy season with the dear brethren," began his optimistic report. "The meeting is to be held near where I formerly lived, and where the brethren are near and dear to me." Burch was referring to the faithful little congregation that met on Oak Creek in Benton County. He had helped to establish this church earlier in the decade.

Although he was leaving on his journey with fond hopes of "enjoying a happy season," Burch was realistic. "Our Indian difficulties are not yet settled," he admitted, "and the minds of the peoples are drawn off from the more weighty matters." Fortunately, the example of many of his fellow-laborers in the territory gave him renewed encouragement. "But notwithstanding the many difficulties that surround us," Burch told Mathes, "I find many good warm-hearted brethren in Oregon, who are fighting for the prince of Peace."[35] Burch himself was one of those more interested in spiritual warfare than carnal warfare.

The meeting at Oak Creek in June 1856 was all that Levi Burch had hoped it would be. There were 19 additions to the church, including 11 added by confession and immersion. "This was truly a happy meeting and will long be remembered," he told Mathes. "The truth is mighty and powerful above all things, and will prevail."[36] The same optimistic spirit was felt next door in Lane County later that summer. The Pleasant Hill Church, though occasionally torn by political strife, was continuing to reap a harvest of souls. John T. Gilfrey penned a note to Daniel Bates in August and said: "The Redeemer's Kingdom is still advancing in this country. During the last month we had 8 or 9 additions by baptism to the Church at this place."[37]

The 1856 Annual State Meeting

The Salem Church requested the privilege of hosting the fifth annual State Meeting in the fall of 1856, and most likely this meeting took place in the new Marion County Court House that was constructed in 1853. The small Salem congregation had been organized in 1855 as a result of the dedicated efforts of two traveling evangelists, A. V. McCarty and John Rigdon, who conducted services in the Court House.[38] The Salem Church had continued to meet weekly in the Court House under the guidance of two dynamic local leaders who were brothers-in-law, Nathan T. Caton and William J. Herren.

Abbott Levi Todd, who was nearing his 36th birthday, came all the way from Lookingglass Valley in Douglas County to attend the annual meeting at Salem. This was an ambitious round trip of more than 300 miles, but Todd was a devout Christian and hungry for fellowship with his brethren. He had been baptized into Christ in Indiana by his cousin, Elijah Goodwin, and he had been influenced by another cousin, Caleb P. Chapman, who was now preaching powerfully throughout Oregon. Todd had preached infrequently for several years, but now he was at a stage in his life where he felt that he ought to give himself more fully to this honorable calling. Consequently, he made his willingness known to the delegates assembled at Salem.

According to Todd's son, "At the State Meeting at Salem in 1856, he was ordained a minister of the gospel of Jesus Christ by Brother Caleb P. Chapman." The son later wrote that, although he "had been preaching for some time before, he now dedicated his life to the saving of souls and pledged his all to that end." When Todd returned home from Salem, he was ready to begin organizing churches, and his son reported:

> He preached at Lookingglass first where a church had already been organized. He organized another in Cole's Valley, one in French Settlement, one in Camas Valley, one at Myrtle Creek and in about 1859 preached at Ten Mile, Canyonville and Cow Creek.[39]

As Caleb P. Chapman, A. L. Todd, John A. Powell, A. V. McCarty and the others left Salem and returned to their home churches in the fall of 1856, there was much for which to be thankful. The cause of primitive Christianity was progressing in many neighborhoods, and the borders of the Restoration Movement in Oregon Territory were continuing to expand. With A. L. Todd in harness, the cause would accelerate rapidly in Douglas County. But there was genuine concern over the fury of the advancing political storm.

Chapter 16

I Love the Good Old *Christian Record* 1857

When we started for Oregon we did not expect to hear any of our brethren preach, at least for years. So we carefully filed all the numbers of the Record, *as we had been taking it since 1843, and brought them with us to Oregon, that we and our children might have something to read from our old home that would refresh our minds concerning the fiery trials through which we had to pass for the truth's sake.*

— Caleb Davis, Lane County

It was fitting that the first news regarding the preaching of the gospel in Oregon Territory should be published in Alexander Campbell's *Millennial Harbinger*. From the moment Campbell launched the *Christian Baptist* in the summer of 1823, periodicals had played a crucial role in chronicling the progress of the Restoration Movement. Campbell's *Christian Baptist* (1823–1830) and *Millennial Harbinger* (1830–1870) had friendly competition from Barton Warren Stone's *Christian Messenger* (1826–1844) and Walter Scott's *Evangelist* (1832–1844) in the early days of the movement, but it was Campbell who commanded the widest editorial patronage in the brotherhood.

Competing for Oregon Readers

Campbell was genuinely interested in America's westward expansion, and he was pleased to run the following notice in the September 1850 issue of the *Harbinger*:

> Agent for Oregon—Professor Mason, late of Bethany College, and a member of the church at Bethany, about to leave for Oregon, is requested to act as agent for the *Millennial Harbinger* in that new country, to which already many of our brethren from other new countries are turning their attention. We cannot, however, send any copies of the *Harbinger*, or any of our works, to Oregon or California, not paid in advance. The distance is too great, and we have paid, in the school of experience, a large price for that branch of education comprehended under the name of PRUDENTIALS, and must, henceforth, practice much more its wholesome precepts. We will always send the *Harbinger* on the receipt of the price . . . Money paid to Brother Mason in Oregon, will be placed to the credit of the parties here.[1]

At the time, it appeared likely that the *Harbinger* would become the dominant paper among Christians in Oregon. Campbell was unquestionably the best-known person in the movement, and his periodical enjoyed a wider circulation throughout the country than any other competing paper. As it turned out, however, the *Harbinger* got off to a slow start in Oregon and never significantly increased in circulation. Perhaps Campbell chose the wrong agent. William Mason did not migrate to Oregon until 1852, and upon arrival in the Territory he rarely traveled beyond the borders of Polk County. The ideal agents were gospel preachers who circulated often among the churches and could collect subscriptions from a wide cross-section of Christian families.

In the decade of the 1850s, two church papers, the *Christian Record* from Indiana and the *Christian Evangelist* from Iowa, filled the vacuum in Oregon created by the *Harbinger*'s slow start. In retrospect, this was not a surprising development. The large majority of Christians migrating to Oregon Territory were from the very states where the *Record* and *Evangelist* were most popular. Christians living in Oregon Territory were eager to receive news from "back home"—and for most, back home was the band of states that included Iowa, Missouri, Illinois, and Indiana. The *Record* and *Evangelist* both contained a wealth of regional news that was of interest to midwestern families who had recently migrated to Oregon. The *Millennial Harbinger* was a larger paper in number of pages, and it contained far more news from places like Canada, the British Isles, and Australia, as well as every corner of America. But Oregonians were interested in "back home," and in that narrower theater the *Christian Record* and the *Christian Evangelist* reigned supreme.

The *Christian Record* was published in Bloomington, Indianapolis, and Bedford, Indiana, from 1843 to 1884 with several interruptions. James Madison Mathes (1808–1892) was the editor from 1843 to May 1859 and again from 1866 to 1884. Elijah Goodwin (1807–1879) was the editor from June 1859 to 1866. The *Christian Evangelist* was published in Mt. Pleasant, Fort Madison, and Davenport, Iowa, from 1850 to 1864. Daniel Bates (?-?) and Aaron Chatterton (1819–1864) shared most of the editorial responsibilities through the years. This journal began as the *Western Evangelist* and changed its name to the *Christian Evangelist* in July 1852. By 1859 it had shortened its name to the *Evangelist*.

The Christian Record

As a result of the tireless efforts of several preachers, the *Christian Record* achieved a wide distribution in the far west in the early 1850s. John Alkire Powell, Caleb P. Chapman, Levi Burch, and A. V. McCarty were primarily responsible for the favorable reception in Oregon Territory, and William Huntington was the main agent in Washington Territory. James Mathes was always careful to praise his hard-working agents in print. "Brother Powell is our authorized agent for the *Christian Record* in all his travels," Mathes wrote at the close of one of John A. Powell's reports. "And we shall be pleased to hear from him and the other proclaimers in Oregon as often as convenient."[2] After a report from Caleb P. Chapman, published in the May 1853 issue, Mathes wrote, "Our thanks are especially due to brethren Chapman, Powell,

Huntington, Burch, McCarty, and many others, for giving the *Record* a general circulation in Oregon Territory. The *Record* is about to become *the paper* of Oregon Territory."[3]

John Alkire Powell probably startled Mathes in November 1853 when he wrote to say that Oregon Christians were not only contemplating opening a school to be known as "Oregon Christian University," but were thinking of establishing a west coast paper as well. "We also think that a periodical devoted to primitive Christianity could be well sustained and be made productive of much good in this 'Far West,'" Powell reported optimistically.[4] Mathes did not comment on this possibility, but he made several shrewd moves to solidify the standing of the *Record* in Oregon homes.

At the Annual Meeting in the fall of 1853, A. V. McCarty and John Rigdon were chosen as traveling evangelists for the next year. James Mathes lost no opportunity to remind his west coast readers that both McCarty and Rigdon were agents for the *Record,* and during the next year the number of subscribers continued to increase. "I forward to you 15 subscribers for the current volume of your valuable *Christian Record,"* McCarty wrote in one typical report. Mathes responded, "Brethren McCarty and Rigdon are Agents for the *Record* in the Willamette Valley. We hope to receive a large addition to our present list of subscribers from the Pacific coast, for the next volume, beginning in January next. We hope these brethren and all others engaged in the work will not fail to report the progress of the good cause among them."[5] Caleb Davis thought he was being helpful when he wrote to Mathes to say, "I would commend to you our beloved Brother Philip Mulkey as a good Agent for the *Record."* But the editor replied immediately, "Brother Philip Mulkey is a good Agent for the *Record."*[6] As far as James Mathes was concerned, all faithful gospel preachers in good standing with the churches were welcomed as Agents for the *Christian Record.*

It was not just the preachers who championed the *Record.* Alpheus Ireland wrote from Douglas County in 1855 to say, "I am delighted with the *Christian Record* which has been sent me by some friend in Indiana. I will do what I can to extend its circulation here." Mathes replied promptly, "Brother A. Ireland will please act as our Agent for the *Record* in his vicinity."[7] In February 1856, David R. Lewis wrote, "The *Christian Record* has come to me regularly for some four years, and has always been a welcome and interesting visitor. Send your prospectus to me for the next volume, earlier next time, and I will try to get up a handsome list."[8] No doubt the readership of the *Record* was greatly enhanced in the Luckiamute district of Polk County because of the efforts of a respected churchman like David Lewis. Lane County's Eliza Ann Smith spoke for many former Midwesterners when she wrote to Mathes:

> I love the good old *Christian Record*, it comes to me as an old friend, always welcome, bearing good and sometimes sad news from afar. I love to read the news from the churches. But the first thing with me is to read the "Obituaries," to see what dear friend, or old acquaintance has crossed the cold Jordan of death, since the last moon. And here alas! I see many familiar names! I then read it all carefully over. Indeed, I should be at a great loss without the *Record*. I have read it ever since it commenced, some fourteen years ago, and I am not willing to give it up yet, for I sometimes read the same number over and over again. And I frequently read former numbers with the deepest interest, because they bring fresh to my mind, loved ones now far away, and thrilling scenes long since passed.[9]

Caleb Davis, another Midwesterner, could certainly identify with Eliza Ann Smith's practice of keeping and re-reading earlier issues of the *Record*. "When we started for Oregon we did not expect to hear any of our brethren preach, at least for years," he informed Mathes. "So we carefully filed all the numbers of the *Record*, as we had been taking it since 1843, and brought them with us to Oregon that we and our children might have something to read from our old home that would refresh our minds concerning the fiery trials through which we had to pass for truth's sake."[10]

The claim made by James Mathes in 1853, that the *Christian Record* was quickly becoming "the paper" among Christians in the far west, was probably true throughout the 1850s and

1860s, but by 1870 it was receiving strong competition from a number of papers, including the *American Christian Review,* the *Christian Standard,* the *Apostolic Times,* and Oregon's own *Christian Messenger.*[11] One Lane County observer wrote to Mathes in 1857 to say, "The *Christian Record* is regarded by the brethren here as the best religious periodical published in the North-West, and deserving of great popularity."[12] As late as 1872, G. W. Richardson was still extolling the virtues of the Indiana paper. "The old *Christian Record* is the most popular, and most generally read, in this part of Oregon of any of our papers," he informed Mathes. "I find it in some families in every place I visit, all seem to be delighted with it because it deals with all subjects pertaining to the religion of Christ, in a style which is adapted to the capacities of the most humble. May it long live to plead the cause of our divine Master."[13]

The Christian Evangelist

Iowa's *Christian Evangelist* provided substantial competition for the *Christian Record* in the 1850s and early 1860s. "We have a large number of subscribers in Oregon and California and some in Washington Territory," the editors reported in 1859, "and we must say, that according to their numbers, they manifest more disposition to pay for their reading matter than do subscribers in the states this side of the mountains."[14] The *Christian Evangelist* was strengthened by the large number of Iowans who migrated to the far west. Dedicated "agents" in Oregon included John Rigdon and James R. Fisher in Lane County and William L. Mascher and Nathan T. Caton in Marion County. Although Rigdon also served as an agent for the *Christian Record,* he had an even greater loyalty to the *Evangelist* due to his strong friendship with Daniel Bates.

New subscribers were not always attributable to hard-working agents. Zephaniah Bryant, a devout Christian living 20 miles out of Hillsboro in Washington County, made his own contact with Daniel Bates in 1853 after reading a copy of the *Evangelist* that was loaned to him by a friend. He wrote:

> I saw one number of the publication conducted by you . . . and I am highly pleased with it. Not being acquainted with any of your Oregon agents, I take this method of introducing myself to you; and believing you to be bold defenders of the Truth, I request you to include me among your list of subscribers for the *Evangelist*. For as there are very few of our brethren in this part of Oregon, I am desirous of knowing how the cause progresses in other places.[15]

Even the slowness of the mail system did not dampen the enthusiasm that Oregonians had for receiving a church paper from back home. "The *Evangelist* is a welcome visitor to my self and family," exclaimed a Christian in Lane County. "The news it contains becomes somewhat old by the time it reaches our part of the globe, but yet we wait for it with patience."[16] Like other Christians who emigrated from Iowa, William and Mary Preston were eager to renew their connection with the *Evangelist* once they had settled in their new home in Oregon's Umpqua Valley. "We have been doing all we could for it, and think by next year we will be able to get many more subscribers for it," Mary reported to Daniel Bates in 1854. "We have been taking it ever since it had an existence, until we started across the 'plains,' and now that we are settled again, I wish to take it while we live, and will do all I can to extend its circulation."

One year later, Mary Preston corresponded with Daniel Bates again to tell him of her interesting exchange with a Baptist woman in the neighborhood. She wrote:

> I will mention one thing more for your encouragement. I was conversing not long since with a Baptist lady, who had lately married a "Campbellite," as she supposed him to be. He brought her to meeting and there she got hold of the *Evangelist*, and examined it and compared its teachings with the Bible, and with the preaching of our brethren; and then said to me: "How is it that you all understand each other, being so far apart. This little book (the *Evangelist*) presents things plainer to my mind than all the Baptist Sermons I ever heard." . . . In conclusion she said, "I must have the *Evangelist*."[17]

In the summer of 1853, Daniel Bates received a significant letter from Dr. James McBride in Oregon. It is unlikely that

Bates and McBride had ever met one another back in the states, but they were aware of each other by reputation and through mutual friends. "We are highly pleased with your valuable periodical," McBride wrote admiringly, "and but for the numerous papers and pamphlets—almost to cloying—which have made their way to Oregon, it would be an easy matter to procure a large list of subscribers."[18]

The phrase "almost to cloying" is very surprising. Could there really have been a glut of church papers cluttering up Oregon in 1853? Apart from the *Harbinger, Record,* and *Evangelist* (all monthlies), it is unlikely that any other papers were circulating among Oregon Christians in the early 1850s. Dr. Carroll Kendrick and L. L. Pinkerton had been co-editing the *Ecclesiastical Reformer* from Harrodsburg, Kentucky, and James W. Goss and Reuben Lindsay Coleman were publishing the *Christian Intelligencer* in Charlottesville, Virginia, but there is no evidence that either publication was circulating in Oregon.[19]

The Christian Magazine

There was one other paper, now long forgotten, which according to McBride "had found a hearty reception" among the Christians in Oregon, and that was Jesse B. Ferguson's *Christian Magazine.* Ferguson was the popular preacher of a 500-member church in Nashville, Tennessee, and still less than 30 years of age when he began editing the *Christian Magazine* in January 1848. The circulation of Ferguson's paper was probably never more than 2,000, but it had subscribers in at least 17 states and in Oregon Territory.[20]

Two of Ferguson's avid readers in Oregon were Dr. James McBride and Glen Owen Burnett, who were both born and reared in Nashville, Tennessee. In an encouraging letter dated May 15, 1851, and published in the September 1851 issue of the *Magazine,* Burnett provided an important West Coast endorsement for Ferguson. "I am glad that the Magazine is finding its way to Oregon," wrote the popular evangelist. "The course you are pursuing is a judicious one." Ferguson knew how valuable Burnett's endorsement was, and he wrote at the end of the correspondence, "Will Brother Burnett accept our thanks for his interest in our behalf and write us more fully of affairs in Oregon?"[21]

Ferguson enjoyed tremendous popularity and prestige until the April 1852 edition of his paper. In that issue he published his interpretation of I Peter 3:18-20 and 4:1-6 in an article entitled "The Spirits in Prison." Alexander Campbell reprinted the article in the June 1852 issue of the *Millennial Harbinger*, and he strongly condemned Ferguson's viewpoint and accused him of Universalism. The controversy raged back and forth in the two periodicals, and Ferguson never recovered. The last issue of the *Christian Magazine* came out in December 1853, and by that time Ferguson had embraced Spiritualism and was on his way out of the Restoration Movement.

Regarding the influence of Jesse B. Ferguson and his monthly publication in Oregon Territory, Dr. James McBride wrote to Daniel Bates:

> The *Christian Magazine* had found a hearty reception here until the editor's exposition of "the spirits in prison" made its appearance; since then it is not so acceptable to any of the brethren with whom I have conversed. We much lament the fantastical course pursued by him. And I doubt not but every one, except himself and a few personal admirers, see with clearness that his usefulness is blighted. The rest of you must work with greater energy to make up for the deficit thus occasioned.[22]

The American Christian Review

With the demise of the *Christian Magazine* in 1853, another paper emerged in the second half of the decade to challenge the *Record, Evangelist,* and *Harbinger*. A gospel preacher named Benjamin Franklin began publishing his monthly *American Christian Review* from Cincinnati, Ohio, in January 1856, and two years later it became the first significant weekly with a national circulation in the history of the Restoration Movement. It did not immediately supplant the big three in the hearts of Christians in the far west, but one Oregon

Christian wrote prophetically to Franklin in December 1857 and said, "I think when once your paper gets a start here there will be many copies ordered. We wish you great success."[23]

From the moment it became a weekly in January 1858, the *Review* was on its way to becoming the most prestigious journal in the brotherhood. "The *Review* is succeeding finely," Franklin editorialized that summer. "It is circulating in all the States and Territories, in Canada and some other parts of the world. It now communicates intelligence pretty generally throughout the brotherhood, and is gaining ground every day."[24] Four years later, one observer wrote, "Probably next to Alexander Campbell, Brother Franklin is more extensively known than any other man connected with the Reformation of the Nineteenth Century."[25]

As the Civil War years approached, Oregon Christians gave their journalistic allegiance to several fine church papers which in turn helped to nurture and strengthen the cause in the territory. In the wake of the decline of the *Christian Magazine*, Dr. James McBride had issued a bold challenge in 1853: "The rest of you must work with greater energy to make up for the deficit thus occasioned." Four exceptional papers answered the challenge and more than made up for the deficit felt by the loss of the Nashville editor. All four papers had loyal friends and supporters among the Oregon Christians, but as 1857 came to a close the *Christian Record* was still "*the paper* of Oregon Territory."[26]

The Labors of G. W. Richardson

After five years of fruitful labor in Marion and Linn counties, in which he organized churches at Scio, Mill Creek, and French Prairie, G. W. Richardson moved to Bethel in Polk County in the fall of 1856. By the spring of 1857 he had "again taken the field of Evangelical labor, and so far, with good success." In the middle of March he was sent to immerse a young man named McKinley who was dying of consumption. The young man did not want his baptism deferred until morning. "So we took him from his bed about midnight,"

Richardson informed Mathes, "and took him in a wagon to the water, where he was buried with his Lord in baptism. From the water he returned home filled with joy." Richardson had more good news to share:

> Not long after this, I was sent for to immerse another young man under nearly similar circumstances. On the day of his baptism, I delivered a short discourse on the subject of the Christian Religion, at the close of which we had the unspeakable pleasure of taking three noble confessions. Great joy and solemnity prevailed throughout the assembly. This was Thursday, and on Sunday following, I preached near the same place where we immersed twelve more. And the night following, twenty-seven brethren and sisters covenanted together to keep house for God. Great harmony and joy prevailed.[27]

Richardson failed to mention which congregation it was that he established in the spring of 1857, but it evidently was in Polk County. "I know but little concerning the prosperity of the cause outside my own field of labor, which is comparatively small," he acknowledged. "But of my own field I can truly say it is ripe, and I believe a good crop will be gathered for the Lord of the harvest."[28]

The Death of a Patriarch

Less than a year before his death, Thomas Crawford McBride penned a lengthy letter to his grandson in Boone County, Missouri. Reflecting on his nine years in Oregon, the aged preacher wrote:

> I emigrated to Oregon in the summer of 1847, not of my own choice, but because all my children then alive, were either in Oregon, or expected to go. I have preached occasionally ever since I first landed in the Territory, but my eye-sight is failing, my memory becoming more treacherous, and the usual feebleness and infirmities of old age, declare to me in terms most positive and certain that my mortal remains will soon return to the dust and my spirit to God who gave it. I have fought the good fight, have finished my course, or nearly so. I have kept the faith and am only waiting to hear the rumblings of Immanuel's chariot for my departing spirit. O, may I be ready! May the law of God burn gloriously and

> triumphantly on the altar of your heart when my change comes. Please present my affectionate remembrances to all my relatives near you, and my Christian love to all the holy brethren wherever you meet them.[29]

The Christians in Oregon lost a truly patriarchal figure when the elderly Thomas McBride died in 1857. He had been a co-laborer with Barton Warren Stone, John Mulkey, and Alexander Campbell among others, and while he lived he was a direct link to the earliest days of the Restoration Movement. "I was the pioneer of the Christian ministry in Missouri," he reminded his grandson. He had not only been the first Christian preacher to locate in Missouri Territory, but he had devoted more than 30 years of his life to nurturing the cause of Bible Christianity in that state.

He was 70 years old and nearly blind when he crossed the Oregon Trail in 1847, but he preached with power on the Oregon frontier for another decade. McBride was three months beyond his 80th birthday when he died peacefully on Wednesday, April 29, 1857, at his residence in Yamhill County. Surrounded by his large family of committed Christians and a host of Christian friends, he was laid to rest in McBride Cemetery.

Two weeks after McBride's death, William Lysander Adams published an obituary account in the *Oregon Argus*. His remembrance of the saintly McBride included these tender lines:

> During his lifetime he was emphatically of that class of men who make it the great business of life to lay up treasures where neither moth nor rust corrupt, nor thieves break through and steal. His precepts were always enforced by his own example, and his long life was marked by a series of blameless acts that made up a Christian character such as seldom pertains to men in the flesh, and it is doubtful whether he had an enemy living. He departed calmly and tranquilly, as an infant gently falls asleep; and as the sun of his natural life went down in full-orbed splendor, the great Son of Righteousness threw a rainbow of glory over his tomb, on which his dim eye rested, and lighted up with luster as it read, "there remaineth a rest for the people of God."[30]

The Cause Is Gaining Ground

Oregon Christians erected several church buildings in the 1850s, but there were still many occasions when church meetings and funerals were conducted in school buildings. In some locations, such as Pleasant Hill, Mill Creek, Monmouth, and Bethel, the school and church shared the same building. In the same month that Thomas Crawford McBride passed away, Dr. James McBride and A. V. McCarty were called to preach the funeral of Mrs. C. A. Hill in Yamhill County. This funeral took place in a school building situated on the Dayton Prairie between Dayton and Amity.[31] McBride and McCarty had probably preached in that schoolhouse before, and they may have used the occasion of Mrs. Hill's funeral to conduct a brief gospel meeting in the schoolhouse.

Unfortunately, Indian hostilities were still a common occurrence that disrupted family life and the work of the church. In a letter dated July 12, 1857, a Monmouth Christian named Edward Ground corresponded with family and friends back in Illinois about the latest disruption. He wrote:

> I have informed you of our Indian difficulties, I believe. I wrote to you that Isaac has returned home from the war safe and sound. He is still at home, but Thomas H. Hutchinson started for the seat of hostilities last Monday, just one week ago. He is first Lieut. in the company and whither he will ever return or not, I cannot tell. Elizabeth is left with three little boys to scuffle for, and if he should fall by the hand of the enemy, as many other has done, she will be left in a bad situation . . . .[32]

Ground and Hutchinson were brothers-in-law, as they had married daughters of Major Peter Butler. Hutchinson was a graduate of a school founded by Illinois Christians called Abingdon College, and he was a member of the board of trustees of Monmouth University. As it turned out, he was unharmed in the Indian hostilities and returned to Monmouth to briefly serve both the church and the college. But he died prior to the recording of the Polk County census in June 1860.

On September 8, 1857, Caleb Davis sent an encouraging letter back home to James Mathes in Indiana. "The cause for which we plead is gaining ground in this far off western land," he wrote with conviction. And then he added, "We have had several valuable additions to our own church during the summer."[33] This note of optimism could have been echoed by Christians living in many different Oregon communities in 1857. With the apparent success of Bethel Institute and Monmouth University, and the continuing proliferation of newly-organized congregations, the future for Oregon Christians appeared bright. In the face of Indian wars and political conflicts, there remained a dedicated cadre of church leaders who were committed to "fighting for the prince of Peace."

Perhaps of even greater significance for the future, there were four powerful church papers equipping the minds of Oregon Christians "concerning the fiery trials" through which they would have to pass "for the truth's sake." James Mathes, Daniel Bates, Alexander Campbell, and Benjamin Franklin were as vital to the spiritual health of the Restoration Movement in Oregon as were any four gospel preachers riding horseback through the Willamette and Umpqua valleys.

Chapter 17

The Autonomy of the Churches

1858–1859

Resolved, that it is the object and purpose of our annual meetings to receive information from the congregations, to extend our acquaintance, and to strengthen the ties of unity and love among the brethren, to afford help to the weak and relief to the destitute, and to advise with the brethren as to such measures as may be conducive to the general welfare of the brotherhood—utterly disclaiming all claim to either legislative or judicial power . . . .

— Minutes, 1858 Oregon Annual Meeting

When Thomas Crawford McBride wrote to his grandson in Boone County, Missouri, on June 28, 1856, he reminded him of a precious principle in the Restoration Movement—the independence of each local church. McBride was grateful that every congregation, regardless of how small and insignificant, was free from "all adventurous meddlings from 'associations,' 'conferences,' etc. . . . of ancient or modern date." To emphasize this point, the old pioneer wrote:

> I now believe that this feature in the Christian church is one of the most conservative principles in it; and but for it—the independency of the churches—we should have been torn and divided into factions long since, as the sects are, who make Protestant popes of their presbyteries, synods, etc. . . . .[1]

Like others in his generation, McBride had little opposition to the practice of annual "state meetings," provided they were limited to worship, preaching, baptizing, and fellowship. As long as they did not control or usurp the authority of the local church, McBride felt that such meetings could serve a useful purpose. What he feared most was the centralizing or concentrating of power in one man or one board or one church or one conference.

The Founding of Monmouth

With the establishment of the town of Monmouth in Polk County in 1856, the center of gravity for the Restoration Movement in Oregon Territory shifted to that new location. Previous to that time the center of numerical strength for the movement was in the district running from the McBride-Adams settlement north of McMinnville in Yamhill County to the Burnett-Harvey farms in the Bethel Hills of northern Polk County. This district was less than 20 miles in length, but a large number of Christians lived within its path.

Other candidates for the center of the movement in the pre-Monmouth years would have been the areas around Bethany in Marion County and around Pleasant Hill in Lane County. But for the quarter-century beginning in 1856, the combined presence of a strong congregation and a fine Christian college secured Monmouth's place at the very center of church activity in Oregon.

It is unlikely that many Oregon Christians realized the long-range significance of the Monmouth venture at its inauguration in 1856. At the time, there were probably many Christians who thought Bethel had a much brighter future. It certainly appeared that way on July 4, 1855, when a large crowd assembled at Bethel to hear the addresses by W. L. Adams and A. V. McCarty and to begin construction on the large two-story school building. By contrast, the first Monmouth school building was not as impressive. It should have been obvious to everyone concerned that the Christians could not support two colleges located in the same county within 15 miles of each other and competing for the patronage of many of the same Christian families.

The Christian Church in Monmouth was organized in July 1856, and the first session of Monmouth University began in November 1856. Within two years, the Monmouth church had become the largest Christian Church in the territory, and the school was off to a good start. In a letter dated December 23, 1857, one Monmouth Christian corresponded with Benjamin Franklin, editor of the *American Christian Review*, and said:

> We have a flourishing Institution of learning here. It is young; but, considering the newness of the country, and the short time it has been here in operation, I think it is doing well. We have only two teachers . . . and seventy-five scholars. One of the teachers is a graduate of Bethany College. We have a church of about one hundred members, and are having accessions frequently, by confession and by letter. Last Lord's day a Presbyterian lady confessed her faith in the Lord and was buried with him in baptism the next day. We have plenty of good preachers in this section of country . . . .[2]

The Bethany College graduate was 24-year-old William Thompson Haley, who had left Polk County in 1853 to enroll in the Virginia college founded by Alexander Campbell. Haley graduated on July 4, 1857,[3] and returned immediately to Oregon where he was warmly welcomed by the organizers of Monmouth University. Levi Lindsay Rowland had graduated from Bethany College in the class of 1856, but he did not return to Oregon until 1859. W. T. Haley was still an eligible bachelor when he began teaching in Monmouth in the fall of 1857, but that soon changed. He married Lucinda Ford, daughter of Nat Ford, at the family residence at Rickreall on June 11, 1858. The wedding was performed by Glen Owen Burnett.

Salem Beginnings

While the Christians were busy establishing Monmouth, they were also making another attempt to organize a congregation in the Methodist stronghold of Salem. Glen Owen Burnett had baptized six converts in Salem as far back as 1847 (see chapter 6), but this little congregation had struggled throughout its history. With the leadership of local Christians like brothers-in-law Nathan T. Caton and William J.

Herren, and the support of outstanding evangelists like A. V. McCarty and John Rigdon, a small group of Christians began meeting on Sundays in 1855 in the Marion County Court House.[4] In the summer of 1858, Caton described the progress:

> All the misrepresentations of the partisans were industriously circulated against us as a religious body. Regardless, however, of every discouragement under which we labored, Brother A. V. McCarty was solicited to take charge of the church; he consented; and from that time up to the present has continued to present the claims of Christianity, as taught by inspired Apostles and Prophets, to the people. The large, attentive and increasing audiences demonstrated unmistakably that the word of God had lost neither its power to attract nor to save. Eleven made the noble confession and ten were otherwise added. The prospect is still flattering. To God and his Son be all the praise.[5]

In addition to the good news emanating from Monmouth and Salem, the churches at Bethany and Pleasant Hill continued to report gains, and G. W. Richardson wrote from Bethel to say, "The churches in this section are in a healthy condition, having occasional accessions."[6] The cause of Christ was gaining ground in the Umpqua Valley through the dedicated efforts of gospel preachers such as A. L. Todd, Samuel Bates Briggs and Edmund Green Browning.

The Mill Creek Church

In the midst of apparent prosperity, the word went out inviting delegates to the seventh Annual Meeting of the Christians in Oregon Territory. The Mill Creek Church in Marion County, in only its fourth year of existence, agreed to host the gathering. This thriving congregation of 62 members was blessed with strong leaders like William Porter, Hiram Alva Johnson, William H. Brayton, George W. Whitney, George M. Whitney, George Richardson, and Jerome B. Greer.

The Mill Creek Church, named for the stream that flows through the district, was organized in 1855 on the property of William Porter. A 16-foot by 20-foot building was constructed on the Porter farm about one mile southeast of Aumsville in the general direction of Stayton. This building was used as a school during the week and for church meetings on Sundays. Sometimes the congregation could not be contained in the small building. One historical record reported that this building was situated in the middle of a large grove of fir trees, and that "many of the meetings were held out of doors in this beautiful grove."[7]

The most frequent guest preacher for the Mill Creek Church in the 1850s was John A. Powell. Among the local elders, George W. Whitney and George Richardson did most of the preaching when one of the circuit-riders was not available. According to one historical record, George M. Whitney, the son of George W. Whitney, began preaching at Mill Creek "about 1860." It is surprising that G. M. Whitney did not begin preaching until near his 30th birthday. It soon became apparent he had a natural gift for preaching, and he was also an outstanding song leader.

W. H. and Lucy Brayton were members of the Mill Creek Church. They had married in Clay County, Kentucky, in 1827, and migrated to Oregon in 1852. On July 28, 1857, their daughter, Henrietta, became the bride of George M. Whitney. When the Mill Creek Church organized a Bible School in April 1859, George M. Whitney was named superintendent. No doubt he was effective as a Bible School superintendent, but Whitney's untapped gifts were in the public proclamation of the gospel of Christ. He was destined to become one of the most powerful preachers in Oregon in the 1860s and 1870s.

The "Organization" of the Churches

Throughout the history of the Restoration Movement, the dialogue on how to effectively organize the churches of a state for evangelistic outreach without infringing on the autonomy of a single local church has always been stormy. Oregon was not an exception in this national debate. The fears and concerns experienced in the Midwestern states over "organization" of the churches for state missionary work were articulated again in the Pacific territories. One historian of the movement, reflecting on those fears, wrote:

> The truth is that the Disciples as a whole were and always have been chary about conventions. They scent ecclesiasticism, popery, and the destruction of their freedom in every attempt to get them together in a single organization, no matter how innocuous the organization may be. They are free churchmen with a bang, and they always intend to remain so.[8]

At the first Annual Meeting of Oregon churches in the fall of 1852, 10 congregations were represented, and they chose John Alkire Powell to evangelize the Willamette Valley, promising to support him. The following year there were 16 congregations represented, and they chose two evangelists—A. V. McCarty for the eastern side of the Willamette River and John Rigdon for the western side. The arrangements for the next four years are not known, but in 1858 there were 20 congregations represented, and they again chose John A. Powell to be the only evangelist. This voluntary system worked with some partial success for a quarter century before it was superseded in 1877 by a separate organization called "The Christian Ministerial Association of the State of Oregon."

The 1858 Annual State Meeting

Fortunately, the "Minutes" for the 1858 Annual Meeting were published by William Lysander Adams in the *Oregon Argus*, and they provide a fascinating window for viewing the Restoration Movement in Oregon at that time. The document covered seven small pages in the *Argus* and was entitled "Minutes of the Annual Meeting of the Christian Church of Oregon, Held September 10, 1858." The meeting was hosted by the Mill Creek Church in Marion County. It took place on Friday and Saturday, September 10 and 11, officially adjourned on the Lord's Day, and met again on Monday and Tuesday, September 13-14. There were 36 delegates in attendance, representing 20 congregations with an aggregate membership of 997.[9] One congregation did not report its membership, so the aggregate membership was more than 1,000. The average membership per church was slightly more than 50. The list of churches, members, and delegates was as follows:

Church	County	Mem	Delegates
Monmouth	Polk	111	Patrick Haley John Ecles Murphy Elijah Davidson
Silver Creek (Bethany)	Marion	105	Thomas C. Shaw Elias Cox Caleb P. Chapman
Pleasant Hill	Lane	98	Gilmore Callison James R. Fisher Samuel Baughman
Bethel	Polk	80	G. W. Richardson John W. Ladd Dr. Wm. C. Warriner
Mill Creek	Marion	62	Wm. H. Brayton Jerome B. Greer Hiram Alva Johnson
Forks Santiam	Linn	55	James Forgey Lewis Stewart
Luckiamute	Polk	52	Dr. Zedekiah Davis
Clackamas	Clackamas	45	Jefferson Huff
Salem	Marion	43	A. V. McCarty Nathan T. Caton William J. Herren
Liberty House	Benton	41	(no delegate)
Monroe	Benton	41	(no delegate)
Salt Creek	Polk	39	Joseph W. Downer F. X. Shoemaker John A. Frazer
McMinnville	Yamhill	38	Isaiah Johns
Clear Lake	Lane	35	(no delegate)
North Fork	Yamhill	35	(no delegate)

Sand Ridge	Linn	34	Joel B. Huston Thomas M. Ward J. Savage
Lower Muddy	Linn	30	Dr. John N. Perkins
Eola	Polk	28	William D. Cole Townsend Waller C. C. Crane
Union Vale	Yamhill	25	Noah Powell Isaiah Matheny
Tualatin	Washington	?	Horace Lindsay

John A. Powell was chosen to be the chairman of the meeting, even though he was not listed as an official delegate for any specific congregation. Perhaps this was by design. They may have wanted the chairman to be a non-delegate. But apparently there was no rule against a preacher being a delegate. Several evangelists were delegates, including John Ecles Murphy, Elijah Davidson, Caleb P. Chapman, Gilmore Callison, G. W. Richardson, A. V. McCarty, Dr. John Nelson Perkins, and Noah Powell. One of the motions that was passed read, "The preaching brethren were invited to participate with the brethren in their deliberations." This could not apply to the preachers who were already approved delegates. There must have been additional preachers in attendance who were invited to join in the deliberations on an equal basis with the approved delegates.

In one of the approved motions, William Dawson "was invited to take a seat with the delegates." Was he joining with Isaiah Johns in representing the McMinnville Church? Or was his membership with another congregation in Yamhill County that was not represented? Or was he simply recognized as a delegate-at-large? As with the inclusion of the non-delegate preachers above, the Dawson addition indicates the relaxed and democratic nature of the proceedings. One gets the impression that no brother in good standing in any congregation would have been denied a voice in these deliberations. The purpose of this gathering was not to exercise control over any church or any Christian, but rather to encourage the individual churches to work together in advancing the cause of Christ in the entire territory.

One motion dealt with the advisability of having a uniformity in the hymn books that were used by the various congregations. After discussion, it was recommended that "the last edition of the *Christian Hymn Book* published by Alexander Campbell" be used exclusively by Oregon and Washington churches. Another motion urged "that preaching brethren be recommended to extend their labors, and hold as many protracted meetings between now and the next annual meeting as possible."

G. W. Richardson submitted a report of the Annual Meeting for the readers of the *Christian Record.* Corresponding with James Mathes, he wrote:

> Our yearly meeting was held in Marion county, including the 2nd Lord's day in September. It was truly a time of rejoicing. We had much good preaching, and the best order that I ever witnessed at so large a meeting. It closed on Tuesday with nine additions by confession and immersion, three from the Baptists, and several by commendation. We thank God and take courage!
>
> . . . the cause of our blessed Master does not seem to prosper as well as in the Atlantic States. But a brighter day for Oregon I think is beginning to dawn. Sectarianism is losing its charm, though its advocates affect not to discover it, and are laboring hard to build it up.[10]

The "Minutes" of the 1858 meeting make clear that not all of the churches were accounted for in the statistics that were gathered. One of the resolutions stated, "That the Clerk take measures to ascertain the numbers in the congregations not represented at the annual meeting, and insert the same in the minutes of this meeting." Unfortunately, those numbers were not included in the minutes that Adams published in the *Argus*.

In addition to the 20 congregations represented at Mill Creek, there were at least 25 additional congregations known to be in existence by the fall of 1858,[11] and they should be included in an assessment of the overall numerical strength of the Restoration Movement in Oregon at that time. An educated guess is that there were approximately 2,000 Christians living in Oregon Territory by the close of 1858. Many of them were represented in the approximately 45 congregations that had been organized, but many others were living in areas where they had no church privileges.

The Report of James R. Fisher

James R. Fisher sent Daniel Bates a report of the Annual Meeting for publication in the *Evangelist*. Among other things, he wrote:

> The annual meeting for this Territory, and that of Washington, was held with the Church at Mill Creek, Marion Co., O. T. The Churches were pretty well represented. The meeting passed off most harmoniously. There were quite a number of very important resolutions passed. The meeting embraced the 2nd Lord's day of September, 1858. 500 copies of the minutes were ordered to be printed in pamphlet form, for general distribution.
>
> From reports that were read at the meeting, I do not think that the cause of primitive Christianity is in as prosperous a condition as it formerly was. This state of things is owing to various causes, that have conspired, as agents of the Wicked One, to blight the fair prospects of Zion's march, and universal prevalence.
>
> Brother John A. Powell was chosen to travel among the Churches, during the ensuing year, and to set in order the things wanting, and to instruct the officers of the congregations how to demean themselves in the House of God. We think him to be a man well suited to the very responsible place which he is called to fill.[12]

Fisher's report raises some interesting questions. How could he claim that "the churches were pretty well represented" when at least half of them were not heard from? Is it possible that churches in distant districts like the ones in Clatsop and Columbia counties to the north and the ones in Douglas County to the south were not in contact with the churches in the heart of the Willamette Valley? But that accounts for only seven churches. How could approximately 18 churches in the Willamette Valley not be represented at the Annual Meeting? Four churches that did not send delegates did send reports. Why did not more churches at least send a report by one of the evangelists? Were some of the congregations uncomfortable with the very concept of an annual meeting of churches? At this early date, were there already some latent fears regarding ecclesiasticism or a loss of autonomy for local churches? This seems unlikely, but again it underscores the inadequate lines of communications between frontier churches and the obvious lack of territorial organization for the Restoration Movement as a whole.

The delegates who were assembled at this Annual Meeting were eager to dispel any criticism of their function. They were prepared not only to explain the specifics of their mission, but to clearly define the limitations of their work. Perhaps with an eye on any potential critics of their assembly, they passed the following resolution:

> Resolved, That it is the object and purpose of our annual meetings to receive information from the congregations, to extend our acquaintance, and to strengthen the ties of unity and love among the brethren, to afford help to the weak and relief to the destitute, and to advise with the brethren as to such measures as may be conducive to the general welfare of the brotherhood—utterly disclaiming all claim to either legislative or judicial power, except such power as pertains to the legality or illegality of delegates to a seat in our annual convention.

As congregational independence was a cherished principle in the Restoration Movement, the delegates were careful to guard the autonomy of each local church. Nevertheless, their most significant action was to send John A. Powell "to visit all the churches in Oregon and Washington Territories, and labor with them, and especially the officers, and set them in order, as far as he can, during the next year." Naturally, they hoped that all of the churches would voluntarily respond with "ample remuneration to Brother Powell" at the time of his visit with them. Before they adjourned, plans were finalized for the next Annual Meeting. It was agreed that the Salem

Church would host the gathering "commencing on Thursday before the second Lord's Day in September."

Two Delegates and Two Perspectives

There was one disturbing note in James R. Fisher's report on the Annual Meeting. "From reports that were read at the meeting," he declared, "I do not think that the cause of primitive Christianity is in as prosperous a condition as it formerly was." It was his opinion that this unfortunate development could be attributed to "various causes" that had "conspired" to "blight" the advance of the movement, but he failed to elaborate on the specific causes. Was his foreboding shared by others at the meeting?

Two weeks before Fisher penned his report, another delegate from the Annual Meeting corresponded with Daniel Bates in a more optimistic mood. Thomas M. Ward wrote:

> The good cause of our common Lord is prospering in this far-off country. Our preaching brethren have been holding several protracted meetings, and they have all been attended with success. Brother A. V. McCarty is located in Salem, and is doing much towards pulling down sectarianism, and he is building up a large Church "on the foundation of the Apostles and Prophets."[13]

Interestingly, Daniel Bates published both of these perspectives in the same issue. Two devout Christians who were both delegates to the Annual Meeting and who lived within a few miles of each other in neighboring counties offered differing opinions on the status of "primitive Christianity" in Oregon. Ward thought it was still "prospering," and Fisher worried that it was not as "prosperous" as it had been. Ironically, allowing for their different vantage points, both were probably correct in their assessments.

Ward could certainly point to several local areas where the cause was prospering. The church papers continued to carry positive reports from Oregon. Kitty Davis wrote to Daniel Bates in October 1858 to say that Daniel Trullinger had just closed a protracted meeting in Yamhill County in which one of those baptized into Christ was her own husband, Jefferson Davis.[14] Eliza Ann Smith wrote to James Mathes a week later to report on a protracted meeting in Lane County. "The result was 7 additions to the army of the faithful; 5 by confession and immersion, one reclaimed, and one by commendation," she wrote happily. "O, what joy it affords to the people of God to see lost sinners returning home to Jesus."[15]

Fisher, on the other hand, was not looking at isolated stories of occasional gospel meetings. He had just listened to 22 church reports at the Annual Meeting. These reports reflected the condition of churches throughout Washington and Oregon Territories, and Fisher concluded that the movement was not as healthy as it had been since his arrival in the Territory in 1854. The progress of the Restoration Movement in Oregon between 1851 and 1857 had been exhilarating. Numerous observers had proclaimed it to be the largest religious movement in the Territory during those years. But the Methodists had caught up and surged ahead with their superior organizational strengths, and the Restoration Movement had been treading water for at least a year. Fisher was looking at the big picture, and he was worried by the trend.

A Disturbing Trend

One trend that Fisher probably was not even aware of yet was the loss of talented proclaimers for Oregon. Beginning in late 1857, seven Oregon preachers would leave for California or Washington during the next six years. Glen Owen Burnett triggered the exodus when he moved his family to northern California near the end of 1857. Although he returned to Oregon for occasional meetings and was once again a resident of Polk County at the time of the 1860 census, Burnett gave the majority of the last 29 years of his ministry to advancing the Restoration Movement in the Golden State.[16] His loss to the Oregon church was incalculable.

In December 1859, A. V. McCarty and Harrison H. Hendrix followed Burnett to California,[17] and in the early 1860s Levi Burch and Charles Bradshaw also chose California over

Oregon. Alfred R. Elder moved across the Columbia River to Washington in 1862, and Dr. John Nelson Perkins followed him to that territory a year or two later. Deepening the tragedy for Oregon Christians was the death of John Rigdon, who died at Pleasant Hill in May 1859.[18]

The Tide Turns in California's Favor

None of the preachers who left Oregon gave any written explanation for their actions, but in the case of the five preachers who moved to California, it may have simply been a matter of greater opportunities for the cause of Christ. Glen Owen Burnett found the California mission field immediately rewarding when he began his gospel labors in the early months of 1858. One California correspondent penned a note to Alexander Campbell on April 27, 1858, and informed him of the new activity in the state. He wrote:

> The cause of Reform is gaining ground in California, and if we had laborers to enter the field, the harvest is ready. Through the labors of Elders White and Burnett, for some time past, we have been made to rejoice over sinners returning to God through Jesus Christ. By the assistance of the above Brethren in the last few months, 22 have confessed and been immersed, 7 reclaimed, 2 from the Baptists, 1 from the Presbyterians. To the Lord be all the glory and us the joy.[19]

Thomas Thompson, one of the leading California preachers, wrote to Daniel Bates on November 13, 1858, and explained what was happening in his area. He reported:

> Within the last 12 months, or from one State Meeting till the next, I baptized 44 persons, and had some 15 additions otherwise. I have traveled considerably . . . we had a most glorious State Meeting: 92 additions—about 70 by immersion. We determined to sustain a paper in California to be styled *Western Evangelist;* 32 pages; and will be edited by Brother Stevenson, assisted by Pendegast and Burnett.[20]

It certainly did not take Burnett long to become involved in California. Oregon had been ahead of California until approximately 1857, but now the cause was taking on new life in several northern California valleys, and the potential for growth was glorious. It may have been the decision to launch the *Western Evangelist* that led Burnett to uproot his family from their home in the Willamette Valley and transplant them in California's upper Sacramento Valley. Whatever the real reason, California's gain was Oregon's loss.

At Oregon's Annual Meeting in September 1858, there were 20 congregations represented with an aggregate membership of more than 1,000. At California's Annual Meeting in the following month there were 29 congregations represented with an aggregate membership of more than 1,200.[21] The tide had turned in California's favor. In the inaugural issue of the *Western Evangelist,* published in November 1858, the editor wrote, "We are gratified to learn that brothers Burnett, Lawson, Thompson and Gill are in the field as evangelists."[22] An eager Burnett had moved into the forefront of church activity in his new home.

From his home in Salem, A. V. McCarty was keeping a close eye on Burnett's progress in California. "Through the kindness of Brother Burnett, I have received the first number of the *Western Evangelist,*" he wrote to the editor on January 26, 1859. "I feel greatly encouraged to find a periodical published so near me devoted to the teachings of the Bible *alone,* in which our real views and understanding of the Scriptures can be sent forth to the world, and no longer be distorted and misrepresented by ignorance or prejudice."[23] Two weeks later, on February 14, 1859, Oregon achieved statehood and the capital city of Salem grew in stature. A strong church in this key city would be important to the Restoration Movement in Oregon, but the church situation in California was looking more and more attractive to McCarty. Another Oregon preacher, Harrison H. Hendrix, was also intrigued with the opportunities that California offered.

When the annual State Meeting adjourned in Salem on September 12, 1859, McCarty and Hendrix had already finalized their plans to cross the state line and get better acquainted with the brethren in California. They proceeded directly to Gilroy in Santa Clara County in order to attend California's annual State Meeting. Arriving for the first session on Thursday, September 22, 1859, the two visitors were greeted as old friends. The "Minutes" of the annual State Meeting record, "Upon motion, Elders H. H. Hendrix and A. V. McCarty, of Oregon, being present, were invited to take seats in the Convention as corresponding members."[24] The Oregon visitors obviously enjoyed their reception at the state meeting. Within three months they had returned to reside and labor in California.

Faithful and True Laborers

Meanwhile, G. W. Richardson and John Alkire Powell worked tirelessly with Oregon churches throughout 1858–59. With the loss of some important co-workers, their task was both more crucial and more difficult. Richardson and Powell traveled widely through the Willamette Valley from Washington County to Lane County in an effort to stimulate the missionary outreach of Oregon churches. Corresponding with James Mathes in September 1858, Richardson wrote:

> I take up my pen to give you a hasty sketch of the progress of the good cause in this part of Oregon. In the latter part of August I held a meeting of some days including the 5th Lord's day, near Harris' Ferry, in Washington county. I found there a few disciples who were called together some three or four years ago, under the labors of Brother H. H. Hendrix.[25] But it may truly be said of them, that they are now as sheep without a shepherd. Our meeting was solemn and impressive for that place. For I assure you that the people there seemed to have lost all confidence in the preachers of all denominations. Farther explanations are unnecessary. Our meeting resulted in the restoration of one erring brother, the strengthening and comforting of the disciples, the removal of some prejudice, and judging from reports a favorable impression was made upon the whole community. O! for laborers! faithful and true laborers, such as Paul would approve.[26]

John Alkire Powell continued his service as a circuit-riding preacher for Oregon churches throughout 1858–59. One church that benefited again from his ministry, as it had in the past, was Pleasant Hill. When he visited them in June, they were still grieving over the death of John Rigdon, who had died the month before, but they rallied to support Powell's evangelistic efforts. Harrison Shelley, one of the elders, sent an encouraging report to the *Evangelist.* With striking imagery, Shelley described the impact of Powell's visit:

> After a gloomy foreboding of more than two years, the clouds that hung over us have at last disappeared, and the Sun of righteousness has arisen with healing in his wings. Zion is again permitted to travail and bring forth sons and daughters to the honor and glory of God. While Angels are made to rejoice, the brethren and sisters are encouraged, edified and built up in the most holy faith. Brother John A. Powell held a meeting here commencing on Friday before the 2nd Lord's day in June and closed Tuesday following with 9 additions—8 by immersion and one reclaimed. Since that time Brother Callison has immersed 6 more, and the prospects are still flattering. To the Lord be all the praise.[27]

It is not immediately clear what Shelley was referring to when he spoke of two years of "gloomy foreboding." He must have been talking about the Pleasant Hill Church in particular and not about the Oregon churches in general. The Pleasant Hill Church often endured periods of turmoil and congregational unrest related to the political battles of the day. Less than two years before the beginning of hostilities in the Civil War, it is interesting to see them so unified.

As the Restoration Movement in Oregon prepared to move into the turbulent 1860s, it was no longer as strong nor as unified as it had been in the middle 1850s. Several outstanding proclaimers had been pulled from the Oregon mission field, and they had not yet been replaced. The friends of Bethel College rejoiced to see Levi Lindsay Rowland return from Bethany College in 1859, but the loss of valued supporters like Glen Owen Burnett and A. V. McCarty was devastating. Monmouth University was in a somewhat stronger position, but it was becoming increasingly obvious that both schools could not survive and prosper. Somehow, they would have to pool their resources.

There were no more discussions about publishing a monthly church periodical in Oregon, and sadly, the Christians in Oregon were not excited about supporting the

Western Evangelist in California. They never felt a sense of ownership in that enterprise. Monmouth hosted the Annual Meeting in the fall of 1859, and Mill Creek's William H. Brayton presided over the meeting. Unfortunately, no one sent a report of this gathering to the church papers. As another decade began, the Oregon Christians seemed far more involved in the intensely divisive issues of election-year politics than they were in the missionary expansion of the church in their new state.

Founders of the Restoration Movement

Thomas Campbell (1763-1854)
courtesy of Disciples of Christ Historical Society

Barton Warren Stone (1772-1844)
courtesy of Disciples of Christ Historical Society

Alexander Campbell (1788-1866)
courtesy of Disciples of Christ Historical Society

John Mulkey (1773-1844)

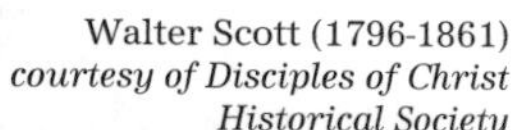

Walter Scott (1796-1861)
courtesy of Disciples of Christ Historical Society

First Casualty on the Oregon Trail

Six-year-old Joel Hembree was fatally injured in July 1843. His is the oldest identified grave along the Oregon Trail.
courtesy of Jim and Reita Lockett

The headstone engraved by William Newby was discovered 118 years later by a Wyoming rancher while clearing his land.
courtesy of Randy Brown

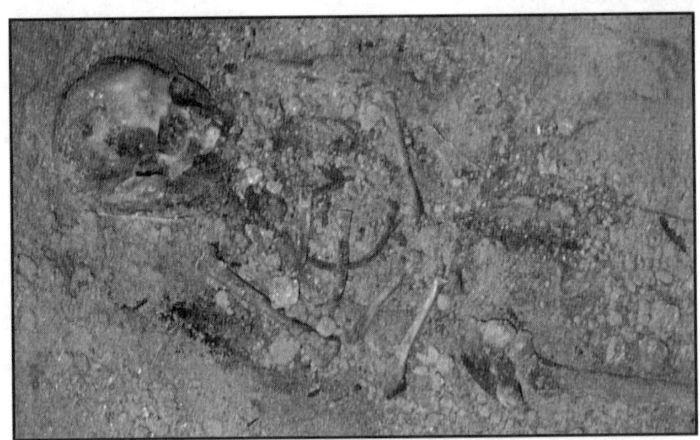

Excavated on March 24, 1962, Joel's skeleton lay on a bed of clay in an excellent state of preservation. His remains were moved a quarter-mile to the west and buried beside the grave of Private Ralston Baker who had been killed in an Indian skirmish in 1867.
courtesy of Leon Chamberlain

The Oregon-California Trails Association erected protective fencing around the two graves.
Photo (left) *courtesy of Randy Brown.*
Photo (above) *courtesy of Jim and Reita Lockett*

Early Yamhill County Settlers

William T. Newby
courtesy of Yamhill County Historical Society

Nancy and Absalom Hembree
courtesy of Yamhill County Historical Society

Amos Harvey

Jane Harvey

courtesy of Amity Church of Christ

Dr. James and Mahala McBride and family
courtesy of Oregon Historical Society

Isaiah Cooper Matheny and Daniel Boone Matheny
courtesy of Don Rivara

Early Oregon Preachers

Dr. James McBride
courtesy of Oregon Historical Society

Glen Owen Burnett
courtesy of Polk County Historical Society

William Lysander Adams
courtesy of Bonnie Miller

Alexander Vance McCarty
courtesy of Vere McCarty

Early Oregon Preachers

Noah Powell
courtesy of Kathryn Notson

John Alkire Powell
courtesy of Kathryn Notson

Philip Mulkey
courtesy of Philip Mulkey Hunt

Sebastian Adams
courtesy of Yamhill County Historical Society

John Ecles Murphy
courtesy of Helen Glodt

Early Polk County Settlers

Lucinda and Nat Ford
courtesy of Polk County Historical Society

Polly and Thomas J. Lovelady
courtesy of Vere McCarty

John and Rosanna McCarty
courtesy of Vere McCarty

William and Betsy Murphy
courtesy of First Christian Church Monmouth

First Settler in Lane County

Elijah Bristow settled at Pleasant Hill in 1846.
courtesy of Lane County Historical Museum

Elijah Bristow Historical Marker at Pleasant Hill

The Pleasant Hill School (left) and the Pleasant Hill Church of Christ (center) were both organized by Elijah Bristow. The Bristow cabin, the local store, and the Robert Callison cabin are included in the cluster of buildings to the right.
courtesy of Marilee Cash

Entrance to Pleasant Hill Cemetery

Elijah Bristow Monument in Pleasant Hill Cemetery

Pioneer Christian Families

Squire S. Whitman Elizabeth Whitman
courtesy of First Christian Church Monmouth

Charles Bisbee and Isabelle Dart
courtesy of Lowell Dart

William Lysander and Frances Adams and family
courtesy of Bonnie Miller

James and Selena Parvin and family
courtesy of Marilee Cash

James Addison and Elizabeth Bushnell and family
courtesy of Lane County Historical Society

Pioneer Homes in Oregon

The McBride cabin on Panther Creek
in Yamhill County was built c1846.
courtesy of Oregon Historical Society

The Elijah Bristow cabin at Pleasant Hill
in Lane County was built c1846.
courtesy of Marilee Cash

The Johnson Mulkey residence at Corvallis in Benton County was built c1848.
These photos were taken around the turn of the century.
courtesy of Philip Mulkey Hunt

The Mac Waller cabin at Eola in Polk County
was built c1860.
courtesy of Polk County Historical Society

The Brunk House at Eola in Polk County
was built c1861.
courtesy of Polk County Historical Society

Christian Editors

Daniel Bates, *The Western Evangelist*
courtesy of Christian Board of Publication

James Madison Mathes, *The Christian Record*
courtesy of Center for Restoration Studies

Alexander Campbell, *The Millennial Harbinger*
courtesy of Disciples of Christ Historical Society

Isaac Errett, *The Christian Standard*
courtesy of Center for Restoration Studies

Benjamin Franklin, *The American Christian Review*
courtesy of Anna Sommer

Bethanys of the West

An 1858 lithograph of Alexander Campbell's Bethany College in Virginia.
courtesy of Bethany College

When Bethel College was erected in 1855, it was the largest building in Polk County.
courtesy of Polk County Historical Society

Monmouth University (later called Christian College) at Monmouth. The original building (background) was erected in the 1850s, and Campbell Hall (foreground) was erected in 1871-1872.
courtesy of Western Oregon University

Historical marker at Bethel
courtesy Polk County Historical Society

Historical plaque at Monmouth
courtesy of Western Oregon University

Pioneer Church Buildings

Amity Church sign in Yamhill County
courtesy of Amity Church of Christ

Bethel Church in Polk County shared the building with Bethel College.
courtesy of Polk County Historical Society

Monmouth Church in Polk County was erected in 1877.
courtesy of First Christian Church Monmouth

Central Church in Linn County was erected in the early 1850s. The spire was added later.
courtesy of First Christian Church Albany

Eola Church in Polk County was erected in the late 1850s.
courtesy of Polk County Historical Society

Bethany Church in Marion County was erected in the late 1850s.
courtesy of Bethany School

Pioneer Church Buildings

Mill Creek Church in Marion County
was erected in 1855.
courtesy of Don Porter

Pleasant Hill Church in Lane County
was erected in 1875.
courtesy of Pleasant Hill Church of Christ

Salem Church in Marion County
was erected in 1867.
courtesy of First Christian Church Salem

Eugene Church in Lane County
was erected during the winter of 1867-1868.
courtesy of First Christian Church Eugene

A. L. Todd's last ministry was with the church he established in Shoestring Valley in northern Douglas County. This building was erected in the early 1880s. When Todd died on April 23, 1886, he was buried in the church cemetery. The building burned to the ground in the 1930s.
courtesy of Douglas County Museum of History

Christians in Salem

Governor George L. Woods was an elder in the Salem Church and he was often called upon to preach for the congregation.
courtesy of Oregon Historical Society

The "little brick church" was erected in Salem in 1867. The photo above shows the church after the steeple was remodeled.
courtesy of First Christian Church Salem

Peter Rogers Burnett, the son of Glen Owen Burnett, preached for the Salem Church in the late 1860s.
courtesy of First Christian Church Monmouth

Levi Lindsay Rowland, former president of both Bethel College and Christian College, preached for the Salem Church in the 1870s.
courtesy of Western Oregon University

Christian Preachers in Oregon

Samuel Bates Briggs
courtesy of Douglas County Museum of History

Gilmore Callison
courtesy of Marilee Cash

A. L. Todd
courtesy of Douglas County Museum of History

Martin Peterson
courtesy of Verna Tucker and Linda Morehouse

Daniel W. Elledge
courtesy of Center for Restoration Studies

George P. Rich
courtesy of Lowell Dart

Allen Jefferson and Sleigh Huddleston and family
courtesy of Douglas County Museum of History

Sarah and Isaac Newton Mulkey and family
courtesy of Philip Mulkey Hunt

Monmouth and Christian College

Jane Eliza Campbell

Thomas Franklin Campbell,
President 1869-1882

Campbell Hall (erected 1871-1872)
with original Monmouth University building in the background
all pictures on this page courtesy of Western Oregon University

David Truman Stanley,
President 1882-1889

Levi Lindsay Rowland,
President 1865-1869

Monmouth and Christian College

Elijah B. Davidson, a deacon in the Monmouth Church, preached in the area in the 1850s and 1860s.

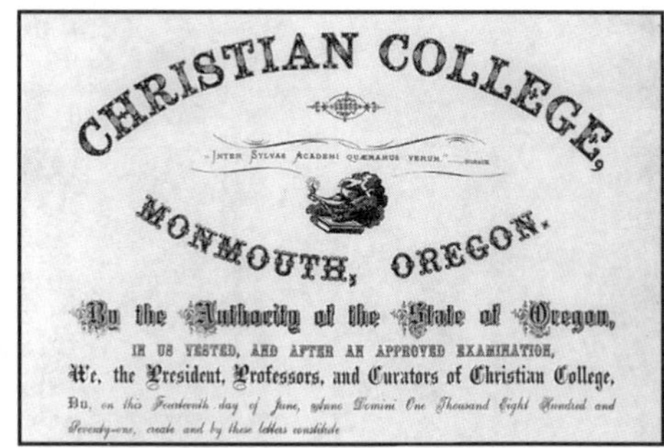

CHRISTIAN COLLEGE,

"Inter Sylvas Academi Quaerimus Verum."—Horace

MONMOUTH, OREGON.

By the Authority of the State of Oregon,

IN US VESTED, AND AFTER AN APPROVED EXAMINATION,

We, the President, Professors, and Curators of Christian College,

Do, on this Fourteenth day of June, Anno Domini One Thousand Eight Hundred and Seventy-one, create and by these letters constitute

Christian College diploma in the 1870s
courtesy of Western Oregon University

A cattle drive moves through the center of the town and past the spire of Monmouth Church.
courtesy of First Christian Church Monmouth

The class of 1876 included Mildred Bedwell whose parents moved to Monmouth to enable her to attend Christian College.
courtesy of Western Oregon University

A. W. Lucas, elder in the Monmouth Church, and a trustee of the College.
courtesy of Western Oregon University

Monuments of Oregon Christians

Cynthia Brown Davie, in the migration of 1842, is buried in Aumsville Cemetery (left). Isaac and Betsy Briggs, founders of the town of Springfield who came to Oregon in 1847, are buried in Laurel Grove Cemetery (below).

The Butlers, Major Peter and Rachel, veterans of the 1853 migration, are buried in Davidson Cemetery west of Monmouth (above) *courtesy of Lotte Larsen*. Alfred Powell came overland in 1851 and preached in Oregon for 30 years. His tombstone declares: "Gone Home" (right).

Mac Waller came overland in 1847 and preached in Oregon for more than 45 years. He is buried in Hilltop Cemetery in Polk County.

John Ecles Murphy preached in Oregon for nearly a quarter century. He is buried in Fir Crest Cemetery in Polk County.

Monuments of Oregon Christians

Samuel Bates Briggs migrated west in 1851. He is buried in the Briggs family cemetery (below) in Canyonville in Douglas County. Caleb P. Chapman preached in Oregon for 44 years. He is buried in Pioneer Cemetery (right) in Salem.

John and Jane Harris (foreground) are buried in Taylor-Lane Cemetery in Lane County. They died within a year of each other. Two other Christian preachers, Henry W. Taylor and Joseph H. Sharp, are buried in this small cemetery near Cottage Grove.

G.W. Richardson preached in Oregon and Washington for 33 years. He is buried in Pioneer Cemetery in Salem.

Martin Peterson preached in Oregon for a quarter century. He is buried in Central Point Cemetery near Medford.

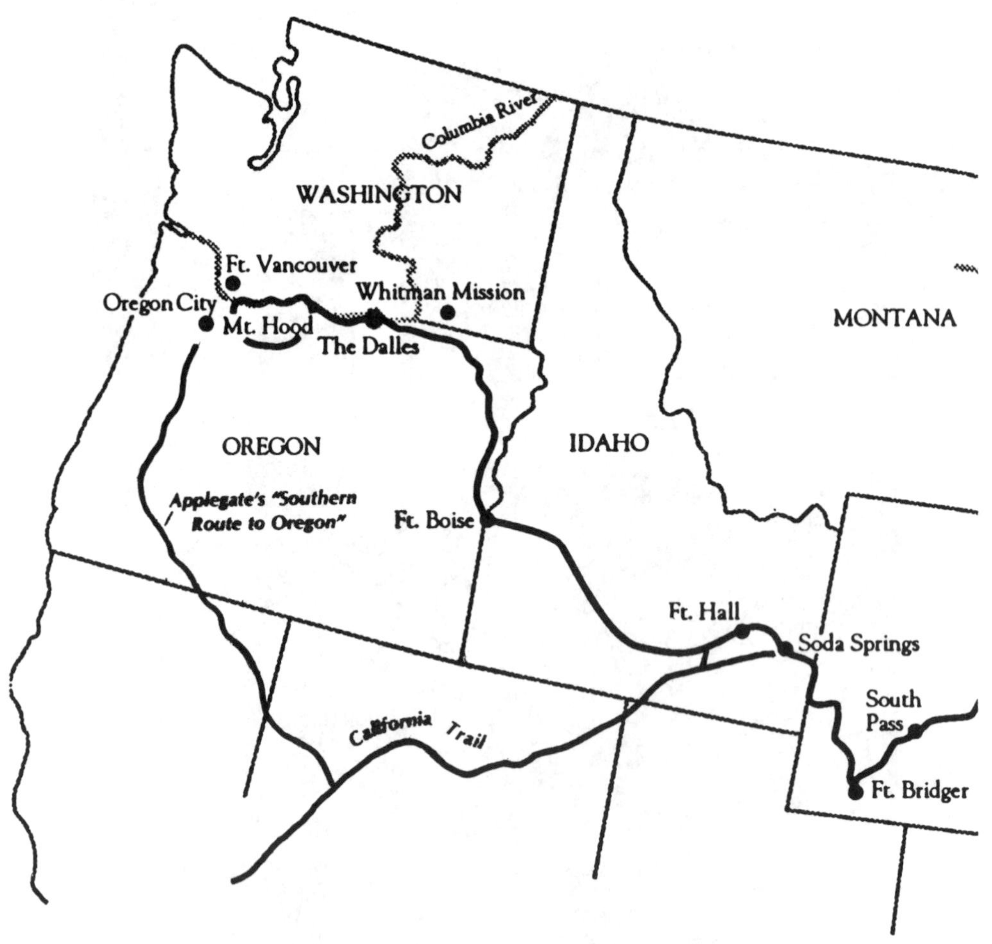
Columbia River
WASHINGTON
Ft. Vancouver
Whitman Mission
Oregon City
Mt. Hood
The Dalles
MONTANA
OREGON
IDAHO
Applegate's "Southern Route to Oregon"
Ft. Boise
Ft. Hall
Soda Springs
South Pass
California Trail
Ft. Bridger

Missouri River
NORTH DAKOTA
MINNESOTA
WYOMING
SOUTH DAKOTA
Independence Rock
Ft. Laramie
Scotts Bluff
NEBRASKA
Chimney Rock
Courthouse Rock
IOWA
California Crossing
Ft. Kearney
Alcove Spring
St. Joseph
Independence
KANSAS
MISSOURI

Settlements Prior to Statehood

Courtesy of William J. Loy, The Atlas of Oregon *(Eugene: University of Oregon Books, 1976).*

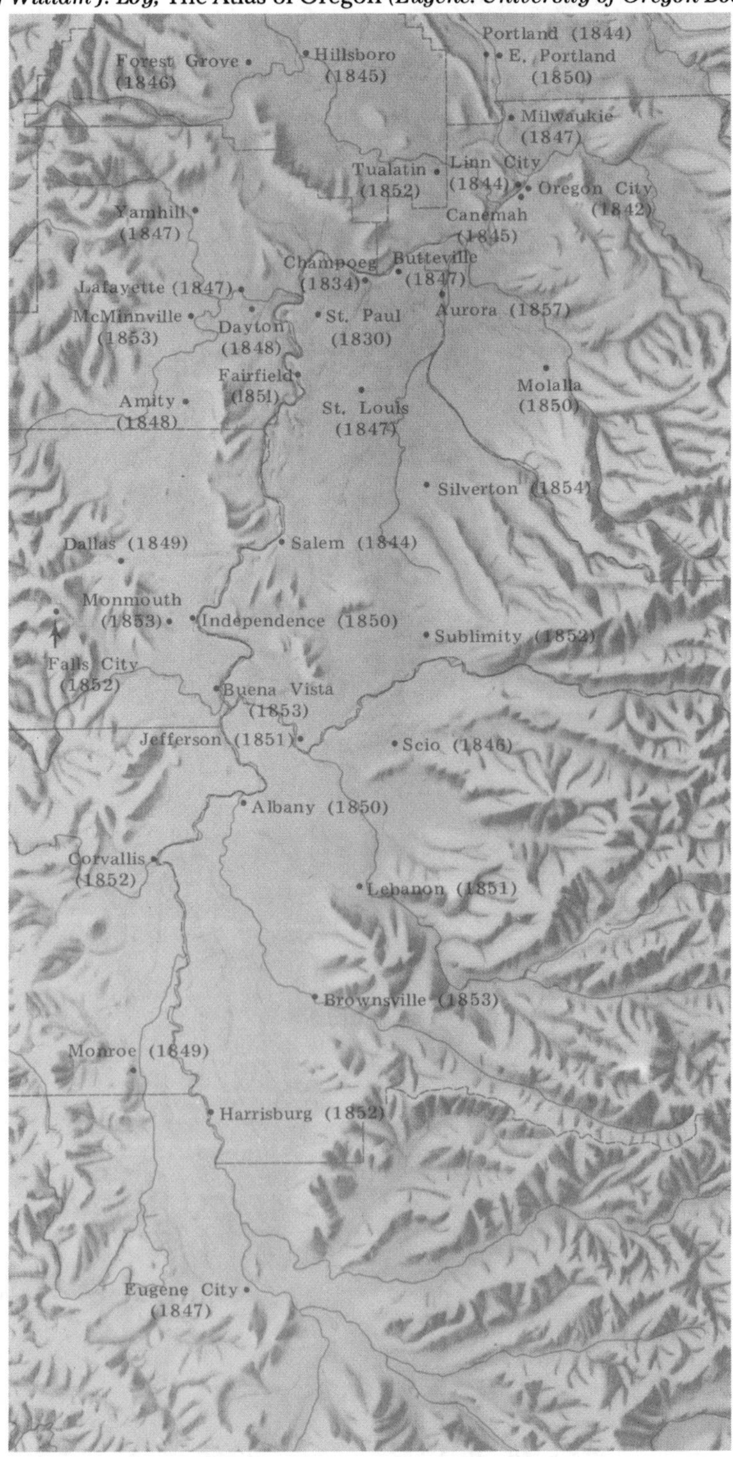

Oregon Settlements 1859–1879

Courtesy of William J. Loy, The Atlas of Oregon *(Eugene: University of Oregon Books, 1976).*

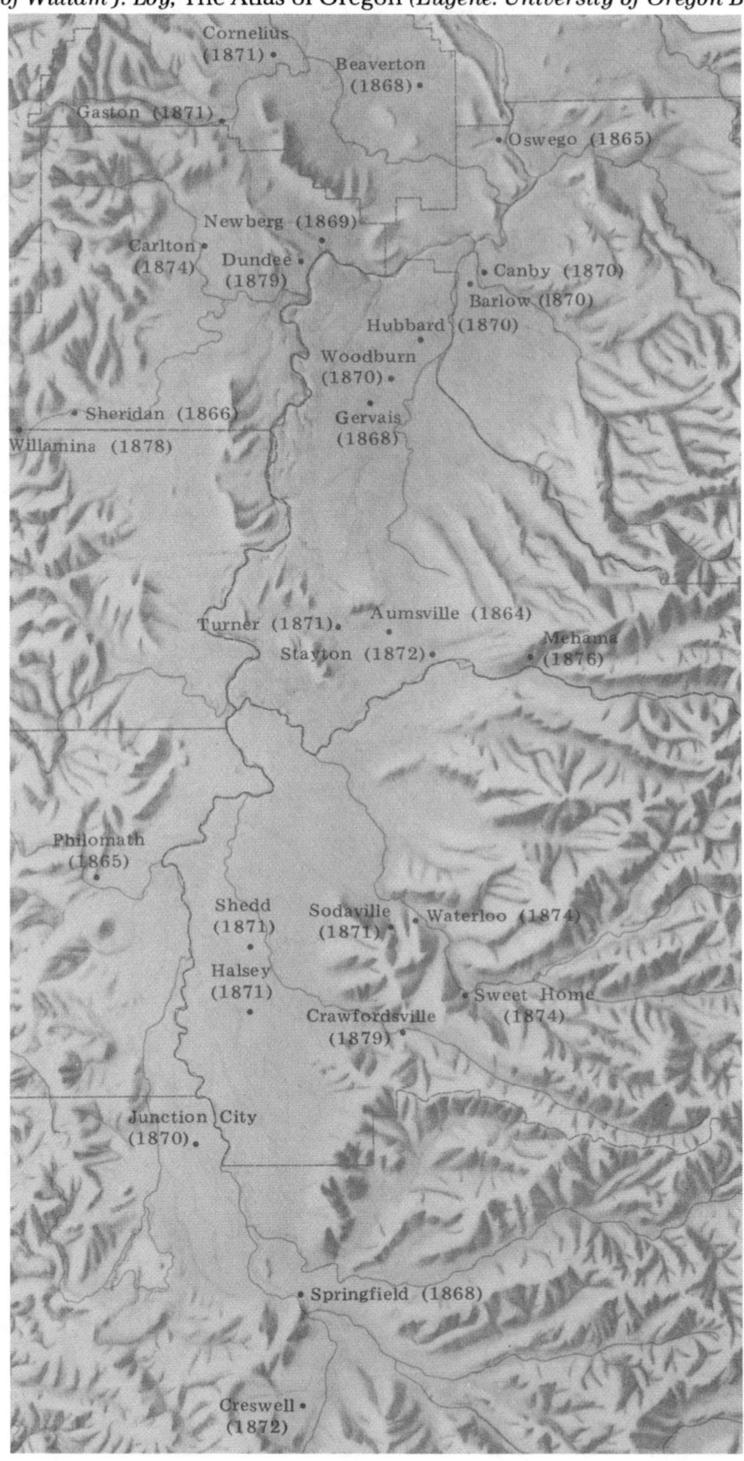

1878 Map of the Willamette Valley

1878 Map of the Umpqua Valley

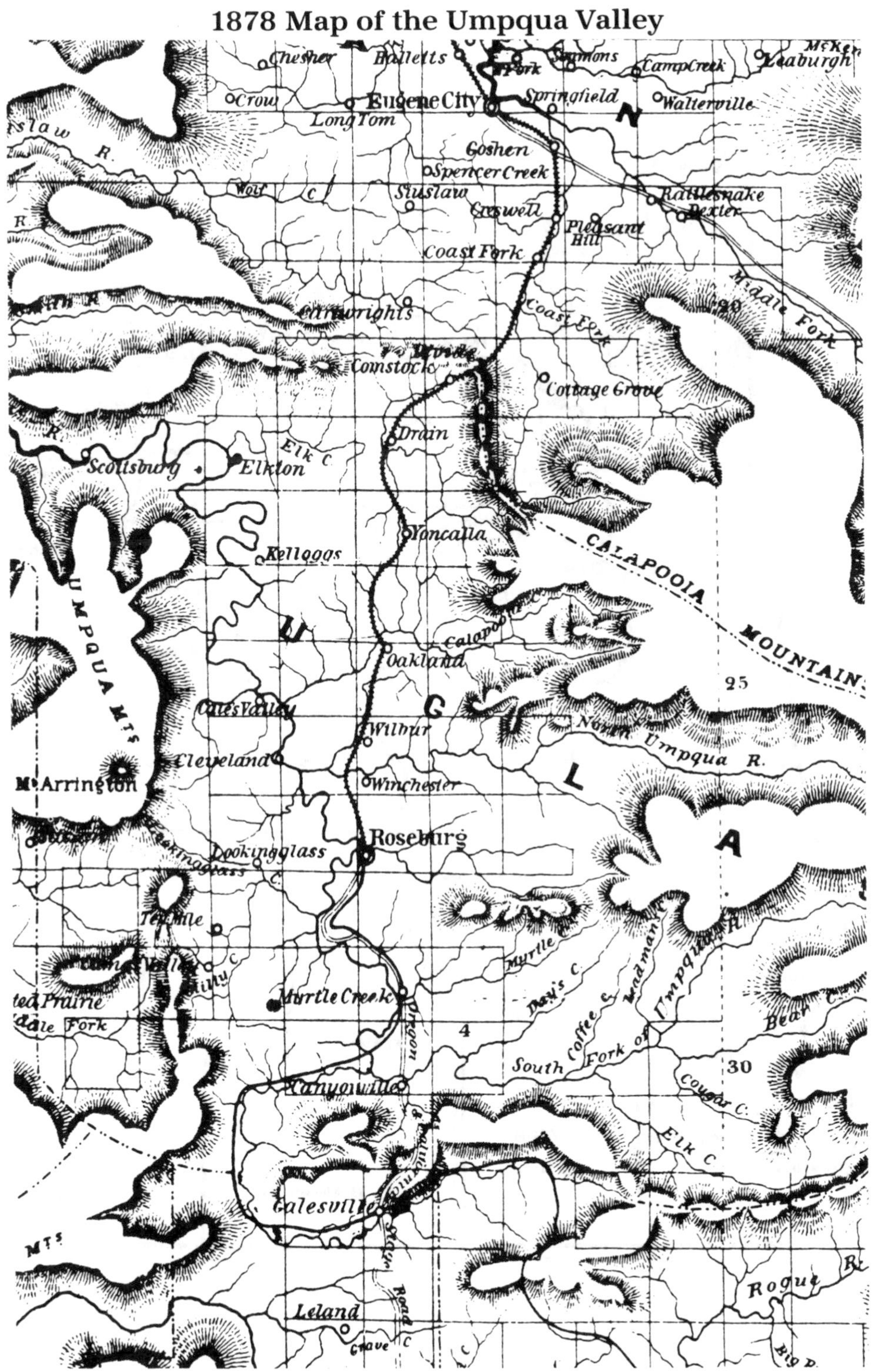

The Baker-Lincoln Friendship

Edward Dickinson Baker was born in London, England, in 1811. Twenty years later he was living in Carrollton, Illinois, and preparing to marry a young Christian widow named Mary Ann Lee. Shortly after his marriage in 1831, he was immersed into Christ and quickly became a leading member of the Church of Christ in Carrollton. His exceptional oratorical abilities and "his sincere devotion to the pure gospel led him to its public proclamation for near a decade." Somewhere between 1831 and 1844, Baker was one of the Restoration Movement's most popular proclaimers of the gospel in Illinois, and "he also baptized some converts."[2] In 1835 he moved to Springfield and became close friends with Abraham Lincoln and pursued a career in politics. He served in the Illinois Legislature from 1837 to 1840 and in the State Senate from 1840 to 1844. In 1843 he and Lincoln were rival candidates for the Whig congressional nomination. Baker won and was elected to the United States Congress in 1844.

At least four different historians have suggested that the decisive factor in Baker's narrow victory over Lincoln was the support of his Christian friends. Albert J. Beveridge wrote, "Baker had all the 'Campbellites,' to whose church he belonged."[3] John Nicolay and John Hay, Lincoln's secretaries, provided this version in their biography:

> Baker and his wife belonged to that numerous and powerful sect which has several times played an important part in Western politics – the Disciples. They all supported him energetically, and used as arguments against Lincoln that his wife was a Presbyterian, that most of her family were Episcopalians, that Lincoln himself belonged to no church, and that he had been suspected of deism . . . .[4]

In a letter to a political friend, Lincoln confided that it was argued during the campaign "that no Christian ought to go for me, because I belonged to no church . . . Baker is a Campbellite, and therefore as I suppose, with few exceptions got all that church . . . with all these things Baker, of course, had nothing to do. Nor do I complain of them."[5] Lincoln and

Baker remained the closest of friends, and Lincoln named his second son Edward Baker.[6]

The Bakers migrated to California in 1852 and then moved on to Oregon in 1860. Within nine months of his arrival in Oregon, Baker became the first Republican elected to represent Oregon in the United States Senate. One month later, Abraham Lincoln won election as the sixteenth president of the United States. Lincoln chose Senator Baker to introduce him at the presidential inauguration in Washington, D.C., on March 4, 1861. The impending Civil War, however, made Baker's career in the Senate very brief. He accepted a military commission from President Lincoln and was killed in the battle of Ball's Bluff on October 22, 1861. He was remembered by Oregonians in the naming of both the city of Baker and Baker County.[7]

The Baker Orbit

When the Bakers moved to Springfield in 1835, they became members of the same congregation that included Alfred and Martha Elder and Alfred's sister and brother-in-law, Sanford and Maria Elder Watson.[8] It is also very likely that they soon became acquainted with John Alkire Powell and his two brothers who were well-known preachers in the counties around Springfield. The Elders and Watsons moved to Oregon in 1849 in a wagon train that was captained by Samuel Baker, Edward Dickinson Baker's brother. Another Brother, Thomas Baker, was married to Cecelia Elder, a sister to Alfred and Maria.[9] Alfred Elder became one of the most active preachers for the Restoration Movement in Oregon Territory, and Sanford Watson became a founding member of the board of trustees of Bethel Institute. The Powell brothers migrated to Oregon in 1851 and made a tremendous contribution to the cause. Did these Illinois Christians harbor hope that their eloquent friend from Springfield would one day join them in evangelistic efforts in the far west?

If Edward Dickinson Baker had remained passionately involved in the growth and progress of the Restoration Movement, his removal to California in 1852 and Oregon in

1860 would have been hailed as a positive development for the church in those distant lands. But the sad truth is that there is no evidence that Baker was ever involved in spiritual concerns after he left Illinois. Politics gradually came to dominate his entire life, and his enormous gift for public address was never again used to preach the unsearchable riches of Christ. His close Christian friends were left wondering what a difference his obvious talents might have made to the cause of Christ in both California and Oregon. His mother, Lucy Baker, remained a devout Christian and a member of the church in Winchester, Illinois. When she died in November 1862, Alexander Campbell published her obituary in the *Millennial Harbinger*.[10]

The Fruits of Victory

The political struggle in Oregon in 1860 was more a fight between the two wings of the Democratic party than it was a clash between Democrats and Republicans. Baker and his political advisors secured their victory with a shrewd coalition of Republicans and Douglas Democrats. The editor of the *Oregonian* later wrote to Lincoln to suggest that Baker's election as United States Senator was the catalyst for Lincoln's surprising victories in both Oregon and California.[11] In the presidential contest the Whigs nominated John Bell and the Democrats split their vote between Stephen A. Douglas and John Breckinridge. The Republicans, in only their second presidential election, unified behind Abraham Lincoln. On November 6, 1860, Oregon gave Lincoln a very narrow plurality of 270 votes. The final vote totals were: Lincoln, 5,344; Breckinridge, 5,074; Douglas, 4,131; and Bell, 212.[12]

Several Christians were significantly involved in the successful campaigns of Edward Dickinson Baker and Abraham Lincoln, but none more than William Lysander Adams, editor of the *Argus*, and the father and son team of Dr. James McBride and John Rogers McBride. In a short time, all three had been handsomely remunerated for their hard work. In the summer of 1861, Adams was appointed by Lincoln to be collector of customs at the port of Astoria.

Lincoln appointed Dr. McBride to be the United States Minister to the Sandwich Islands (Hawaii), and John Rogers McBride won election to the United States Congress as an Oregon Republican in 1862. McBride's two-year term in Washington, D.C., began on March 4, 1863, about the same time his parents were preparing to move to Honolulu to begin a four-year commitment of service to their country.

The 1860 Annual State Meeting

At the very peak of political excitement in early September of 1860, before the fate of Baker and Lincoln was known, the Christians met in Eola in Polk County for their annual State Meeting. Mac Waller was the regular preacher for this church, and this was one of the few Oregon congregations that had its own meetinghouse. Most Oregon churches were still meeting in the local schoolhouse or courthouse. A report in the *Evangelist* said that "messengers from most of the congregations of the Christian Church in Oregon" were in attendance at the meeting, and that Brother Alfred R. Elder had "preached from the fourth chapter of Ephesians, urging the brotherhood to keep the unity of the Spirit in the bond of peace."[13] This was certainly an appropriate text, given the political volatility of the times.

James R. Fisher from Pleasant Hill Church in Lane County was elected president for the meeting, and William Porter from Mill Creek Church in Marion County was chosen to serve as secretary. Porter began by announcing the death of William H. Brayton, who had presided over the previous state meeting. "Letters were then read from the various congregations, and verbal statements made in reference to the condition of the churches," continued the report, "from which it appeared that the churches are not all in a prosperous condition." Nevertheless, the meeting itself was a grand success. "During the progress of the meeting, the ministering brethren preached the gospel of Christ frequently to the large number of persons who were in attendance," concluded the report, "and seventeen persons made confession, and were immersed."

This was an encouraging meeting for Oregon Christians, but it paled in comparison to what was experienced by California Christians two weeks later in their annual State Meeting near Santa Rosa. It was not only the 33 California churches represented, with an aggregate membership of 1,400, but the large attendance of people who knew very little about the plea of the Restoration Movement. One Christian leader enthused, "The number present upon the first Lord's day was estimated at five thousand—a very prudent estimate we presume, as many gave us a margin for one or two thousand above that number."[14] During the meeting, there were 95 additions to the church, including 83 immersions. "It was without doubt the largest religious meeting ever held in the State," boasted one California Christian, "and has been so published in several political sheets."[15]

One contributing factor to the success of the 1860 annual State Meeting in Oregon was its location in Polk County. This was unquestionably the strongest county, from the perspective of church leadership, for the Christians in Oregon. Not only were Bethel College and Monmouth University located in the county, but 14 of the 20 preachers listed in the 1860 Polk County Census were from the Restoration Movement.[16] The 14 preachers were: Glen Owen Burnett, John Ecles Murphy, Mac Waller, Alfred R. Elder, Levi Lindsay Rowland, William Thompson Haley, Elijah Davidson, Elijah B. Davidson, Charles Bradshaw, John Burris Smith, William Ruble, G. W. Richardson, Daniel Boone Matheny and Orlando Alderman. The last two named, 30-year-old Daniel Boone Matheny and 27-year-old Orlando Alderman, had not been preaching long. The percentage of Christian preachers in Polk County had even been higher. Two outstanding preachers who were recent residents in the county, A. V. McCarty and Levi Burch, were now residing in California.[17]

Beyond the Willamette and Umpqua Valleys

The Christians living in the Rogue River Valley in southern Oregon were heard from for the first time in the summer of 1860. Margaret Chambers wrote to the *Western Evangelist* to say, "There are a few Disciples here, and no doubt if we could be visited by some of the preaching brethren, that many could be added to the saved."[18] Around the same time, Wasco County was heard from for the first time. Absalom and Olivia Bolton moved there some time before 1862.[19] Evidently the Boltons had moved to The Dalles in Wasco County, as a congregation in that city was mentioned in the "Minutes" of the 1863 annual State Meeting.[20]

Bethel College

Two months after the State Meeting, and less than a week after Lincoln's election, Glen Owen Burnett wrote to W. W. Stevenson, editor of the *Western Evangelist* in California, and enclosed a news release about the opening of Bethel College. It read:

> The Institution at Bethel, Polk County, is about to enter upon a new era in its history. It will be opened as a College, with all the regular departments and professorships, on the third Wednesday in November. Levi Rowland, A. M., late a graduate of Bethany College, Virginia, and a most estimable man, will be inaugurated as President.[21]

William Lysander Adams published the same news release in the *Argus* on October 27, 1860, and then commented on the good news. "We have been familiar with the history of this Institution since it was first set on foot through the indefatigable exertions of a few noble souls as Glen O. Burnett, Amos Harvey and Dr. Warriner," Adams wrote, "and since the day it was determined to establish an Institution of learning at Bethel, we have seen it struggle onwards and upwards, through storm and sunshine, till, contrary to the predictions of many, it has become an entire success."[22]

In the Shadow of the Civil War

On the eve of the Civil War, the Christians in Oregon appeared unified in most places and even prosperous in some areas. John Foster's congregation on the Clackamas River in Clackamas County, the second oldest congregation in the state, was demonstrating renewed life. On February 28, 1861, James Henry Pedigo sent an encouraging report back home to Iowa. He wrote:

> We have a congregation here, on the Clackamas River, numbering something over 50 members. The congregation here, as well as at many other places in Oregon, has been rather luke-warm during two years past; but, thank God, they are now rousing up! We had 2 accessions by immersion on the first Lord's day in February. May the Lord enable us to move on.[23]

One week later, Dr. James McBride submitted another positive report to the *Evangelist*. The ministerial labors of G. W. Richardson had resulted in 26 additions for the McMinnville church, including 19 immersions. A month later William Dawson wrote to say that Richardson's ministry had led to 11 more additions at McMinnville. In addition, Richardson had preached at Lafayette on the fifth Sunday in March and baptized 11 more persons into Christ. "We have had a season of refreshing," Dawson exulted. "The good cause is prospering. There is yet a great work to be done." But he closed on a sobering note: "The Methodists and Presbyterians do all they can against the cause."[24]

Four days after Dawson wrote about the "season of refreshing," Fort Sumter was fired on in South Carolina, and the nation was abruptly engaged in a Civil War. Over the next four agonizing years, the unity of Christians in Oregon would be severely tested. One Oregon Christian wrote to the respected editor of the *Evangelist* in Iowa to ask where his loyalties were in the tragic conflict. "A brother in Oregon wishes to know for himself and others, whether I have any sympathy with the secession movement," replied Daniel Bates. "I have as little as anybody can have; for I have none at all. Any one who sincerely deplores war, will just as sincerely disapprobate the overt acts by which war was set on foot—such as taking possession of government property, and firing into United States vessels and forts."[25]

In the spring of 1861, just as the Civil War was beginning to threaten the fragile peace in the border state of Missouri, Keathley and Sarah Bailes and their children began the arduous trek across the plains on the Oregon Trail. They traveled by ox team with other families, and one account noted that the trip was "a slow, long and weary one." True to his calling, Keathley Bailes "preached every Sunday" to the circled wagon train during the six-month journey.[26]

The Bailes family spent their first winter in Oregon on Wildhorse Creek in Umatilla County, near the present location of Athena. The winter was so severe that they lost all their livestock. In the spring of 1862 they pushed on to a new home in Marion County, where Keathley began to preach for the Bethany Christian Church, west of Silverton, and for the Rock Creek Church of Christ, south of Molalla. This was the beginning of a lengthy preaching ministry for Keathley Bailes in Oregon and Washington that would span more than half a century.[27]

The Church in Wartime

Less than three months after the firing on Fort Sumter, a meeting in support of the Union cause was held in the Yamhill County town of Wheatland on the Willamette River. Three Christians, George Lemuel Woods, John Rogers McBride, and Samuel M. Gilmore, were featured prominently on the program. Under the banner headline of "UNION MEETING AT WHEATLAND," the *Oregon Statesman* published an article on the event. Among other things, the article reported:

> On Saturday, June 29th, the people of Wheatland and vicinity assembled for the purpose of a flag raising and barbecue in the beautiful grove near the ferry. The people gathered in from every direction; by 12 o'clock some four hundred persons having assembled, the meeting was called to order. A. A. Skinner was chosen President . . . a beautiful national flag was then presented in behalf of the ladies of the vicinity by G. L. Woods, Esq., accompanied by a thrilling and eloquent speech, to which the President replied, pledging the gallantry and patriotism of the meeting to defend from dishonor that emblem of our national sovereignty whenever and wherever imperiled. The procession was then formed by S. M. Gilmore, marshall of the day, and marched to the flag staff, where the "Stars and Stripes" were raised amidst the

firing of a national salute and the enthusiastic shouts of the people . . .[28]

After the flag-raising there was a dinner, and following the dinner there were five patriotic speeches. Woods and McBride were included among the speakers, all of whom, according to the newspaper, declared "their unswerving attachment to our glorious and indivisible Union."

The reality of war in other parts of the nation did not necessarily serve as a deterrent to evangelistic outreach in Oregon in 1861. The Silver Creek Church (Bethany) in Marion County hosted the annual State Meeting as planned in September. The Coast Fork Church in Lane County was the site for an exciting ten-day meeting in October-November that resulted in 42 additions, including 31 immersions. John Alkire Powell, Gilmore Callison, and Joseph H. Sharp were the three evangelists who shared the preaching responsibilities. That same fall, Powell reported that he labored with G. W. Richardson in a meeting at "Christian Chapel in my own neighborhood" that saw 13 persons baptized into Christ.[29]

People on both sides of the conflict thought that the Civil War would surely be over by the end of the first summer. In this hopeful prediction, they were sadly mistaken. By the springtime of 1862, as the war approached its first anniversary, there was no end in sight. The two-day battle at Shiloh Church, fought on April 6 and 7, 1862, was the bloodiest battle ever fought on the North American continent up to that time. The two armies suffered a combined loss of 24,000 men in just two days of fighting.

For some unknown reason, the annual State Meeting in 1862 was moved to June instead of remaining at its usual time in September. The Pleasant Hill Church hosted the event, but no report on the meeting was ever published in the church papers. The only information released was the announcement that the 1863 annual State Meeting would be hosted by the Central Church in Linn County, and that it would begin on Thursday, October 1.[30] The news from Oregon churches was extremely meager in 1862. One reference to Mac Waller in 1862 is in the diary of a 26-year-old carriage maker named Lot

Livermore. After attending church on February 23, 1862, Livermore wrote: "I heard Mr. Waller preach today. By way of criticism, I would say that his sermons are too long—he preached about 2 hours and a half."[31]

A vivid commentary on the lack of church work accomplished during the wartime year of 1862 is seen in Glen Owen Burnett's brief note to the *Western Evangelist,* dated July 2, 1862, and sent from his California home at Grand Island in the northern Sacramento Valley. "I have not been able to visit any of the Congregations this summer, save the one on the Island," he explained. "My circumstances, so far as this world's goods are concerned, have fallen so immeasurably below par, that I am unable to defray expenses of travel, and hence my confinement. But of this I do not wish to complain, as I have had the society of my family, and raised a tolerable crop of wheat and barley for their use."[32]

Several members of the Christian Church who were living in southern Yamhill County, including the Faulconers and Graves families, established a new townsite around 1863. Since they were strongly supportive of the Union cause, they named their village after General Philip Sheridan. A church building was constructed for the congregation, and for several years it was the only church in the town. As late as 1871, the Christian Church was the only church in Sheridan.[33]

Dissension in the Family

It was natural that Oregon Christians mirrored the growing sectional controversy between North and South, as Christians had migrated to Oregon from both regions. However, the majority of Oregon Christians reflected the mentality of the inhabitants of the border states who rejected both the defenders of slavery in the Deep South and the fiery abolitionists in the North. Most Oregon churches maintained an uneasy and fragile peace during the Civil War years, but a few were torn asunder by activists on both sides. According to the records of the Mill Creek Church in Marion County, one member was dropped from the church roll for refusing to extend the right hand of fellowship to "a rebel and a bush whacker."[34]

The Grand Prairie Church of Christ northwest of Eugene in Lane County was a tragic example of a church devastated by the outspoken actions of its leaders. Philip Mulkey and James Addison Bushnell were two gifted church leaders with profoundly different viewpoints on the sectional conflict. Mulkey, 24 years older, was the son of one of the pioneer founders of the Restoration Movement. Although he had come to Oregon from western Missouri, he had deep and lasting associations with the southern Kentucky and middle Tennessee roots of the movement.

J. A. Bushnell, born in New York and reared in Ohio, had migrated to Oregon from Hannibal, Missouri. He was an unapologetic defender of the Union. Both Mulkey and Bushnell arrived in Lane County in 1853, and they worked together to establish the Grand Prairie Church of Christ in the spring of 1855. Mulkey baptized Bushnell's wife, Elizabeth, and Bushnell was chosen to be a deacon in the congregation. When Bushnell helped construct the Grand Prairie school house in the spring of 1856, the church began meeting in that facility. Although Gilmore Callison, John Alkire Powell, John Rigdon, and John Ecles Murphy all preached on occasion for this church, the regular preacher for several years was Philip Mulkey.[35]

When the Civil War broke out, most Oregon Christians refrained from inflammatory statements and actions and concentrated on maintaining the peace in their respective congregations. Unfortunately, this was not true of the Mulkey and Bushnell factions. Philip Mulkey's son, John Thomas Mulkey, took the lead in flying a confederate flag from a prominent oak tree in his district. Then he came "swaggering into town offering to fight any so-and-so who didn't like it."[36] On another occasion he paraded through Eugene at night shouting "Hurrah for Jeff Davis." He was eventually arrested in Eugene because of his speeches in favor of Jefferson Davis. Because he had so enraged some local citizens, the authorities spirited him by ferry to Coburg and incarcerated him in the

Vancouver barracks for his own safety. His armed friends were preparing to intervene and recapture their leader, but soldiers dispatched from the Vancouver barracks took down the rebel flag and put an end to the local disturbance.[37]

Adding to the turmoil in Philip's life, was the death of his wife, Martha, on October 24, 1862, just prior to their 42nd wedding anniversary.[38] Meanwhile, Bushnell and other northern sympathizers from both the community and the church were not willing to overlook the brash actions of young John Mulkey. "A great many, myself among the number raised a liberty pole to show where we stood," Bushnell wrote. "We also organized a company of cavalry of which I was first sergeant, but there was fortunately no fighting to do. We went into camp at Salem the summer of 1864 and took the prize given by the state for the best drilled and finest equipped company in the state."[39]

With such strong actions from both sides of the church, it was only a matter of time before their precious unity in Christ was destroyed. Many years later, when writing his memoirs, Bushnell reflected on the tragic division in the church. But even at that distance, he found it difficult to be charitable and accept part of the blame for the inflamed feelings aroused during wartime. Putting the stigma of division squarely on the Mulkey family, and Philip in particular, "Sergeant" Bushnell wrote:

> The Christian Church on Grand Prairie was split in two by the war, uncle Philip Mulkey and all his children and connections who were all Democratic leaving the church in a body. The old man who had been preaching all his life the gospel of peace, denied that he ever was a preacher and declared if he was in Missouri he would take his gun and help shoot down abolitionists. To such an extent did party spirit lead astray one of the best men. He lived to see and deplore his conduct in this crisis of our country's history.[40]

Presumably, Bushnell did not see any inconsistency in his own military posturing and his willingness to shoot down secessionists: he only saw fault with Mulkey's willingness to shoot down abolitionists. No doubt Philip Mulkey's account of why the Grand Prairie Church was divided would be somewhat different, but no less tragic. Fortunately for all concerned, when the war finally came to an end, the breach in the church family was repaired, and the two brothers labored together again in proclaiming the gospel of peace. Mulkey and Bushnell were two of the most talented and energetic leaders in the Restoration Movement, and Oregon Christians could not afford to lose either one.

Trouble in Mill Creek

Another congregation torn by sectional strife was the one meeting at Mill Creek in Marion County. The uneasy peace and harmony that prevailed through the early war years was broken with the arrival of a gospel preacher from Missouri named Daniel W. Elledge in the fall of 1864. Elledge was a gifted preacher, but it soon became apparent that he favored the south in the national conflict.

According to church records, Elledge preached at Mill Creek for the first time on October 9, 1864. On November 13, 1864 he preached to "a large congregation" assembled at the church building. Nevertheless, despite the apparent revival of the Mill Creek Church under the labors of the veteran preacher, there were murmurs of discontent. The troubles came to a head when the Elledge family submitted a formal letter requesting membership in the church. The two elders of the Mill Creek Church, William Porter and George M. Whitney, were divided on how to handle the request.

William Porter thought the timing of the letter was unfortunate. Knowing that several families in the congregation were disturbed by the political views of the new preacher, he advised Elledge to delay his request. Elledge was apparently offended by this suggestion, and he continued to press his right to be recognized as a member in good standing of the Mill Creek Church. Unfortunately, the Porter-Elledge standoff became public knowledge, and members of the congregation began to take sides. Porter also served as the church clerk, and in his notation for January 12, 1865 he wrote:

> The congregation met for the purpose of settling a difficulty in the church, but failed to accomplish said object. Said difficulty came from a request by W. Porter for D. W. Elledge to postpone offering his letter for membership on account of suspected disloyalty—said suspicions resting on various rumors that said Elledge is a secessionist.[41]

The situation escalated in the next month, and on February 12, 1865, George M. Whitney went before the church and publicly disfellowshipped his fellow elder, William Porter. The church records contain Porter's terse accounting of this action. He wrote:

> Had meeting at the church house and William L. Mascher preached on Christian Union. G. M. Whitney went through the farce of turning William Porter out of the church for Heresy—said Heresy being brought to light by said W. Porter asking D. W. Elledge to postpone offering his letter for membership on the ground of rumored Disloyalty to the U. S. Government.[42]

Whitney would not have had the support of the entire congregation in this action, and there is no evidence that Porter ever left the church. As it turned out, the Elledge family soon left the community and moved to another county. April brought news of the cessation of the Civil War and the assassination of President Lincoln, but the Mill Creek Church remained hopelessly divided. For the next two and a half years the congregation only met sporadically, and there was no rapprochement of the Porter and Whitney factions.

On September 15, 1867, Porter noted in the church records: "Congregation met at the usual place of meeting, and unanimously voted to withdraw fellowship from G. M. Whitney for disorderly conduct."[43] It had taken nearly three years, but William Porter and his friends had reestablished control of the Mill Creek Church. There is no evidence that Whitney was adversely affected by this action. He soon moved to Lane County where he was welcomed enthusiastically by the Christian Church in Eugene. It is not known for certain if the friendship between Porter and Whitney was ever restored, but it is assumed that they must have labored together again in Marion County in the 1870s when Whitney was preaching in meetings.

Like Mulkey and Bushnell, William Porter and George M. Whitney were two of the most energetic leaders in the church and Oregon Christians could not afford to lose the talents of either one. Fortunately, both men remained in the harness. Porter lived to 1899 and was a prominent church leader in Marion County for the rest of his life. Whitney continued to live in Eugene until his death in 1895. He became one of the most effective evangelists in Oregon.

The Changing of the Guard

Oregon did lose several preachers during the war years. Glen Owen Burnett, A. V. McCarty, H. H. Hendrix, and Levi Burch had already moved to California prior to the war, and by 1862 the Charles Bradshaw family had joined them. William Thompson Haley would soon follow them. Alfred R. Elder moved to Washington Territory in 1862, and Dr. John Nelson Perkins followed him there a year or two later. William Lysander Adams and Dr. James McBride were now serving political appointments, although Adams may have done some preaching in Clatsop County. Thomas Crawford McBride and John Rigdon had died prior to the war, and James R. Fisher died at Pleasant Hill on March 22, 1864, when he was only 45 years old.[44]

From the perspective of available preachers, there was a partial changing of the guard for Oregon churches in the middle of the Civil War. Adjusting to the loss of so much preaching talent was difficult, but Oregon Christians were cheered with the emergence of some younger preachers such as George M. Whitney, Joseph H. Sharp, William L. Mascher, Daniel Boone Matheny, and Orlando Alderman. Equally encouraging was the wartime migration of three outstanding preachers to their state. Keathley Bailes and Daniel W. Elledge in Marion County and Martin Peterson in Jackson County would have been great additions in any decade, but their arrival between 1862 and 1864 was of vital importance to the renewed spiritual health of Oregon churches.[45]

1858–1863

1858		1863	
1. Monmouth (Polk)	111	1. McMinnville (Yamhill)	117
2. Silver Creek (Marion)	105	2. Monmouth (Polk)	111
3. Pleasant Hill (Lane)	98	3. Silver Creek (Marion)	96
4. Bethel (Polk)	80	4. Pleasant Hill (Lane)	82
5. Mill Creek (Marion)	62	5. Bethel (Polk)	80
6. Central (Linn)	55	6. Eola (Polk)	73
7. Luckiamute (Polk)	52	7. Central (Linn)	70
8. Clackamas (Clackamas)	45	8. Grand Prairie (Lane)	54
9. Salem (Marion)	43	9. Luckiamute (Polk)	43
10. Monroe (Benton)	41	10. Scio (Linn)	43
11. Liberty House (Benton)	41	11. Mill Creek (Marion)	40
12. Salt Creek (Polk)	39	12. Upper Muddy (Lane)	40
13. McMinnville (Yamhill)	38	13. Salt Creek (Polk)	39

The most striking fact about the annual State Meetings in 1858 and 1863 was that approximately half of the functioning congregations did not send a representative or a written report. The lack of effective communication between congregations was continuing to hamper the overall progress of the Restoration Movement in the state. In an effort to organize the state more effectively for both intra-congregational communication and evangelism, chairman John Ecles Murphy appointed a five-man committee to divide the state into districts. The five members of this crucial committee were: John Alkire Powell (Linn County), Samuel Bates Briggs (Douglas County), Philip Mulkey (Lane County), William Thompson Haley (Polk County), and Hiram Alva Johnson (Marion County).

This committee divided Oregon into the following seven districts: (1) Douglas and Coos counties; (2) Lane and Benton counties; (3) Linn and Marion counties and Lane County north of the McKenzie River and east of the Willamette River; (4) Clackamas County and Multnomah County east of the Willamette River; (5) Polk, Yamhill, and Washington counties; (6) Columbia, Clatsop and Tillamook counties, and Multnomah west of the Willamette River; and (7) Wasco County and all territory east of the Cascade Mountains.[49]

When John A. Powell submitted a report of this annual State Meeting for the readers of the *Evangelist,* he was obviously much encouraged by the results. He wrote:

> The business part of the meeting was conducted with great harmony and good feeling throughout . . . . The meeting closed on Tuesday with thirty-three or thirty-four additions . . . . The attendance at the meeting was large throughout, with marked attention, and was one of the most happy meetings that I ever attended. The brethren were much edified and stirred up.[50]

Hope for the Future

On this optimistic note the delegates adjourned, pledging to meet again at McMinnville in a little more than eight months. The date had been set for Thursday, June 17, 1864.[51] John Ecles Murphy and G. W. Richardson traveled and preached through Polk and Yamhill counties during the last three months of the year and reported "twenty-six additions to the army of the faithful." When they preached in Monmouth in December 1863, "fifteen made the good confession and were buried with their Lord in the liquid grave."[52] In April 1864, they preached together in Amity and baptized eight more persons into Christ.[53]

A. L. Todd was also very busy in Douglas County during the last years of the war. According to his son, in 1864–65 Todd organized churches at Deer Creek, Pine Grove Schoolhouse, Cox Schoolhouse, Robert's Creek, and Green's Schoolhouse. Soon after, he organized churches at Oakland, Camas Swale, Calapooia, and Fair Oaks. Todd was the first Christian preacher to evangelize in Coos County, and he was most likely the first Christian preacher to travel in Curry County as well.[54]

Confronting the demoralizing reality of a nation engulfed in a prolonged conflict, the Oregon preachers were discovering that their war-weary neighbors were again interested in hearing the gospel of the prince of peace. A young 27-year-old preacher named William L. Mascher, whose father had been a leader in the Bethany Church for the past 14 years, sensed that a new chapter of opportunity was opening for the Restoration Movement in Oregon. Corresponding with the readers of the *Evangelist*, he declared, "Never have the prospects for pure and primitive Christianity been any brighter in Oregon than they are at present."[55]

The prospects may have been bright, but preaching the gospel was not without its dangers. The oldest daughter of A. L. Todd remembered a time when she accompanied her father to his regular preaching appointment at Myrtle Creek in 1865. On this particular Saturday afternoon, after he had preached his sermon, a woman indicated that she was ready to be baptized into Christ. Years later, Cynthia Todd, who was just a teenager at the time, described the subsequent events. She wrote:

> Just as we started to the river, which was near by, a woman came to me and said, "I am afraid for your father to baptize that woman, for her husband says he will shoot the man who baptizes her." Of course I was frightened. I hurried on and caught up with my father and told him what the woman had said, and begged him not to baptize her. He said, "It is the Lord's work and I am not afraid to do it." On arriving at the river bank, my fears were intensified by seeing the man, the husband of the candidate, sitting on the bank of the river with his rifle in his lap.[56]

Thankfully, the husband refrained from shooting the preacher, and A. L. Todd lived to preach in Douglas County and the surrounding counties for another 20 years. Todd felt he had no choice but to fulfill the obligations of his calling as a minister of the gospel of Christ. As one of his children has written, "It seemed that if he could not preach the gospel, he could not live."[57]

Oregon Christians had survived the war years. They could not know it at the time, but they were about to enter an exciting 20-year period of growth and unification that future historians would refer to as the "Golden Age" of the Restoration Movement in Oregon.

Chapter 19

A Christian in the Governor's Mansion

1866-1869

We have many good and able brethren in the church here who labor in the word and doctrine from time to time. Of that number is the talented Governor of the State, Brother G. L. Woods. If he could devote his entire time to the ministry, he would have but few equals; but he is a politician, and has too many duties to perform to do much preaching at present.

— Joseph Warren Downer, Salem, Oregon,
December 27, 1869

When the delegates assembled for the annual State Meeting in Linn County in October 1863, they were worried about the future of Christian education in their state. Bethel College, after a promising beginning, had become a casualty of the Civil War. It was forced to terminate its college work in 1862. A published history of the college explained the predicament that forced the trustees to act:

> When the war came on, the sale of lots diminished and collections on those previously sold were likewise affected. All things taken together including financial difficulties for the individuals who were bearing the responsibility reduced the income to such an extent that they felt they could carry it no further with any degree of satisfaction. They still had plenty of land but it was not readily convertible into legal tender under wartime conditions.[1]

Christian College

The trustees of Monmouth University were struggling to keep their own doors open, but the future looked increasingly bleak. Haunted by the specter of Oregon being without a church-related college for Christian youth, a committee of delegates at the State Meeting put forward the following resolution: "We recommend to the favorable consideration of the brotherhood in the annual meeting convened, the propriety of establishing an institution of learning to be called The Christian College, to be located by a board of trustees to be appointed by the annual meeting."[2] There is no direct evidence that this specific resolution was carried into action, but as one historian has noted, "the annual meeting set in motion a series of events that resulted, in 1865, in the creation of Christian College at Monmouth out of the materials of both Bethel College and Monmouth University."[3]

The friends of Bethel College were disappointed that Christian College would not be housed in their fine two-story facility, but the Monmouth location had several advantages. To begin with, Monmouth University had managed to stay open throughout the war years and the Monmouth Church was in a healthier condition at the moment. Perhaps more significant for the future of Christian College, the Monmouth site had 540 acres of land and the Bethel site was limited to 261 acres. On December 18, 1865, the charter of Monmouth University was amended to change the name to Christian College.[4]

The charter that was adopted for Bethel Institute in February 1856, listed nine men on the board of trustees. The charter that created Monmouth University a month later listed 11 men on the board of trustees.[5] Nineteen of these 20 board members were known to be strong church leaders in the Restoration Movement. Interestingly, not one of these 19 men was represented on the new 11-member board of trustees that created Christian College in December 1865. It appears that church leaders wanted a fresh beginning for Christian College, and they deliberately selected persons who would be well received by constituents from both of the former colleges.

The new board included: William Dawson, Sebastian C. Adams, Alfred Stanton, William Murphy, G. W. Richardson, Levi Lindsay Rowland, Nathaniel Hudson, John A. Frazer, B. F. Whitson, A. W. Lucas, and Daniel Holman. Of these 11 men, only Nathaniel Hudson was not a Christian.[6] Their first order of business was to agree on a president for the college. The president would need to be a strong churchman who could inspire all Oregon Christians to feel a sense of ownership and pride in their new college at Monmouth.

The unanimous choice to head the new institution was Levi Lindsay Rowland. This graduate of Bethany College had served as president of Bethel College during its two years of operation, and he was one of the most highly-respected men in the church in Oregon. His wife, Emma Sanders, had been educated at Tolbert Fanning's Franklin College in Nashville, Tennessee. The Rowlands accepted the challenge of the board of trustees and moved to Monmouth in 1866. When Christian College began its first session in the fall of 1866, Levi Lindsay Rowland was just celebrating his 35th birthday. He guided the progress of the young college for three crucial and formative years, and then he moved to Salem to join the medical college faculty at Willamette University. After Rowland's second year as president, one Christian preacher wrote that Christian College was "in a more prosperous condition than ever before."[7]

The McBride-Woods-Adams Connection

Thomas Crawford McBride (1777-1857) was a grand patriarchal figure in the Restoration Movement. Two of his children, James and Margaret, were strong Christians in Missouri and Oregon, and two of their sons, John Rogers McBride and George Lemuel Woods, were born within three weeks of each other in the summer of 1832. These first cousins, and proud grandsons of Thomas Crawford McBride, were reared together and were the best of friends. When George married John's sister, Louisa, they became brothers-in-law in addition to being first cousins. When William Lysander Adams, a graduate of Bethany College, came to Oregon and opened his "Yamhill University," John and George and their good friend, Levi Lindsay Rowland, sat at his feet. The three teenagers were inspired by Adams to dream big dreams for their vocational futures.

Sebastian Adams, younger brother of William Lysander Adams and older brother of Eunice, arrived in Oregon in 1850. He fell in love with Martha McBride, John's older sister, and married her in 1851. John, in turn, married Eunice Adams in 1852, and George Woods married Louisa McBride in the same year. The McBride-Woods-Adams connection was now complete, and within two years, William Lysander Adams had launched his editorial career with the *Oregon Argus,* and the three strong Christian families were working together to change the political map of Oregon Territory. From their united efforts, as well as from the assistance of Christian friends like Amos Harvey and Samuel M. Gilmore, came the birth of the Republican Party in Oregon.[8]

Will Adams claimed that he started the *Oregon Argus* because he was afraid the "Slavocrats" would persuade the people of Oregon to adopt a pro-slavery position. It was Adams who called together the first Republican Convention at Albany in February 1857. Abraham Lincoln was a subscriber to the *Oregon Argus* and an admirer of the writings of Adams, and Adams reciprocated with unabashed support for Lincoln. One of the friends of Adams observed, "There are two subjects he never allows to be assailed in his hearing without speaking in their defense—'Abe Lincoln and the New Testament.'"[9] Another contemporary said that Adams was "the chief informer, energizer, and rally center of the distinctly anti-slavery forces of that day and generation."[10] Because of his stature as a popular preacher for Oregon Christians and his frequent moralizing in the *Oregon Argus,* Adams was often called "Parson Billy" by the rival *Oregon Statesman.*[11]

John Rogers McBride and George Lemuel Woods were proud of their heritage in the Restoration Movement. Toward the end of his life, George Woods reflected on the spiritual heritage of his parents and wrote:

> My parents were life-long members of the Christian church, and I was borne along upon its bosom from early boyhood, accepting its faith and obeying its precepts as best I could. From across the threshold of its temple, my mother, whom I loved with an idolatrous devotion, passed full of faith and hope to her eternal reward. And my venerable father, still with me in manly courage and unfaltering footsteps, "has fought the fight and kept the faith," and in Christian cheerfulness is awaiting a home and a crown. To me they and their lives and the Christian church are inseparable.[12]

McBride and Woods were shaped by powerful preaching models during their young professional years. Their grandfather was legendary, and Dr. James McBride was one of the leading proclaimers of the gospel of Christ in Oregon. The Adams brothers were equally strong in the pulpit. Young McBride and Woods probably did some public speaking at church gatherings, but they really cut their oratorical teeth on the political stump of the Republican Party. Hubert Howe Bancroft has written:

> Another who began his public speaking with the formation of the Republican Party in Oregon was George L. Woods. His subsequent success in public life is the best evidence of his abilities. He was cousin to John R. McBride . . . both were friends and neighbors of W. L. Adams, and the three, with their immediate circle of relatives and friends, carried considerable weight into the Republican ranks.[13]

McBride's political career blossomed quickly. He served in the legislature and then was elected twice to the state senate. In 1862 he won election to the United States House of Representatives. Following his stay in the nation's capital, he was given a presidential appointment as chief justice of Idaho Territory. Woods was admitted to the bar in 1858, and by 1863 he had become probate judge of Wasco County and was helpful to the small congregation of Christians meeting at The Dalles. Sebastian Adams was elected county clerk of Yamhill County in 1862, and after serving six years, he won election as a state senator. Levi Lindsay Rowland had returned from Bethany College to be president of Bethel College and later Christian College.

Meanwhile, William Lysander Adams had accepted his appointment from Abraham Lincoln and was serving as Collector of the Port at Astoria, and Dr. James McBride had accepted his presidential appointment and was serving as United States Minister to the Sandwich Islands (later, the Hawaiian Islands). It was during his stay in Hawaii that McBride became friends with Admiral Enquist, the commander of the Russian fleet that was stationed in Honolulu. Convinced by frequent conversations with this officer that Russia was willing to dispose of Alaska Territory, McBride began writing a series of persuasive letters to William Henry Seward, Lincoln's Secretary of State, urging this acquisition. Of this correspondence initiated by McBride, the author of *History of the Pacific Northwest* has written:

> Nor were his efforts wasted. In Secretary Seward he found a statesman capable of sympathizing with his patriotic desire to extend the area of his country; and, as soon as the storm of the Civil War had spent its force, the purchase was consummated, and the greatest acquisition since the Louisiana Purchase added to our national domain. It may be fairly said that Doctor McBride was the author of the Alaska purchase . . .[14]

The Watershed Year of 1866

Historians of the Restoration Movement have long noted the significance of the first full calendar year following the end of the Civil War and the assassination of President Lincoln. The death of Alexander Campbell on March 4, 1866, removed the man who had been the most celebrated leader in the movement's pioneer generation. His passing alone would have made 1866 significant, but several other developments combined to make this a dramatic turning point in the history of the movement. In this year Benjamin Franklin, editor of the *American Christian Review*, changed his editorial policy and began to oppose the concept of missionary societies. For the next 12 years (until his death in 1878) he inherited the mantle of Campbell and became the most influential leader in the movement. In the same year of 1866, Isaac Errett established the *Christian Standard,* and through his support of the missionary society concept, he became the most visible competitor to Franklin's editorial dominance of the movement.

In the war-torn South, Tolbert Fanning and David Lipscomb resurrected the *Gospel Advocate* in 1866. This significant journal, begun in 1855, had been forced to cease publication during the war years. It would become the leading voice for southern Christians for the remainder of the century and beyond. Perhaps more significant for Oregon Christians was the announcement by James Madison Mathes in Indiana that he would begin to edit the *Christian Record* again. Samuel Denny wrote to Mathes from Albany and said that he rejoiced when he learned that Mathes "had again taken the great and glorious responsibility of editing that very welcome visitor, the *Christian Record,* of which [he had] now received five numbers." Denny continued, "It comes to us like a good father to his children, or like a good shepherd to feed his flock, or to see that no harm should come to them."[15]

The watershed year of 1866 witnessed a turning point for the Restoration Movement in Oregon as well. At the end of 1865 and the beginning of 1866, an Indiana preacher named John M. Harris, who had just arrived in the state, "rode through the entire rainy season, and did not lose a single appointment" in the Willamette Valley. His powerful preaching resulted in 256 additions to the church.[16] On the second Lord's Day in January, Mac Waller preached for the church in Dallas and had nine additions. "One lady, upwards of seventy years old, who had taken a solemn oath that she would never hear Waller preach, was prevailed upon to hear him," commented one observer. "She did so, and was buried with the Lord in baptism."[17]

A. V. McCarty had moved back to Oregon in the summer of 1865, and he was surprised to find that he was drawing larger audiences than he had in California. "There appears to be a great anxiety and readiness among the people," he noted, "to hear the pure, limpid gospel as it gushed from the hearts and poured from the tongues of inspired men." When he preached in Corvallis, the county seat of Benton County, in January 1866, he was "really surprised at the interest taken in the ancient gospel."[18]

On the last Sunday in January, McCarty preached at Buena Vista in Polk County "and a young Methodist minister came out boldly, made the good confession, and was buried with his Lord." McCarty wrote admiringly, "He had no change of clothes, but still he demanded immersion without delay. He said that he would rather ride home in wet clothes than go without a good conscience."[19] McCarty returned to Corvallis in February and immersed seven converts. "I have also hunted up the scattered sheep of that place, who have been without a shepherd," he told a California friend, "and have collected forty together into a congregation."[20] The new church had asked him to preach for them, and McCarty informed his California correspondents that he was now living in Corvallis.

When the new year of 1866 dawned in Oregon, two of the most talented young preachers in the state, William L. Mascher and Peter R. Burnett, were laboring together in several meetings in Marion County. Their efforts resulted in "thirty-five additions to the Church, mostly by confession and baptism."[21] It was a good omen of things to come. These second-generation Oregon Christians were eager to follow the example of church involvement and leadership set by their dedicated fathers, C. Frederick Mascher and Glen Owen Burnett.

Another second-generation Oregon Christian was ready to move onto center stage. George Lemuel Woods became the Republican candidate for governor of Oregon in the spring of 1866. He was just 33 years old when he won the closely contested election in June, but he had turned 34 by the time his four-year term began on September 12. The election of George Woods was a boon to the small and struggling congregation of Christians in Salem. Within the first year of his arrival, Woods had persuaded the congregation to erect a $7,000 brick church building on the corner of Center and North High Streets and to call Peter Rogers Burnett to be their preacher. This 25-year-old son of Glen Owen Burnett was a multi-talented preacher, and even though he remained in the capital city for only two years, they were years of solid organization and growth for the Salem Church.

August 2, 1867, was a mountaintop experience for the little band that Peter Rogers Burnett called "The Church of Christ in Salem." The assembled congregation selected elders and deacons for the first time, and the ministry of Peter Burnett officially began. The four elders appointed were: Governor George Woods, Caleb P. Chapman (who had preached in Oregon for nearly 20 years), Thomas Ladd, and Hezekiah Burford. Alfred Stanton and Joseph Warren Downer were chosen as deacons, and William P. Murphy, a son of John Ecles Murphy, was named clerk of the congregation. When the congregation dedicated the "Little Brick Church" on September 22, 1867, there were 75 active members on the church roll. In just one year of residence in the Governor's Mansion, the grandson of Thomas Crawford McBride had made a substantial contribution to the cause of Christ in Oregon's capital city.

Trying to establish a strong congregation in the Methodist stronghold of Salem, even with the assistance of devout Christians in state government, was an uphill battle. In September 1868, halfway through the term of Governor Woods, Peter Burnett described the situation to James Mathes:

> The Church of Christ in Salem was organized in the summer of 1867, a little over one year ago . . . we have kept up our meetings from that time to the present, and we now number nearly one hundred members . . . . About two years ago the brethren determined to erect a meeting house, where they could worship God according to the Primitive manner. After many delays and disappointments, the house was built, and the brethren thanked the Lord and took courage. Meanwhile sectarianism had been at work until it seemed the city was "wholly given to idolatry." But by the blessing of our kind Heavenly Father we shall succeed in firmly establishing the cause in this city of the West.[22]

The return of Peter R. Burnett to Oregon, following his graduation from Hesperian College in Woodland, California, was applauded by Oregon Christians everywhere—and with good reason. His father had been one of the hardest working and most beloved preachers in the state, and Peter showed promise of following in the same tradition. For the next half-century, until his death in Eugene, Oregon in 1922, Peter Rogers Burnett would be a prince in the pulpit for the Restoration Movement in California and Oregon.

John M. Harris and Daniel W. Elledge

It was not only the arrival of young Peter R. Burnett that made the future look bright. At the conclusion of the Civil War, Oregon Christians welcomed several new evangelists to their state. Among the most valuable were two veteran preachers: 62-year-old John M. Harris from Indiana and Illinois and 52-year-old Daniel W. Elledge from Illinois and Missouri. For the next 15 years, the contagious evangelistic spirit and wise counsel of these soldiers of the cross would bring a much-needed spiritual maturity to the advancement of primitive Christianity in the Pacific states.

John Moses Harris was born in Stanford, Kentucky, on April 1, 1803. One record noted: "He was fourteen years of age when his father joined the Shakers at Shakertown, Kentucky, there spending the remainder of his life, as also did his daughter."[23] John remained with the Shakers four years, and then he ran away to Indiana. In 1827 he married Jane Wilson, whose family were all devout Christians. John Harris was baptized into Christ in 1827 and began preaching in 1828. He preached in Indiana for nearly 30 years before moving to Adams County, Illinois, around 1857. He crossed the plains to Oregon in 1865.

Daniel W. Elledge was born in Bourbon County, Kentucky, in 1813. His parents, who were "Hardshell Baptists," moved to Edgar County, Illinois in 1816. Soon after his marriage in 1831, Daniel Elledge became affiliated with the Restoration Movement. He was baptized into Christ by an Indiana preacher named Michael Combs, and he began to preach almost immediately. For the next 20 years his ministry was confined mainly to Edgar, Clark, and Cole counties in Illinois.

He sold his Clark County farm in 1853 and moved to Putnam County, Missouri within three miles of the Iowa state line.[24] Concerning his ministry in Illinois, Missouri, and Iowa, he wrote, "I had with my own hands immersed over three thousand persons."[25] Elledge preceded John M. Harris on the Oregon Trail. He came across the plains in the spring and summer of 1864.

A Renaissance for Oregon Christians

The end of the Civil War brought a change of fortune for Churches of Christ in Oregon. After years of treading water, the Restoration Movement began to show signs of moving forward again. John M. Harris arrived in the Willamette Valley in September 1865 and "commenced riding and preaching the first of October." In less than 10 months of labor, his ministry resulted in 256 additions to the church. It was the harbinger of good things to come.

When he preached the funeral of Elizabeth Barger, the daughter of Philip Mulkey, in July 1866, there were a thousand persons present. He used the occasion to proclaim the gospel of Christ, and "five noble souls confessed and obeyed the Lord, our King." On the following Sunday he preached at Pleasant Hill in the same county and had seven additions. One week later he returned to preach in Eugene on Saturday and Sunday and immersed 10 more persons into Christ.[26]

In the summer of 1867, Peter R. Burnett reported to James Mathes:

> The cause of Christ in the State is still making some progress. Several meetings have lately been held over the country, resulting in a number of additions to the church. At a meeting held by Brother Callison in the Umpqua Valley, there were some twenty immersed. Brother Richardson immersed about half-a-dozen not long since, during a meeting held by him. At a meeting held in Salem, the capital of the State, there were five additions. Brother K. Bailes and myself lately held a meeting at which there were fifteen added by immersion, and one who had been a member of the Church of Christ before.[27]

Gradually the wartime wounds of sectional strife were healed. When John M. Harris paid a visit to the Pleasant Hill Church of Christ after the war, he "found it in a very cold situation—divided on the war question." Nevertheless, "they came together as brethren ought" for their gospel meeting with Harris, and there were 52 additions to the church.[28] Harris held a meeting with the Dallas Church in Polk County in February 1868, and there were not only eight persons added to the church, but church unity was restored. "They had been divided on account of some difficulty growing out of politics, for about three years," Harris explained to Mathes.[29]

The situation was similar at Grand Prairie in Lane County where inflamed political feelings had destroyed the unity of Christians during wartime. Both church unity and renewed growth returned to the churches of Lane County in the post-war years, and one resident of the county proudly informed Mathes in 1869, "The Church of Christ predominates in this county, notwithstanding the opposition we have to meet from all the sects."[30]

John M. Harris was persuaded that the Restoration Movement in Oregon would not accomplish all that it should until there were strong congregations in Portland and Oregon City. With Samuel Bailey as a co-laborer in the spring of 1868, Harris set out to establish churches in both of these urban centers. The preachers discovered "some thirty or forty members" in Portland, and after preaching for five evenings, they would have organized a congregation except for two reasons: "1st. The brethren had no place to meet in for worship. 2nd. We made a proposition to the Baptists for union upon the Bible *alone*, and they had some thought of accepting it. We deferred the organization to give them time to think over the matter, and to determine the question." In Oregon City they preached five discourses and organized a congregation of sixteen members.[31]

The potential merger of Christians and Baptists in Portland was never consummated, but the very fact that it was considered is a commentary on the fraternal feelings between the two immersionist groups in the post-war years. This was partially attributable to their work together in the American Bible Union, and to their mutual longing for a more accurate English translation of the Bible. C. A. Buckbee, a noted Baptist and an agent of the American Bible Union, visited Oregon in 1868 and was given a good reception by both Christians and Baptists. Buckbee corresponded with W. K. Pendleton, Alexander Campbell's son-in-law and the new editor of the *Millennial Harbinger*:

> I am now attending . . . a meeting at Sheridan with Elder G. W. Richardson of Bethel. Elder G. O. Burnett, of California, is also here. The word preached has been mixed with faith in some hearers. Three have yielded to Christ, and the immersion of two Methodists today has ended their doubts on the subject of baptism. The cause of the Bible Union all along this coast meets a cordial welcome by the Christian and Baptist churches.[32]

Buckbee also attended the annual State Meeting of Christians in June, and once again he was warmly embraced as a brother. In a report on the meeting published in the *Christian Record,* John M. Harris wrote:

> We had with us our beloved brother, C. A. Buckbee, of Bible Union notoriety. He is laboring earnestly to promote union between the Baptists and ourselves. He is a host in himself. And a great amount of sectarian prejudice was removed during the meeting, and a very large amount of Christian love and affection was manifested, and we feel sure that the cause of our blessed Master received an onward impulse in Oregon.[33]

The "onward impulse" of the cause in 1868 was well documented in the *Christian Record.* Gilmore Callison, Daniel Elledge, and John M. Harris organized a church of 16 members in Lane County, 25 miles southwest of Eugene, in May. "Here is the best prospect for doing good I have seen for months," enthused Harris.[34] During the course of the annual State Meeting in June, there were 41 additions, including 37 immersions.[35] G. W. Richardson reported in July, "During the past year, the churches for which I labored have had about 80 additions, mostly by immersion. And the prospect was never better than now."[36] Harris organized a church of 12 members in Brownsville in Linn County in September, and in a short time it numbered more than 20.[37] Near the close of the year James W. Butler, the president of Abingdon College in Illinois, visited Monmouth and preached in a meeting. There were 20 additions, and most of those were immersions.[38] Not surprisingly, Richardson's assessment of the progress of the movement in 1868 was upbeat and optimistic: "I rejoice to say that the cause of the Lord is now advancing in Oregon."[39]

The cause in Oregon was indeed flourishing, but the shortage of laborers was a matter of great concern. Peter R. Burnett used the columns of the *Christian Record* in the fall of 1868 to make an impassioned plea for more preachers to move to Oregon. Sounding like the president of the local chamber of commerce, the young preacher wrote persuasively:

> Salem is beautifully located on the right bank of the Willamette River, and is a great field for preaching the gospel—in truth there is no better field, in my opinion for faithful laborers, than the young State of Oregon. If two or three able, earnest, faithful preachers, men of influence, would come to this country, they could accomplish great good for our Lord. The harvest, indeed, is plentiful, but the laborers are very, very few.
>
> Oregon offers superior advantages to any who may wish to come. It possesses, in many respects, a delightful climate, the most beautiful scenery in the world, beautiful vales, and rippling brooks, a rich soil, good schools, and everything conducive to the happiness of all. Who will come?[40]

The Growth of the State Meetings

The annual State Meetings served to unify the Christians. "Cut off as we are from all the rest of the world," noted one preacher, "our State Meetings are a necessity, in order to preserve the unity of the faith."[41] These events were not only occasions for gathering information on the current progress of the cause, but they were opportunities for younger Christians to mingle with the pioneer preachers who had planted primitive Christianity in Oregon soil. Dr. James McBride and

Glen Owen Burnett were reunited at the 1868 State Meeting. McBride had returned to Oregon after four years in Honolulu, and Burnett was now a resident of California. Twenty-two years earlier they had preached together on the Oregon Trail. They were joined in preaching at the 1868 State Meeting by Elijah Davidson, John Alkire Powell, and John Ecles Murphy. "Their tender and fatherly exhortations and admonitions seemed as a voice from the tomb," wrote G. W. Richardson, "And well did the people seem to feel their solemn appeal."[42]

One veteran preacher missing from the 1868 State Meeting was John Foster, who had died just three months earlier on March 22 in Clackamas County. This pioneer of 1845 had been the first preacher from the Restoration Movement to arrive in Oregon Territory. For more than 20 years he had preached for and nurtured his little congregation on the Clackamas River about seven miles out of Oregon City. One church historian wrote, "Foster continued to preach for this church until he was an old man. When he finally gave up preaching he could talk for only a few minutes at a time."[43]

The Restoration Movement lost another dedicated proclaimer of the gospel in 1868 when Alexander Vance McCarty died on October 10. He was only 43 years old. McCarty had returned to California and was preaching for the church in Vacaville when he contracted a fever and died within a few months.[44]

Two other pioneer preachers, Daniel Trullinger of Clackamas County and Gilmore Callison of Lane County, died in early 1869. Trullinger was 68 and had been preaching in Oregon for 20 years. Twelve years later his widow, Elizabeth Trullinger, submitted a letter to the *Pacific Christian Messenger* in which she recalled the impact of her husband's ministry in Oregon. She wrote:

> I was immersed into Christ in 1818, and have lived in the Christian Church ever since, for nearly forty years. My companion was an evangelist, traveling and preaching, and I went as often as I could with him, and when I could not go, my prayers went with him that our Father in heaven would be as a wall of fire around him to shield him from all harm, and present himself faultless before His throne, and it

> was seldom that he returned without sheaves. The last time he was at Monmouth he gathered in fourteen. He preached through six counties in Oregon, and immersed in every stream in Oregon from the Calapooia to the Columbia river.[45]

Gilmore Callison was only 60 and had been very active in gospel meetings and was preaching for the church in Eugene until shortly before his death.[46] At the State Meeting in June 1869, G. W. Richardson observed, "But many hearts were made sad, and eyes to fill with tears, when we found not our beloved Brother Callison present. This devoted servant of Christ had been called to his reward since our last meeting."[47]

From its beginning in 1852, the annual State Meeting moved to a different location every year until the establishment of the "Christian camp ground" ten miles west of Salem sometime around 1866 or 1867.[48] G. W. Richardson wrote in 1869, "Our State Meetings are now uniformly held at the same place, on the banks of the Rickreall, near a little town called Dixie."[49] The town that Richardson called "Dixie" was also known as Rickreall. This was the area in Polk County where Nat Ford and David Goff had settled in 1845. One record confirmed, "During the Civil War and for some time thereafter Rickreall village was frequently referred to as Dixie because of Southern sentiment in the community. The name Dixie was used colloquially for several decades . . ."[50]

In the earlier years, the State Meeting was designed as a four-day event, beginning on a Friday and closing on a Monday. Usually the attendance was limited to the host church and to delegates and leaders from other congregations. However, not long after the move to the Christian camp ground at Rickreall the meetings grew to become 12-day family encampments. These meetings traditionally would begin on a Thursday or Friday and embrace two Lord's days and close on Monday. The attendance at these family encampments increased dramatically in the post-war years. When the 1868 State Meeting resulted in 37 immersions and a total of 41 additions to the church, Richardson commented, "Take our State Meeting altogether, it was the nearest a perfect success of any that have ever been held in the state;

though some of our former meetings have resulted in great good."[51]

The attendance at the 1869 State Meeting was the largest to that time. The audience for the Sunday sessions was estimated at between 5,000 and 6,000. Richardson called it "one of the most happy meetings that I ever attended," and he was amazed that "notwithstanding the vast concourse of people, we had good order."[52] John M. Harris was equally impressed with the 1869 encampment, and he called it "the most remarkable meeting that I ever attended."[53] It is certain there were not 5,000 members of the Restoration Movement in Oregon. The State Meetings had become social and spiritual phenomena that drew large crowds of interested spectators, many of whom had very little knowledge of what the Christians believed. With so many non-Christians in attendance, it is not surprising that there were a large number of immersions each summer in Rickreall Creek. There were 33 immersions during the 1869 encampment.[54]

The Progress of the Cause

Sebastian Adams became a state senator in 1868, but he continued to preach often for the Christians. On his visit to Washington Territory in May 1869, the *Vancouver Register* published the following item:

> Honorable Sebastian C. Adams, Senator from Yamhill County, Oregon, is in the city . . . . He is a Campbellite preacher of fine abilities and bears the reputation before the public of a worthy Christian gentleman. He thinks of soon taking charge of a congregation in Salem, Oregon. Mr. Adams is a brother of W. L. Adams, formerly editor of the Oregon City *Argus* . . . .[55]

Dr. James McBride was not pleased with this description of his son-in-law as a "Campbellite," and he refused to let it pass. Writing from his home in St. Helens, Oregon, on June 10, Dr. McBride attempted to set the record straight. He wrote:

> In your paper for May 22nd, I find a very respectful notice of Honorable S. C. Adams, of Yamhill County, Oregon, in

> which you call him a "Campbellite" preacher etc. . . . The honorable bearings of your notice, very clearly evince your high respect for the man with no intentions to disparage his church. Yet, I have a right to object to the epithet, "Campbellite!"
>
> Mr. Campbell was neither the Father, nor lawgiver of the church . . . hence, the invidious epithet, *Campbellite,* is inappropriate and untrue.
>
> We are, however, proud to say that Mr. C. was one of us, from the time he united with us, until his death, and was an able defender of the Bible alone—a distinctive characteristic of our church.
>
> We only ask, and we do ask it as a courtesy due us, to be known and called by the name which we have chosen, and that is "Christian."
>
> If Mr. C. was our leader and lawgiver, it would be appropriate enough to call us *Campbellites*: yet, even at that, it would bear the marks of an invidious discourtesy, when it is known that we disown the name and take another.
>
> But as we take *Christ* for our leader and our only lawgiver, and take his word as our discipline, confession of faith, rules of decorum etc. . . . it is peculiarly appropriate that we should call ourselves *Christians*.
>
> As that improper epithet was used by you, (innocently, I doubt not), I regard this correction and defense through the same channel, as a privilege which you would not deny to anyone.[56]

Good reports abounded for 1869. John M. Harris and John Burris Smith had 29 additions, including 24 immersions, when they preached at Coast Fork in May.[57] In the middle of July, Harris reported from Albany: "During the last two months there have been sixty persons immersed in this part of Oregon, that I know of. And I think the prospect in Oregon is better now than for a year past."[58] Harris widened his circuit that fall and obtained 7 additions in the Rogue River Valley and 14 additions in the Umpqua Valley.[59] In November, George M. Whitney conducted a meeting at Oak Hill in Lane County that resulted in 40 additions. He followed that by teaming with John Ecles Murphy in a meeting at Springfield in the same county that resulted in 42 additions, "nearly all by confession and immersion."[60]

George M. Whitney rapidly was developing into one of the most effective evangelists in Oregon. When he and Philip Mulkey traveled to neighboring Benton County to preach in a meeting, there were 40 additions to the church.[61] "Brother Whitney is devoting his entire time to the ministry of the Word," marveled one of his friends, "having lost sight of every world interest, he is only intent in saving sinners and building up the Church."[62] Whitney gave all the credit to his mentor, the aged Philip Mulkey. "Our beloved old Brother, Philip Mulkey, is my exemplar and standard-bearer in all these meetings. The Lord spare him to this work, leaning upon his staff, till a strong young man be raised up to bear aloft the banner of truth."[63] Another Lane County Christian said of the veteran preacher, "Brother Mulkey is doing all that a man of his advanced age can do, and is greatly beloved by all who are acquainted with him. He is laboring with good success."[64]

The church at Oak Hill in Lane County met near the residence of Philip Mulkey and had been planted by him in 1867. Following Whitney's meeting in 1869, it had grown to include 120 members and was "in a very prosperous condition." One of Mulkey's friends called this church "the pride of his declining years."[65] Mulkey was also ministering to the church at Grand Prairie again. He and James Addison Bushnell had been reunited following the war, and the church in that community now numbered 40 members.

The church in the state capital was continuing to prosper, and there were 103 members by the fall of 1869. The "Little Brick Church" did not have a baptistry in the early years, and the congregation made use of the mill stream near the South Commercial Street bridge.[66] Although Peter R. Burnett had moved to California to preach in its capital city of Sacramento, the Salem Church was enjoying the ministry of Sebastian Adams, who was now a state senator. Levi Lindsay Rowland had also become a resident of Salem and was often available to preach for the church. He was beginning a new career in the medical college of Willamette University. One of the deacons, Joseph Warren Downer, wrote to James Mathes and gave an update on the situation in Salem:

> We have many good and able brethren in the church here, who labor in the word and doctrine from time to time. Of that number is the talented Governor of the State, Brother G. L. Woods. If he could devote his time to the ministry, he would have but few equals; but he is a politician, and has too many duties to perform to do much preaching at present.[67]

Three months later, Downer reported that the $7,000 brick church building in Salem was completely debt-free. "We are still prospering here," he informed Mathes, "twenty-two added since my last." One of the reasons for the growth was undoubtedly the ministry of Sebastian Adams. "He is a good speaker," declared Downer, "and one of the most devoted Christian brothers in the Lord." But Adams was struggling with his health, and Governor Woods and Levi Lindsay Rowland were often pressed into service.[68]

With the resignation of Levi Lindsay Rowland from the presidency of Christian College in the summer of 1869, the board of trustees began an aggressive search for a suitable replacement. The inspired choice of Thomas Franklin Campbell led Oregon Christians into a decade and more of unparalleled achievement in both Christian education and Christian journalism.

Chapter 20

Thomas Franklin Campbell of Monmouth

1870-1874

Men who have half a dozen irons in the fire, are not the ones to go crazy. It is the man of voluntary or compelled leisure who mopes and pines and thinks himself into the mad-house or the grave. Motion is in all of nature's laws. Action is man's salvation, physical and mental . . . he only is wise who lays out his work to life's latest hours.

— Thomas Franklin Campbell, *Christian Messenger,* September 16, 1871

When the board of trustees of Christian College began looking for a new president in 1869, their search led them to an energetic 47-year-old educator in Helena, Montana, named Thomas Franklin Campbell.[1] Reared in a Christian home in Mississippi, he had traveled to Bethany College to study under Alexander Campbell in 1848. Although unrelated to the Campbells, he had solidified his ties to the prominent family by marrying Jane Eliza Campbell, a first cousin to Alexander.

A New Leader for Oregon

Following his graduation from Bethany College in 1852, Thomas Franklin Campbell had preached and worked for Christian schools in Texas, Kansas, Missouri, and Montana for 17 years. In Helena he was preaching for the Christian Church and serving as its only elder. He was also conducting a boys school in his log cabin, and he had been appointed the territorial superintendent of schools by the governor of Montana.

Upon graduation from Bethany, Campbell had moved to East Texas to become president of church-related Mt. Enterprise Academy in Rusk County.[2] Alexander Campbell provided some publicity for this Christian school in the March 1855 *Millennial Harbinger*. "Its President is one of our best graduates of Bethany College," Campbell wrote proudly, "a brother of indomitable energy, who was recommended by us for that place, and whose talents, industry, and devotion to his duties, have equaled, as we learn, our highest anticipations of his capacity for such a position."[3] In the summer of 1857, Thomas Franklin Campbell returned to his alma mater to receive the honorary A.M. degree at the annual Bethany commencement ceremonies.[4]

Campbell was flattered by the offer from the representatives of Christian College, and he made the decision to move his family to Oregon. One history of the college noted: "In a Holladay Concord coach which had been used for stagecoach purposes, he placed his family and all his earthly possessions, and behind four white ponies made the one thousand mile journey to Monmouth."[5] Campbell initially may have been disappointed at the size of Christian College.[6] Although 540 acres of land had been donated for the college, there was only one two-story wood frame building on the campus, and this was used for both church and college purposes.

If Campbell had any misgivings about the decision to move his family to Monmouth, he never expressed them. He evidently saw enormous potential in both the church and the college, and he immediately threw himself into the task to which he had been called. At the close of his first year in Monmouth he summed up his labors in the following report:

> We arrived at Monmouth on the last day of August, 1869. We commenced preaching on the 4th of September, and opened the Christian College, at this place, on the 6th of the same month. Since that time up to the 1st of September, 1870, we made one hundred and seventy-five sermons, on fifty-three different texts and topics, made four lectures on

> education, and one temperance address. The immediate result of our preaching was sixty-three added to the church at the several points where we preached, besides the thirty-nine added at the annual meeting under the joint labors of the brethren present. The Lord has preserved and blessed us abundantly, and has given us health and strength to serve our generation, we trust yet more abundantly in the twelve months upon which we have now entered. May His kingdom spread and His name be exalted above every name, until every knee shall bow, and every tongue shall confess to his glory![7]

The Rowland-Calloway Debate on Baptism

Oregon may have had a new president at the helm of Christian College, but the former president was still very involved in the progress of the Restoration Movement. As a professor in the medical school at Willamette University and a leader in the Salem Church, Levi Lindsay Rowland continued to be one of the most respected church leaders in the state When an opportunity arose in the summer of 1870 for a public debate on the action and subject of baptism with a presiding elder in the Methodist Church, the Christians chose Rowland to represent their cause.

The debate was announced for June 13-16 near the city of Dallas in Polk County. The date was deliberately set between the annual meetings of the Methodists and the Christians, both of whom used the facilities of the "Christian camp ground" near Rickreall. With hundreds of church-going visitors in the county, a large attendance was assured. It is quite probable that the debate took place at the camp ground in order to accommodate the large crowds that would be interested in the discussion.

One account of the debate said of Rev. J. B. Calloway, Rowland's opponent: "Mr. Calloway is an experienced debater, and enjoys the hearty endorsement of his denomination as 'chief of his Conference.' He labored earnestly and faithfully, and was supported by two prominent ministers of his church." Calloway began the four-day discussion with "much courage," according to a report published in the *Millennial Harbinger*, but after his first few speeches "he exhibited thorough discomfort, which soon changed into depressing discouragement and finally culminated in chagrin, venting itself in vulgar and insulting epithets."[8]

The person who submitted the account to the *Harbinger* was persuaded that a great victory had been obtained for the Christian cause. The writer declared that "this was one of the most complete successes we ever witnessed." Of Rowland's efforts, it was reported:

> Prof. Rowland wielded the sword of truth with veteran skill. His characteristic suavity of address, fairness in debate, earnestness of manner, well-timed repartee and irresistible logic, won and controlled the audience through the entire debate. That portion of the congregation which would scatter abroad during the efforts of his opponent, would, on his rising, gather in from the outskirts and listen with mute attention till the closing word.

The Christians were especially pleased with Rowland's defense of immersion as the proper mode of baptism. "His arguments for immersion from the original Greek," declared the reporter to the *Harbinger*, "were the most satisfactory that I ever heard." Not surprisingly, the four-day event ended with the crowds lining the banks of Rickreall Creek. "After the close of the debate, three intelligent and prominent persons (one a member of the Methodist Church) were immersed," noted the correspondent, "and, from the most reliable indications, many more will soon follow."

The Oregon correspondent knew that Rowland's former teachers at Bethany College would be pleased to hear of his development as a debater. Therefore, the report was sent as a personal letter to President W. K. Pendleton, the successor and son-in-law of Alexander Campbell. The article ended by extolling the merits of the most famous college in the Restoration Movement:

> Prof. Rowland is a graduate of Bethany College, which is an impressive illustration of the great good which that noble institution is doing for the cause of general science and

> primitive Christianity. Be not surprised if many more of Oregon's sons shall soon seek the same blessings of Bethany.[9]

The Christian Messenger

At the annual State Meeting in June 1870, the vigorous new president of Christian College convinced his brethren that the time was right for Oregon Christians to have their own church paper. The proposed journal would be called the *Christian Messenger,* and it would be issued weekly from Monmouth. In addition to his duties as president of Christian College and preacher for the Monmouth Church, T. F. Campbell would take on the added responsibilities of editor and publisher of the church paper. This proposed venture met with the wholehearted approval of those in attendance, and more than $12,000 was raised during the course of the State Meeting to purchase the steam press and other equipment necessary to launch the project.[10]

The inaugural issue of the *Christian Messenger* rolled from "one of the first steam presses used in the Willamette Valley"[11] on Saturday, October 8, 1870. It was a proud day for Oregon Christians. The Methodists had been publishing the *Pacific Christian Advocate* since 1856, and now Oregon would have a second church-related newspaper.[12] California Christians had supported a church paper since November 1858, but they were temporarily without a periodical in the fall of 1870.[13] Campbell used his first editorial to defend the need for a journal that could command the patronage of the entire Restoration Movement in the great American West, and he wrote:

> A numerous, wealthy and influential Christian community, dispersed throughout California, Oregon, and Washington Territory, without any organ of communication, or facilities for co-operation in the important reformation in which it is engaged, seems to give rise to a necessity imperious in its demands, and fully justifying the effort to establish such an organ. The importance of this measure has long since been recognized by the Church, and efforts have been made to meet it; but, hitherto, without success. Passion over the causes of failure, and looking to that vast territory,

extending from Puget Sound, on the north, to the Gulf of California, on the south; and from the coast of the Pacific to the base of the Rocky Mountains, occupied, in part, by a Christian brotherhood numbering many thousands in its memberships, "contending earnestly for the faith"—for pure Christianity, read in the Bible, not proven out of it—a Christianity aggressive in spirit as it was in the days of the Apostles, showing no quarter to error, but boldly attacking it and exposing its deformity under the searching light of Truth—we see this community, in all this vast region, without any medium through which to correspond and co-operate in this great and good work.[14]

Although the *Millennial Harbinger* had announced that it would suspend publication with the December 1870 issue, after more than 40 years of service, there were still four church papers enjoying a wide circulation among Oregon Christians. These were: *Christian Record,* a monthly edited by James Madison Mathes in Bedford, Indiana; *American Christian Review,* a weekly published by Benjamin Franklin from Cincinnati; *Christian Standard,* another weekly published by Isaac Errett from Cincinnati; and *Apostolic Times,* a third weekly edited by J. W. McGarvey, Moses E. Lard, and three others from Lexington, Kentucky. Campbell disavowed any competitiveness with these papers, and he wrote in his first editorial:

It is certainly true, that many valuable papers and periodicals from the East circulate extensively amongst us; nor is it desirable that their circulation should be curtailed by a single copy; but they cannot meet our local wants, foster our local institutions, nor elicit and develop the talents, varied and diversified, found in our churches. These ends can be met only by a paper in our midst.[15]

Two West Coast Christians were publicly thanked for their assistance in making the *Messenger* a reality. "Governor George L. Woods of Salem, and Elder Charles Vinzent of San Francisco, will please accept our thanks for valuable services rendered in the purchase of our press," wrote the grateful editor. "The former in connection with the transmission of the money and placing it in the hands of a competent agent. The latter, in purchasing and shipping the press without charges."[16] When the "Agents for the *Christian Messenger*" were listed on page one, Charles Vinzent was "our only authorized agent in San Francisco." [17]

The Golden Age

With the strengthening of Christian College, the birth of the *Christian Messenger,* and the continuing growth of the annual State Meeting, the Restoration Movement entered its most productive decade in Oregon. "If ever there was a Golden Age for Disciples in Oregon," wrote one church historian, "the 70s was it."[18] The preachers were reaping a great harvest everywhere they traveled. "Brother Whitney still labors faithfully in the upper counties," noted one observer, "and is, perhaps, doing as much, or more good than any two or three other preachers in the State. But we greatly fear that he is over-taxing his constitution."[19] When John M. Harris sat down with pen in hand on December 28, 1870, and totaled the number of additions to the church for that year he was very pleased. "There have been over 400 accessions to the churches in this country during the last year," he informed James Mathes, "under the labors of brethren J. E. Murphy, G. M. Whitney, myself, and others."[20]

One of the most spectacular aspects of this post-war period of growth and expansion in American society was the building of railroads. The dramatic completion of the transcontinental railroad in 1869 signaled the opening of a new chapter in the American West. Actual construction in Oregon began in 1868, and by 1872 the tracks extended from Portland through the length of the Willamette Valley and down to Roseburg. Roads of every kind were being laid out and surfaced. Oregon's population nearly doubled (there was a 93 percent growth rate) in the decade between 1870 and 1880.[21]

When "the messengers of the Churches of Christ met at their camp grounds near Dixie"[22] in the summer of 1871, they were filled with optimism. J. J. Maxey, a member of the Albany Church, described the results of the annual State Meeting:

> Our annual meeting commenced June 16th, and continued twelve days. We had a good time together. On the last Lord's day of the meeting the audience was estimated at five or six thousand. It was the largest crowd I ever saw at any one time in Oregon. And the beauty of the matter was, that everything went off in the best of order. During the meeting, there were 42 added to the army of the Lord, 36 of them by immersion and 6 from the sects, who had been immersed.[23]

Levi Lindsay Rowland was chosen to be chairman of the 1871 State Meeting, and Peter R. Burnett served as the secretary. In the midst of the proceedings, two Christian young people were joined in marriage on June 20. Troy Shelley, a young preacher, and Annie Lewis were wed by Levi Lindsay Rowland, who was assisted in this joyful task by Glen Owen Burnett. The Shelleys moved to The Dalles in Wasco County where Troy taught school during the week and preached for the Christian Church on Sundays. He maintained an active ministry in eastern Oregon for over half a century.[24]

Statistics were shared from 64 congregations in the state with a net membership of 2,842. When "scattered" members from areas with no organized churches were added, it was estimated that there were 3,250 baptized believers in Oregon. However, there were a number of congregations in existence (perhaps 10 to 20) that were not included in the list of 64.[25] When the members of those churches are added to the total, the actual number of baptized believers affiliated with the Oregon Christians was probably close to 3,500. When children and other adherents (non-members who were regular attenders) are added, the round figure of 4,000 for the total size of the Restoration Movement in Oregon in 1871 is an accurate estimate. The 64 churches reported at the State Meeting, arranged according to their size, were as follows:[26]

Church	County	Members
1. Salem	Marion	160
2. Bethel	Polk	160
3. Monmouth	Polk	140
4. Pleasant Hill	Lane	125

Church	County	Members
5. Harrisburg	Linn	100
6. Central	Linn	83
7. McMinnville	Yamhill	80
8. Oak Hill	Lane	80
9. Bethany (Silver Creek)	Marion	75
10. Damascus	Clackamas	72
11. Tualatin	Washington	65
12. Mt. Pleasant	Linn	61
13. Mt. Pleasant	Douglas	61
14. Amity	Yamhill	60
15. Cottage Grove (Coast Fork?)	Lane	60
16. Springfield	Lane	60
17. Hillsboro	Washington	57
18. Eugene	Lane	55
19. Scio	Linn	50
20. Manzanita	Jackson	50
21. Grand Ronde	Union	50
22. Antioch	Marion	50
23. Dallas	Polk	48
24. Sheridan	Yamhill	48
25. Fifteen Mile Creek	Wasco	45
26. White Oak Grove	?	45
27. Corvallis	Benton	40
28. Grand Prairie	Lane	40
29. Concord	Clackamas	40
30. Mill Creek	Marion	38
31. Sand Ridge	Linn	35
32. Splawn's School House	Linn	34
33. Canyonville	Douglas	30
34. Brownsville	Linn	30
35. Rock Creek	Clackamas	30
36. Hopewell	Yamhill	30
37. Portland	Multnomah	30
38. Oak Creek	Linn	28
39. Lookingglass	Douglas	27
40. Camas Swale	Douglas	26
41. Mohawk	Lane	25

Church	County	Members
42. Monroe	Benton	25
43. Oak Plain	Linn	24
44. Buena Vista	Polk	23
45. Oakland	Douglas	22
46. Coquille	Coos	20
47. Lewisville	Polk	20
48. Eola	Polk	20
49. Lone Rock Valley	Wasco	20
50. Yoncalla	Douglas	19
51. West Chehalem	Yamhill	18
52. Applegate	Josephine	17
53. Myrtle Creek	Douglas	17
54. St. Helen's	Columbia	16
55. Salt Creek	Polk	15
56. Oregon City	Clackamas	14
57. Soda Springs	Linn	14
58. Deer Creek	Douglas	12
59. Jefferson	Marion	12
60. Albany	Linn	12
61. Ashland	Jackson	12
62. Cole's Valley	Douglas	11
63. Antioch	Jackson	11
64. Panther Creek	Yamhill	10

The 34-member church that was meeting in Splawn's School House near present-day Holley in Linn County had just been established. Among the charter members were Christians named Riggs, Crawford, Shanks, Fields, Finley, Hamilton, Cary, Splawn, Newton, Lewis, Barr, Fuller, Earl, Stewart, Hughes and Powell.[27]

The Christians returned home from Dixie much encouraged. "The cause of our Master is onward in this State," wrote Lane County's John T. Gilfrey, "and according to the reports from the congregations in the State to the General State Meeting, we out number any denomination in the State, and we are still advancing, and will continue to advance, as long as our brethren continue to preach the old

Jerusalem gospel, and live it out."[28] Gilfrey's optimism was understandable, but the Methodists were most likely the largest church group in Oregon in 1871. However, the Christians were the second largest group followed closely by the Baptists.[29]

Campbell Hall

Thomas Franklin Campbell did not often take time for vacations, and one biographer noted, "As a substitute for a summer vacation, Mr. Campbell was in the habit of traveling about the country delivering lectures, preaching, founding congregations of the Christian Faith, raising money for the college, and recruiting its student constituency."[30] On August 6, 1871, Campbell preached for the Fir Grove congregation in Lane County. The announcement that the popular president of Christian College would be visiting their neighborhood prompted a larger than usual attendance that Lord's day. Campbell found himself "so surrounded with brethren and friends" that he was "obliged to adjourn from the large school-house to the grove, where, with ample room and every comfort, we enjoyed the day in a pleasant manner not soon to be forgotten."[31]

In the course of his tour through Lane County, Campbell was appalled by the level of gossip and the wild rumors with which the members of the Restoration Movement had to contend, and he wrote:

> The Disciples in Lane County have a bright future before them, for they are really enjoying the sweets of Christian love and unity, and are being more firmly bound together by the shafts of malice and jealousy hurled by a few restless spirits and superannuated sectarian preachers, who have no flock to lead nor bell to jingle. . . . Though these rumors never had any foundation in fact, they show how, in a sinking cause, the imagination will be put upon the rack, and subjected to torture by men who are alarmed at the increasing numbers and growing strength of the Disciples of Jesus.[32]

One week later, while still traveling in Lane County, Campbell preached for the Christians in Springfield, a pleasant little village situated on the opposite side of the

Willamette River from Eugene. "During our stay in Springfield," he informed his readers, "we enjoyed the hospitalities of Bro. Dr. Owsley and his amiable lady and interesting family." This was a reference to William and Mariah Owsley. Campbell was pleased to report that the Springfield congregation had erected a stone foundation on "a beautiful site overlooking the village for a frame building which when finished will be the largest church building in the county—probably the largest in the state."[33]

Meanwhile, the fund-raising for Christian College was going well. By the late summer of 1871, Campbell had accumulated enough cash and pledges to justify starting construction on the first brick building for the college. The inspiration for its design, of course, would be the main building at Bethany College. The cornerstone was laid and dedicated on September 5, 1871, and the former president, Levi Lindsay Rowland, was summoned to Monmouth to give the dedication address.[34] When the three-story, brick structure was completed in 1872, it was named Campbell Hall by the board of trustees, in honor of President Thomas Franklin Campbell. The enrollment at Christian College for the school year of 1871-72 was 237 students. Of this number, 126 were in the collegiate department (86 men and 40 women), and the remainder were either in the preparatory department or were special music students.[35]

The laying of the cornerstone for Campbell Hall, like the launching of the weekly *Christian Messenger*, was another proud achievement for President Campbell. In the short space of two years, traveling and preaching throughout the state, he had become a household name among families affiliated with the Restoration Movement. He had mobilized Oregon Christians as no one had before him, and he had motivated them to believe in the nobility of their cause. Lesser men were amazed at the sheer industry he brought to every task before him. One week after the cornerstone ceremony, Campbell offered an insight into his philosophy of life when he editorialized in the *Messenger*:

> Men who have half a dozen irons in the fire, are not the ones to go crazy. It is the man of voluntary or compelled leisure who mopes and pines and thinks himself into the mad-house or the grave. Motion is in all of nature's laws. Action is man's salvation, physical and mental . . . he only is wise who lays out his work to life's latest hours.[36]

Among the constant "irons" that Campbell had in the fire were his daily duties as a lecturer in the college. One of the most famous features of Bethany College in Virginia had been Alexander Campbell's morning lecture on "Sacred History." T. F. Campbell had been in attendance at those morning lectures for several years, and now he was determined to carry on the tradition at Christian College. "I cannot refrain from paying a tribute to the wonderful personality of President T. F. Campbell," one student wrote years later. "The more you saw of him the more you were impressed with his nobility of character, his high ideals and his forceful way of teaching. His Bible lectures each morning, during the school years, made a lasting impression on all those who had the good fortune to be his pupils."[37]

Another "iron in the fire" for Campbell, although a brief one, was in the world of political debate. The high visibility that Christian College and the *Christian Messenger* achieved for him, along with his constant travels and speaking engagements around the state, made him a desirable political candidate. In the election year of 1874, Campbell threw his hat into the gubernatorial contest. His friends persuaded him to carry the banner of the newly-formed Grange Party against the Democrats and Republicans, and his years of preaching and lecturing served him well during the campaign. Charles Henry Carey, president of the Oregon Historical Society, said that Campbell was ". . . a man of great originality and force, whose natural gift for disputatious oratory greatly enlivened the campaign."[38]

The Democratic incumbent, L. F. Grover, won the election over the Republican candidate, J. C. Tolman, by the narrow margin of 9,713 to 9,163. However, Campbell made a respectable showing by polling 6,532 votes. Campbell not only won in his home county of Polk, but he was also victorious in Benton, Douglas, Grant and Washington counties. His political skills were so surprisingly strong that a movement developed to make him a candidate for the United States Senate, but Campbell refused all future opportunities to seek public office.

The Rogue River Valley

Martin Peterson first came overland in 1850 and lived in California for three years. When he returned across the trail in 1863, it was as the leader of a 30-member "Church on Wheels" that made quite an impact when they arrived during the annual State Meeting in Vacaville, California, that fall. By the spring of 1864, Peterson had decided to leave California and carve out a home in southern Oregon. With his wife, Elizabeth, and several children, Peterson settled on "Mound Ranch" at Sticky Flat a few miles north of present-day Medford. He gave land to build the first school house in the area. He was the first preacher from the Restoration Movement to preach in southern Oregon, and he established his first congregation within a year of his arrival. For the next quarter century, until his death in 1889, Martin Peterson roamed through Jackson and Josephine counties planting and nurturing several small congregations.

Peterson labored in isolation for the first few years, but once he had established some small churches he began to receive help from traveling evangelists. In the fall of 1870, John M. Harris came to his assistance. "I have lately returned from a preaching tour through Jackson County, Oregon," Harris told James Mathes. "Had twenty-three additions; sixteen by confession and baptism."[39] In the early spring of 1871, Peterson organized a congregation of ten members at Ashland. A few months later, Glen Owen Burnett and his son, Peter, visited Peterson on their way from California to attend the Oregon State Meeting. Glen Owen Burnett remained only four days, but Peter Burnett preached for three weeks in the Rogue River Valley and had seven additions to the church, including five immersions. Some of these additions were at Ashland.[40]

When Peter R. Burnett left for the State Meeting, Peterson continued to preach along the Rogue River. In a report sent to T. F. Campbell for publication in the *Christian Messenger*, Peterson wrote:

> Brother Campbell—As the friends of Jesus are ever pleased to hear of the prosperity of Zion, I take this method to give a synopsis of our work in Rogue River Valley . . . .
>
> I preached two discourses yesterday on the north side of Rogue River. One made the good confession there, and then we came some six miles to the Bybee ferry, on the river, where we had agreed to meet with the people to immerse two young ladies who had made the good confession. Here we met with the largest congregation we ever have had together to witness an immersion in this valley. Mr. Robinson, the ferryman, allowed us the use of his yard and porch as an audience chamber, and let us have lumber to make seats for our women and children under the majestical oak tree that stood in the yard. The men occupied the fence and ground for seats, while we spoke to them for about three-quarters of an hour, from the sixth chapter of Romans, 17th and 18th verses, to which they listened with profound attention. We then went to the water near by, where I immersed the three young sisters in the presence of the large and solemn audience, which was said to be the most quiet and orderly that had ever been seen together on such an occasion here . . . . We are on the gaining ground in this section. If the members will only live their religion all the time, we need fear no evil . . . .[41]

When a visiting evangelist named John Sutherland came through the Rogue River Valley in the 1880s, he was impressed with the self-sacrificing efforts of Martin Peterson. Writing to the *American Christian Review*, Sutherland reported, "Brother Peterson is an old settler in Jackson County, and works inveterately for the Master; preaches all the time and at his own expense; has built up some four churches in Jackson and Josephine counties . . ."[42] After Peterson's death in the summer of 1889, a fellow-Christian tried to describe his appeal to the common man. "Brother Peterson was emphatically a pioneer preacher—a self-made man, a hard student, as a glance at his well-thumbed, well-selected library will attest," he wrote. "A man of positive convictions and fearless in his exposures of errors. The immense concourse of citizens that followed him to his last resting place testified to the hold he had upon the popular heart."[43]

On the Road with A. L. Todd

The children of A. L. Todd always knew that their father's "greatest desire in life was to win souls to Christ." They could not remember any occasion when he had failed to fulfill a preaching appointment. "He never missed an appointment that it was possible for him to attend," his daughter wrote with certainty. His son echoed that statement and said that he could "not remember of father ever spending a single Sunday without preaching, if he was well enough to do it."[44] After Todd's death in 1886, his children wrote down their memories of his constant travels to advance the cause of Christ.

Coming home one winter's day in the late 1860s from a preaching tour in Coos County, Todd found the upper Coquille River swollen from recent rains. Despite the rapid current, Todd attempted to ford the dangerous river. Before he reached midstream, the current had swept the feet from under his horse and in an instant they were adrift in the icy stream. Todd grabbed the horse by her tail and down the river they went, their heads sometimes above the water and sometimes under. The horse finally swam to shore with her exhausted companion still clutching her tail. They rested for awhile on the river bank, and then pushed on toward home. The thoroughly soaked preacher was suffering severely from the cold, but they rode for 15 miles before they came to the next house.[45]

Todd's oldest daughter remembered another dangerous preaching trip when an accident almost led to a fatality. Writing the story as she must have heard it later from her father, she explained:

> At another time he was going to Camas Swale; on the road between Wilbur and Oakland night had fallen and it was a dark winter night. Taking a cut-off to avoid mud, his horse missed the road and came out on the railroad track; he followed it a little way, when the horse, stepping into a cattle

> guard, fell and caught father's foot under the horse; all efforts to free Himself seemed of no avail and the south bound train from Portland to Roseburg, then due, came in sight, he lying on the track in his helpless condition. All he could do to make the horse move did not free him, but as the train thundered down on to them with its gleaming headlight, the engineer blew his whistle and the frightened horse with one supreme effort, freed father's foot and rolled off to one side of the track and father rolled off on the other, barely missing the locomotive as it dashed past him with its train.[46]

One Sunday morning before church, Todd was in his pasture taking care of his sheep and trying to determine what had been attacking them. Suddenly, his dogs treed a panther. Rushing back to the farmhouse, Todd yelled at the top of his voice for his gun. One of his daughters ran to meet him with the gun and he returned to the tree and shot the panther. He returned to the house, dressed for church, and then hurried off to fulfill his appointment and preach his sermon.

A. L. Todd traveled far and wide in pursuit of souls for Christ, and often his audiences were very small. On one preaching tour through Coos County he sent word ahead that he would be preaching at Burton Prairie school house. It was a rainy afternoon in the wintertime, and only four persons came out to hear him preach. All four of his hearers were men, and none of them had thought to bring any matches for the candles. There was not enough time for any of the men to return home, so Todd began preaching in the fading light of a winter evening. The school house was cold, damp and dark, and as he preached the darkness deepened.

"He therefore preached the light of the gospel in the darkness of that winter night, while the rain fell outside," wrote his daughter, "his voice being all that could be distinguished." One of the four hearers obeyed the gospel soon after that experience, and he developed into a song leader and a gospel preacher. Several years later he told Todd's daughter about the sermon in the dark. "That earnest voice coming out of the darkness that night, I could not resist," he admitted, "and if ever any good comes from my work in the preaching of the gospel, it will be on account of that sermon delivered in the dark, in that little old school house at Burton Prairie."[47]

All of Todd's children treasured those occasions when it was their turn to accompany their father on a preaching tour. Levi Todd remembered going to Myrtle Creek when it was six or eight degrees below zero. Fording the rivers with their large bodies of mushy ice was hazardous, and after making it across the Umpqua River at Dillard's Ford they decided to detour and take a trail that led over the mountains. The difficult journey took the entire day, but the 15-year-old boy remembered the reaction when they arrived. He wrote:

> Arriving at Myrtle Creek late in the evening, we stopped at Brother Ady's house. Sister Ady met us at the gate, and grasping father's hand, said, "Oh, Brother Todd, I knew you would come; they told me I needn't look for you this time, but I told them you would come."
>
> We warmed ourselves at the fire and pushed on about three miles further, and stayed all night with a Brother Cornelius. Next morning we went to church. The weather being so cold, there were only about ten persons present; but father preached just as earnestly as if the house had been crowded. After church we went about six miles on the road home, and stopped for the night. The next day we reached home late in the afternoon.[48]

A. L. Todd continued to ride his circuit in southwestern Oregon for more than 30 years. No weather was too severe, and no appointment was too far, if at the end of the trail there were a few people hungering to hear the gospel of Christ. "Of Hell and its horrors he had little to say," his son remembered, "but of the unbounded love of Jesus Christ for fallen and suffering man, he never tired of telling, never wearied in calling sinners to accept that love and to live under the banner of the Heavenly King."[49]

The Progress of the Cause

As the decade of the 1870s began, G. W. Richardson was rotating his efforts between a handful of churches in North Polk, Yamhill and Washington counties. He had been riding this circuit for at least a decade, and with encouraging results.

In a letter to James Mathes, dated January 20, 1870, Richardson wrote:

> As to Church News, I will just say that since my last to you there have been about forty accessions to the Lord's army at the various points where I labor. About half that number by immersion. Our audiences are larger in Oregon than they were in the States when I left there. At Dallas we have a good meeting house, about thirty-two by forty-five feet, which seldom fails to be full when we have a preacher. At Bethel our house is thirty-six feet square; at McMinnville our house is thirty-six by fifty-six feet, and at all these places our houses are well filled, and in good weather they often overflow. Other places in the bounds of my labors are about as the above.[50]

Richardson wrote to Mathes later in that same year with exciting news about the arrival in Yamhill County of an outstanding preacher from Iowa named Peter Shuck. Richardson was not wanting to relinquish his responsibilities, he was just looking for a co-laborer.[51] Peter Shuck served the church in Oregon for many years. John M. Harris toured Douglas County in the spring of 1870 and had eight additions at Yoncalla, two at California, and one at Camas Swale.[52] Two co-laborers in the fall of 1870 were Keathley Bailes and William L. Mascher. Together they held six protracted meetings that resulted in 18 additions to the church.[53] When Mascher wrote again the next year, it was to say that his preaching had resulted in 32 additions to the church and that he had organized a new congregation.[54]

In the summer of 1870 a 71-year-old preacher of the gospel from Indiana named D. D. Weddle, accompanied by his 67-year-old wife, crossed the continent and settled in Oregon. A decade later, Weddle recalled how warmly he was welcomed to Oregon by the busy man who served as president of Christian College and editor of the *Christian Messenger*. Weddle remembered:

> Yes, my dear brother, you were the first brother that visited me and my companion when we first came to this coast, ten years ago. You never will know the comfort you gave us in that visit, Bro. Campbell. We were strangers, and

> you gave us a hearty welcome, and I feel that you were a brother in deed and in truth.[55]

It did not take D. D. Weddle long to become involved in the evangelistic outreach of the church in his new home. He corresponded with James Mathes in 1871 to submit an account of his first 10 months of labor in Oregon. "You may say to the brotherhood," he wrote, "that since the 19th of September, 1870, I have taken into the church some 43 persons—31 of them by confession and immersion."[56] Daniel Elledge moved to Summerville in Union County in the fall of 1871, and less than a year later he wrote to say that there were 75 members of the church living in that valley.[57] The good reports continued from G. W. Richardson. His letter in September 1872 gave the locations for 39 additions to the church, and his letter three months later provided information on 18 more additions.[58]

The church in Oregon was weakened by the deaths of two preachers in 1872, and then in turn strengthened by the arrival of two new proclaimers. The death of 67-year-old Samuel Bates Briggs in Douglas County was expected, as he had been ill for a few months. But the sudden death of 36-year-old William L. Mascher in Marion County was a severe blow to the church. He had been preaching in meetings throughout the state with increasing effectiveness, and it was thought that his most productive years were just ahead.[59]

Regarding the new arrivals, Professor James C. Campbell was recruited from Kentucky in 1872 to be a faculty member at Christian College. However, it was soon discovered that he would be a powerful addition to the corps of gospel preachers in Oregon. Equally significant in 1872 was the arrival of John Engard Roberts in the Marion County town of Aumsville. One year into his new ministry, Roberts submitted the following progress report to the *Christian Record*:

> The cause of Christ is progressing in this part of the world. I commenced my labors at this place a little over a year ago. At that time the Church was in rather a low condition; but the brethren are now much revived, and I have immersed about 30 persons and received several from the

sects, and several have been reclaimed. We had three immersions last night.[60]

John M. Harris celebrated his 70th birthday on April 1, 1873, but he showed no signs of slowing down. His meetings in Brownsville and Harrisburg in February 1873, resulted in 19 additions to the church.[61] Near the close of the year his meeting on the McKenzie River in Lane County resulted in 11 additions to the church, and his meeting at Pleasant Hill in the same county closed with 26 additions. "Brother Harris has on the whole armor, and knows how to wield the Sword of the Spirit," one member at Pleasant Hill wrote admiringly, "and as a teacher of the Word he is second to no one that I have heard here, and he is doing a vast amount of good . . . . May he long live to plead the Redeemer's cause." At the close of the meeting with Harris the Pleasant Hill Church had "about two hundred" members and was the oldest and largest of the nine Christian congregations in Lane County.[62]

The good news continued into the summer of 1874. On July 15, Andrew Kelley of the Salem Church sent a report to the *Christian Standard* in Cincinnati, Ohio. "The cause of Christ is progressing rapidly in Oregon," he wrote excitedly. "During the last two months there have been about two hundred and fifty conversions at different points."[63] One week later, an Oregon preacher named William Manning wrote to the same periodical to report on a 12-day gospel meeting at Mill Creek Church in Marion County that had resulted in 50 additions to the church. Manning had been assisted in the preaching by John M. Harris, Keathley Bailes, Mac Waller and John Engard Roberts. He concluded: "The cause is being advanced in this part of the State, and our brethren are doing a good work here."[64]

Times Have Greatly Changed

The Restoration Movement in Oregon was in its "Golden Age" in the 1870s and there was much to be encouraged about, but one brother in Lane County was worried about what he saw as a serious decline of strong opposition to the movement. In a very significant letter to James Mathes, penned on November 3, 1873, Caleb Davis reflected on the old pioneers he had known in the 1840s and 1850s and on the "great and bitter opposition" they had endured. Comparing the church leaders of that generation with those of his own, Davis wrote:

> Then we used to carry the word of God with us as we followed the plow, and when we sat down to rest we would try to gather all the knowledge we could from its sacred pages, that we might be "strong in the Lord and in the power of his might." But times have greatly changed. The opposition to the cause we plead has nearly ceased, and we have to some extent dropped back upon our oars and are floating in comparative ease down the stream of time, while many of these old leaders have crossed the river to where the mansions rise up in full view.[65]

Caleb Davis worried that the Restoration Movement might be a victim of its own success. It had arrived. It was becoming popular.

Thomas Franklin Campbell would not have agreed with this dire assessment. He was not resting on his oars. He taught the Bible every day to a room full of eager students, and when he traveled around the state he was grieved by the amount of opposition to the great principles inherent in the Restoration plea. Campbell may have regarded himself as one of many second-generation leaders in the Restoration Movement who had inherited a portion of the mantle of leadership of Alexander Campbell himself.

Like the sage of Bethany, T. F. Campbell was proud to be the president of a fine Christian college and the editor of an influential church paper. He was not aware that anything relative to the Restoration Movement had "greatly changed." Rather than focusing on some imagined weakness in the movement, the most prominent citizen of Monmouth and a candidate for the State of Oregon's highest office was more interested in chronicling the numerical gains of the movement. From Campbell's perspective, the impressive gains were an accurate barometer of a "Golden Age" for Oregon Christians.

Chapter 21

Requiem for the Pioneer Generation

1875-1880

It mortifies me to see the old faithful brethren who planted and established the cause in this country, and wore out the frame of their lives in preaching, ignored and set at naught by these hirelings . . . . There are a few of them still lingering on the shores of time – G. O. Burnett, the brothers Powell, and others, who went out without price, proclaimed the unsearchable riches of Christ, and prepared the fields. Shall they be set at naught and their memories be forgotten?

– Philip Mulkey, May 19, 1880

One history of Christian College confirms that in the mid-1870s "more and more of President Campbell's time and energy were spent in travel to raise money to pay off the indebtedness of the building fund and for support of the college."[1] Added to the demands on his time was the increasingly grave illness of his wife. Jane had not been well when they first arrived in Monmouth in the fall of 1869, and through the decade of the 1870s her health gradually deteriorated until her death in the fall of 1881. Shortly after Jane died, Campbell made a brief reference to her long illness in the *Messenger*:

> Our labor, too, has been coupled with anxious care and the deep unmitigated grief which has its source only in the slow, but sure decline toward the portals of death, under an incurable malady of body and mind, of one dear as life itself.[2]

The Pacific Christian Messenger

By the mid-1870s, it was clear that Thomas Franklin Campbell could no longer shoulder all of his responsibilities alone. Beginning with volume VI of the *Messenger,* in March 1876, David Truman Stanley became editor and Campbell assumed the role of associate editor. Stanley was a fine gospel preacher and a graduate of Bethany College. He had been summoned to Oregon for this very purpose, and he threw himself into his work with great energy. The new editor doubled the size of the weekly from four pages to eight pages, beginning with the September 8, 1876, issue. With the May 31, 1877, issue, Stanley changed the name of the journal to the *Pacific Christian Messenger* and added Glen Owen Burnett and Levi Lindsay Rowland to the slate of associate editors.

The most significant change took place with the October 18, 1877, issue when Thomas Porter, preacher for the church in Colusa, California, came on board as co-editor with Stanley. Campbell, Burnett, and Rowland remained as associate editors. California was without a church paper at this time, and it was hoped that the addition of the two popular Californians, Porter and Burnett, would increase the circulation in the Golden State. It was further decided to simultaneously publish the weekly *Pacific Christian Messenger* from two locations, Monmouth, Oregon, and Sacramento, California.

This was the most ambitious attempt ever made to merge the strengths of the Oregon and California churches, but the distance was still too great, and the project was doomed to failure. In less than a year Thomas Porter returned to his former home in Australia, and the Christians in California decided to start their own paper rather than continue the arrangement with Monmouth. In the spring of 1879, after three years of trying to put the *Messenger* on a self-sustaining basis, David Truman Stanley chose to relinquish the editorial reins. Once again Thomas Franklin Campbell found himself sitting in the editor's chair and responsible for keeping the paper afloat. This time he brought Mary Stump into the partnership as "office editor and publisher."[3]

The editorial team of Thomas Franklin Campbell and Mary Stump worked together effectively for three years. However, after the death of his wife in the fall of 1881, Campbell felt the need to close the Monmouth chapter of his life, and he resigned from both the college and the paper. David Truman Stanley was chosen to replace Campbell as president of the college, and at the same time he reassumed his involvement with the weekly journal. Beginning in 1882, the name of the paper changed from the *Pacific Christian Messenger* to the *Christian Herald,* and the new co-editors were David Truman Stanley and Bruce Wolverton. Campbell left Monmouth to travel and preach for three years, but he returned home in 1885 and married Mary Stump.[4] They lived together in Monmouth until his death in January of 1893.

The Demise of the State Meeting

The "Golden Age" for Oregon Christians was centered in the first years after the close of the Civil War. With the return of A. V. McCarty and Peter R. Burnett in the summer of 1865 and the arrival of John M. Harris and Daniel W. Elledge in the fall of 1865, the church in Oregon enjoyed a period of evangelistic revival that lasted for at least a decade. Fueled by evangelists like George M. Whitney, William L. Mascher, G. W. Richardson, Philip Mulkey, Martin Peterson, D. D. Weddle, A. L. Todd, Thomas Franklin Campbell, and Keathley Bailes, the Restoration Movement enjoyed an unprecedented advance in Oregon. Nowhere was this seen more vividly than in the rising attendance patterns at the annual State Meetings. The crowds at these 12-day family encampments increased dramatically from the late 1860s to the mid-1870s, with more than 5,000 in attendance at the larger assemblies on Sundays. However, the "Golden Age" of annual State Meetings had clearly peaked by the summer of 1876.

A sister from the Salem Church named Clara Whitehead attended the 1875 State Meeting "at the old camp ground near Dixie," and then sent her impressions to the *Christian Record.* During her visit she had become "acquainted with many intelligent brethren and sisters," and she was pleased to see "a great many members here, and some very good preachers." She reported that the largest crowds were estimated at 6,000 and that the meeting had resulted in 29 additions to the church, including 27 "by confession and baptism." But the large crowds had seemed somewhat undisciplined, and she was bothered that "only about one fourth of the multitude sat down quietly to hear the preaching."[5] Nevertheless, on balance it appeared that the annual State Meeting for Oregon Christians was alive and well in 1875.

However, for some unknown reason, the decision was made to move the encampment away from Dixie in 1876—although it did not move very far. Ellen Scott Lyle, a charter member of the church in Dallas, offered her property for the use of the State Meeting and the offer was accepted.[6] A "shed" was constructed on the grounds for the preaching services, and advertisements were sent off to the papers. Evidently not everyone agreed with the decision to change locations, and there were predictions that the meeting would suffer a decline. President Campbell defended the move, and after the encampment he published the following positive evaluation of the program in the *Christian Messenger*:

> Notwithstanding the gloomy forebodings of many, the meeting was, in many respects, quite successful. There was a good attendance of preaching brethren, while the audiences were fair in numbers nearly all of the time, and too large on Lord's days. The shed would seat comfortably some two thousand persons, but from one-third to one-half of the people were unable to find seats either Lord's day. In the main, the preaching was good, the audiences attentive, but the results in the way of confessions, not so great as on former occasions. Much credit is due the police force of Dallas for constant attendance and preventing all rowdyism on the grounds. Brother L. L. Rowland, of Salem, was chief engineer of the meetings during the greater part of the time, and greatly enhanced the interest of the meeting by his persistent efforts to have things done decently and in order.[7]

This was putting the best possible face on the encampment, but it could not mask the disappointing results. After at least eight (and perhaps nine or ten) consecutive State Meetings at

Dixie, with Sunday attendance peaking at from 5,000 to 6,000, the annual gathering had suffered a significant decline. From an estimated Lord's day attendance of 6,000 the year before, the 1876 meeting dropped to between 3,000 and 4,000. Campbell's surprising remark that the audiences were "too large on Lord's days" did not fool anyone. When it came to preaching the gospel to non-Christians, the higher attendance was always preferred. Even more telling, the large numbers of immersions that usually punctuated the event, were noticeably absent. Campbell thought it best not to publicize the number.

The published statistics on churches and members, so exciting in previous State Meetings, were also disappointing. Only 22 congregations submitted statistics, and there were no reports of new congregations being established. "It was greatly desired that we should have full reports from *all* our congregations in the State this year," Campbell lamented, "but in this we were not successful. The report as found in another column, does not make as good a showing for the cause as is desirable." The feeling was now gaining acceptance that the State Meeting format was an inefficient way of organizing a state for evangelistic outreach, and that a change was needed soon. The State Meeting format had served Oregon's pioneer generation well for a quarter century, but it had become a nostalgic event for an aging constituency.

From that perspective it was still valuable. "As a reunion, it was altogether a success," noted Campbell. "From all parts of the State were gathered the lovers of the Lord who had met in former years, with some who were here for the first time, and the clasping of hands and the many words of greeting and good cheer, showed that the occasion was not one to be soon forgotten." But the emphasis was on the past and not on the future, and in particular there was a great deal of attention focused on those who had recently died. Two of the most powerful proclaimers, Dr. James McBride and John Ecles Murphy, had died since the last State Meeting and "many were the tears of sorrow shed at the remembrance of our fallen heroes." Campbell wrote sadly, "Often was our attention called to the fact that many had gone to their reward during the past year, and we parted wondering who would be gathered home from our number, ere we meet on a like occasion again."

But were there compelling reasons for planning another State Meeting? "Doubtless a course might be pursued which would make the Annual Meeting far more beneficial to the cause in general," admitted Campbell, "but this is not the proper time for suggesting any particular method of procedure. The sentiments of the brethren themselves are preparing the way for improvements that will certainly be beneficial."[8] By the time the State Meeting convened again on Ellen Scott Lyle's property in June 1877, "an earnest and decided conviction seemed resting upon the messengers and brethren there assembled, that *something must be done* at this very meeting, if ever, toward adopting some plan or system by which the evangelizing of the State might be inaugurated . . . ."[9]

It was agreed to bring the annual State Meeting to a close and to replace it with a different strategy. "The Annual State Camp-meeting of the Church of Christ in Oregon is no more," editorialized Campbell in the *Messenger*. "The brethren have done wisely, we think, by discontinuing the State Meetings as heretofore conducted, and replacing them with county meetings and an annual cooperation of delegates."[10] When the "Minutes" of this historic meeting were published and made available for general distribution among the churches, they contained the following declaration: "This meeting will long be remembered not only as the last general State meeting, but as the inaugural of a better state of affairs in the church."[11] Not everyone agreed with the sentiments expressed in the last half of the sentence. There were many who had never made their peace with the missionary society concept, and they prized the autonomy of the churches as one of the finest achievements of the Restoration Movement.

The Ministerial Association

The decision to encourage annual county meetings proved to be popular, and over the next few years several of these meetings were very large.[12] But the decision to form "an annual cooperation of delegates" for the purpose of organizing the state for mission work was not unanimously accepted. During the 1877 State Meeting a separate organization, with a complete slate of officers, was voted into existence with the imposing name of "The Christian Ministerial Association of the State of Oregon." The officers elected were: Thomas Franklin Campbell, president; J. J. Moss, vice-president; Sebastian C. Adams, secretary; and Hiram Alva Johnson, treasurer.[13]

The association was designed to be composed of "such preachers or evangelists, elders and deacons of the Church of Christ in this State" who would be willing to meet three modest requirements. Each church leader was required to sign the agreement that chartered the organization. In addition, they agreed to a 50 cent initiation fee, and a 25 cent annual fee every year thereafter. All monies raised were to go to fund mission work in the state.

There were 33 men who signed the document during the State Meeting,[14] and it was announced that the first annual meeting of the organization would take place at the Salem church building in late October of that year. Copies of the agreement (called the "Basis of the Oregon Christian Ministerial Association") were sent to all church leaders with the following urgent appeal:

> Beloved Brother: You are requested as soon as this falls into your hands to send your name with the initiation fee to S. C. Adams, of Salem, secretary of the association, and to use your influence to get every preacher, elder and deacon within your reach to do the same. We believe the objects, as set forth in the basis association, will commend themselves to every good man, and we trust you will earnestly engage in the work, and that you and all the preachers and officers of the churches of the entire State will come up to Salem next October 29th, and be ready to commence early on the morning of the 30th, and continue till November 2nd at night. If we do so we shall inaugurate a new era for our cause in the State. That something must be done and that right soon we think you must see and feel, or we as a people shall soon be dead and buried.[15]

This strongly-worded statement was signed by Thomas Franklin Campbell and Sebastian C. Adams, two of the most respected leaders among Oregon Christians. Two months later, in an editorial in the *Pacific Christian Messenger* entitled "Our Missionary Effort," David Truman Stanley continued to beat the drum for the Ministerial Association. "In looking over the few weeks that have passed since our Annual Meeting, we have reason to thank God and take courage," he wrote. "The movement that was then inaugurated for a more systematic effort to spread the Gospel, has awakened a new interest and a new life that does not diminish as time passes, but is increasing." Stanley was gratified to report that "there have been no grumblers to hinder the work. All seem rejoiced to see the good seed being sown on the rich fallow now before us."[16]

This was wishful thinking on Stanley's part, and he knew it. There had been opposition to the missionary society concept of evangelism from the very beginning, but no one was eager to be critical in print. Now Martin Peterson decided to break the silence. Writing to T. F. Campbell on October 1, 1877, Peterson protested that the creation of a Ministerial Association was a "movement not toward Jerusalem but toward Babylon." In other words, he was persuaded that this was a movement headed in the direction of sectarianism and denominationalism and not in the direction of a restoration of primitive Christianity. Peterson was one of those who even worried about the scripturalness of State Meetings, and he was strongly opposed to missionary societies. In the letter to Campbell, he wrote:

> I have written to the *Messenger* in years gone by showing that Missionary Societies, State Meetings, and also now Ministerial Associations are things unknown in the ancient order of things. Those introducing any of these are introducing among the brethren seeds of discord and causes of alienation, and not only this, but are virtually acknowledging to our opponents that our plea that was made by the pioneers of this great reformation is false, for these pioneers made their record against associations and every thing that looked in that direction.

> Now if we turn away from this solemn protest and inaugurate systems similar to our sectarian neighbors without producing a thus saith the Scripture, then how shall we meet our opponents, and further, how shall we meet our Lord when he shall say, who required this at your hands. I am well aware, Brother Campbell, that you and those good brethren associated with you have formed this association with the best of motives, but I am equally confident that the great and good men that formed the Methodist discipline did it with just as pure motives as you formed this association . . . I would say to you, and those good brethren associated with you in this new society, which is unknown in the divine pattern, to destroy it, abandon it, absolve it, do away with it, let it be among the things of the past, while it is under your control, lest by age it gets control of you and the dear brethren, and binds you and takes you where you do not wish to go.[17]

Peterson agreed that Oregon churches needed to be encouraged to do more mission work. "Then how shall we go to work to accomplish this much-desired state in our midst?" he asked. "You say by our Ministerial Association. I say no, but by the word of the Lord which liveth and abideth forever." This was a serious criticism from a respected churchman, and it could not be disregarded. Campbell himself replied in the same issue, agreeing with much that Peterson said but defending the legitimacy of the Ministerial Association. J. J. Moss responded to Peterson in the next issue of the *Messenger,* and he disagreed with the premise that "the pioneers of this great reformation" were opposed to organizations like the Ministerial Association. He reasoned:

> I know that they are misrepresented when it is said that they were opposed to preachers meetings and cooperation. That they were opposed to all ecclesiastical associations, synods, assemblys, conferences and everything else that had delegated authority, or authority in any other way, to lord it over the churches and over men's consciences, or over their faith, or even their opinions is true; and it is equally true that our modern preachers are just as much opposed to this as the pioneer preachers were; but that the pioneer preachers were any more opposed to the cooperation of churches for their mutual benefit and protection, and for the spread of the Gospel, or to minister's meetings to help each other in their

> growth in grace and in the knowledge of the truth, and to mutually help each other to better understand their duties and responsibilities, and how best to discharge them than modern preachers is not true.[18]

The first annual meeting of the Ministerial Association convened on schedule in Salem on Monday evening, October 29, and Thomas F. Campbell delivered an address on the subject of "Power." On Thursday morning, November 1, a motion was entertained that "the sister-wives of the members of the Association be eligible to membership." This motion was opposed by J. J. Moss and favored by Levi Lindsay Rowland. Moss admitted that he had no difficulty with women praying or even preaching, but he argued that "in all matters pertaining to authority" women should "not usurp authority." This was a stunning admission of the Association's true function, given that its most vocal supporters had repeatedly stated that they had no interest in exercising authority over any local church or individual.

Rowland replied that the Association was not set up "for the purpose of legislating or exercising authority over the brethren or churches," and therefore the women should be eligible for membership. He argued that the Association was not "surrounded by the primitive customs and prejudices of the semi-civilized people composing the early churches." Rowland reminded his listeners that "in Christ there is neither male nor female." The motion carried, and when the meeting dismissed on November 2, the total number of signers had risen to 58.

This was a membership gain of only 25 since the week of the annual State Meeting in June, and given the high profile of the leaders of the association and the amount of pressure exerted on all church leaders to join, it must have been disappointing.[19]

T. F. Campbell continued his policy of opening the columns of the *Pacific Christian Messenger* to reasonable voices on both sides of this difficult issue. In the December 15, 1877, issue of the paper he published a strong dissenting article from the pen of Charles H. Hining, the respected preacher for the Christian Church in Modesto, California. Under the heading of "Preachers' Meeting, Conventions, Committees for Settlement of Church Difficulties, and Evangelists," Hining issued a warning about the direction in which the church was moving. "These meetings are very dangerous," he began. "They are extremely useful, if their action is confined to legitimate subjects. But this is the difficulty. It is almost impossible to do it."

Hining was primarily concerned with the abuse of power. "As these conventions become strong and popular, they will almost certainly assume powers and subjects beyond their jurisdiction," he reasoned. "Transcending their proper bounds, such bodies have issued decrees, established rules, published bulls of excommunication, and made creeds. Each one of these steps, taken separately, may not be long; but all of them together, takes a people outside of the Bible; and thus they reject God's law, and establish their own."

What really alarmed Hining, and others like him, was the potential for groups of preachers and evangelists to band together in some kind of "committee" or "convention" that would be unaccountable to anyone else in the church. "There is no safety for the cause of Christ," he warned, "except in strict accountability to the congregation, of both preachers and private members." Like Martin Peterson before him, Hining saw these new developments as a departure from the pioneers. "I think it will result in great evil, and should be strenuously opposed," he said bluntly. "It is a new doctrine. The fathers of this restoration neither knew nor taught any such thing. It is a departure from the old land marks, and promises only evil."

Hining knew that his warning would be scoffed at by many, but he was adamant in his views. "If we may go an inch beyond the Divine teaching, express or implied," he concluded defiantly, "we may go anywhere—everywhere—there is no limit."[20]

Nevertheless, despite the uneasiness of readers like Peterson and Hining, the *Messenger* continued to carry positive references to the Ministerial Association, including the announcement that the second annual meeting of the association would take place in Monmouth in November 1878. One historian, commenting on the ineffectiveness of the Ministerial Association, wrote, "During the second year a reaction set in, and at the third meeting of the Cooperation in 1879, again held at Monmouth, there was consternation. Practically nothing had been contributed."[21]

The Instrumental Music Question

At the same time Oregon Christians were struggling with the pros and cons of establishing a state missionary society, another issue emerged that proved to be distracting and ultimately divisive. This was the practice of introducing musical instruments into the public worship of the church. It began gradually in a handful of urban churches, but it was met with immediate opposition from a number of conservative spokesmen.

As with the debate over the scripturalness of the Ministerial Association, Thomas Franklin Campbell managed to occupy the middle ground. And once again, he opened the columns of the *Pacific Christian Messenger* to sweet-spirited Christians on both sides of the issue. "We have never believed there is any Scriptural reason why it may not be used in worship," Campbell editorialized in May 1878, "but the argument of expediency which has been the main argument in its favor, will finally put it out of nearly every church."

Campbell announced that he had been carefully observing "the result of instrumental music in our churches," and now he was prepared to offer some conclusions. He wrote:

> 1. Churches that have an organ for a considerable length of time, have less spiritual activity than those that have only good vocal music.
>
> 2. The music which is at first improved by the introduction of the instrument deteriorates as the congregation gets to depending more on the instrument and finally they stand far behind sister churches that have not had an instrument, in really good music.
>
> These conclusions may be questioned by some but we give it as the result of several years observation both in the east and the west. It is only necessary to compare our

congregations on this coast to prove both our conclusions correct.

The editor declared that at one time in his career he had been so strongly in favor of instrumental music that he had furnished his own instruments in the churches he served, but now he admitted that "experience has worked a thorough change in our convictions on the subject." From his conversations with other church leaders in Oregon, Campbell knew that he was not the only one whose thinking on the subject had come full circle. "We feel confident that time will work in the minds of many of our brethren the conclusions it has worked in ours," he wrote optimistically, "until finally it will be scarcely known among us as a people."

It clearly bothered Campbell to admit that the discussion of the organ question in the Restoration Movement had "given us more trouble than the hosts of sectarianism and infidelity combined." He was glad to get this issue behind him. He concluded: "We believe the instrument in our churches has reached the zenith of its glory and already begins to wane." In fact, he confidently entitled his editorial "The Organ Waning."[22]

Sadly, Campbell's hopeful prediction was wrong. The same brethren who favored the establishment of a state missionary society favored the introduction of musical instruments into the public worship of the church. Those who struggled with the scripturalness of establishing an organization, separate from the local church, to oversee missionary work, were the same people who were questioning the scripturalness of adding musical instruments to the public worship of the church. The problem was far more serious than Campbell wanted to admit. In less than 20 years, there would be a parting of the ways.

Preaching in the 1870s

As far as can be determined now, Isaac Newton Mulkey (called "Newt" most of his life) was the first Oregon preacher to travel to his new home on the transcontinental railroad that had been completed in 1869. Along with his wife, Sarah, and their young family, Newt made the journey in 1871, traveling all the way to San Francisco by rail. They continued their journey on a boat from San Francisco to Portland, and then traveled by steamboat from Portland to Eugene. They were greeted in Eugene by Newt's uncle, Philip Mulkey, and they spent their first winter in Oregon at Philip's residence on Spencer Creek, southwest of Eugene.

In the spring of 1872, Newt moved his family to nearby Pleasant Hill where he took up farming and blacksmithing. He built a home and three other buildings and became an active member of the Pleasant Hill Church of Christ. One biographical record noted: "In his blacksmith shop, Newt set the iron tires and shod the horses for the freighters. In a second shop building he built buggies, wagons and hacks. The grist mill in the third building was powered by a water wheel—a stream ran down through the pasture and drove the wheel."[23]

Beginning around 1875, when he was in his mid-30s, Newt followed the example of his uncle and began preaching occasionally for area churches. On Sunday, August 5, 1877, he was formally set apart by the Pleasant Hill Church of Christ for the work of an evangelist. One member of the congregation submitted a brief account of the event to the *Messenger*:

> On last Lord's day morning, we listened to a very interesting discourse from Brother Peter Burnett on the duties of an evangelist to the people, and the duty of the church to the evangelist. At the close of the usual morning services, he ordained Brother I. N. Mulkey as an evangelist. The audience was large and attentive.[24]

Newt Mulkey preached for congregations at Mohawk, Trent, Irving, Halsey, Dexter, and Drain in addition to frequently preaching at Pleasant Hill. He was particularly active in preaching in protracted meetings, and he was often paired with his uncle in these meetings. Typical of the reports in the *Messenger* was this one in 1881 from a Christian at Trent:

> Brothers Philip Mulkey and I. N. Mulkey commenced a meeting at Lost Valley school house, near this place, on Friday evening, May 20th, continuing until the following Wednesday evening. The immediate result being ten additions to the church (at Trent); nine by baptism, and one (Sister Ida Panter) reclaimed. Surely we have good reasons to rejoice, and, indeed, we have been made to rejoice to see so many bow to the will of heaven while in their youth.
>
> Brother I. N. Mulkey has been filling his monthly appointments at the place of said meeting for about two years, and he is now permitted, at least in part, to enjoy the fruits of his efficient labors. Truly some prophets have honor and success in their own country.[25]

Like Newt Mulkey, most preachers migrating to Oregon in the 1870s came by train. But there were a few poorer ones who were still compelled to travel overland on the Oregon Trail. Among the latter was Civil War veteran George P. Rich and his wife, Nancy, who lived very close to the trail in Nemaha County, Kansas. In 1875, George and Nancy decided to move their growing family (they would eventually have 13 children) to far-away Oregon. They arrived in May of that year and settled in the northern reaches of Clackamas County between Kelso and Pleasant Home.

George was not well-educated, and he was personally embarrassed at his poor grasp of English grammar. Nevertheless, soon after his arrival in Oregon, the 27-year-old preacher found that his humble gifts were in demand. He began preaching on a regular basis for Churches of Christ in Clackamas County—most often at Damascus and Rock Creek. An anonymous correspondent from Damascus reported to the *Pacific Christian Messenger*, "Brother Rich preaches for us on the second and fourth Lord's days. He is a young man, but he uses the Word of God with power."[26]

The Damascus Church was undoubtedly the outgrowth of the John Foster congregation on the Clackamas River. This was the second oldest church established by the Christians in Oregon, and it was celebrating its 30th anniversary when George P. Rich began preaching for them twice a month in 1876. One member enthused about the young preacher, "Since the 1st of last June, by Brother Rich's preaching, there have been six confessions by baptism, one by relation, and one reclaimed; total number of members at present sixty, prospects bright ahead for more."[27]

Despite his own self-consciousness about his lack of formal education, George Rich was clearly loved by the common people who populated the rural churches in Clackamas County. After hearing Rich preach in a gospel meeting in Cherryvale, one church leader wrote:

> Brother Rich is indeed a workman that needeth not to be ashamed, rightly dividing the word of truth, and has such an earnest, sympathetic way of presenting the plain unvarnished truths of the Bible, that his hearers are led to see their duty to God, and many are led to obey their Savior.[28]

Two other young preachers who moved to Oregon in the 1870s were C. H. Hodges and S. C. Espy. The little congregations at St. Helens and Scappoose in Columbia County were the beneficiaries of their youthful energy. Columbia County, above Portland on the Washington border, had been virtually neglected by the Restoration Movement until Dr. James McBride and his wife retired to St. Helens in 1867. Before McBride's death in 1875, he had been able to organize congregations in both St. Helens and Scappoose. In describing his own ministry in this region, Espy wrote in May 1877:

> I plead guilty of proclaiming the glad tidings at Scappoose and elsewhere in Columbia County, Oregon, and of baptizing a few of the disciples of that county; but the building of the congregation there is not my work, it is the result of the labor of Brother McBride deceased, and I am sure that if any person will visit the county they will find thirty or more disciples "anchored firm on the rock." . . . When I left Columbia County about one year ago, the brethren at Scappoose and elsewhere in Columbia County were in the care of Jesus the "Shepherd and Bishop" of souls. Brother Walker was their elder, Brother C. Wood and Brother Harris deacons, and Brother Hodges, a graduate of Bethany College, was laboring among them in word and doctrine. Brother L. L. Rowland has also labored among some during the last year; both of these brethren are good preachers or proclaimers of the glad tidings . . . .[29]

Sebastian Adams, the son-in-law of the McBrides, had often visited the church in St. Helens while his in-laws were still living. Following their deaths, he continued to make periodic visits to strengthen the band of believers in that area. Corresponding with David Truman Stanley from St. Helens in July 1877, Adams wrote:

> Permit me through the columns of the *Messenger* to report that I preached twice on Sunday the 15th, and also on the 22nd, at this place, to large and attentive congregations. Three very excellent and noble women and one old gentleman of 75 believed with their heart, made confession with their mouth, and were buried by baptism into the likeness of Christ's death, in the grand and beautiful waters of the Columbia River. I feel impressed that other precious sheaves will yet be garnered.[30]

At the other end of the state, a new resident in Douglas County named Edward A. Chase was finding it difficult to answer all the calls for preaching. His calendar was full in the fall of 1876. "We expect to commence a meeting in Camas Swale on Friday before the second Lord's day in September," he wrote to a friend. "One at Yoncalla, commencing on the Saturday before the first Lord's day in October; each meeting to continue over two Lord's days provided my strength will hold out that long." Others were pleading for his attention. "The call comes up from Lookingglass, Myrtle Creek, Canyonville and other places," he informed his friend. "May the Lord strengthen us all to do our whole duty."[31]

Chase was especially pleased that he had been able to strengthen the 15-member church in the isolated Douglas County district that bordered Day's Creek. "I first met with this congregation last November," he informed the readers of the *Messenger* in May 1877. "There were four or five members scattered over a distance of fifteen or twenty miles, but all rallied to the support of the truth, and are now in a condition to make their influence felt. It is 50 miles from my place to their place of meeting," he admitted, "yet I have managed to meet them each month so far." Chase had assisted in organizing the small band of believers, and now he wrote proudly, "Brothers Andrew McCabe and Dillard Strode were elected elders. Brethren J. C. Harris and J. R. Jennings, deacons, and Brother William Briggs, clerk."[32]

But the good news was tempered with reality. None of the small congregations in Douglas County were in a position to support Chase in such a way that he could devote all of his energy to preaching and organizing churches. He had achieved fine results within a limited schedule, and he would accomplish more in the future, but now it was time to confront his debts. He described his predicament to the editor of the *Messenger*:

> But I regret to inform you that I am compelled to suspend preaching and go to work. We have had some sickness and my debts must be paid, and there seems no other way to do but to go to work. Times are hard here, consequently I have not done much for the *Messenger*. I think after harvest we can do more.[33]

For more than 30 years the Restoration Movement in Oregon had depended on the sacrificial labors of an heroic band of dedicated proclaimers of the gospel. Without the promise of any financial remuneration, this pioneer generation of farmer-preachers had left their plows standing and gone forth on faith to plant the standard of the cross throughout the territory.

But a new generation of young preachers, most of them college-trained, were arriving in Oregon in increasing numbers in the late 1870s. They were gravitating to the larger and wealthier urban churches who were looking for full-time ministers. Those preachers shaped by the pioneer mold, who would willingly preach without salary, were increasingly relegated to the little rural churches that dotted the Oregon back country.

68,000 Miles on Horseback

A. L. Todd always felt uncomfortable when he was offered money for preaching the gospel of Christ. His wife, Angeline Tate Todd, shared his discomfort. On one occasion he closed a protracted meeting at Myrtle Creek by baptizing 15 people at one time, and afterwards a grateful congregation took up a collection. But his wife did not want him to accept the offering. "I felt like it was begging," she confided to her daughter. "I wanted him to preach for the saving of souls, not for money." When the church at Canyonville tried to give him some money, Todd stood up and said: "That is against my wish; I do not wish a collection taken for me."[34]

It was not that Todd was independently wealthy. His resources were so limited that he often could not afford the candles that were necessary to light his log cabin. He cut blazes in the pine trees on his farm and then regularly collected the balls of pitch that formed at the base of each slashed tree. He burned these pitch deposits at night so that he could have enough light to study his Bible and write the outlines for his sermons.

For many years Todd maintained a full calendar of preaching appointments. His normal routine was to preach the first Sunday of every month at Canyonville (60 miles round-trip); the second Sunday at Calapooia (50 miles round-trip); the third Sunday at Myrtle Creek (44 miles round-trip), and the fourth Sunday for his home congregation at Lookingglass (6 miles round-trip). On the four "fifth Sundays" in every year's calendar, he would preach at Camas Valley. His daughter remembered:

> At each of these appointments away from home he often preached Saturday afternoon and Saturday night, Sunday at eleven and also at one or three in the afternoon, and at night; making from one to four sermons each trip, sometimes more; for he held protracted meetings of about two weeks' duration, at least once each year, at each of these places, and sometimes more.[35]

How many sermons did A. L. Todd preach during his 31-year ministry in Oregon? His children researched this question and concluded that the number exceeded 4,000 and was probably closer to 5,000. In addition, he officiated at a large number of weddings and preached many funerals. As to how many people he immersed into Christ, his children thought that "no one save his Master will ever know." All they knew for certain was that "he baptized nearly everywhere he preached."[36]

To answer the question of how far their father had traveled on horseback to proclaim the gospel, his children calculated the round-trip mileage of all his preaching appointments and then added all of his annual preaching tours to places like the Willamette Valley and Coos County. After carefully adding the totals for 31 years, they concluded that he had traveled more than 68,000 miles on horseback over muddy roads and mountain trails as a messenger for Jesus Christ.

A. L. Todd was a friend of preachers, both young and old. He assisted in commissioning and setting apart at least five young men for the preaching ministry, including Edward A. Chase and Isaac N. Muncy. Older preachers were always honored guests at the Todd farmhouse in Lookingglass Valley. One of his daughters wrote:

> Our home was the resting place for all tired preachers. They came often to rest with him from their work; were always welcome and stayed as long as they cared to stay. Old Brother [Israel] Clark,[37] when he knew his end was near, came and was cared for and died there. Father and Mother watched over him as they would have done for their own parent, and when his spirit took its departure for the other world, they gave his remains a respectable burial.[38]

Toward the end of his life, Todd began to worry that he had set a bad example by never accepting financial support for his preaching. When he urged young men to preach the gospel, they responded by saying they would not be able to support their families. He decided to invest in some mercury ("quicksilver") mines in order to raise money to help educate and support young men for the ministry. He wrote out his last will and testament and pasted it in the family Bible. It read, "This, my last will and testament shows that it is my desire that all money made in the mines over and above enough to make my family a living shall be used to educate and pay young men for the ministry."

In the judgment of his children, A. L. Todd was a faithful example of a self-sacrificing Christian preacher who devoted his entire life to the cause of Christ. "For of all the sermons that he ever preached in life," his son wrote, "there is none so eloquent to his children and those who knew him best as the one he lived."[39]

The Prudence Papers

It was inevitable that the columns of the *Pacific Christian Messenger* would begin to reverberate with discussions pro and con on the advisability of "hiring" preachers. As the decade of the 1880s dawned, Sebastian Adams published a rebuke directed toward members of the church who were opposed to hiring preachers. As far as he was concerned, such members were like dead limbs that needed to be pruned in order for the tree to achieve new growth.

Elderly Aaron Payne, now in his 90s, responded for the pioneer generation. Since his arrival in Oregon in 1847, he had preached whenever and wherever, without regard to recompense. He reminded Adams that there was a time when the Restoration Movement had "universally opposed" a hired ministry. Payne was only too aware that the current generation referred to the pioneers as "old fogies," and he was keenly cognizant of the fact that he could not alter the drift of the movement. He was "very thankful that those that oppose the hiring of the clergy, for the good of the church and the world, are nearly all dead, and gone to heaven."[40]

An anonymous young Christian from Coos County, with the pen name "Celsus," entered the fray. He held Payne and "all our old and long tried soldiers of the Cross" in the highest esteem, but he disagreed with their interpretation of Paul's teaching. He argued:

> Paul, by his example, would, as far as example can go, enjoin upon the ministry to be diligent and do all they can to keep from being an encumbrance to the church; but by his precepts he enjoins upon the churches to remunerate the labors of those who reap for them the harvest and make themselves the instruments under God of building up the church militant, and I am satisfied that no church whose hands grip too closely the filthy lucre, and thereby starve out or drive off to other fields able and faithful preachers, will ever be prosperous, or ever attain any eminence in spirituality, but will have souls dwarfed by parsimony, and

> no enlarged and outspreading conceptions of this most glorious gospel, proclaimed by such men as Paul and his co-laborers.[41]

Beginning with the March 26, 1880, issue, the *Pacific Christian Messenger* published a series of anonymous articles by "Silas, Jr." under the title of "Prudence Papers." Silas was clearly in sympathy with "Celsus" and Sebastian Adams, and in his article in the April 9 issue he issued a challenge to the pioneer way of doing things. "There are only two methods of filling a pulpit," he argued. "A person must be either called or sent." Regardless of whether a preacher was "called" or "sent," both methods presupposed that the church would support his labors.

Then Silas used blunt language to drive home his point. "These good nice preachers," he wrote sarcastically, "who are so liberal as to preach for nothing—volunteer workers. Beware of them." Pressing his point further, he argued: "I once heard of a preacher who said he had preached for twenty years and had never charged anything for his labor . . . . Beware of the man who works for nothing."[42]

An anonymous correspondent calling himself "James the Elder" replied to say that he had not been prepared to read such a bold charge "that one who would preach for nothing was to be totally driven out of the field as a suspicious and unworthy character." He wrote:

> Silas should have waited a little longer before avowing such sentiments. Should have waited at least till all those old pioneer preachers are dead who went forth without scrip or purse to fight the battles of the Reformation, and without being called or sent, pushed the Word into destitute places, and whose labors were crowned with such glorious results—results which have never been equaled, not even by all the "called" "sent" paid preachers of subsequent times . . .
>
> If the cause of Christ, in the past, had depended upon the work of a paid ministry, it had long since drooped and died. And I humbly conceive that its future success does not depend on a "called" or "sent" paid ministry. I am inclined to think that the poorest paid preachers of whom we have any account have been the most successful; while on the other hand I believe that the love of money, the root of all evil, has

> had more to do in corrupting the ministry and the church of God, than all other influences combined.[43]

"James the Elder" was so upset by the charge of Silas that he felt "like paraphrasing his words and saying: Beware of the good, nice preachers who will not preach without money. Beware of them. Beware of the man who will not work in the cause of Christianity without pay." James went further: "And I am almost ready to add, Beware of the able bodied man who depends solely upon the church for his food and raiment, and will not work with his hands."

The more James wrote, the angrier he got. "It is not the man that will preach for nothing that is really to be dreaded, but the one who will not preach without money," he thundered. "For the difference between the two is simply this, one preaches through love for Christ and trusts him for his pay, while the other preaches through love for money and takes no trust of any, but must be paid if 'sent' or 'called.' He never moves otherwise."[44]

Philip Mulkey had been reading the exchange between Silas and James the Elder with extreme interest. "I simply want to acknowledge my appreciation of James' article," he wrote in a letter to T. F. Campbell. "If it had not been for men who were neither called nor sent, there would have been no congregations to call or send: consequently there would have been no place for Silas and his kind." Then the aging son of John Mulkey, looking backward over a lifetime devoted to the glorious cause of primitive Christianity, eloquently expressed the fears of his pioneer generation:

> It mortifies me to see the old faithful brethren who planted and established the cause in this country, and wore out the frame of their lives in preaching, ignored and set at naught by these hirelings; and the people warned to *beware of them*. There are a few of them still lingering on the shores of time—G. O. Burnett, the brothers Powell, and others, who went out without price, proclaimed the unsearchable riches of Christ, and prepared the fields. Shall they be set at naught and their memories be forgotten?[45]

It was the anguished cry of a pioneer generation that had labored courageously to proclaim the ancient gospel in

Oregon Territory and did not want to be forgotten. The few who were "lingering on the shores of time" were soon gone. Noah Powell and Dr. James McBride had already died in 1875, followed by John Ecles Murphy in 1876, and Amos Harvey in 1877.

John Alkire Powell died in 1880, one month after Mulkey penned these words. Alfred Powell and John M. Harris died in 1881. Aaron Payne passed away in 1883, Alfred R. Elder in 1884 and G. W. Richardson in 1885. Glen Owen Burnett and A. L. Todd both died in 1886, followed by Edmund Green Browning and Elijah B. Davidson in 1888. Martin Peterson died in 1889, Daniel W. Elledge in 1890, and Caleb P. Chapman in 1892. When Thomas Franklin Campbell, Mac Waller, and Philip Mulkey all died in 1893, it pulled the final curtain on an exciting era that had witnessed the planting of the "glorious cause of primitive Christianity in the wilds of Oregon."

Chapter 22

A Preacher in the White House

1881

That President Garfield was more than a man of strong moral and religious convictions – that he was also a man of conscientious and fervid spiritual life, would scarcely be questioned . . . . In my judgment, there is no more interesting feature of his character than his loyal allegiance to the body of Christians in which he was trained, and the fervent sympathy with which he shared in their Christian communion.

– President Noah Porter, Yale College, 1881

The *Pacific Christian Messenger* estimated that in 1879 there were approximately 4,000 members of the church in Oregon, and the following year there was another published account that reported 4,750 adherents to the Restoration Movement in Oregon.[1] However, despite the encouraging numbers, the Christians were not very well known to the church-going populace and even less well-known to the general public. For nearly forty years they had labored in relative obscurity – characterized as "Campbellites" if characterized at all. But all of that was about to change.

1880 Republican National Convention

Chicago, Illinois, was hosting the Republican National Convention in June 1880, and for more than a week the windy city had been "a swirling, hectic madhouse." One account noted, "Each incoming train disgorged a fresh load of Republicans who scrambled for hotel rooms, roamed the corridors looking for familiar faces, crowded the lobbies spreading the latest rumors and sampled the local liquors . . . ."[2] In the midst of the uproar, a congressman from Ohio named James Abram Garfield quietly checked into room 108 in the Grand Pacific Hotel and prepared for a busy week.[3] The former Civil War general had been tapped to be the floor manager for Ohio's favorite son, John Sherman.

Sunday, June 6 was an exceedingly stormy morning in Chicago, with a cold rain blowing in from Lake Michigan. Very few of the out-of-town guests in the city ventured forth from their comfortable hotels on such a miserable morning. But in spite of the inclement weather, Congressman Garfield briskly exited the ornate lobby of the Grand Pacific Hotel, hailed a carriage, and rode more than three miles to the meetinghouse of the Christian Church. Once there, he listened appreciatively to the preaching of his old friend, Otis A. Burgess.[4] There was nothing unusual about Garfield going to great lengths to find an opportunity to worship with his brethren. Unless he was ill, the congressman from northeastern Ohio seldom missed attending a church service on the Lord's day.

Earlier in his career, James A. Garfield had been "a favorite preacher" for the Restoration Movement in northeastern Ohio, and he had also served for several years as president of a fine Christian school called Western Reserve Eclectic Institute (later Hiram College) in the same region. Garfield had enjoyed a very close friendship with Alexander Campbell in the 1850s and 60s, and he had been a member of the board of trustees at Bethany College for the past 14 years. Over a 17-year period he had been a very active member of the Vermont Avenue Christian Church in the nation's capital.

The balloting for the Republican nomination began on Monday, June 7, and continued into Tuesday. The three leading candidates, Ulysses S. Grant, James G. Blaine, and John Sherman, struggled mightily to gain a majority, but after more than 30 ballots it became increasingly clear that none of the three would be able to secure the nomination. On the 34th ballot the name of James A. Garfield received support from Wisconsin for the first time, and on the 35th ballot Indiana wheeled into line behind Wisconsin. On the 36th ballot it became a landslide as state after state in the exhausted and deadlocked convention, including Oregon, threw their support to the 48-year-old former Christian preacher.

A Preacher for President

The news of Garfield's nomination was received with pleasure and surprise by Christians in most parts of the country. Only in the South, where some church leaders had not forgiven him for his strong military involvement in the Civil War, was there opposition to Garfield's candidacy from Christian editors.[5] John F. Rowe, editor of the *American Christian Review* in Indianapolis, Indiana, spoke for the majority of Christians when he editorialized:

> General James A. Garfield, recently nominated by the Chicago Republican Convention for the Presidency of the United States, is a member of the Church of Christ, and has been for about thirty years . . . besides being a statesman of acknowledged ability, his private life has been pure, and . . . his Christian character is without a stain . . . . We have known Brother Garfield personally for twenty-five years, and during all that time have known him as an humble Christian . . . . The last time we were in Washington city we found him teaching a Bible class in the Sunday-school . . . . We have spoken these few words in praise of Brother Garfield as a Christian citizen . . . because we think our brethren at large feel pleased that so distinguished an honor has been conferred on one of our brethren.[6]

On November 2, 1880, ten million Americans went to the polls and elected James A. Garfield to be the twentieth president of the United States. But Garfield's victory over the Democratic candidate, General Winfield Scott Hancock, was no landslide. He squeaked by with a popular plurality of only 7,368 votes, or less than one tenth of one percent of the total votes cast. As expected, Garfield failed to carry a single southern state, and he lost in Texas by nearly one hundred thousand votes. Each party carried nineteen states, but the Republicans won the important ones.[7]

The majority of Oregon Christians supported Garfield's candidacy, and it is not difficult to make the case that their loyal support provided the difference in Oregon's very close election. Garfield defeated Hancock in Oregon by a narrow vote of 20,619 to 19,955. The slim majority of only 664 votes out of more than 40,000 cast gave Garfield his closest state victory in the election.[8]

Stirring the Church with Great Power

Garfield was deluged with congratulatory letters in the first week after his election, but none more significant than the one penned by Burke Hinsdale, the president of Hiram College. This good friend wrote:

> I have been astonished . . . at the hold that your candidacy took of the religious mind of the country. It has stirred the Disciples with great power, but has reached out beyond them and embraced all the Protestant bodies. "Now we are going to have a religious man for President" is a thought that has swelled in the hearts of thousands of religious men.[9]

In his response to this letter, the president-elect carefully defined his relationship with his religious brethren. "Our people must remember that they are not a very large percent of the whole Republican party and a still smaller percent of the whole American people," he reasoned with Hinsdale, "and it would not be difficult for me to injure the administration by giving undue prominence to the Disciples in matters of appointment. Let us not flaunt ourselves in the face of the American people as though we had made a special conquest, but by modesty and moderation bear our part worthily and take whatever resulting advantages may come."[10]

The Presidential Inaugural took place on Friday, March 4, 1881. Two days later the attention of the nation was focused on the obscure meetinghouse of the Vermont Avenue Christian Church in Washington, D.C. This was an opportunistic Sunday for the Christians, and they made the most of it. A special program was arranged, with Garfield's approval, that included several nationally-known ministers from the Restoration Movement. Under a headline that read, "President Garfield At Church," the Associated Press reported the next day:

> It seemed as if everybody took a sudden interest yesterday in the doctrines of the Disciples. Before ten o'clock in the morning crowds of people were concentrating in the Christian Church on Vermont Avenue, where President Garfield worships. The church, with its gallery and Sunday-school rooms, was speedily filled to overflowing, and disappointed thousands were unable to obtain admission.[11]

The responsibility for the sermon fell on Chaplain George G. Mullins of the United States Army, one of Garfield's good friends. Mullins preached on a portion of the third verse of Jude: ". . . ye should earnestly contend for the faith which was once delivered unto the saints." The sermon was entitled "The Faith of the Disciples," and its contents were widely published in newspapers across America that week. In Oregon, excerpts of the sermon were published in several newspapers and Oregon Christians were recipients of an unprecedented period of good will that focused attention on the main themes of the Restoration Movement. During Garfield's first frenetic months in office, he remained constant in his Sunday attendance at the Vermont Avenue Christian Church. The press snidely referred to the Vermont meetinghouse as the "Campbellite shanty," but after Garfield's election its seats were always filled hours ahead of time.

Assassination of the President

On Saturday morning, July 2, 1881, four months after he entered office, Garfield was shot twice at point-blank range as he walked through the Baltimore and Potomac Railroad depot in Washington, D.C. The assassin was a deranged man named Charles Guiteau who was a disappointed office-seeker. The mortally wounded president was immediately rushed to the White House where it was thought that he might not live through the first night. For three days, Garfield's life hung in the balance. But to the surprise of everyone, he rallied and for eleven agonizing weeks, through the heat of the summer, he fought valiantly for his life.

The Restoration Movement continued to receive worldwide publicity during Garfield's courageous battle. One church historian recalled:

> The President's religion was the chief thing prominently brought to light during the entire time of his illness, and when it became generally known that he was identified with the religious people known as "Disciples of Christ," or "Churches of Christ," this fact of itself drew special attention to their principles and aims, and gave their religious movement an importance which it had never attained before.[12]

This was just as true in Oregon as it was in other parts of the world. As a result of Garfield's election and assassination, the principles and history of the Restoration Movement became more widely known and appreciated than ever before. After years of strident "opposition from the sects," Oregon Christians enjoyed a brief chapter in their history in which they basked in the glow of public approval. The grandson of Glen Owen Burnett, Thomas J. Graves, and his wife, Martha Shelton, welcomed a son into their Yamhill County home in the summer of 1881 when the eyes of the nation were on the sick room in the White House. These Christians were proud of their spiritual connection to the dying president, and they promptly named their son Herbert Garfield Graves.

Lament for a Fallen Hero

Garfield's suffering ended quietly on Monday evening, September 19, 1881. The shock had been lessened somewhat by long weeks of anxiety, but the news of the president's death triggered the greatest outpouring of grief since the death of Abraham Lincoln.

On Saturday, September 24, the Portland *Daily Oregonian* had its usual full page detailing all of the church services and sermon titles for the next day. One title that undoubtedly caught the attention of many readers was the one submitted by Bruce Wolverton, the preacher for the Christian Church that met on the corner of Columbia and Park. The title of Wolverton's 11:00 a.m. sermon was, "Lessons from the Faithful Life and Sad Death of our Brother in Christ, James A. Garfield, drawn by the Lamp of Truth."[13] Given the unique spiritual ties between America's 20th President and the Restoration Movement, no other church in Portland could have used the expression "Our Brother in Christ, James A. Garfield" in quite the same way. Bruce Wolverton was probably not the only Christian preacher in Oregon to claim a special relationship with America's slain President on the Sunday following his death.

The public funeral was held at Lakeview Cemetery in Cleveland, Ohio, on Monday, September 26. In honor of this occasion President Chester Arthur called for a day of fasting and prayer throughout the land. Isaac Errett, editor of the *Christian Standard* and Garfield's friend of many years, was chosen by the family to deliver the eulogy.

More than 250,000 people were in the public park or nearby vicinity when Errett began his 40-minute address. He reviewed Garfield's conversion to Christ and his budding career as a Christian preacher. "You are within a few miles of the spot," Errett informed the throng, "where the great congregations . . . hung upon words that fell from his lips, with admiration, wonder and enthusiasm." In the course of his remarks, Errett drove one point home with unusual clarity. "James A. Garfield went through his whole public life," Errett insisted, "without surrendering for a single moment his Christian integrity, his moral integrity, or his love for the spiritual."[14]

One prominent Oregon Christian was a participant in the trial of Charles J. Guiteau, the assassin of President Garfield. Dr. James H. McBride, the son of Dr. James McBride, was the superintendent of the Oregon Insane Asylum in Milwaukie for many years. As one of the leading nerve specialists in the country, he was summoned by the government to examine Guiteau and offer an opinion on his sanity. During the course of the trial, Dr. McBride was one of the government witnesses called to give testimony.[15]

In the months following the president's death, there were continuous memorial services and addresses across the country. Churches affiliated with the Restoration Movement were particularly active in this regard, and in Oregon there were memorial services for the slain president at several Christian churches including ones in Portland, Monmouth, and Eugene. In later years, historical stained glass windows in tribute to America's preacher-president were installed in the Christian churches in Portland and Eugene.

In Chicago, Illinois, the four Christian churches cooperated in a memorial service for Garfield, and they chose Otis A. Burgess to deliver the memorial address. In defending the appropriateness of such a memorial service, Burgess commented:

> And certainly for us, in whose communion he stood for more than thirty years, part of the time as one of our most honored preachers, and always as one of our most active and earnest members, it is fitting to give whatever expression to our deep feelings that words and tears can give as we say our sad goodbye over the grave of our distinguished, our beloved, brother.[16]

So Heroic a Faith

It was not only the community of Christians that gloried in Garfield's commitment to the Restoration Movement. Outsiders had also been impressed with his tenacious loyalty to the Christians with whom he had been reared. Noah Porter, president of Yale College and a Congregational clergyman, spoke for many when he observed:

> That President Garfield was more than a man of strong moral and religious convictions—that he was also a man of conscientious and fervid spiritual life, would scarcely be questioned . . . . In my judgment, there is no more interesting feature of his character than his loyal allegiance to the body of Christians in which he was trained, and the fervent sympathy with which he shared in their Christian communion . . . President Garfield adhered to the church of his mother, the

> church in which he was trained, and which he had served as a pillar and an evangelist, and yet with the largest and most unsectarian charity for all "who love our Lord in sincerity."[17]

Most Christians agreed with that assessment. "The lesson of his religious life will not be lost," said Otis Burgess. "His Church will cherish it as a part of their precious heritage, and unbelievers, touched by the glory of so heroic a faith, will be moved to inquire whence the fountains of such inspirations."[18] As Burgess rightly predicted, the Garfield saga continued to draw attention to his church connection. After Garfield's election, the Vermont Avenue Church had launched a national campaign to build a new church building in the nation's capital. Following his death, contributions continued to pour in, and the church announced that it would soon begin construction. Thomas Franklin Campbell gave frequent publicity and ample space to this national campaign in the pages of the *Pacific Christian Messenger*.

President Garfield and the Christians

On July 2, 1882, the first anniversary of the shooting of Garfield, the cornerstone was laid for the new meetinghouse on Vermont Avenue in Washington, D.C. More than 5,000 people, including President Chester Arthur, attended the ceremony, and newspapers across the country published accounts of the event. On January 20, 1884, the prestigious new home of the Vermont Avenue Christian Church was officially dedicated in a special three-hour service. Among those present were President Arthur again and many members of Congress. W. K. Pendleton, a son-in-law of Alexander Campbell and the current president of Bethany College, delivered the dedication address.[19] Once again, the Restoration Movement was the recipient of generous publicity in the nation's press.

Several years later, a respected church historian reflected back on the impact of Garfield's election and assassination on the Restoration Movement and concluded:

> It may seem almost sacrilegious to some to suggest that his death was much more powerful for good than his life

> could have been, even if it had continued for many years. Nevertheless, it is believed that this was true in his case. To use his own language, when another martyred president fell, the Lord still reigned, and the country was saved, even if Garfield died, and not only was this so, but the Church was saved also, and a new force entered into it from Garfield's death chamber when it was told everywhere that he died the death of a Christian, and that his Christianity consisted in a simple faith in, and obedience to, the Lord Jesus Christ, without any additions such as belong to the creeds of Christendom. At any rate, it is certain that through his death the plea of the Disciples was practically made known to the civilized world.[20]

At the beginning of 1880, the Restoration Movement in Oregon was continuing to demonstrate spiritual vitality on many fronts and there were more than 4,000 adherents to "the glorious cause" scattered throughout the state. The election and assassination of President James A. Garfield did nothing to diminish these statistics. Like their brethren in other parts of the world, Oregon Christians were stirred with "great power" by Garfield's political prominence, and they found a sustaining strength in retelling the saga of the life and death of "The Preacher President."[21]

Epilogue

That the Cause May Be Preserved

My fear is that this reformation contended for by Thomas Campbell and Alexander Campbell, father and son, B. W. Stone and Walter Scott, is to be divided. But my prayer is that the cause may be preserved, and that we may all be willing to adopt the motto of these noble men; that is, "Where the Word of God speaks, we speak; where it is silent, we are silent.

— Caleb Davis, Lane County, Oregon, 1873

Caleb Davis was born in Ohio in 1820 and reared in west-central Indiana. He married Ann Chrisman in Boone County, Indiana, in 1842, and they raised a large family of 11 children. Caleb and Ann were devout Christians, and when James Madison Mathes launched the monthly *Christian Record* from Bloomington, Indiana, in July 1843 they were among the first subscribers. They named their second child Barton Warren Davis in honor of the beloved Kentucky reformer, Barton Warren Stone, who had recently died.

When the Davis family migrated to Oregon Territory in 1858, they brought with them a passionate love for the Restoration Movement and a complete set of well-thumbed back issues of the *Christian Record.* Upon arrival in Oregon they renewed their subscription to the *Record* and looked for ways to strengthen the cause of primitive Christianity in the new land. They settled first in the Linn County neighborhood of John Alkire Powell and were members of his Central congregation. Later they moved south to Lane County in March 1866, settled in the Pleasant Hill district, and became very active members of the Pleasant Hill Church of Christ. Occasionally, Caleb would send encouraging reports on the progress of the cause in Oregon back to Indiana for publication in the *Record.*

Caleb Davis was typical of those members of the Restoration Movement who were disappointed when the American Christian Missionary Society was organized in Cincinnati, Ohio, in the fall of 1849. Davis was convinced that there was no scriptural justification for missionary societies or any other kind of man-made organizations doing the work of the church, and he was worried about what he considered an alarming concentration of power in the position of corresponding secretary of the ACMS. It particularly bothered Davis that the *Christian Record,* which he greatly respected, had endorsed the ACMS from the beginning and had continued to give it unconditional support for almost a quarter century.

In a significant letter to J. M. Mathes, penned from Lane County on November 3, 1873, Davis chided Mathes for his vigorous advocacy "of a cause I think without foundation in the Word of God." He continued, "I refer of course to the missionary cause, of which Thomas Munnell[1] is Corresponding Secretary." Then giving expression to his greatest concerns, Davis wrote prophetically:

> My fear is, that this reformation contended for by Thomas Campbell and Alexander Campbell, father and son, B. W. Stone and Walter Scott, is to be divided. But my prayer is that the cause may be preserved, and that we may all be willing to adopt the motto of these noble men, "Where the Word of God speaks, we speak; where it is silent, we are silent".[2]

Mathes was quite sure that his old friend was guilty of overreacting to the situation when he talked about "the Reformation being divided by missionary work." The veteran editor confidently admitted that he personally had "no fears of the Reformation being divided by the missionary work." But in this cavalier judgment, subsequent events would prove him tragically wrong. A full decade and more before many others realized it, Oregon's Caleb Davis had accurately predicted the nature of the coming division. The division would be centered in a changing view of the nature of scripture, and in particular, it would focus on how to interpret the silence of scripture when confronting doctrinal disagreements. To the progressive mindset, the silence of scripture signaled permission. To the conservative mindset, it cautioned restraint.

When Caleb Davis wrote to James Mathes in the fall of 1873, Oregon Christians had at least 70 congregations in the state with an average membership of 50 in each. There were 3,500 baptized believers, not counting children and other adherents. Christian College had moved into Campbell Hall, and the school was growing in numbers and prestige. The *Christian Messenger* was increasing in circulation, and the annual State Meeting was drawing Sunday crowds of 6,000. Several dedicated evangelists were traveling and preaching through the Oregon countryside with encouraging results, and many new congregations were being established. A number of church buildings were under construction, and the churches were at peace. It was truly a "Golden Age" for the cause of primitive Christianity in Oregon, and it had been since the end of the Civil War.

And yet, incredibly, Caleb Davis worried that the movement had lost its way and was on the brink of a disastrous division. Within a decade, some others would begin to agree with his dire prediction. The annual State Meeting, after ten successive years of large attendance and multiple baptisms, was discontinued after 1877 and replaced with a Ministerial Association that never had more than 100 dues-paying members. Christian College was turned over to the State of Oregon and renamed "Oregon State Normal School." The *Pacific Christian Messenger* folded its tent and was replaced by a journal, the *Christian Herald*, that was not able to command the wide patronage in the church that its predecessor had enjoyed.

During the heralded Garfield era of 1880-1881, the Restoration Movement in Oregon appeared to be outwardly unified, but in less than five years, there were significant changes. One major turning point was the death of Jane Campbell and the subsequent decision by Thomas Franklin Campbell to resign from both Christian College and the *Pacific Christian Messenger* and leave Oregon.

It was Campbell's suggestion that the *Messenger* become the property of a joint-stock company, and that the company be composed of West Coast Christians and "be published in the interest of primitive Christianity and the promotion of the Christian church on this coast." One anonymous reader of the *Messenger,* calling himself "A Wayworn Disciple," corresponded with Campbell and expressed the concerns of many conservatives in the church when he asked:

> If the money is subscribed to the endowment of a paper, what kind of a paper may it be? Into whose control will it fall? Will "progressions" or "old fogies" control it? Will it go in for "organs," "church fairs," "pastors," and the other "new departures," or will it stand firm for the primitive order of things; or, will it be neither hot nor cold on any of those things, but merely a passive "nancy nobody?"

"Wayworn Disciple" was clearly worried about the future direction of both the *Messenger* and the cause that it championed. At the end of the letter he wrote:

> And now, in conclusion, let me say to you, Bro. Campbell, that it is with some degree of sorrow that I see in the future a time when your fingers will cease to wield the pen, and your mind control the columns of the church paper; and I feel that we are about to enter upon a critical experiment which will effect the cause of Christianity for good or evil, probably for many, many years in our midst. I hope and pray our conclusions and resolves in the matter may be guided and directed by the divine spirit, and result for good to them that love the Lord, and have the cause of Christianity at heart.[3]

In 1926, one historian reflected back on the significance of Thomas Franklin Campbell's departure from Christian College forty-four years earlier and wrote:

> It is not necessary to assume that the departure from Monmouth in the summer of 1882 of T. F. Campbell . . . caused the death of Christian College, severe as the loss of the elder man at that time was felt to be. Yet, it is a coincidence

> that the college, under its old name and character, did not long survive. Within a year its name was changed to the Oregon State Normal School and from that time the institution was familiarly known as the Monmouth Normal.[4]

It would be unfair to blame the succeeding president, David Truman Stanley, for the death of Christian College. Like his predecessors, Rowland and Campbell, Stanley was a graduate of Bethany College and a strong churchman. He would have been comfortable at the helm of a prosperous and growing church-related college. In reality, the Christian churches of Oregon did not have the financial resources or the requisite number of young people to support a growing college. Stanley believed the only hope for the continuation of the school was through state-supported funding, and he quickly moved the college in that direction. Nevertheless, the loss of Christian College was emotionally devastating to the Christian families of Oregon.

Other issues began to tear at the fabric of unity in the Oregon Restoration Movement. The Oregon Christian Missionary Society became a reality in the early 1880s, a logical outgrowth of the Ministerial Association. As expected, this new organizational development was not welcomed by all Christians. Nevertheless, in October 1882, when the "Christian Missionary Convention of the State of Oregon" convened at the brick meetinghouse of the Christian Church in Eugene, it enjoyed widespread support from a majority of Oregon Christians. The popular George M. Whitney gave the welcoming address for the 4-day event, and Sebastian Adams was chosen to preside over the convention. Philip Mulkey led the closing prayer at the Saturday morning session.[5]

Musical instruments were gradually introduced into the public worship assemblies of some of the larger urban churches in the early 1880s, but once again the practice was not universally accepted. The introduction of employing full-time "hired" ministers for the same urban churches became common practice, but some conservative Christians deplored "the one-man Pastor system" that was replacing the plurality of elders that had fed and nurtured the churches for years.

Caleb Davis had prayed in 1873 that "the cause" would be "preserved," but a progressive-conservative rift in the Oregon Restoration Movement became apparent in the mid-1880s. George P. Rich looked back to that time period as the watershed years when the church began to divide. Writing to a church paper in Indiana in 1895, Rich said:

> Ten years ago the Church of Christ in western Oregon was in peace and enjoying a good degree of prosperity in numbers at least. Such men as Waller and Bailes had baptized their thousands, and yet they worked at manual labor to support those who were dependent on them. In those days there was unity and love in all the congregations of the disciples of the Lord. It is true the great majority of the elders and teachers were unlearned and ignorant men, outside of the Word of the Lord. But they knew and could and did teach successfully in the face of the most bitter opposition.[6]

Albert Whitfield Lucas, an elder in the Monmouth Church, was another observer who felt that the Restoration Movement in Oregon began to lose its identity in the mid-1880s. In the summer of 1885 he sent an article on "The Cause in Oregon" to the *Christian Evangelist* in St. Louis, Missouri, in which he complained that the cause was not as prosperous as it had been. "A number of old pioneer preachers have died, some moved to other parts," he wrote sadly, "and with their departure much zeal has taken swift wings and flown away."

There was another practice that bothered Lucas. "Some preachers have been received from the sects about us," he noted, "and put to preaching immediately before learning the way of the Lord more perfectly." These were the same preachers who were excited when the celebrated Congregational minister from Brooklyn, Henry Ward Beecher, visited Oregon. Lucas was not enamored of the gospel that Beecher preached in Oregon, and he concluded:

> This is certainly a grand field, and I am confident the people are beginning to hunger and thirst for some good solid gospel preaching, such as Christ and Him crucified, and raised, and no Beecherism.[7]

To those most intimately involved in the progressive-conservative tensions buffeting the Oregon Restoration

Movement in the 1880s and 1890s, the reality of an unavoidable schism was evident by 1890. Most conservatives had always preferred the designation "Church of Christ"—or "Churches of Christ" when referring to more than one congregation—and now they began adopting this term exclusively. Most progressives had always been comfortable with all three of the most frequently used terms: "Disciples of Christ," "Christian Church," and "Church of Christ," and they continued for a time to make use of all three. However, with the conservatives using "Church of Christ" exclusively, the progressives gravitated toward the other two terms.

In their religious census of 1906, the United States Census Bureau gave official recognition for the first time to the division between Disciples of Christ and Christian Churches on one side and Churches of Christ on the other side. However, this was a belated recognition of a situation that had existed for at least a decade or more. It is generally conceded by historians that the statistics gathered for Churches of Christ in 1906 were inaccurate and therefore not very helpful, but there is no mistaking the fact that the Christian Churches had significantly higher numbers.

The census revealed that the Christian Churches had 8,293 churches and 982,701 members nationwide, while the Churches of Christ could account for only 2,649 churches and 159,658 members. Ten years later, in the more reliable 1916 census, it was discovered that the Christian Churches had 8,408 churches and 1,226,028 members nationwide, and the Churches of Christ had 5,570 churches and 317,937 members. In Oregon the differential was even more dramatic, and the conservatives were left with only a handful of churches and very few members at the time of the 1906 census. The situation had not changed much by the time of the 1916 census, when Churches of Christ in Oregon were represented as having just 23 congregations and 1,133 baptized believers.[8]

Beginning in the 1920s, the Christian Churches went through another gradual division between progressives (who became the Disciples of Christ) and moderates (who became the Independent Christian Churches and Churches of Christ).[9]

Today in Oregon there are approximately 45 churches affiliated with the Disciples of Christ, approximately 180 churches affiliated with the Independent Christian Churches and Churches of Christ, and approximately 120 churches affiliated with the Churches of Christ. In other words, there are nearly 350 Oregon churches today that can claim to be the spiritual offspring of the original 13-member church that began meeting on the banks of the Yamhill River in March of 1846. The combined Sunday morning worship attendance for these nearly 350 Oregon churches is more than 40,000 every Sunday.

Although separated by 150 years of tumultuous history, the modern-day heirs of the Restoration Movement have much to learn from their spiritual ancestors who came overland on the Oregon Trail. The first generation of Oregon Christians not only participated in the settling of the great Oregon Territory, they laid the foundation for what they proudly called "Bible Christianity." Above all, they died in the knowledge that they had been active participants in a "glorious cause" to restore "primitive Christianity" in their own day. One of their finest preachers, Dr. James McBride, spoke for them all when he said: "Some of the richest and most refreshing seasons from the presence of the Lord, ever witnessed by me, have been in the wilds of Oregon."

Some books are written to achieve fame, and others are written to make money. This book was written to rescue from oblivion the names of some humble Bible-believing men and women who were proud to wear the name of Christ. They never once thought of themselves as heroes or heroines, but they lived the most heroic of lives. We owe a debt of gratitude to the first generation of Oregon Christians. They laid the foundation for the beginnings of the Restoration Movement in Western America. May their story be remembered, cherished and retold by each succeeding generation of Oregon Christians.

Christian Preachers in Oregon

Beginning with the arrival of John Foster in the fall of 1845, and continuing to the inauguration of George Lemuel Woods as the third governor of Oregon in the fall of 1866, there were approximately 75 preachers from the Restoration Movement who preached in Oregon. Unfortunately, it is not possible to identify all of these preachers and the year they began preaching. However, the list below indicates that the largest number of Christian preachers came to Oregon in the 24 months between the fall of 1851 and the fall of 1853. By the last half of the 1860s and throughout the 1870s there were increasing numbers of Christian preachers who settled in Oregon. Although some of them were included in this volume, there was not sufficient space to mention all the preachers who served between 1866 and 1882.

1.	John Foster (1792-1868)	1845
2.	Dr. James McBride (1802-1875)	1846
3.	Glen Owen Burnett (1809-1886)	1846
4.	John Burris Smith (1816-1901)	1846
5.	Thomas Crawford McBride (1777-1857)	1847
6.	Aaron Payne (1789-1883)	1847
7.	Hugh McNary "Mac" Waller (1817-1893)	1847
8.	Alexander Vance McCarty (1825-1868)	1847
9.	Daniel Trullinger (1801-1868)	1848
10.	Caleb P. Chapman (1810-1892)	1848
11.	William Lysander Adams (1821-1906)	1848
12.	Alfred R. Elder (1806-1884)	1849
13.	Elijah A. Davidson (1783-1870)	1850
14.	Elijah Banton Davidson (1819-1888)	1850
15	Sebastian C. Adams (1825-1898)	1850
16.	Samuel Bates Briggs (1805-1872)	1851
17.	John Alkire Powell (1807-1880)	1851
18.	Noah Powell (1808-1875)	1851
19.	Alfred Powell (1810-1881)	1851
20.	Dr. John Nelson Perkins (1816- ?)	1851
21.	George W. Richardson (1824-1885)	1851
22.	Levi Burch (1824- ?)	1851
23.	John Rigdon (1796-1859)	1852
24.	John Ecles Murphy (1806-1876)	1852
25.	Gilmore Callison (1808-1869)	1852
26.	Henry W. Taylor (1808-1890)	1852
27.	Lewis Casteel (1813-1867)	1852
28.	Edmund Green Browning (1816-1888)	1852
29.	Abbott Levi James Todd (1820-1886)	1852

30.	Charles Bradshaw (1822-1898)	1852
31.	Harrison H. Hendrix (1823- ?)	1852
32.	George R. Caton (c1828- ?)	1852
33.	Israel L. Clark (1790- ?)	1853
34.	Patrick Rivers Haley (1802-1884)	1853
35.	Philip Mulkey (1802-1893)	1853
36.	Stephen Guthrie (1802-1865) (settled in W. T., but occasionally preached in Oregon)	1853
37.	William Huntington (1816-1894) (settled in W. T., but occasionally preached in Oregon)	1853
38.	William Ruble (1823- ?)	1853
39.	John F. Mulkey (1830-1903)	1853
40.	James R. Fisher (1819-1864)	1854
41.	Joel Vail (1828-1907) (arrived in 1853, and converted to the Christians in 1857)	1857
42.	William Thompson Haley (1833- ?) (returned to Oregon from Bethany College in November 1857)	1858
43.	Levi Lindsay Rowland (1831-1908) (returned to Oregon from Bethany College in 1859)	1859
44.	George M. Whitney (1830-1895) (arrived in Oregon earlier, and began preaching in 1860)	1860
45.	Daniel Boone Matheny (1829-c1891) (arrived in Oregon in 1843, and began preaching around 1860)	1860?
46.	Isham Burnett (1830-1916) (arrived in Oregon earlier, and began preaching around 1860)	1860?
47.	Joseph H. Sharp (1834-1913) (arrived in Oregon in 1852 and began preaching in 1861)	1861
48.	Keathley Bailes (1829-1915) (arrived in Oregon in 1861, and began preaching in 1862)	1862
49.	George Lemuel Woods (1832-1890) (arrived in Oregon in 1847, and began preaching in the 1860s)	1862?
50.	Orlando Alderman (1833-1903) (arrived in Oregon in 1848, and began preaching in the 1860s)	1862?
51.	Martin Peterson (1820-1889) (arrived in California in 1863, moved to southern Oregon in 1864)	1864
52.	William L. Mascher (1836-1872) (arrived in Oregon in 1850, and began preaching in the 1860s)	1864?
53.	Daniel W. Elledge (1813-1890)	1864
54.	John M. Harris (1803-1881)	1865
55.	Peter Rogers Burnett (1842-1922) (arrived in Oregon in 1846, and began preaching in 1865)	1865

56.	Samuel Y. Bailey (may have preached in Oregon as early as the 1850s)	1865?
57.	A. W. Flint (may have preached in Oregon as early as the 1850s)	1865?
58.	Francis Dillard Holman (1831-1899) (arrived in Oregon in 1845, and began preaching after the Civil War)	1866?
59.	Rufus Gilmore Callison (1839-1915) (arrived in Oregon in 1852, and began preaching after the Civil War)	1866?
60.	Jasper Vincent Crawford (1839-1915) (arrived in Oregon in 1851, and began preaching after the Civil War)	1866?
61.	Ephraim W. Barnes (arrived in Oregon in 1852, and began preaching after the Civil War)	1866?
62.	James A. Campbell (1847-1916) (arrived in Oregon in 1852, and began preaching in 1866)	1866

Church Leaders Who Preached

Some Oregon church leaders presented lessons at church or performed weddings occasionally but did not really consider themselves to be preachers. Included in this category were: Elijah Bristow (1788-1872); Amos Harvey (1799-1877); Christian Deardorff (1805-1884); Thomas J. Lovelady (1806-1890); William Porter (1812-1899); Ira F. M. Butler (1812-1909); Harrison Linville (1813-1893); David R. Lewis (1814-1894); Vincent Scott McClure (1815-1893); William Murphy (1816-1874), a brother to John Ecles Murphy; William Dawson (1816-1889); Hiram Alva Johnson (1819-1896); Charles Bisbee Dart (1820-1902); Thomas C. Shaw (1823-1898); Elias Cox (1823-1907); William John Herren (1824-1891); William Wilshire Bristow (1826-1874); James Addison Bushnell (1826-1912); Albert Whitfield Lucas (1827-1893); James F. Amis (1828-1912); William P. Murphy (1831- ?), a son of John Ecles Murphy; Nathan T. Caton (1832-1916); Elijah Weddle (1834-1912); George S. Downing (1836- ?); P. P. Underwood (c1836- ?); and Reuben Doty (1838-1899).

Oregon Preachers in the 1870s

In addition to many of the preachers listed above, some of the Christian preachers who served in Oregon in the 1870s were: Thomas Franklin Campbell, William Lane, Troy Shelley, Peter Shuck, D. D. Weddle, Isaac Newton Mulkey, Jasper Jesse Moss, Rufus H. Moss, Calvin Adams, W. W. Watson, John Engard Roberts, Henry Clay Fleming, Allen Jefferson Huddleston, Charles W. H. Smith, James C. Campbell, Ephraim Nott, Thomas McBride Morgan, W. D. Owens, James H. Moore, Edward A. Chase, Isaac N. Muncy, William Manning, H. T. Morrison, Amos Buchanan, Leo Willis, Bruce Wolverton, Charles Wright, George W. Smith, George Pew Rich, C. H. Hodges, S. C. Espy, David Truman Stanley, Prince Lucien Campbell, R. L. Shelley, Dr. R. M. Doty, J. W. Spriggs, George H. Barnett, J. F. Floyd, S. Monroe Hubbard, Ephraim Badger, John L. Wigle, and L. B. Trullinger. Three Christian preachers from northern California, John Provines McCorkle, James W. Webb and Alexander Johnston, labored with Oregon churches at different times in the late 1870s and early 1880s.

Unsolved Problems

1. On p. 364 of T. P. Haley's *Historical and Biographical Sketches of the Early Churches and Pioneer Preachers of the Christian Church in Missouri*, published in 1888, the author reported that three Missouri preachers, Dr. James McBride, James Lovelady and James Cox, moved to Oregon in 1840. It is true that Dr. McBride came overland in 1846, but there is no evidence that Lovelady or Cox ever visited Oregon.

2. In his 1878 article in the *Pacific Christian Messenger* entitled "A Visit to Tualatin Plains," Glen Owen Burnett recalled his labors with Dr. James McBride in Washington County in the summer and fall of 1847. As a result of their efforts, a Baptist minister identified as "Dr. Evans" was among those who "threw off all human appendages and gave adherence to Christ alone and to the word of his grace." Unfortunately, Dr. Evans died a short time later "in the infancy of his usefulness to the cause." Nothing more is known about this preacher who "had been a Baptist minister for a number of years, and was a man of fine abilities and moral worth."

3. On p. 251 of Sarah Hunt Steeves' *Book of Remembrance of Marion County, Oregon, Pioneers 1840-1860*, there is a reference to "Rev. Begley" who is described as "a Campbellite preacher" in the 1852 migration. There was a "Rev. Daniel Bagley" who came to Oregon around that time and settled briefly in Polk County. However, it is almost certain that he was a Methodist preacher. He married Ann Mulkey in Douglas County in 1860, and he died in Seattle in 1905.

4. On p. 6 of Victor Emanuel Hoven's 1918 master's thesis entitled "The Beginnings and Growth of the Church of Christ in Oregon," the author mentioned a pioneer Oregon preacher named Patrick Haley. He identifies this preacher as a brother to William Thompson Haley. His source for this identification is his interview with 75-year-old Peter Rogers Burnett who may have known the Haley family. However, it can not be established that W. T Haley had a brother named Patrick. In all probability, this is a reference to Patrick Rivers Haley, the father of W. T. Haley.

5. In a letter penned July 24, 1866 and published in the *Christian Standard*, John M. Harris listed eleven preachers who were his co-laborers in the Willamette Valley, and then added "and brethren Crossly, Sherwood and Watson." These names are not familiar, although the middle one could refer to John Sherwood in Marion County and the last one could refer to Sanford Watson in Polk County. Harris implies that these three brethren were vitally involved in the evangelistic efforts that were taking place in the Willamette Valley.

6. A news release published in the *Christian Messenger* listed all of the preachers who were present at the annual State Meeting in 1872. Most of the names were familiar, but three of the preachers, identified by last name only, were new. The last names of the preachers were: Owens, Hamilton and Boly. Owens was most likely a reference to W. D. Owens who was preaching for the Eugene Church, but nothing more is known about him. Subsequent references indicated that Hamilton and Boly were both preaching in eastern Oregon, but no other information has been discovered on these preachers.

7. On p. 65 of the article on his father entitled "Rev. A. L. J. Todd: Pioneer Circuit Rider," Aurelius Todd provided the names of 16 preachers who assisted his father in gospel meetings. Eleven of those names were well-known, but five were unfamiliar. Three of the unfamiliar names were identified with last names only. The five preachers were: Isaac Hughes, Robert Paris, Brother Johnson, Brother Ford and Brother MacCallister. Nothing more is known about the ministries of these five men.

8. Among the church records for the Pleasant Hill Church in Lane County there is a document entitled "Names of Ministers who have preached at the Pleasant Hill Church of Christ since its organization." In the listing for the early years, all of the names are familiar with the exception of a "Brother Davis" who was one of the very first preachers to visit the Pleasant Hill Church. There are no other references to a Christian preacher named Davis in early Oregon.

9. On p. 102 of C. F. Swander's *Making Disciples in Oregon,* he mentions a "lay preacher" named S. D. Evans who was caring for a small church in Winchester in Douglas County as early as 1856. This is a reference to Dr. Samuel D. Evans who settled a claim 5 miles north of Winchester in 1852 and then moved to Nevada in 1859. Swander quotes an 1856 letter in which Evans writes: "We have great need of help here. We have no preacher at all in the Umpqua Valley; and a large field lies unoccupied. Will not someone come and occupy it? Why is it that other denominations have teachers here and we have none, especially when the cause we plead flourishes so well wherever it is faithfully preached." However, Swander does not document this reference and nothing more is known about the families that comprised this early congregation.

10. A history of the Junction City Church in Lane County reports that a church of 14 members "was begun at the home of B. Bryant" on the 4th Lord's day in June 1855. There was a 30-year-old man named Brown Bryant living in Marion County in the 1850 census, but there is no available information on the elusive "B. Bryant" in Lane County in 1855.

Oregon Christians

Beginning with the first typical wagon train on the Oregon Trail in the spring of 1842 and continuing on to the election of a former Christian preacher named James Abram Garfield as 20th President of the United States in the fall of 1880, there were several thousand Christians who migrated to Oregon. Glen Owen Burnett estimated that there were already about 1,200 Christians in Oregon Territory by the fall of 1851. That number swelled to more than 4,000 in the 1870s. Only a small percentage of those families can now be identified by name. The following list of more than 600 families is far from complete. It is offered as a sampling of the determined Christians who chose to endure the rigors of the trail in order to establish a new life for themselves and their children and to plant primitive Christianity in a distant land of promise called Oregon.

Adams, Gaines Melanchthon (6/26/1856 – 8/?/1922) **1856**
Anna Liza Paslay (8/20/1866 – 2/?/1951) m. 1/13/1884
Son of William Lysander & Frances Adams. She was related to the Ruble family. They moved to Pateros, Washington in 1889 and are buried in Pateros Cemetery. Two of their sons, Cecil and Francis, became preachers in the Church of Christ in Washington.

Adams, Sebastian C. (7/28/1825 – 1/5/1898) **1850**
Martha E. McBride (5/12/1831 – 12/16/1882) m. 2/6/1851 **1846**
Martha Rhael (? – 12/8/1886) m. 3/?/1884
Sarah A. Baker Babcock (1840 – 4/17/1904) m. 6/12/1890
Younger brother of William Lysander Adams. Married a daughter of Dr. James & Mahala McBride. Served in the state senate, and preached for the Salem Church for many years. They are buried in Pioneer Cemetery in Salem.

Adams, William Harmon (3/12/1850 – 11/14/1917) **1850**
Olive S. Pagett (? – 1/17/1903) m. 10/13/1875
Son of William Lysander Adams and a graduate of Christian College in Monmouth. Admitted to the Oregon State Bar in 1874, and later appointed a judge. Agent for the *Pacific Christian Messenger*. Charter members of the Christian Church in Portland when it was established in 1879.

Adams, William Lysander (2/5/1821 – 4/26/1906) **1848**
Frances Olivia Goodell (10/5/1821 – 6/23/1886) m. 8/25/1844
Mary Susan Mosier (1/22/1855 – 12/11/1922) m. 10/22/1881
Graduate of Bethany College and one of the best-known preachers among the Christians in Oregon. He preached the first sermon at the organization of the Pleasant Hill Church of Christ in Lane County in 1850, and he was one of the original 9 board members for Bethel Institute in Polk County. Editor of the *Oregon Argus* and one of the founders of the Republican Party in Oregon.

Adkins, Edward Stringer (3/5/1825 – 7/15/1888) **1853**
Helen Augusta Bushnell (5/24/1831 – 1927) m. 1/13/1848
She was a sister to James Addison Bushnell, and he was a brother to Elizabeth Adkins Bushnell. With the Bushnells, they became charter members of the church established in the Clear Lake (Junction City) area of Lane County in 1855. Her mother, Ursula Bushnell, lived with them in Oregon for nearly 30 years.

Alderman, Orlando Singleton (4/7/1833 – 4/2/1903) **1847**
Isabella Baker (4/1/1836 – 1/23/1916) m. 7/3/1851 **1845**
He came to Oregon as a teenager and began preaching in the 1860s. Members of the Monmouth Church in the late 1850s and early 1860s. Moved to Spring Valley in 1865. Buried in the Alderman Family Cemetery in northeastern Polk County.

Allen, William Franklin 10/30/1834 – 5/12/1902) **1853**
Mary Catherine Lewis (1/3/1841 – 5/27/1920) m. 1/3/1856 **1845**
Daughter of David R. & Mary Lewis. Married on her 15th birthday, and the ceremony was performed by John Ecles Murphy. In the 1860 census they were still living in Polk County, but they moved later to Benton County. They may have been members of the Philomath Church. They are buried in Pleasant Valley Cemetery in Benton County.

Amis, James F. (2/6/1828 – 8/29/1912) **1852?**
Elizabeth McCollum Bailey (1/1/1833 – 5/15/1912) m. c1854
She was a widow when they married around 1853-54. They lived in the Eugene area for nearly 60 years. He represented Lane County in the state legislature in 1870-1872. When the division occurred in the church in Eugene in the 1890s, they remained with the conservatives who identified with the Churches of Christ. They are buried in Mulkey Cemetery in Eugene.

Applegate, Jesse A. (1836 – ?) **1843**
Virginia Watson (9/4/1840 – 2/9/1909) m. 5/25/1858 **1849**
They were married by Glen Owen Burnett. Virginia was a daughter of Sanford & Maria Jane Watson and a member of the Bethel Church. It is not known if Jesse became a Christian.

Arthur, William (4/9/1796 – 8/14/1866) **1843**
Milley (Millie) Malone (c1792 – 9/30/1861) m. 8/11/1818
Catherine Ayres Hicks (c1825 – ?) m. 10/29/1862
They were in "The Great Migration" of 1843 and were among the first converts of John Foster in Clackamas County. They hosted Dr. James McBride and Glen Owen Burnett during their gospel meeting in that district in November 1846. Their daughter, Mary, married Isaac Foster, a son of John Foster.

Atterbury (Attebery), John (c1835 – ?) **1850s**
Rachel Mulkey (2/23/1838 – 1914) m. 7/26/1856 **1847**
She was a daughter of Luke & Rutha Mulkey and her wedding was performed by Philip Mulkey, Christian preacher and relative. Her younger sister, Eliza, married John Henry Hawley 2 years later on 5/6/1858. John & Rachel were early members of the Monmouth Church. After his death, she married Thomas O. Waller, a brother of Mac Waller. Rachel & Thomas are buried in Fir Crest Cemetery south of Monmouth.

Badger, Ephraim (8/3/1852 – 1/8/1936) **1856**

Nancy Octavia (Favia) Lovelady (2/7/1861 – 4/?/1956) m. 9/30/1877

Son of Ephraim & Elma Badger and younger brother of Thomas Ruble Badger. His father died and his mother married Andrew Jackson Rose. He was just 4 years old when they came overland, and he began preaching in the 1870s. She was a daughter of Preston & Lovina Lovelady. When the Restoration Movement suffered a division in the 1890s, they remained with the Churches of Christ. Buried at Missouri Flats Cemetery in Jackson County.

Badger, Thomas Ruble (10/20/1845 – 9/?/1921) **1856**

Martha Ellen Bounds (10/15/1851 – 4/14/1923) m. 9/30/1867

Son of Ephraim & Elma Badger and older brother of Ephraim Badger. She was a daughter of John Bird Bounds. They settled in Linn County. After 1886 he was a correspondent in the *Christian Leader*, a Cincinnati periodical that represented the viewpoint of the Churches of Christ. He became a leader in the Churches of Christ after the gradual division with the Disciples of Christ in the 1890s.

Bagby, William R. (5/15/1823 – 6/15/1902) **1852**

Harriet Wright (8/10/1830 – 8/10/1921) m. 4/13/1848

She was a member of the Rock Creek Church of Christ south of Molalla in Clackamas County, but it is not certain that he ever became a Christian. At least six of their children became members of the Rock Creek congregation. William & Harriet are buried in Molalla Pioneer Cemetery.

Bailes, Keathley (10/14/1829 – 3/17/1915) **1861**

Sarah Marshall (? – 1919) m. 1/30/1847

Preached in Oregon, Washington and northern California for more than half a century. Remained with Churches of Christ after the division in the 1890s. One daughter married Edward Axel Pedigo. In the 1910 census they were living near London in Lane County, and Isham Burnett was residing with them. The Bailes are buried in Ellensburg, Washington.

Bailey, Samuel Y. **1850s**

wife's name unknown

Not much is known about this elusive gospel preacher in Oregon church history. He was preaching in Oregon in the 1860s, and perhaps earlier.

Baker, Edward Dickinson (2/24/1811 – 10/22/1861) **1859**

Mary Ann Lee m. 4/27/1831

E. D. Baker had formerly been a Christian preacher in Illinois, but there is no indication that he was involved in church activities in Oregon. However, Mary Ann may have remained faithful in church attendance while living in Salem.

Baker, Isaac (1817-1862) **1847**

Eliza T. Ash (c1818 – ?) m. 10/12/1838

Overland in 1847 in train captained by Wiley Chapman. Their 4-year-old daughter, Elizabeth, died on the trail and was buried at Fort Bridger. They settled near Salem.

Baker, John Gordon (10/17/1818 – 3/4/1887) **1843**
Catherine Blevins (6/1/1823 – 1/16/1912) m. 10/9/1839
In "The Great Migration" of 1843. John Gordon Baker may not have been a church member as he was not listed with her as a charter member of the Blackhawk congregation in Yamhill County in 1847. However, he was one of the contributors to the fund to bring a Christian preacher, A. V. McCarty, to Oregon in 1847. They are buried in Masonic Cemetery in McMinnville.

Baker, John W. (1/10/1846 – ?) **1853**
Lucretia Ann Martin (8/9/1850 – ?) m. 1868 **1850**
She was a daughter of Franklin & Anna Burnett Martin and a member of the McMinnville Church. It is not known if John became a Christian.

Barger, William B. (1823 – 9/22/1895) **1853**
Elizabeth Margaret Mulkey (? – 7/?/1866) m. 9/11/1851
Harriet Bailey (1822 – 6/8/1871) m. 6/16/1868
Elizabeth was a daughter of Philip Mulkey. They were charter members of the congregation established in the Clear Lake district (Junction City) of Lane County in 1855. Harriet's obituary was published in the *Christian Messenger*.

Barlow, William (10/26/1822 – 6/13/1904) **1845**
Laura C. (? – 10/18/1849) m. 8/?/1849
Martha Ann Partlow Allen (c1822 – 4/20/1901) m. 4/26/1852
His first wife's funeral was preached by Dr. James McBride on 10/18/1849. He and his second wife were baptized into Christ by Glen Owen Burnett and John Ecles Murphy in 1855. They made their spacious residence near present-day Canby in Clackamas County available for 2 gospel meetings in summer of 1855. A. V. McCarty preached in both meetings which resulted in 13 additions to the church in that area.

Barnes, Ephraim W. **1852**
Georgia Annie Mason (6/21/1857 – ?) m. 6/15/1874
By the decade of 1870s he was preaching throughout Oregon, Washington and northern California. He was living in Jackson County at the time of his marriage. She was a daughter of Eli & Susan Mason, Christians living in New Pine Creek on the Oregon-California border. He served as agent for *Pacific Christian Messenger* in 1870s. He remained with Churches of Christ following the division with Disciples of Christ.

Barnes, William T. (12/14/1828 – ?) **1852**
Sarah A. Blaine m. 9/12/1849
They were listed first among the 16 charter members of the Hillsboro Christian Church in Washington County. It was established on 10/17/1862. Moved to Walla Walla County in W. T. in 1864. In 1877 they were members of the Dixie congregation in Walla Walla County. In that same year he was chosen chairman of the annual meeting for the Christians living in eastern Oregon and eastern W. T.

Barnett, George Hays (8/25/1829 – 11/10/1900) **1853**
Barbara E. Martz (11/26/1831 – ?) m. 9/19/1852
They were living in Wasco County in the 1870s and 1880s. He was preaching for the Fifteen Mile Creek Church in that county when the P. P. Underwood family arrived in 1878. Underwood shared the preaching responsibilities with Barnett.

Barr, Jesse (10/18/1818 – 1/3/1893) **1853**
Anna Kirk (1825 – ?) m. 2/5/1842
Overland from Mercer County, Missouri. They settled in Linn County. In 1871 they were charter members of the church that was established in Splawn's School House near present-day Holley.

Barrows, John W. (11/15/1823 – 5/23/1854) **1847**
Eliza Marien Hooker (8/18/1821 – 5/13/1856) m. 12/9/1849 **1848**
He came overland with Mac Waller, Hiram Alva Johnson and other Illinois Christians. She came overland with her parents, Ira & Sarah Hooker. They were married in Polk County by Mac Waller, and they are buried near her parents in Burch Pioneer Cemetery in Polk County.

Baskett, George Johnston (2/25/1818 – 1/4/1883) **1848**
Catherine Bristow (9/21/1828 – 3/5/1913) m. 9/8/1850
She was a daughter of Elijah & Susanna Bristow. Their wedding was performed by William Lysander Adams at Pleasant Hill in Lane County, but they lived most of their married life on the Baskett donation land claim in Polk County. They are buried in City View Cemetery in Salem.

Baughman, Samuel (7/9/1814 – 6/3/1903) **1852**
Elizabeth McCall (7/28/1813 – 1/24/1874) m. 8/28/1836
For many years he was an elder in the Pleasant Hill Church of Christ. She was an older sister to William McCall. They are buried in Pleasant Hill Cemetery in Lane County.

Baughman, William Howard (10/20/1847 – 10/4/1902) **1852**
Lucetta Callison (6/7/1855 – 3/28/1942) **1848**
Son of Samuel & Elizabeth Baughman and daughter of Robert & Polly Callison. They were members of the Pleasant Hill Church of Christ, and they are buried in Pleasant Hill Cemetery.

Beal, Philip (3/4/1835 – ?) **1847**
Clarinda Noland m. 1862 **1852**
On 10/17/1862 she was a charter member of the Hillsboro Church in Washington County. Later, they were members of the Forest Grove Church in Washington County, and he served as an elder in this church.

Bean, Obadiah Roberts (2/2/1830 – 3/15/1890) **1851**
Julia Ann Sharp (2/25/1838 – 2/19/1908) m. 10/20/1853
They became members of the Grand Prairie Church (Junction City area) in Lane County in 1859. She was a younger sister to Joseph H. Sharp who preached for this church in the 1860s. They are buried in the Masonic Cemetery in Eugene.

Beauchamp, Stephen A. (1779 – after 1869 in California) **1845**
Elizabeth Ann Stone (c1781 – 7/29/1865) m. 1799
He was baptized into Christ by Glen Owen Burnett back in Missouri. Two of their daughters married sons of John Foster. Adeline married John T. Foster in November 1848, and Letha married Isaac M. Foster on 8/10/1849. They settled near the Fosters in Clackamas County, but by the 1850 census they were living in Yamhill County. She is buried in Masonic Cemetery in McMinnville. He died in California.

Bedwell, Elisha (9/9/1819 – 5/9/1896) **1847**

Sarah Ann Davis

America Minerva Shelton (2/18/1831 – 12/5/1916) m. 6/18/1850

Accompanied Thomas Crawford McBride on his westward journey in 1847. Baptized into Christ on 4/14/1848 and married into a Christian family. She was a daughter of Zebedee & Lavina Shelton and older sister to John W. Shelton. They lived in Yamhill County until 1874. Moved to Monmouth so their children could attend Christian College. He served on board of trustees of Christian College in 1870s and early 1880s.

Berry, Charles (3/15/1820 – 8/1/1865) **1850**

Rebecca Lemasters (1/14/1836 – 11/18/1924) m. 5/18/1853

He was a younger brother to John H. Berry. Both brothers and their families were members of the McMinnville Church. Following the death of Charles, Rebecca married John J. Calhoon who later became an elder in the McMinnville Church.

Berry, John H. (1818 – ?) **1850**

Narcessa (Narcissa) J. (5/21/1822 – 3/30/1866) m. 4/20/1842

He was an older brother to Charles Berry. Both brothers and their families were members of the McMinnville Church. She was born in McMinnville, Tennessee and was a sister of William T. Newby. She is buried in Masonic Cemetery in McMinnville, but there is no record of his burial.

Bird, William Allen (7/24/1812 – 11/29/1885) **1847**

Harriet Bird (6/16/1818 – ?) m. 10/9/1836

Illinois Christians who came overland in 1847 with a party that included the Robert Crouch Kinney family and the various McCarty families. They settled at Shucks Mills on Butte Creek in Marion County. They are buried in the Robert Bird Cemetery (formerly called the Stafford Cemetery) in Clackamas County.

Blackerby, Dr. Joseph Monroe (4/17/1806 – 1/19/1878) **1848**

Cassandra Coffey (c1810 – 1885) m. 1/1/1834

She was a daughter of Nebuzardan & Elizabeth Coffey and a sister-in-law to William Porter and William Wilshire Bristow. They became members of Bethany Church in 1863. Buried near the Coffeys and Porters in Aumsville Cemetery in Marion County.

Blaney, Ambrose **1878**

Catherine B.

These Ohio Christians arrived in Oregon in April, 1878. They had been members of the Richmond Street Christian Church in Cincinnati, and they became charter members of the Christian Church in Portland in 1879. Ambrose Blaney was a building contractor. Their son, Dr. O. C. Blaney, was also one of the charter members. Ambrose Blaney and John T. Dickinson were the first two elders in the Portland Church.

Blaney, Dr. O. C. **1878**

wife's name unknown

Charter member of Christian Church in Portland. Son of Ambrose & Catherine Blaney.

Bohna, Thomas J. (3/14/1840 – 1926) **1866**
Luvena Osburn (1851 – 1915) m. 2/11/1868
He was a successful dairyman. She was a daughter of Albert & Mary Osburn. They were members of the Damascus Church in Clackamas County for many years. He served as a deacon in this church in the late 1870s and 1880s. They reared a family of 11 children, and they are buried in Damascus Pioneer Cemetery near her parents.

Bolton, Absalom D. (2/2/1822 – 2/20/1903) **1852**
Olivia (9/6/1822 – 2/19/1908) m. 3/4/1852
They were newlyweds when they came overland from Cedar County, Iowa. Settled first in Lane County, but moved to Wasco County in the early 1860s and made their home there for the next 40 years. They are buried in Rice Cemetery in Wasco County.

Bond, Allen (12/5/1833 – 10/22/1902) **1853**
Rachel Robinson (11/1/1831 – 9/14/1900) m. 3/23/1853
Left for Oregon Territory with his bride of one day. Traveled with the McClures and his brother, Isaac William. Settled on a claim in Lane County next to Isaac. He represented Lane County in the state legislature in 1876. They are buried close to Isaac's family in Luper Cemetery near Irving in Lane County.

Bond, Isaac William (12/19/1827 – 5/22/1915) **1853**
Hettie McClure (8/19/1835 – 4/14/1901) m. 10/9/1851
Married eldest daughter of Vincent McClure. They came west together and settled on adjoining claims. One record notes that Isaac William Bond "served as deacon for many years in the Christian Church." He was an older brother to Allen Bond. They are buried in Luper Cemetery near Irving in Lane County.

Bonney, Bradford Sherwood (8/30/1825 – 7/10/1904) **1846**
Alzina Clarinda Dimick (4/2/1832 – 4/2/1897) m. 1/29/1848
Agnes G. Fisher (Frisbie) m. 12/4/1898
Son of Truman & Pemelia Bonney. After marriage, he settled on a 422-acre farm near Woodburn in Marion County. Served as an elder in the church in the 1880s and 1890s. One of his sisters married John Sherwood.

Bonney, Truman Lawrence (4/24/1796 – 10/27/1868) **1846**
Pemelia (Pelena) Townsend (3/8/1801 – 8/28/1884) m. 8/3/1818
Migrated from Illinois to California in 1845 and then continued on to Oregon in 1846. Settled on French Prairie in Marion County. He was a member of board of trustees of Rickreall Academy in 1854. One of their sons, Bradford Sherwood, became an elder in the church. A daughter, Hannah, married John Sherwood.

Boothby, Reason Rounds (5/15/1812 – 10/30/1884) **1849**
Mary Ann Waller (c1819 – 5/21/1863) m. 2/12/1834
Margaret McFadden (1/4/1829 – 2/15/1891) m. 1877
Overland from Illinois. Traveled across the plains with Harrison Brunk family of Troy, Missouri. On the crowded trail in the summer of '49, they were among the few who were bound for Oregon instead of California. Boothby and Brunk married sisters of Mac Waller, Townsend Waller and T. O. Waller. They settled near the Waller families in Polk County. The matriarch of this family, Jane Waller, also lived in Polk County. He was a delegate for the Eola Church at the annual State Meeting in 1863.

Bounds, John A. (?/?/1836 – 3/30/1915) **1846**
Nancy J. McBride (7/31/1843 – 5/21/1871)
Son of John Bird & Elizabeth Bounds. Settled in Polk County but later moved to Benton County. Served as an agent for the *Pacific Christian Messenger* for several years. His sisters were married to Harrison Linville, Alexander Vance McCarty and Edward Wilburn McCarty. His aunt Polly was married to Thomas J. Lovelady. He served as an agent for the *Christian Messenger*.

Bounds, John Bird (1800 – ?) **1846**
Elizabeth Lovelady (? – 11/13/1846)
M. A. Brink m. 11/21/1850
Elizabeth died on the Applegate Trail after arriving in Oregon Territory. She was the mother of John A. Bounds, Nancy Bounds Linville, Jane Bounds McCarty, and Amanda Bounds McCarty. She was a sister to Thomas J. Lovelady, who married her husband's sister.

Bowen, Joshua (1835 – 12/4/1914) **1853**
Louise Elizabeth Cox (1840 – 1920) m. 3/22/1858 **1846**
Joshua and Peter were teenagers when their mother died just prior to the overland journey to Oregon. Their father died on the trail. Joshua and Peter continued on to Oregon and settled near Bethany in Marion County. They married sisters. Their wives were daughters of Gideon & Susanna Cox. Both weddings were performed by Caleb P. Chapman. Both families were members of the Bethany Church, and they are all buried in Bethany Pioneer Cemetery.

Bowen, Peter Wood (1837 – 5/14/1916) **1853**
Permilla Cox (1839 – 1913) m. 8/10/1859 **1846**
He was a younger brother of Joshua Bowen, and she was a daughter of Gideon & Susanna Cox. Members of Bethany Church and buried in Bethany Pioneer Cemetery.

Bowman, William (1814 – 4/24/1879) **1848**
Polly (c1823 – 5/30/1907) m. 11/29/1838
They came overland from Iowa with 5 children. Charter members of the Pleasant Hill Church of Christ in 1850. They are buried in Davidson Cemetery in Polk County.

Boyle, Dr. James Whitten (Whiton) (4/15/1815 – 7/4/1864) **1845**
Josephine Pauline Ford (12/5/1830 – 6/21/1916) m. 5/1/1846 **1844**
Daughter of Nat & Lucinda Ford. She had been a student at the church-related "Female Seminary" in Columbia, Missouri. She was baptized into Christ in Rickreall Creek by Glen Owen Burnett in January 1847. There is no evidence that her husband became a Christian. He was the first physician in Polk County. Following his death, she was a member of the Salem Church for many years.

Bradley, William Pollard (3/22/1833 – 1/16/1915) **1852**
Permelia Ann (11/21/1848 – 1/29/1939) m. 3/4/1869
She was a daughter of Reason & Mary Ann Boothby. Their wedding was performed at Eola by her uncle, Mac Waller. They were members of Eola and Independence churches in Polk County and later of the Eugene Church in Lane County. Buried in Pioneer Cemetery in Eugene.

Bradshaw, Charles (1822 – 2/23/1898) **1852**

Malvina E. (8/29/1824 – 11/8/1893) m. 12/?/1841

Came overland from Warren County, Illinois. Settled near Pleasant Hill in Lane County, but later moved to Polk County. He preached throughout Oregon for 9 years before moving his family to California in 1861. He preached in Ventura, California in the 1870s and 1880s. They are buried at Rosedale Cemetery in Los Angeles.

Brayton, William H. (1804 – 1860) **1852**

Lucy Ann (8/3/1807 – 4/20/1887) m. 12/16/1827

Members of the Mill Creek Church in Marion County. William was an orchardist by vocation. He presided over the 1859 annual State Meeting which was hosted by the Monmouth Church. His death was announced at the 1860 annual State Meeting hosted by the Eola Church. Their daughter, Henrietta, married George M. Whitney in Marion County on 7/28/1857.

Briedwell, John W. (2/17/1832 – 11/30/1904) **1852**

Nancy Edmonston (1/20/1831 – 4/28/1889) m. 10/13/1851

Came overland from Iowa and settled for 5 years near Wheatland in Yamhill County. Moved to 160-acre farm one mile west of Amity in 1857, and expanded farm to 430 acres. Erected a large warehouse on their property next to the railroad tracks and became extensive grain dealers. Members of the Amity Church. Their eldest daughter married James St. Clair McCarty. They are buried in Amity Cemetery.

Briggs, Elias M. (1824 – 1/17/1896) **1847**

Mary Johnson m. 5/18/1847

Son of Isaac & Betsy Briggs. Both families came overland from Iowa via the Applegate Trail and settled near Elijah Bristow at Pleasant Hill. Charter members of Pleasant Hill Church of Christ in 1850. Founded the town of Springfield (the spring was in his field), and established a church in the town. Elias operated a ferry service across the Willamette River. In the 1880 census they were still living in Springfield.

Briggs, Isaac (1802 – 1/28/1891) **1847**

Elizabeth (Betsy) Morris (1805 – 1890) m. 3/23/1823

Devout Christians from Iowa. Charter members of the Pleasant Hill Church of Christ in Lane County in 1850. Founded the town of Springfield and worked with their son and daughter-in-law in building up a congregation in that area. It is not known if they were related to the Briggs families in Douglas County. In the 1880 census they were still living in Springfield. Buried in Laurel Grove Cemetery in Springfield.

Briggs, John Alexander (1834 – 12/25/1861) **1851**

Sarah Jane Veatch (c1841 – ?) m. 1855 or 1857 **1853**

Son of Samuel Bates & Susanna Phillips Briggs. He and his brother, William, married sisters. Both families remained in Douglas County. He drowned in the South Umpqua River on Christmas day 1861 while navigating a ferry crossing.

Briggs, Nathaniel Phillips (1/28/1826 – 10/22/1898) **1853**

Mary M. Preston (c1833 – 4/11/1870) m. 8/13/1850 or 1852

Mahala J. St. Clair (1/30/1834 – 8/19/1892) m. 2/6/1876

Son of Samuel Bates & Susanna Phillips Briggs and daughter of William & Mary Preston. He was an older brother of John Alexander Briggs and William Fernando Briggs, and she was a sister to William P. Preston. Moved to Corvallis in Benton County. Nathaniel served as an agent for the *Pacific Christian Messenger*.

Briggs, Samuel Bates (1805 – 12/27/1872) **1851**
Susanna S. Phillips (1805 – 7/28/1880) m. 4/28/1825 or 1828
He was one of the prime movers in the organization of Douglas County and served as county commissioner for several years. A mechanic by vocation, and a gospel preacher in Oregon for more than 20 years. He was a delegate from the Canyonville Church at the annual State Meeting in 1863. They are buried in the Briggs Cemetery north of Canyonville.

Briggs, William Fernando (9/18/1837 – ?) **1851**
Elizabeth Veatch (3/2/1846 – ?) m. 10/22/1860 **1853**
Son of Samuel Bates & Susanna Phillips Briggs. County surveyor for Douglas County for 18 years. They were owners of Overland Hotel (later Briggs Hotel) in Canyonville.

Bristow, Abel King (1/6/1819 – 5/31/1881) **1848**
Almira K. Gooch (5/30/1826 – 3/8/1917) m. 1/26/1843
Son of Elijah & Susanna Bristow. Charter members of the Pleasant Hill Church of Christ in Lane County in 1850. They lived at Pleasant Hill throughout their married life and they are buried in Pleasant Hill Cemetery. She was the last surviving charter member of the Pleasant Hill Church, having been a member for nearly 67 years.

Bristow, Darwin (12/21/1862 – 1951) **1862**
Mary L. Medley (1864 – 1928) m. 3/16/1885
Son of William Wilshire & Elizabeth Coffey Bristow. His paternal grandfather was Elijah Bristow. President of First National Bank and 5-term mayor of Cottage Grove before moving to Eugene. He was a member of the Christian Church in Eugene. Darwin and his son, Darwin Darrel, are buried in Masonic Cemetery in Eugene.

Bristow, Elijah (4/28/1788 – 9/19/1872) **1846**
Susanna Gabbart (Gabbert) (8/23/1791 – 3/7/1874) m. 3/7/1812 **1848**
Patriarch and matriarch of the Bristow clan. He migrated from Illinois to California in 1845 and then continued on to Oregon the next spring. Founded the town of Pleasant Hill in Lane County and built the first cabin in the county. Donated property for Pleasant Hill Church of Christ, Pleasant Hill School and Pleasant Hill Cemetery. They are buried in Pleasant Hill Cemetery near several of their children.

Bristow, Dr. John Kennedy (King) (3/26/1814 – 1/28/1887) **1852**
Emeline Hatch (9/2/1825 – died on plains in '52) m. 11/?/1846
Mary A. Crow (1822 – 1901) m. 3/21/1857
Eldest son of Elijah & Susanna Bristow. His wife died during the journey across the plains in 1852. He settled briefly in Pleasant Hill, but soon moved to Eugene. John & Mary are buried in Pleasant Hill Cemetery near his parents.

Bristow, William L. (1/10/1859 – 2/8/1929) **1859**
Luella Handsaker (2/5/1868 – ?) m. 7/23/1890
Son of Abel & Almira Bristow. Born in Oregon Territory. William became a strong leader in the church. He is buried in Pleasant Hill Cemetery, but there is no record of her burial there.

Bristow, William Wilshire (7/18/1826 – 12/8/1874) **1848**

Elizabeth Coffey m. 10/17/1850 **1848**

Martha McCall m. 4/27/1865 **1852**

Mary Jane Wells (c1819 – 12/25/1898) m. 9/16/1869

Son of Elijah & Susanna Bristow and daughter of Nebuzardan & Elizabeth Coffey. His second wife was a daughter of William & Matilda McCall. He taught at Pleasant Hill School. Elected to the State Senate in the 1850s and again in the 1870s. He was a gifted church leader, first with the congregation at Pleasant Hill, and later with the congregation at Eugene. He and all 3 wives are buried in Pleasant Hill Cemetery.

Brock, Levi (3/11/1816 – 3/1/1885) **1852**

Mary Downing (9/20/1830 – 3/26/1903) m. 3/12/1848

Came overland from Missouri and settled about 4 miles west of present-day McMinnville in Yamhill County. They were members of McMinnville Church, and he served as a deacon in that church. Buried in Masonic Cemetery in McMinnville.

Brown, Charles (1/16/1813 – 1/23/1887) **1845**

Margaret May (7/8/1826 – 2/28/1903) m. 6/21/1845

Daughter of John & Elizabeth Lewis and younger sister of David R. Lewis and Nancy Jane Cook. Married near the Platte River on the Oregon Trail. He may not have been a Christian. Lived near Oregon City 5 years and near Portland 12 years before moving to W.T. She was a member of the Christian Church in Waitsburg in Walla Walla County. One of their sons became a preacher. They are buried in Waitsburg.

Brown, Gabriel (1789 – 6/?/1870) **1842**

Elizabeth Ashe King (c1795 – 3/25/1866) m. 1/3/1827

They were in the first wagon train of 1842. Employed Reuben Lewis as their hunter. Their daughter, Cynthia, married Allan Davie on 3/19/1844. The Browns were Christians but it is not known which congregation they were members of. Their daughter was a member of the Aumsville Church.

Brown, William C. (11/30/1824 – 5/10/1909) **1847**

Martha J. Townsend (11/10/1826 – 11/19/1899) m. 8/6/1848

Settled in Polk County near present-day Dallas. He was an early Dallas merchant and was known for his generosity to penniless early settlers in the area. He represented Polk County in the 1874 legislature. They are buried in the William C. Brown Cemetery between Dallas and Polk Station.

Browning, Dr. Edmund (Edmond) Green (8/19/1816 – 3/28/1888) **1852**

Nancy Callison (9/19/1812 – died on plains in '52) m. 1840

Nancy Allen (Allyn) m. 1/24/1853 **1852**

Overland from Illinois with the Callison train. Nancy Callison Browning was a sister to Gilmore and Robert Callison of Pleasant Hill. Like many others that summer, she died on the trail from the effects of cholera. Dr. Edmund Green Browning practiced medicine and preached the gospel of Christ for more than 35 years in Douglas County. He is buried in Pioneer Cemetery in Myrtle Creek.

Bruce, James J. (1828 – ?) **1851**
Elizabeth Simmons m. 4/15/1864
Both James and William Bruce are listed as early members of the Grand Prairie Church in Lane County. Most likely they were brothers of the wives of Vincent Scott McClure and James F. McClure. They preceded the McClure-Bond-Bruce train of 1853. James arrived in 1851 and William in 1852.

Bruce, William Perry (1824 – ?) **1852**
Caroline Adelia O'Neal m. 2/10/1850
Older brother of James J. Bruce. He may have been a brother to both Sallie Bruce McClure & Nancy Bruce McClure. Member of Grand Prairie Church in Lane County.

Brunk, Harrison (4/17/1812 – 10/23/1895) **1849**
Emily C. Waller (11/18/1820 – 12/19/1888) m. 7/29/1839
Overland from Missouri with the Reason Round Boothby family. Emily Waller Brunk and Mary Ann Waller Boothby were sisters. They settled in Polk County near their mother, Jane Waller, and near their brothers, Mac Waller, Townsend Waller and Thomas O. Waller.

Bryant, B. **1850s**
wife's name unknown
A history of the Junction City Church in Lane County says that a church of 14 members "was begun at the home of B. Bryant" on the 4th Lord's day in June 1855. There was a 30-year-old man named Brown Bryant living in Marion County in the 1850 census, but there is no available information on the elusive "B. Bryant" in Lane County in 1855.

Bryant, Zephaniah S. (1813 – ?) **1852**
Sarah Ann Brown (c1817 – ?) m. 3/23/1845
They came overland from Van Buren County, Iowa and settled in Washington County. He sent some informative letters back home to Daniel Bates for publication in Iowa's *Christian Evangelist.*

Buffum, William Gilbert (6/25/1804 – 3/25/1899) **1845**
Caroline Thurman (3/19/1804 – 11/5/1895) m. 11/8/1828
They settled in Amity in Yamhill County and lived in that community for 40 years. They were charter members of the Amity Church, and are buried in Amity Cemetery.

Bullock, Charles J. (1822 – ?) **1853**
Nancy Ellen m. 3/7/1850
In the mid-1860s they were active members of the Hillsboro Christian Church in Washington County. He was chosen to be a deacon in this church on June 16, 1866.

Burch, Benjamin S. (1830 – ?) **1850?**
Mary Ann Comegys m. 8/27/1851
He came overland from Missouri, possibly as early as the 1840s, and settled in Yamhill County. She was a sister to Presley Comegys and Ellen Scott Lyle was her aunt. They were married in Yamhill County by Glen Owen Burnett.

Burch, Levi (1824 – ?) **1851**
Elizabeth m. 2/12/1845
He preached in Oregon for 7 years, most often in Linn and Polk counties, and then moved to California in 1858. He lived in Santa Barbara for 2 years in the late 1860s, and was living in Santa Rosa in Sonoma County in 1873.

Burford, Hezekiah (7/6/1811 – 6/12/1884) **1852**
Levina Sears (10/12/1813 – 5/29/1884 m. 2/20 or 25/1830
Early members of the Monmouth Church in Polk County. One daughter married Alexander B. Davidson, and another married John W. Shelton. Their son, Thomas J. Burford, was also in Monmouth Church. Hezekiah Burford was one of the delegates from the Monmouth Church at the annual State Meeting in 1863. In November 1864 they moved to Salem. In 1867 he was appointed an elder in the Salem Church along with Caleb P. Chapman, Thomas Ladd and Governor George Woods.

Burford, Thomas Jefferson (8/12/1834 – 5/15/1905) **1852**
Virginia E. Pitman (c1843 – ?) m. 8/26/1858
S. E. Thompson m. 10/20/1899
Came overland from Illinois. Son of Hezekiah & Levina Burford. Early member of the Monmouth Church, and he later served as a deacon and elder in various congregations in Oregon, Washington and California. He died in Santa Barbara, California.

Burnett, George William (10/18/1811 – 12/25/1877) **1846**
Sidney Ann Younger (2/25/1817 – 10/26/1907) m. 11/10/1831
Younger brother of Glen Owen Burnett. Charter members of the church at Blackhawk schoolhouse in Yamhill County in 1847. Their daughter married Jefferson Nelson, who became an elder in McMinnville Church. G. W. served in legislature 1868-1870, and his obituary in *Pacific Christian Messenger* was written by Collin Austin Wallace, an elder in McMinnville Church. They are buried in Masonic Cemetery in McMinnville.

Burnett, Glen Owen (11/16/1809 – 1886) **1846**
Sarah M. Rogers (c1815 – 1889) m. 1/6/1830
He preached in Missouri for several years before coming overland with the McBrides. Preached in Oregon and California for 40 years. He was a member of the board of trustees of both Bethel Institute and Christian College, and he was associate editor of *Pacific Christian Messenger*. Their son, Peter Rogers Burnett, was a preacher in Oregon and California for 55 years. They are buried in Santa Rosa, California.

Burnett, Horace G. (1832 – ?) **1846**
Margaret A. Lovelady (c1835 – ?) m. 8/28/1851 **1846**
Son of Glen Owen & Sarah Burnett and daughter of Thomas & Polly Lovelady. Their wedding was performed by Mac Waller.

Burnett, Isham (12/9/1830 – 9/1/1916) **1840s**
Minerva (Manerva) Griffith (1/29/1838 – 1/26/1909) m. 7/21/1859
He was born in Tennessee and related to Glen Owen Burnett. He began preaching in the years following the Civil War. He remained with the Churches of Christ following the division in the 1890s. They were living in Lane County at the time of the 1900 census, and she died in 1909. In the 1910 census he was residing with Keathley & Sarah Bailes at their home near London in Lane County.

Burnett, James White (2/3/1821 – 11/21/1884) **1867**
Sarah Jane Turner (1/4/1828 – 2/1/1909) m. c1845
Younger brother of Glen Owen Burnett. He traveled overland to California in 1849 and lived there 18 years. Moved to Oregon in 1867 and settled first in Washington County and then in Polk County. He died in Yamhill County.

Burnett, Peter Hardeman (11/15/1807 – 5/17/1895) **1843**
Harriet Mary Walton Rogers (2/21/1812 – 9/19/1879) m. 8/20/1828
He and his brother, Glen Owen Burnett, married sisters. Peter converted to Roman Catholicism in 1846. Dr. John McLoughlin was his godfather when he was baptized into the Catholic church. He moved to California and was elected the first governor of California in 1850.

Burnett, Peter Rogers (4/9/1842 – 11/22/1922) **1846**
Mary Elizabeth Todd (2/8/1849 – 7/19/1916) m. 10/14/1866
Son of Glen Owen & Sarah Rogers Burnett. Studied at Hesperian College 1861-1864, a Christian college in Woodland, California. One record noted: "In 1865 he began preaching for the Church of Christ." Among the Oregon churches he served were: Salem, Eugene, Pleasant Hill, Monmouth, and McMinnville. She was a daughter of Jonathan & Patsy Todd. They are buried in Masonic Cemetery in McMinnville.

Bushnell, James Addison (7/27/1826 – 4/8/1912) **1853**
Elizabeth Crawley Adkins (2/22/1831 – 1868) m. 9/6/1849
Sarah Ferrel Powell Page m. 1870
Charter members of the Grand Prairie Church in Lane County in 1855. His mother, Ursula Bushnell, lived with his sister and brother-in-law, Helen & Edward Adkins. His strong support of the Union cause clashed with Philip Mulkey's southern sympathies, but they were reunited after the war. In 1895 he was one of the founders of Eugene Divinity School which is known today as Northwest Christian College.

Bushnell, Daniel (? – 1/17/1843)
Ursula Griswold Pratt (5/28/1785 – 3/15/1883) m. 9/?/1816 **1853**
Mother of James Addison Bushnell and Helen Bushnell Adkins. Her husband died before she migrated to Oregon Territory with her children. She resided with her daughter and son-in-law, Helen & Edward Adkins, for nearly 30 years.

Butler, Benjamin D. (1819 – ?) **1850**
Elvira Josephine McBride m. 11/23/1851 **1846**
She was a daughter of Dr. James & Mahala McBride. In the 1860 census they were living with their 3 children in the Salt Creek district of Polk County.

Butler, Elijah D. (4/16/1824 – 1/25/1858) **1852**
Sarah Elizabeth Lucas m. 8/26/1846
He was a son of Major Peter & Rachel Butler, and she was a sister to Thomas Hartzwell Lucas and Albert Whitfield Lucas. He died in 1858 and is buried in Davidson Cemetery in Polk County, but there is no record of her burial. In the 1860 census she was living alone in Polk County with her 2 small daughters.

Butler, Ira Francis Marion (5/20/1812 – 1/16/1909) **1853**

Mary Ann Davidson (4/22/1814 – 6/29/1888) m. 11/5/1835

Son of Major Peter & Rachel Butler and daughter of Elijah & Margaret Davidson. He was captain of his wagon train. Served on board of trustees for Monmouth University and Christian College, and as an elder in Monmouth Church. Represented Polk County in the legislature in 1850s and 1860s and was elected speaker. Elected judge of Polk County in 1878. They are buried in Davidson Cemetery in Polk County.

Butler, Isaac (6/13/1820 – 6/1/1904) **1845**

Tabitha Jane Tucker (1/31/1831 – 1869) m. 3/14/45

Polly Caroline Moore m. 8/15/1869

They were newlyweds when they came overland in 1845. Settled 4 miles east of Hillsboro in Washington County. They became members of the Hillsboro Church in 1863. Isaac was the second person baptized into Christ after the organization of the Hillsboro Church in the fall of 1862. His second marriage was performed by Keathley Bailes.

Butler, Isaac M. (12/2/1831 – 5/6/1913) **1850**

Sarah A. Webb (1840 – 1906) m. 5/11/1856

Son of Major Peter & Rachel Butler. They were married in Polk County by Mac Waller, and they became members of the Monmouth Church. They are buried in Hilltop Cemetery in Polk County.

Butler, Joseph Bradley Varnum (9/18/1809 – 10/18/1879) **1849**

Elizabeth Ingalls (8/6/1821 – 5/27/1900) m. 5/9/1839

Settled in Polk County near Eola, but moved to Monmouth in the late 1850s. They were strong supporters of Christian College and members of the Monmouth Church. They are buried in Fir Crest Cemetery south of Monmouth in Polk County.

Butler, Major Peter (3/9/1789 – 6/24/1856) **1853**

Rachel Murphy (4/2/1788 – 1/10/1874) m. 7/25/1811

Patriarch and matriarch of the Butler clan. Their sons, Ira Francis Marion Butler, Elijah D. Butler and Isaac Butler, were Christians. Their daughters married Edward Ground, Isaac Smith and Thomas H. Hutchinson. She was one of the 35 charter members of the Monmouth Church, but he died less than a month before the church was organized. They are buried in Davidson Cemetery in Polk County.

Butts, John (1810-1890) **1845**

Catherine (? – 10/2/1845) m. c1836

Jane McKinley Evans (c1806 – ?) m. 7/17/1850

Catherine died soon after they arrived in Oregon Territory. She died while descending a hill to the Deschutes river in October 1845, and she was buried at the peaks known as "The Three Sisters" in the Cascade range in Wasco County. John Butts secured a donation land claim in the vicinity of Forest Grove in Washington County. Their son, Lewis Butts, became a leader in the Christian Church in Washington County.

Butts, Lewis (1832-c1880) **1845**

Elizabeth (Mary) Constable (? – c1870) m. 11/29/1862

Son of John & Catherine Butts. He settled in Washington County and secured a homestead in the Forestdale Valley. He was prominent in the Christian Church in that county, and his son, Charles Butts, was also active in the Christian Church.

Byerly (Byerley), Absalom (2/27/1833 – 8/3/1917) **1852**
Mary Florence Allen (9/16/1842 – 9/24/1892)
Son of Martin & Elizabeth Byerly. They were members of the Christian Church in Dallas, and they are buried in Salt Creek Cemetery.

Byerly (Byerley), Martin (10/18/1809 – 5/12/1888) **1851**
Elizabeth Sears (? – 11/12/1852)
Mary (11/3/1810 – 4/21/1902)
Charter Members of the Christian Church in Dallas in Polk County. He served as an elder in this church for several years, and they are buried in Salt Creek Cemetery.

Cagle, William (c1824 – ?) **1840s**
Mary A. (c1829 – ?)
In the 1850 census they were living in Clackamas County. They became members of the Mill Creek Church in Marion County in the fall of 1863.

Caldwell, Alexander P. (10/1/1825 – 3/15/1876) **1846**
Sarah Ann McKinney (c1827 – ?) m. 2/14/1850 **1848**
She was a daughter of Stephen & Louisa McKinney. He may have been an older brother of James R. Caldwell. They were living by her parents in Washington County in the 1850 census, but in the early 1850s they moved to property that encompassed both Yamhill and Polk counties. He is buried in Bethel Cemetery, but there is no record of her burial.

Caldwell, James R. (5/4/1827 – 11/26/1887)
Celia (12/4/1834 – 2/17/1913)
He was chosen to be a deacon in the Carlton Church in Yamhill County at the time of its organization in the summer of 1877. He became an elder of the Carlton Church in January 1880. They are buried in Yamhill-Carlton Cemetery.

Calhoon, John J. (8/7/1833 – 9/29/1902) **1858**
Rebecca Lemasters Berry (1/14/1836 – 11/3/1924) m. 9/27/1866 **1852**
She was the widow of Charles Berry. They were members of the McMinnville Church and John served for a time as an elder in that church. They are buried in Masonic Cemetery in McMinnville.

Callison, George Harden (2/24/1842 – 7/13/1931) **1852**
Mary Ellen Fisher (c1851 – ?) m. 1/1/1868 **1854**
Son of Gilmore & Elizabeth Callison and daughter of James Robb & Sarah Fisher. Their fathers were Christian preachers, and they became members of the Pleasant Hill Church of Christ. Harden was a deacon in the Pleasant Hill Church in the 1870s and 1880s. They died in the state of Washington and are buried there.

Callison, Gilmore (12/22/1808 – 3/22/1869) **1852**
Elizabeth McClure (11/5/1807 – 11/4/1852 m. 10/29/1829
Eliza Fleenor Linder (4/5/1817 – 2/11/1876) m. 5/15/1853
Older brother to Robert Callison. Settled near him at Pleasant Hill in Lane County. He preached in Oregon for more than 15 years, and helped to establish the Eugene Church. Their son, Rufus Gilmore Callison, preached in Oregon for nearly 50 years. Gilmore & Elizabeth are buried in Pleasant Hill Cemetery. After Gilmore died, Eliza married Michael Shelley.

Callison, Robert (6/5/1818 – 1/16/1906) **1848**

Mary Ann "Polly" Bristow (10/28/1820 – 3/24/1911) m. 12/5/1839

Younger brother of Gilmore Callison and daughter of Elijah & Susanna Bristow. They were charter members of the Pleasant Hill Church of Christ and Robert served as an elder in that church for many years. They were members of Pleasant Hill Church for more than half a century, and are buried next to her parents in Pleasant Hill Cemetery.

Callison, Rufus Gilmore (12/24/1839 – 7/7/1915) **1852**

Martha Willis (5/8/1849 – 6/10/1912) m. 5/15/1868

Sarah J. Adamson Hastings (c1836 – ?) m. 10/6/1914

Son of Gilmore & Elizabeth Callison. He preached in Oregon for nearly 50 years and died while preaching at the annual State Meeting in the tabernacle at Turner in July 1915. They are buried in Pleasant Hill Cemetery in Lane County.

Callison, William Thomas (10/14/1832 – 12/5/1869) **1852**

Rebecca Jane Linder (11/17/1837 – 1/11/1913) m. 9/22/1853

Son of Gilmore & Elizabeth Callison. He married the daughter of his stepmother. Members of the Pleasant Hill Church of Christ until they moved to northern California in 1866. They settled at Burgettville (now Glenburn) in Shasta County. Three of their children died in this village, followed by the death of William in December 1869. He died of an intestinal disorder.

Campbell, James A. (? – 3/6/1879) **1852**

Nancy (5/3/1803 – 2/13/1881)

The came overland from Illinois and settled 5 miles south of Hillsboro in Washington County. They established the Farmington (Bridgeport) congregation in that county. Their son, also named James A. Campbell, became a Christian preacher. They are buried near their son in Lewis Cemetery in Washington County.

Campbell, James A. (10/3/1847 – 4/15/1910 or 1916) **1852**

Martha (Mattie) E. Stinson (c1854 – 7/23/1890) m. 1875

He was just an infant when his family came overland and settled in Washington County. The Campbell family started the Farmington (Bridgeport) Church, and James began preaching for this congregation when he was 18 years old. Attended Christian College. Preached for the Salem Church in the mid-1870s. He preached in Oregon for nearly 50 years. They are buried beside his parents in Lewis Cemetery.

Campbell, James C. **1871**

Mary J.

Graduate of Bethany College. Principal of Pleasant Hill Seminary in Pennsylvania & Paris Female Seminary in Missouri. Moved from Hopkinsville, Kentucky to teach mathematics & astronomy at Christian College. Honorary M.A. degree conferred by Bethany on 6/19/1873. Their 27-year-old daughter developed mountain fever and died at their residence on 10/17/1873. He was a brother-in-law of Thomas Franklin Campbell, and he assisted him as assoicate editor of the *Christian Messenger*.

Campbell, James Givens (3/29/1810 – 3/16/1886) **1853**

Elizabeth Amanda Black (4/15/1811 – 10/23/1867) m. 1/3/1833

Alta A. Armstrong (c1828 – ?)

Came overland from Iowa and settled in Polk County. He was a delegate for the Salt Creek congregation at the annual State Meeting in 1863. In the 1870s he was a member of the board of trustees of Christian College. They are buried in Salt Creek Cemetery.

Campbell, Prince Lucien (10/6/1861 – 8/14/1925) **1869**
Eugenia J. Zieber (? – 2/?/1891) m. 9/12/1887
Susan Campbell Church (1857 – 9/6/1932) m. 8/20/1908
Son of Thomas F. & Jane Eliza Campbell. Graduate of Christian College in Monmouth. He succeeded David Truman Stanley as president of Oregon Normal School (1889-1902), and then became president of the University of Oregon in Eugene. He was a vital member of both the Monmouth Church and the Eugene Church.

Campbell, Thomas Franklin (5/22/1822 – 1/17/1893) **1869**
Jane Eliza Campbell (1/1/1822 – 10/23/1881)
Mary S. Stump (3/12/1851 – 8/19/1927) m. 1885
Graduate of Bethany College. President of Christian College 1869-1881. Editor of *Christian Messenger* and then of *Pacific Christian Messenger* from 1870-1882. He was the most admired and respected leader of the church during the post-war "Golden Age" of the Restoration Movement in Oregon. Candidate for Governor of Oregon in 1874.

Carlin, John (12/25/1820 – 3/10/1889) **1846**
Martha Ellen Rogers Garrison (2/18/1823 – 1904) m. 10/20/1850 **1845**
They were members of the congregation that met at Blackhawk schoolhouse in Yamhill County beginning in 1847, and they were charter members of the McMinnville Church. He is buried in Masonic Cemetery in McMinnville, but there is no record of her burial.

Cary, Miles (6/5/1811 – 9/26/1858) **1843**
Cyrene (Cyrena) B. Taylor (7/24/1815 – 9/1/1911) m. 1831
They came overland from Missouri in "The Great Migration" with Hembrees, Newbys and Chesley B. Gray. Settled in Yamhill County where he was a merchant. They are buried in Lafayette Pioneer Cemetery.

Cary, Miles (1826 – ?) **1850**
Nancy Jane Robinette m. 11/24/1851
They settled in Linn County near the Riggs, Fields, Lewis, and Shanks families. In 1871 they were among the charter members of the church established at Splawn's School House near present-day Holley.

Casteel, Lewis (2/4/1813 – 2/6/1867) **1852**
Eliza Caroline (Carolina) (9/28/1820 – 11/6/1873) m. 7/3/1836
Preached in Oregon and Washington for 15 years. The wife of George R. Caton may have been their daughter. They are buried in Bethel Cemetery in Polk County.

Caton, George R. (c1828 – ?) **1852**
Jerrusha Casteel (c1828 – ?) m. 9/29/1853
Son of George W. & Sarah Caton. She may have been a daughter of Lewis & Caroline Casteel. He preached in Oregon for more than a decade and possibly longer. He was auditor of Lane County in 1852 and performed weddings in Lane County in the 1850s. He performed weddings in Marion County in 1863. His brother, Nathan T. Caton, was a leader in the Salem Church. His sister, Susan Sebena Caton, married Daniel S. Herren.

Caton, George Washington (1801 – ?) **1852**
Sarah H. Moore (c1804 – 1894) m. 5/12/1822
Their children, George R. Caton, Nathan T. Caton and Susan Sebena Caton Herren, were Christians, and George R. was a preacher.

Caton, Nathan Thomas (1/6/1833 – 1916) **1852**
Martha Ann Herren (9/30/1837 – 1904) m. 4/14/1853 **1845**
Son of George R. & Sarah Caton and daughter of John & Theodosha Herren. Nathan's sister, Susan Sebena, married Martha's brother, Daniel S. Herren. Nathan and his brother-in-law, William John Herren, were delegates for the Salem Church at the 1858 annual State Meeting. The Catons are buried in the state of Washington.

Chapman, Caleb P. (10/3/1810 – 7/14/1892) **1848**
Elizabeth Smith (12/15/1819 – 7/4/1906) m. 6/9/1842
Came overland from Indiana and settled in Marion County. He preached throughout Oregon for more than 40 years. He organized the Bethany Church in Marion County in 1851. In 1867 he was chosen as one of the elders of the Salem Church along with Thomas Ladd, Hezekiah Burford and Governor George Woods. Caleb & Elizabeth are buried in Pioneer Cemetery in Salem.

Chapman, Wiley (1814 – 1884) **1847**
Ruhamah Stockton Farmer (died on trail in '47) m. 1833
Ellen Matlock (8/2/1829 – 7/11/1891) m. 1/13/1854
Captain of his wagon train. His wife died on the trail. He settled in Marion County and served in the territorial legislature in 1851-52. His second wife was the eldest daughter of William & Betsy Matlock. Wiley Chapman died in Clackamas County.

Chase, Edward A. (c1839 – ?) **1860s**
Annie E. (c1834 – ?)
Settled in Oakland in Douglas County and preached throughout the county in the 1870s and early 1880s. His mentor was A. L. Todd. While living in Oakland he served as an agent for the *Pacific Christian Messenger*. In 1882 he moved from Oakland to Camas Prairie in Idaho Territory, and in 1887 he was living in Grangeville, Idaho.

Chenoweth, Francis A. (1819 – 1889) **1849**
Hannah Logan m. 1842
Elizabeth A. Finley (1833 – 1911) m. 1850
When A. V. McCarty preached in Corvallis in January-February 1866, he was able to organize a congregation of 40 members. One of the community leaders who most encouraged McCarty in this effort was F. A. Chenoweth. However, it is not certain that he became a member of the church.

Churchill, James Madison **1853**
wife's name unknown
Eldest son of Lewis & Mary Churchill. He was a devout Christian and a leader in the Oak Creek Church of Christ in Linn County. During the gradual process of division between Disciples of Christ and Churches of Christ in the 1890s, he became a spokesman for the Churches of Christ.

Churchill, L. Arthur (3/20/1857 – ?) **1857**
Son of Lewis & Mary Churchill and younger brother of James Madison Churchill. He never married. He inherited the family farm 10 miles southeast of Albany, and he completed medical studies and became a doctor.

Churchill, Lewis (1806 – 1/13/1869) **1853**

Mary A. Cooper m. 1834

Lewis came across the plains in 1847, but soon returned home to Iowa. The entire family came overland in 1853. Located in Douglas County for 3 years, and then moved to Linn County in 1856. Settled 10 miles southeast of Albany. Of Lewis & Mary, one record noted: "Both were devout and faithful members of the Christian Church."

Churchill, William (1825 – 5/?/1912) **1851**

Sarah Elizabeth Lemon (1827 – after 1912) m. 11/17/1846

They traveled overland in the same train with the Powell brothers. Became members of the Monmouth Church in June 1866, and transferred their membership to the Independence Church in September 1879. In the early 1870s he was treasurer of the board of trustees of Christian College.

Churchill, Wiloby (Willoughby) (1809-1895) **1851**

Elizabeth J. Humphreys (? – 1851) m. 1834

Matilda Ann Price (c1830 – ?) m. 8/11/1852

Charter members of the Harrisburg Christian Church in 1863. When the church purchased property in November 1867, Wiloby Churchill was one of the four trustees.

Clark, Israel L. (3/8/1790 – ?) **1853**

Hannah Willis (? – 7/5/1855) m. 3/28/1815

He was described as "a Stonite from Cane Ridge, Kentucky" when he was preaching in Benton and Iowa counties in Iowa in the 1840s. He may have been the Israel Clark whose wife and son were killed by Indians in Yamhill County in 1855. He was preaching in Lane County in 1865. He preached throughout Oregon for many years and died at the home of A. L. Todd in Lookingglass Valley in Douglas County.

Cochran, Thomas (10/13/1811 – 6/3/1882)

Nancy (12/31/1810 – 1/18/1895)

Lived in Ohio and Michigan before coming across the trail. Settled in Yamhill County and became members of the Amity Church. They are buried in Amity Cemetery.

Coffey, J. B. (c1837 – ?) **1860s**

Mary E. (c1848 – ?)

Elder of the Church at Scio in Marion County in late 1870s and early 1880s.

Coffey, Nebuzardan (1790 – ?) **1848**

Elizabeth Easley (c1787 – 1/?/1880) m. 9/11/1810

Their sons-in-law included William Porter, Dr. Joseph Monroe Blackerby and William Wilshire Bristow. The Coffeys are buried next to the Porter and Blackerby families in Aumsville Cemetery in Marion County

Coffey, Thomas C. (1815 – ?) **1852**

Lucille J. Baker (? – 7/1/1859) m. 4/26/1838 or 1839

They were members of the Mill Creek Church in Marion County.

Cole, William D. (1823 – ?) **1845**

Rosanna McNary (1/4/1827 – ?) m. 3/25/1847

Along with Townsend Waller and C. C. Crane, he was a delegate from the Eola Church at the 1858 annual State Meeting. Rosanna was a cousin of Mac Waller.

Comegys, Presley (7/2/1830 – 12/7/1917) **1851**

Melzena (Meloma) Duncan (1834 – 4/30/1868) m. 6/15/1863

Malinda J. Clearwater (7/27/1842 – 10/30/1914) m. 7/21/1872

He crossed the plains with ox-teams and went to California in 1850, and continued on to Oregon in 1851. He settled 3 miles northeast of Springfield and lived there 37 years. His mother, Lucinda Scott Comegys, was a daughter of Felix & Ellen Scott and a sister of Ellen Scott Lyle. His sister, Mary Ann, married Benjamin S. Burch. Presley Comegys served as an elder in the Christian Church for several years.

Connor, Job (12/3/1827 – 11/10/1887) **1845**

Polly Ann Riggs (4/13/1834 – 4/13/1871) m. 3/29/1855 **1851**

Martha Hicklin (9/27/1842 – 1913) **1849**

He was not affiliated with the Restoration Movement. She was a daughter of Zadok & Jane Riggs. Her father died at Independence Rock during the overland crossing. She was a Christian, and her son, Roswell, was also a Christian.

Cook, James W. (1/28/1808 – 1/4/1879) **1845**

Nancy Jane Lewis (1818 – 1894) m. 10/11/1839

She was a daughter of John & Elizabeth Lewis, and a sister to David R. Lewis. They settled in Corvallis in Benton County and they were members of the Corvallis Church. His obituary noted: "Almost with his expiring breath, he praised the Lord, and exhorted his wife, children, and attending friends, to prepare to meet him in heaven."

Cooper, Harben M. (1828 – ?) **1853**

Ann Jane (c1832 – ?) m. 2/20/1851.

They came overland from Missouri and settled in Polk County. He was a younger brother to James Lindsey Cooper. They were early members of the Monmouth Church in Polk County.

Cooper, James Lindsey (1824 – 12/3/1864) **1852**

Hester Ann Moxley (c1821 – ?) m. 12/25/1843

They came overland from Missouri and settled in Polk County. They were early members of the Monmouth Church in 1856. His younger brother, Harben M. Cooper, was also a member of the Monmouth Church.

Cornelius, Absalom Hiet (1/2/1839 – ?) **1845**

Lavina Powell (1/14/1850 – ?) m. 9/20/1868 **1851**

She was the youngest daughter of Noah and Mary Powell. He was a Baptist who had studied at McMinnville College. They lived at Jefferson in Marion County.

Cornett, William M. (10/29/1821 – 1909) **1853**

Nancy Jane McCarty Pigg (1/22/1832 – 1915) m. 3/19/1854 **1847**

This blacksmith was elected captain of a train of 40 wagons that crossed the plains. Married the widow of John R. Pigg. She was a sister to A. V. McCarty. They lived near Bethel in Polk County until 1880 and then moved to Condon in Gilliam County. One record referred to him as "a pillar in the Christian Church."

Cowls, Judge J. W. (11/3/1823 – 11/24/1896) **1852**

Lucretia Martin (9/23/1827 – 2/4/1892) m. 5/16/1861

Lucy Elizabeth Graves Bewley (4/?/1838 – ?) m. 8/24/1893

She was formerly married to Franklin B. Martin who died in 1860. Judge J. W. Cowls was a leader in the McMinnville Church for many years, and he was a state senator representing Yamhill County in the 1870s. He was an agent for the *Pacific Christian Messenger* in the 1870s and for the *Christian Herald* in the 1880s.

Cox, Elias (1823 – ?) **1846**

Jemima Griffin (died on trail in '46) m. 11/23/1843

Lucia Tucker m. 11/27/1851

Son of Peter & Jane Cox and nephew of Gideon Cox. The Cox families came overland from Fountain County, Indiana. Lucia was a daughter of Samuel & Sarah Tucker, and she and Elias were charter members of Bethany Church in 1851. The Bethany meetinghouse was built on their property. Elias preached on occasion, and one obituary noted: "For 50 years Mr. Cox preached the gospel of the Christian religion."

Cox, Gideon S. (1806 – 1/17/1890) **1846**

Susanna W. Coffenberry (1808 – 1869) m. 2/8/1825

Fanny Raines m. 10/17/1875

He was younger brother to Peter Cox and uncle to Elias Cox. Two of their sons, John T. and Peter Jackson, became elders in the church. Three of their daughters married church leaders. Marcilla married Wilburn King, Elizabeth married Joshua Bowen and Permilla married Peter Wood Bowen. They are buried in Bethany Pioneer Cemetery.

Cox, John T. (1828 – 5/1/1910) **1846**

Mary Jane Pitman (c1837 – ?) m. 10/27/1853

Son of Gideon & Susanna Cox. He was a volunteer in the Cayuse Indian War in 1848. John & Mary Jane were members of the Bethany Church, and he served as an elder in the church in later years. They are buried in Bethany Pioneer Cemetery.

Cox, Peter (1802 – 12/14/1876) **1846**

Jane Raines m. 6/20/1820

Isabella Marlatt (1801 – 8/10/1851) m. 12/25/1834

Emily Crabtree (1817 – 1881) m. 1/8/1854

Came overland from Fountain County, Indiana and settled just west of Silverton in Marion County. Charter members of the Bethany Church in 1851. He served as an elder in the Bethany Church for many years. Peter, Isabella and Emily are buried in Bethany Pioneer Cemetery.

Cox, Peter Jackson (12/27/1846 – after 1903) **1846**

Christie Hadley

Son of Gideon & Susanna Cox and younger brother of John T. Cox. His older sisters were married to Wilburn King, Joshua Bowen and Peter Wood Bowen. He was born on Howell Prairie in Marion County. He and Christie were members of the Bethany Church, and he served as an elder in the church in later years.

Cox, Samuel Standfield (10/5/1819 – 6/26/1900) **1848**
Harriet Cox (5/6/1824 – 5/1/1862) m. 8/4/1842
Elizabeth (Betsy) Bailes (12/22/1811 – 5/28/1883) m. 5/7/1863
Samuel & Harriet were cousins, but it is not known how they were related to the other Cox families living in the Bethany area. They came 2 years after the other Cox families, and they settled on a donation land claim south of Silver Creek in Marion County. They were charter members of the Bethany Church in 1851. Betsy was the mother of Keathley Bailes. She and Samuel moved to Kittitas Valley in W.T. in 1880.

Crabtree, James Isaiah (12/5/1834 – 3/18/1905) **1853**
Martha Ann Shelton (? – 1874) m. 1865
Selecta Gardner Stayton (1851 – 4/11/1925) m. 9/8/1878
Son of Washington Crabtree. Settled in Marion County. His funeral was at Stayton Christian Church and he is buried in Lone Oak Cemetery.

Crabtree, Washington (10/1/1808 – 9/13/1901) **1853**
Susannah (2/14/1810 – 2/3/1892) m. 2/24/1831
Along with John Richardson, he was a leader in the Scio Church in Linn County for many years. One of the delegates from this church at the 1863 annual State Meeting.

Crabtree, Zimri (8/4/1817 – 6/8/1884) **1853**
Mary (Mariah) Jane (4/20/1821 – 10/?/1873) m. 12/25/1837
They came overland from Missouri. Probably traveled in the same train with the Philip Mulkey family. Became members of the Grand Prairie Church in Lane County in May 1859. Their daughter, Louisa, was married to Welcome Hayes Mulkey, a son of Philip & Martha Mulkey.

Crane (Crain), C. C. (c1824 – ?) **1850?**
S. M. (c1828 – ?)
They came overland from Illinois and they were in Oregon by 1851 and probably earlier. They settled in Polk County. He was a delegate for the Eola Church at the 1858 annual State Meeting.

Crawford, Jasper Vincent (8/7/1839 – 12/10/1915) **1851**
Elizabeth N. Dunlap (1/28/1848 –?) m. 6/11/1867
He was just 12 years old when he arrived in Oregon. He began preaching after the Civil War, and he preached in Oregon and Washington for nearly 50 years. Most of his ministry was devoted to the northeastern Oregon counties of Gilliam, Morrow, Umatilla, Union, and Wallowa.

Crawford, Philemon Vawter (9/24/1814 – 2/1/1901) **1851**
Lettitia (Lilitia) Smith (8/31/1817 – 6/13/1896) m. 12/18/1833
Came overland from Indiana and settled briefly in Yamhill County. However, they soon moved and gave their name to the settlement of Crawfordsville in Linn County. They were still living in Crawfordsville in the late 1870s and Philemon was serving as an agent for *Pacific Christian Messenger.* Their son, Jasper Vincent Crawford, became a gospel preacher in eastern Oregon. They are buried in Crawfordsville Cemetery.

Crocker, Abner T. (c1825 – ?) **1860s**
Margaret (c1828 – ?)
Along with William Evermont Pedigo, he was chosen to be an elder of the Hillsboro Christian Church in Washington County on 6/16/1866.

Crowley, Thomas Leland (1802 – 12/4/1846) **1846**
Catherine Linville (8/28/1803 – 5/31/1884) m. 8/3/1820
Daughter of Richard & Mary Linville and a sister to Harrison Linville and Margaret Vanderpool. During the overland journey to Oregon she suffered through the deaths of 5 of her children, most from typhoid fever, the tragic drowning of her mother, and finally the death of her husband to pneumonia. She settled in Polk County with her 5 remaining children and married James M. Fulkerson.

Crump, Turner (1799 – 3/18/1862) **1846**
Tabitha (c1812 – 5/12/1879) m. 10/28/1834
He was not a Christian, but she was an early member of the Salem Church. They are buried in the IOOF Rural Cemetery in Salem.

Crystal, Richard Sharpe (4/20/1817 – 4/9/1882) **1864**
Delilah Morrow m. 2/23/1838
Mary Ann Mitchell (c1834 – ?) m. 4/9/1854
They were members of the Dallas Church in Polk County and he was superintendent of the Sunday School program. He was a state senator representing Polk County in 1874-1878. He served as an agent for the *Pacific Christian Messenger* in the 1870s. At the time of his death, he was county treasurer of Polk County. He is buried in Dallas Cemetery, but there is no record of the burial of either wife.

Dart, Charles Bisbee (1/20/1820 – 5/7/1902) **1852**
Isabella Eleanor Kean (8/26/1824 – 4/10/1911) m. 6/22/1843
Overland from Mt. Pleasant, Iowa. A son, Thomas Lee, died on trail 6/19/1852. Settled near Rock Creek, 3 miles below Molalla. Charter members of Rock Creek Church of Christ. Meetinghouse built on their property in 1863. Charles was a spiritual leader of this church for nearly 50 years. Their sons, Will and Edward, were also leaders at Rock Creek Church. The Darts are buried in Molalla Pioneer Cemetery.

Dart, Charles William (1846 – ?) **1852**
Arena (c1851 – ?) m. c1866
Eldest son of Charles & Isabella Dart. He was known as Will Dart. They were members of the Rock Creek Church of Christ in Clackamas County until 1900 when they moved to Stayton in Marion County.

Dart, Edward Kean (1856 – 1944) **1856**
Alice Rich (? – 5/25/1895) m. c1892 **1875**
Clara Hatton
Son of Charles & Isabella Dart. His first wife was a daughter of a Christian preacher in Oregon named George P. Rich. The Darts were members of the Rock Creek Church of Christ in Clackamas County, and they are buried in Molalla Pioneer Cemetery.

Davidson, Alexander B. (c1828 – ?) **1850**
Elizabeth Ann Burford (c 1839 – ?) m. 3/15/1860 **1852**
Son of Elijah & Margaret Davidson and daughter of Hezekiah & Levina Burford. They were married in Polk County by his brother-in-law, Ira F. M. Butler, who was married to his older sister, Mary Ann Davidson. He gave a $50 contribution to Monmouth University in 1855.

Davidson, Carter T. (10/26/1802 – 11/30/1881) **1852**
Elizabeth Shirley (c1805 – 2/9/1899) m. 5/8/1828
Eldest son of Elijah & Margaret Davidson and an older brother of Henry, Elijah Banton and Alexander. His sisters married I. F. M. Butler, William Mason, Squire S. Whitman and Thomas H. Lucas. Elizabeth may have been a sister to Ethan Allen Shirley. They are buried in Fir Crest Cemetery south of Monmouth in Polk County.

Davidson, Elijah A. (2/23/1783 – 4/24/1870) **1850**
Margaret Murphy (8/19/1785 – 3/2/1864) m. 2/23/1802
Patriarch and matriarch of the Davidson clan. Overland from Warren County, Illinois. Elijah preached in Illinois for many years before moving to Oregon, and he preached in Oregon for nearly 20 years. Their sons, Carter, Henry, Elijah Banton and Alexander were Christians. Daughters married I. F. M. Butler, William Mason, Squire S. Whitman, and Thomas H. Lucas. They are buried in Davidson Cemetery which was located on their donation land claim about 2 miles southwest of Monmouth.

Davidson, Elijah Banton (2/3/1819 – 1/16/1888) **1850**
Salome Jones (8/13/1822 – 8/22/1909) m. 10/22/1840
Son of Elijah & Margaret Davidson. Like his father, he was a gospel preacher, and he preached in Oregon for more than 35 years.

Davidson, Henry (5/28/1818 – 2/19/1894) **1852**
Sarah Montgomery (12/27/1824 – 5/17/1918) m. 4/22/1840
Son of Elijah & Margaret Davidson, and brother to Alexander B. and Elijah Banton. He served as a deacon and then an elder in the Halsey Church in Linn County.

Davidson, Hezekiah (2/1/1789 – 2/25/1876) **1847**
Melissa Ann "Lucy" Page (12/14/1804 – 5/5/1877) m. 9/27/1820
This family was not closely related to the other Davidsons in Polk County. They were baptized into Christ in 1851 by their son-in-law, Mac Waller. He had married their daughter in 1850. Their son married a daughter of Harrison & Nancy Linville. Hezekiah & Elizabeth are buried in Buena Vista Cemetery in Polk County.

Davidson, James O. (10/12/1825 – 7/16/1899) **1847**
Mary E. Linville (9/2/1838 – 10/29/1914) m. 7/30/1851
Son of Hezekiah & Melissa Davidson and daughter of Harrison & Nancy Bounds Linville. Members of the Luckiamute Church. They are buried in Buena Vista Cemetery in Polk County near both sets of parents.

Davie, Allan Jones (2/28/1816 – 9/17/1874) **1842**
Cynthia Brown (1/5/1829 – 3/28/1903) m. 8/30/1843
First wedding of Christians in Oregon Territory? Allan may not have been a Christian. She was a member of the Aumsville Church. They are buried in Aumsville Cemetery.

Davis, Caleb (9/27/1820 – 1/21/1890) **1853**
Ann Maria Chrisman (3/25/1822 – 2/10/1865) m. 3/20/1842
Winna Cummings (c1821 – ?) m. 10/26/1876
Devout Christians from Indiana. Settled first in Linn County, but moved to the Pleasant Hill district of Lane County in the mid-1860s.

Davis, Charles A. (11/6/1855 – ?) **1855**

Narcissa Rutelidge (Ruttledge) (1858 – 1910) m. 6/22/1876

He was a son of Caleb & Ann Davis. They were members of the Pleasant Hill Church of Christ in Lane County.

Davis, Drury (c1829 – ?) **1850s**

Frances (c1841 – ?)

In the 1860 census they were living in the Salt Creek precinct of Polk County. They were charter members of the Dallas Church in the 1860s. A history of the church notes that they were "quiet people and consistent members." They moved to Philomath in Benton County in the 1870s and became members of the Philomath Church. He served as an agent for the *Pacific Christian Messenger* and the *Christian Herald.*

Davis, Isaac (2/12/1825 – 2/28/1882) **1852**

Margaret Ledgerwood

Sarah C. Hines Buckingham (3/4/1829 – 9/7/1886)

Younger brother of Thomas C. Davis. Settled in Yamhill County. In the 1870s they were members of the North Yamhill congregation and Isaac was an agent for the *Pacific Christian Messenger*. He became an elder of the Carlton Church in Yamhill County at the time of its organization in 1877. He and Sarah are buried in Pike Cemetery.

Davis, Jefferson (11/23/1826 – 6/8/1890) **1851**

Kittie (Kitty) Robinson (5/28/1829 – 12/6/1902) m. 11/13/1853

They were married in Yamhill County and lived in southern half of the county. Kitty was a Christian prior to their marriage. Her husband was baptized into Christ by Daniel Trullinger during a gospel meeting in Yamhill County in October 1858.

Davis, Leander S. (1826 – 6/29/1874) **1847**

Mary Cox (c1832 – ?) m. 7/5/1848

They became members of Bethany Church in June 1863. According to church record book, Leander was baptized into Christ at that time and Mary was accepted into fellowship because she was already a Christian. He served in state legislature in 1866.

Davis, Levi (2/2/1818 – 11/15/1900) **1853**

Matilda A. Cline (7/2/1824 – 2/28/1899) m. 2/8/1846

Charter members of the Rock Creek Church of Christ south of Mollala in Clackamas County. Along with Charles Bisbee Dart, Levi Davis became an elder of the Rock Creek Church of Christ on 5/12/1867. They are buried in Russellville Cemetery in Clackamas County.

Davis, Thomas C. (10/19/1821 – 12/6/1887) **1847**

Nancy Ann Himes (Hines) (9/21/1830 – 9/2/1891) m. 8/29/1850

Older brother of Isaac Davis. Thomas and Isaac married sisters. They lived in Yamhill County for all of their married life and were members of the North Yamhill and Carlton congregations. They are buried in Pike Cemetery. Their daughter, Elizabeth Jane, married Charles Vos Kuykendall.

Davis, Dr. Zedekiah (1/17/1804 – 7/9/1878) **1846**

Virginia (died on trail in '46) m. 1824

Huldah Ann (7/25/1824 – 8/3/1905) m. 11/30/1851

His wife died on the Oregon Trail. He settled near Buena Vista in Polk County and remarried five years later. He served as an agent for the *Pacific Christian Messenger* from its beginning until his death. Buried in Buena Vista Cemetery.

Dawson, William (12/21/1816 – 1889) **1845**

Mary E. Searcy (5/13/1823 – 8/3/1862) m. 12/28/1842

Mary Baker Rash (Rush) (10/24/1833 – 4/16/1898) m. 1/or 7/17/1864

She may have been a sister to Evaline Searcy Martin, the wife of Hardin D. Martin, and they may have come overland together. Both families settled in Yamhill County. Charter members of the church that met in Blackhawk schoolhouse in 1847. Members of the McMinnville Church. He was on the board of regents for Christian College and was an agent for the *Christian Messenger.* Buried in Masonic Cemetery in McMinnville.

Deardorff, Christian (1/15/1805 – 12/14/1884) **1850**

Matilda Landess (Landers) (8/31/1802 – 4/30/1891) m. 1/23/1824

They settled in Christilla Valley (now Happy Valley) east of Milwaukie near Sunnyside in Clackamas County. They were members of John Foster's congregation that met in a schoolhouse near present-day Damascus. She may have been a younger sister to Abraham Landess. Their sons, John M. Deardorff and David H. Deardorff, were strong leaders in the church.

Deardorff, David H. (5/11/1827 – ?) **1852**

Lucinda A. Armentrout (1831 – 1897) m. 2/1/1846 or 2/10/1848

Son of Christian & Matilda Deardorff and younger brother of John M. Deardorff. They settled near Sunnyside in Clackamas County and they were members of the Damascus Church He was an agent for the *Pacific Christian Messenger* in the 1870s.

Deardorff, John M. (10/10/1824 – 12/7/1902) **1850**

Rachel Ingram (1837– 7/28/1901) m. 1/5/1854 **1852**

Son of Christian & Matilda Deardorff and older brother of David H. Deardorff. They settled near Sunnyside in Clackamas County and were members of Damascus Church.

Dickinson, John P. **1870s**

Sally T.

Charter members in the Christian Church in Portland (1879). He was one of the first elders, and the church originally met in their home.

Doty, Dr. D. M.

wife's name unknown

He was a dentist-preacher. He preached for the McMinnville Church in the 1870s, the Amity Church in the 1880s and the Dallas Church in the 1890s. It is not known if he was related to Reuben Doty.

Doty, Reuben (8/18/1838 – 3/26/1899) **1853**

Sarah Jane Ray (6/30/1848 – 8/24/1936) m. 6/30/1864

He came overland from Illinois and settled in Polk County where he found employment as a carpenter. He was recording secretary at the 1863 annual State Meeting and he preached on occasion. He died at his home in Lorane in Lane County.

Dougherty, Winn **1875**

Martha Boyd (? – 1/?/1936)

They came overland from Missouri and settled briefly in Summerville in Union County. The next year they continued on to the town of Wallowa in Wallowa County. The William Boyd and Doll Johnson families had arrived in Wallowa the previous year, and they had established the Wallowa Church of Christ. The Dougherty's were leaders in this church for the next 60 years.

Downer, Joseph Warren (1825 – 3/10/1904) **1847**

Eleanor Ann Pigg (c1833 – 6/?/1854) m. 8/27/1850

Ann Dennison m. 2/1/1855

Overland with Isaac and Elias Briggs via the Applegate Trail. Settled south of Ballston in Polk County. Mac Waller performed his first marriage to daughter of Reuben Pigg. Served on board of trustees of Bethel College 1855-1861. A saddler by trade, he moved to Salem for business reasons. Deacon in Salem Church. Moved to Portland in 1870s and became a charter member of Portland Church. He died in Yakima, Washington.

Downing, George S. (10/28/1836 – ?) **1853**

Missouri A. Evans (c1842 – 10/13/1865) m. 6/25/1857

Mary C. Evans Smith (9/17/1844 – 7/22/1882) m. 2/14/1867

Elizabeth A. Rossiter m. 6/6/1883

Younger brother of John Downing. Settled in the Waldo Hills near Sublimity in Marion County. When his first wife died he married her widowed sister. He was a deacon in the church for many years.

Downing, John (11/1/1828 – 9/16/1887) **1847**

Temperance Elizabeth Hunt (1/16/1834 – 9/16/1876) m. 4/12/1849

Mary Jane "Jennie" Carpenter (1850 – 4/14/1927) m. 10/4/1877

He met Temperance on the overland journey and they were married 2 years later. Settled in Marion County near Sublimity. He represented Marion County in the state legislature in 1872-74. One record noted: "He was a devout member of the Christian Church and a deacon until his death."

Downing, William Henry (5/7/1858 – ?) **1858**

Henrietta McKinney (? – 2/20/1884) m. 1/20/1881

Deliah H. Bower (? – 2/17/1900) m. 6/30/1886

Augusta Newton m. 3/11/1903

He was a son of George & Missouri Downing and a nephew of John Downing. She was a daughter of William & Matilda McKinney, and their marriage was performed by Sebastian C. Adams. His second marriage was performed by a Christian preacher named James W. Webb.

Drinkwater, William (1811 – ?) **1853**

Nancy (? – 11/1/1870) m. 5/22/1836

They were members of the Mill Creek Church in Marion County as were three of their married daughters, Amanda Drinkwater Megee, Barthena Drinkwater Hodkins and Martha Drinkwater Megee.

Earl, Joseph (1825 – ?) **1845**
Jemima Powell (11/6/1834 – 7/26/1894) m. 12/4/1851 **1851**
Two Earl brothers married two daughters of John Alkire Powell. Joseph & Jemima were charter members of the Albany Church in February 1882.

Earl, Robert (c4/30/1835 – 8/27/1915) **1845**
Lourana Powell (10/15/1836 – 8/24/1916) m. 9/16/1852 **1851**
Two Earl brothers married two daughters of John Alkire Powell.

Eby, David **1851**
Elizabeth Barger
He was a deacon in the Christian Church. They moved often, and they lived in Astoria, Portland, Oregon City, Linn County, and Lane County.

Elder, Alfred R. (1806 – 2/13/1882) **1849**
Martha P. Baker (c1810 – 2/13/1868) m. 1/16/1827
Mrs. H. H. Lord m. 8/28/1868
Came overland from Illinois and settled in Yamhill County. They were living in Polk County in the 1860 census. He preached in Oregon for more than 12 years before moving to Washington Territory in 1862. Died near Olympia in Thurston County.

Elledge, Daniel W. (1813 – 1890) **1864**
Catharine (Katie) Goodman (7/27/1810 – 3/13/1875) m. 12/22/1858
Nancy W. (? – 8/27/1881)
He preached in midwestern states for many years before coming overland, and then in Oregon/Washington for nearly a quarter-century. Katie died at Summerville in Union County, funeral by L. L. Rowland. He lived with William H. & Hannah Wilson at Yoncalla in Douglas County in the 1880s, and he died there. One account noted: "He fought a good fight, he kept the faith, and he finished his triumphant course."

Evans, Samuel D. (1827 – 8/1/1861) **1852**
Louisa Thompson (1832 – 4/27/1912) m. 3/2/1851
Came overland from Illinois and settled a claim 5 miles northwest of Winchester in Douglas County. They may have established a small congregation in that area, and Swander referred to him as a "lay preacher." They moved to Virginia City, Nevada in 1859 to pursue mining interests. He was murdered by Indians in California's Modoc County while driving cattle from Oregon to Nevada.

Faulconer, Absalom B. (6/8/1816 – 1/20/1899) **1846**
Mary Ann Graves (c1826 – 8/27/1854) m. 12/10/1840
Mary J. Cutting Trullinger (9/30/1833 – 3/12/1886) m. 3/13/1856
Came overland in 1846 and settled in Yamhill County. Laid out the townsite of Sheridan in 1865-66. Charter members of the Sheridan Church. At the time of the 1870 census, the Christian Church was the only church in the town of Sheridan.

Faulconer, Marcellas (Marcellus (10/30/1822 or 1823 – 4/20 or 30/1907) **1850**
Caroline G. Baunbridge (5/8/1827 – 10/7/1911) m. 1/?/1854
He settled by his older brother in Yamhill County. The Faulconer families became charter members of the Sheridan Church.

Faulconer, O. M. (9/2/1859 – ?) **1859**
Ida Bower (? – 1893) m. 1886
Claudia Steward m. 1899
He was the son of Marcellas & Caroline Faulconer, charter members of the Sheridan Church in Yamhill County. O. M. Faulconer served as a deacon in the church.

Faulconer, Thomas N. (1830 – ?) **1851**
Lucy A. (3/23/1844 – 10/19/1907)
He settled by his brothers in the Sheridan district of Yamhill County. They became charter members of the Sheridan Church. In the 1870s he was still living in Sheridan and serving as an agent for the *Pacific Christian Messenger*. He represented Yamhill County in the state legislature in 1882-84.

Fenton, William David 6/29/1853 – 5/15/1925) **1865**
Katherine (Katie) Lewis Lucas (7/6/1859 – 9/14/1930) m. 10/16/1879
Graduates of Christian College. She was a daughter of A. W. & Elizabeth Lucas and a granddaughter of John Ecles Murphy. He was a lawyer, state legislator and agent for the *Pacific Christian Messenger* in the 1870s. Wedding performed by T. F. Campbell.. They lived in Lafayette until 1885 and then moved to Portland. Members of Lafayette Church and Portland Church. He was an agent for the *Christian Herald* in the 1880s.

Fields, Thomas (5/4/1809 – 7/1/1875) **1847**
Rebecca Jane Riggs (1/24/1812 – 1/29/1874) m. 1/22/1829
She was a daughter of Thomas & Leah Hunt Riggs and a sister to Rachel Riggs, Elizabeth Lewis, Mary Shanks, Timothy A. Riggs, and Thomas Riggs. Her father and brother-in-law died on the trail. Thomas & Rebecca were living in Linn County at the time of the 1850 census.

Fisher, Frederick (1/5/1796 – 9/27/1883) **1850s**
Mary (7/29/1796 – 6/19/1880) m. 4/16/1818
Came overland from Indiana and settled in Lane County. His obituary was published in the *Christian Herald* and it noted: "He obeyed the Lord in 1840 and has lived a consistent Christian life ever since . . . [he] leaves two sons and one daughter to mourn his absence. They are all members of the Church of Christ."

Fisher, James Robb (6/30/1819 – 3/24/1864) **1854**
Sarah McCall (3/29/1826 – 3/26/1867) m. 10/10/1844
He preached in Iowa for several years before they came overland to Oregon. She may have been a younger sister of William McCall and Elizabeth McCall Baughman who lived at Pleasant Hill. The Fishers settled at Pleasant Hill in Lane County and are buried in Pleasant Hill Cemetery. Two of their daughters, Mary and Minerva, married sons of Gilmore Callison.

Fisher, John Smith (10/10/1824 – 2/22/1910) **1854**
Dolly Catherine Pedigo (6/22/1830 – 1/10/1917) m. 5/10/1846
She was a daughter of Edward & Lettice Pedigo. They came overland from Iowa with other members of the Pedigo family and settled near Damascus in Clackamas County. They moved to Washington Territory with her parents in the 1870s. They are buried in Vineland Cemetery in Clarkston, Washington.

Flanery, Elijah (1/?/1819 – 6/9/1866) **1853?**
Talitha (9/27/1822 – 5/10/1896)
They came overland from Missouri and settled in Polk County. He was a delegate from Bethel Church at 1863 annual State Meeting. They are buried in Bethel Cemetery.

Fleming, Henry Clay (7/15/1842 – 9/29/1930) **1872**
Winnie Marchbanks (9/26/1841 – 9/14/1908) m. 7/21/1867
Reared in Tennessee and fought 4 years with the Confederate Army in Civil War. They moved to northern California in 1869 and to Ashland, Oregon in 1871. He was county school superintendent, farmer and gospel preacher. They moved to Lake County in 1888 and he preached for the Church of Christ at New Pine Creek. They remained with Churches of Christ after the division with Disciples of Christ. They are buried in New Pine Creek Cemetery.

Flint, A. W. **1850s**
wife's name unknown
Not much is known about this evangelist. He may have been preaching in Oregon as early as the 1850s.

Ford, Marcus Aurelius (4/18/1823 – 1/1/1850) **1844**
Amanda Thorp (? – 12/19/1848) m. 1/24/1847
Son of Nat & Lucinda Ford and daughter of John & Lucy Thorp. He was a graduate of Bacon College in Harrodsburg, Kentucky, the first college established by the Restoration Movement. Amanda died in San Francisco. Marcus was drowned (or murdered by Indians) at Shoalwater Bay.

Ford, Colonel Nathaniel (1/22/1795 – 1/9/1870) **1844**
Lucinda Duncan Embree (11/18/1799 – 1/14/1874) m. 7/11/1822
Captain of his wagon train. Settled on Rickreall Creek in Polk County. His sister and brother-in-law, Kezziah & David Goff, settled on the adjacent claim. Members of the Rickreall Church. One of their daughters married a Christian preacher named W. T. Haley. Nat Ford was elected to represent Polk County in the state senate on several occasions. They are buried in Burch Pioneer Cemetery in Polk County.

Forgey, James (1825 – ?) **1852**
Mary E. m. 5/7/1847
Elizabeth Young m. 11/30/1859
Harriet Ray m. 5/12/1863
He was a delegate from the Forks Santiam Church in Linn County at the 1858 annual State Meeting. He served as an elder in the Scio Church in Linn County in the 1860s and 1870s. He moved to Washington Territory in the 1880s.

Foster, Ambrose D. (1816 – 1/22/1860) **1845**
Zerelda Emma Redding (Reddin) (c1817 – ?) m. 2/3/1836
Eldest son of John & Nancy Foster. Their daughter, Martha Ann, married James Henry Pedigo on 3/26/1858.

Foster, Isaac M. (5/7/1819 – 11/2/1893) **1845**
Letha Jane Beauchamp (8/10/1834 – 10/?/1879) m. 8/10/1849
Mary Jane Arthur m. 11/29/1872
Son of John & Nancy Foster and daughter of Stephen & Elizabeth Beauchamp. His second wife was a daughter of William & Millie Arthur.

Foster, John (1792 – 3/22/1868) **1845**
Nancy (1797 – 6/7/1870) m. 8/15/1814
The pioneer preacher for the Restoration Movement in Oregon Territory. He established a congregation near present-day Damascus in 1846. This was the second congregation established by the Restoration Movement in Oregon. He preached in Oregon for more than 20 years.

Foster, John T. (1822 – ?) **1845**
Adaline Beauchamp (c1815 – ?) m. 11/?/1848 **1845**
Son of John & Nancy Foster and daughter of Stephen & Elizabeth Beauchamp. They were members of the Mill Creek Church in Marion County.

Fouts, John Thomas (6/23/1839 – 6/3/1912) **1852**
Frances Eliza Sappington (12/1/1843 – 10/3/1907)
He was chosen to be an elder in the Carlton Church in Yamhill County at the time of its organization in the summer of 1877.

Frazer, John A. (1828 – 7/?/1866) **1853**
Mary Louise Riggs (2/28/1839 – 7/13/1856) m. 9/22/1855 **1845**
Sarah J. Nicklin (Nicklaus) (? – 3/?/1866) m. 6/1/1858 **1852**
Overland from Kentucky with younger brother, Lucien. Settled in Salt Creek district of Polk County. First wife was daughter of James Berry Riggs. Marriage performed by G. O. Burnett. Second marriage performed by G. W. Richardson. One of the delegates for Salt Creek Church at the annual State Meeting in 1858. Represented Polk County in state legislature in 1864, and died in Salem in July 1866 four months after death of his wife. Their 4 small children were raised by relatives.

Frazer, Lucien B. (9/24/1833 – 8/18/1900) **1853**
Elizabeth A. Campbell (2/4/1839 – 12/15/1911) m. 7/31/1856
Younger brother of John A. Frazer. Settled first in Yamhill County 5 miles north of Willamina, but moved to Bethel district in Polk County in 1866. Served as an elder and taught Sunday School at Bethel Church. Member of the board of trustees of Bethel College. They are buried in Bethel Cemetery.

Frazer, William B. (c1824 – ?) **1847?**
Delilah (c1832 – ?)
They were members of the Mill Creek Church in Marion County. They moved to California in 1859.

Frier, Absalom H. (1814 – ?) **1845**
Elizabeth McCulloch (c1820 – 3/8/1896) m. 4/?/1838
Along with several other families of Christians, such as the Fosters, Dawsons, Riggs, and Herrens, they followed Stephen Meek on his ill-fated short cut. They ran a hotel and conducted a ferry service near Oregon City for a time. In 1850 census they were living in Washington County, but moved to the Bethel area of Polk County soon after. He was first president of board of trustees of Bethel Institute, serving from 1855-1859.

Garrett, Thomas (1831 – ?) **1852**
Parmelia Ann (c1832 – ?) m. c 10/22/1850
Charter members of Rock Creek Church of Christ south of Molalla in Clackamas County. On 5/12/1867 he and Elijah Weddle were appointed deacons in this church. On the same day, Charles Bisbee Dart and Levi Davis were chosen to serve as elders in the Rock Creek Church.

Gerking, Jonathan R. (12/17/1812 – 7/12/1882) **1862**
Nancy Myers (c1818 – ?) 11/3/1834
Settled in Marion County and became members of Bethany Church. Moved to Weston in Umatilla County in 1871. He was one of the elders of the Wild Horse congregation. A report in the *Pacific Christian Messenger* in 1877 noted: "Father Gerking, an old and faithful soldier in the Lord's army, talked for us." The Gerking family was a large one, and many of them were active in the Restoration Movement in Oregon.

Gilfrey (Gilfry), John T. (1818 – 1896) **1852**
Delilah C. Bristow (1/26/1822 – 1887) m. 6/2/1840
She was a daughter of Elijah & Susanna Bristow. He was elected county judge in Lane County in September 1852. He was one of the founders of Creswell in Lane County, and he operated a store there for many years. He was an agent for the *Pacific Christian Messenger* in the 1870s and for the *Christian Herald* in the 1880s.

Gill, Dr. Joseph P. (c. 1818 – ?) **1860s**
Margaret (c. 1833 – ?)
They settled in Lane County and became active members of the Eugene Church. In the 1870 census they were living with the George M. Whitney family. Along with Rufus Gilmore Callison, son of Gilmore Callison, he served as an elder in this growing church in the late 1870s and the early 1880s. In the 1880 census they were neighbors of Dr. William Owsley, Rufus Gilmore Callison and S. Monroe Hubbard.

Gill, Matthew Cooper (1/23/1842 – ?) **1864**
Nancy Elizabeth Howell (1848 – ?) **1848**
They settled in Scio in Linn County and became members of the Scio Church. Matthew served as an elder in this church. He ran a blacksmith shop for 20 years and then established a hardware business.

Gilliland, Samuel Pinckney (10/15/1827 – 12/4/1883) **1854**
Betsy (Betsey) Ann Pedigo (8/27/1833 – 2/4/1897) m. 9/16/1848
She was a daughter of Edward & Lettice Pedigo and a sister to Zerelda Jane Pedigo Hendrix. Her brothers were William Evermont Pedigo, James Henry Pedigo and Edward Axel Pedigo. The Gillilands settled around Damascus in Clackamas County, and he represented the county in the 1857-58 legislature. They moved to Washington Territory in 1871. They are buried in Eden Valley Cemetery in Whitman County.

Gilmore, Samuel M. (3/17/1815 – 11/5/1893) **1843**
Martha Ann (9/11/1818 – 2/27/1909) m. 2/5/1837
Veterans of "The Great Migration" of 1843. Came overland from Buchanan County, Missouri. Settled in Yamhill County about 3 miles east of Amity. Along with William Lysander Adams and others, he was one of the founders of the Republican Party in Oregon. Member of the board of trustees of Bethel College 1855-1862.

Githens, George (3/15/1828 – ?) **1852**
Jane Stout (? – 2/8/1853) m. 8/4/1848
Mary A. Howlett m. 1855
Overland from Indiana. Cholera attacked the train and 6 in their company died. George & Jane arrived safely in October, but she died 4 months later. He settled on a farm in Clackamas County with a magnificent view of Mt. Hood.

Goff, David (6/26/1795 – 2/6/1875) **1844**

Kezziah Ford (4/28/1798 – 2/22/1866) m. 8/11/1819

The Goffs and the Fords traveled together in the 1844 migration and settled on adjacent claims near Rickreall Creek in Polk County. Kezziah Goff was a sister to Nat Ford. They were members of the Rickreall Church, and they are buried near the Fords in Burch Pioneer Cemetery in Polk County.

Graves, Charles B. (1/28/1824 – 1/23/1892) **1846**

Mary H. Burnett (1834 – 1897) m. 1/15/1851 **1846**

Son of James & Diana Graves. He settled on a donation land claim near Sheridan in Yamhill County. In 1849 he mined for gold in California and returned about $2,000 richer. He married a daughter of Glen Owen & Sarah Burnett in 1851, and 13 years later they returned to Bethel and bought the old Burnett homestead. They were members of the Bethel Church and they are buried in Bethel Cemetery.

Graves, James (1796 – 1882) **1847**

Diana Newton (12/6/? – 3/23/1848)

Catherine Bewley (c1803 – 1867) m. 8/26/1849

James & Diana were parents of Charles B. Graves. They followed him to Oregon in 1847 and settled near him in the Sheridan district of Yamhill County. James served in the territorial government and according to one account he "became prominent in Republican politics." They were members of the Sheridan Church. Buried on private property on their old donation land claim north of Sheridan.

Graves, Thomas J. (10/24/1855 – 1944) **1855**

Martha E. Shelton (3/29/1854 – 7/7/1881) m. 1878 **1854**

Mary Ella Wilcox (6/21/1861 – 1924) m. 1885

Son of Charles & Mary Graves and daughter of John W. & Mary Jane Shelton. He was a grandson of Glen Owen Burnett and she was a granddaughter of Zebedee Shelton & Hezekiah Burford. He graduated from Christian College in 1874. They were members of the Bethel Church. Thomas and both wives are buried together in Bethel Cemetery.

Gray, Chesley B. **1843**

In "The Great Migration" of 1843. Erroneously listed as Chesley B. Gray by both Lenox and Bancroft. He traveled in same train with William & Sarah Newby, and he drove one of the wagons for Elijah Millican. Settled in Yamhill County. In the fall of 1846 he rode with Joel Jordan Hembree to assist McBride-Burnett party when they reached The Dalles. He may have died or returned home. He was not mentioned in 1850 census.

Greenwood, William (9/13/1806 – 5/18/1869) **1848**

Elizabeth Jane Branael (6/16/1814 – 8/7/1875) m. 8/12/1828

Overland from Iowa. Settled on a donation land claim on Howell's Prairie in Marion County. He was a member of the state senate in 1862. They were members of the Bethany Church and they were buried in Bethany Pioneer Cemetery.

Greer, Jerome B. (1810 – ?) **1850**

Matilda J. m. 3/15/1832

He was a delegate from the Mill Creek Church in Marion County at the 1858 annual State Meeting.

Ground, Edward (1809 – 1885) **1853**

Eliza Ann Butler (1816 – 12/24/1864) m. 10/29 or 11/1/1834

She was a daughter of Major Peter & Rachel Murphy. They settled on a donation land claim eight miles south of Monmouth on the Luckiamute River in Polk County. They were members of the Luckiamute Church, and he was one of the delegates from this church at the annual State Meeting in 1863. They are buried in Davidson Cemetery.

Guthrie, Stephen (9/6/1802 – 12/7/1865) **1853**

Amy Harper (1/12/1804 – 5/23/1873) m. 12/24/1824 or 12/22/1825

They lived in Meigs County, Ohio and Adams County, Illinois before coming overland. They settled in Thurston County in Washington Territory. He was a delegate from the Thurston congregation in W.T. at the 1858 annual State Meeting at Mill Creek Church in Marion County. He died at Chambers Prairie in Thurston County.

Hackleman, Abraham (7/29/1829 – ?) **1847**

Elenore B. Davis m. 3/20/1849

Vira Anthrom McKinnon

He came overland from Rush County, Indiana and settled in Linn County. He was living in Linn County when he married his first wife.

Haley, Bedford (1832 – ?) **1853**

Mary E. m. 1/24/1858

Son of Patrick Rivers Haley and older brother of William Thompson Haley and Maximillian Haley. They were members of the Monmouth Church, but he was withdrawn from in December 1865 for disorderly conduct.

Haley, Maximillian (1837 – 1914) **1853**

Caroline C. Boothby (1845 – 1914) m. 10/25/1863

Son of Patrick Rivers Haley and daughter of Reason Rounds & Mary Ann Boothby. He was a carpenter in Monmouth and they were members of the Monmouth Church. They are buried in Fir Crest Cemetery in Polk County.

Haley, Patrick Rivers (2/17/1802 – 9/13/1884) **1853**

Martha Jane

Jane McWhorter (5/25/1808 – 6/29/1890) m. 10/23/1845

Father of Bedford, William Thompson and Maximillian Haley. He was a preacher and they were members of Monmouth Church. He was one of the delegates from the Monmouth Church at the annual State Meeting in 1863. They are buried in Davidson Cemetery about 2 miles southwest of Monmouth.

Haley, William Thompson (1833 – ?) **1853**

Lucinda Miller Ford (10/28/1840 – 5/19/1867) m. 7/22/1858 **1844**

Son of Patrick Rivers Haley and daughter of Nat & Lucinda Ford. Following his graduation from Alexander Campbell's Bethany College in 1857, he returned to Oregon and found employment in the Christian schools at Bethel and Monmouth. He moved to California in the 1860s.

Hampton, John Jacob (10/15/1804 – 8/19/1882) **1845**
Elizabeth Fickle (9/8/1809 – 4/2/1880) m. 11/9/1828
Came overland from Missouri and settled 6 miles below Sheridan in Polk County. They were in the group of Christians who gave money to bring A. V. McCarty to Oregon in 1847. Their daughter, Eliza, married Milton Scott Riggs on 8/5/1851. In the 1850s they were living on a ranch 6 miles south of Eugene in Lane County.

Hardesty, Charles (1815 – ?) **1852**
Mary Jane m. 12/15/1836
Katherine (Catherine) Alkire m. 1/22/1857
He came overland from Illinois and settled near Springfield in Lane County. He assisted Isaac Briggs in rescuing B. F. Owen and other members of the "lost" wagon train of 1853. In the 1860 census he was living in the Mohawk area of Lane County.

Hardesty, Charles Henderson (c1812 – ?) **1852**
Lusena (Lurania) (c1815 – ?)
They came overland from Illinois with 4 children and a 5th was born on the plains. They settled in Clackamas County and became charter members of the Rock Creek Church of Christ south of Molalla. It is not known if they were related to the other Charles Hardesty in Lane County or to S. W. & Margaret Hardesty who settled near them several years later.

Hardesty, S. W. (11/4/1843 – ?) **1864**
Margaret Sconce (7/3/1849 – 1/17/1893) m. 1870 **1853**
Union soldier. Wounded at battle of Prairie Grove. Lost sight in one eye and the other eye seriously damaged. Crossed the plains from Missouri and settled 3 miles south of Needy in Clackamas County. Totally blind by 1873. Opened a general merchandise store at Needy in 1877 and a branch store in Molalla. Margaret served as postmistress at Needy. She is buried in Rock Creek Cemetery, but there is no record of his burial.

Hardwick, George Washington (? – 1893) **1877**
Mary Sisk (? – 1866)
Mary Majors
He fought for the Union army in the Civil War. His wife died in Missouri after the war and he brought his 5 children to Oregon. They settled in the Chehalem Valley in northeastern Yamhill County and they were members of the West Chehalem Church. He served as an agent for the *Christian Herald* in the 1880s.

Harlan, James (c1817 – ?) **1870s**
He was evidently a bachelor. There is no record of a wife and children. He was a charter member of the church that was organized at Drain Station in Douglas County in the 1870s, and he served as an agent for the *Christian Herald* in the 1880s.

Harpole (Harpool), James V. (8/31/1820 – 9/23/1885) **1853**
Margaret Scollard (1825 – ?) m. 12/?/1843
During the overland crossing his aunt was killed when a wagon ran over her, and his cousin died in childbirth. James & Margaret settled near Silverton in Marion County. They were evidently members of the Bethany Church, but their names are not in the church record book. When the Bethany meetinghouse was constructed in 1858, he made all the shingles by hand as his personal donation to the church.

Harris, David Rice (11/15/1840 – 11/21/1920) **1865**
Rebecca Elnora Grimes (3/5/1838 – 3/11/1914) m. 5/22/1862
He was a son of John M. & Jane Harris. They were married in Illinois and came overland with his parents. They settled in Lane County and he became an elder in the Hebron Church in 1880. Later, he served as an elder in the London Church. They are buried in Taylor-Lane Cemetery near his parents. His older sister was Martha Harris Powell, and his younger brother was Dr. Thomas W. Harris.

Harris, John C. (1826 – ?) **1851**
Cinderella Smith (c. 1840 – ?) m. 6/19/1853
They were married in Polk County and they became charter members of the Monmouth Church in 1856. She was the eldest daughter of a Christian preacher named John Burris Smith. The Smiths were also members of the Monmouth Church.

Harris, John Moses (4/1/1803 – 9/16/1881) **1865**
Jane Wilson (11/10/1810 – 11/15/1880) m. 11/6/1828
Preached for many years in Indiana and Illinois before moving to Oregon at the end of the Civil War. He was one of the most effective Christian preachers in Oregon in the years after the Civil War. Preached throughout Oregon for 16 years. They are buried at Taylor-Lane Cemetery near Cottage Grove in Lane County.

Harris, John William (3/2/1856 – ?) **1865**
Mary Rosetta Shortridge (1857 – ?) m. 6/6/1875 **1857**
He was a son of John M. & Jane Harris and he was educated at Christian College in Monmouth and at the medical department of Willamette University. She was a daughter of James & Amelia Shortridge. Following marriage they lived in Cottage Grove and Eugene and he pursued a medical career. She remained a faithful member of the Christian Church, but he did not maintain any church membership.

Harris, Thomas W. (12/27/1849 – ?) **1865**
Laura Agnes Cattron (c1856 – ?) m. 10/24/1872
He was a son of John M. & Jane Harris. He was educated at Christian College in Monmouth and at the Medical College of Ohio. He took up residence in Eugene in 1878 and became a prominent physician and mayor of the city. It is not certain that he shared the Christian commitment of his parents.

Harvey, Amos (3/24/1799 – 1/11/1877) **1845**
Jane H. Ramage (4/25/1811 – 9/10/1866) m. 4/20/1832
Ursula Post m. 7/23/1868
Came overland from Illinois with their relatives, James & Sarah Ramage. Established a 13-member congregation in Yamhill County in March 1846. This was the first church organized by the Restoration Movement in Western America. They were prominent supporters of Bethel College, and he served on the board of trustees. John D. Kelty was their son-in-law. They are buried in Bethel Cemetery.

Hastings, John C. (3/18/1833 – ?) **1852**
Melissa Wood (c1841 – ?) **1853**
He was born in Tennessee and she was born in Arkansas. They settled in the Airlie district of Polk County.

Hawley, Cyrus B. (1812 – 11/?/1863) **1844**
Elizabeth Smith (2/22/1813 – 4/17/1887) m. 5/6/1833
The Hawleys were married in London, Ontario, Canada. They lived in Detroit, Michigan; Farmington, Iowa; and Sparta, Missouri prior to coming overland. Settled on a 640-acre donation land claim 3 miles southeast of present-day McMinnville in Yamhill County. He died in Idaho on a mining expedition and was buried there. She is buried in Bethel Cemetery beside her son and his family.

Hawley, John Henry (3/10/1835 – 8/24/1911) **1844**
Eliza E. Mulkey (7/27/1840 – 5/6/1924) m. 5/6/1858 **1847**
Son of Cyrus & Elizabeth Hawley and daughter of Luke & Rutha Mulkey. He was a member of the board of trustees of Bethel College for many years, and an agent for the *Pacific Christian Messenger* in the 1870s. Postmaster, store owner and justice of the peace in Bethel. State legislator in 1882. Later he was a bank president in Monmouth and mayor of Monmouth. They are buried in Bethel Cemetery.

Headrick, Isaac (11/16/1800 – 1881) **1847**
Margarette Fisher (1/10/1802 – 1883) m. 2/14/1823
Charter members of Bethany Church in 1851. Their daughter married Thomas C. Shaw on 11/28/1850. Margarette was called "a woman of deep religious convictions." One account noted of Isaac: "He was a member of the Christian Church and a man of deep piety, tender hearted and kind. It was said of him that the story of Christ's crucifixion always brought tears to his eyes and his Bible was his daily solace."

Heater, Benjamin (c1821 – ?) **1850**
Mary Jane Adams (c1830 – ?) m. 2/18/1847
Traveled overland from Iowa with 2 small daughters. Settled in the Chehalem Valley in northeastern Yamhill County and were members of the West Chehalem Church.

Hembree, Absalom Jefferson (12/14/1813 – 4/10/1856) **1843**
Mary Nancy Dodson (6/22/1813 – 1/12/1886) m. 1/14 or 22/1834
In "The Great Migration" of 1843. He was a younger brother of Joel Jordan Hembree. Represented Yamhill County in the legislature in the 1840s and 1850s, and provided Glen Owen Burnett with a horse to travel to preaching appointments in 1846-47. Volunteered for service in Yakima Indian War and was killed near Toppenish in W.T. They are buried in the Hembree Family Cemetery 4 miles north of Lafayette.

Hembree, Andrew T. (1805 – ?) **1843**
Martha Lorinda McCoy (6/24/1814 – ?) m. 1833
Veterans of "The Great Migration" of 1843. He was an uncle to Joel Jordan Hembree and Absalom Jefferson Hembree, and he settled near them in Yamhill County. Glen Owen Burnett remembered that he and Dr. James McBride were accompanied by "Brother Andrew Hembree" when they began preaching in Oregon in the fall of 1846.

Hembree, Isham N. (8/24/1838 – 8/23/1910) **1872**
Christena J. (Tena) Gibson (1858 – 1913) m. 1881
Fought in the Civil War. First Lieutenant in the Confederate army. Moved to Oregon in 1872 and settled 12 miles northwest of Eugene and became a member of the Fern Ridge Christian Church. Served as county commissioner for Lane County. Not closely related to the Hembrees in Yamhill County.

Hembree, James Thomas (9/13/1825 or 1826 – 1/12/1919) **1843**

Malvina (Melvina) Ann Millican (1832 – 1916) m. 9/24/1845

Son of Joel Jordan & Sally Hembree and daughter of Elijah & Lucinda Millican. He drove one of the family wagons across the Oregon Trail in 1843. His parents were Christians and her parents may have been Christians. James & Malvina were members of the Lafayette Church and they are buried in Lafayette Masonic Cemetery.

Hembree, Joel Jordan (12/7/1807 – 9/8/1865) **1843**

Sally Payne (3/2/1809 – 3/15/1854) m. 10/20/1825

Letitia Woolery (1810-1888)

Veterans of "The Great Migration" of 1843. He was an older brother of Absalom Jefferson Hembree and a nephew of Andrew Hembree. A small son died along the Oregon Trail, and a daughter was born a week later. Three of their sons, James Thomas, Wayman and Lafayette became leaders in the church. Joel Jordan & Sally are buried in Masonic Cemetery in McMinnville.

Hembree, Lafayette M. (12/1/1830 – 9/8/1895) **1843**

Eliza E. Ruble m. 1/27/1859

Son of Joel Jordan & Sally Hembree and younger brother of James Thomas and Wayman Clark.

Hembree, Wayman (Waman) Clark (3/7/1829 – 3/22/1920) **1843**

Nancy Ann Garrison (7/29/1843 – 9/7/1892) m. 6/?/1861 **1845**

Nancy J. Beagle Crisp (1835 – 4/16/1914)

Son of Joel Jordan & Sally Hembree. He was 14 years old when he drove one of the wagons in "The Great Migration" of 1843. A brother died on the trail that summer and a sister was born a week later. The Hembrees settled in Yamhill County. Wayman & Nancy became members of the McMinnville Church and he later served as an elder in this church. They are buried in Masonic Cemetery in McMinnville.

Hendricks, James M. (2/5/1809 –3/20/1878) **1848**

Elizabeth (Betsy) Bristow (10/9/1815 – 1/11/1878) m. 9/7/1834

She was a daughter of Elijah & Susanna Bristow. They were charter members of the Pleasant Hill Church of Christ in 1850, and they are buried in Pleasant Hill Cemetery. Their son, Thomas G. Hendricks, became an elder in the Eugene Church.

Hendricks, Thomas G. (6/17/1838 – 12/12/1919) **1848**

Mary J. Hazelton (? – 1866) m. 10/20/1861

Martha A. Stewart (? – 2/4/1939) m. 1/3/1869

Son of James M. & Betsy Hendricks and grandson of Elijah Bristow. Charter member of the Christian Church in Eugene and served as one of the first two deacons. In later years he became an elder. Also church treasurer for many years. Served as state senator 1880-1884. Second wife was not a Christian when they married, but she was baptized into Christ in May 1889. They are buried in the Masonic Cemetery in Eugene.

Hendrix, Harrison H. (1823 – ?) **1852**

Zerelda Jane Pedigo (8/5/1827 – ?) m. 6/15/1846

Gloriunda Geisy (? – 5/9/1886) m. 6/20/1885

Overland from Wapello County, Iowa. She was a daughter of Edward & Lettice Pedigo. He preached in Iowa for several years prior to their overland journey, and he preached throughout the Willamette Valley before moving his family to northern California in December 1859. Hendrix preached in northern California in the 1860s.

Herren, Daniel S. (1829 – ?) **1845**
Susan Sebena Caton m. 12/1/1852
Son of John & Theodosha Herren and daughter of George R. & Sarah Caton. He was a brother to William John Herren and she was a sister to Nathan T. Caton.

Herren, John Daniel (9/30/1799 – 3/2/1864) **1845**
Theodosha Ann Robbins (5/20/1804 – 9/15/1881) m. 6/13/1822
Came overland from western Missouri with a large family. Followed Stephen Meek in his disastrous attempt to find a short cut to the Willamette Valley. Settled 4 miles east of Salem in Marion County. Made $2,000 in the California gold mines. Moved to a new claim 6 miles southeast of Salem. William John Herren and Daniel S. Herren were their sons. A daughter was married to Nathan T. Caton.

Herren, William John (1/17/1824 – 4/13/1891) **1845**
Nancy Evaline Hall (9/22/1830 – 11/17/1905) m. 10/14/1847
Son of John & Theodosha Herren and brother of Daniel S. Herren and Martha Ann Herren Caton. Along with A. V. McCarty and his brother-in-law, Nathan T. Caton, he represented the Salem Church at the 1858 annual State Meeting.

Himes, Tyrus (1818 – 4/22/1879) **1853**
Emeline Holcombe (12/27/1821 – 10/28/1898) m. 5/1/1843
They helped plan the exodus of families from Monmouth, Illinois to Monmouth, Oregon, and they participated in the discussions that led to the founding of Monmouth University. However, when they finally came overland, they settled in Washington Territory about 5 miles east of Olympia in Thurston County.

Hodges, Charles Hubbell (10/29/1847 – 12/1/1912) **1875**
Annie Temple m. 5/4/1886
He graduated from Bethany College in the class of 1873, and he preached in Oregon from 1875 to 1883. Among the Oregon churches he served were Stayton, St. Helens, Scappoose, Springfield, Halsey, Chehalem, and Glencoe. Later he preached in Washington and Alaska.

Hogue, Jesse Monroe (2/19/1826 – 11/16/1908) **1873**
Mary Ellen Baker
Came by railroad to San Francisco and by boat to Oregon. Settled at Hardman in Morrow County and established a church in that community. Later moved to London in Lane County and were members of the London Church. Their son, Jasper Newton Hogue (1855-1931) became a leader in the London Church. Jesse is buried in Bemis Cemetery near London, but Mary Ellen died in Morrow County and was buried there.

Holman, Daniel Saunders (11/15/1822 – 3/15/1910 **1843**
Martha E. Burnett (12/11/1830 – 1913) m. 8/21 or 31/1847 **1846**
He was a veteran of "The Great Migration" of 1843. She was a daughter of Glen Owen & Sarah Burnett. He was an older brother to a gospel preacher named Francis Dillard Holman who married a daughter of Dr. James McBride. The Holmans were members of the McMinnville Church and they are buried in Masonic Cemetery in McMinnville.

Holman, Francis Dillard (5/23/1831 – 12/2/1899) **1845**
Mary McBride m. 9/25/1856 **1846**
She was a daughter of Dr. James & Mahala McBride. He was a younger brother to Daniel Saunders Holman. He began preaching after the Civil War, and he preached in Oregon for more than 30 years.

Hood, Andrew (9/2/1802 – 3/5/1874) **1845**

Ann McCann (8/5/1805 – 7/10/ or 7/16/1886) m. 1827

Former Roman Catholics who converted to the Restoration Movement. Glen Owen Burnett preached in their home in Oregon City in 1847.

Hooker, Cyrenus Clark (12/1/1818 – 2/12/1852) **1848**

Came overland from Scott County, Illinois, with his parents, Ira & Sarah Hooker. Brought with him a letter of recommendation from the Union Christian Church back home. He was an older brother of Eliza Barrows, and Demetrius Hooker. He never married. Lived with the Barrows at Rickreall in Polk County. He was murdered at the age of 33, and he is buried in Burch Pioneer Cemetery.

Hooker, Demetrius Dionitious (3/21/1826 – 7/20/1908) **1848**

Annie Margaret Lewis (3/13/1845 – 1/23/1924) m. 4/11/1861 **1846**

He was a son of Ira & Sarah Hooker, and she was a daughter of Stewart & Elizabeth Riggs Lewis. They were married one day before the Civil War began. They lived in the Airlie district of Polk County.

Hooker, Ira Allen (4/2/1781 – 8/1/1857) **1848**

Sarah Taylor (1/11/1786 – 4/12/1869) m. 8/16/1807

They lived in Scott County, Illinois for 30 years before coming overland to Oregon. They settled southwest of Lewisville in Polk County. They brought a letter of recommendation from the Union Christian Church back home in Illinois.

Howell, John (12/6/1787 – 10/4/1869) **1843**

Temperance Midkiff (4/29/1796 – 3/22/1848) m. 10/14/1811

Frances R. (c1805 – ?) m. 2/17/1850

Veterans of "The Great Migration" of 1843. They gave their name to "Howell Prairie" east of Salem in Marion County. His obituary, submitted by Thomas C. Shaw, confirmed: "He had been an exemplary Christian for more than forty years, and he was perfectly willing to meet death." Elizabeth Brooks McCorkle was their daughter.

Hubbard, S. Monroe (c1843 – ?) **1879**

Sarah (c1849 – ?)

This gospel preacher arrived in Oregon around 1879 and settled in Eugene in Lane County. He was one of the leaders in the establishment of the missionary society in Oregon in 1882.

Huddleston, Allen Jefferson (6/6/1834 – 10/8/1920) **1872**

Sleigh (Seleigh) Smith (9/24/1836 – 10/29/1921) m. 7/29/1855

Corporal in Union Army under General Sherman. Married the daughter of an Indiana Christian preacher named Charles W. H. Smith. Both families settled on Bell Mountain, 3 miles east of Elkton in Douglas County. Huddleston was a circuit-riding preacher in the Umpqua Valley for more than 40 years. Buried in Lone Oak Cemetery in Stayton in Marion County.

Huff, Jefferson (1809 or 1810 – ?) **1852**

Lutilda (? – 10/3/1857) m. 7/12/1831

Emeline E. Sellick Johnson m. 2/24/1859

He was a delegate from the Clackamas Church at the 1858 annual State Meeting. Moved to Washington Territory.

Humphrey, Alfred **1850s**
Mary
Charter members of the Harrisburg Church in Linn County 11/7/1863. Alfred Humphrey was one of the four trustees of the congregation when they purchased property on which to build in November 1867.

Humphrey, Thomas Dabney (2/4/1822 – 5/1/1898) **1847**
Elizabeth Ann Taylor (4/10/1836 – 2/8/1875) m. 10/7/1849
Came overland with Mac Waller, Hiram Alva Johnson and other Illinois Christians. Settled in Washington County. In the 1870s he was a member of the board of trustees of Christian College. He became an elder in the Hillsboro Church in the 1880s. They are buried in Hillsboro Pioneer Cemetery.

Huntington, William (1816 – 1894) **1853**
Eliza Jane Koontz m. 6/23/1839
They settled near Castle Rock in Cowlitz County in Washington Territory. He was a delegate from the Monticello congregation in Washington Territory at the 1858 annual State Meeting at Mill Creek Church in Marion County. He sometimes preached on the Oregon side of the Columbia River, and he established a congregation in Columbia County in the 1850s.

Huntley, Nathaniel C. (1827 – ?) **1848**
Mary Jane (c1832 – ?) m. 2/17/1847
They settled in Lookingglass Valley 10 miles southwest of present-day Roseburg. They became Christians through the ministry of their neighbor, A. L. Todd, who taught them how to read. In the 1870 census they were living in Coos County with their 18-year-old son, Enoch Huntley. Enoch was later baptized into Christ by A. L. Todd.

Huston, Joel Bradshaw (12/22/1810 – 3/20/1879) **1853**
Catherine Huston (cousin) (10/8/1811 – 4/23/1895) m. 8/31/1829
Came overland from Henderson County, Illinois with 9 children and settled 12 miles south of Albany in Linn County. He was a delegate from the Sand Ridge Church in Linn County at the 1858 annual State Meeting. Two of their sons, Walter and Worth, became church leaders.

Huston, Walter (3/18/1839 – 1/18/1931) **1853**
Susan E. Smith (? – 1876) m. 5/7/1868
Lodema A. Shelley (10/?/1855 – ?) m. 11/1/1877
Son of Joel Bradshaw & Catherine Huston. His second wife was a daughter of Michael & Sena Shelley. He lived near Harrisburg in Linn County for many years.

Huston, Worth (11/2/1854 – ?) **1854**
Lucy Dannals
Son of Joel Bradshaw & Catherine Huston. He was born on his parent's donation land claim south of Albany in Linn County. He was the youngest in a family of 10 children and the only one born in Oregon. He served as the sheriff of Linn County for many years. One record noted: "For many years he has been an active member of the Christian Church, and is a deacon therein."

Hutchinson, Thomas Hanna (5/5/1824 – 2/10/1860) **1853**
Elizabeth H. Butler (4/9/1829 – 1/2/1866) m. 7/1/1851
She was a daughter of Major Peter & Rachel Butler. He was a member of the board of trustees of Monmouth University.

Hutton, Dr. Albert G. (8/31/1809 – 9/11/1877) **1851**
Mary W. (2/16/1817 – 6/3/1892) m. 11/14/1832
They became members of the Bethany Church in Marion County on 11/4/1865. That they had already been baptized into Christ is indicated by the language in the church record book which reports that he was accepted into membership by "restoration" and she was accepted by "letter."

Ireland, Alpheus (1/10/1808 – 2/5/1868) **1853**
Sophia (c1819 – 5/12/1887) m. 12/6/1831
Settled near Myrtle Creek in Douglas County. Charter members of the Myrtle Creek Church. He represented Douglas County in the state legislature in the mid-1860s. They are buried in Pioneer Cemetery in Myrtle Creek.

Ireland, David (10/22/1819 – 2/10/1892) **1864**
Mary Ann Sanderson (3/29/1824 – 9/13/1881)
Parents of Theron A. Ireland & William P. Ireland. They lived in Indiana for several years and then in Iowa for a year before coming overland. Settled in Polk County. They are buried in Fir Crest Cemetery south of Monmouth in Polk County.

Ireland, Theron A. (12/10/1842 – 1/23/1908) **1864**
Nancy L. Brummett (12/15/1845 – 10/29/1905) m. 3/17/1864
They were newlyweds when they came overland. Settled in Polk County. He was a son of David & Mary Ann Ireland and an older brother of William P. Ireland. They were members of the Monmouth Church. Buried in Fir Crest Cemetery.

Ireland, William P. (4/16/1846 – 1/17/1918) **1864**
Cornelia J. Staats (1/11/1851 – 2/11/1912) m. 2/9/1869
Son of David & Mary Ann Ireland and younger brother of Theron A. Ireland. One account reported that they were "active in the Christian Church." They are buried in Fir Crest Cemetery south of Monmouth in Polk County.

Johns, Isaiah M. (1821 or 1822 – ?) **1847**
Mary Sophia Martins (c1832 – ?) m. 1/24/1850
He settled in Yamhill County on the Yamhill river southeast of present-day McMinnville, and he became a well-known blacksmith in the area. He was a delegate from the McMinnville Church at the 1858 annual State Meeting. In the early 1870s he was a member of the board of trustees of Christian College in Monmouth In 1877 they were living in Walla Walla in Washington Territory

Johnson, Hiram Alva (Alvah) (2/18/1819 – 2/4/1896) **1847**
Elizabeth Jane Whitley (8/26/1819 – 2/26/1897) m. 7/25/1841
Came overland with Mac Waller, Abraham Landess and other Illinois Christians. Settled in Marion County. Delegate from the Mill Creek Church at the 1858 and 1863 annual State Meetings. He was a deacon in the Salem Church in 1870s and 1880s.

Johnson, Melchior (Melchi) (4/17/1807 – 7/14/1875) **1850**
Delilah Leavensworth Ware (3/10/1820 – 1900) m. 12/28/1834 or 1835
Overland from Missouri. Settled first in Yamhill County but moved to Polk County before the 1860 census. Delegate from the Bethel Church in Polk County at the 1863 annual State Meeting.

Johnson, Travis **1850**
He was a black slave who drove an ox team for a Presbyterian family named Glover. A few years after his arrival in Oregon, he purchased his freedom. He was a member of the Mill Creek Church in Marion County and he lived with the Reuben Lewis family.

Jones, Joseph M. (2/5/1814 – 3/23/1891) **1853**
Mary Polly Davis (7/31/1822 – 8/10/1890) m. 4/4/1839
Members of the Mill Creek Church in Marion County. They lived near Sublimity and they are buried in Lone Oak Cemetery.

Kelley (Kelly), Andrew (1833 – 3/23/1886) **1852**
Lydia A. Hawley
He was a deacon in the Salem Church and mayor of Salem in the 1870s.

Kelty, John D. (1831 – 1914) **1852**
Sarah E. Harvey (1838 – 1867) m. 9/?/1855
Jane Harvey (1847 – 1918) m. 8/5/1868
Married a daughter of Amos & Jane Harvey. When she died, he married her sister. Lived at Bethel in Polk County. Treasurer and member of the board of trustees for Bethel College. From 1864 to 1875 he operated a store in Bethel in partnership with John Henry Hawley. Postmaster of Bethel. Post office was located in Kelty & Hawley store. They were members of Bethel Church and they are buried in Bethel Cemetery.

Keyt, Ebenezer Connet (11/10/1827 – 2/17/1904 **1851**
Susan J. Kump (Kemp) (1/30/1829 – 9/27/1855) m. 12/7/1853
Amanda Doty (2/19/1840 – 12/19/1913) m. 7/17/1859
They settled south of present-day Perrydale in Polk County. They may have supported the churches at Bethel or Salt Creek in the early years, but they were among the families who were instrumental in establishing a congregation in Perrydale sometime after 1870. Susan Keyt is buried in Etna Cemetery and Ebenezer & Amanda are buried in Bethel Cemetery.

Kimsey, Edson Ross (4/20/1826 – 4/26/1906) **1847**
Melinda Jane Walker (2/25/1835 – 1917) m. 5/26/1852
Members of the Mill Creek Church in Marion County. They are buried in Macleay Cemetery. Her parents, Gilliam & Rhoda Walker, were members of the Mill Creek Church. Her sister was Mary Nash.

King, Wilburn (1822 – 7/?/1885) **1846**
Marcilla (Marcilia) Cox (5/1/1828 – 5/17/1896) m. 11/?/1846
Charter members of Bethany Church in 1851. Daughter of Gideon & Susanna Cox and an older sister of Elizabeth Bowen and Permilla Bowen. Two of her brothers, John T. and Peter Jackson, became elders in the church. Wilburn traveled overland from Missouri in same train with the Cox families. Romance must have blossomed along the trail as he and Marcilla were married soon after they arrived in Marion County.

Kinney, Robert Crouch (7/4/1813 – 3/2/1875) **1847**
Eliza Lee Bigelow (5/1/1813 – 5/30/1890) m. 7/?/1833
They may have traveled overland with the McCarty families. They were among the families who contributed to the fund to assist A. V. McCarty to move to Oregon. The Kinneys settled near Lafayette in Yamhill County, but moved to Salem in the 1870s.

Kramer, John A. (1797 – 8/23/1857) **1853**
Mary Ann (c1801 – after August 1870) m. 9/6/1822
They were among the 35 charter members in the Monmouth Church in 1856. Several of their sons were members of the Monmouth Church, including George M., Lewis P., Samuel G., and William T. Two of their daughters, Mary Jane Kramer and Margaret Kramer Murphy, the wife of Calvin L. Murphy, were also charter members of the Monmouth Church. They are buried in Davidson Cemetery in Polk County.

Kuykendall, Charles Vos (1851 – 1926) **1870**
Elizabeth (Eliza) Jane Davis (1855 – 1931) **1855**
She was a daughter of Thomas C. & Nancy Ann Davis. He was an agent for the *Christian Herald* in the 1880s. They are buried in Pike Cemetery in Yamhill County.

Ladd, James L. (8/20/1804 – 5/16/1867) **1853**
Sarah H. Ritchey (8/20/1811 – 5/16/1867) m. 11/27/1835
Settled 3 miles south of Bethel in Polk County. He was chairman of the building committee that supervised the construction of the Bethel Institute building in 1855, and with others he platted the town of Bethel in the mid-1850s. His son was also named James L. Ladd, and it is easy for historians to confuse the two of them.

Ladd, James L. (2/10/1836 – 5/9/1905) **1853**
Mary A. (3/18/1841 – 3/10/1914)
Son of James & Sarah Ladd. In the early 1870s he was a member of the board of trustees of Christian College in Polk County and he was living in St. Helens in Columbia County. Assisted Dr. James McBride in establishing a church in St. Helens. He moved his family to Amity in mid-1870s. They are buried in Amity Cemetery.

Ladd, John W. (1813 – ?) **1846**
wife's name unknown
Settled on the Yamhill-Clackamas county line about 6 miles east of Newberg. He developed a nursery business and moved it to Bethel around 1853. He was one of the delegates from the Bethel Church at the annual State Meeting in 1858.

Ladd, Thomas B. (1811 – ?) **1853**
Elizabeth m. 8/9/1831 or 1832
In 1867 he was chosen to be an elder in the Salem Church in Marion County along with Caleb P. Chapman, Hezekiah Burford and Governor George Woods.

Lancefield, Robert J. (3/12/1817 – 12/27/1881) **1846**
Sarah Henderson (? – 7/18/1849) m. 4/5/1835
Sarah Carpenter Mulkey (4/1/1812 – 12/25/1856) m. 4/30/1850
Eliza Allen (5/16/1817 – 9/7/1885) m. 5/31/1863
After his first wife died, he married the widow of a Christian preacher named Thomas Mulkey. Robert & Sarah Mulkey were members of the Amity Church. She died on Christmas day 1856. He waited 7 years before marrying again. He is buried in Amity Cemetery between his last two wives.

Landess, Abraham (3/18/1790 – 3/29/1855) **1847**
Elizabeth Conkrite (1793 – 11/20/1870) m. 12/?/1810
Former Baptists who embraced the Restoration Movement in Adams County, Illinois in February 1843. Their 3 sons and 2 daughters also became Christians. They came overland with Mac Waller, Hiram Alva Johnson and other Illinois Christians. Settled in Washington County.

Landess, Abraham (1825 – 1854) **1847**
Diana (Dinah) m. 1/19/1843
Son of Abraham & Elizabeth Landess. Came overland with Mac Waller, Hiram Alva Johnson and other Illinois Christians. Settled in Washington County.

Landess, Felix (10/1/1820 or 1821 – 3/1/1903) **1847**
Elizabeth Jane White (c1821 – ?) m. 11/8/1840
Son of Abraham & Elizabeth Landess. Came overland with Mac Waller, Hiram Alva Johnson and other Illinois Christians. Settled in Washington County.

Landess, William (1833 – ?) **1847**
Elizabeth Caroline m. 2/17/1853
Laura F. Boone m. 2/19/1871
Son of Abraham & Elizabeth Landess. Came overland with Mac Waller, Hiram Alva Johnson and other Illinois Christians. Settled in Washington County.

Large, E. P.
wife's name unknown
He was an elder of the Fern Ridge Church in Linn County and later of the Crawfordsville Church in the same county. He was an agent for the *Christian Herald* in the 1880s.

Lewis, Abner (12/10/1846 – 12/3/1934) **1846**
Margaret A. Baker m. 12/12/1869
Son of Reuben & Polly Lewis. He was born near Aumsville in Marion County, and following his marriage in 1869 he settled on a farm in that district. Members of the Aumsville Church. They lived on that farm for nearly 50 years before moving to Salem. He represented Marion County in the state legislature 1898-1900. When they celebrated their golden anniversary on 12/12/1919, they were living in Salem.

Lewis, David R. (3/9/1814 – 12/8/1894) **1845**
Mary Redden (3/19/1810 – 4/19/1897) m. 10/4/1832
Son of John & Elizabeth Lewis. Settled in Polk County and founded the settlement of Lewisville. Member of the board of regents of Rickreall Academy and Monmouth University. Served as an elder in the church and as an agent for the *Pacific Christian Messenger*. They are buried in New Smith Cemetery adjacent to Fir Crest Cemetery south of Monmouth.

Lewis, David William (1/11/1845 – 7/8/1925) **1845**
Susan A. Williams (11/6/1853 – 7/26/1915) m. 12/30/1869 **1853**
Son of David R. & Mary Lewis. He was less than a year old when he came across the trail. His family settled at Lewisville in Polk County. He ran a successful blacksmith business in Lewisville. At different times they were members of the Monmouth Church and the Lewisville Church. They are buried at the New Smith Cemetery in Polk County beside his parents and other family members.

Lewis, Francis Marion (2/5/1847 – 3/9/1923) **1847**
Flora McLeod (5/13/1850 – 8/28/1907) m. 5/30/1869
Son of John & Elizabeth Lewis. Born on his parents donation land claim at Lewisville in Polk County and died at the same place. At different times they were members of the Monmouth Church and the Lewisville Church. They are buried at the New Smith Cemetery in Polk County beside his parents and other family members.

Lewis, James Henry (1/24/1849 – 10/8/1923) **1849**
Mary Martisue (Marty) Roberts (6/9/1857 – 4/7/1933) m. 12/25/1877
Son of David R. & Mary Lewis and daughter of John Engard & Mary Jane Roberts. Mac Waller joined them in marriage on Christmas day 1877. They settled in Polk County and they are buried with other Lewis family members in the New Smith Cemetery adjacent to Fir Crest Cemetery south of Monmouth.

Lewis, John Douglas (10/8/1782 – 8/7/1854) **1845**
Elizabeth R. Stout (1787 – 3/2/1852) m. 8/27/1811
Patriarch and matriarch of the Lewis clan. Among their children were David R. Lewis, Nancy Jane Cook and Margaret May Brown.

Lewis, Reuben (3/20/1814 – 4/6/1886) **1842**
Polly Frazier (c1827 – 7/14/1862) m. 2/14/1844 **1843**
Catherine Van Nuys m. 4/9/1868
Came overland in the first wagon train. He was employed by Gabriel & Elizabeth Brown to be their hunter on the overland journey.

Lewis, Stewart (11/3/1818 – 11/25/1899) **1846**
Elizabeth Riggs (12/22/1818 – 1/2/1898) m. 12/3/1843
Overland from Ray County, Missouri. She was a daughter of Thomas & Leah Hunt Riggs. Her father died on the trail. She was a sister to Rachel Riggs, Rebecca Fields, Mary Shanks, Timothy A. Riggs, and Thomas Riggs. They lived at Foster near Sweet Home in Linn County.

Lindsay, Horace (1/18/1818 – ?) **1850**
Mary Ritchey (c1822 – ?) m. 10/3/1847
Living in Clackamas County in 1850 census. At the 1858 annual State Meeting he was a delegate from Tualatin Church in Washington County. Moved to Bethel prior to 1860 census, and then located in Monmouth in mid-1860s. Store-owner and deacon in Monmouth Church. In 1872 he was president of the board of trustees of Christian College. She was a sister of Emily Ritchey Warriner, wife of Dr. William C. Warriner.

Linville, Harrison (9/22/1813 – 12/7/1893) **1846**
Nancy Bounds (1819 – 1/29/1856) m. 11/20/1837
Clarissa L. Downer Frederick (6/22/1823 – 1/4/1899) m. 9/6/1857
Overland from Missouri via the Applegate Trail. Settled on Luckiamute River in Polk County. Charter members of Luckiamute Church organized by Mac Waller in 1848. Ran ferry service, store, hotel, and stagecoach stop. Served as legislator, postmaster, justice of the peace, and elder in Luckiamute Church. Appointed agent for Malheur Indian Reservation in 1873 and served 3 years. Buried in Buena Vista Cemetery.

Linville, Richard (8/25/1773 – 3/17/1856) **1846**
Mary Yount (9/2/1774 – 11/22/1846) m. 1792
Residents of Missouri 1820-1846. Parents of Harrison Linville, Catherine Crowley and Margaret Vanderpool. Their train suffered great losses during the overland journey. Came into Oregon via the Applegate Trail and Mary was drowned in a tragic accident while attempting to ford a river in present-day Douglas County.

Linville, Willard Stone (5/19/1849 – ?) **1849**
Hannah C. Nash (1/20/1852 – 3/14/1884) m. 1/8/1871 **1864**
Son of Harrison & Nancy Linville. He was in the mercantile business most of his life. Government clerk on the Malheur Indian Reservation in 1873-74 during his father's tenure as government agent of the reservation. He lived at Buena Vista and Independence and served as an agent for the *Pacific Christian Messenger*. Her funeral was preached by Mac Waller and her obituary was published in the *Christian Herald*.

Lovelady, Preston W. (1828 or 1829 – ?) **1846**
Lovina (Lavina) McBride (5/8/1837 – ?) m. 9/5/1852 **1846**
He was the eldest son of Thomas J. & Polly Lovelady and she was a daughter of Thomas & Martha Ann McBride and a granddaughter of Thomas Crawford McBride. Their daughter, Nancy, married Ephraim Badger.

Lovelady, Thomas J. (3/19/1806 – ?) **1846**
Mary Elizabeth (Polly) Bounds (c1811 – 1878) m. 8/9/1827
Charter members of the Rickreall Church. He was an elder in this church for many years. Their son married a daughter of Thomas McBride and their daughter married a son of Glen Owen Burnett. They are buried in Dallas Cemetery in Polk County.

Lucas, Albert Whitfield (10/24/1827 – 4/6/1893) **1852**
Elizabeth Francis Murphy (10/28/1832 – 11/17/1914) m. 3/13/1851
He was a younger brother to Thomas Hartzwell Lucas and she was a daughter of John Ecles & Frances Murphy. He was secretary of the board of trustees for Christian College, and he served as an elder in the Monmouth Church for many years. A daughter married William D. Fenton. They are buried in Fir Crest Cemetery south of Monmouth in Polk County.

Lucas, Thomas Hartzwell (8/27/1824 – 4/26/1908) **1850**
Sarah H. Davidson (5/23/1825 – 11/10/1882) m. 12/11/1844
He was an older brother to Albert Whitfield Lucas and she was a daughter of Elijah & Margaret Davidson. They settled in Polk County and played important roles in the establishing of Monmouth University and Monmouth Church. He was a member of the board of trustees of Monmouth University. They are buried in Davidson Cemetery 2 miles southwest of Monmouth. Mac Waller preached her funeral.

Lyle, John Eakin (1/13/1815 – 9/9/1862) **1845**
Ellen Scott (1826 – 1890) m. 11/3/1846
He drove one of the wagons for Amos & Jane Harvey on the overland journey. She was a daughter of Felix & Ellen Scott. Their marriage was performed by Glen Owen Burnett. He may not have been a Christian, but she was a prominent member of the Rickreall Church and later of the Dallas Church in Polk County.

Maddox, George A. (1823 – 1906) **1860s**
Caroline (1819 – 1918)
Settled in Amity in Yamhill County. By 1870 he was serving as an elder in the Amity Church and he continued to serve for many years. They are buried in Amity Cemetery.

Markham, Samuel (1792 – 1878) **1847**
Elizabeth Winchell (c1805 – ?) m. 1/8/1829
He may not have been a Christian., but one record noted: "The Markhams moved from Michigan to Oregon in 1847 with a company of Campbellites." Their son, Charles Edwin Markham, was born in Oregon City on April 23, 1852 and was baptized into Christ as a teenager before enrolling in Christian College in Santa Rosa, California. He became "the Dean of American Poets."

Martin, Franklin (4/15/1824 – 1/24/1882) **1846**
Anna M. Burnett (8/28/1835 – ?) m. 7/8/1849
He was a delegate from the McMinnville congregation at the 1863 annual State Meeting. He is buried in Lafayette Masonic Cemetery, but there is no record of her burial in that cemetery.

Martin, Franklin B. (12/17/1811 – 7/11/1860) **1846**
Lucretia m. 4/?/1844
Charter members of the church organized by Aaron Payne at Blackhawk schoolhouse in Yamhill County in 1847. He may have been a brother to Hardin D. Martin, as they were born in Knox County, Kentucky one year apart. Franklin was a territorial legislator in 1852. Following his death, Lucretia married J. W. Cowls on 5/16/1861. She is buried in Masonic Cemetery in McMinnville with her two husbands.

Martin, Hardin D. (1810 – 1882) **1845**
Evaline (Eveline) Searcy (c1811 – 2/11/1884) m. 11/1/1838
He may have been an older brother of Franklin B. Martin. She may have been a sister of Mary Searcy Dawson, the wife of William Dawson, and the two families may have come overland together. Both families followed Stephen Meek on his ill-fated short cut, and then settled in Yamhill County. The Martins later lived in California, Idaho and Washington Territory. They died in W.T.

Mascher, Christ Frederick (12/29/1811 – 1898) **1850**
Sarah Eisenhardt (1807 – 1883) m. 7/?/1836
Charter members of the Bethany Church in Marion County in 1851. Their son, William L. Mascher, preached in Oregon for nearly a decade before his untimely death in 1872. They are buried in Bethany Pioneer Cemetery.

Mascher, Lawrence Frederick (12/6/1850 – ?) **1850**
Alwilda (Allie) J. Allen m. 6/7/1875
Son of Christ Frederick & Sarah Mascher and younger brother (by 14 years) of William Lewis Mascher. His parents settled on a 640-acre donation land claim 3 miles south of Silverton in Marion County and lived there the rest of their lives. Frederick was born on this farm, and he in turn lived there throughout his lifetime. They were members of Bethany Chuch and they helped organize the Silverton Church in 1887.

Mascher, William Lewis (11/14/1836 – 3/22/1872) **1850**

Ann Moore (Moons) (11/24/1833 – 4/24/1890) m. 6/30/1855

Son of Christ Frederick & Sarah Mascher and older brother of L. F. Mascher. He was a devout Christian and he began preaching in the early 1860s. He preached for a decade before his untimely death at the age of 35. His wife outlived him by 18 years. They are buried near his parents in Bethany Pioneer Cemetery west of Silverton.

Mason, Eli Craven (9/5/1825 – 10/4/1901) **1869**

Susan E. Thomas (1833 – 1923) m. 1853

Settled at New Pine Creek, just north of California state line, in Lake County, and then moved to Jackson County. He represented Jackson County in the state legislature 1872-1874. Their daughter, Georgia Annie, married a Christian preacher named Ephraim W. Barnes on 6/15/1874. The Masons later returned to live at New Pine Creek and were members of the Church of Christ in that town.

Mason, William (1812 – 1/27/1900) **1852**

Margaret Davidson (c1816 – 2/?/1887) m. 12/11/1834

He was a professor at Alexander Campbell's Bethany College in Virginia. She was a daughter of Elijah & Margaret Davidson. Charter members of the Monmouth Church in the summer of 1856. They were enthusiastic supporters of Monmouth University and Christian College. He was a member of the board of trustees.

Matheny, Daniel Boone (1/5/1829 – c1891) **1843**

Margaret E. McDonald (? – 5/24/1863) m. 7/18/1850

Jennie (Louisa) McDonald

He preached in Oregon for several years before moving his family to northern California in 1867-68. He was a younger brother to Isaiah Cooper Matheny.

Matheny, Isaiah Cooper (12/2/1826 – 9/3/1906) **1843**

Emiline (Emeline) Allen (1833 – 10/11/1903) m. 3/14/1850

Older brother to Daniel Boone Matheny. He was a delegate from the Union Vale Church in Yamhill County at the 1858 annual State Meeting. He served on the board of trustees of Bethel College from 1857 to 1862.

Matlock, John I. (6/20/1858 – ?) **1858**

Annie Johnson (? – 1887)

Olive Pendleton m. 10/12/1891

Oldest son of William & Nancy Matlock and younger brother of Amanda Matlock Splawn. They lived in the Crawfordsville district of Linn Counties.

Matlock, William (1825 – 1875) **1851**

Nancy Shields m. 3/12/1852

Settled in Linn County by the Riggs, Fields, and Shanks families. A daughter married Greenbury Splawn. Their son, John I., was active in the Christian Church.

Matlock, William T. (c1806 – ?) **1847**

Elizabeth (Betsy) Ballard (3/9/1807 – 4/12/1884)

They came overland from Indiana in the wagon train that was captained by Wiley Chapman. Their daughter, Ellen, married Wiley Chapman on 1/13/1854. W. T. Matlock was elected to the territorial legislature 1849-1854 and later served as a county judge in Clackamas County.

Mays, Elijah (1809 – ?) **1852**

Mary Bradshaw (7/10/1812 – 11/1/1880) m. 3/12/1829

She became a Christian in Illinois in 1835. He may not have been a Christian. They settled in Lane County. In the 1860 census they were living next to Elijah & Susanna Bristow at Pleasant Hill. Her obituary was published in the *Pacific Christian Messenger*, and at that time they were living south of Monroe near the Lane-Benton county line.

McBride, George Wickliff (3/13/1854 – 6/18/1911) **1854**

Laura W. Walter m. 5/24/1902

Son of Dr. James & Mahala McBride. Studied 2 years at Christian College. While a merchant in St. Helens in Columbia County in the 1870s, he assisted his parents in establishing a congregation. State legislator 1882-1886, secretary of state 1886-1894, and United States Senator from Oregon 1895-1901.

McBride, Dr. James A. (2/9/1802 – 12/17/1875) **1846**

Mahala Woods Miller (9/24/1811 – 2/23/1876) m. 6/20/1830

Overland from Missouri with G. O. Burnett. Son of Thomas Crawford McBride and a powerful Christian preacher like his father. Their talented family of 14 children helped plant the church in Oregon. Five daughters married George Woods, Sebastian Adams, Francis Dillard Holman, Ben Butler, and William Morse. Sons included John Rogers, James H., Thomas Allen, and George Wickliff. Dr. McBride served 4 years as Lincoln's ambassador to the Sandwich Islands.

McBride, Dr. James H. (? – 12/8/1912) **1846**

Ella Ackley

Son of Dr. James & Mahala McBride. Superintendent of the insane asylum in Milwaukie in Clackamas County. Specialist in nervous and mental diseases. Called to testify at the much-publicized Washington D. C. trial of President Garfield's assassin, Charles Guiteau.

McBride, John Rogers (8/22/1832 – 7/20/1904) **1846**

Eunice Marie Adams (1/22/1830 – 7/8/1904) m. 12/4/1852

He was the eldest son of Dr. James & Mahala McBride, and she was a sister to William Lysander Adams and Sebastian C. Adams. He was elected to serve in the Oregon legislature and the state senate and in 1862 was elected representative to Congress. Appointed chief justice of Idaho Territory in 1865.

McBride, Thomas (1806 – 6/23/1853) **1847**

Martha Ann Brink m. 12/13/1835

Son of Thomas Crawford McBride. Brother to Dr. James McBride. He drowned in the Willamette River near Albany. His daughter married Preston Lovelady.

McBride, Thomas Allen (11/15/1847 – 9/9/1930) **1847**

Mary E. Merrill (? – 8/24/1925) m. 2/7/1875

Lottie May Chappell m. 4/8/1927

Son of Dr. James & Mahala McBride. Named for a Missouri Christian preacher. Practiced law in St. Helens in Columbia County 1872-1876, and served in state legislature 1876-1878. Helped his parents establish a church in St. Helens. Elected circuit judge in 1892. Appointed justice of the Oregon Supreme Court in 1909. Elevated to chief justice in 1913. Served on the Oregon Supreme Court for 21 years.

McBride, Thomas Crawford (7/25/1777 – 4/29/1857) **1847**
first wife's name unknown (? – c1846)
Ann (c.1796 – ?) m. 9/28/1851
Pioneer preacher for the Restoration Movement in Missouri. This patriarch of the McBride clan was a 70-year-old widower with failing eyesight by the time he migrated westward in 1847, but he preached in Oregon Territory for a decade. Dr. James McBride and Margaret McBride Woods were 2 of his children. His grandson, George Lemuel Woods, was the third governor of Oregon. He is the only member of the McBride family buried in the McBride Cemetery in Yamhill County.

McCabe, Andrew
wife's name unknown
Charter members of the Day's Creek Church in Douglas County in 1877. Andrew McCabe served as one of the elders of this church.

McCall, William (7/23/1815 – 4/6/1877) **1852**
Matilda (10/16/1820 – 3/19/1909) m. 10/27/1837
Elizabeth McCall Baughman was his older sister, and Sarah McCall Fisher was possibly a younger sister. A daughter of the McCalls married William Wilshire Bristow on 4/27/1865. The McCalls lived in Lane County and William served as an elder in the Church of Christ for several years. Buried in Pleasant Hill Cemetery.

McCarty, Alexander Vance (1825 – 10/3/1868) **1847**
Jane Bounds (1827 – 1908) m. 5/1/1846
Son of John & Rosanna McCarty and daughter of John Bird & Elizabeth Bounds. He preached in the Willamette Valley for more than 12 years before moving his family to northern California in December 1859. He returned to preach in Salem and Corvallis in 1865-66. She outlived her husband by 40 years. They are buried in Vacaville Cemetery in Solano County, California.

McCarty, Edward Wilburn (9/15/1827 – 12/6/1895) **1847**
Amanda Bounds (c1832 – ?) m. 8/26/1850 **1846**
Son of John & Rosanna McCarty and daughter of John Bird & Elizabeth Bounds. He was a younger brother of Alexander Vance McCarty and she was a younger sister of Jane Bounds McCarty. Their marriage was performed by Thomas J. Lovelady.

McCarty, James St. Clair (1844 – ?) **1847**
Sarah M. Briedwell (1851 – 1920)
Son of John & Rosanna McCarty and daughter of John W. & Nancy Briedwell. They were members of Amity Church for many years. They are buried in Amity Cemetery.

McCarty, John (12/10/1798 – 1891) **1847**
Rosanna Wilburn (3/11/1806 – 9/15/1872) m. 1/11/1824
Patriarch and matriarch of the McCarty clan. Parents of Alexander Vance, Edward Wilburn, William Rucker, John Granville, and James St. Clair. Their daughter married William M. Cornett. They are buried in Bethel Cemetery in Polk County.

McCarty, John Granville (9/29/1837 – 11/29/1901) **1847**
Cynthia Walling (c1850 – ?) m. 11/29/1868 **1854**
Son of John & Rosanna McCarty and daughter of John R. & Mary Walling. They were married in Amity and they became members of the Amity Church.

McCarty, William Rucker (12/4/1829 – 12/3/1888) **1847**

Eliza Ann Lovelady (c1837 – 5/22/1892) m. 9/17/1851

Son of John & Rosanna McCarty and daughter of Thomas J. & Polly Lovelady. Settled below Amity near Polk County line, but moved to Douglas County in 1863 and homesteaded in Lookingglass Valley near A. L. Todd. He is buried in Echo Cemetery in Umatilla County. She is buried by her parents in Dallas Cemetery in Polk County.

McClure, James F. (2/25/1821 – 9/5/1862) **1853**

Mary Ann (Nancy) Bruce (11/15/1824 – 8/9/1907) m. 3/10/1842

Charter members of the Grand Prarie Church in Lane County. He was a younger brother to Vincent Scott McClure and she was a younger sister to Sallie Bruce McClure. Their daughter, Jane Curry, married Benjamin Franklin Owen on 9/1/1859. James is buried in Luper Cemetery near Irving in Lane County.

McClure, Vincent Scott (8/30/1815 – 5/18/1893) **1853**

Sarah (Sallie) H. Bruce (11/15/1815 – 4/26/1858) m. 11/13/1834

Sarah (Sallie) Scott Tandy Benson (c1824 – 1/20/1899) m. 10/16/1859

Charter members of the Grand Prarie Church in Lane County. He was an older brother to James F. McClure and she was an older sister to Nancy Bruce McClure. He served in the state legislature in the 1860s. When the Eugene Church was established in March 1866, he and Thomas G. Hendricks were asked to serve as deacons. Buried in Luper Cemetery near Irving in Lane County.

McClure, William Henry Harrison (10/6/1840 – ?) **1853**

Amanda Elizabeth Callison (7/26/1848 – 12/9/1938) m. 11/13/1864

Eldest son of Vincent & Sallie Bruce McClure and youngest daughter of Gilmore & Elizabeth Callison. Their fathers were leaders in organizing Eugene Church, and they became charter members of that congregation. They were members of the Pleasant Hill Church of Christ in the 1870s and they were living in W.T. in the 1880s.

McCorkle, George F. McCorkle (9/10/1819 – 7/26/1891) **1843**

Elizabeth Brooks Howell (4/24/1822 – 9/26/1900) m. 2/6/1840

They were in "The Great Migration" of 1843. George may not have been a Christian. Her parents were John & Temperance Howell, for whom "Howell Prairie" was named in Marion County. They settled at Howell Prairie and they are buried in Howell Prairie Cemetery. Her obituary noted: "She became a member of the church in her early youth and remained a Christian until her death."

McElroy, Ebenezer Burton (9/17/1842 – 5/4/1901) **1873**

Agnes C. McFadden m. 1869

She was a niece of Alexander Campbell, and they were married near Bethany College. They settled at Corvallis in Benton County where he occupied the chair of literature at the school that became Oregon State University. He was promoted to Oregon State superintendent of public instruction in the 1870s.

McFadden, William (1825 – ?) **1851**

Theresa Powell (1/28/1829 – 8/11/1851) m. 11/25/1847

Margaret Earl (1/4/1829 – 2/15/1891) m. 1/24/1852

Married the oldest daughter of John Alkire Powell. She died on the Oregon Trail. His second wife was a sister to Joseph Earl and Robert Earl, both of whom also married daughters of John Alkire Powell. When William died, Margaret married Reason Rounds Boothby in 1877.

McKinney, Stephen M. (1796 – ?) **1848**

Louisa Anderson (c1806 – 2/19/1919) m. 11/?/1826

In the 1850 census they were living in Washington County next to their son-in-law and daughter, Alexander P. & Sarah McKinney Caldwell. Both families moved to new locations in the early 1850s that included property in both Yamhill and Polk counties. A. V. McCarty conducted a gospel meeting at the McKinney's residence in May 1855.

McKinney, William W. (1820 – 10/20/1875) **1847**

Matilda Darby (c1831 – 8/28/1921) m. 4/25/1847

Soon after their wedding they came overland from Jackson County, Missouri and settled in Marion County. He built the first mill in Marion County. They were members of the Scio Church and they donated property for the church building in 1863. A daughter married William Henry Downing.

Menifee, William R. (12/5/1823 – 6/19/1906) **1852**

Nancy Jane Benefiel (10/30/1831 – 2/11/1907) m. 2/8/1849

Charter members of the Dallas Church in Polk County. He was a delegate from the Dallas Church at the annual State Meeting in 1863. In the early 1880s they were living at Kingsley in Wasco County, and he was serving as an agent in that district for the *Christian Herald*.

Miller, Christian (10/10/1810 – 7/15/1874) **1848**

Mary Ann Coddington (5/9/1806 – 9/2/1892) m. 8/5/1832

Younger brother of Isaac Miller and younger sister of Elizabeth Coddington. The Miller brothers married the Coddington sisters. Christian & Mary Ann were members of the Central Church in Linn County, and they are buried in Central Cemetery.

Miller, Isaac Sr. (2/8/1806 – 2/26/1878) **1848**

Elizabeth Coddington (1/18/1805 – 2/26/1878) m. 12/20/1827

Lived in Marion, Clackamas and Linn counties before moving to Jackson County in 1867. Resided in Medford for over 20 years. They died at their residence within 3 hours of each other. Buried in the same grave in the IOOF Cemetery in Ashland. An obituary noted: "For more than 30 years they had been exemplary members of the Christian Church, and both died in the hope of a happy immortality."

Miller, Richard (1803 – ?) **1847**

Margaret Stanton (c1804 – 8/9/1856) m. 2/5/1824

Mary Hardman m. 2/28/1858

Settled on the Abiqua River in the Silverton district of Marion County. Charter members of the Bethany Church in Marion County in April 1851. He is most likely the "R. Miller" who was one of the 16 members of the board of trustees of Rickreall Academy in 1854.

Millican, Elijah (1804 – ?) **1843**

Lucinda Crisp (7/29/1811 – 4/23/1877) m. 4/1/1827

They were in "The Great Migration" of 1843, and they hired Chesley B. Gray to drive one of their wagons. They traveled in the same party with the Hembrees and Newbys. Their daughter, Melvina Ann, married James Thomas Hembree on 9/24/1845. He was a son of Joel Jordan & Sally Hembree. The Millicans settled near Lafayette and she is buried in Lafayette Masonic Cemetery.

Mitchel, James G. (8/?/1818 – 1894) **1852**

Miranda Shelley (1825 – ?) m. 11/29/1846

They were members of the Pleasant Hill Church of Christ in Lane County. She may have been a younger sister of Michael and Harrison Shelley. In 1855 James G. Mitchel was a member of the 5-man committee that placed ads in church papers regarding the need for a Christian teacher at Pleasant Hill Academy. They are buried in Pleasant Hill Cemetery.

Morgan, Thomas McBride (? – 5/10/1908) **1875**

Rachael Barnes m. 1863

Born to Missouri Christians and named for Thomas Crawford McBride. He had been preaching in Kansas for more than a decade when he moved his family to Oregon in 1875. Preached in Oregon, Washington, Idaho and California for more than 40 years. He preached for churches at Amity, Bethel, Pleasant Hill, Junction City, Roseburg and Cottage Grove. He died at Santa Cruz, California and was buried there.

Morse, William B. (10/24/1828 – 4/22/1883) **1855**

Nancy E. McBride m. 12/13/1857

He became a Christian in 1854 and was a member of the McMinnville Church when he married a daughter of Dr. James & Mahala McBride. They were members of the Salem Church in the 1860s and he was appointed first warden of the state penitentiary by Governor George Woods. They lived at St. Helens in 1870s. His obituary noted: "He assisted much in church work, always maintaining a firm Christian character."

Moss, Jasper Jesse (7/13/1806 – 5/?/1895) **1870?**

wife's name unknown

Raised Presbyterian. Baptized into Christ in September 1829. Preached in Ohio and surrounding states 40 years. Vice-president of American Christian Missionary Society in 1849. Chaplain in Union army. With his son, Rufus H. Moss, he moved to Oregon around 1870. Organized the Carlton Church in Yamhill County in the summer of 1877. Preached in W.T. in 1880s & 90s. Died in Seattle, 2 months before his son.

Moss, Rufus H. (c1836 – 7/12/1895) **1870?**

wife's name unknown

Son of Jasper Jesse Moss. Student at Hiram College in Ohio. Fought with James A. Garfield in the Civil War. As a result of war wounds he was nearly blind. Began preaching after the war and moved to Oregon around 1870. By the 1880s he was preaching in W.T. Preached in Seattle for 6 years and died there in 1895.

Mulkey, Isaac Newton (2/9/1840 – 3/26/1917) **1871**

Sarah Frances Randolph (7/12/1846 – 4/2/1923) m. 9/?/1861

Nephew to Philip Mulkey. He preached in Oregon for more than 45 years. They are buried in Pleasant Hill Cemetery in Lane County.

Mulkey, James Houston (11/24/1848 – 6/29/1932) **1848**

Emily J. Porter m. 6/15/1871

He was a son of Luke & Rutha Mulkey, and was born at the family home 4 miles west of Corvallis in Benton County. She was a daughter of Samuel & Frances Porter. He served as a deacon in the church for several years.

Mulkey, John F. (3/14/1830 – 9/25/1903) **1853**

Sarah Ann Sirus (Cyrus) (12/31/1841 – 2/5/1869) m. 2/12/1859
Louisa Honig m. 2/11/1872

He was a grandson of John Mulkey (1773 – 1844) and a nephew of Philip Mulkey. He preached in Oregon for more than 40 years, and he is buried in West Point Cemetery near Harrisburg in Linn County. At the time of the division between Disciples of Christ and Churches of Christ, he identified with Churches of Christ.

Mulkey, Johnson (1/?/1808 – 2/?/1862) **1845**

Susan Brown Roberts (1819 – ?) m. 2/17/1835 or 2/1/1836 **1847**

Younger brother of Thomas Mulkey and older brother of Luke Mulkey. On Christmas day 1847, he and his wife settled on a Benton County donation land claim west of the present-day campus of Oregon State University in Corvallis.

Mulkey, Luke (5/9/1810 – 8/31/1894) **1847**

Rutha Allison Reed (12/28/1812 – 9/23/1858) m. 12/18/1832
Narcissa A. Brents (? – 1865)
Sarah H. Caton (1804 – 1894) m. 3/13/1866

Younger brother of Thomas and Johnson Mulkey. Their daughter, Rachel, married John Atterbury on 7/26/1856, and their daughter, Eliza, married John Henry Hawley on 5/6/1858. They were members of the Monmouth Church and they are buried in Fir Crest Cemetery south of Monmouth. His third wife was the widow of George Washington Caton.

Mulkey, Monroe (1/11/1839 – 5/11/1912) **1847**

Margaret E. Garrison (6/13/1843 – 8/23/1895) m. 1858
Sarah Martin

He was a son of Thomas & Sarah Carpenter Mulkey. After his father died at Laurel Hill in 1847, his mother married Robert Lancefield who lived at Amity in Yamhill County. His mother died in Amity on Christmas day 1856. Monroe & Margaret were married in 1858 and became members of the Amity Church. He was serving as a deacon in this church in the 1870s. They are buried in Amity Cemetery.

Mulkey, Philip (1802 – 12/3/1893) **1853**

Martha H. Martin (5/15/1804 – 10/24/1862) m. 11/?/1820
Phebe Broshear (c1814 – ?) m. 4/5/1863

Son of John Mulkey, one of the pioneer preachers in the Restoration Movement, and a close associate of Barton Warren Stone. Philip Mulkey preached in Oregon for 40 years. His nephews, John F. Mulkey and Isaac Newton Mulkey, also preached in Oregon for more than 40 years. His son, Welcome Hayes Mulkey, was a leader in the church, and his daughter, Elizabeth married William B. Barger.

Mulkey, Thomas (1807 – 1847) **1847**

Sarah Carpenter (4/12/1812 – 12/25/1856)

He died of mountain fever after entering Oregon and was buried at Laurel Hill. She married Robert Lancefield, a member of the Amity Church, on 4/30/1850. She died on Christmas day 1856 and is buried in Amity Cemetery.

Mulkey, Welcome Hayes (4/29/1830 – 8/31/1899) **1853**
Louisa Crabtree (12/27/1838 – 12/1/1931) m. 11/13/1855
Son of Philip & Martha Mulkey and daughter of Zimri & Mariah Crabtree. At the time of the division between Disciples of Christ and Churches of Christ, they identified with Churches of Christ. They are buried in Mulkey Cemetery in Eugene.

Muncy, Isaac Newton (4/16/1844 – ?) **1852**
Julia Dyer (1/19/1846 – ?) m. 9/?/1871
He preached in Douglas and surrounding counties in the 1870s. His mentor was A. L. Todd. In the late 1870s he was living in Canyonville in Douglas County and serving as an agent for *Pacific Christian Messenger*. He served in the state legislature in 1909-1910.

Murphy, Calvin L. (1824 – ?) **1852**
Margaret E. Kramer m. 3/9/1848
Charter members of the Monmouth Church in 1856. He was a cousin of John Ecles Murphy and she was a daughter of John A. & Mary Jane Kramer. He was a strong supporter of editor Benjamin Franklin and the *American Christian Review*.

Murphy, Henderson Warren (2/3/1835 – ?) **1852**
Rebecca Lucretia Davidson (1843 – 7/21/1917) m. 11/18/1863
Son of John Ecles & Frances Murphy and daughter of Henry & Sarah Davidson. They were members of the Monmouth Church. He was a member of the board of trustees of Christian College.

Murphy, John Bunyan (1/2/1829 – c1860) **1852**
Mary Ann Whitman (c1830 – 2/2/1870) m. 8/28/1853 or 1854 **1850**
He was a cousin of John Ecles Murphy. She was the eldest child of Squire & Elizabeth Whitman, and a granddaughter of Elijah A. Davidson. They were among the 35 charter members of the Monmouth Church in 1856. After the death of John Bunyan Murphy, she married Charles Wood (1820 – 1905) on 7/14/1861.

Murphy, John Ecles (10/16/1806 – 5/7/1876) **1852**
Frances Wright Doughty (11/14/1810 – 12/30/1891) m. 3/?/1827
He preached in Illinois for several years before moving to Oregon, and he preached in Oregon for nearly a quarter-century. He was prominent in the establishing of Monmouth University and Monmouth Church. Member of the board of trustees of Monmouth University and later of Christian College. They are buried in Fir Crest Cemetery south of Monmouth in Polk County.

Murphy, William (12/18/1816 – 1/4/1874) **1852**
Elizabeth (Betsy) Roundtree (12/23/1823 – 2/28/1889) m. 5/20/1841
He was a younger brother to John Ecles Murphy, and she was a sister to Dr. James Harrison Roundtree and to Polly Roundtree Shirley. They settled briefly in Washington Territory but soon returned to the Monmouth district in Polk County. He was a member of the board of trustees of Christian College and an agent for the *Christian Messenger*. They are buried in Fir Crest Cemetery south of Monmouth.

Murphy, William Preston (1831 – 3/11/1904) **1852**
Sarah J. Taylor (c1840 – ?) m. 12/13/1855
Sarah E. Stanton Stover (7/23/1840 – ?) m. 9/27/1866
Son of John Ecles & Frances Murphy. He was an early member of the Monmouth Church, but in 1867 he was the clerk for the Salem Church. His second wife was a daughter of Alfred & Phoebe Stanton.

Nash, John (c1830 – 1858) **1853**

Mary Katherine Walker (? – 8/15/1864) m. 7/9/1854

Members of the Mill Creek Church in Marion County. She was a daughter of Gilliam & Rhoda Walker and a sister of Melinda Kimsey.

Neal, William (1819 – ?) **1852**

Emily Jane Sneed m. 3/18/1837

They were members of the Mill Creek Church in Marion County.

Nelson, Andrew Jefferson (5/28/1827 – 12/17/1899) **1852**

Lucretia Burnett (4/30/1837 – 1/5/1904) m. 4/2/1854

He traveled overland from Adams County, Illinois to the California gold fields in 1850, and then moved on to Yamhill County, Oregon in 1852. She was a daughter of George William & Sidney Burnett and a niece of Glen Owen Burnett. They were members of the McMinnville Church, and he served as an elder in that church for many years. They are buried in Masonic Cemetery in McMinnville.

Newby, William Thompson (3/25/1820 – 10/22/1884) **1843**

Sarah Jane McGary (12/23/1823 – 1/29/1887) m. 10/11 or 14/1841

Veterans of "The Great Migration" of 1843 and founders of the city of McMinnville in Yamhill County. Charter members of the McMinnville Church. He represented Yamhill County in the state senate 1870-1872. They are buried in Masonic Cemetery in McMinnville.

Nichols, Benjamin F. (1825 – ?) **1845**

Sarah Ann Gilliam m. 12/13/1850 **1844**

She was a daughter of Colonel Cornelius Gilliam who was killed during the Cayuse Indian War on 3/24/48. Nichols was not a Christian and they were later divorced. She was a charter member of the Dallas Church in Polk County.

Nott, Ephraim **1873**

Elizabeth

He was preaching and performing weddings in Marion County in the 1870s.

Orchard, Pleasant (1831 or 1832 – ?) **1851**

Elizabeth A. Miller (1831 – 1/14/1881) m. 10/14/1851 **1851**

She became a Christian in Illinois when she was 15, but her husband may not have been a Christian. She was a member of the Dallas Church in Polk County and it was one of the elders of that church, Martin Byerly, who submitted her obituary to the *Pacific Christian Messenger*.

Osburn, Albert (12/18/1803 – 3/3/1880) **1865?**

Mary Ann Haggard (2/20/1825 – 9/12/1883) m. 3/10/1844

One record noted, "he united with the Church of Christ in 1841." He was an elder in the Damascus Church in Clackamas County. One of their daughters married Thomas H. Bohna who became a deacon in that church. Albert's funeral was preached by his good friend, George P. Rich. Albert & Mary were buried in Damascus Pioneer Cemetery, and later the Bohna and Rich families were buried near them.

Owen, Benjamin Franklin (11/24/1828 – 1/7/1917) **1853**
Jane Curry McClure (12/8/1842 – 4/15/1887) m. 9/1/1859
Met the McClures on the overland journey and married their daughter 6 years later. Along with her parents, they were members of the Grand Prairie Church in Lane County in the late 1850s. They are buried near Wren in Benton County.

Owsley, Dr. William M. (c1819 – ?) **1866**
Mariah L. (c1835 – ?)
They were living in California in 1860, in Nevada in 1862, and in Idaho in 1865. They moved to Oregon around 1866-67. They were members of the Springfield Church in Lane County. Thomas Franklin Campbell was a guest in their home during a preaching tour in August 1871. In the 1880 census they were still living in Springfield.

Pagett, Christopher C. (1824 – ?) **1852**
Urania Pinto m. 6/3/1856 **1853**
Came overland from Missouri with the Harry L. Woodford family. His sister, who was married to Woodford, died on the trail. C. C. Pagett moved to W.T. in the mid-1850s.

Parvin, James (5/2/1831 – 12/17/1908) **1853**
Selena Parker (1834 – 1913) m. 2/5/1854
They met on the Oregon Trail during the overland journey and were married less than a year later. They settled at Dexter in Lane County where he found employment as a carpenter, cabinet maker and building contractor. He served as postmaster and ran a store in Dexter for 11 years. He operated a threshing machine for 25 years and was the clerk of the Dexter Church for many years.

Payne, Aaron (12/30/1789 – 5/19/1883) **1847**
May Murphy (? – 1/18/1846) m. 10/24/1815
Veteran gospel preacher from Illinois. Father of Caleb Payne. He preached in Oregon for more than 35 years. He organized a congregation near his home at Blackhawk schoolhouse in Yamhill County in 1847. He is buried in Yamhill-Carlton Cemetery.

Payne, Caleb J. (5/24/1821 – 9/18/1858) **1845**
Malinda (Melinda) Toney (3/24/1829 – 1/26/1898) m. 9/19/1850
Son of Aaron & May Payne and daughter of James & Patsy Toney. He came overland with Amos & Jane Harvey and James & Sarah Ramage, and he settled on Deer Creek east of present-day Sheridan in Yamhill County.

Pedigo, Edward (4/15/1805 – 9/4/1894) **1854**
Lettice Gill (11/23/1806 – 6/20/1879) m. 11/2/1824
Married in Barren County, Kentucky. Relatives are buried in cemetery at Mulkey Meetinghouse. Came overland from Wapello County, Iowa. Settled in Clackamas County. He named the town of Damascus. Moved to Washington Territory in 1871 and established Eden Valley Church of Christ in Whitman County. Buried at Eden Valley Cemetery in Garfield, Washington.

Pedigo, Edward Axel (8/19/1845 – ?) **1854**
Mary Ann Bailes m. 9/9/1866
Son of Edward & Lettice Pedigo. Prior to his marriage, he was one of the 16 charter members of the Hillboro Christian Church when it was established on 10/17/1862 in Washington County. She was a daughter of Keathley & Sarah Bailes.

Pedigo, James Henry (8/2/1837 – 1915) **1854**
Martha Ann Foster m. 3/26/ or 4/3/1858 **1845**
Son of Edward & Lettice Pedigo and daughter of Ambrose & Zerelda Foster. Their wedding was performed at Damascus in Clackamas County by her grandfather, John Foster, the first preacher from the Restoration Movement to preach in Oregon Territory.

Pedigo, William Evermont (12/5/1828 – ?) **1854**
Sarah Ann Hanna (c1828 – ?) m. 7/1/1850
Along with his brother, Edward Axel Pedigo, they were among the 16 charter members of the Hillsboro Christian Church when it was established on 10/17/1862 in Washington County. In the early 1880s he was an elder in the Monmouth Church in Polk County. His sister, Zerelda Jane, was married to a Christian preacher named Harrison H. Hendrix.

Perkins, Dr. John Nelson (1816 – ?) **1851**
Derissa Matsler m. 11/3/1839 or 1840
Preached in Oregon for more than 15 years before moving to W. T. after 1866. He was elected to the state legislature from Linn County in 1864. One record noted: "For several years he traveled over Linn, Lane and Benton counties, treating both the bodies and the souls of the people." When he moved to eastern Washington he engaged in stock-raising and became well-known as a cancer doctor.

Peterson, Martin (9/29/1820 – 7/2/1889) **1864**
Elizabeth (12/20/1822 – 5/26/1891)
First preacher from the Restoration Movement to locate in southern Oregon. He preached in Jackson and Josephine counties for a quarter-century. He was an agent for the *Pacific Christian Messenger* in the 1870s and for the *Christian Herald* in the 1880s.

Pettyjohn, Lewis (11/25/1820 – 10/9/1900) **1847**
Sarah Ann Rains (c1827 – ?) m. 3/22/1844
They came overland from Missouri with 2 small daughters. He may not have been a Christian, but she was an early member of the Salem Church in Marion County.

Pigg, John R. (1828 – 11/5/1852) **1849**
Nancy Jane McCarty (1832 – ?) m. 3/6/1851
Son of Reuben & Adeline Pigg and daughter of John & Rosanna McCarty. They were members of the Bethel Church. She was a sister to Alexander Vance McCarty. When John R. Pigg died, Nancy Jane married William M. Cornett.

Pigg, Reuben (c1799 – ?) **1849**
Adeline (c1805 – ?)
They came overland from Missouri with 6 children and settled in Polk County. They were members of the Bethel Church. Their eldest son married a sister of Alexander Vance McCarty.

Pigg, Reuben (2/19/1839 – 1/17/1878) **1849**
Emma S. Graves m. 5/12/1870
Son of Reuben & Adeline Pigg and younger brother of John R. Pigg. He was a member of the Bethel Church and his obituary was published in the *Pacific Christian Messenger*. Emma was a daughter of Charles B. Graves and a granddaughter of Glen Owen Burnett.

Porter, Henry C. (11/24/1850 – ?) **1850**
Minnie F. Welch (1858 – ?) m. 11/24/1877
Son of William G. & Martha Porter. He was a justice of the peace for 8 years in the Aumsville district of Marion County, and he was superintendent of the Sunday School program at the Aumsville Church for 20 years.

Porter, Samuel (5/12/1819 – 12/29/1909) **1853**
Frances Virginia Chrisman (12/14/1825 – 12/7/1877) m. 2/12/1843
He was a younger brother to William D. Porter. One account mentions that he was a member of the Church of Christ for 70 years and an elder in the Halsey Church for 12 years. Their daughter, Emily, married James Houston Mulkey at The Dalles on 6/15/1871. The Porters are buried in Pine Grove Cemetery in Linn County.

Porter, Stephen (1819 – ?) **1848**
Catherine Jane Coffey m. 9/1/1844
Susan Gibson Turner m. 8/15/1851
Younger brother of William G. Porter and a member of the Mill Creek Church in Marion County. His first wife was most likely a daughter of Nebuzardan & Elizabeth Coffey.

Porter, William G. (12/14/1812 – 3/30/1899) **1848**
Sarah Coffey (? – 1848) m. 1840
Martha Coffey (c1813 – 5/17/1903) m. 10/4/1849
Married two daughters of Nebuzardan & Elizabeth Coffey. His first wife died of mountain fever and was the first person buried in Aumsville Cemetery. William was a prominent church leader in Marion County for 50 years. Presided over the annual State Meeting in 1860. Served in state legislature 1876-78. They were the parents of Henry C. Porter. Buried in Aumsville Cemetery near the Coffeys and the Blackerbys.

Porter, William D. (6/6/1811 – 2/16/1892) **1853**
Elizabeth Nott (Knott) (12/17/1814 – 11/11/1887) m. 10/15/1835
Members of the Harrisburg Church in Linn County. He was an older brother to Samuel Porter. They are buried in Masonic Cemetery in Harrisburg.

Powell, Alexander Hamilton (12/8/1834 – 3/12/1915) **1851**
Mary Anne McKnight (4/4/1844 – 5/31/1912) m. 2/25/1864
Son of Alfred & Sarah Bracken Powell. He was baptized into Christ in November 1851 by his uncle, John Alkire Powell. He was a deacon in the Central Church in Linn County for 7 years, and he was an elder in the Hebron Church in Lane County for 36 years. The Hebron church building was located on their farm. They are buried in Taylor-Lane Cemetery southeast of Cottage Grove in Lane County.

Powell, Alfred (7/10/1810 – 12/18/1881) **1851**
Sarah Bracken (11/30/1815 – 1/?/1837) m. 1834
Hannah Goble Shirrill (1812 – 5/18/1859) m. 7/?/1837
Abigail Lane (1808 – 12/13/1873) m. 10/4/1860
Mary Cooper Churchill
Younger brother of John Alkire Powell and Noah Powell. He preached in Oregon for 30 years. He is buried in Central Santiam Cemetery in Linn County.

Powell, Augustus Steuben (8/17/1831 – 3/17/1907) **1851**
Ruhama Marshall (1833 – 3/22/1880) m. 4/14/1853
Son of John Alkire & Savilla Powell. One account described him as "a devoted member of the Christian Church." They were members of the Albany Church in Linn County in the 1880s, and he served as an agent for the *Christian Herald*.

Powell, Franklin Smith (3/20/1830 – 12/4/1916) **1851**
Louisa Jane Peeler (4/29/1830 – 1926) m. 3/20/1850
Eldest son of John Alkire & Savilla Powell. She was the daughter of Abner Peeler, a prominent Christian preacher in Illinois. They were living in Albany in the 1870s and he was serving on the board of trustees of Christian College. He won election to the state legislature in the 1880s.

Powell, James Henry (1/9/1837 – 12/?/1880) **1851**
Martha Harris (9/30/1838 – 8/17/1929) m. 1/4/1866 **1865**
He was a son of Alfred & Sarah Powell, and brother of Alexander Hamilton Powell and Joseph Goble Powell. She was a daughter of John M. & Jane Harris and a sister of David R. Harris and Thomas W. Harris. He was a deacon in the Hebron Church in Lane County in the 1870s. She married Daniel C. Baughman on 1/29/1884. He died 11/28/1919. All 3 are buried in Taylor-Lane Cemetery.

Powell, John Alkire (2/20/1807 – 6/18/1880) **1851**
Savilla Smith (9/28/1810 – 1/7/1889) m. 4/3/1828
He preached in Illinois for 18 years before moving to Oregon, and he preached in Oregon for nearly 30 years. He was an older brother to Noah and Alfred, who were also preachers. Charter members of the Central Church in Linn County. Their sons and daughters were all devout Christians. He was a member of the board of trustees of Christian College. They are buried in Central Santiam Cemetery in Linn County.

Powell, Joseph Goble (6/1/1841 – 9/9/1924) **1851**
Melissa Ann Ramsey (8/29/1846 – 8/8/1925) m. 9/25/1862 **1852**
Son of Alfred & Hannah Powell. He and his wife lived in Linn County until 1889 when they moved to Lane County. They were members of the Central Church in Linn County and he was a justice of the peace for their precinct. Members of Hebron Church and London Church in Lane County. They are buried in Bemis Cemetery south of London.

Powell, Noah (9/24/1808 – 3/6/1875) **1851**
Mary Smith (7/28/1812 – 1/27/1893) m. 11/5/1830
Younger brother to John Alkire Powell and older brother to Alfred Powell. Noah and John were married to sisters. He settled on Howell Prairie in Marion County, but he lived near Amity in Yamhill County for 5 years (1853-58) before returning to Marion County. He preached in Oregon for 24 years. They are buried in Hunsaker Cemetery in Marion County.

Powell, Stephen Dodridge (5/11/1833 – 5/5/1910) **1851**
Margaret Ann Umphlet (9/17/1840 – ?) m. 5/23/1858
Son of John Alkire & Savilla Powell and daughter of Stanley & Jane Umphlet. He was an agent for the *Christian Messenger* in the early 1870s while living at Tillamook.

Powell, William H. (1/21/1837 – 1900) **1851**

Alameda Maxwell (? – 1873)

Mary Maxwell

Son of Noah & Mary Smith Powell. He was a carpenter, wagon-maker and cabinet worker. When they lived in Aumsville in Marion County they were members of the Aumsville Church and he was justice of the peace and postmaster. When they lived in Stayton in Marion County for 9 years they were members of the Stayton Church. They lived in Portland in the early 1890s and moved to California in 1894.

Preston, William (3/21/1797 – 10/20/1873) **1853**

Mary White (6/1/1808 – ?) m. 11/17/1822

Parents of William P. Preston and Mary Preston Briggs. Originally from Indiana, but they came overland from Iowa.

Preston, William P. (3/14/1826 – ?) **1853**

Mary Ann White (1830 – ?) m. 11/26/1849

Overland from Iowa. Son of William & Mary White Preston and older brother of Mary Preston Briggs. His sister was married to the eldest son of Samuel Bates & Susanna Briggs. The Prestons settled in Canyonville in Douglas County and assisted Samuel Bates & Susanna Briggs in establishing a congregation in that community. They were living in Peoria in Linn County in 1875.

Propst, Anthony (9/22/1810 – 9/19/1852) **1852**

Lucinda Powell (2/19/1817 – 8/19/1852) m. 1836

Sister to the three Powell brothers who were gospel preachers. She and her husband died on the Oregon Trail, one month apart.

Propst, Franklin (4/10/1832 – 1917) **1852**

Mary Powell (10/18/1838 – 12/18/1914) m. 6/18/1855

Nephew to Anthony & Lucinda Propst. Married a daughter of John A. Powell.

Propst, James Marion (1843 – 6/14/1901) **1852**

Ann Eliza Guliford

After his parents died on the Oregon Trail, he was raised by his first cousin, Franklin S. Powell. In the 1870s he was living in Albany and serving as an agent for the *Pacific Christian Messenger*.

Propst, John Wesley (4/12/1837 – 5/24/1939) **1852**

Margaret Jane Cole (5/7/1843 – 12/24/1918) m. 11/1/1860

He was baptized into Christ in Silver Creek in Marion County in June 1853. In later years, he served as an elder in the Central Church in Linn County. This church was established by his uncles, John Alkire Powell and Alfred Powell, in the fall of 1851. In the 1880s he was living in Albany and serving as an agent for the *Christian Herald*.

Pugh, William David (c1790 – 1/3/1846) **1845**

Sarah White m. c1811

Jeanette Donelson (12/28/1798 – ?) m. 2/14/1815

These Indiana Christians experienced many difficulties on their journey to Oregon. Their eldest son buried his wife and 2 children at the Big Sandy River in Wyoming. After arriving in Oregon, William David and two of his younger children died at Forest Grove. Jeannette continued on to Marion County and settled on a donation land claim near Chemawa.

Pulaski, Daniel Benjamin (c1811 – ?) **1857**
Elizabeth (1825 – 9/18/1880) m. 1853
She became a Christian in Knox County, Indiana. Her obituary records that she "remained such, witnessing a good profession and died in the triumphs of a living faith." He may not have been a Christian. They settled in Coos County and she was "one of the first white women to brave the trials of pioneer life in the valley of the Coquille." She was a charter member of the Coquille Church established by A. L. Todd in the mid-1860s.

Putman, David H. (1834 – ?) **1847**
Catherine (c1838 – ?) m. 7/30/1854
They were married in Linn County and they were charter members of the Brownsville Church in that county. He was a carpenter in Brownsville, and he served as an agent for the *Pacific Christian Messenger* in the 1870s and for the *Christian Herald* in the 1880s.

Quinn, Joseph H. (1817 – ?) **1852**
Polly m. 7/?/1836
They were charter members of the Rock Creek Church of Christ south of Molalla in Clackamas County.

Ramage, James (1789 – 10/21/1851) **1845**
Sarah Jane Harvey (c1793 – 5/28/1863) m. c1810
He was a brother to Jane Harvey and she was a sister to Amos Harvey. The two families came overland together from Illinois in 1845. Two young bachelors, Caleb Payne and John Eakin Lyle, were hired as wagon drivers for the overland journey. James & Sarah settled near the Joel Jordan Hembree family in Yamhill County.

Read, Clifton Kitridge (1813 – 10/20/1875) **1852**
Martha S. (1811 – 4/1/1891) m. 1/1/1834 or 1835
They were members of the Mill Creek Church in Marion County, and he was a delegate from this church at the 1867 annual State Meeting. He served for a time as state senator in the Oregon legislature.

Rich, George Pew (8/16/1847 – 11/9/1908) **1875**
Nancy Hickey (1852 – 1922) m. 3/29/1868
Civil War veteran. He preached in Oregon for 33 years. Throughout their Oregon years they lived in Clackamas County. He was an agent for the *Christian Herald* in the 1880s. When the division gradually occurred between Disciples of Christ and Churches of Christ in the 1890s, he became the most visible leader among the Churches of Christ. They are buried in Damascus Pioneer Cemetery in Clackamas County.

Richardson, Enoch (c1816 – ?) **1852?**
Jane Mackey (c1816 – ?)
Came overland from Illinois and settled in the Salt Creek district of Polk County. He was one of the founders of the Perrydale Christian Church in northern Polk County. Served as an agent for the *Pacific Christian Messenger* in the 1870s.

Richardson, George Washington (9/26/1824 – 1/22/1885) **1851**
Mary Ann (7/4/1828 – 10/18/1868) m. 2/1/1844 or 1845
Martha Lucy Durham m. 10/19/1869
Son of John & Orpha Richardson. Indefatigable evangelist in Oregon and Washington for more than 30 years. President of the board of trustees of Bethel College. Elected to state legislature in 1862 and 1864. His first wife and 3 sons were buried in Bethel Cemetery. He moved to W.T. in 1877 and continued to preach often. He is buried in Pioneer Cemetery in Salem with his second wife and other children.

Richardson, Gideon (5/14/1790 – 6/26/1871) **1848**
Mary (Margaret) Morrow (c1796 – c1870s)
Settled along the Long Tom river in northern Lane County and lived there over 22 years. His obituary in the *Christian Messenger* noted that he had "been a member of the Christian Church about fifty-five years."

Richardson, I. N. **1870s**
Florence Gerking m. 10/11/1878
He was one of the young leaders in the Weston Church in Umatilla County in the 1870s, and she was a member of one of the strongest families in the Weston Church. During the late 1870s and early 1880s, he frequently sent news items about the Weston Church to Thomas F. Campbell for publication in the *Pacific Christian Messenger*.

Richardson, John G. (1/28/1797 – 4/14/1873) **1851**
Orpha Thompson (1802 – 1863)
Plua Bonney m. 6/22/1869
Overland from Adams County, Illinois. Settled at "Richardson's Gap" near Scio in Linn County. Along with Washington Crabtree, he was a leader in the Scio Church for many years. He was a delegate for this church at the 1863 annual State Meeting. Their sons, George Washington, Lewis Clark, and John Wesley, were strong leaders in the church.

Richardson, John Wesley (1/1/1832 – 1914) **1851**
Mary Ann Conkrite (Cronkite) (10/14/1836 – 1922) m. 7/23/1854
Son of John & Orpha Richardson and younger brother of G. W. Richardson and L. C. Richardson. He settled at "Richardson's Gap" near Scio in Linn County. He served as a deacon in the Scio Church for many years.

Richardson, Lewis Clark (1826 – 1869) **1851**
Eliza A. Whitley m. 8/15/1852
He was a son of John & Orpha Richardson and a brother of G. W. Richardson and John Wesley Richardson. She was a daughter of Samuel & Catherine Whitley and a sister of Elizabeth Jane Whitley Johnson. He was an elder in the Scio Church in Linn County in the 1860s.

Richardson, Nathaniel C. (1808 – ?) **1847**
Anna H. Bushnell (1807 – 1/3/1858) m. 3/9/1829
Catherine L. Cox m. 1/23/1873
Came overland with Mac Waller, Hiram Alva Johnson and other Illinois Christians. Settled near Oregon City in Clackamas County, and then moved in 1852 to a farm 3 miles south of Hillsboro in Washington County.

Riches, George P. S. (4/1/1821 – 5/9/1891) **1847**
Mary Shotwell Hunt (? – 7/17/1852) m. 5/22/1851
Mary Jane Watkins Walker (4/12/1835 – 11/6/1904) m. 12/12/1852 **1852**
She came overland from Wayne County, Indiana. Buried both her parents and her husband on the journey across the plains. Married George P. S. Riches on 12/12/52. He may not have been a Christian, but she was an active member of the Christian Church for more than 50 years. They were married for nearly 40 years until his death in 1891, and they are buried in Mt. Hope Cemetery in Marion County.

Rigdon, John (10/15/1796 – 3/13/1859) **1852**
Catherine Logan (6/12/1798 – 6/15/1834) m. 12/8/1818
Mary Bell m. 7/27/1837
Preached for many years in Ohio, Illinois and Iowa before coming to Oregon. Settled in Polk County for 2 years and then moved to a farm 5 miles southeast of Pleasant Hill in Lane County. His son married a daughter of Elijah & Susanna Bristow. John Rigdon was a circuit-riding evangelist in Oregon for more than 6 years. John & Mary are buried in Pleasant Hill Cemetery in Lane County.

Rigdon, Stephen (5/11/1829 – 8/13/1904) **1853**
Zilphia Etna Bristow (9/9/1834 –5/11/1903) m. 4/23/1854 **1848**
Son of John & Catherine Rigdon and daughter of Elijah & Susanna Bristow. They lived at Pleasant Hill in Lane County for a half-century and are buried in Pleasant Hill Cemetery. Devout members of Pleasant Hill Church of Christ.

Rigdon, Thomas Jefferson (9/16/1824 – 1852) **1850**
Anna Townsend (c1825 – ?) m. 1842
One record noted: "This family were Baptist as to their faith until Alexander Campbell personally visited them and they joined . . . the Christian Church." Came overland from Iowa and settled in Jackson County where Thomas died. She moved to Marion County and married a man named Orondo Beardsley.

Riggs, James Berry (3/21/1802 – 8/15/1870) **1845**
Nancy C. Anderson (7/20/1803 – 3 or 5/11/1859) m. 4/28/1824
Margaret Taylor m. 6/10/1860
Older brother of Zadok Riggs. Settled in Polk County. Charter members of Salt Creek Church. Buried in Salt Creek Cemetery. His parents were Scott & Hannah Riggs, well-known Christians in Illinois. One record noted of Scott Riggs: "He had been reared in the Baptist faith, but in early life he espoused the views of Alexander Campbell, and devoted much time and thought to the dissemination of those views . . ."

Riggs, Milton Scott (1/18/1825 – ?) **1845**
Eliza J. Hampton (8/?/1835 – 2/17/1923) m. 8/5/1851 **1845**
Son of James Berry & Nancy Riggs and daughter of John Jacob & Elizabeth Hampton. He was an older brother of Rufus Anderson Riggs. In the 1860 census they were living in Polk County with their 5 children.

Riggs, Reuben (died on the trail) **1846**

Rachel Riggs (c1811 – ?)

Daughter of Thomas & Leah Hunt Riggs and sister of Rebecca Riggs Fields, Mary Riggs Shanks, Elizabeth Riggs Stewart, Timothy A. Riggs, and Thomas Riggs. Although her husband died on the trail, she continued on to Oregon and settled in Clackamas County with her 4 children.

Riggs, Rufus Anderson (11/27/1827 – 4/3/1898) **1845**

Evelina Mary Hames Nicklin (9/1/1830 – 2/1/1903) m. 11/20/1851

Son of James Berry & Nancy Anderson Riggs and younger brother of Milton Scott Riggs. They were members of the Salt Creek Church in Polk County and they are buried in Salt Creek Cemetery.

Riggs, Thomas (c1787 – 1846) **1846**

Leah Hunt (? – 9/27/1857) m. 1807

He died on the overland journey and was buried on the west bank of the Missouri River at Iowa Point in northeast Kansas. One account noted that he was a Baptist minister who "adopted the theological views of Alexander Campbell." One daughter married a relative named Reuben Riggs, who died on the trail. Three other daughters married Thomas Fields, Stewart Lewis and Noah Shanks. Their sons were Timothy A. and Thomas.

Riggs, Thomas (1/5/1828 – 10/4/1868) **1846?**

Mary Newton

Son of Thomas & Leah Hunt Riggs and younger brother of Rachel Riggs, Rebecca Riggs Fields, Mary Riggs Shanks, Elizabeth Riggs Stewart, and Timothy Ambrose Riggs. He was living in Clackamas County at the time of the 1850 census.

Riggs, Timothy Ambrose (1825 – 1902) **1846**

Cecelia (Celia) Russell (c1830 – ?) m. 6/10/1849

Son of Thomas & Leah Hunt Riggs and an older brother of Thomas Riggs. He was a younger brother of Rachel Riggs, Rebecca Riggs Fields, Elizabeth Riggs Stewart, and Mary Riggs Shanks. They settled in Linn County and became members of the Holley Church. They were still living in Holley in 1875.

Riggs, Zadok T. (7/12/1811 – 7/5/1851) **1851**

Jane Leib (8/21/1814 – 3/1/1874)

Younger brother of James Berry Riggs. He was captain of his wagon train in the 1851 migration, but died at Independence Rock near Sweetwater River. She continued on to Oregon with her children and settled in Polk County near her husband's brother. She was a member of Salt Creek Church and is buried in Salt Creek Cemetery. She erected a memorial stone to her husband in that cemetery. A daughter married Job Connor.

Ritchey, Samuel Caleb (Cable) (6/28/1807 – ?) **1853**

Elizabeth m. 11/5/1845

Charter members of the Christian Church in Portland when it was organized in 1879. They had been living in the Portland area for many years. He may have been an older brother (or cousin) of Sarah Ritchey Ladd, Mary Ritchey Lindsay, Lydia Ritchey Morgan and Emily Ritchey Warriner.

Roach, Thomas (1807 – ?) **1852**

Maraetta (Maryetta) m. 6/8/1833

Charter members of the Harrisburg Church in Linn County 11/7/1863. Thomas Roach was one of the four trustees of the congregation when they purchased property on which to build in November 1867.

Robb, John H. (1/1/1814 – 11/19/1861) **1846?**

Elizabeth G. Garwood (10/14/1817 – 6/16/1902) m. 9/4/1835

They settled near McCoy in northern Polk County. He was a member of the board of trustees of Bethel Institute and served on the building committee. One account referred to him as, "a faithful member of the Christian Church." He is buried in Bethel Cemetery, but there is no record of her burial.

Roberts, John Engard (6/27/1831 – 4/1/1906) **1872**

Mary Jane Linville

Spokesman for the Restoration Movement in Oregon for more than 30 years. He preached for the Halsey Church in Linn County in the 1870s and for the Mill Creek Church in Marion County in the 1880s. Their daughter, Mary Martisue, married a son of David R. & Mary Lewis on Christmas day 1877. The wedding ceremony was performed by Mac Waller at their residence in Halsey.

Rogers, Henry M. (1827 – 4/26/1924) **1853**

Paulina (1833 – 9/23/1899) m. 3/28/1852

They were married in Des Moines County, Iowa. They settled in Lane County in 1854, and they were active in the Hebron Church. Henry was described as "a zealous worker in the Christian Church." One of their daughters, Elizabeth (Lizzie), married Levi Geer on 9/13/1877. The Rogers and Geers moved to Moscow, Idaho in 1880. When the Geers returned to Lane County, Levi became an elder in the London Church.

Rose, Andrew Jackson (c1820 – 1893) **1856**

Elma Ruble Badger (12/21/1824 – 2/2/1914) m. 1855

She was a daughter of Thomas & Elizabeth Ruble and a sister of William and David Ruble. She married Ephraim Badger on 11/28/1844, and their son, Thomas Ruble Badger, was born on 10/20/1845, and their other son, Ephraim Badger, was born on 8/3/1852. When her husband died, Elma married Andrew Jackson Rose in 1855. They came overland in 1856 and settled at Lebanon in Linn County.

Roth, Charles (1815 – ?) **1847**

wife's name unknown m. 1834

Martha Conovert (c1834 – ?) m. 1867

Charter members of the Harrisburg Church in Linn County 11/7/1863. Charles Roth was one of the trustees of the congregation when property was purchased on which to build in November 1867. He served as an elder of the Harrisburg Church and he donated some of the timbers for the church building that was constructed in 1869-70.

Roundtree, Dr. James Harrison (11/23/1815 – 1/25/1895) **1852**

Emeline Cole Riddle (12/8/1818 – 1892) m. 3/28/1838

Came overland from Henry County Illinois with the Murphy-Davidson train. Remained in Oregon only one year and then settled in Washington. One of his sisters married William Murphy and another married Ethan Allen Shirley. The Roundtrees are buried in Centralia, Washington.

Rowland, Green Loyed (5/6/1827 – 1910) **1844**

Sufronia (Sophronia) Fouts (11/25/1835 – 5/10/1900) m. 4/28/1853

Son of Jeremiah Rowland and brother of John B. Rowland and Levi Lindsay Rowland. She was an older sister of John Thomas Fouts. They were charter members of the Carlton Church when it was organized in the summer of 1877, and Green helped in the construction of the church building. They are buried in Yamhill-Carlton Cemetery.

Rowland, Judge Jeremiah (11/23/1805 – 6/22/1879) **1844**

Mary Ann Sappington (12/2/1820 – 11/22/1905) m. 6/15/1847 **1845**

He was already twice a widower when he crossed the plains with his 8 children. Appointed probate judge of Yamhill County in 1846 and served for 7 years. He was the father of John B. Rowland, Green L. Rowland and Levi Lindsay Rowland. He moved to McMinnville in 1865 and was a member of the McMinnville Church for 14 years. Buried in Masonic Cemetery in McMinnville.

Rowland, John B. (6/10/1824 – 1/?/1854) **1844**

Patricia Stillwell m. 7/27/1845

Son of Jeremiah Rowland and older brother of Green Rowland and L. L. Rowland. He was a volunteer in the Cayuse Indian War in 1848. He died early and was the second person buried in the Yamhill-Carlton Cemetery.

Rowland, Levi Lindsay (9/17/1831 – 1/19/1908) **1844**

Emma Sanders (5/1/1839 – ?) m. 11/18/1858

He was a graduate of Alexander Campbell's Bethany College, and she was a graduate of Tolbert Fanning's Franklin College. Returned to Oregon in 1859. He was a Christian preacher and president of both Bethel College and Christian College. He was a medical professor at Willamette University and Oregon's first Superintendent of Public Instruction. Associate editor of *Pacific Christian Messenger.* Elder in the Salem Church for several years. They are buried in City View Cemetery in Salem..

Rowland, Dr. William H. (c1833 – ?) **1870**

Sarah M. (c1837 – ?)

He was a physician and druggist in Brownsville in Linn County. He was one of the leaders of the Brownsville Church in the 1870s, and he was an agent for the *Christian Messenger*. In the 1880s they were living in Umatilla County and he was serving as an agent for the *Christian Herald*.

Ruble, David (12/11/1831 – 11/17/1907) **1853**

Orlena Russell (5/28/1834 – 2/15/1911) m. 4/22/1853

Younger brother of William Ruble. Their families traveled overland together and settled near each other in the Eola Hills. They were members of the Eola Church. In 1871 David moved his family to Alcea in Benton County and built the first saw mill and grist mill in that area. In 1879 he continued on to the coast and founded the town of Waldport in Lincoln County. They are buried near Waldport.

Ruble, Thomas (1/6/1797 – 9/?/1857) **1856**

Elizabeth Irons (10/27/1795 – 7/20/1870) m. c1820

Parents of William and David Ruble and Elma Badger Rose. They followed their sons to Oregon in 1856. Thomas died a year later. In the 1860 census, Elizabeth was living with the family of David Ruble She was a member of the Eola Church. Thomas & Elizabeth are buried in City View Cemetery in Salem.

Ruble, William (3/22/1823 – ?) **1853**

Ruth Russell m. 11/20/1844

Overland from Barry County, Missouri. Settled on a donation land claim 5 miles west of Salem in the Eola Hills of Polk County. Members of Eola Church. William preached on occasion and was a member of the board of trustees of Christian College. Moved to Josephine County in 1880s and established the church at Golden in 1890. His sister was Elma Badger Rose, and his nephew, Ephraim Badger, became a gospel preacher.

Ruddell, Stephen D. (1816 – ?) **1851**

Winaford (4/26/1816 – 1/6/1856)

They were among the first Christian families to settle north of the Columbia River in Washington Territory. When he wrote to Daniel Bates, editor of the *Christian Evangelist*, on 5/7/1854, they were living at Olympia in Thurston County.

Russell, Abel (1805 – ?) **1848**

Elizabeth (1813 – ?) m. 11/29/1830

Came overland from Iowa with 9 children. Along with their eldest son, John, they were charter members of the Pleasant Hill Church of Christ in Lane County in 1850.

Russell, John (c1831 – ?) **1848**

Margaret m. 10/1/1855

Son of Abel & Elizabeth Russell and a charter member of the Pleasant Hill Church of Christ in Lane County in 1850.

Scholl, Peter (10/20/1809 – 11/23/1872) **1847**

Elizabeth Cowhick (Cowbick) (5/7/1808 – 2/1/1872) m. 8/21/1828

Came overland with Mac Waller, Hiram Alva Johnson and other Illinois Christians. Settled in Washington County.

Scott, Felix Sr. (1788 – 1860) **1846**

Ellen Cansley (1805 – 1882) m. 4/5/1821

Migrated to California in 1845 in the same train with Elijah Bristow. They accompanied Bristow when he moved north to Oregon in the spring of 1846. They settled in present-day Lane County. Their daughter, Ellen, married John Eakin Lyle on 11/3/1846 in a ceremony performed by Glen Owen Burnett.

Shaff, G. W. (? – 4/8/1880)

Betsy M. (c1832 – ?)

He was baptized into Christ by George M. Whitney on 4/20/1862 and she was baptized into Christ by Whitney on 5/11/1862. They became members of the Mill Creek Church in Marion County.

Shanks, Noah (9/22/1822 – 3/14/1900) **1851**

Mary Riggs (1823 – 1/2/1899) m. 5/30/1843

Settled near Crawfordsville in Linn County. She was a daughter of Thomas & Leah Hunt Riggs and a sister of Rachel Riggs, Rebecca Riggs Fields, Elizabeth Riggs Lewis, Timothy Ambrose Riggs and Thomas Riggs. They traveled overland with the Crawford-Vawter train. They were still living near Crawfordsville in 1875.

Shannon, Davis (4/19/1811 – 11/2/1889) **1845**
Came overland with his nephew, Wesley Shannon, and with Elijah Bristow. The Shannons may not have been Christians, but Bristow mentions them in a letter back to his wife in Illinois. She evidently knew both of them, and it may have been through a church connection. Davis Shannon never married.

Shannon, Wesley (5/9/1820 – 11/12/1890) **1845**
Elizabeth Simmons (3/3 or 3/19/1830 – ?) m. 7/15 or 18/1847
Came overland with his uncle, Davis Shannon, and with Elijah Bristow. Wesley Shannon may not have been a Christian, but he praised Elijah Bristow for being a strong Christian. Elizabeth was the daughter of Samuel & Mahala Simmons.

Sharp, Joseph H. (11/28/1834 – 4/1/1913) **1852**
Phebe Jane White (7/28/1844 – 9/8/1922) m. 9/28/1865
He began preaching in Lane County in 1861. He may have been a cousin of Julia Ann Sharp Bean, the wife of Obadiah Bean. They were all members of the Grand Prairie Church in Lane County in the 1860s. Joseph & Phebe are buried in Taylor-Lane Cemetery southeast of Cottage Grove in Lane County.

Shaw, Judge Thomas C. (2/23/1823 – 8/31/1898) **1844**
Josephine Headrick (c1827 – 8/26/1905) m. 11/28/1850 **1847**
Charter members of the Bethany Church in Marion County in 1851. She was a daughter of Isaac & Margarette Headrick, who were also charter members of the Bethany Church. He was elected county commissioner of Marion County in 1864, assessor in 1870, sheriff in 1874 and county judge in 1880. He served as an elder in the Bethany Church for many years, and they are buried in Bethany Pioneer Cemetery.

Shelley, Harrison (1821 – ?) **1848**
Ruth Jane (c1825 – ?) m. 4/30/1843
Charter members of the Pleasant Hill Church of Christ in Lane County in 1850. He was an elder in the Pleasant Hill Church for many years. He was a younger brother to Michael Shelley.

Shelley, James Monroe (5/22/1843 – ?) **1848**
Lydia A. Baxter (? – 1884) m. 1874
Nancy Johnson Applegate (4/26/1850 – ?) m. 1/26/1898
Son of Michael & Sena Shelley, and older brother of Troy and Roswell. Attended Christian College. Elected sheriff of Lane County in 1880, and elected to the state legislature in 1902. He was a deacon in the Eugene Church and an agent for the *Pacific Christian Messenger.* One record noted that he was "an influential member of the Christian Church." His second wife was a daughter of Melchi Johnson.

Shelley, Michael (12/6/1814 – 10/24/1894) **1848**
Sena Mays (4/13/1814 – 3/2/1861) m. 6/22/1835
Martha Cooper Branson (10/?/1814 – 12/30/1869)
Eliza Fleenor Linder Callison (4/5/1817 – 2/11/1876) m. 11/4/1872
Charter members of Pleasant Hill Church of Christ in Lane County in 1850. He was an older brother to Harrison Shelley. Four of their sons, James Monroe, Troy, Roswell, and R. L., became prominent church leaders, and Troy and R. L. were preachers. One daughter married Doc Sitton, and another married Walter Huston. They are buried in Davidson Cemetery in Polk County, where the last name on their tombstone is spelled "Shelly." His third wife was a widow of Gilmore Callison.

Shelley, R. L. (c1852 – ?) **1852?**
Mary Gross m. 5/7/1876
Youngest son of Michael & Sena Shelley and a brother of James Monroe, Troy and Roswell. His wedding in 1876 was performed by Peter Rogers Burnett at the Pleasant Hill Church of Christ. He became a gospel preacher and he preached for the Drain and Elk Creek Christian Churches in Douglas County in the 1880s.

Shelley, Roswell (1846 – ?) **1848**
Mary Tatom m. 1878
Son of Michael & Sena Shelley and brother of James Monroe Shelley, Troy Shelley, and R. L. Shelley.

Shelley, Troy (1/6/1845 – 7/4/1928) **1848**
Annie Holland Lewis (2/15/1851 – 8/27/1936) m. 6/20/1871
Son of Michael & Sena Shelley. Their marriage was performed by Levi Lindsay Rowland and Glen Owen Burnett during the 1871 annual State Meeting. He began preaching in 1869 and he preached for more than 50 years. Most of his ministry was in eastern Oregon. From childhood he suffered with infantile paralysis. His younger brother, R. L., was a Christian preacher.

Shelton, John W. (5/1/1833 – 3/29/1922) **1846**
Mary Jane Burford (1836 – 12/17/1878) m. 7/10/1853 **1852**
Mary Matthews Mattoon m. 9/6/1882
He was a son of Zebedee & Sophronia Shelton, and she was a daughter of Hezekiah Burford. He was chosen to be a deacon in the Carlton Church in Yamhill County at the time of its organization in the summer of 1877. He was an agent for the *Pacific Christian Messenger* in the 1870s.

Shelton, Zebedee (4/13/1804 – 11/22/1857) **1846**
Sophronia Miller
Lavina Miller (10/22/1808 – 12/12/1894) m. 10/11/1839
Overland from Franklin County, Missouri. Two of their children died on the trail. Lavina was a sister to Mahala Miller McBride, wife of Dr. James McBride. The two families traveled together and settled near each other in Yamhill County. Their son, John W. Shelton, became a leader in Carlton Church. Buried in McBride Cemetery, Thomas Crawford McBride and Zebedee Shelton were among first to be buried there.

Sherwood, John (1815 – ?) **1850**
Hannah S. Bonney (c1820 – ?) m. 7/27/1837
She was a daughter of Truman & Pemelia Bonney and an older sister of Bradford Sherwood Bonney. He may have been the "Brother Sherwood" who was a co-laborer with John M. Harris in the Willamette Valley (see unsolved problems).

Shirley, Ethan Allen (6/20/1826 – 6/27/1903) **1850**
Mary (Polly) Turner Roundtree (1826 – 1914) m. 9/27/1853 **1852**
Came overland with the Elijah Davidson party in 1850. He married a Christian in 1853 and was baptized into Christ by John Ecles Murphy in June 1855. She was a sister to Dr. James Harrison Roundtree. In the early 1870s they were living in Monmouth and he was a member of the board of trustees of Christian College.

Shoemaker, Frederick X. (1823 – ?) **1852**
Ann (c1824 – ?) m. 2/20/1847
They came overland from Iowa with 2 small children and settled in the Salt Creek district of Polk County. Charter members of the Salt Creek Church. He was a delegate from the Salt Creek Church at the 1858 annual State Meeting.

Shortridge, James Henderson (7/18/1831 – 10/25/1916) **1851**
Amelia Savannah Adams (2/12/1835 – 7/31/1919) m. 3/13 or 18/1853 **1852**
He came overland from Mercer County, Illinois and she came overland from Iowa. They had "been sweethearts back east." After marriage they settled in Lane County. He ran blacksmith shop for Oregon and California stage line for 40 years and served as a deacon in the Hebron Church. A daughter, Mary, married John William Harris, a son of John M. & Jane Harris.

Shuck, Andrew J. (6/19/1815 – 2/10/1894) **1847**
Mary Conlee (3/15/1818 – 2/22/1907) m. 2/8/1838
Son of Jacob & Susannah Shuck. Overland from Iowa and settled in Yamhill County. Charter members of church established at Blackhawk schoolhouse in 1847, and later members of McMinnville Church. He was the first sheriff of Yamhill County and served 5 terms in state legislature. One daughter married Collin Austin Wallace, an elder in McMinnville Church. Buried in Masonic Cemetery in McMinnville.

Shuck, Jacob (1/17/1784 – 1/18/1856) **1847**
Susannah Jones (12/8/1785 – 1/26/1868) m. 3/14/1805
They came overland from Iowa and settled in Yamhill County. They were the parents of Andrew Shuck and Peter Shuck.

Shuck, Peter **1870**
Mary (4/?/1828 – ?)
Son of Jacob & Susannah Shuck and younger brother of Andrew Shuck. He preached in Iowa for several years before moving to Oregon in 1870. In 1861 he was preaching for the Eddyville Church in Wapello County, Iowa. He preached in Oregon through the 1870s and 1880s. In 1887 he was preaching for the Monitor and Bethany congregations in Marion County.

Shupe, (**Shoupe**) Michael R. (1810 – 1884) **1853**
Margaret W. VanNostern (12/?/1811 – /2/12/1870) m. 6/?/1843
Members of the Oakland Church in Douglas County. She died of typhoid fever, and an obituary notice reported: "Sister Shoup has been a member of the Church of Christ thirty-two years." Her funeral was preached by A. L. Todd.

Simmons, Samuel (2/3/1802 – 11/6/1882) **1845**
Mahala Amy Bunch (1/1/1801 – 11/6/1879) m. 12/?/1822
Settled on Howell's Prairie 11 miles east of Salem. Former Quakers. A daughter married Wesley Shannon in July 1847. Samuel was a nurseryman. He was on board of trustees of Rickreall Academy in 1854, vitally involved in beginning of Bethel Institute in 1855, and elected to original 9-man board of trustees of Monmouth University in 1856. One account called him a "prominent member of the Christian Church."

Sitton, Mary Shelley Laughlin (12/8/1839 – 7/1/1904) **1848**
Nathan "Doc" Sitton (9/2/1825 – 7/10/1902) m. 1/31/1871
He was not a Christian but "strongly endorsed his wife's efforts" to teach the Bible to neighborhood children. She was a daughter of Michael & Sena Shelley, and a sister to James Monroe Shelley, Troy Shelley, R. L. Shelley, Roswell Shelley, and Lodema Huston. She was a charter member of the Carlton Church. Buried in McBride Cemetery in Yamhill County.

Smith, Charles W. H. (M) (c1814 – ?) **1872**
P. (c1815 – ?)
Christian preacher from Indiana. Their daughter married a preacher named Allen Jefferson Huddleston. Both families settled on Bell Mountain, 3 miles east of Elkton in Douglas County. He helped to organize the church at Drain Station in Douglas County, and he served as an agent for the *Christian Herald* in the 1880s.

Smith, George Henry (c1805 – ?) **1846**
Margaret Copple (c1809 – ?) m. c1829
Came overland from Missouri with 6 children (and a 7th born on the trail) and settled near Hillsboro in Washington County. They were charter members of the Hillsboro Church on 10/17/1862. He served as a trustee of the church and was one of the first 2 deacons chosen in 1866.

Smith, Henry (1818 – 2/10/1885) **1846**
Suzannah (Susan) T. Wright (c1820 – ?)
They were members of the Mill Creek Church in Marion County. He served in the state legislature in the early 1880s. One record said of Henry: "He was a strong supporter of the church by his faithful attendance and financial aid, his pocketbook having been converted with him." He built the church building in Aumsville.

Smith, Isaac (2/12/1816 – 4/29/1897) **1853**
Margaret Butler (2/4/1822 – 12/8/1871) m. 12/9/1840
She was a daughter of Peter & Rachel Butler, and a sister to Ira F. M. Butler, Eliza Butler Ground and Elizabeth Butler Hutchinson. They settled on a farm at Luckiamute in Polk County, and were members of the Luckiamute Church. He served 2 terms in the state legislature and served 1 term as county judge. Buried in Davidson Cemetery 2 miles west of Monmouth in Polk County.

Smith, John Burris (1816 – 1901) **1846**
Emily Thorp (c1824 – ?) m. 2/6/1840
He was one of the first Christian preachers to travel overland to Oregon Territory. They settled in Polk County and she died there in the mid-1860s. She may have been a daughter of John & Lucy Thorp and a sister of Amanda Thorp Ford. John Burris Smith moved to Douglas County in 1870 and lived and preached there for the last 31 years of his life. He lived 9 miles north of Myrtle Creek.

Smith, John H. (2/18/1824 – 1/13/1893) **1846**
Martha Jane Lewis (9/11/1835 – 11/7/1913) m. 10/3/1850
She was a daughter of David R. and Mary Lewis, and they were members of the Lewisville Church. John H. Smith was described in one record as "a quiet, unobtrusive man and consistent member of the Christian Church." They lived in the Luckiamute (Lewisville) district of Polk County all their married life, and they are buried in New Smith Cemetery adjacent to Fir Crest Cemetery south of Monmouth in Polk County.

Snodgrass, David (1817 – ?) **1852**

Mary Ann m. 2/7/1839

David was a charter member of the Hillsboro Church in Washington County when it was organized on 10/17/1862. Mary Ann was not listed among the charter members.

Splawn, Greenbury (6/19/1847 – ?) **1850**

Amanda (Mandy) E. Matlock (c1853 – ?) m. 3/28/1869

It is not known if his parents, Moses & Ann Splawn, were Christians. His father died on the trail in 1850. She was a daughter of William & Nancy Matlock. They were among the charter members of the church that was established in 1871 at Splawn's School House near present-day Holley in Linn County.

Spriggs, J. W. **1870s**

wife's name unknown

He preached for the Salem Church in the 1870s and 1880s. Resigned on 5/17/1885 because he knew the members were openly "dissatisfied with my liberal teaching." At issue were his views on the inspiration of the scriptures.

Springer, Barney D. (1803 – 10/23/1863) **1850**

Susan (1/9/1805 – 3/10/1865)

Came overland from Iowa and settled briefly in Washington County. Moved to Amity in Yamhill County. Members of the Amity Church. Buried in Amity Cemetery

Springer, Barney H. (9/26/1829 – 1/25/1902) **1850**

Eliza Warren (3/16/1836 – 5/13/1912) m. 5/17/1855

Son of Barney & Susan Springer and younger brother of G. W. Springer. Settled in Amity. They were members of Amity Church and they are buried in Amity Cemetery.

Springer, George Washington (2/10/1822 – 8/14//1880) **1850**

Sarah A. Clark m. 2/?/1848

Son of Barney & Susan Springer and older brother of Barney H. Springer. An obit of George noted: "In the summer of 1844, under the preaching of Elder Israel L. Clark, he made confession of his faith, and was by him immersed and received into the Christian congregation, then just being organized in Benton County, Iowa." Members of Amity Church and supervisor of the Sunday School. They are buried in Amity Cemetery.

Stafford, William (3/11/1814 – 6/30/1888) **1852**

Priscilla Jane Ramsey (1818 – 1/23/1903) m. 2/20/1836

Overland from Missouri. Settled in the Mohawk Valley in Lane County. The Staffords were baptized into Christ one year after arriving in Oregon Territory. They were cited in one account for "both working zealously thereafter for the promotion of the cause of truth and morality." They moved to Halsey in Linn County in 1866 and became members of the Halsey Church.

Stanley, David Truman **1876**

wife's name unknown

Graduate of Bethany College. Preached for Oregon churches in the 1870s. Became associated with *Christian Messenger* in June 1876 and changed name to *Pacific Christian Messenger.* Succeeded Thomas F. Campbell as president of Christian College in 1882, and served until 1889. Co-editor of the *Christian Herald* in the 1880s.

Stanton, Alfred (7/23/1808 – 6/11/1892) **1847**
Phoebe Fail (5/11/1815 – 3/11/1886) m. 1/9/1831
Laura Convers m. 3/8/1887
Phoebe was pregnant when they came overland from Indiana with 5 children. Their 6th child was born in Oregon. They settled on 640 acres just east of Salem in Marion County. Alfred ran a nursery business. Charter members of the Salem Church. He served on board of trustees for Christian College.

Stanton, Benjamin (c1814 – 10/18/1888) **1853**
Matilda Baldwin (3/15/1816 – 1/14/1906) m. 1835
Overland from Tennessee. Settled on Butte Creek about 3 miles north of Sublimity in Marion County. He represented Marion County in the state legislature 1882-1884. They are both buried in Macleay Cemetery.

Steeples, Perrin (8/8/1828 – ?) **1852**
Mary Eleanor Lafferty (? – 10/3/1889) m. 3/26/1852
They were newlyweds when they came overland from Clark County, Illinois. They settled in Washington County and eventually moved to a farm 2 miles southeast of Hillsboro. Charter members of the Hillsboro Christian Church in Washington County when it was organized on 10/17/1862.

Stewart, Lewis (11/18/1819 – ?) **1847?**
Nancy Neal (c1829 – ?) m. 10/?/1849
They settled in Linn County. He was a delegate from the Forks Santiam Church in Linn County at the 1858 annual State Meeting.

Stout, Jonathan L. (9/29/1812 – 3/4/1896 **1850**
Abigail E. Beckwith m. 12/31/1843
Alice Gearhart
They came overland from Ohio and settled in Yamhill County. He contributed to the fund to send the *Pacific Christian Messenger* to the inmates in the Oregon Penitentiary. He is buried in McBride Cemetery beside several of his children, but there is no record of burial for either of his wives.

Strode, Dillard A. (1835 – 1911)
Mellissa (1843 – 1920)
Charter members of the Day's Creek Church in Douglas County in 1877. Dillard Strode served as one of the elders of this church.

Stump, David (10/29/1819 – 2/21/1886) **1845**
Catherine Elizabeth Chamberlin (2/23/1835 –?) m. 3/10/1850 **1844**
Settled on Luckiamute river 6 miles south of Monmouth. Prominent supporters of Monmouth University, Christian College, and *Pacific Christian Messenger.* Moved to Monmouth in the 1870s. Members of Monmouth Church. He represented Polk County in the state legislature 1874-1876. Their daughter, Mary, married Thomas Franklin Campbell in 1885. Buried in Fir Crest Cemetery south of Monmouth.

Sullins, (Sullens), Isaac M. (1822 – ?) **1853**
Elizabeth C. Tomlinson m. 7/12/1849
They were charter members of the Mill Creek Church in Marion County, and Isaac was one of the first two deacons chosen to serve the church.

Taylor, Felix M. (1816 – ?) **1847**
Rachel (c1818 – ?) m. 3/23/1837
They were members of the Mill Creek Church in Marion County.

Taylor, George Washington (3/5/1831 – ?) **1852**
Mary Whetstone
Julia Ann (Julyane) Parker m. 5/15/1853
They were members of the Mill Creek Church in Marion County.

Taylor, Henry Wells (2/18/1808 – 5/4/1890) **1852**
Charlotte (Charlotta) Peterson (10/?/1810 – 3/28/1883) m. 11/28/1829
Settled south of Cottage Grove in Lane County. He preached in Lane and surrounding counties for many years. Theirs is the first monument in Taylor-Lane Cemetery, and the cemetery is evidently named for them and their family. It is located on the edge of their donation land claim. Two other Christian preachers and their wives, John M. Harris and Joseph H. Sharp, are buried in Taylor-Lane Cemetery.

Taylor, John (3/27/1792 – 10/25/1870) **1847**
Elizabeth Murphy (c1794 – 1874) m. 12/?/1813
He was a veteran of the War of 1812. They came overland from Missouri with teen twins, Melville and Milsena. They were members of the Mill Creek Church, and they are buried in Aumsville Cemetery.

Taylor, Joseph Peterson (7/27/1830 – 3/9/1912) **1852**
Mary Angeline Small (9/25/1837 – 5/23/1917) m. 12/24/1857
Oldest son of Henry & Charlotte Taylor and first white settler in Lane County village that would be called Hebron. Joseph & Mary became teachers in Coast Fork Union Sabbath School that was organized on 5/24/1857 and were married later that year. They lived in the community all their lives and were active in the Hebron Church. Buried in Taylor-Lane Cemetery near his parents.

Taylor, Melville (1/22/1829 – ?) **1847**
Cyrena (Serena) McDonald m. 12/9/1853 **1852**
Members of the Mill Creek Church in Marion County. His parents were John & Elizabeth Taylor.

Taylor, Oliver Perry (1823 – ?) **1850**
Sarah Greenstreet (c1825 – ?) m. 10/31/1844
He may have been a son of John & Elizabeth Taylor, as they settled on adjoining farms in Marion County. They were charter members of the Mill Creek Church and he served as a deacon for many years.

Thorp, John (10/13/1796 – 1/9/1881) **1844**
Lucy Embree (? – 1832)
Parents of Emily Thorp Smith, the wife of John Burris Smith, and of Amanda Thorp Ford, the wife of Marcus Ford. Each of these families were living in Polk County in the late 1840s. He represented Polk County in the territorial legislature in the early 1850s.

Thurston, Hiram **1860s**
wife's name unknown
He settled on the North Fork of the Coquille River in Coos County. He wrote to the editor of the *Christian Messenger* in the 1870s and begged for his support in persuading some Christian preachers to come into his remote area and establish a church.

Todd, Abbott Levi James (10/12/1820 – 4/23/1886) **1852**
Louvina Gaither (? – 1843) m. 1842
Martha Gaither (? – 1846) m. 1845
Angeline Lorraine Tate (1/5/1832 – 12/7/1917) m. 10/12/1848
One of the most indefatigable preachers in Oregon church history. He lived in Lookingglass Valley and traveled horseback more than 68,000 miles in a ministry that spanned 30 years in Douglas and surrounding counties. Mentor to younger preachers such as Edward A. Chase and Isaac N. Muncy. Agent for *Pacific Christian Messenger* and *Christian Herald*. He is buried in a small cemetery in northern Douglas County next to the former site of Shoestring Valley Church that he helped build in the 1880s.

Todd, Jonathan (2/12/1816 – 8/29/1905) **1865**
Patsey A. Brock (5/26/1825 – 2/11/1899)
Members of the McMinnville Church in Yamhill County. He served as an elder in this church in the 1880s and 1890s. Their daughter, Mary Elizabeth, married Peter Rogers Burnett on 10/14/1866. They are buried in Masonic Cemetery in McMinnville.

Toney, James (1798 – 4/?/1891) **1847**
Martha (Patsy) Thornton (1798 – 1863) m. 4/20/1822
Mary Minor m. 9/1/1890
Came overland from Missouri and settled in Yamhill County. Their daughter and son-in-law, Melissa & Owen Turner, settled on an adjacent claim. Another daughter, Malinda, married Caleb Payne. William L. Toney was their son.

Toney, William L. (1/30/1827 – 8/19/1923) **1847**
Elsie (Elcey) (Alcy) Ann (7/?/1837 – 1916) m. 3/4/1851 **1850**
Came overland from Missouri with his parents, James & Patsy Toney. He contributed to the fund that enabled A. V. McCarty to move to Oregon. His older sister married Owen P. Turner and his younger sister married Caleb Payne. William & Elcey were members of the McMinnville Church and they are buried in Masonic Cemetery in McMinnville.

Townsend, Gamaliel George (8/12/1803 – c1884) **1850**
Mariam Sampson (1809 – c/1891) m. 5/8/1822
They came overland from Illinois and settled 3 miles southeast of Woodburn in Marion County. They raised a large family of 16 children. One historical record commented on Gabriel's "religious enthusiasm" for the cause of the Christian Church. Although the meetinghouse of the Christian Church was 10 miles from their home, they were devoted to the church and regularly made the 20-mile round-trip journey for worship.

Townsend, Washington R. (11/27/1846 – ?) **1850**
Nancy Emeline Stephens (12/21/1857 – ?) **1852**
He was only 3 years old when his parents started across the plains. Despite limited educational opportunities, he became a teacher. Following his marriage, he settled on a farm in Marion County.

Trullinger, Daniel (2/6/1801 – 1/23 or 29/1869) **1848**
Elizabeth Johnson (1807 – 1887 or 1888) m. 4/27/1823
He had preached for many years in the area around Fountain County, Indiana, before moving to Oregon Territory. They settled near Rock Creek in southwestern Clackamas County, and they were charter members of the Rock Creek Church of Christ. He preached in Oregon for 20 years. After his death, his wife wrote: "He immersed in every stream in Oregon from the Callipooia to the Columbia river."

Trullinger, L. B. **1860s**
Alice Flinn m. 6/17/1891
This descendant of Daniel Trullinger was preaching in Oregon in the 1880s, and he may have begun preaching as early as the 1870s.

Tucker, Samuel (4/18/1782 – 1867) **1848**
Sarah Black (2/14/1804 – 1867) m. 8/2/1836
They were members of the Mill Creek Church in Marion County. Their daughter, Lucia, married Elias Cox 11/27/1851. Elias & Lucia were members of the Bethany Church. Most likely, Rebecca Caroline Tucker Wright was also their daughter. The Wrights were members of the Mill Creek Church.

Tucker, Thomas (1810 – ?) **1853**
Hester Lemon m. 4/21/1831
Overland from Illinois with 3 children. Charter members of the Grand Prairie Church in Lane County. Their document, dated November 28, 1858, began: "We whose names are hereunto annexed agree to unite ourselves together as a Church of Christ. To take the Bible as our only rule of faith and practice and to be known as the Grand Prairie Congregation." He was a delegate for this church at the annual State Meeting in 1863.

Tucker, Walter H. (1816 – ?) **1840s**
Mary Coffee (1818 – 1870) m. 4/24/1838
They were members of the Mill Creek Church in Marion County, and he was a delegate from this church at the 1867 annual State Meeting.

Turner, Henry L. (1810 – ?) **1852**
Judith (Julia Ann) Sharp (1/16/1803 – 7/26/1882) m. 7/5/1835
Gave their name to the town of Turner in Marion County. On 5/17/1878 they deeded 8 acres of land as a site for an annual camp meeting. County meetings were held there in 1878-1884. An annual State Meeting has been held on the site every year since 1885. The Turner children erected a large tabernacle on the property as a memorial to their parents in 1891. The Turners are buried in Twin Oaks Cemetery in Turner.

Turner, Owen P. (12/10/1813 – 5/11/1895) **1847**
Melissa (Mazella) B. Toney (12/21/1823 – ?) m. 3/21/1842
She was a daughter of James & Patsy Toney and an older sister of William L. Toney. They were among the contributors to the fund to bring A.V. McCarty to Oregon. They came overland from Missouri with the Toneys and settled in Yamhill County.

Turner, Thomas (1/16/1835 – 2/7/1900) **1852**
Mahala F. Cochran Rice (7/14/1846 – ?) **1846**
They were members of the Harrisburg Church in Linn County in the 1870s, and Thomas served as one of the elders of the church.

Umphlet, Stanley (1810 – 3/17/1893) **1845**

Frances (Fanny) Jane Earl (1/1/1815 – 4/?/1847) m. 6/?/1839

Serena Cook (12/21/1833 – 3/21/1919) m. 10/20/1849 **1850**

Jane died in childbirth and was buried at Miller's Gap. A daughter of Stanley & Jane married Stephen Dodridge Powell on 5/23/1858. After Stanley's marriage to Serena they settled in Amity in Yamhill County. Members of the Amity Church. She is buried in Amity Cemetery but there is no record of his burial.

Underwood, P. P. (c1846 – ?) **1878**

Annie E. (c1851 – ?)

They moved from Gilroy in Santa Clara County, California to Wasco County. They became members of the Fifteen-Mile Creek Church near Dufur. He shared some of the preaching responsibilities with a minister named George H. Barnett. In the mid 1880s they were living in Boyd in Wasco County and he was an agent for the *Christian Herald.*

Vail, Joel (1828 – 10/14/1906) **1853**

Mary Isabel Bramwell (? – 6/17/1854) m. 8/14/1853 **1847**

Mary Elizabeth Lee (3/2/1839 – 1/1/1931) m. 5/7/1857

He was a Baptist, but shortly after his marriage to Mary Elizabeth Lee he embraced the Restoration Movement. That was in September 1857. He was employed as a teacher at Pleasant Hill School in Lane County and began preaching for Oregon Christians in Lane and surrounding counties. They moved to Linn County in 1866.

Vanderpool, Medders (1799 – 1896) **1846**

Margaret E. Linville (2/23/1818 – 5/22/1888) m. 2/?/1842

She was the daughter of Richard & Mary Linville, and a sister to Harrison Linville and Catherine Linville Crowley. They settled in Polk County.

Vawter, Cyrus (9/28/1830 – 2/11/1864) **1851**

Sarah Jane Finley (5/18/1840 – ?) m. 12/10/1856

He was the son of Beverly Vawter, a well-known Christian preacher in Indiana. He came overland with the Philemon Vawter Crawford family to whom he was related. They were members of the Crawfordsville Church in Linn County. Cyrus found employment as a miller at the R. C. Finley flour mill owned by his father-in-law, and he is buried at the old Finley Family Cemetery a short distance west of Crawfordsville.

Vernon, George Washington (1812 – ?) **1853**

Rebecca Greenway (1808 – 8/19/1891) m. 11/13/1828

Missouri Christians who migrated to Texas in 1847. They moved from Texas and settled at Tangent, near Albany, in Linn County. She was baptized into Christ by Thomas M. Allen in Missouri in 1837. One account described her as "a devoted Christian." Her funeral was preached by Mac Waller to "a large audience." They are buried in Albany Cemetery.

Vickers, Andrew J. (1816 – ?) **1845**

Ann Engle (11/20/1824 – 4/20/1865) m. 11/15/1838

Came overland with 3 small daughters, 2 of whom died of measles and were buried at Fort Laramie. They settled in Clackamas County. Ann was a charter member of the Rock Creek Church of Christ south of Molalla, but Andrew may not have been a Christian. He is not mentioned in the church record book.

Walker, Gilliam H. (1800 – ?) **1851**

Rhoda Finley (Findley) (1/25/1799 – 8/28/1892) m. 3/27/1832

Their daughters were married to Edson Kimsey and John Nash. All three families were members of the Mill Creek Church in Marion County.

Wallace, Collin Austin (1/17/1834 – ?) **1852**

Eliza J. Shuck (3/23/1839 – 5/31/1922) m. 1857 **1847**

She was a daughter of Andrew & Mary Shuck. In the 1860 census they were living along the south fork of the Yamhill river in Yamhill County. They were members of the McMinnville Church, and he served as an elder with this church in the 1880s.

Wallace, William T. (1813 – 1899) **1845**

Susannah R. (Susan) Herren (1826 – 1906) m. 5/25/1841

She was a daughter of John & Theodosha Herren and a sister to William John Herren and Daniel S. Herren. Along with her parents and many others, they mistakenly followed Stephen Meek on his short cut in 1845. In the 1850 census William was listed as a carpenter, and they were living in Yamhill County. Later, they lived in southern Oregon and California.

Waller, George Townsend (9/24/1830 – 12/24/1893) **1847**

Mary Jane Doty (7/18/1835 – 1/22/1906) m. 6/24/1855

Son of Jane Waller. Brother of Mac Waller, Thomas O. Waller, Mary Ann Waller Boothby, and Emily Waller Brunk. She may have been a younger sister of Reuben Doty. They were members of the Eola Church, and he was a delegate for this church at the 1858 annual State Meeting. Buried in Fir Crest Cemetery south of Monmouth.

Waller, Hugh McNary "Mac" (9/9/1817 – 2/25/1893) **1847**

Mary E. Davidson (2/26/1833 – 12/7/1889) m. 8/18/1850 **1847**

He had preached in Illinois for a few years before moving to Oregon. He arrived in Oregon City on his 30th birthday. It is estimated that he baptized more than 7,000 persons in his lifetime. His ministry in Oregon spanned 45 years. She was a daughter of Hezekiah & Melissa Davidson. They are buried in Hilltop Cemetery in Polk County.

Waller, Jane L. McNary (11/23/1792 – 11/23/1869) **1847**

Widowed mother of Mac Waller, Townsend Waller, T. O. Waller, Mary Ann Waller Boothby, and Emily Waller Brunk. She came overland with her sons in 1847 and settled with them in Polk County. She died on her 77th birthday. She is buried in Fir Crest Cemetery south of Monmouth.

Waller, Thomas O. (11/20/1823 – 1913) **1849**

Maria Livermore (5/31/1828 – 3/9/1863) m. 3/26/1847

Rachel A. Mulkey Atterbury (2/23/1838 – 1914) m. 7/5/1879

Son of Jane Waller. He was a brother of Mac Waller, Townsend Waller, Emily Waller Brunk, and Mary Ann Waller Boothby. They all lived in Polk County. Maria was buried in Shaw Cemetery in Polk County, and Thomas & Rachel are buried in Fir Crest Cemetery south of Monmouth. Rachel was a daughter of Luke & Rutha Mulkey, and she had formerly been married to Jonathan Atterbury.

Walling, Judge Jerome B. (1810 – ?) **1847**
Sarah (c1814 – ?) m. 3/4/1829
They came overland from Iowa with other members of the Walling family. He represented Yamhill County in the territorial legislature in 1849-1850, and then served as a county judge.. Dr. James McBride immersed "Judge Walling and his amiable lady" during a gospel meeting with the Amity Church in Yamhill County in May 1855. He was an older brother to Jesse Dutton Walling.

Walling, Jesse Dutton (4/1/1816 – 1870) **1847**
Elizabeth Ann Wise (1822 – 1893) m. 12/1/1839
They may not have been Christians, but several members of the Walling and Wise families were affiliated with the Restoration Movement. They sent their children to school at Bethel Institute.

Ward, Thomas M. (8/15/1815 – 4/5/1888) **1847**
Mary Hannah Morgan (4/25/1822 – 12/26/1901) m. 11/14/1844
They settled in Linn County. He was a delegate for the Sand Ridge Church in Linn County at the 1858 annual State Meeting.

Warriner, Dr. William C. (1814 – ?) **1853**
Emily Ritchey (c1825 – ?) m. 2/22/1848
Settled southeast of Bethel in Polk County. She was a younger sister of Mary Ritchey Lindsay, wife of Horace Lindsay. The Warriners were members of the Bethel Church. He was a delegate for the Bethel Church at the 1858 annual State Meeting, and he was a member of the board of trustees of Bethel College. In 1872 he was a member of the board of trustees of Christian College.

Watson, Sanford (1/28/1801 – 7/6/1870) **1849**
Betsy Ann Stevenson (? – 9/?/1835) m. 6/3/1833
Maria Jane Elder (5/24/1809 – ?) m. 3/18/1839
Maria Jane was a younger sister of Alfred R. Elder, and the two families came overland together from Illinois. The Watsons settled 2 miles southeast of Bethel in Polk County. Strong supporters of Bethel College, where he was a member of the board of trustees. They were members of the Bethel Church, and he was a delegate for that church at the 1863 annual State Meeting.

Watt, Ahio Scott (1/15/1824 – 5/15/1909) **1848**
Mary Elizabeth Elder (c1829 – ?) m. 7/23/1850 **1849**
The Watt family were Baptists but they had numerous contacts with the Restoration Movement. Ahio was the son of John & Mary Watt and a younger brother of Joseph Watt. Mary Elizabeth was a daughter of a Christian preacher named Alfred R. Elder. Ahio was a surveyor for Yamhill County, and they lived near Lafayette. He served in the state senate 1876-1880. They may have attended the Lafayette Church.

Watt, John (11/11/1792 – 7/19/1854) **1848**
Mary Scott (2/1/1802 – 11/21/1855) m. 1816 or 1817
Overland from Ohio. She was a younger sister of Felix Scott, Sr. Their sons were Joseph and Ahio. The Watt family was Baptist but they had a number of ties to the Restoration Movement. They settled in Amity in Yamhill County, and they may have attended the Amity Church. They are buried in Amity Cemetery.

Watt, Joseph (12/17/1817 – 8/30/1900) **1844**

Levina (Lavina) A. Lyons (1833 – 1914) m. 6/28/1860

It was at his residence near Amity that Glen Owen Burnett performed the marriage ceremony for John Eakin Lyle & Ellen Scott on 11/3/1846. Joseph Watt was related to Ellen Scott. He was the son of John & Mary Watt and an older brother of Ahio Scott Watt. They may have attended Amity Church. Their 8-year-old daughter's obituary was published in *Christian Messenger* 8/12/1871. They are buried in Amity Cemetery.

Weddle, D. D. (8/10/1799 – ?) **1870**

wife's name unknown.

Baptized into Christ in October 1829 in Monroe County, Indiana. Began preaching in 1845 and, by his own accounting, led "many thousands" to become Christians. He and his wife followed their son to Oregon in 1870 and settled in Lane County. Members of the Mohawk Church. In the 1880 census they were still living in the Mohawk district of Lane County.

Weddle, Elijah (1834 – 4/27/1912) **1853**

Margaret Ann Slover (1837 – 11/23/1915) m. 12/27/1855

Son of a Christian preacher named D. D. Weddle. On 5/12/1867 he became a deacon in the Rock Creek Church of Christ south of Molalla in Clackamas County. Later he moved to Stayton in Marion County where he performed several marriages as a justice of the peace. He and his wife are buried in Lone Oak Cemetery in Stayton.

Westerfield, Dr. Alexander B. (3/9/1822 – 11/10/1869 **1853**

Rebecca Ann Chrisman (2/17/1837 – 7/4/1895)

He was one of the contributors to the fund that enabled A. V. McCarty to move to Oregon in 1847. He came across the plains six years later. They settled in the Lafayette district of Yamhill County and became members of the Lafayette Church. He served in the territorial legislature in the 1850s. They are buried in Lafayette Masonic Cemetery.

Whitley, Samuel P. (12/25/1784 – 9/28/1868) **1847**

Catherine L. Miller McNary (5/27/1791 – 11/20/1869) m. 3/30/1817

Came overland with Mac Waller and other Illinois Christians, including their son-in-law, Hiram Alva Johnson. Settled in Marion County.

Whitman, Squire Stoten (5/1/1818 – 5/22/1892) **1850**

Elizabeth Davidson (5/29/1823 – 10/18/1896) m. 2/26/1839

They came overland with other Christians from Illinois. She was a daughter of Elijah & Margaret Davidson. They were strong supporters of Monmouth University and Christian College, and he served on the board of trustees of both institutions. The Whitmans were among the 35 charter members of Monmouth Church. They are buried in Davidson Cemetery in Polk County.

Whitney, George Miller (2/29/1830 – 12/4/1895) **1853**

Henrietta B. Brayton (1834 – 6/13/1917) m. 7/28/1857 **1852**

He was Sunday School superindentent for the Mill Creek Church in Marion County in the late 1850s. She was a daughter of William H. & Lucy Brayton. He began preaching around 1860 and became one of the most effective evangelists in the Restoration Movement in Oregon. His name was put forward as a candidate for Congress in the mid-1870s. They were residents of Eugene in Lane County, and they are buried in the pioneer cemetery adjacent to the University of Oregon campus.

Wigle, John L. (10/17/1838 – ?) **1852**
Eliza E. White m. 2/12/1862
Eva Norton m. 10/16/1906
He was just turning 14 when his family arrived in Oregon. It is known that he was preaching for Christian Churches in Oregon in the 1870s, and it is likely that he began preaching in the late 1860s.

Wilbur, Fones **1850s**
Very little is known about this man. He was a trustee of the Bethany Church in Marion County and the foreman of the building committee. He was a delegate to the Republican State Convention in 1860 and a teacher at Bethany School in the 1860s. He evidently remained a bachelor and he resided with the Thomas J. Wilcox family for several years.

Wilcox, Thomas James (4/8/1822 – 8/17/1892)) **1853**
Elizabeth Jane Johnson (8/22/1826 – 2/13/1873) m. 10/12/1845
Pauline E. Hargrove (c1842 – ?) m. 4/20/1877
Came overland with the Mulkeys, Bargers and Crabtrees. Elizabeth Wilcox was a niece to Philip Mulkey. They settled in the Silverton area of Marion County and became members of the Bethany Church. He was a delegate for the Bethany Church at the 1863 annual State Meeting. In the 1870s they were living in Aumsville and he was an agent for *Pacific Christian Messenger*. They are buried in Aumsville Cemetery.

Williams, Enos C. (9/24/1818 – 2/24/1890 **1845**
Willamina Craig Mealy (4/17/1817 – 1/15/1883) m. 2/24/1848
Charter members of the Amity Church. He was an agent for the *Pacific Christian Messenger* in the 1870s. They are buried in Amity Cemetery.

Willis, Leo (c1831 – 4/10/1899)
Carolina (c1839 – ?)
He was pastor of a Baptist congregation in Salem when he chose to affiliate with the Restoration Movement in the mid-1870s. He became a leader in the Christian Church in Salem.

Wilson, William H. (12/18/or 12/28/1822 – 2/11/1902) **1843**
Hannah R. Dickinson Gilliam (11/5/1832 – 5/27/1919) m. 10/1 or 10/22/1849 **1847**
He was in "The Great Migration" of 1843. Settled at Yoncalla in Douglas County. They were married 52 years. He represented Douglas County in the state legislature in the 1860s. They were members of the Yoncalla Church. One record called her "a consistent Christian," and said of him: "He was a consistent member of the Christian Church and his religion constituted a vital force in his career."

Wisecarver, Jacob (2/5/1825 – 4/12/1887) **1862**
Jane McCormick (10/11/1824 – 3/12/1907) m. 3/?/1845
They were among the contributors to the fund to bring A. V. McCarty to Oregon in 1847, but they did not follow him to Oregon for another 15 years. They were members of the McMinnville Church and he served as a deacon in that church. They are buried in Masonic Cemetery in McMinnville.

Witzel, Benjamin A. (1/8/1822 – 2/27/1905) **1854**

Lavila Hendrix (Hendricks (c1817 – 8/10/1880) m. 1840

Located near Aumsville in Marion County, and lived there for more than half a century. He represented Marion County in the state legislature 1866-1868. One record calls Benjamin "a devout member of the Christian Church."

Wolverton, Bruce (1853 – ?) **1853**

Mary Ann Humphreys (10/16/1856 – 10/8/1935) m. 11/16/1880 **1856**

Son of John & Mary Jane Wolverton. He was born on the Oregon Trail and was 7 weeks old when his family arrived in the Willamette Valley. His parents were former Quakers who converted to the Restoration Movement in 1868. He graduated from Christian College and was the first preacher for the Christian Church in Portland in the early 1880s. Co-editor of the *Christian Herald* in the 1880s with David Truman Stanley.

Wolverton, John (12/4//1822 – 12/30/1902) **1853**

Mary Jane Nealy (Neeley) (5/1/1825 – 9/20/1907) m. 11/24/1847

Settled in Polk County and became Christians in 1868. John was baptized into Christ on December 4, 1868 during a gospel meeting in Monmouth with James W. Butler of Abingdon, Illinois. In the early 1870s he was a member of the board of trustees of Christian College and served as a deacon in Monmouth Church. Their son, Bruce Wolverton, graduated from Christian College and became a well-known preacher.

Woodford, Alonzo M. (10/25/1844 – 12/11/1920) **1852**

Eliza A. Dyer (3/5/1857 – 6/2/1911) m. 12/27/1873 **1865**

Son of Harry L. Woodford. Overland from Ray County, Missouri. His mother died on the Oregon Trail, and his father returned to Missouri 5 years later. Alonzo remained in Oregon and moved to Medford in Jackson County where he became postmaster. Members of the Medford Church. One account noted of Alonzo & Eliza: "In matters of faith the family are Christians and take an active interest in the work of that church."

Woodford, Harry L. (c1827 – 1894) **1852**

? Pagett (died on trail in '52)

His wife died on the trail but he continued on to Oregon with his children. Settled in Douglas County and remained 5 years. Returned to Missouri in 1857.

Woods, Caleb (1/12/1806 – 2/4/1896) **1847**

Margaret McBride (5/29/1809 – 1/28/1871) m. 1/11/1828 or 1829

She was a daughter of Thomas Crawford McBride and a sister to Dr. James McBride. Their son, George Lemuel Woods, was elected third governor of Oregon in 1866. They are buried in Buena Vista Cemetery in Polk County.

Woods, George Lemuel (7/30/1832 – 1/14/1890) **1847**

Louisa A. McBride (3/18/1835 – 10/2/1924) m. 4/25/1852 **1846**

Son of Caleb & Margaret McBride Woods and grandson of Thomas Crawford McBride. Married his first cousin. She was a daughter of Dr. James & Mahala McBride. John R. McBride was her brother. George was educated under William Lysander Adams and at Bethel Institute. Became a lawyer but also did some preaching. At the age of 34 he was elected third governor of Oregon in 1866. He was an elder in the Salem Church.

Woods, James Caleb (1/11/1838 – 4/18/1912) **1847**
Charlotte L. Caples m. 1/31/1860 **1850**
He was a son of Caleb & Margaret Woods, a younger brother of Governor George Woods, and a grandson of Thomas Crawford McBride. They were married at Lafayette in Yamhill County by his uncle, Dr. James McBride. They were members of the Lafayette Church for many years, but in later years they were members of the First Christian Church in Portland.

Woolen, George (1820 – 6/15/1892) **1850**
Julia (Juliann) Eisenhardt (c1824 – ?) m. 1/15/1840
Charter members of the Bethany Church in Marion County in 1851. She was most likely a sister to Sarah Eisenhardt Mascher, the wife of Christ Frederick Mascher. Both of these families were from Baltimore, Maryland, and they probably came overland together in 1850. George Woolen served as an elder in the Bethany Church in the 1880s. They are buried in Bethany Pioneer Cemetery.

Wright, Isaac W. (1828 – ?) **1852**
Rebecca Caroline Tucker m. 7/4/1858 **1848**
He was baptized into Christ in September 1862 during a 4-day gospel meeting at Mill Creek Church in Marion County. His wife, Rebecca Caroline, was already a member of this church. She was most likely a daughter of Samuel & Sarah Tucker, and a younger sister of Lucia Tucker Cox.

Key: m. (date of marriage)
bold date (year arrived in Oregon)

NOTES

NOTES TO PROLOGUE

1. This statement was made by Thomas Campbell (1763-1854) on September 7, 1809, just prior to the first public reading of his *Declaration and Address*. This document, long considered the Magna Carta of the Campbell movement, was a 56-page pamphlet when it first came from the press in 1809. Now generally accepted as one of the great classics of Christian literature, it has been described by William Warren Sweet as one of the greatest religious documents ever produced in America. Thomas Campbell was a faithful minister in the Seceder Presbyterian Church in Ireland before his immigration to America in 1807. By 1809 he had decided to withdraw from his ancestral church, and he published to the world his reason for this action in the *Declaration and Address*. By the time it had left the press, his son, Alexander, had joined him in America and his greater aggressiveness and platform eloquence caused his father to surrender to him the leadership of the reform movement which the *Declaration and Address* had initiated. The *Declaration and Address* was a comprehensive statement of the restoration and unity principles which were to become the central themes in the plea of the Restoration Movement.
2. This quotation is taken from the text of the *Last Will and Testament of the Springfield Presbytery*. This document, originally issued on June 28, 1804, was one of the first statements of religious freedom ever proclaimed in the Western Hemisphere. Its authorship is uncertain since it was signed by five men, but it has generally been accepted that Barton Warren Stone (1772-1844) was the man responsible for its publication. The document denounced all human creeds and appealed to the Bible as the only rule of faith and practice. It also declared in favor of the name "Christian" as the only proper name for the followers of Christ. The reading of the *Last Will and Testament* on June 28, 1804, initiated a movement of independent "Christian" churches. Along with the *Declaration and Address*, the *Last Will and Testament of the Springfield Presbytery* is considered to be one of the great religious charters that gave direction to the Restoration Movement.
3. Two antecedent movements in the Eastern states were led by James O'Kelly and two brothers, David and Rice Haggard (beginning in Virginia in 1794), and by Abner Jones and Elias Smith (beginning in New England in 1801). These movements

felt a kinship with Barton Stone, and they referred to each other as "Christians East" and "Christians West." When Elias Smith began editing the *Herald of Gospel Liberty* in the fall of 1808, he gave attention in his paper to both "Christians East" and "Christians West." The O'Kelly-Haggard and Jones-Smith movements entered into a merger in 1811 and became known as the "Christian Connexion," but soon after this time David and Rice Haggard migrated west and began working with the Stone movement. The "Christian Connexion" included the Stone-Mulkey churches from 1811 to 1832, and whenever the eastern Christians moved west they naturally affiliated with Stone and Mulkey. However, portions of the "Christian Connexion" north of the Ohio River did not agree with some of the teachings of Alexander Campbell (particularly his rational interpretation of the Word of God and his view of baptism for the forgiveness of sins). Consequently, when the Stone-Mulkey and Campbell movements merged in 1832 it signaled the parting of the way between portions of the "Christian Connexion" north of the Ohio River and the Stone-Mulkey churches.

4. For information on Benjamin Lynn embracing the Stone movement and influencing John Mulkey in the same direction, see C. P. Cawthorn and N. L. Warnell, *Pioneer Baptist Church Records of South-Central Kentucky and the Upper Cumberland of Tennessee, 1799-1899*, 1985. For information on the relationship between Lewis Byram and John Mulkey, see *An Autobiography of Abner Hill, Pioneer Preacher of Tennessee, Alabama, and Texas.* This unpublished 43-page typescript is in the possession of R. L. Roberts in Abilene, Texas.
5. Thomas Crawford McBride (1777-1857) was preaching for a Baptist church in Jackson County, Tennessee, just across the state line from John Mulkey's Mill Creek meetinghouse, when he followed Mulkey's lead in 1810. Other preachers in the Stockton Valley Baptist Association who followed John Mulkey's example included his brother, Philip Mulkey, Abner Hill, Corder Stone, Thomas Stone, Martin Trapp, Martin Trapp, Jr., and William Randolph.
6. *An Autobiography of Abner Hill*, 13.
7. Beginning in 1825, Alexander Campbell (1788-1866) wrote a series of 30 articles in the *Christian Baptist* entitled "A Restoration of the Ancient Order of Things." It was an attempt to evaluate the practices of Protestantism by the light of the New Testament pattern. The spirit of these articles was strongly

iconoclastic, and Campbell mercilessly attacked the clergy, creeds, and authoritative councils of Protestantism.

8. Walter Scott (1796-1861) was educated at the University of Edinburgh. He immigrated to America in 1818, and became associated with the Campbell movement in the winter of 1821-1822. Along with the Campbells and Stone, Scott is generally considered to be one of the four "founding fathers" of the Restoration Movement in America. Scott suggested the name *Christian Baptist* to Campbell and was a frequent contributor to that periodical. He submitted his articles under the pseudonym of "Philip" and saw his relationship to Alexander Campbell as being the same as Philip Melanchthon bore to Martin Luther. His greatest contributions to the Restoration Movement were his work as an evangelist of the Mahoning Association (1827-1830) and his authorship of a book entitled *The Gospel Restored* (1836). The source for the statement on the Western Reserve being "the principal theater" of the "Disciples" movement is A. S. Hayden, *Early History of the Disciples in the Western Reserve* (Cincinnati: Chase & Hall, Publishers, 1875), iii.
9. See William E. Tucker and Lester G. McAllister, *Journey in Faith: A History of the Christian Church (Disciples of Christ)* (St. Louis: The Bethany Press, 1975), 26. Tucker noted: "about 12,000 Disciples and 10,000 Christians united in the 1830s." Bill Humble wrote: "The united movement probably had between 20,000 and 25,000 members in 1832." See Bill Humble, *The Story of the Restoration* (Austin: Firm Foundation Publishing House, 1969), 36. R. L. Roberts is of the opinion that the united movement had at least 25,000 members in 1832, and that the Stone-Mulkey movement was significantly larger at this time than the Campbell movement.
10. A good discussion of the differences between Campbell and Stone on the question of the proper name for the followers of Jesus can be found in William Garrett West, *Barton Warren Stone* (Nashville: The Disciples of Christ Historical Society, 1954), 153-57.
11. Tucker and McAllister, *Journey in Faith*, 26.
12. The first national organization in the Restoration Movement was the American Christian Bible Society (ACBS), which was established by a prominent Cincinnati preacher named David S. Burnet in 1845. With the encouragement of Alexander Campbell (although he was not present), a separate meeting was held in Cincinnati, Ohio, October 23-26, 1849, in conjunction with the

annual meeting of the ACBS to explore the possibility of organizing a national missionary society. Ten states were represented by the 156 people present for the meeting. The result of their four-day meeting was the establishment of the American Christian Missionary Society (ACMS), with Alexander Campbell as president and twenty others as vice-presidents. Among the vice-presidents were: Walter Scott, David S. Burnet, John O'Kane, W. K. Pendleton (Campbell's son-in-law), Tolbert Fanning (who was not present and later became an opponent of the ACMS), and Jasper Jesse Moss (who would later move to Oregon and be instrumental in the establishing of a missionary society in that state). Campbell's approval of this development was a repudiation of his position in the 1820s (although he did not think it was) when he strongly opposed any man-made societies that usurped the authority and work of the local church. The ACMS became controversial during the Civil War when it passed loyalty resolutions favoring the North. After the war it was strongly opposed by influential Christian editors such as Tolbert Fanning and David Lipscomb in the *Gospel Advocate* and Benjamin Franklin in the *American Christian Review.* Eventually, the missionary society controversy became one of the central issues that led to a tragic division in the ranks of the Restoration Movement. This was also the pattern in Oregon, where a division over missionary societies and other issues was clearly evident by 1890.

NOTES TO INTRODUCTION

1. *Millennial Harbinger,* January 1840, 19.
2. Ibid., January 1840, 20-21.
3. *Christian Baptist,* November 6, 1826, 288.
4. Benjamin Lyon Smith, *Alexander Campbell* (St. Louis: The Bethany Press, 1930), 174.
5. Ibid.
6. *Millennial Harbinger,* March 1830, 118.
7. Ibid.
8. Ibid.
9. *Christian Evangelist,* November 1854, 428.
10. *Christian Record,* May 1873, 234.
11. Hubert Howe Bancroft, *History of Oregon,* Vol. II, 1848-1888 (San Francisco: The History Company, 1888), 677-88.

12. Joseph Gaston, *The Centennial History of Oregon*, Vol. I (Chicago: S. J. Clarke Publishing Company, 1912), 580.
13. Joseph Schafer, "William Lysander Adams," in *Dictionary of American Biography*, Vol. I, 102.
14. *Vancouver Register*, May 22, 1869, and June 19, 1869.
15. George O. Goodall, "The Upper Calapooia." *Oregon Historical Quarterly*, Vol. LXXII, No. 1 (March 1972), 4.
16. John B. Horner, *Oregon, Her History, Her Great Men, Her Literature* (Portland: J. K. Gill, 1921), 158.
17. Jonas A. Jonasson, *Bricks Without Straw: The Story of Linfield College* (Caldwell, Idaho: The Caxton Printers, 1938), 24.
18. Other historians have recognized the historical accuracy of calling these people "Christians." See James DeForest Murch, *Christians Only: A History of the Restoration Movement* (Cincinnati: The Standard Publishing Company, 1962). See also Richard T. Hughes and C. Leonard Allen, eds., *Illusions of Innocence: Protestant Primitivism in America, 1630-1875* (Chicago: The University of Chicago Press, 1988). Allen's chapter on this movement is entitled "From Freedom to Constraint: The Transformation of the 'Christians in the West.'" See also D. G. Hart, ed., *Reckoning With The Past: Historical Essays on American Evangelicalism from the Institute for the Study of American Evangelicals* (Grand Rapids, Michigan: Baker Books, 1995). The article on this movement by Nathan O. Hatch is entitled "The Christian Movement and the Demand for a Theology of the People."
19. *Millennial Harbinger*, October 1850, 592-93. *Christian Evangelist*, November 1853, 407-08.
20. *Millennial Harbinger*, December 1848, 702.
    Christian Record, February 1849, 254-55.

NOTES TO FOREWORD

1. *Millennial Harbinger*, February 1846, 67.
2. Ibid., 68-69.
3. Ibid., February 1853, 72.
4. Ibid., 71.
5. In a letter written on October 23, 1851, from Yamhill County in Oregon Territory, Glen Owen Burnett noted: "From the best information I have been able to get, we have in Oregon about 1200 disciples, but mostly in a disorganized condition." See *Millennial Harbinger*, February 1852. Campbell published the

letter on page 117. The non-Indian population in Oregon Territory in 1850 was just 11,873.

6. Swander, *Making Disciples in Oregon* (by the author, 1928), 39.
7. Sarah Fisher Henderson, Nellie Edith Latourette, Kenneth Scott Latourette, eds., "Correspondence of the Reverend Ezra Fisher," *Oregon Historical Quarterly*, Vol. XVII, No. 1, (March 1916), 64. Ezra Fisher made this observation in his diary entry for October 20, 1847.
8. The American Bible Union had been formed in 1850 for the express purpose of producing a new translation of the Bible that would supplant the King James Version. The Restoration Movement was one of the nine religious groups sponsoring the project, and Alexander Campbell was one of the vice-presidents in the organization. Campbell would soon be thoroughly involved in his own assignment of translating the Book of Acts for this project.
9. When William Lysander Adams (1821-1906) arrived in Oregon Territory in 1848, he may have been the first Bethany College student to make the journey. Levi Lindsay Rowland (1831-1908) was just 13 years old when he came west with his father in 1844. He returned to enroll at Bethany in 1853, graduated in 1857, and came back to Oregon in 1859. William Thompson Haley (1833-?) also left Oregon to enroll at Bethany in 1853, graduated in 1857, and returned to Oregon immediately. A Bethany College faculty member, William Mason (1812-1900), along with his wife, Margaret, and their children, migrated to Oregon in 1852. He became a deacon in the Monmouth church, and he was a strong supporter of the Christian College that was established in that town. One source claims that John Rigdon (1796-1859), a cousin to Sidney Rigdon and a powerful preacher of the gospel, had studied under Alexander Campbell. He arrived in Oregon in 1852. Both James C. Campbell, who graduated from Bethany College in the mid-1840s, and Thomas Franklin Campbell (1822-1893), who graduated in the class of 1852, would later give several years to strengthening Christian College in Monmouth.

NOTES TO CHAPTER 1

1. Hubert Howe Bancroft, *History of Oregon*, Vol. I, 1834–1848 (San Francisco: The History Company, 1886), 29.
2. Ibid., 54–103. Charles H. Carey, *A General History of Oregon Prior to 1861*, Vol. I. (Portland: Metropolitan Press, 1935), 181–92. Thomas D. Yarnes, *A History of Oregon Methodism*, ed. Harvey E.

Tobie (Portland: The Parthenon Press, 1957), 11–21. Erle Howell, *Methodism in the Northwest*, ed. Chapin D. Foster (Portland: The Parthenon Press, 1966), 17–31.

3. Yarnes, *A History of Oregon Methodism*, 23–33.
4. Bancroft, *History of Oregon*, 104–39.
5. Yarnes, *A History of Oregon Methodism*, 33–35. Howell, *Methodism in the Northwest*, 32–41.
6. Samuel N. Dicken and Emily F. Dicken, *The Making of Oregon: A Study in Historical Geography* (Portland: Oregon Historical Society, 1979), 64–72. Charles Wilkes, *Narrative of the United States Exploring Expedition* (Philadelphia: 1845), Vol. 4, 141, 292, 296, and 306.
7. Carey, *A General History of Oregon*, Vol. II, 420–21.
8. Bancroft, *History of Oregon*, 203–11. Dicken and Dicken, *The Making of Oregon*, 72.
9. Sarah Hunt Steeves, *Book of Remembrance of Marion County, Oregon, Pioneers, 1840–1860* (Portland: The Berncliff Press, 1927), 8.
10. Ibid., 10. See also Carey, *A General History of Oregon*, 328–29. Carey confirmed, "May 2, 1843, is a red letter day in Oregon's calendar." See also Bancroft, *History of Oregon*, 303–04. Bancroft concluded, "The object for which so much striving and scheming had been carried on for two years was at last accomplished. The people had consented to a provisional government."
11. Bancroft, *History of Oregon*, 340–45. Carey, *A General History of Oregon*, Vol. I, 307–11.
12. Nicholas Perkins Hardeman, *Wilderness Calling: The Hardeman Family in the American Westward Movement, 1750–1900* (Knoxville: The University of Tennessee Press, 1977), 153ff.
13. Peter H. Burnett, *Recollections and Opinions of an Old Pioneer* (New York: A. Appleton and Company, 1880), 98–99.
14. Edward Henry Lenox, *Overland to Oregon in the Tracks of Lewis and Clark: A History of the First Emigration to Oregon in 1843* (Oakland: 1904), 10.
15. Ibid., 10–13.
16. John Minto, "Antecedents of the Oregon Pioneers and the Light These Throw on Their Motives," *Oregon Historical Quarterly*, Vol. IV, No. 1 (March 1904), 40.
17. Burnett, *Recollections*, 95.
18. Lenox, *Overland to Oregon*, 13.

19. Glen Owen Burnett was two years younger than Peter, and he and Peter married the Rogers sisters, the only daughters of Peter Rogers. Peter married Harriet, and Glen married Sarah. Peter and Glen also ran a store together at one time, and they were close friends during their years in Missouri. Two of their younger brothers, George William Burnett and James White Burnett, were also Christians. Glen and George William migrated to Oregon in 1846, and James White moved to California in 1849 and to Oregon in 1867.

NOTES TO CHAPTER 2

1. Quoted in Lloyd W. Coffman, *Blazing a Wagon Trail to Oregon: A Weekly Chronicle of the Great Migration of 1843* (Springfield, Oregon: Echo Books, 1993), 7–8. See also Verne Bright, "The Folklore and History of The 'Oregon Fever,'" (*Oregon Historical Quarterly,* Vol. LII, No. 4 (December 1951). This quotation appeared in the *Niles National Register,* May 6, 1843, and it was reprinted from the *Ohio Statesman,* April 26, 1843.
2. Hubert Howe Bancroft, *History of Oregon,* Vol. I, 1834–1848 (San Francisco: The History Company, 1886), 370–81. What most immigrants of 1843 did not know was that although Senator Linn's bill had narrowly passed in the Senate, it failed in the House. It would be 1850 before the United States Congress passed the Donation Land Claim Act.
3. Charles H. Carey, *A General History of Oregon Prior to 1861,* Vol. II (Portland: Metropolitan Press, 1936), 420–21. Samuel N. Dicken and Emily F. Dicken, *The Making of Oregon: A Study in Historical Geography* (Portland: Oregon Historical Society, 1979), 72.
4. Peter H. Burnett, *Recollections and Opinions of an Old Pioneer* (New York: D. Appleton and Company, 1880), 102.
5. The list of persons traveling in the 1843 migration party was published in Bancroft, *History of Oregon,* 394–95. See also Edward Henry Lenox, *Overland to Oregon in the Tracks of Lewis and Clark: A History of the First Emigration to Oregon in 1843* (Oakland, 1904), 63–69.
6. *Oregon Spectator*, October 16, 1869.
7. Stephenie L. Flora, *Howell Prairie Cemetery* (Salem, Oregon: by the author, 1988), 23.
8. Julie Fanselow, *The Traveler's Guide to the Oregon Trail* (Helena, Montana: Falcon Press, 1992), 1–4.

9. Lenox, *Overland to Oregon*, 29.
10. Reg P. Duffin, "The Grave of Joel Hembree," *Overland Journal*, Spring 1985, 7.
11. Charlotte Matheny Kirkwood, *Into the Eye of the Setting Sun: A Story of the West when it was New* (McMinnville: The Family Association of Matheny, Cooper, Hewitt, Kirkwood and Bailey, 1991), 17.
12. Ibid.
13. Ibid., 16.
14. Joel Justin Hembree was born on March 2, 1837, in Warren County, Tennessee, and he died on July 19, 1843. His death was the first fatality in "The Great Migration" of 1843. His death occurred at a place about 11 miles west of present-day Douglas, Wyoming.
15. Squaw Butte Creek is known today as La Prele Creek.
16. James W. Nesmith, "Diary of the Imigration of 1843," *Oregon Historical Quarterly*, Vol. VII, No. 4 (December 1906), 341.
17. Duffin, "The Grave of Joel Hembree," 9.
18. Ibid., 6–16. See also *Graves and Sites on the Oregon and California Trails* (Independence, Missouri: Oregon-California Trails Association, 1991), 16–17. Because of projected irrigation plans, in 1962 it was decided to move Joel's grave to higher ground. His remains were removed from the original grave and the bones were examined by Dr. William Hinrichs. It was his opinion that Joel's skull had been "seriously fractured" when the wheels of the wagon passed over him. Joel's remains were moved 1,625 feet to the west and buried beside the grave of Private Ralston Baker, a U. S. cavalryman who was killed in an Indian skirmish on May 1, 1867.
19. The current owners of the property, Butch and Jody White, are gracious in allowing visitors to see Joel Hembree's gravesite. However, they only request that you first stop at their residence, Natural Bridge Ranch, and ask for permission and receive directions to the site.
20. Reminiscences, *Portland Evening Telegram*, October 23, 1884.
21. Samuel M. Gilmore, "Documents," *Oregon Historical Quarterly*, Vol. IV (1903), 282.
22. Jesse Applegate, "A Day with the Cow Column in 1843," *Oregon Historical Quarterly*, Vol. I, No. 4 (December 1900), 371–83.
23. Coffman, *Blazing a Wagon Trail to Oregon*, 147.
24. Ibid., 160–62.
25. Reminiscences, *Portland Evening Telegraph*, October 23, 1884.

26. Joel Palmer, *Journal of Travels Over the Oregon Trail in 1845* (Portland: Oregon Historical Society, 1993), 173. Palmer did not spell the Hembree name correctly. He wrote: "The Yam-hill plains is called the Hemerey settlement, from a family of this name there settled."
27. Flora, *Howell Prairie Cemetery,* 19, 23.
28. Coffman, *Blazing a Wagon Trail to Oregon,* 168.

NOTES TO CHAPTER 3

1. Hubert Howe Bancroft, *History of Oregon,* Vol. I, 1834–1848 (San Francisco: The History Company, 1886), 26–32.
2. Peter Burnett and a trail companion, General M. M. McCarver, founded the settlement of "Linnton" for speculative reasons and named it after Senator Lewis Linn of Missouri. They thought Linnton would become the head of navigation on the Willamette River, but they were mistaken. The head of navigation would be located at Oregon City a few miles upstream. Within a short time Burnett gave up on Linnton and settled on the Tualatin Plains in Washington County.
3. Bancroft, *History of Oregon,* 10.
4. Ibid., 30.
5. Peter H. Burnett, *Recollections and Opinions of an Old Pioneer,* (New York: D. Appleton and Company, 1880), 143.
6. Ibid., 143.
7. Glen Owen Burnett, "Our Meeting in Oregon City in 1847," *Pacific Christian Messenger,* February 23, 1878, 4–5.
8. Bancroft, *History of Oregon,* 31.
9. Ibid.
10. Charles H. Carey, *A General History of Oregon Prior to 1861,* Vol. I (Portland: Metropolitan Press, 1935), 299–300.
11. Ibid., 300.
12. Bancroft, *History of Oregon,* 323–27. It is probable that Pierre-Jean DeSmet was the Catholic priest who conducted the Christmas Eve service that Burnett attended at Fort Vancouver in 1843.
13. Peter H. Burnett, *The Path which led A Protestant Lawyer to the Catholic Church,* (New York and Cincinnati: Benziger Brothers, 1968), v–vi.
14. Most of the members of the Restoration Movement had settled in Yamhill County, but Burnett displayed no interest in settling near them. His roots were not deep in this religious tradition,

and he may have had no desire to exercise any leadership in establishing the movement in Oregon Territory. Perhaps Burnett was already conscious of being independent of this church family.

15. Burnett, *Recollections of an Old Pioneer*, 188.
16. Vincent Snelling was born on March 15, 1797. He was 47 years old when he arrived in Oregon Territory, and he was ten years older than Peter Burnett.
17. George H. Himes, "Beginnings of Christianity in Oregon," *Oregon Historical Quarterly*, Vol. XX, No. 2 (June 1919), 170–71.
18. Clifford R. Miller, *Baptists and the Oregon Frontier* (Ashland, Oregon: by the author, 1967), 25ff.
19. Albert W. Wardin, Jr., *Baptists in Oregon* (Portland: Judson Baptist College, 1969), 34.
20. *Religious Expositor*, May 6, 1856, 3. Ibid., May 20, 1856, 2. *Christian Evangelist*, November 1854, 428–29. *Millennial Harbinger*, April 1846, 237.
21. Burnett, *Recollections of an Old Pioneer*, 189.
22. John Joseph Hughes (1797–1864) became Bishop of New York in 1842 and archbishop in 1850. John Baptist Purcell (1800–1883) also became an archbishop in 1850. Debating Alexander Campbell solidified Purcell's fame, and one account described Purcell's status after the debate: "Aside from John Hughes, Purcell had now become the most influential figure in the American hierarchy, and probably no bishop was better known in Rome." See *Dictionary of American Biography*, Vol. VIII, 267.
23. These are the words of his father, Thomas Campbell, in the *Millennial Harbinger*, January 1840, 19. But they are an accurate summary of Alexander's own commitment to restoring primitive Christianity.
24. *A Debate on the Roman Catholic Religion* (St. Louis: Christian Board of Publication, 1837), 2.
25. Ibid., 25.
26. Burnett, *Recollections of an Old Pioneer*, 188.
27. Ibid., 189.
28. Was there any significance to the timing of Burnett's conversion? He became a Catholic three months before his two brothers, both strong Christians, arrived in Oregon City. It may have been that he was hurrying to avoid a confrontation with his family, knowing they would never approve of his decision.
29. Joseph Gaston, *The Centennial History of Oregon*, Vol. IV (Chicago: S. J. Clarke Publishing Co.), 1076–78.

30. Ibid.
31. Bancroft, *History of Oregon,* 282.
32. Gaston, *Centennial History,* 1077.
33. Sarah Hunt Steeves, *Book of Remembrance of Marion County, Oregon, Pioneers, 1840–1860* (Portland: The Berncliff Press, 1927), 10.
34. C. F. Swander, *Making Disciples in Oregon,* (by the author, 1928), 25.
35. See Bancroft, *History of Oregon,* 448. He reported that Dr. John McLoughlin estimated the number of immigrants in 1844 at 1,475. See also John D. Unruh, Jr., *The Plains Across: The Overland Emigrants and the Trans–Mississippi West* (Urbana: University of Illinois Press, 1979). Unruh estimated that about 1,500 people reached Oregon that year.
36. See Thomas A. Rumer, *The Wagon Trains of '44: A Comparative View of the Individual Caravans in the Emigration of 1844 to Oregon* (Spokane, Washington: The Arthur H. Clark Company, 1990). For a listing of the immigrants of 1844, see Bancroft, *History of Oregon,* 465–66.
37. John T. Ford, "Colonel Nathaniel Ford," *Polk County Pioneer Sketches* (Dallas, Oregon: The Polk County Observer, 1927), 36–38.
38. Rumer, *The Wagon Trains of '44,* 127.
39. Ibid.

NOTES TO CHAPTER 4

1. Samuel N. Dicken and Emily F. Dicken, *The Making of Oregon: A Study in Historical Geography* (Portland: Oregon Historical Society, 1979), 72.
2. Hubert Howe Bancroft, *History of Oregon,* Vol. I, 1834–1848 (San Francisco: The History Company, 1886), 496.
3. John T. Ford, "Marcus A. Ford: A Forgotten Young Pioneer," *Polk County Pioneer Sketches* (Dallas, Oregon: The Polk County Observer, 1927), 33–35. Mark Ford graduated from Bacon College in Harrodsburg, Kentucky, in 1843. Bacon College began in Georgetown, Kentucky, in 1836 before moving to Harrodsburg in 1839. There were approximately 100 students in the early 1840s. One student that Mark Ford may have known was Carroll Kendrick, who later devoted most of his life to preaching in Texas and California. James Shannon (1799-1859) was president of the college when Mark Ford was a student. He

had previously been president of the College of Louisiana at Baton Rouge, and in 1850 he would move from the presidency of Bacon College to the presidency of the University of Missouri in Columbia. Shannon was an outspoken leader among proslavery advocates in the Restoration Movement. One account noted of him: "Probably no other man in the first generation history of the Disciples came as close to rivaling Alexander Campbell in education, intellectual capacity, and sheer force of personality as Shannon." See David Edwin Harrell, Jr., *Quest for a Christian America* (Nashville: The Disciples of Christ Historical Society, 1966), 121–25. The passion of President Shannon's proslavery position might have influenced the Ford family. When the Fords migrated to Oregon in 1844, they brought with them six black slaves. Five of these were members of one family.

4. Bancroft, *History of Oregon*, 496. See also Nicholas Perkins Hardeman, *Wilderness Calling: The Hardeman Family in the American Westward Movement, 1750–1900* (Knoxville: University of Tennessee Press, 1977), 184.
5. See Donna M. Wojcik, *The Brazen Overlanders of 1845* (Portland: by the author, 1976). This is the most detailed history of the 1845 migration ever published. See also Bancroft, *History of Oregon*, 508–31, for his discussion of the 1845 migration and for his listing of the immigrants.
6. G. W. Richardson, "Obituary on the Death of Amos Harvey," preached at Bethel, Polk County, Oregon, January 15, 1877. This is MSS #728 in the Oregon Historical Society collection.
7. John E. Smith, *Bethel, Polk County, Oregon* (by the author, 1941), 56.
8. Richardson, "Obituary on the Death of Amos Harvey."
9. Julia Veazie Glen, "John Lyle and Lyle Farm," *Oregon Historical Quarterly*, Vol. XXVI, No. 2, (June 1925), 132.
10. John Foster (1792–1868) was born in South Carolina, and Nancy Foster (1797–1870) was born in Kentucky. They were traveling on this journey with several children, including one married son. Their oldest son, Ambrose Foster, was married to Zerelda Redding. Their next two sons, Isaac M. and John T., would marry daughters of Stephen and Elizabeth Beauchamp in Clackamas County, Oregon.
11. Joel Palmer, *Journal of Travels over the Rocky Mountains* (Cleveland: The Arthur H. Clark Company, 1906), 53–54. See also W. A. Baldwin, *History of Churches of Christ in Nebraska*

(Lincoln: Nebraska Christian Missionary Society, no date), 2. Baldwin refers to this diary entry and calls this "the first sermon" by a Christian preacher in Nebraska Territory.
12. Glen, "John Lyle and Lyle Farm," 133.
13. A. G. Walling, *Illustrated History of Lane County, Oregon* (Portland: by the author, 1884), 331–32.
14. This letter is in the possession of the Lane County Historical Society, Eugene, Oregon. In the letter, Bristow informs his family that he is writing from the "North Fork of Laplatto, 556 miles west of Independence." The letter was taken by courier on June 18 and postmarked in St. Joseph, Missouri, on July 8. A note on the letter indicates that it was received in Laharpe, Hancock County, Illinois, on July 23.
15. William Gilbert Buffum, *Oregon Pioneer Association Transactions,* 1889, 42–44.
16. Ibid.
17. See the description of this experience in Palmer's *Journal of Travels,* 125–57. See also Buffum, *Oregon Pioneer Association Transactions,* 42–44.
18. Palmer, *Journal of Travels,* 150–51. At this point, the Hoods were still 80 miles from Oregon City and could have reasoned that they did not have enough to share with anyone else. But the nine people in the two needy families included four small children. Palmer wrote: "Mr. Hood kindly furnished us with a wagon cover, with which we constructed a tent, under which we rested for the night." The next day they caught up with the Buffums. This may have been the first meeting of the Buffums and the Hoods. In later years, when they met at church gatherings, they probably relived this wet introduction on the Barlow Road.
19. "Lewis Family Papers" in possession of Justine Lewis Jones of Salem, Oregon. Justine Jones is a great, great granddaughter of David R. Lewis. Concerning the "measles" story and other early stories about the family in Oregon, the "papers" record this observation: "The foregoing is tradition that has been passed down, orally, 'from father to son' in the Lewis family for many generations."
20. Ibid.
21. *Polk County Itemizer,* April 30, 1897.
22. See Keith Clark and Lowell Tiller, *Terrible Trail: The Meek Cutoff, 1845* (Bend, Oregon: Maverick Publications, Revised Edition,

1993). This is the most detailed discussion ever published about the families that decided to follow Stephen Meek.

23. Twenty-one year old William John Herren was traveling with his parents. Several other family members were also Christians. William later became a leader in the Salem Church. It is thought that another family who followed Meek may have been affiliated with the Restoration Movement. This was John and Catherine Butts and their seven children. Catherine Butts was a casualty of the Meek cut-off. She died on October 2 at the crossing of the Deschutes River. Her oldest son, Lewis Butts, was later affiliated with the Restoration Movement. It cannot be positively established whether the Pugh family followed Meek or remained on the main trail. It is known that the wife and two sons of William Porter Pugh died at the Big Sandy River in Wyoming Territory prior to the decision to follow Stephen Meek. It is also known that David Pugh died on January 3, 1846, not long after arriving in Washington County, and that his two youngest children died around the same time.
24. Julie Fanselow, *The Traveler's Guide to the Oregon Trail* (Helena, Montana: Falcon Press, 1992), 149.

NOTES TO CHAPTER 5

1. John E. Smith, *Bethel, Polk County, Oregon* (by the author, 1941), 56. *Millennial Harbinger*, December 1848, 702.
2. More research needs to be done on the precise location of the Harvey land claims. How long were they in the Lafayette area? When did they move to Bethel? Bethel was named by Glen Owen Burnett who arrived there in the fall of 1846, but Burnett does not mention that the Harveys were neighbors at that time. This calls into question the Amity claim that it is the inheritor of the first congregation "on the banks of the Yamhill." The first congregation of 13 members could have been near Lafayette and could have included the Hembrees, Newbys, and Dawsons among others. If, on the other hand, the first church was a few miles up river toward Amity, it could have included the Buffums, Gilmores, and Enos Williams among others. The accepted position since the centennial celebration in 1946 is that the first church met near Whiteson between Amity and McMinnville. If so, then the Amity claim is legitimate. See "*History of the Amity Church of Christ*," compiled by William F. Morse for the centennial in 1946. His main source was an elderly woman named Alice Taylor who told him "that the

Amity Church was first started on the banks of the Yamhill River near the place now known as Whiteson." This printed history led the *Christian Standard* to report in its April 20, 1946, issue: "The Amity Church of Christ celebrated its one hundredth anniversary on March 17. This is the oldest church in the Oregon Country, and is the direct descendant of that tiny church of thirteen members organized 'on the banks of the Yamhill River,' by Amos Harvey, in 1846." But, the question remains, if the Harveys were living near Lafayette surrounded by Christians like the Hembrees and Rowlands, why did they travel more than seven miles to call together a congregation near Whiteson? Tradition has it that this first congregation met in homes. Poring over a map of this area to see where the Christians settled reveals that the only families whose property literally bordered "the banks of the Yamhill" were Cyrus and Eliza Hawley close to Whiteson, William and Sarah Newby east of present-day McMinnville, and Andy and Martha Hembree between present-day McMinnville and Carlton. This problem may not be solvable, but since this was the first Church of Christ established in all of Western America it is of more than passing interest. If only Amos Harvey would have provided the names of the first thirteen members.

3. *Millennial Harbinger*, December 1848, 702.
4. Moses E. Lard (1818–1880) was 27 years old when he wrote this article and older than most of the other students at Bethany College. When he entered Bethany in 1845 he was already married and had two children. Lard graduated with distinguished honors in Bethany's sixth graduating class on July 4, 1849, and he gave the valedictory address on that occasion. He preached in Missouri in the 1850s and early 60s, and then moved to Lexington, Kentucky, where he edited *Lard's Quarterly* for five years (1863–1868). Beginning in 1869 he was one of the editors of the *Apostolic Times* for several years.
5. *Millennial Harbinger*, April 1846, 236–38.
6. Ibid.
7. Ibid., December 1848, 702.
8. Ibid.
9. Douglas Dornhecker doubted the accuracy of this story because the name of Vincent Snelling, the first Baptist preacher in Oregon, was connected with it. But as we have seen, Snelling had already participated in at least one protracted meeting with Peter H. Burnett, and this early in the settlement of the territory

he may have had fraternal relations with an immersionist group like the Christians. Or perhaps his name was included in error. Green Rowland (1827–1910) is a strong source that is hard to dismiss. He was a leader in the Christian Church at Carlton until his death in 1910. F. M. York, the man to whom he entrusted the story, was also a leader in the Christian Church in Carlton. Swander knew the veracity of both men, and he accepted the accuracy of the story.

10. Hubert Howe Bancroft, *History of Oregon*, Vol. I, 1834–1848 (San Francisco: The History Company, 1886), 552–53. Bancroft noted: "From the best evidence I can gather, about twenty-five hundred persons left the Missouri frontier this year for the Pacific Coast. Of these, from fifteen to seventeen hundred went to Oregon; the remainder to California." See pages 567–72 for Bancroft's listing of the names belonging to the immigration of 1846.
11. John Rogers McBride, "Overland 1846" in the *McBride Family Papers*. This 95-page typed document is manuscript #458 in the Oregon History Center collection.
12. Ibid., 8.
13. Ibid., 9–12.
14. Ibid., 18.
15. Fred Lockley, *Conversations with Bullwhackers, Muleskinners, Pioneers, Prospectors, '49ers, Indian Fighters, Trappers, Ex-Barkeepers, Authors, Preachers, Poets & Near Poets & all sorts & conditions of Men* (Eugene: Rainy Day Press, 1981), 35.
16. McBride, "Overland 1846."
17. Ibid.
18. Two Burnett brothers and their families were traveling together. Glen Owen Burnett (1809–1886) and George William Burnett (1811–1877) were younger brothers to Peter Hardeman Burnett (1807-1895), who had migrated to Oregon three years earlier and was now judge of the supreme court for Oregon Territory. A third brother, James White Burnett (1821-1884), came overland in 1849 and settled in California. He moved to Oregon in 1867.
19. McBride, "Overland 1846."
20. Robert Horace Down, *A History of The Silverton Country* (Portland: The Berncliff Press, 1926), 32.
21. A. G. Walling, *Illustrated History of Lane County, Oregon* (Portland: by the author, 1884), 324–25. Dorothy Velasco, *Lane*

County: An Illustrated History of the Emerald Empire (Northridge, California: Windsor Publications, 1985), 24–25.

22. Walling, *Illustrated History of Lane County, Oregon*, 325. Julia Veazie Glen, "John Lyle and Lyle Farm," *Oregon Historical Quarterly*, Vol. XXVI, No. 2 (June 1925), 134–39. When the Scotts arrived in Oregon they were grieving over the recent death of their daughter, Harriet. She died of typhoid at Sutter's Fort in January 1846.
23. Glen, "John Lyle and Lyle Farm," 138.
24. John H. Wallace, *The Riggs Family Genealogy*, Vol. I (New York: by the author, 1901), 53.
25. Ibid., Four of the married daughters of Thomas Riggs came to Oregon. Rachel (born about 1811) married a relative named Reuben Riggs who died on the way to Oregon, but the year of his death is not recorded. Rebecca (born about 1812) married Thomas Fields, and they migrated to Oregon in 1847. Elizabeth (born in 1818) married Stewart Lewis in 1843 and migrated to Oregon in 1846. Mary (born in 1823) married Noah Shanks in 1843, and they migrated to Oregon in 1851. Two unmarried sons, Timothy (born 1825) and Thomas (born 1828) also came overland in 1846. They both married in Oregon.
26. Bert Webber, *Over the Applegate Trail to Oregon in 1846* (Medford, Oregon: Webb Research Group Publishers, 1996), 7.
27. Bancroft, *History of Oregon*, 559.
28. *History of Polk County Oregon* (Monmouth: Polk County Historical Society, 1987), 155.
29. Webber, *Over the Applegate Trail*, 109–13. Once she was settled in Polk County, Catherine married James M. Fulkerson.
30. Glen Owen Burnett, "Our Meeting on the Clackamas in 1846," *Pacific Christian Messenger*, November 9, 1877, 5.
31. John Eakin Lyle and Ellen Scott were married by Glen Owen Burnett at the residence of Joseph Watt, her relative, near present-day Amity. Lyle was a Presbyterian, and some accounts say he was never affiliated with the Restoration Movement, but Ellen was a lifelong member of the Christian Church in Dallas, Oregon. In 1854 Lyle was selected to the board of trustees for Rickreall Academy, and all of the members of that board were active members of a Christian Church or Church of Christ. Lyle may have chosen to attend church with his wife on various occasions in his married life.
32. *Pacific Christian Messenger*, December 8, 1877, 1. When Burnett penned this article in 1877 he was looking back over 30 years to

a dinner with Thomas and "Aunt Polly" Lovelady in the winter of 1846–47. He recalled this dinner with the Loveladys as "the first fashionable dinner party I had seen in Oregon."

33. Lewis Family Papers, 21. These papers are in the possession of Justine Lewis Jones of Salem, Oregon.
34. Dr. Davis (1804–1878) remarried in 1851. He provided great leadership for Oregon Christians until his death.
35. Burnett, "Our Meeting on the Clackamas in 1846."
36. Ibid.
37. Of the Arthurs, Burnett wrote: "In the immediate neighborhood lived an old preacher by the name of Foster, of pious memory, who had been instrumental in converting brother Arthur to the simplicity of the truth as it is in Christ Jesus." Stephen Beauchamp's wife was Elizabeth, but Burnett does not say if she came with him to the meeting. In the 1850 census, the Beauchamps had moved from Clackamas County and were living in Yamhill County close to the McBrides. The sons of John Foster married the daughters of Stephen Beauchamp. John T. Foster married Adeline Beauchamp in November 1848, and Isaac M. Foster married Letha Beauchamp less than a year later on August 10, 1849.
38. Burnett, "Our Meeting on the Clackamas in 1846."

NOTES TO CHAPTER 6

1. Glen Owen Burnett, "A Visit to Tualatin Plains," *Pacific Christian Messenger*, January 5, 1878, 5.
2. Ibid.
3. Ibid.
4. John Holman's son, Daniel Holman, married Glen Owen Burnett's daughter, Martha, later that year. Burnett performed the wedding at the Burnett house in Bethel on August 21, 1847. Daniel and Martha were affiliated with the Restoration Movement for the rest of their lives. They were members of the McMinnville Church. John Holman may have remained with the Baptists. William Beagle was one of the trustees of Jefferson Institute and a good friend of Nat Ford. Beagle probably remained with the Baptists as well.
5. Burnett, "A Visit to Tualatin Plains."
6. Glen Owen Burnett, "It Is Still Fresh in Memory," *Pacific Christian Messenger*, December 22, 1877, 5.
7. E. Ruth Rockwood, "Diary of Rev. Geo. H. Atkinson, D.D., 1847-1858," *Oregon Historical Quarterly*, Vol. XL, No. 4

(December 1939), 348–49. Nat Ford and David Goff were brothers-in-law.

8. Burnett, "It Is Still Fresh in Memory."
9. Ibid., Burnett wrote this article 30 years later, and one wonders if the events described actually took place in 1847 or sometime later. The Church of Christ was not organized in Salem until the 1850s. But Burnett seems clear that he baptized those six converts in the 1840s, and he implies that it was as early as 1847. Perhaps they formed a housechurch.
10. Charles Henry Carey, "Diary of Rev. George Gary," *Oregon Historical Quarterly*, Vol. XXIV, No. 4 (December 1923), 405.
11. In 1846 a treaty with Great Britain ended the controversy over ownership and fixed the northern boundary of Oregon at the 49th parallel, which is the current boundary between Washington state and British Columbia. This new boundary encouraged settlement in the Pacific Northwest, especially north of the Columbia River on land that had previously been controlled by the Hudson's Bay Company.
12. Hubert Howe Bancroft, *History of Oregon,* Vol. I, 1834–1848 (San Francisco: The History Company, 1886), 623. When Oregon became an official territory of the United States in 1848, there was renewed pressure on Congress to recognize the existing land claims. But it was not until 1850 that Congress passed a special bill for Oregon Territory called the Donation Land Law.
13. Ibid., 625.
14. J. H. Painter, ed., *The Iowa Pulpit of the Church of Christ* (St. Louis: John Burns Publishing Co., 1884), 441.
15. Philip Mulkey Hunt, *The Mulkeys of America* (Portland: by the author, 1982), 642–91.
16. Sarah Hunt Steeves, *Book of Remembrance of Marion County, Oregon, Pioneers, 1840–1860* (Portland: The Berncliff Press, 1927), 113–14.
17. John E. Smith, *Bethel, Polk County, Oregon* (by the author, 1941), 53. A. C. Vail, "Obituary of Joseph Warren Downer," *Pacific Christian,* March 10, 1904, 15.
18. *The Dictionary of American Biography.*
19. Jerry Rushford, "Edwin Markham and the Restoration Movement," *Firm Foundation* (June 2, 1981), 340.
20. The family Bible of Jane Bounds McCarty has been preserved and contains a wealth of information. The second McCarty son, Edward Wilburn, married Jane's sister, Amanda Bounds, in Polk County, Oregon in 1850. The third McCarty son, William

Rucker, also married a Christian. He wed Eliza Ann Lovelady, daughter of Thomas and "Aunt Polly" Lovelady, in Polk County in 1851. The other McCarty sons who married Christians were John Granville who married Cynthia Walling, and James St. Clair who married Sarah Briedwell.

21. There are various versions of this story, but all are substantially the same. Reverend Samuel Allen was in the same train. His version is in the *Allen Genealogy Book.* See also Charlotte Matheny Kirkwood, *Into the Eye of the Setting Sun: A Story of the West when it was New* (McMinnville, Oregon: The Family Association of Matheny, Cooper, Hewitt, Kirkwood and Bailey, 1991), 31.
22. Jane Bounds McCarty family Bible.
23. See Fred Lockley, "Observations and Impressions of The Journal Man," *Oregon Daily Journal,* April 22, 1922, 4. This is Lockley's interview with Walter Lloyd Hembree, son of Wayman Clark Hembree, and grandson of Joel Jordan Hembree. Lockley quotes Hembree as saying: "Here is another interesting document I found among my father's papers. It is a list of those who paid for bringing the Rev. McCarty's family to Oregon." He then provides the list of the 19 contributors along with the amount they gave. The list is dominated by Yamhill County Christians, and it appears that the Hembree family was responsible for collecting the funds. Although most of these families were already in Oregon, some came overland that summer.
24. C. F. Swander, *Making Disciples in Oregon* (by the author, 1928), 34.
25. See the series of "Reminiscences of H. M. Waller" by G. M. Weimer that ran in the *Christian Standard* in 1893. The series began on February 4 and ran six issues through March 11.
26. Ibid., March 11, 1893, 188.
27. James and Betsy Toney migrated to Oregon in 1847. Their 20-year-old son, William Toney, was one of the contributors to the fund that enabled the A. V. McCarty family to come to Oregon. Their daughter, Melissa, was married to a Christian named Owen P. Turner. The Turners accompanied the Toneys to Oregon in 1847, and they were also contributors to the McCarty fund. Malinda Toney married Caleb Payne on September 19, 1850. Their marriage was relatively brief, as Caleb died in 1858.
28. Elisha Bedwell married America Minerva Shelton, the daughter of Zebedee and Sophronia Shelton, on June 18, 1850, in Yamhill

County. His first wife, Sarah Ann Davis, was a sister to Thomas and Isaac Davis and a granddaughter of Thomas Crawford McBride. She died in Texas prior to 1847.

29. Sarah Fisher Henderson, Nellie Edith Latourette, Kenneth Scott Latourette, eds., "Correspondence of the Reverend Ezra Fisher," *Oregon Historical Quarterly*, Vol. XVII, No. 1, (March 1916), 64.
30. Glen Owen Burnett, "Our Meeting in Oregon City in 1847," *Pacific Christian Messenger*, February 23, 1878, 5. It cannot be established that Jesse Applegate was ever affiliated with the Christians. But he was a neighbor to the Burnetts in Missouri, was close friends with many of the Christians, served on the board of trustees at Bethel College, and was always favorably inclined toward the progress of the Christian movement in Oregon. His nephew, Jesse A., married into a Christian family.
31. Ibid.
32. The Christian Church in Oregon City is a puzzle to historians. It is never mentioned again in this time period, and evidently it was never fully organized. There were Christian families living in Oregon City in the 1850s, but there is no record of a church being established. When John M. Harris organized a church in Oregon City in the 1860s, there was no mention of a congregation having met there before.
33. Julia Veazie Glenn, "John Eakin Lyle," *Polk County Pioneer Sketches* (Dallas, Oregon: The Polk County Observer, 1927), 14.
34. *Millennial Harbinger*, December 1848, 702.

NOTES TO CHAPTER 7

1. *Christian Record*, May 1853, 336–37.
2. *Millennial Harbinger*, December 1848, 702. *Christian Record*, February 1849, 254–55.
3. G. M. Weimer, "Reminiscences of H. M. Waller: The Oldest Evangelist of the Church of Christ on the Pacific Slope," *Christian Standard*, March 11, 1893, 189.
4. Ibid.
5. Ibid.
6. C. F. Swander, *Making Disciples in Oregon* (Portland: by the author, 1928), 39.
7. E. Ruth Rockwood, ed., "Diary of Reverend George H. Atkinson, D.D., 1847–58," Part IV, *Oregon Historical Quarterly*, Vol. XL, No. 4 (December 1939), 348.
8. Ibid., No. 2, (June 1939), 177.

9. Ibid., No. 4, (December 1939), 355.
10. *Millennial Harbinger*, October 1850, 592–93.
11. Ibid.
12. Weimer, "Reminiscences of H. M. Waller."
13. Inez Eugenia Adams Parker, "Early Recollections of Oregon Pioneer Life," *Transactions of the Oregon Pioneer Association* (1928), 23.
14. Charles H. Carey, *A General History of Oregon Prior to 1861*, Vol. II (Portland: Metropolitan Press, 1936), 478.
15. Hubert Howe Bancroft, *History of Oregon*, Vol. II, 1848–1888 (San Francisco: The History Company, 1888), 43.
16. Ibid., 43–44.
17. Catherine would soon marry George Johnston Baskett and settle in Polk County, and Zilphia would marry Stephen Rigdon and remain in Lane County.
18. Parker, "Early Recollections of Oregon Pioneer Life," 17.
19. Caleb P. Chapman was a cousin to the Indiana preacher, Elijah Goodwin, who was instrumental in his conversion to Christ. Chapman wrote: "I was a proselyte from the Methodist Church. I went trying to preach as soon as I could get on dry clothes, such as it was, but suffice it to say, I have done my best . . ." The Chapmans are buried in the Pioneer Cemetery in Salem.
20. Daniel Trullinger was born on February 6, 1801, and he died on January 23, 1869. He was a preacher of the gospel of Christ for about 45 years. Elizabeth Trullinger was a niece to President Andrew Johnson.
21. See page 38 of the biographical sketch on Adams by George N. Belknap in his 1968 edition of William Lysander Adams, *Treason, Stratagems & Spoils*.
22. Fred Lockley, *Oregon Journal*, June 20, 1923, 6.
23. Bonnie Miller, "Restoration Pioneer in Oregon: William Lysander Adams," (unpublished manuscript, 1993), 10.
24. Ibid., 11.
25. Elwood Evans, *History of the Pacific Northwest, Oregon & Washington*, 2 Vols. (Portland: North Pacific History Company, 1889), 187.
26. Inez Eugenia Adams Parker, "Early Recollections of Oregon Pioneer Life," 20.
27. Carey, *A General History of Oregon*, 704.
28. John Rogers McBride, "Overland 1846," in the *McBride Family Papers*. This 95-page typed document is manuscript #458 in the Oregon History Center collection.

NOTES TO CHAPTER 8

1. Quoted in Dan Luckenbill, *California Collections: Catalog of an Exhibit*, (Los Angeles: Department of Special Collections, University Research Library, University of California, 1990).
2. Quoted in Andrew F. Rolle, *California: A History* (New York: Thomas Y. Crowell Company, 1963), 210.
3. Hubert Howe Bancroft, *History of Oregon*, Vol. II, 1848–1888 (San Francisco: The History Company, 1888), 43.
4. Ibid., 45.
5. It is not known if the McDonalds were Christians.
6. William Gilbert Buffum, "Reminiscences," *Transactions of the Oregon Pioneer Association* (1889), 42–44.
7. John Rogers McBride, "Overland 1846" in the *McBride Family Papers*. This 95-page typed document is manuscript #458 in the Oregon History Center collection.
8. Robert Glass Cleland, *From Wilderness to Empire: A History of California* (New York: Alfred A. Knopf, 1959), 126.
9. John Walton Caughey, *California* (Englewood Cliffs: Prentice-Hall, Inc., Second Edition, 1953), 242.
10. Hubert Howe Bancroft, *History of California*, Vol. VI 1848–1859 (San Francisco: The History Company, 1888) 75.
11. Inez Eugenia Adams Parker, "Early Recollections of Oregon Pioneer Life," *Transactions of the Oregon Pioneer Association* (1889), 20–21.
12. Bonnie Miller, "Restoration Pioneer in Oregon: William Lysander Adams" (unpublished manuscript, 1993), 13, 26.
13. John E. Smith, *Bethel, Polk County, Oregon* (by the author, 1941), 63.
14. Sarah Hunt Steeves, *Book of Remembrance of Marion County, Oregon, Pioneers, 1840–1860* (Portland: The Berncliff Press, 1927), 145.
15. Ibid., 151.
16. See John T. Ford, "Marcus A. Ford," *Polk County Pioneer Sketches* (Dallas, Oregon: The Polk County Observer, 1927), 33–35.
17. *Oregon Spectator*, January 26, 1850.
18. There were probably other members of the legislature from the Christian movement, but they cannot be positively identified at this time. Among the possibilities are: W. D. Holman and Gabriel Walling from Clackamas County (several members of the Holman and Walling families were Christians), William S.

Matlock from Champoeg County (his daughter married Wiley Chapman), and John Thorp from Polk County (his daughter, Amanda, married Marcus Ford, the son of Nat Ford).

19. Bancroft, *History of Oregon,* Vol. II, 78.
20. George R. Stewart, *The California Trail* (Lincoln: University of Nebraska Press, 1962), 217ff. Caughey, *California,* 245–52. Bancroft, *History of Oregon,* Vol. II, 63–65.
21. The congregation at Eola was organized in 1856. The large house the Brunks built near there in 1861 is still standing and is one of the "showplaces" of the Polk County Historical Society.
22. H. K. Hines, *An Illustrated History of the State of Oregon* (Chicago: Lewis Publishing Company, 1893), 1002–3.
23. Thomas Thompson (1797–1872) had preached for a quarter-century in Missouri. For more information on Thompson see T. P. Haley, *Historical and Biographical Sketches of the Early Churches and Pioneer Preachers of the Christian Church in Missouri* (Kansas City, Missouri: J. H. Smart & Co., 1888), 107–12. See also Jerry Rushford, "A Pioneer Preacher in California," *Firm Foundation,* September, 2, 9, 16, 23, 1981. William Wilson Stevenson (1797–1886) was a former Cumberland Presbyterian preacher who had converted to the Restoration Movement in Little Rock, Arkansas, in 1832. He had been preaching for the Christians in Little Rock for 17 years. See Lester G. McAllister, *Arkansas Disciples: A History of the Christian Church (Disciples of Christ) in Arkansas* (by the author, 1984), 6–8. John G. Parrish (1817–1871) was baptized into Christ in Fredericksburg, Virginia, in 1838. Later, he moved to Bowling Green in Caroline County, Virginia. He had only been preaching a few years when he migrated to California. See Frederick Arthur Hodge, *The Plea and the Pioneers in Virginia* (Richmond: Everett Waddey Company, 1905), 254–64.
24. McBride," Overland 1846," 14.
25. *Millennial Harbinger,* October 1850, 592.

NOTES TO CHAPTER 9

1. *Christian Magazine,* September 1851, 286.
2. *Millennial Harbinger,* February 1852, 117.
3. Ibid., October 1850, 593.
4. George H. Himes, "Beginnings of Christianity in Oregon," *Oregon Historical Quarterly,* Vol. XX, No. 2 (June 1919), 171–72.
5. Ibid.

6. Inez Eugenia Adams Parker, "Early Recollections of Oregon Pioneer Life," *Transactions of the Oregon Pioneer Association* (1928), 25-26.
7. Joseph Gaston, *The Centennial History of Oregon,* Vol. IV (Chicago: S. J. Clarke Publishing Company, 1912), 64–65.
8. W. L. Bristow, "History of the Pleasant Hill Church." (unpublished typed manuscript, June 20, 1926, at Lane County Historical Society, Eugene, Oregon). Nathaniel S. Haynes, *History of the Disciples of Christ in Illinois, 1819–1914* (Cincinnati: The Standard Publishing Company, 1915), 277–78.
9. "Elijah Bristow," Anonymous unpublished eight-page typed manuscript in Lane County Historical Society, Eugene, Oregon. W. H. Baughman, "History of the Pleasant Hill Church," *Pacific Christian,* January 31, 1901.
10. William Wilshire Bristow (1826–1874) was born in Kentucky but moved to Illinois when he was a young boy. When he came overland in 1848, he traveled in the same train that included the Coffeys, Porters, and Blackerbys. He married Elizabeth Coffey on October 17, 1850, at her parents' home in Aumsville. They had four children before Elizabeth died in 1863. Later, W. W. Bristow married Martha McCall, daughter of William McCall, an elder of the church in Lane County. Bristow sold his farm at Pleasant Hill and moved to Eugene in 1865 to become a partner in a mercantile business known as Bristow & Company. In June 1858 he was elected one of the first state senators from Lane County. He was elected again to the state senate in 1872. As a state senator, he played the leading role in having the University of Oregon established in Eugene.
11. This list of 25 charter members may be off by one. There are several competing lists. Some do not include the wife of W. W. Bristow, which would be correct. They were not married until October 17 of that year. Some do not include Mary Briggs, but this is confusing. She and Elias were married in 1847. One surprising omission in the list is Betsy Briggs, the wife of Isaac Briggs. Every list includes Katie Bristow, but she was married to George Johnston Baskett in September and left to live in Polk County. Or, if they lived briefly in Lane County, why was George Johnston Baskett not listed as a charter member since he was a Christian? Another surprise is that 17-year-old Elijah Lafayette Bristow was not listed as a charter member. Was he not a Christian yet? Or was he away from home at that time? It is possible that he never became a Christian.

12. One record noted that George and Katie were married on September 8, 1850. Did W. L. Adams remain at Pleasant Hill for more than a month to perform that ceremony? See *Polk County, Oregon Cemeteries, Volume Four: Small Cemeteries in North Polk County* (Dallas, Oregon: Polk County Genealogical Society, 1991), 7.
13. *Christian Evangelist,* July 1853, 249. *Millennial Harbinger,* October 1834, 506–08. Bristow recorded that one man objected to using this model from the *Harbinger* because he thought it was longer than necessary. Later, "one brother who lived at a distance" from the congregation said that "although he believed every word of our preamble and agreement, that he could not join the congregation because the sects would say we had a confession of faith." The Christians were always sensitive to any charge that they had a creed.
14. This was the language of Alexander Campbell from the model he offered in October 1834.
15. Beulah Harden Carrothers, "History of the Pleasant Hill Christian Church," in *Lane County Historian* (Eugene, Oregon: Lane County Historical Society, June 1959), 26.
16. Haynes, *History of the Disciples of Christ,* 422–23.
17. Ibid., 424–25.
18. Ellis A. Stebbins, *The OCE Story* (Monmouth, Oregon: Oregon College of Education, 1973), 1.
    Helen Butler Jones, "The Contribution of Certain Leaders to the Development of the Oregon Normal School, 1850 to 1930." (unpublished master's thesis, University of Oregon, 1947), 6–8.
19. Elijah Davidson (1783–1870) was now 67 years old, and he was traveling with his wife, Margaret. Squire S. Whitman (1818–1892) was married to Elizabeth Davidson, and Thomas H. Lucas (1824–1908) was married to Sarah Davidson. Elijah B. Davidson (1819–1888) was traveling with his wife, Saloma. Others in the party included Ethan A. Shirley, Elijah Jones, William McWhorter, and Levi McWhorter.
20. Although Elijah Davidson, Sr., was already 67 years old upon arriving in Oregon, he lived for another 20 years, and one record reported he was "hale and hearty and preaching till the end." A biographer, attempting to account for his longevity, wrote, "During his whole life, Mr. Davidson practiced temperance and was an early riser." Elijah B. Davidson spent the last 22 years of his life (1866 to 1888) preaching and farming in Josephine County in southern Oregon.

21. Jones, "The Contribution of Certain Leaders," 8–9.
22. John Udell, *Incidents of Travel to California, across the Great Plains; together with the Return Trips through Central America and Jamaica; to Which are Added Sketches of the Author's Life* (Jefferson, Ohio: by the author, 1856), 9–10.
23. Ibid., 17.
24. Ibid., 21.
25. Silas Higgins was an adopted son of George Townsend, the father of Anna Rigdon. She considered him to be a younger brother. The Rigdons were traveling in a company of seven wagons that were all related to the Townsend family, but it is not known if any of these other families were Christians.
26. Sarah Hunt Steeves, *Book of Remembrance of Marion County, Oregon, Pioneers, 1840–1860* (Portland: The Berncliff Press, 1927), 197.
27. *History of Polk County Oregon* (Monmouth, Oregon: Polk County Historical Society, 1987), 199.
28. Steeves, *Book of Remembrance*, 197–98.
29. Joel E. Ferris, *The Pacific Northwesterner*, Vol. 5, 5–6. Bonnie Miller, "Restoration Pioneer in Oregon: William Lysander Adams." (unpublished manuscript, 1993), 13–14.
30. Inez Eugenia Adams Parker, "Early Recollections of Oregon Pioneer Life," *Transactions of the Oregon Pioneer Association* (1889), 21.
31. Sebastian Adams (1825–1898) was one of the founders of the town of McMinnville in Yamhill County, and of the college in that town that became Linfield College. Adams served three terms as county clerk of Yamhill County before being elected a state senator. The *Register*, a newspaper in Vancouver, Washington Territory, once said of Sebastian Adams: "He is a Campbellite preacher of fine abilities and bears the reputation before the public of a worthy Christian gentleman."

NOTES TO CHAPTER 10

1. Commodore Wesley Cauble, *Disciples of Christ in Indiana: Achievements of a Century* (Indianapolis: Meigs Publishing Company, 1930), 38–39.
2. Madison Evans, *Biographical Sketches of the Pioneer Preachers of Indiana* (Philadelphia: J. Challen & Sons, 1862), 173.
3. *Christian Leader*, May 3, 1887, 3.
4. Ibid.

5. *Millennial Harbinger*, July 1852, 418.
6. *Christian Record*, August, 1852, p. 62. This letter was written by Caleb Chapman on April 5, 1852, from Marion County.
7. Robert Glass Cleland, *From Wilderness to Empire: A History of California* (New York: Alfred A. Knopf, 1959), 136.
8. Robert Horace Down, *A History of The Silverton Country* (Portland: The Berncliff Press, 1926), 32.
9. Marceil Middlemiss, *A History of the Christian Church in Silverton, 1851–1976* (by the author, 1976), 1–2.
10. Ibid., 3–5.
11. John (1807–1880), Noah (1808–1875), and Alfred (1810–1881) were 18, 17 and 15 when they moved to Illinois. They all began preaching in the early 1830s.
12. John married Savilla Smith in 1828, and Noah married Mary Smith in 1830. Alfred married Sarah Bracken in 1834.
13. James Madison Powell, *Powell History: An Account of the Lives of the Powell Pioneers of 1851 – John A., Noah and Alfred – Their Ancestors, Descendants and other Relatives* (Portland: by the author, 1922), 41–42, 76–77.
14. Ibid., 77.
15. Nathaniel S. Haynes, *History of the Disciples of Christ in Illinois, 1819–1914* (Cincinnati: The Standard Publishing Company, 1915), 324.
16. Powell, *Powell History*, 43.
17. Ibid., 37.
18. Ibid., 39.
19. *Christian Record*, December 1852, 186.
20. Ibid.
21. Ibid.
22. Robert Earl, "Reminiscences," 68. This 113-page handscript and typescript is Manuscript #793 at the Oregon History Center. Two of the Earl brothers, both of whom were Christians, married two of the Powell sisters. Joseph Earl married Jemima Powell on December 4, 1851, and Robert Earl married Lourana Powell on September 16, 1852. The Earls had migrated to Oregon in 1845, and their father had died on the way. Both daughters of John A. Powell remained faithful Christians, but it is not known if their husbands were ever Christians.
23. Powell, *Powell History*, 46.
24. Ibid., 101.
25. Ibid., 120–21.
26. Ibid., 310–11.

27. John E. Smith, *Bethel, Polk County, Oregon* (by the author, 1941), 62.
    Elwood Evans, *History of the Pacific Northwest,* 2 Vols. (Portland: North Pacific History Company, 1889), 535.
28. *Christian Herald,* August 24, 1883, 6.
29. *Christian Record,* October 1857, 298–99.
30. Victor Emanuel Hoven, "The Beginnings and Growth of the Church of Christ in Oregon," (unpublished master's thesis, University of Oregon, June 1918), 5.
31. John H. Wallace, *The Riggs Family Genealogy,* Vol. I (New York: by the author, 1901), 54.
32. Haynes, *Disciples in Illinois,* 590.
33. John O. Fry, "John O. Fry's Trip Across the Plains," 15. This 35-page typescript is Manuscript #427 in the Oregon History Center. In *Platte River Road Narratives,* Merrill Mattes wrote of John O. Fry: "Skulking Indians stayed clear of this train when two of them were bitten by Fry's dog. The reputation of the ferocious animal 'went ahead of him for 500 miles.'"
34. C. F. Swander, *Making Disciples in Oregon* (by the author, 1928), 33.

NOTES TO CHAPTER 11

1. Glen Owen Burnett, "Reminiscence of a Rainy Sunday," *Pacific Christian Messenger,* September 6, 1877, 5.
2. Ibid., Levi Lindsay Rowland and Emma J. Sanders were married at her home in Marvin, Alabama. Bethel College was established by leaders of the Restoration Movement in Oregon in 1855. In later years it was merged with Monmouth University in nearby Monmouth to form a new school known as Christian College. Levi Lindsay Rowland became the first president of Christian College and served in that position from 1866 to 1869. He was minister of the Christian Church in Salem from 1869 to 1876. Along the way he completed his medical training. He served as state superintendent of public instruction from 1874 to 1878 and was professor of physiology in the medical department of Willamette University from 1870 to 1878. He, with others, organized the State Medical Society in 1874.
3. Alexander Campbell, "Conventions," *Millennial Harbinger,* November 1851, 601–05.
4. C. F. Swander, *Making Disciples in Oregon* (by the author, 1928), 48.

5. Douglas B. Dornhecker, "A History of Annual Meetings of Disciples of Christ in Oregon to 1877." (Johnson City, Tennessee: unpublished M.Div. thesis, Emmanuel School of Religion, 1979), 41.
6. *Christian Record,* December 1852, 186.
7. Ibid.
8. The ten Christian preachers migrating to Oregon in 1852 were: Abbott Levi James Todd (1820–1886) Henry W. Taylor (1808–1890), John Rigdon (1796–1859), Harrison H. Hendrix (1823–?, Lewis Casteel (1813–1867), John Ecles Murphy (1806–1876), Gilmore Callison (1808–1869), Edmund Green Browning (1816–1888), Charles Bradshaw (1822–1898), and George R. Caton (c1828-?). Rigdon, Callison and Bradshaw settled in the Pleasant Hill area of Lane County, and Caton and Casteel settled in the Eugene area of Lane County. Taylor located south of Cottage Grove in Lane County. Murphy settled in Polk County near the future site of Monmouth. Hendrix settled briefly in Clackamas and then removed to Washington County. Todd spent one winter at Howell's Prairie and then moved to Lookingglass Valley in Douglas County. Browning settled in the Myrtle Creek area of Douglas County.
9. *Christian Record,* December 1852, 186.
10. James Madison Powell, *Powell History* (Portland: by the author, 1922), 310.
11. Lucinda Powell Propst was just 35 when she died. Anthony was nearing his 42nd birthday. Their oldest child, 16-year-old John Wesley Propst, was baptized into Christ in June 1853. In later years he became an elder of the Central Church that had been established by his uncles.
12. Sarah Hunt Steeves, *Book of Remembrance of Marion County, Oregon, Pioneers, 1840–1860* (Portland: The Berncliff Press, 1927), 251–53. Begley's first name is not mentioned. He is referred to as "a Campbellite preacher" by Sarah Adamson who submitted the article on Mary Watkins. No further information is available on this Christian preacher who was traveling in the same train with the Watkins family. He is never mentioned in Oregon. Exactly one year earlier to the day before the Walker-Watkins wedding, a Christian named Zadok Riggs died and was buried at Independence Rock (see chapter 10).
13. Calvin Walker died at Philip Foster's place on the Barlow Road.
14. Steeves, *Book of Remembrance,* 252–53. There is a road called "Riches Road" half way between Silverton and Sublimity, and

this was probably the location of their farm. It cannot be determined which congregation Mary attended. She was about equi-distant between Bethany and Mill Creek. Both Mary and her husband are buried at Mt. Hope Cemetery in Marion County.

15. John Udell, *Incidents of Travel to California, across the Great Plains, together with the Return Trips through Central America and Jamaica; to Which are Added Sketches of the Author's Life* (Jefferson, Ohio: by the author, 1856), 54. Udell spelled the name "Paget," but other sources give "Pagett" and "Padgett" as the correct spelling. The best evidence favors "Pagett" or "Padgett."
16. Joseph Gaston, *The Centennial History of Oregon, 1811–1912,* Vol. II (Chicago: The S. J. Clarke Publishing Company, 1912), 989. Woodford remained in Douglas County until 1857, and then he returned east. His middle son, Alonzo Woodford, remained in Oregon for the rest of his life. Gaston wrote of Alonzo Woodford: "In matters of faith the family are Christians and take an active interest in the work of that church, among whose membership they number many friends."
17. Leland G. Jackson, *Early Castle Rock and North Cowlitz County, Washington,* Second Edition (Castle Rock, Washington: by the author, 1992), 70–73. See also Orval D. Peterson, *Washington-Northern Idaho Disciples* (St. Louis: Christian Board of Publication, 1945), 39–40.
18. *Portrait and Biographical Record of the Willamette Valley, Oregon: Containing Original Sketches of many well-known Citizens of the Past and Present* (Chicago: Chapman Publishing Company, 1903), 1507–08.
19. Ibid.
20. Ibid., 1243–44. See also Fred Lockley, *History of the Columbia River Valley from The Dalles to the Sea,* Vol. III, (Chicago: The S. J. Clarke Publishing Company, 1928), 348–51. See also Fred Lockley, *Conversations with Bullwhackers, Muleskinners, Pioneers, Prospectors, '49ers, Indian Fighters, Trappers, Ex-Barkeepers, Authors, Preachers, Poets & Near Poets & All Sorts & Conditions of Men* (Eugene, Oregon: Rainy Day Press, 1981), 235–37.
21. Nathaniel S. Haynes, *History of the Disciples of Christ in Illinois, 1819–1914* (Cincinnati: The Standard Publishing Company, 1915), 218. Included in the group that planted the church was Elizabeth's brother, James McClure, and Gilmore's brother, Josiah, and his father, Joseph Callison. The two Callison brothers preached for this church for many years.

22. "Elijah Lafayette Bristow Letters, 1857–1864," (Eugene, Oregon: Lane County Historical Society, 1959). A section entitled "A Genealogy of the Bristow Family" mentions that Emeline died on the plains during the crossing of 1852.
23. Julie Fanselow, *The Traveler's Guide to the Oregon Trail* (Helena, Montana: Falcon Press, 1992), 3.
24. *Diary of John J. Callison: Oregon Trail, 1852.* (Eugene, Oregon: Lane County Historical Society, 1959), 7.
25. Theresa Powell McFadden, oldest child of John A. Powell, died on August 10, 1851, and was buried at Meacham Station in Umatilla County, Oregon. Lucinda Powell Propst, younger sister of John A. Powell, died on August 19, 1852, and was buried at Butler Creek in Umatilla County, Oregon. John Joseph Callison died on August 23, 1852, and was buried at LaGrande in Union County. The sites in Umatilla County are very close together, and LaGrande is just 25 miles distant.
26. Ethel L. Briggs, *A History and Genealogy of Gilmore Callison and his Descendants* (Yucaipa, California: by the author, 1962), 18–19.
27. Ibid., 20.
28. Charles Bisbee Dart (1820–1902) and Isabelle Eleanor Kean Dart (1824–1911) remained in the Rock Creek area for the rest of their lives, and Edward Pedigo (1805–1894) and Lettice Gill Pedigo (1806–1879) remained in the Damascus area for many years before moving to Washington Territory.
29. *Christian Record,* May 1853, 336.
30. Ibid., February 1853, 255.
31. George H. Himes, "Beginnings of Christianity in Oregon." *Oregon Historical Quarterly,* Vol. XX, No. 2 (June 1919), 171–72.

NOTES TO CHAPTER 12

1. Andrew S. McClure, "Journal of Andrew S. McClure, 1853." (Eugene, Oregon: Lane County Historical Society, 1959 and 1978). The original publication in 1959 contained entries from May 8 to October 1853. The earlier portion of the diary, from March 21, 1853, to May, came to the attention of the Historical Society in 1978. Today, the entire diary is published as one document.
2. Benjamin Franklin Owen, "My Trip Across the Plains, March–October 1853." (Eugene, Oregon: Lane County Historical Society, second printing, 1967), 3.
3. Ibid., 23.
4. Ibid., 24.

5. The Bushnell-Adkins party had originated in Kirksville, Adair County, Missouri. Among the Christians were Ursula Bushnell and her daughter-in-law, Elizabeth Bushnell. They were unaware that James Addison Bushnell, Elizabeth's husband who had been mining in California, was on his way back to Missouri to get his family. Traveling with the Bushnells were Elizabeth's brother, Edward Adkins, and his large family. Edward was married to Helen Bushnell, the sister of James Addison. The two Preston families were related. William and Mary Preston, the parents, were traveling with William P. and Mary Ann, their son and daughter-in-law. All four were Iowa Christians.
6. Leah Collins Menefee and Lowell Tiller, "Cutoff Fever, III," *Oregon Historical Quarterly*, Vol. LXXVIII, No. 2 (June 1977), 147.
7. Ibid., 49–50. Isaac Briggs was born in 1802. He was a pioneer leader of the Restoration Movement in Iowa, and he was a charter member of the second congregation established in that state. This was the "Lost Creek" congregation that was organized five miles north of Fort Madison in the summer of 1836. One record noted of this church: "The growing congregation, needing more room decided to move to the double room log cabin owned by Isaac Briggs and used by him for a home. This cabin stood on the north bank of Lost Creek in a beautiful glade; in front of it was an ever living spring . . . In a few years, Isaac Briggs felt the need of a larger house so on the hill above the spring, where he could look down on the old double room log cabin he erected a two-story house, giving the old home to the congregation to be used as a church house. So far as we know, this was the first building in Iowa to be used exclusively as a church house. . . . Lost Creek is generally looked to as being the Mother church of all Iowa churches." See Francis M. Roberts, *100 Years of History of the Christian Church (Disciples of Christ) in Marion County, Iowa, 1846–1946* (by the author, 1946), 9–10. Isaac Briggs had married Elizabeth Morris in Floyd County, Kentucky, in 1823, and their oldest son, Elias M. Briggs, was born in 1824 in that same county. . Isaac and Elizabeth Briggs and their son and daughter-in-law, Elias M. and Mary Briggs, migrated to the Pleasant Hill area in 1847, and they became pioneer members of the Pleasant Hill Church of Christ when it was organized in 1850. Later they founded the town of Springfield, across the Willamette River from Eugene. This is where they were living when they came to the rescue of

several members of the "Lost Wagon Train" in 1853. Charles Hardesty (spelled Hardisty in the 1860 census for Lane County) was a native of Illinois. He was 38 years old in 1853 when he assisted Isaac Briggs in the rescue of Owen and McClure. At that time he was living at Springfield near Isaac Briggs, but in the 1860 census he had moved a short distance away to the Mohawk community.

8. *Christian Record,* May 1853, 336–37. This letter was written on December 28, 1852.
9. *Christian Evangelist,* June 1852, 196–97. Elias and Mary Briggs had first settled in the Pleasant Hill district of Lane County, and they were charter members of the Pleasant Hill Church. But by now they had moved down to the Willamette River and founded the town of Springfield (named for the spring in the Briggs' field) across the river from Eugene. Isaac and Elizabeth Briggs, the parents of Elias, had moved with them and were co-founders of the town. Elias was now operating a ferry service across the river. Less than 3 months before he wrote this letter, Elias and his wife had suffered through the deaths of their two oldest children. Jasper (age 4) and Susannah (age 2) had died within 10 days of each other in October 1852. See *Christian Evangelist,* June 1855, 292. When Isaac Briggs wrote to Daniel Bates to report on the death of his two grandchildren, he noted: "These children were the offspring of our only child, Elias M. Briggs, and we had flattered ourselves that we would be cheered by their presence while we were permitted to continue in this world. But the monster death has hurried them to the spirit-land, and blasted that hope; though we are assured that, if we do the will of our Heavenly Father while we live, we shall join their company in Heaven to part no more."
10. Ibid., April 1853, 143–45. This letter was written on November 27, 1852, from Rickreall in Polk County. Rigdon had settled in the neighborhood of the Fords, Goffs and Loveladys. He was suffering from a disease in his eyes which "had become so serious as to render me nearly blind." Despite this handicap, he was eager to preach again.
11. Ibid., 145–46.
12. Ibid., August 1853, 296–97. This letter was written to John G. Haley.
13. Ibid., 297.
14. C. F. Swander, *Making Disciples in Oregon* (by the author, 1928), 96.

15. *Christian Record,* October 1853, 123–24.
16. Mina Davis Hargis, "The History of the Disciples of Christ in Iowa before the Civil War" (Iowa City: unpublished M.A. thesis, State University of Iowa, 1937), 69.
17. *Christian Evangelist,* March 1853, 119.
18. Ibid., December 1853, 442–44. As soon as Rigdon saw the editorial notice in the March issue (which would have reached him in May), he sat down and wrote his response on May 25, 1853. The *Evangelist* could have printed his letter as early as the July or August issue, but it did not appear until the December issue.
19. Ibid., November 1853, 406–07. This letter was written on June 14, 1853.
20. Ibid., July 1854, 275–76. This letter was written on March 22, 1854.
21. Inez Eugenia Adams Parker, "Early Recollections of Oregon Pioneer Life," 23.
22. Ibid., January 1854, 40. This letter was written on October 7, 1853.
23. Ibid., 30–31. This letter was written on October 9, 1853.
24. Ibid., November 1853, 407–08. This letter was written July 14, 1853.
25. *Christian Record,* February 1854, 61. This letter was written by John Powell from his home in Linn County on November 3, 1853. He does not mention where the annual meeting was, which would seem to indicate that it was most likely hosted again by his own Central Church in Linn County. C. F. Swander is of the opinion that the second meeting was at Rickreall, but he offers no support for this view.
26. Ibid., This letter was written on November 3, 1853.
27. Ibid., May 1854, 156. This letter was written on November 28, 1853.
28. Ibid., 156.
29. Among the Christian families arriving in 1853 were those headed by Joel B. Huston, James L. Ladd, James V. Harpool, and James Parvin.
30. Zillah Paeth, "Early Letters . . . Pioneers Describe Life in Monmouth," *Historically Speaking,* Vol. IX (Polk County Historical Society, September 1990), 16. The information on "47 persons in the train" was found in a letter from Peter Butler to family and friends back home in Illinois, dated August 14, 1853.

31. Kenneth L. Holmes, ed., *Covered Wagon Women: Diaries & Letters from the Western Trails, 1840–1890,* Vol. VI (Spokane, Washington: The Arthur H. Clark Company, 1991), 18.
32. Ibid., 16.
33. Patrick Rivers Haley (1802–1884) and his wife, Jane (1808–1890), lived in Illinois for several years. They were accompanied on their journey west by his two sons from a previous marriage, Bedford and William Thompson. William Thompson Haley moved his family to California in the 1860s, and his wife, Lucinda, died there on May 19, 1867.
34. Paeth, "Early Letters," 17.
35. Joshua Bowen (1835–1914) married Elizabeth Cox (1840–1920), and Peter Bowen (1837–1916) married Permilla Cox (1839–1913).
36. See "A Brief Synopsis of the William Ruble Family History," by D. R. Ruble in *Compilation of the History of the Ruble Family* (by the family, 1935), 17–18.
37. Sarah Hunt Steeves, *Book of Remembrance of Marion County, Oregon, Pioneers, 1840–1860* (Portland: The Berncliff Press, 1927), 261.
38. Ibid., 260.
39. See the Lewis Family Papers. Nancy Cook was a younger sister to David R. Lewis. In the 1850 census, the Cooks were living in Clackamas County, and Abram Cuffy was listed as a 50-year-old member of their household. In the 1860 census, the Cooks were living in Benton County, and Abram Cuffy was no longer listed as a member of their household.
40. See Scott McArthur, "The Polk County Slave Case," *Historically Speaking,* Vol. II (Polk County Historical Society, 1970), 1–10. This is a well-written and balanced account. See also Lenwood G. Davis, "Sources for History of Blacks in Oregon," *Oregon Historical Quarterly,* Vol. LXXIII, No. 3 (September 1972), 197–203. See also Fred Lockley, "The Case of Robin Holmes vs. Nathaniel Ford," *Oregon Historical Quarterly,* Vol. XXIII, No. 2 (June 1922), 111–37.
41. Ralph Friedman, "Holmes Vs. Ford: A Chapter in Ebony," *This Side of Oregon* (Caldwell, Idaho: The Caxton Printers, 1983), 141–67.
42. McArthur, "Polk County Slave Case," 3.
43. Pauline Burch, "Pioneer Nathaniel Ford and the Negro Family." This 12-page typescript is Manuscript #707 in the Oregon History Center.

44. *Oregon Statesman*, March 31, 1857. See also Walter Carleton Woodward, *The Rise and Early History of Political Parties in Oregon, 1843–1868* (Portland: The J. K. Gill Company, 1913), 103, 128.
45. McArthur, "Polk County Slave Case," 8.
46. James Addison Bushnell, *The Autobiography of James Addison Bushnell, 1826–1912*. (Eugene, Oregon: Lane County Historical Society, 1959), 20.
47. Ibid., 25–29.
48. *Millennial Harbinger*, March 1854, 175–76.

NOTES TO CHAPTER 13

1. Joseph Gaston, *The Centennial History of Oregon, 1811–1912*, Vol. IV (Chicago: The S. J. Clarke Publishing Company, 1912), 1076–78.
2. *Christian Evangelist*, November 1854, 427. It appears from the way Daniel Bates set this in type that the letter was much longer and that he was only publishing some excerpts that would be of interest to his readers. Mary was about 24 years old when she wrote this letter, and her husband was 28. The *Christian Evangelist* began publication in 1850. The parents of William P. Preston were also named William and Mary. They were in the same wagon train with their son and his family.
3. *Christian Messenger*, September 1843, 160.
4. Browning married so quickly after arriving in Myrtle Creek that he must have already known the family of Nancy Allen (sometimes spelled Allyn). They were married in Clackamas County, which is not close to Douglas County. This would seem to be another indication that he must have already known the family before he traveled to Clackamas County to ask for her hand in marriage. In addition to preaching and farming, Browning served his community as a physician. One record refers to him as a "noted pioneer physician."
5. *Christian Evangelist*, October 1855, 478. This information is found in a letter from E. G. Browning to Daniel Bates written on July 9, 1855.
6. Ibid.
7. Ibid., November 1855, 526. "Brother Chapman from Willamette" refers to Caleb P. Chapman who was living in Marion County. Chapman often traveled to preach in gospel meetings. He was probably invited to Lookingglass Valley by

his cousin, Abbott Levi Todd. This letter was written by Mary Preston on June 29, 1855.

8. Alpheus Ireland was born in Wayne County, Indiana in 1808. He and his wife, Sophia, were married in Cass County, Michigan on December 6, 1831, and they came overland to Oregon in 1853.
9. *Christian Record*, December 1855, 379. This letter was written on August 20, 1855. It is very unlikely that the church in Lookingglass and the one in Myrtle Creek are the same congregation, as these two locations are 15 miles apart. That was a significant distance in 1855, when the transportation options were horses, horse-drawn buggies and walking.
10. *Christian Evangelist*, October 1855, 478. This letter was written on August 20, 1855.
11. Ibid., 570. This letter was written on September 6, 1855.
12. In 1842 Todd married Louvina Gaither, but she died the next year, leaving him with a 9-month-old daughter. He then married Louvina's sister, Martha Gaither, in 1845, but she also died a year later after bearing a second daughter for Todd.
13. Angeline Tate Todd gave birth to a daughter (Todd's third) while they were still living in Arkansas. Elijah Todd was the first son in the family, and he was most likely named for both Elijah Goodwin (Todd's cousin who baptized him into Christ) and Elijah Chapman (Todd's uncle who taught him the potter's trade).
14. Aurelius Todd, "Rev. A. L. J. Todd, Pioneer Circuit Rider," *The Umpqua Trapper*, Vol. VI, No. 3, Fall 1970), 61. A. L. Todd would have been very disappointed with the attachment of "Rev." in front of his name. Like other Christian preachers in the 19th century, he refused to adopt this practice that was so common among denominational preachers. Todd believed that the term "Reverend" was a title reserved for God alone.
15. Ibid., Vol. VI, No. 2, Summer 1970, 46–47. See also Vol. VI, No. 3, Fall 1970, 59.
16. There is no record of John Foster (1792–1868) ever preaching outside of Clackamas County, and John Burris Smith (1816–1901) did not preach outside of Polk County in the early years of his residence in Oregon. Dr. James McBride (1802–1875) and Glen Owen Burnett (1809–1886) represented the preaching force for Oregon Christians at the beginning of 1847.
17. Thomas D. Yarnes, *A History of Oregon Methodism*, ed. Harvey E. Tobie (Portland: The Parthenon Press, 1957), 97.

18. A young Baptist preacher named Joel Vail, who later preached for the Christians, had been in Oregon Territory since 1853. However, he did not become affiliated with the Restoration Movement until 1857. Two other Christian preachers, Thomas Mulkey and Dr. Evans, died in Oregon before 1850. A Christian preacher whose last name was Begley came overland in 1852, but it is not known if he remained in the territory. One history of the Restoration Movement in Missouri recorded that two Missouri preachers, James Lovelady and James Cox, migrated to Oregon. See T. P. Haley, *Historical and Biographical Sketches of the Early Churches and Pioneer Preachers of the Christian Church in Missouri* (Kansas City, Missouri: J. H. Smart & Co., 1888), 364. Haley wrote: "In 1840, James Lovelady, James Cox and James McBride moved to Oregon." McBride came in 1846, but there is no evidence that Lovelady and Cox ever came to Oregon.
19. *Christian Record,* October 1853, 124.
20. *Christian Evangelist,* February 1854, 78–79.
21. Ibid., December 1854, 462.
22. Ibid., November 1854, 427–29.
23. *Christian Record,* September 1854, 286.
24. Ibid., 287.
25. *Christian Evangelist,* November 1854, 428.
26. *Millennial Harbinger,* February 1855, 117.
27. Ibid., Amos Harvey's letter was dated October 8, 1854, and James McBride's letter was written on November 6, 1854.
28. *Christian Evangelist,* December 1854, 462. This letter was written on August 13, 1854.
29. Ibid., November 1854, 428. This letter was written on July 24, 1854.
30. *Millennial Harbinger,* January 1855, 57. This letter was written on November 24, 1854.
31. Margaret Standish Carey and Patricia Hoy Hainline, *Sweet Home in the Oregon Cascades.* (Brownsville, Oregon: Calapooia Publications, 1979), 42.
32. The Reverend J. A. Cornwall was born in Georgia in 1798 and migrated to Oregon the same year Glen Owen Burnett did in 1846.
33. *Christian Evangelist,* February 1855, 90–91. This information is in a letter from James McBride to Daniel Bates, dated November 2, 1854. The debate took place in the middle of October.
34. Ibid.

35. Ibid., September 1854, 351–52. This letter was written along the trail on June 6, 1854, from a location "Near Fort Laramie."
36. Ibid., June 1855, 282–83. This letter was written on January 28, 1855.
37. Dr. James Harrison Roundtree (1815-1895) and his wife, Emeline Cole Riddle Roundtree (1818–1892), were in the group of Christians who migrated from Monmouth, Illinois (Warren County), in the western part of the state in 1852. They were actually from neighboring Knox County. William Murphy (1816–1874) was a younger brother to John Ecles Murphy, and he was married to Elizabeth (Betsy) Roundtree (1823–1889), a younger sister to Dr. James Harrison Roundtree. The Roundtrees and Murphys both settled in Lewis County. The Roundtrees remained in Washington, but the Murphys returned to Oregon and joined the other Illinois families who had founded the town of Monmouth. William Murphy was a member of the board of trustees for Christian College, and he was an elder in the Monmouth Church. William Huntington (1816–1894) and his wife, Eliza Koontz Huntington, settled in the Castle Rock area of Cowlitz County. The Henry Jackson family settled near the Huntingtons on Arkansas Creek southwest of Castle Rock.
38. Minnie Roof Dee, *From Oxcart to Airplane: A Biography of George H. Himes* (Portland: Binfords & Mort, Publishers, n.d.), 29.
39. *Christian Evangelist,* September 1854, 351. This letter was written on May 7, 1854.
40. *Millennial Harbinger,* January 1855, 57. This letter was written on November 24, 1854.
41. *Christian Evangelist,* February 1855, 90–91. This letter was written on November 2, 1854.
42. Ibid., November 1854, 429. This letter was written on July 24, 1854.

NOTES TO CHAPTER 14

1. D. Duane Cummins, *The Disciples Colleges: A History* (St. Louis: CBP Press, 1987), 23–43.
2. Ibid., 33.
3. *Millennial Harbinger,* November 1856, 649.
4. Ibid., January 1855, 9.
5. Ellis A. Stebbins, *The OCE Story* (Monmouth, Oregon: Oregon College of Education, 1973), 1.

6. C. F. Swander, *Making Disciples in Oregon* (by the author, 1928), 49. Douglas B. Dornhecker, "A History of Annual Meetings of Disciples of Christ in Oregon to 1877" (Johnson City, Tennessee: unpublished M. Div. thesis, Emmanuel School of Religion, 1979), 42.
7. Ruth Stoller, "Lafayette—The First Town," *Old Yamhill: The Early History of its Towns and Cities* (Portland: Binfords & Mort Publishing, 1989), 36.
8. *Christian Evangelist,* November 1855, 513–14. This advertisement was sent on June 26, 1855.
9. Ibid., November 1855, 513–14.
10. Eleanor Wilson, "A History of Bethany School" (unpublished typescript). The Bethany School is still in existence, and it occupies buildings on property donated by Elias Cox in 1886. This site is less than half a mile from the Bethany Pioneer Cemetery and the original site of the meetinghouse of the Bethany Christian Church. When visitors inquire about the history of the school, they are given the five-page article by Eleanor Wilson.
11. Robert Horace Down, *A History of the Silverton Country* (Portland: The Berncliff Press, 1926), 213. See also Robert Carlton Clark, *History of the Willamette Valley* (Chicago: S. J. Clarke, 1927), 594. See also H. Earl Pemberton, "Early Colleges in Oregon," *Oregon Historical Quarterly,* Vol. XXXIII, No. 3 (September 1932), 231–32.
12. Wilson, "A History of Bethany School."
13. *Christian Evangelist,* April 1854, 163.
14. Jonas A. Jonasson, *Bricks Without Straw: The Story of Linfield College* (Caldwell, Idaho: The Caxton Printers, 1938). Kenneth L. Holmes, ed., *Linfield's Hundred Years: A Centennial History of Linfield College, McMinnville, Oregon* (Portland: Binfords & Mort, Publishers, 1956). Reverend A. J. Hunsaker, "The Early History of McMinnville College" (unpublished document, written in January 1912, and housed in the archives of the library at Linfield College).
15. Hubert Howe Bancroft, *History of Oregon,* Vol. II (San Francisco: The History Company, 1888), 684. See also Joseph Gaston, *The Centennial History of Oregon, 1811–1912,* Vol. I (Chicago: The S. J. Clarke Publishing Company, 1912), 603. Gaston noted of Sebastian Adams: ". . . as he and most of the settlers in that vicinity were members of the Christian church, the school became a Christian or Campbellite institution."

16. Jonasson, *Bricks Without Straw*, 24.
17. John E. Smith, *Bethel, Polk County, Oregon* (by the author, 1941), 13.
18. Ibid., 19.
19. Ibid., 15.
20. *Christian Record*, April 1856, 121–22. This letter was written on January 28, 1856.
21. Bancroft, *History of Oregon*, 686.
22. Stebbins, *The OCE Story*, 7.
23. Gaston, *Centennial History*, 580.
24. *Christian Evangelist*, May 1855, 229–30. This letter was written on January 21, 1855.
25. Ibid., August 1855, 381. Letter from Dr. James McBride written on May 14, 1855. *Christian Record*, August, 1855, 250. Letter from A. V. McCarty written on May 28, 1855. Ibid., April 1856, 121–22. Letter from A. V. McCarty written on January 28, 1856.
26. *Christian Evangelist*, October 1855, 478. This letter was written on July 3, 1855.
27. *Christian Record*, January 1856, 24. This letter was written on November 15, 1855.
28. *Christian Evangelist*, September 1855, 433. This letter was written on May 27, 1855.
29. Ibid., August 1855, 381. This letter was written on May 14, 1855.
30. *Christian Record*, April 1856, 121–22. This letter was written on January 28, 1856.

NOTES TO CHAPTER 15

1. *Christian Record*, April 1857, 122. This letter was written on December 26, 1856.
2. *Christian Evangelist*, December 1854, 461–62. This letter was written on August 13, 1854.
3. *Christian Record*, May 1855, 146–47. This letter was written on February 18, 1855.
4. Ibid., This letter was written on February 18, 1855.
5. Ibid., October 1855, 313. This letter was written on June 14, 1855.
6. Ibid., April 1856, 121–22. This letter was written on January 28, 1856.
7. *Oregon Statesman*, July 7, 1855.
8. *Christian Evangelist*, July 1854, 276. This letter was written on March 22, 1854.

9. Ibid., January 1854, 40. This letter was written on October 7, 1853.
10. Ibid., August 1854, 316. This letter was written on April 12, 1854.
11. Clifford C. Miller, "The Religious Expositor: Oregon Pioneer Journal," *Oregon Historical Quarterly,* Vol. LXIV, No. 2 (June 1963), 130.
12. Joseph Schafer, "William Lysander Adams," *Dictionary of American Biography,* Vol. I (New York: Charles Scribner's Sons, 1957), 102.
13. Inez Eugenia Adams Parker, "Early Recollections of Oregon Pioneer Life," 23.
14. *Oregon Statesman,* March 20, 1855.
15. Sarah Hunt Steeves, *Book of Remembrance of Marion County, Oregon, Pioneers, 1840–1860* (Portland: The Berncliff Press, 1927), 260–61 and 145.
16. Gary Burlingame, Julie Jones, and Don Rivera, *The Cooper-Hewitt-Matheny History* (by the authors, 1996), 22.
17. "Elijah Lafayette Bristow Letters, 1857–1864," (Eugene, Oregon: Lane County Historical Society, 1959), 4–9. In a letter dated May 4, 1857, and sent to a friend in the midwest, E. L. Bristow commented on the political situation. With little regard for accurate spelling, he wrote: "Our Teritory is in quite a ferment just now — Politicly Speaking. We are endeavoring to form a State Constitution during this summer. The Slavery question is being interduced. And will perhaps be the only question at isue among us. The Democratic party have held there convention & published thire platform. Which obligates ther candidates, (provided they are elected) to form the "State" constitutions, with two separate Schedules, One for Slavery, and the other against which must then be submitted to a Special vote of the people. But the oposition — free State party they call themselves — are going it On a one-side plan; that is formeing it for free-state only. But the Democrats have a fare show to elect ther Candidates, to the State Constitutional convention. Though I think that in the end, that this will become a free state. Though my own sympathies are with the pro Slavery Side-party." In a later letter to his wife's parents in California, dated June 17, 1857, he laments that some Democrats have "turned Black-Republican." He appears to be talking about his brother, William Wilshire Bristow, who in the following year was elected to the state senate.

18. Walter Carleton Woodward, *The Rise and Early History of Political Parties in Oregon, 1843–1868* (Portland: The J. K. Gill Company, 1913), 103, 128. The "independents" called a convention of "National Democrats" to meet in Eugene in April 1858. The regular Democrats lashed out at Ford, Shuck and their friends and all others who would join "this Eugene Negro equality movement." The Nationals were referred to as "certain malcontents" and "traitors" who were moving in the direction of "the Black Republican Camp.
19. *Oregon Statesman*, March 31, 1857.
20. *Republican League Register: A Record of The Republican Party in the State of Oregon* (Portland: The Register Publishing Company, 1896), 23.
21. Oregon Historical Society *Scrap Books*, Vol. 77, 130.
22. Joseph Gaston, *Portland, Oregon: Its History and Builders*, Vol. I, (Portland: S. J. Clarke Publishers, 1911), 666.
23. Robert W. Johannsen, *Frontier Politics on the Eve of the Civil War* (Seattle: University of Washington Press, 1955), 46.
24. Samuel N. Dicken and Emily F. Dicken, *The Making of Oregon: A Study in Historical Geography* (Portland: Oregon Historical Society, 1979), 89.
25. Jim and Reita Lockett, *Settling the Land of Promise: Stories of Pioneer Men, Women and Children who laid a Firm Foundation for Generations to Come* (McMinnville: by the authors, 1994), 71.
26. Ibid.
27. John Rogers McBride, "Overland 1846" in the *McBride Family Papers*. This 95-page typed document is manuscript #458 in the Oregon History Center collection.
28. Glen Owen Burnett, "Our Meeting on the Clackamas in 1846," *Pacific Christian Messenger*, November 9, 1877, 5.
29. Fred Lockley, "Observations and Impressions of the Journal Man," *Oregon Daily Journal*, April 17, 1922, 8. This was Lockley's interview with Joel Jordan Hembree.
30. Lockett, *Settling the Land of Promise*, 73.
31. *Christian Record*, March 1856, 91–92. This letter was written on February 5, 1856.
32. Ibid., 91. This letter was written on February 23, 1856.
33. Lockett, *Settling the Land of Promise*, 73–74.
34. Lockley, "Observations and Impressions of the Journal Man." See also William P. Bonney, "Monument to Captain Hembree," *Pacific Northwest Quarterly*, Vol. 11. A footnote recorded: "On Sunday June 20, 1920, an interesting ceremony was held in

Toppenish, Yakima County, Washington. The Washington State Historical Society had placed a marker on the battlefield where Captain Hembree was killed by the Indians."

35. *Christian Record,* August 1856, 254. This letter was written on May 22, 1856.
36. Ibid., 256. This letter was written on June 21, 1856.
37. *Christian Evangelist,* December 1856, 566. This letter was written on August 23, 1856.
38. Opal and Leslie Carson, *First Christian Church, Salem, Oregon: The Centennial Story, 1855–1955* (Salem, Oregon: n. p., 1955), 5.
39. Aurelius Todd, "Rev. A. L. J. Todd, Pioneer Circuit Rider," *The Umpqua Trapper* (Publication of the Douglas County Historical Society, Fall 1970), 63.

NOTES TO CHAPTER 16

1. *Millennial Harbinger,* September 1850, 539–40.
2. *Christian Record,* December 1852, 186.
3. Ibid., May 1853, 336.
4. Ibid., February 1854, 61. This letter was written on November 3, 1853. As it turned out, it would be 17 years before Oregon Christians were strong enough to support their own paper. Thomas F. Campbell established the *Christian Messenger* in Monmouth, Oregon, in October 1870.
5. Ibid., September 1854, 286.
6. Ibid., January 1858, 21.
7. Ibid., December 1855, 379. Alpheus Ireland wrote on August 20, 1855.
8. Ibid., March 1856, 91. David R. Lewis wrote on February 23, 1856.
9. Ibid., April 1857, 122–23. This letter was written on December 26, 1856.
10. Ibid., December 1873, 568.
11. In the years after the Civil War, Benjamin Franklin's *American Christian Review,* published in Indianapolis, and Isaac Errett's *Christian Standard,* published in Cincinnati, became powerful weeklies that enjoyed a national circulation among Christians. Both had devoted supporters in Oregon. Beginning in 1869, the *Apostolic Times,* edited by J. W. McGarvey, Moses Lard, and others in Lexington, Kentucky, also competed favorably for a share of the readers on the west coast. However, Oregon Christians could finally boast of having their own paper when

Thomas F. Campbell began editing the *Christian Messenger* from Monmouth in October 1870.

12. *Christian Record,* January 1858, 21. This letter was written from Lane County by Caleb Davis on September 8, 1857.
13. Ibid., November 1872, 521. This letter was written from Polk County by G. W. Richardson on September 28, 1872.
14. *Evangelist,* October 1859, 468–69.
15. *Christian Evangelist,* January 1854, 30–31. This letter was written October 9, 1853.
16. Ibid., June 1855, This letter was written by James R. Fisher on January 28, 1855.
17. Ibid., November 1855, 521.
18. Ibid., November 1853, 407. This letter was written on July 14, 1853.
19. Carroll Kendrick (1815–1891) and L. L. Pinkerton (1812–1875) published the *Ecclesiastic Reformer* from Harrodsburg, Kentucky, for five years (1848–1852), but that periodical had ceased publication by the time of McBride's letter. Reuben Lindsay Coleman (1807–1880) and James W. Goss (1812–1870) began editing the *Christian Publisher* in 1836, and it became the *Christian Intelligencer* in 1843. It continued to be published by John G. Parrish (1817–1871) and others until 1864. Parrish was a "49er" who lived and preached in California for a few years, and through his connection there could have been some California circulation of this journal. But it is very doubtful that it had any Oregon readers.
20. See James Brooks Major, "The Role of Periodicals in the Development of the Disciples of Christ, 1850–1910" (Nashville: unpublished Ph.D. dissertation, Vanderbilt University, 1966). This includes an entire chapter (52–84) on the Jesse B. Ferguson controversy.
21. *Christian Magazine,* September 1851, 286.
22. *Christian Evangelist,* November 1853, 407.
23. *American Christian Review,* February 23, 1858, 31. This letter was written by Calvin L. Murphy on December 23, 1857. He wrote from Monmouth in Polk County, Oregon Territory.
24. Ibid., June 8, 1858, 90.
25. Ibid., November 25, 1862, 7. This was the opinion of David Walk in "Brief Sketches of Noticeable Characters, No. II."
26. After the failure of *Christian Magazine* in 1853, Tolbert Fanning began editing the *Gospel Advocate* in Nashville in 1855, but it was years before this journal began to have any influence in Oregon.

Of more significance for Oregon Christians, W. W. Stevenson began editing the *Western Evangelist* in northern California in November 1858. This was the first church paper published by the Restoration Movement on the West Coast, and it occasionally carried news from Oregon churches.

27. *Christian Record,* October 1857, 298–99. This letter was written on April 20, 1857.
28. Ibid., October 1857, 299.
29. *American Christian Review,* April 30, 1867, 139. This letter was written by Thomas Crawford McBride from his home in Yamhill County, Oregon Territory, on June 28, 1856. He died 10 months later. More than a decade later, this letter was reprinted by Benjamin Franklin for the readers of his *American Christian Review.*
30. *Oregon Argus,* May 9, 1857.
31. Ruth Stoller, *Schools of Old Yamhill* (Lafayette, Oregon: Yamhill County Historical Society, 1982), 15.
32. Zillah Paeth, "Early Letters . . . Pioneers Describe Life in Monmouth," *Historically Speaking,* Vol. IX, 17–18.
33. *Christian Record,* January 1858, 21. This letter was written on September 8, 1857.

NOTES TO CHAPTER 17

1. *American Christian Review,* April 30, 1867, 139.
2. Ibid., February 23, 1858, 31.
3. *Millennial Harbinger,* August 1857, 467. At the same graduation ceremony, Thomas Franklin Campbell received an honorary Master's degree. Twelve years later he would move to Monmouth to assume the presidency of Christian College.
4. There are various accounts for the beginning of the Salem Church, some as early as 1855. But Caton wrote that it began "last Spring." He evidently is referring to the spring of 1857, as he made the statement on July 3, 1858. A beginning date for Salem in 1855 must be correct, because the Salem Church hosted the 1856 annual State Meeting, and that decision would have been announced at the 1855 annual State Meeting. The Salem Church was fragile in the beginning. It may have met in 1855 and 1856, disbanded in the winter of 1856–57, and then had a new beginning in the spring of 1857.
5. *American Christian Review,* September 28, 1858, 155. This letter was written on July 3, 1858.

6. *Christian Record,* May 1858, 155.
7. "Church of Christ History Told; Building Plan Set," *Stayton Mail,* September 25, 1958.
8. Frederick D. Kershner, "Stars, Chapter VI—The Message of Isaac Errett (Continued)," *Christian Standard,* July 13, 1940, 669.
9. There were two congregations from Washington Territory represented, and they each had a delegate present. So there were actually 22 congregations and 38 delegates at the meeting. The two delegates from Washington Territory were William Huntington from the Monticello congregation (38 members) and Stephen Guthrie from the Thurston congregation (number of members not recorded).
10. *Christian Record,* January 1859, 27. This letter was written on September 24, 1858.
11. Among the other congregations established by 1858 were: Rainer in Columbia County; Hillsboro in Washington County; Lafayette, Chehalem, Sheridan, and Amity in Yamhill County; Rock Creek in Clackamas County; Howell's Prairie in Marion County; Spring Valley and Rickreall in Polk County; Scio and French Prairie in Linn County; Oak Creek and Mary's River in Benton County; Big Muddy, Grand Prairie, Wallace Butte, Springfield, and Coast Fork in Lane County; and Coles Valley, Winchester, Lookingglass Prairie, Myrtle Creek, and Canyonville in Douglas County. There may have been Christians meeting on the Clatsop Plains in Clatsop County, but that cannot be verified. In addition, Stephen Powell and Margaret Umphlette had married on May 23, 1858, and moved to Tillamook County. They were devout Christians and they probably organized a church in their house.
12. *Evangelist,* February 1859, 82–84. This letter was written on November 14, 1858.
13. Ibid., 91. This letter was written on November 1, 1858. The report from James R. Fisher was written on November 14, 1858.
14. Ibid., This letter was written on October 12, 1858.
15. *Christian Record,* February 1859, 60. This letter was written on October 21, 1858.
16. Elias Benton Ware, *History of the Disciples of Christ in California* (Healdsburg, California: F. W. Cooke, 1916), 66–71.
17. Ibid., 104.
18. *Evangelist,* August 1859, 383.
19. *Millennial Harbinger,* September 1858, 537. This letter was written by James Anderson from Santa Clara, California, on

April 27, 1858. The preacher that Burnett was teamed with was John O. White from Missouri. Burnett and White had known each other for many years, and they had preached together back in Missouri. White had not moved to California permanently. Following these meetings with Burnett, he returned to his home in Missouri.

20. *Evangelist,* February 1859, 91. This letter was written on November 13, 1858.
21. *Western Evangelist,* November 1858, 18–19.
22. Ibid., 2.
23. Ibid., March 1859, 157–58.
24. Ibid., November 1859, 6.
25. Either Richardson or Mathes misspelled the name of H. H. Hendrix. It was printed as H. H. Hendricks, which was a common mistake.
26. *Christian Record,* January 1959, 26–27. This letter was written on September 24, 1858.
27. *Evangelist,* November 1859, 526. This letter was written on August 11, 1859.

NOTES TO CHAPTER 18

1. Walter Carleton Woodward, *The Rise and Early History of Political Parties in Oregon, 1843–1868* (Portland: The J. K. Gill Company, 1913), 167.
2. Nathaniel S. Haynes, *History of the Disciples of Christ in Illinois, 1819–1914* (Cincinnati: The Standard Publishing Company, 1915), 466–69.
3. Albert J. Beveridge, *Abraham Lincoln, 1809–1858,* Vol. I. (Boston and New York, 1928), 360.
4. John G. Nicolay and John Hay, *Abraham Lincoln: A History,* Vol. I. (New York: The Century Company, 1890), 221.
5. Roy P. Basler, ed., *The Collected Works of Abraham Lincoln* (New Brunswick, New Jersey: University Press, 1953), Vol. I, 319-21. This is in a letter from Lincoln to Martin S. Morris, dated March 26, 1843. See also Charles L. Woodall, "Lincoln's Religion and the Disciples," *Discipliana,* Winter 1980, 51–54; 59–61.
6. Edward A. Dickson, "Lincoln and Baker: The Story of a Great Friendship," *Historical Society of Southern California Quarterly,* September 1952, 229–42. See also James H. Matheny, "A Modern Knight Errant—Edward Dickinson Baker," *Journal of the Illinois State Historical Society,* April 1916, 23–42. See also John

P. Snigg, "Edward Dickinson Baker—Lincoln's Forgotten Friend," *Lincoln Herald*, Summer 1951, 33–37.

7. William C. Boyd, "Edward Dickinson Baker, Alien Senator," *Oregon Historical Quarterly*, Vol. XLIII, No. 2 (June 1941), 139–44. (Note misprint on the *Quarterly* cover, it reads 1941, but year was 1942.)
8. Charles Foster McElroy, *Ministers of First Christian Church (Disciples of Christ) Springfield, Illinois, 1833–1962* (St. Louis: The Bethany Press, 1962), 28–29, 34.
9. Lillian Applegate, "Biography of Maria Elder Watson." This is Mss #1089/Dye Coll. Box 1 in the Oregon History Center. Lillian Applegate, granddaughter of Maria Watson, calls Edward Dickinson Baker and his wife "old friends" and "life long friends" of her grandparents. See also John E. Smith, *Bethel, Polk County, Oregon* (by the author, 1941), 65-66.
10. *Millennial Harbinger*, April 1863, 191.
11. Simeon Francis, editor of the *Oregonian* wrote to Lincoln on November 23, 1860. This letter was cited in Robert W. Johannsen, *Frontier Politics on the Eve of the Civil War* (Seattle: University of Washington Press, 1955), 148.
12. Johannsen, *Frontier Politics on the Eve of the Civil War*, 128–53. Woodward, *The Rise and Early History of Political Parties*, 166–88.
13. *Evangelist*, January 1861, 37–38. This report was submitted by William Porter, the secretary of the annual State Meeting. It was sent from Sublimity, Oregon, in September 1860.
14. *Millennial Harbinger*, December 1860, 695–97. This report was submitted by Oscar L. Matthews on October 8, 1860. See also the *Evangelist*, December 1860, 564–66, for editorial comments on the large California meeting by Aaron Chatterton. See also *Western Evangelist*, October 1860, 369–71, for the report of this meeting by the California editor, W. W. Stevenson.
15. *Millennial Harbinger*, December 1860, 695. This statement was made by Oscar L. Matthews. He was a recent graduate of Bethany College and was about to become the founding president of Hesperian College in Woodland, California, the first college established by the Restoration Movement in the state.
16. Some of these preachers had moved to Polk from other counties, including: Alfred Elder from Yamhill County, Charles Bradshaw from Lane County, and Orlando Alderman from Marion County.

17. *1860 Polk County, Oregon, Census.* Transcribed by Harley Haskins. Publisher: End of Trail Researchers. Along with the strongest preaching contingent in the state, Polk County in 1860 was home to a wide array of talented laymen including: Amos Harvey, Nat Ford, David Goff, Thomas Lovelady, Harrison Linville, Hezekiah Burford, David R. Lewis, Dr. Zedekiah Davis, Dr. William C. Warriner, Ira F. M. Butler, Reuben Doty, Squire S. Whitman, Thomas H. Lucas, A. W. Lucas, William Murphy, William Mason, John Bounds, Sr., John A. Bounds, James Berry Riggs, John McCarty, Carter Davidson, Harrison Brunk, Ebenezer Connet Keyt, Townsend Waller, William D. Cole, C. C. Crain, Absalom B. Faulconer, Luke Mulkey, John W. Ladd, James L. Ladd, John D. Kelty, George Johnston Baskett, Michael Shelley, David Stump, John Henry Hawley, Joseph Warren Downer, Edward Ground, John D. Frazer, Lucien B. Frazer, William Cornett, Horace G. Burnett, James G. Campbell, Melchi Johnson, Elezar Flannery, Frederick X. Shoemaker, and Jesse Dutton Walling. Some of the more prominent Christian women were also residents of Polk County in 1860 including: Ellen Scott Lyle, Jane Waller, Jane Riggs, Polly Lovelady, Lucinda Ford, Catherine Bristow Baskett, Jane Ramage Harvey, Maria Elder Watson, and Martha Burnett Holman.
18. *Western Evangelist,* July 1860, 287. This letter was written on June 8, 1860.
19. See the *Evangelist,* July 1862, 336. The Boltons wrote to report the death of their nine-year-old daughter, Sarah Elizabeth, as a result of lung fever.
20. "Minutes of the Oregon Annual Meeting," 1863.
21. *Western Evangelist,* January 1861, 29.
22. Editorial, *Oregon Argus,* Saturday, October 27, 1860.
23. *Evangelist,* June 1861, 329. This letter was written on February 28, 1861.
24. Ibid., 329–30. McBride wrote on March 4, 1861, and Dawson wrote on April 8, 1861.
25. Ibid., January 1862, 48.
26. *Pacific Tidings,* April 9, 1915, 5. This information is in the Keathley Bailes obituary account written by J. N. Hogue of London, Oregon. Bailes was born October 14, 1829, and died March 17, 1915.
27. The use of "Christian Church" and "Church of Christ" was synonymous at this time. The Bethany Christian Church was often referred to as the Bethany Church of Christ. The Bethany

Church has been discussed before. Its leaders included: Thomas C. Shaw, C. F. Mascher, William L. Mascher, Elias Cox, Peter Cox, Gideon Cox, Isaac Headrick, Joshua Bowen, Peter Bowen, and Fones Wilbur. The preacher for this church for many years was Caleb P. Chapman, but he also traveled frequently in evangelistic work. The leaders of the Rock Creek Church of Christ were Charles Bisbee Dart, Daniel Trullinger, and Levi Davis. The Bethany Church was in Marion County, and the Rock Creek Church was in Clackamas County, but the meetingplaces of the two congregations were less than 15 miles apart.

28. *Oregon Statesman,* July 8, 1861. See also Gary Burlingame, Julie Jones, and Don Rivera, *The Cooper-Hewitt-Matheny History* (by the authors, 1996), 21–22.
29. *Evangelist,* July 1862, 334. The Coast Fork Church was probably in the neighborhood near Cottage Grove. Powell's reference to "Christian Chapel in my own neighborhood" must be a reference to the Central congregation seven miles east of Albany in Linn County.
30. Ibid., December 1862, 575. James R. Fisher sent this announcement to the Iowa paper.
31. "Diary of Lot Livermore," Oregon Pioneer Association *Transactions,* 1915, 246.
32. *Western Evangelist,* August 1862, 615. This letter was written July 2, 1862.
33. See Ruth Stoller, "Sheridan— A. B. Faulconer's Town" in *Old Yamhill: The Early History of its Towns and Cities*. (Portland: Binfords & Mort Publishing, 1989), 71-76.
34. "Church of Christ History Told; Building Plan Set," *Stayton Mail,* September 25, 1858.
35. See "Autobiography of James Addison Bushnell, 1826–1912" (Eugene, Oregon: Lane County Historical Society, 1959). This is a 68-page typed manuscript. The material on the founding of the Grand Prairie Church of Christ is on pp. 29–30. In later years, this congregation was referred to as the Grand Prairie Christian Church. At different times in its history it has also been called Clear Lake Christian Church and Junction City Christian Church. Bushnell called it Grand Prairie Church of Christ in the 1850s, and when describing his first attachment to it he wrote, "I united with the Church of Christ and Elizabeth also uniting by confession and immersion." He does not specifically confirm that Philip Mulkey baptized his wife, but it

is implied in the narrative. Mulkey was responsible for organizing the church.

36. Lucia W. Moore, Nina W. McCornack and Gladys W. McCready, *The Story of Eugene* (Eugene, Oregon: Lane County Historical Society, 1995), 76–77.
37. Philip Mulkey Hunt, *The Mulkeys of America* (Portland: by the author, 1982), 192–93.
38. Of Philip and Martha Mulkey's eleven children, nine had lived to maturity. Most of these children and their spouses were strong Christians, and most of them lived around Philip in Lane County.
39. "Autobiography of James Addison Bushnell," 33.
40. Ibid.
41. "Chronicles of Mill Creek Church, Aumsville, Oregon," as recorded by William Porter, church clerk, 13.
42. Ibid., 14.
43. Ibid., 14-15.
44. *Evangelist,* June 1864, 200. Harrison Shelley submitted the obituary on James R. Fisher. He wrote: "He died as he had lived, firm in the faith of the Gospel . . . He was an affectionate husband, an indulgent father, and a consistent Christian-contended earnestly for the faith, was an able advocate of the cause of truth; but that well-known and beloved voice is now stilled in death." Fisher was survived by his wife and six children.
45. Keathley Bailes (1829–1915) has already been mentioned. He arrived in Marion County in 1862 and served Churches of Christ in the Great Northwest for the next half-century. Martin Peterson (1820–1889) came overland to California in 1863 and continued on to Oregon in 1864. He lived and preached around Jackson County for the next quarter-century until his death in 1889.
46. Margaret Standish Carey and Patricia Hoy Hainline, *Sweet Home in the Oregon Cascades* (Brownsville, Oregon: Calapooia Publications, 1979), 42.
47. G. M. Weimer, "Reminiscences of H. M. Waller, The Oldest Evangelist of the Church of Christ on the Pacific Slope," *Christian Standard,* April 29, 1893, 328–29.
48. The statistics for Pleasant Hill were not submitted in the "Minutes" for 1863 even though W. W. Bristow was a delegate to the meeting. The membership total of 82 is from 1862 when Pleasant Hill hosted the annual State Meeting.

49. "Minutes of the Oregon Annual Meeting," 1863. It is puzzling that there is no report from Pleasant Hill Church, since William Wilshire Bristow was present at the meeting. It is also confusing that there is no report on the Salem Church, since Alfred Stanton was present at the meeting. One encouraging item in the "Minutes" is the realization that A. L. Todd and Samuel Bates Briggs had traveled all the way from Douglas County to be in attendance. It is also interesting to note the presence of George M. Whitney and Keathley Bailes. Their most productive years for preaching in Oregon were just beginning. Nine congregations appear only in the 1858 minutes: Liberty House, Monroe, Clackamas, Clear Lake (this is referred to as Grand Prairie in 1863), Lower Muddy, Sand Ridge, Union Vale, Tualatin, and North Fork Yamhill. Eleven churches appear only in the 1863 minutes: Canyonville, Grand Prairie (this was Clear Lake in 1858), Lower Fork Willamette, Upper Muddy, Scio, Dallas, Antioch, The Dalles, Butte Creek, Harris Bridge, and Lookingglass Prairie.
50. *Evangelist*, January 1864, 31–34.
51. There must have been some advantages to a June meeting. Following McMinnville in June 1864, the Bethel Church hosted the annual meeting in June 1865, two months after Lincoln's assassination.
52. *Evangelist*, March 1864, 101.
53. Ibid., June 1864, 199.
54. Aurelius Todd, "Rev. A. L. J. Todd, Pioneer Circuit Rider," *The Umpqua Trapper*, Vol. VI, No. 3, Fall 1970, 64–65.
55. Ibid., March 1864, 102. Mascher made this comment on January 4, 1864.
56. Todd, "Rev. A. L. J. Todd," No. 4, Winter 1970, 88.
57. Ibid., No. 3, Fall 1970, 71.

NOTES TO CHAPTER 19

1. John E. Smith, *Bethel, Polk County, Oregon* (by the author, 1941), 38.
2. *Evangelist*, January 1864, 32. The *Evangelist* suspended publication after the June 1864 issue. This was a disappointment to Oregon Christians who had faithfully supported this journal. The demise of the *Evangelist* was due to the death of Aaron Chatterton, who by that time was carrying most of the editorial responsibilities. The health and age of Daniel Bates, plus the upheaval of the Civil War, were other factors that contributed

to the suspension of publication. Barton Warren Johnson began editing the *Evangelist* in Oskaloosa, Iowa, in October 1865.

3. Douglas B. Dornhecker, "A History of Annual Meetings of Disciples of Christ in Oregon to 1877" (unpublished M.Div thesis, Emmanuel School of Religion, 1979), 74.
4. Ellis A. Stebbins, *The OCE Story* (Monmouth, Oregon: Oregon College of Education, 1973), 7.

John E. Smith, *Christian College* (by the author, 1953), 7.

5. The nine original board members for Bethel Institute were: Glen Owen Burnett, Amos Harvey, Joseph Warren Downer, William Lysander Adams, Samuel M. Gilmore, John H. Robb, A. V. McCarty, A. H. Frier, and Sanford Watson. The 11 original board members at Monmouth were: Ira F. M. Butler, John Ecles Murphy, David R. Lewis, Squire S. Whitman, John B. Smith, Reuben P. Boise, William Mason, Thomas H. Lucas, Samuel Simmons, Hezekiah Burford, and Thomas H. Hutchinson. Ten of those 11 were well-known church leaders among the Christians, and the other, Reuben Boise, was a prominent community leader.
6. Ten of the new 11 board members were strong Christians. Nathaniel Hudson was a Presbyterian. He was chosen, not for his church affiliation, but for his academic strengths. He had taught at Bethel College, and he was widely respected as an educator. William Dawson was from the McMinnville Church. Sebastian Adams was a brother to William Lysander Adams and a fine preacher, and William Murphy was a brother to John Ecles Murphy and an elder in the Monmouth Church. Daniel Holman was the son-in-law of Glen Owen Burnett. Richardson was the preacher at Bethel. Stanton was an elder in the Salem Church, and Lucas and Whitson were leaders in the Monmouth Church. Rowland was a talented educator with ties to Bethel, and Frazer was a leader in the Salt Creek congregation in Polk County.
7. *Christian Record,* October 1868, 309. This letter was written by John M. Harris on July 1, 1868.
8. See Bonnie Miller, "Restoration Pioneer in Oregon: William Lysander Adams," (unpublished manuscript, 1993). See also Walter C. Woodward, *Political Parties in Oregon, 1843-1868* (Portland: The J. K. Gill Company, 1913). See also Robert W. Johannsen, *Frontier Politics on the Eve of the Civil War* (Seattle: University of Washington Press, 1955).
9. Elwood Evans, *The West Shore,* May 1876, 4.

10. T. W. Davenport, "Slavery Question in Oregon," *Oregon Historical Quarterly*, Vol. IX, No. 3 (September 1908), 246.
11. This observation is from George N. Belknap, in his edition of *William Lysander Adams, Treason, Stratagems & Spoils*, 1868, 38.
12. Portland *Oregonian*, January 13, 1890. 5.
13. Hubert Howe Bancroft, *History of Oregon*, Vol. II (San Francisco: The History Company, Publishers, 1888), 431.
14. Elwood Evans, *History of the Pacific Northwest: Oregon and Washington*. 2 Vols. (Portland: North Pacific History Company, 1889), 446-47.
15. *Christian Record*, September 1867, 274.
16. *Christian Teacher*, September 1866, 283. This letter was written by John Harris on July 24, 1866. This California periodical was the successor to the *Western Evangelist*, edited by W. W. Stevenson, which had run from November 1858 through 1863. The *Christian Teacher* was a monthly, edited by J. N. Pendegast for the three years of 1864 through 1866.
17. Ibid., March 1866, 85-88. This information is in a lengthy letter from A. V. McCarty dated February 5, 1866, and sent from Buena Vista in Polk County.
18. Ibid., 86-87.
19. Ibid., 88.
20. Ibid., April 1866, 122. A. V. McCarty wrote this letter to John N. Pendegast, the editor of the *Christian Teacher*, on February 18, 1866.
21. Ibid., March 1866, 95.
22. *Christian Record*, November 1868, 345-46.
23. Joseph Gaston, *The Centennial History of Oregon*, Vol. II (Chicago: S. J. Clarke Publishing Company, 1912), 660.
24. Nathaniel S. Haynes, *History of the Disciples of Christ in Illinois, 1819-1914* (Cincinnati: The Standard Publishing Company, 1915), 506-08.
25. *Pacific Christian Messenger*, May 14, 1880, 1.
26. *Christian Teacher*, September 1866, 283-84. John M. Harris wrote this letter on July 24, 1866.
27. Ibid., October 1867, 319.
28. Ibid., April 1874, 160. This information is in a letter written by Caleb Davis to James Mathes on January 27, 1874. He was reflecting back on the impact of John M. Harris at Pleasant Hill.
29. Ibid., May 1868, 146.
30. Ibid., January 1870, 40.
31. Ibid., July 1868, 213.

32. *Millennial Harbinger*, September 1868, 535.
33. *Christian Record*, October 1868, 308-09.
34. Ibid., July 1868, 213-14.
35. Ibid., September 1868, 278.
36. Ibid., 279.
37. Ibid., April 1869, 179.
38. Ibid., 179. Abingdon College was one of the colleges affiliated with the Restoration Movement. James W. Butler was president of this college from 1860 to 1874. His son, A. D. Butler, taught briefly at Christian College. About this time (December 1868) or soon after, it must have become known that Levi Lindsay Rowland was thinking of resigning his position as president of Christian College. One record noted that James W. Butler was offered the presidency of Christian College and that he turned it down. This opened the door for an offer to be made to Thomas Franklin Campbell.
39. Ibid., September 1868, 279.
40. Ibid., November 1868, 346.
41. Ibid., September 1869, 427. This statement was made by G. W. Richardson in a letter written July 6, 1869.
42. Ibid., September 1868, 278-79. G. W. Richardson wrote this letter on July 8, 1868.
43. C. F. Swander, *Making Disciples in Oregon*, (by the author, 1928), 26.
44. Two of McCarty's daughters were ill at the same time, and they may have contracted the same fever that killed their father. Twenty-one-year-old Elizabeth Ann ("Betty") died in June 1868, and 5-year-old Ellen died in July. Betty was the little six-month-old child who nearly drowned in the Platte River crossing when the McCarty's came overland in 1847. See Charlotte Matheny Kirkwood, *Into the Eye of the Setting Sun: A Story of the West when it was New* (McMinnville, Oregon: The Family Association of Matheny, Cooper, Hewitt, Kirkwood and Bailey, 1991), 31. Charlotte Matheny knew the McCarty family. She mentions the death of A. V. McCarty and his oldest daughter, and she noted Betty was "brilliant like her father." McCarty's wife, Jane Bounds McCarty, outlived her husband by 40 years. When she died in 1908, her body was brought back to Vacaville, California and buried beside her husband and children.
45. *Pacific Christian Messenger*, February 27, 1880, 5. This letter was written from Salem on February 20, 1880.

46. See *Index to Clackamas County Probate Records, 1845-1910,* 119. For Daniel Trullinger it recorded: "No date of death shown in file." But it confirms that his estate was settled by his widow and his children in March 1869. The record in the Trullinger Family Bible recorded that Daniel was born on February 6, 1801, in Ohio and died on January 23, 1869, in Molalla, Oregon. If so, he died just prior to his 68th birthday. Daniel was a pioneer of 1848 and had preached in Oregon for 20 years. Gilmore Callison had arrived in Pleasant Hill in Lane County in 1852. He preached often for the Pleasant Hill Church of Christ and was one of the founders of the Christian Church in Eugene. He was elected to the state legislature in 1864. He moved to Eugene in 1866 and encouraged the congregation to build the brick meetinghouse on the corner of Ninth (Broadway) and Pearl. It was dedicated shortly after his death. Callison died of lung fever and was buried near other members of his family in Pleasant Hill Cemetery. See Ethel L. Briggs, *A History and Genealogy of Gilmore Callison and his Descendants* (Yucaipa, California: by the author, 1962). See also *A History of First Christian Church of Eugene, Oregon in Observance of its Centennial, 1866-1966,* (Eugene, Oregon, n. p.), 7-9.
47. *Christian Record,* September 1869, 426-27. G. W. Richardson wrote this letter on July 6, 1869.
48. In the decade of the 1860s, the State Meeting was held at Eola (Polk) in 1860; Bethany (Marion) in 1861; Pleasant Hill (Lane) in 1862; Central (Linn) in 1863; McMinnville (Yamhill) in 1864; and Bethel (Polk) in 1865. Records are not extant for the 1866 and 1867 meetings, but they were probably the first ones held at the "Christian camp ground" near Rickreall. Every State Meeting was held at this site near Rickreall through 1875. The meeting rotated again between 1876 and 1884. It has been held at Turner in Marion County every year since 1885.
49. *Christian Record,* September 1869, 427. G. W. Richardson wrote this letter on July 6, 1869.
50. Lewis A. McArthur, *Oregon Geographic Names,* 4th Edition, Revised and Enlarged (Portland: Oregon Historical Society, 1974), 616-17.
51. *Christian Record,* September 1868, 279.
52. Ibid., September 1869, 426.
53. Ibid., 429.
54. Ibid., August 1869, 366. Ibid., September 1869, 427.
55. *Vancouver Register,* May 22, 1869.

56. Ibid., June 19, 1869.
57. *Christian Record,* August 1869, 367. This letter was written by John M. Harris on May 20, 1869.
58. Ibid., September 1869, 429. John M. Harris wrote this letter on July 14, 1869.
59. Ibid., November 1869, 519. John M. Harris wrote this letter on October 8, 1869.
60. Ibid, January 1870, 39-40. Caleb Davis wrote this letter on November 22, 1869. Ibid., February 1870, 85. George M. Whitney wrote this letter on December 24, 1869.
61. Ibid., March 1870, 139. This information is from Joseph Warren Downer in a letter written on December 27, 1869.
62. Ibid., January 1870, 39. This observation is from Caleb Davis of Lane County. In a letter to the *Christian Standard* in Cincinnati, Ohio, dated January 25, 1870, Davis wrote: "Bro. Whitney is a fine speaker, has a good education, and is the finest singer that I have ever heard. The people generally come in crowds to hear him."
63. Ibid., February 1870, 85. George M. Whitney made this statement on December 24, 1869.
64. Ibid., January 1870, 39. This viewpoint was expressed by Caleb Davis.
65. Ibid., 40. This information is from Caleb Davis.
66. Opal and Leslie Carson, *First Christian Church, Salem, Oregon: The Centennial Story, 1855-1955,* (Salem, Oregon: n.p., 1955), 10. Although not blessed with a baptistry in the beginning, the "Little Brick Church" did possess a red Brussels carpet and padded pews. This printed history of the church reports that the building cost $4,000 and the lot cost $600 and a later addition to the building cost $1,000. But Joseph Warren Downer, one of the original deacons, told James Mathes that the building cost $7,000.
67. *Christian Record,* March 1870, 139. This letter was written by Joseph Warren Downer from Salem on December 27, 1869.
68. Governor Woods was not only an elder, but he served as clerk of the church for a time. The published history of the Salem Church stated: "There are many records in the first record book of the church signed by him." Early Bible School records show that he was also deeply interested in the Bible School.

NOTES TO CHAPTER 20

1. Thomas Franklin Campbell (1822-1893) was an older student when he enrolled in Bethany College in 1848, and he was 30 years old when he graduated in 1852. Jane Eliza Campbell was a first cousin to Alexander. Her father, Archibald Campbell, was a brother to Thomas Campbell. During his student days at Bethany, Thomas Franklin Campbell boarded for a time in the Campbell residence, as had William Lysander Adams before him.
2. At Mt. Enterprise Academy, Campbell was associated with Charles Vinzent, a wealthy benefactor, and Carroll Kendrick, an outstanding evangelist. In the 1870s, Campbell would be reunited with both men on the West Coast. Vinzent was an elder in the San Francisco Church and later in the Oakland Church, and it was at his invitation that Kendrick moved to California in 1876 to become the preacher at Oakland. For more information on Campbell at Mt. Enterprise Academy see Colby Hall, *Texas Disciples* (Fort Worth: Texas Christian University Press, 1953), 249-50. See also Nimmo Goldston, "The Beginnings of the Disciples of Christ in East Texas" (Fort Worth: unpublished B.D. thesis at Texas Christian University, Brite Divinity School, 1948).
3. *Millennial Harbinger*, March 1855, 174.
4. Ibid., August 1857, 467. At the time of his graduation, Campbell was no longer with Mt. Enterprise Academy. He was preaching for the church in Leavenworth, Kansas. In the 1860s he served as superintendent of Camden Point Female Academy in Missouri for a time. He moved to Helena, Montana, in the summer of 1864. See Harvey C. Hartling and Merrill G. Burlingame, *Big Sky Disciples: A History of the Christian Church (Disciples of Christ) in Montana* (Great Falls: Christian Church in Montana, 1984), 1-4, for information on T. F. Campbell in Montana.
5. Ellis A. Stebbins, *The OCE Story* (Monmouth, Oregon: Oregon College of Education, 1973), 14.
6. It is reported in one of the published histories of the college that when Campbell arrived in Monmouth the following dialogue took place between him and the board of trustees: "Where is the College?" "You are to build it." "Where is the money?" "You are to raise it." See Stebbins, *The OCE Story*, 14.
7. *Christian Messenger*, October 8, 1870, 2.

8. *Millennial Harbinger,* August 1870, 455-56. This article was entitled "Debate at Dallas City, Oregon." The author of the article was only identified with the initials of M.A.M.
9. Ibid.
10. *Christian Record,* August 1870, 373. In a letter written June 30, 1870, John M. Harris wrote: "Our great Annual Convocation has closed, and it was a grand success. There were some five or six thousand persons on the ground. . . . About forty additions were obtained, mostly by confession and immersion. Over twelve thousand dollars were subscribed to buy a press and fixtures to print our paper, the *Christian Messenger*. We want to issue the first number about the first of September."
11. John E. Smith, *Christian College* (by the author, 1853), 8.
12. J. S. Griffin, a Congregational minister, published for a brief time in 1848 the *Oregon American and Evangelical Unionist,* and Charles H. Mattoon, a Baptist minister, published the *Religious Expositor* for a few months in 1856. William Lysander Adams, a Christian preacher, began publishing the *Oregon Argus* in 1855. This primarily was a political sheet, but it occasionally carried news about Bethel Academy and other church-related events of interest to Christians. The *Argus* did not carry church items after Adams relinquished his editorial duties in 1859.
13. *Western Evangelist,* a monthly periodical, had been established by W. W. Stevenson in November 1858. It was edited by Stevenson and J. N. Pendegast through 1863. Pendegast edited the monthly *Christian Teacher* for three years (1864-1866), and then Samuel K. Hallam and J. W. Craycroft issued the first weekly paper for California Christians. Their *Pacific Gospel Herald* began in January 1867, but by the fall of 1870 its financial difficulties forced it to suspend publication. Alexander Johnston launched a monthly periodical in California, the *Biblical Expositor,* in January 1871. It ceased publication in 1875.
14. *Christian Messenger,* October 8, 1870, 2. Campbell's desire to edit a journal that would gain the support of the entire Pacific slope was dealt a blow when Alexander Johnston began editing the *Biblical Expositor* in Santa Rosa, California, in January 1871. Californians preferred their own paper, and it was difficult for Campbell to gain much support in that state.
15. Ibid., In addition to the four main periodicals listed here, there were some other papers with limited circulation in Oregon. These included the *Gospel Advocate,* edited by David Lipscomb in Nashville, Tennessee; the *Evangelist,* edited by Barton Warren

Johnson in Oscaloosa, Iowa; and the *Gospel Echo,* edited by James Harvey Garrison in Macomb, Illinois.

16. Ibid.
17. In addition to Vinzent, Campbell listed 12 other "Agents" and then concluded by writing that "all Christian Preachers everywhere" were considered "Agents" of the *Messenger*. The 12 names included four preachers: John M. Harris, A. L. Todd, George M. Whitney, and Daniel W. Elledge (who was then living at Walla Walla in Washington Territory). The other eight church leaders serving as "Agents" were: James Monroe Shelley at Portland; John A. Bounds at Starr's Point; Enos Williams at Amity; William Dawson at McMinnville; Levi Lindsay Rowland at Salem; Martin Byerly at Dallas; Dr. Zedekiah Davis at Buena Vista; and David R. Lewis at Lewisville. Within the first year of publication, Campbell added several other "Agents" to his list including: J. S. Churchill at Independence; Charles Woods at Salem; T. B. Newman at Dallas; W. A. Whitman at Umatilla; William Murphy at Jackson; Stephen Dodridge Powell at Tillamook; Troy Shelley at The Dalles; Nathaniel Phillips Briggs at Corvallis; J. M. Smith at Harrisburg; Dr. William H. Rowland at Brownsville; and John W. Shelton at North Yamhill. Within the first year, Campbell dropped "The" from the title of his periodical, and the journal became *Christian Messenger*. Sometime during the first year, the quote on the masthead changed from "Peace on Earth—Good Will to Man" to "Peace on Earth—Good Will Among Men."
18. Douglas B. Dornhecker, "A History of Annual Meetings of Disciples of Christ in Oregon to 1877" (Johnson City, Tennessee: unpublished M.Div. thesis, Emmanuel School of Religion, 1979), 88.
19. *Christian Record,* October 1870, 473. This letter was written by Joseph Warren Downer, a deacon in the Salem Church, on July 10, 1870.
20. Ibid., February 1871, 83. Harris is actually quoted as saying "county" instead of "country," but it is unlikely that there were more than 400 additions in one county.
21. Oregon's population grew from 91,000 to 175,000 during that decade.
22. *Christian Messenger,* July 1, 1871, 2. This is the language of T. F. Campbell.
23. *Christian Record,* August 1871, 377. This letter was written by J. J. Maxey on July 7, 1871.

24. Fred Lockley, *History of the Columbia River Valley: From The Dalles to the Sea,* Vol. III (Chicago: The S. J. Clarke Publishing Company, 1928), 348-52.
25. Among the congregations not reported on at the 1871 State Meeting were: Aumsville (Marion), North Yamhill (Yamhill), Lafayette (Yamhill), Luckiamute (Polk), Independence (Polk), Tillamook (Tillamook), The Dalles (Wasco), Farmington (Washington), Halsey (Linn), London (Lane), and a large number of congregations in Douglas, Coos, and Jackson counties.
26. *Christian Messenger,* July 1, 1871, 2. When they totaled their numbers they came up with 2,842, but there are actually 2,807 (a discrepancy of 35).
27. Margaret Standish Carey and Patricia Hoy Hainline, *Sweet Home in the Oregon Cascades,* (Brownsville, Oregon: Calapooia Publications, 1979), 42.
28. *Christian Record,* September 1871, 427. This letter was written by John T. Gilfrey on July 29, 1871.
29. The numbers for the Methodists are not available for 1871, but they claimed to have 4,349 members in 1873. See Thomas D. Yarnes, *A History of Oregon Methodism,* ed. Harvey E. Tobie (Portland: The Parthenon Press, 1957), 305. See also Albert W. Wardin, Jr., *Baptists in Oregon* (Portland: Judson Baptist College, 1969), 173-74. The author suggests that the Methodists had the largest membership in the 1870s and 1880s followed by the Christians (he calls them Disciples), and then the Baptists and Presbyterians.
30. Joseph Schafer, *Prince Lucien Campbell* (Eugene: University of Oregon Press, 1926), 35.
31. *Christian Messenger,* August 19, 1871, 1.
32. Ibid.
33. Ibid., August 26, 1871, 2.
34. Ibid., September 9, 1871, 2. Among those present for the laying of the cornerstone were John Ecles Murphy, Sebastian C. Adams, Dr. Zedekiah Davis, and Glen Owen Burnett. Burnett had moved back to Oregon in 1871 and was living in Monmouth. He remained two years and then returned to live in California.
35. Smith, *Christian College,* 11.
36. *Christian Messenger,* September 16, 1871, 2.
37. Helen Butler Jones, "The Contribution of Certain Leaders to the Development of the Oregon Normal School, 1850 to 1930"

(Eugene: unpublished Master's thesis, University of Oregon, 1947), 28-29. The student who made this observation was Katherine Lucas Fenton, a daughter of A. W. and Elizabeth Lucas.

38. Stebbins, *The OCE Story*, 17.
39. *Christian Record*, January 1871, 36. This letter was written by John M. Harris on November 2, 1870.
40. *Christian Messenger*, July 1, 1871, 4. This letter was written by Martin Peterson on June 12, 1871.
41. Ibid.
42. *American Christian Review*, April 2, 1885, 110. This letter was written on February 24, 1885.
43. *Octographic Review*, December 19, 1889, 3. This was written by A. B. Wade on August 5, 1889.
44. Aurelius Todd, "Rev. A. L. J. Todd: Pioneer Circuit Rider," *The Umpqua Trapper*, Vol. VI, No. 4, Winter 1970, 93.
45. Ibid., 91.
46. Ibid., 89.
47. Ibid., 93.
48. Ibid., 92.
49. Ibid., 96.
50. *Christian Record*, April 1870, 180. This letter was written by Richardson on January 20, 1870.
51. Ibid., April 1871, 184. This letter was written by Richardson on December 29, 1870.
52. Ibid., August 1870, 373. This letter was written by John M. Harris on June 30, 1870.
53. Ibid., February 1871, 85. This letter was written by William L. Mascher on January 6, 1871.
54. Ibid., March 1872, 136-37. Mascher submitted this report on December 6, 1871.
55. *Pacific Christian Messenger*, October 29, 1880, 7.
56. Ibid., September 1871, 428. D. D. Weddle wrote this letter on August 1, 1871.
57. Ibid., May 1872, 232. This letter was written by Daniel Elledge on March 7, 1872. Ibid., 235. This letter was written by Daniel Elledge on April 1, 1872. Ibid., August 1872, 375. This letter was written by Daniel Elledge in the summer of 1872.
58. Ibid., November 1872, 520-21. Richardson wrote this letter on September 28, 1872. Ibid., May 1873, 234. Richardson wrote this letter on December 30, 1872.

59. In addition to the deaths of Briggs and Mascher in 1872, Oregon Christians were saddened by the death of Elijah Bristow, the founder of Pleasant Hill in Lane County.
60. *Christian Record,* November 1873, 521. J. E. Roberts wrote this letter on August 9, 1873.
61. Ibid., April 1873, 186. John M. Harris wrote this letter on March 6, 1873.
62. Ibid., April 1874, 159-60. This information is found in a letter written by Caleb Davis on January 27, 1874.
63. *Christian Standard,* August 8, 1874, 255.
64. *Christian Standard,* August 15, 1874, 263.
65. *Christian Record,* December 1873, 568-70. This letter was written by Caleb Davis from his home in Lane County on November 3, 1873.

NOTES TO CHAPTER 21

1. Ellis A. Stebbins, *The OCE Story* (Monmouth, Oregon: Oregon College of Education, 1973), 26.
2. *Pacific Christian Messenger,* December 12, 1881.
3. Mary Stump was the daughter of David Stump, a devout Christian and a generous benefactor of Christian College. She was one of T. F. Campbell's first students at Christian College.
4. Mary was 34 years old at the time of her wedding, and she had never been married before. Campbell was 29 years older than his new bride, and he had several grown children. Nevertheless, he began a second family with Mary, and the couple had 3 children before his death.
5. *Christian Standard,* May 15, 1875, 157. This was an advance notice giving the dates of the meeting. See also *Christian Record,* August 1875, 502. This letter was written by Clara Whitehead on July 5, 1875.
6. *First Christian Church, Dallas, Oregon: The Heritage of a Hundred Years, 1856-1956* (n. p., 1956), 5.
7. *Christian Messenger,* June 30, 1876, 2.
8. Ibid.
9. *Christian Standard,* July 21, 1877, 226.
10. *Christian Messenger,* June 28, 1877, 4.
11. *Minutes of the Christian Co-Operation in the State of Oregon, in Annual Meeting,* Dallas, June 15-25, 1877 (Monmouth, Oregon, Messenger Publishing Company, 1877), 2.

12. Some counties had already been holding annual meetings for a few years. The annual meeting for Linn County in 1877 was deliberately scheduled to begin in the week following the State Meeting at Dallas. The attendance on the second Sunday (July 8) was estimated to be 1,500 to 2,000. Peter R. Burnett and Ephraim W. Barnes did most of the preaching, and Philip Mulkey "was present most of the time and delivered one or two warm exhortations to the people." There were 21 additions to the church, including 16 immersions. See the *Pacific Christian Messenger*, July 26, 1877, 7.
13. *Pacific Christian Messenger*, July 26, 1877, 2.
14. In addition to the 4 officers, the 29 church leaders who signed on to become members of the Ministerial Association were: Rufus H. Moss, Peter R. Burnett, Isaac N. Muncy, John M. Harris, Peter Shuck, David Truman Stanley, Leo Willis, William Manning, Mac Waller, Levi Lindsay Rowland, David R. Lewis, G. A. Maddox, M. Morrison, William E. Pedigo, Franklin S. Powell, James S. McCarty, William Ruble, Albert W. Lucas, William Dawson, Collin A. Wallace, Andrew Kelley, Jonathan Todd, Lucien B. Frazer, J. M. Campbell, Marcellas Faulconer, T. Morrison, Horace Lindsay, John Henry Hawley, and William Burt.
15. *Pacific Christian Messenger*, July 26, 1877, 2.
16. Ibid., August 30, 1877, 4.
17. Ibid., October 11, 1877. This letter was written by Martin Peterson from Mound Ranch, Jackson County, on October 1, 1877.
18. Ibid., October 18, 1877.
19. Ibid., November 16, 1877, 2.
    Christian Standard, November 24, 1877, 373.
20. *Pacific Christian Messenger*, December 15, 1877, 2, 7.
21. C. F. Swander, *Making Disciples in Oregon* (Portland: by the author, 1928), 54. Swander recorded that the first year of the Ministerial Association was "successful beyond their hopes," but this may have been attributed to the positive slant put on all of the news releases in the *Messenger*. The actual mission work undertaken by the association was modest in scope, but the association was very significant in preparing the way for the acceptance of a state missionary society in 1882.
22. *Pacific Christian Messenger*, May 11, 1878, 4.
23. Philip Mulkey Hunt, *The Mulkeys of America* (Portland: by the author, 1982), 109.

24. *Pacific Christian Messenger,* August 16, 1877, 5. This information is found in a letter from A. H. Beckwith to David Truman Stanley, written from Pleasant Hill on August 11, 1877.
25. Ibid., June 10, 1881, 4. This information is found in a letter written to T. F. Campbell by D. W. Bridges from Trent, Lane County, on May 29, 1881.
26. Ibid., May 31, 1877, 7. This letter was written from Damascus on May 19, 1877, and signed by "Disciple."
27. Ibid., June 14, 1877, 7. This letter was written from Damascus on May 29th, 1877, and signed by " A Disciple."
28. *Octographic Review,* January 29, 1891, 3. This letter was written by D. W. Parker from Cherryvale in Clackamas County on January 1, 1891.
29. *Pacific Christian Messenger,* May 17, 1877. This letter was written from La Center, Washington, on the other side of the Columbia River opposite St. Helens and Scappoose. It was written on May 1, 1877. Espy had preached briefly in Oregon, but he was to give the majority of his years of ministry to the church in Washington, and he was one of those who helped plant the church in Seattle in 1882-83.
30. Ibid., August 2, 1877. This letter was written by Adams on July 23, 1877.
31. *Christian Messenger,* September 8, 1876, 4.
32. *Pacific Christian Messenger,* May 31, 1877, 2. This letter was written by E. A. Chase from his home in Oakland, Douglas County, on May 23, 1877.
33. Ibid.
34. Aurelius Todd, "Rev. A. L. J. Todd: Pioneer Circuit Rider," *The Umpqua Trapper,* Vol. VI, No. 4, Winter 1970, 88.
35. Ibid., 93-94.
36. Ibid., 94.
37. Mina Davis Hargis, "The History of the Disciples of Christ in Iowa Before the Civil War," (Iowa City: State University of Iowa, unpublished M. A. thesis, August, 1937), 80-81. Mina Davis Hargis includes an "e" on the end of his name. She wrote: "Israel Clarke, a 'Stoneite' who had been converted at Cane Ridge, Kentucky, was the pioneer preacher in Iowa County." She also noted: "His sermons were long, but many people were converted by them." Clark may have migrated to Oregon as early as 1853. It is known that he was preaching at the Court House in Eugene in December 1865.
38. Todd, "Rev. A. L. J. Todd", 90.

39. Ibid.
40. *Pacific Christian Messenger,* February 20, 1880, 1. This letter was written on February 9, 1880.
41. Ibid., March 12, 1880, 1. This letter was written on February 27, 1880.
42. Ibid., April 9, 1880, 1.
43. Ibid., May 14, 1880, 1.
44. Ibid.
45. Ibid., June 4, 1880, 1. This letter was written on May 19, 1880.

NOTES TO CHAPTER 22

1. These were the statistics published by the American Christian Missionary Society in 1880. See Earl Irvin West, *The Search for the Ancient Order,* Vol. II (Indianapolis: Religious Book Service, 1950), 167. See also *Gospel Advocate,* February 24, 1881, 114.
2. Allan Peskin, *Garfield* (Kent, Ohio: Kent State University Press, 1978), 460.
3. Harry James Brown and Frederick D. Williams, eds., *The Diary of James A. Garfield,* Vol. IV, 1878-1881 (East Lansing, Michigan: Michigan State University Press, 1981), 424.
4. F. M. Green, *A Royal Life: The Eventful History of James A. Garfield* (Chicago: Central Book Concern, 1882), 174. Otis A. Burgess, *President Garfield* (Chicago: Central Book Concern, 1881), 18. Otis A. Burgess (1829-1882) graduated from Bethany College in 1854. He was a prominent educator and preacher in the Restoration Movement. As president of North Western Christian University (later Butler University) in Indianapolis, Indiana, Burgess played a leading role in securing the support of Indiana Christians for Garfield's candidacy. Burgess was given a great deal of credit for Garfield's narrow victory in that state. Garfield won Indiana by a margin of less than 7,000 votes.
5. The three Christian editors in the South who opposed Garfield's nomination for political reasons were: David Lipscomb, editor of the *Gospel Advocate* in Nashville, Tennessee; C. M. Wilmeth, editor of the *Christian Preacher* in Dallas, Texas; and Thomas R. Burnett, editor of the *Christian Messenger* in Bonham, Texas.
6. *American Christian Review,* July 10, 1880, 186.
7. Herbert J. Clancy, *The Presidential Election of 1880* (Chicago: The Loyola Press, 1958).

8. *Republican League Register: A Record of The Republican Party in the State of Oregon* (Portland: The Register Publishing Company, 1896), 167.
9. Mary L. Hinsdale, ed., *Garfield-Hinsdale Letters: Correspondence Between James Abram Garfield and Burke Aaron Hinsdale* (Ann Arbor: University of Michigan Press, 1949), 462-66. This letter was written from Hiram College on November 9, 1880.
10. Garfield's reply was written on November 17, 1881.
11. Chaplain G. G. Mullins, *My Life is an Open Book* (St. Louis: John Burns, Publisher, 1883), 229.
12. W. T. Moore, *The Life of Timothy Coop* (London: The Christian Commonwealth Publishing Company, 1889), 404-05.
13. *Daily Oregonian*, September 25, 1881.
14. For Errett's full address, see *Isaac Errett, Linsey-Woolsey and Other Addresses* (Cincinnati: The Standard Publishing Company, 1893). For descriptions of the various Garfield funerals, see Henry J. Cookinham, ed., *In Memoriam: James A. Garfield, Twentieth President of the United States* (Utica, New York: Curtiss and Childs, Publishers, 1881), and J. S. Ogilvie, *The Life and Death of James A. Garfield* (New York: J. S. Ogilvie, 1881).
15. *Oregon Journal*, July 2, 1911, 3.
16. Burgess, President Garfield, 4-5.
17. Green, *A Royal Life*, 189-90.
18. Burgess, *President Garfield*, 22.
19. Frederick D. Power, *Life of William Kimbrough Pendleton* (St. Louis: Christian Publishing Company, 1902), 412. The old "Garfield pew" was retained in the new church building.
20. William Thomas Moore, *A Comprehensive History of the Disciples of Christ* (New York: Fleming H. Revell Company, 1909), 731-32.
21. A wide variety of volumes have referred to Garfield as "The Preacher President." See Barbara Barclay, *Our Presidents* (New York: Bowmar Publishing Corporation, 1976). The chapter on James Garfield is entitled "The Preacher President."

NOTES TO EPILOGUE

1. Thomas Munnell (1823-1898) was an honors graduate of Bethany College in 1850. He taught ancient languages and literature at Western Reserve Eclectic Institute (later Hiram College) in Hiram, Ohio, for several years before serving churches in Cincinnati, Ohio, and Mt. Sterling, Kentucky. He was the corresponding secretary of the Kentucky Missionary

Society for several years before being elected to the same post in the American Christian Missionary Society in 1868. He served in this influential position for nine years from 1869 through 1877. Prior to Munnell the most significant occupants of this office had been David S. Burnet serving 1852-1856 and 1862-1863 and Isaac Errett serving 1858-1861.

2. *Christian Record,* December 1873, 568-70.
3. *Pacific Christian Messenger,* August 26, 1881, 5.
4. Joseph Schafer, *Prince Lucien Campbell* (Eugene: University of Oregon Press, 1926), 89.
5. *Christian Herald,* November 3, 1882, 2.
6. *Octographic Review,* March 19, 1895, 1.
7. *Christian Evangelist,* July 9, 1885, 439.
8. *Religious Bodies 1906* (Washington: Government Printing Office, 1910). *Religious Bodies 1916* (Washington: Government Printing Office, 1919).
9. Beginning in the 1940s, the Churches of Christ also suffered a division in their ranks when some conservative congregations (sometimes characterized as non-institutional or anti-cooperation) emerged as a separate fellowship of churches. Of the 120 Churches of Christ in Oregon today, approximately 30 are affiliated with this separate fellowship of churches.

A NOTE ON THE SOURCES

The most important source materials for this study of Oregon Christians were the nineteenth century religious periodicals produced by editors in the Restoration Movement. The two periodicals that enjoyed the widest distribution among the Christians in early Oregon were the *Christian Record* edited by James Madison Mathes in Indiana, and the *Evangelist* edited by Daniel Bates and Aaron Chatterton in Iowa. The two other periodicals that enjoyed a wide readership in Oregon were Alexander Campbell's *Millennial Harbinger*, published in Virginia, and Benjamin Franklin's *American Christian Review*, published in Ohio.

Beginning in the fall of 1870, Oregon Christians were given their own monthly periodical when Thomas Franklin Campbell began editing the *Christian Messenger* from Monmouth. This periodical changed its name to the *Pacific Christian Messenger* in 1877 and to the *Christian Herald* in 1882, but it continued to be published in Monmouth and it was widely distributed throughout the state. David Truman Stanley served as editor of the *Pacific Christian Messenger* for a few years in the late 1870s, and he was one of the founding editors of the *Christian Herald* in 1882.

Listed below are the twenty periodicals, all publications produced by the Restoration Movement, that were consulted in researching information on Oregon Christians. For some of these periodicals, only scattered issues are extant. The title of each periodical is included along with one place of publication, the years consulted, and one editor. The location of most of these cities would be recognizable, but the location of some of the smaller towns are: Santa Rosa, California; Bonham, Texas; Woodland, California; Mt. Pleasant, Iowa; Macomb, Illinois; and Bethany, Virginia.

BIBLIOGRAPHY

I. PERIODICALS

The American Christian Review (Cincinnati) 1856-86, Benjamin Franklin
The Apostolic Times (Lexington) 1869-1885, Lard & McGarvey
The Bible Expositor (Santa Rosa) 1871-1875, Alexander Johnston
The Christian (St. Louis) 1873-1882, James Harvey Garrison
The Christian Herald (Monmouth) 1882-1889, David T. Stanley
The Christian Leader (Cincinnati) 1886-1897, John F. Rowe
The Christian Magazine (Nashville) 1848-1853, Jesse B. Ferguson
The Christian Messenger (Bonham) 1875-1892, Thomas R. Burnett
The Christian Messenger (Monmouth) 1870-76, Thomas F. Campbell
The Christian Record (Indianapolis) 1843-1884, James M. Mathes
The Christian Standard (Cincinnati) 1866-1888, Isaac Errett
The Christian Teacher (Woodland) 1864-1866, John N. Pendegast
The Evangelist (Mt. Pleasant) 1850-1864, D. Bates & A. Chatterton
The Gospel Advocate (Nashville) 1866-1890, David Lipscomb
The Gospel Echo (Macomb) 1863-1872, James Harvey Garrison
The Millennial Harbinger (Bethany) 1830-70, Alexander Campbell
The Octographic Review (Indianapolis) 1886-1900, Daniel Sommer
The Pacific Christian (Portland & S.F.) 1894-1910, W. B. Berry
The Pacific Christian Messenger (Monmouth) 1877-82, T. F. Campbell
The Western Evangelist (San Francisco) 1858-63, W. W. Stevenson

II. BOOKS

A Debate on the Roman Catholic Religion. St. Louis: Christian Board of Publication, 1837.

A History of First Christian Church of Eugene, Oregon in Observance of its Centennial, 1866-1966. Eugene, Oregon, n.p.

Adams, W. L. *Lecture on the Oregon and the Pacific Coast*. Boston: n.p., 1869.

Applegate, Jesse Sr. *A Day with the Cow Column in 1843*. Chicago: Caxton Club, 1934.

Baldwin, W. A. *History of Churches of Christ in Nebraska*. Lincoln: Nebraska Christian Missionary Society, n.p.

Bancroft, Hubert Howe. *History of Oregon*. 2 vols. San Francisco: The History Company, 1888.

Barrows, William. *Oregon: The Struggle for Possession*. Boston: Houghton, Mifflin and Company, 1892.

Barth, Gunther P., ed. *All Quiet on the Yamhill: The Civil War in Oregon: The Journal of Corporal Royal A. Bensell*. Eugene; University of Oregon Books, 1959.

Bates, Carol. *Scio in the Forks of the Santiam*. By the author, 1989.

Beck, Warren A. and Ynez D. Haase. *Historical Atlas of the American West*. Norman: University of Oklahoma Press, 1989.

Belknap, George N. 1968 edition of William Lysander Adams, *Treason, Strategems & Spoils*.

Beveridge, Albert J. *Abraham Lincoln, 1809-1858*. Vol. I. Boston and New York, 1928.

Black, Melba, Anne Dashiell, Dr. Guy Wright, and Peggy Corpion. *First Christian Church, Dallas, Oregon: The Heritage of a Hundred Years, 1856-1956*. n.p., 1956.

Bourke, Paul, and Donald DeBats. *Washington County: Politics and Community in Antebellum America*. Baltimore: The Johns Hopkins University Press, 1995.

Bowen, William A. *Willamette Valley: Migration and Settlement on the Oregon Frontier*. Seattle: n.p., 1978.

Bowers, Fidelia March, ed. *The Organizational Journal of an Emigrant Train of 1845, Captained by Solomon Tethrow, with an Account of the Wagon Train*. Eugene: Lane County Pioneer Historical Society, 1960.

Boyd, Robert G. *Wandering Wagons: Meek's Lost Emigrants of 1845*. Bend, Oregon: The High Desert Museum, 1993.

Brandt, Patricia, and Nancy Guilford, eds. *Oregon Biography Index*. Corvallis: Oregon State University Press, 1976.

Briggs, Ethel L. *A History and Genealogy of Gilmore Callison and his Descendants*. Yucaipa, California: by the author, 1962.

Bristow, Elijah Lafayette. *Elijah Lafayette Bristow Letters, 1857-1864*. Eugene, Oregon: Lane County Historical Society, n.d.

Burlingame, Gary, Julie Jones, and Don Rivera. *The Cooper-Hewitt-Matheny History*. By the authors, 1996.

Burnett, Peter H. *The Path which led A Protestant Lawyer to the Catholic Church*. New York and Cincinnati: Benziger Brothers, 1868.

________. *Recollections and Opinions of an Old Pioneer*. New York: Appleton, 1880.

Bushnell, James Addison. *Autobiography of James Addison Bushnell, 1826-1912*. Eugene: Lane County Pioneer Historical Society, 1959.

Bushnell, John C. *Narrative of John C. Bushnell*. Eugene: Lane County Pioneer Historical Society, 1959.

Callison, John J. *Diary of John J. Callison*. Eugene: Lane County Pioneer Historical Society, 1959.

Carey, Charles H. *A General History of Oregon Prior to 186l*. 2 vols. Portland: Metropolitan Press, 1936.

Carey, Margaret Standish and Patricia Hoy Hainline. *Sweet Home in the Oregon Cascades*. Brownsville, Oregon: Calapooia Publications, 1979.

Carson, Opal and Leslie. *First Christian Church, Salem, Oregon: The Centennial Story, 1855-1955*. Salem: by the First Christian Church, 1955.

Cauble, Commodore Wesley. *Disciples of Christ in Indiana: Achievements of a Century*. Indianapolis: Meigs Publishing Company, 1930.

Clancy, Herbert J. *The Presidential Election of 1880*. Chicago: The Loyola Press, 1958.

Clark, Keith and Tiller, Lowell. *Terrible Trail: The Meek Cutoff, 1845*. Bend, Oregon: Maverick Publications, Revised Edition, 1993.

Clark, Robert Carlton. *History of the Willamette Valley*. Chicago: S. J. Clarke, 1927.

Coffman, Lloyd W. *Blazing a Wagon Trail to Oregon: A Weekly Chronicle of the Great Migration of 1843*. Springfield, Oregon: Echo Books, 1993.

Compilation of the History of the Ruble Family. By the family, 1935.

Cookinham, Henry J., ed. *In Memoriam: James A. Garfield, Twentieth President of the United States*. Utica, New York: Curtiss and Childs, Publishers, 1881.

Corning, Howard McKinley, ed. *Dictionary of Oregon History*. Portland: Binfords & Mort, 1956.

Cummins, D. Duane. *The Disciples Colleges: A History*. St. Louis: CBP Press, 1987.

Dee, Minnie Roof. *From Oxcart to Airplane: A Biography of George H. Himes*. Portland: Binfords & Mort, Publishers, n.d.

Dicken, Samuel N., and Emily F. Dicken. *The Making of Oregon: A Study in Historical Geography*. Portland: Oregon Historical Society, 1979.

Dimon, Elizabeth F. *'Twas Many Years Since: 100 Years in the Waverly Area 1847-1947.* Milwaukie, Oregon: by the author, 1981.

Down, Robert Horace. *A History of the Silverton Country.* Portland: The Berncliff Press, 1926.

Emerson, William. *The Applegate Trail of 1846: A Documentary Guide to the Original Southern Emigrant Route to Oregon.* Ashland, Oregon: Ember Enterprises, Publishers, 1996.

Evans, Elwood. *History of the Pacific Northwest, Oregon & Washington.* Portland: North Pacific History Company, 1889.

Evans, Madison. *Biographical Sketches of the Pioneer Preachers of Indiana.* Philadelphia: J. Challen & Sons, 1862.

Fanselow, Julie. *The Traveler's Guide to the Oregon Trail.* Helena, Montana: Falcon Press, 1992.

Flora, Stephenie L. *Howell Prairie Cemetery.* Salem, Oregon: by the author, 1988.

Franzwa, Gregory M. *Maps of the Oregon Trail.* Gerald, Missouri: Patrice Press, 1982.

________. *The Oregon Trail Revisited.* Tucson: The Patrice Press, 1988.

Gaston, Joseph. *Portland, Oregon: Its History and Builders.* Vol. I. Portland: S. J. Clarke Publishers, 1911.

________. *The Centennial History of Oregon.* Vol. I, II, and IV. Chicago: S. J. Clarke Publishing Company, 1912.

Geer, Marie Gilham. *They Called it Hebron.* By the author, 1996.

Genealogical Material in Oregon Donation Land Claims. 5 Vols. Portland: Genealogical Forum of Portland, 1957-1975.

Graves and Sites on the Oregon and California Trails. Independence, Missouri: Oregon-California Trials Association, 1991.

Haley, T. P. *Historical and Biographical Sketches of the Early Churches and Pioneer Preachers of the Christian Church in Missouri.* Kansas City, Missouri: J. H. Smart & Co., 1888.

Hall, Colby. *Texas Disciples.* Fort Worth, Texas Christian University Press, 1953.

Hardeman, Nicholas Perkins. *Wilderness Calling: The Hardeman Family in the American Westward Movement, 1750-1900.* Knoxville: University of Tennessee Press, 1977.

Harpham, Josephine Evans. *Doorways into History: The Early Houses and Public Buildings of Oregon.* Seattle: The Shorey Book Store, 1993.

Harrell, David Edwin Jr. *Quest for a Christian America.* Nashville: The Disciples of Christ Historical Society, 1966.

________. *The Social Sources of Division in the Disciples of Christ 1865-1900*. Atlanta and Athens, Georgia: Publishing Systems, Inc., 1973.

Hart, D. G., ed. *Reckoning With The Past: Historical Essays on American Evangelicalism from the Institute for the Study of American Evangelicals*. Grand Rapids, Michigan: Baker Books, 1995.

Hartling, Harvey C. and Merrill G Burlingame. *Big Sky Disciples: A History of the Christian Church (Disciples of Christ) in Montana*. Great Falls: Christian Church in Montana, 1984.

Haskins, Harley, transcriber. *1860 Polk County, Oregon, Census*. Publisher: End of Trail Researchers.

Haynes, Nathaniel S. *History of the Disciples of Christ in Illinois, 1819-1914*. Cincinnati: The Standard Publishing Company, 1915.

Helfrich, Devere and Helen, and Thomas Hunt, compilers. *Emigrant Trails West*. Klamath Falls, Oregon: n.p., 1984.

Hines, Harvey K. *An Illustrated History of the State of Oregon*. Chicago: Lewis Publishing Company, 1893.

Hinsdale, Mary L., ed. *Garfield-Hinsdale Letters: Correspondence Between James Abram Garfield and Burke Aaron Hinsdale*. Ann Arbor: University of Michigan Press, 1949.

History of Polk County Oregon. Monmouth: Polk County Historical Society, 1987.

Hodge, Frederick Arthur. *The Plea and the Pioneers in Virginia*. Richmond: Everett Waddey Company, 1905.

Hodgkin, Frank E. and J. J. Galvin. *Pen Pictures of Representative Men of Oregon*. Portland: Farmer and Dairyman Publishing Company, 1882.

Holmes, Kenneth L., ed. *Covered Wagon Women: Diaries & Letters from the Western Trails, 1840-1890*. Spokane, Washington: The Arthur H. Clark Company, 1991.

________, ed. *Linfield's Hundred Years: A Centennial History of Linfield College, McMinnville, Oregon*. Portland: Binfords & Mort, Publishers, 1956.

Horner, John B. *Oregon, Her History, Her Great Men, Her Literature*. Portland: J. K. Gill, 1921.

Howell, Erle. *Methodism in the Northwest*. (Chapin D. Foster, ed.) Portland: The Parthenon Press, 1966.

Hughes, Richard T., and C. Leonard Allen. *Illusions of Innocence: Protestant Primitivism in America, 1630-1875*. Chicago: The University of Chicago Press, 1988.

Hughes, Richard T. *Reviving the Ancient Faith: The Story of Churches of Christ in America.* Grand Rapids: Wm. B. Eerdmans Publishing Company, 1996.

Hunt, Philip Mulkey. *The Mulkey's of America.* Portland: by the author, 1982.

Index to Clackamas County Probate Records, 1845-1910.

Jackson, Leland G. *Early Castle Rock and North Cowlitz County, Washington.* Second Edition. Castle Rock, Washington: by the author, 1992.

Johannsen, Robert W. *Frontier Politics on the Eve of the Civil War.* Seattle: University of Washington Press, 1955.

Jonasson, Jonas A. *Bricks Without Straw: The Story of Linfield College.* Caldwell, Idaho: The Caxton Printers, 1938.

Kirkwood, Charlotte Matheny. *Into the Eye of the Setting Sun: A Story of the West when it was New.* McMinnville: The Family Association of Matheny, Cooper, Hewitt, Kirkwood and Bailey, 1991.

Kuykendall, George B. *History of the Kuykendall Family . . . With Sketches of Colonial Times, Old Log Cabin Days, Indian Wars, Pioneer Hardships, Social Customs, Dress and Mode of Living of the Early Forefathers.* Portland: n.p., 1919.

Lacy, Ruby, compiler. *Oregon Territory 1850 Census.* Ashland: Ruby Lacy, 1984.

Lang, Herbert O. *History of the Willamette Valley.* Portland: George H. Himes, 1885.

Lavender, David. *Westward Vision: The Story of the Oregon Trail.* Lincoln: University of Nebraska Press, 1963.

Lenox, Edward Henry. *Overland to Oregon in the Tracks of Lewis and Clark: A History of the First Emigration to Oregon in 1843.* Oakland: 1904.

Lockett, Jim and Reita. *Settling the Land of Promise: Stories of Pioneer Men, Women and Children who laid a Firm Foundation for Generations to Come.* McMinnville, Oregon: by the authors, 1994.

Lockley, Fred, ed. *Captain Sol. Tethrow, Wagon Train Master: Personal Narrative of His Son . . . Who Crossed the Plains to Oregon, in 1845.* Portland: n.d.

________. *History of the Columbia River Valley: From The Dalles to the Sea.* Vol. III. Chicago: The S. J. Clarke Publishing Company, 1928.

________. *Oregon's Yesterdays*. New York: The Knickerbocker Press, 1928.

________. *Conversations with Bullwhackers, Muleskinners, Pioneers, Prospectors, '49ers, Indian Fighters, Trappers, Ex-Barkeepers, Authors, Preachers, Poets and Near Poets & all sorts & conditions of Men*. Eugene: Rainy Day Press, 1981.

________. *Conversations with Pioneer Women*. Eugene: Rainy Day Press, 1981.

Loy, William G. *The Atlas of Oregon*. Eugene: The University of Oregon Books, 1976.

Maffly-Kipp, Laurie F. *Religion and Society in Frontier California*. New Haven: Yale University Press, 1994.

Mattes, Merrill J. *The Great Platte River Road*. Lincoln, Nebraska State Historical Society, 1969.

________. *Platte River Road Narratives*. Urbana and Chicago: University of Illinois Press, 1988.

May, Dean L. *Three Frontiers: Family, Land, and Society in the American West, 1850-1900*. Cambridge, United Kingdom: Cambridge University Press, 1994.

McAllister, Lester G. *Arkansas Disciples: A History of the Christian Church (Disciples of Christ) in Arkansas*. By the author, 1984.

________. *Bethany: The First 150 Years*. Bethany, West Virginia: Bethany College Press, 1991.

McArthur, Lewis A. *Oregon Geographic Names*. 4th edition, Revised and Enlarged. Portland: Oregon Historical Society, 1974.

McElroy, Charles Foster. *Ministers of First Christian Church (Disciples of Christ) Springfield, Illinois, 1833-1962*. St. Louis: The Bethany Press, 1962.

McLagan, Elizabeth. *A Peculiar Paradise: A History of Blacks in Oregon, 1788-1940*. Portland: The Georgian Press, 1980.

Middlemiss, Marceil. *A History of the Christian Church in Silverton, 1851-1976*. By the author, 1976.

Milam, Loy R. *Old Mulkey: A Pioneer Plea for the Ancient Order (History of Mill Creek Church of Monroe County, Kentucky)*. Tompkinsville, Kentucky: by the author, 1996.

Miller, Clifford R. *Baptists and the Oregon Frontier*. Ashland, Oregon: by the author, 1967.

Mintz, Lannon W. *The Trail: A Bibliography of the Travelers on the Overland Trail to California, Oregon, Salt Lake City, and Montana during the Years 1841-1864*. Albuquerque: University of New Mexico Press, 1987.

Moore, Lucia W., Nina W. McCornack, and Gladys W. McCready. *The Story of Eugene*. Eugene: Lane County Historical Society, 1995.

Moore, William Thomas. *A Comprehensive History of the Disciples of Christ*. New York: Fleming H. Revell Company, 1909.

Morgan, Dale L., ed. *Overland in 1846: Diaries and Letters of the California Trail*. 2 vols. Georgetown: Talisman Press, 1963.

Morse, William F., compiler. *"History of the Amity Church of Christ."* n.p., 1946.

Murch, James DeForest. *Christians Only: A History of the Restoration Movement*. Cincinnati: The Standard Publishing Company, 1962.

Nicolay, John G. and John Hay. *Abraham Lincoln: A History*. Vol. I. New York: The Century Company, 1890.

Overholser, Marguariete. *A Man is a Man: A Hooker Family Saga*. Portland: Binfords & Mort Publishing, 1993.

Owen, Benjamin Franklin. *My Trip across the Plains March – October 1853*. Eugene: Lane County Pioneer Society, n.d.

Paine, Lauran. *Conquest of the Great Northwest*. New York: Robert M. McBride Company, 1959.

Painter, J. H., ed. *The Iowa Pulpit of the Church of Christ*. St. Louis: John Burns Publishing Co., 1884.

Palmer, Joel. *Journal of Travels Over the Oregon Trail in 1845*. Portland: Oregon Historical Society, 1993.

Peterson, Orval. *Washington-Northern Idaho Disciples*. St. Louis: Christian Board of Publication, 1945.

Polk County, Oregon Cemeteries, Volume One: Dallas Cemetery. Dallas, Oregon: Polk County Genealogical Society, 1987.

Polk County, Oregon Cemeteries, Volume Two: The Southwest Fourth. Dallas, Oregon: Polk County Genealogical Society, 1988.

Polk County, Oregon Cemeteries, Volume Three: Hilltop Cemetery District. Dallas, Oregon: Polk County Genealogical Society, 1989.

Polk County, Oregon Cemeteries, Volume Four: Small Cemeteries in North Polk County. Dallas, Oregon: Polk County Genealogical Society, 1991.

Polk County, Oregon Cemeteries, Volume Five: More Cemeteries. Dallas, Oregon: Polk County Genealogical Society, 1995.

Porter, H. C. *The Mill Creek Church of Christ Now Aumsville Church of Christ*. By the author, 1921.

Portrait and Biographical Record of the Willamette Valley, Oregon: Containing Original Sketches of many well-known Citizens of the Past and Present. Chicago: Chapman Publishing Company, 1903.

Powell, James Madison. *Powell History: An Account of the Lives of the Powell Pioneers of 1851 – John A., Noah and Alfred – Their Ancestors, Descendents and Other Relatives.* By the author, 1922.

Preston, Ralph H., compiler. *Historical Early Oregon.* Corvallis, Oregon: Western Guide Publishers, 1972.

Primus, Ted J., Narlene Althaus, Sharon Cochran, Bill Creighton, A. A. Rodakowski, Mrs. William Mack, Florence Williams, and Jo McElroy. *A Century of Polk County History.* Dallas, Oregon: Curry Print Shop, 1959.

Reflections of Carlton: From Pioneer to Present: The Story of Carlton, Oregon. Carlton, Oregon: Carlton Elementary School Bicentennial Club, 1976.

Republican League Register: A Record of The Republican Party in the State of Oregon. Portland: The Register Publishing Company, 1896.

Richardson, Earle. *Polk County Pioneer Sketches,* Vol. I. Dallas, Oregon: Polk County Observer, 1927.

________. *Polk County Pioneer Sketches,* Vol. II. Dallas, Oregon: Polk County Observer, 1929.

Riddle, George W. *Early Days in Oregon: 1851-1861 History of the South Umpqua Valley.* Canyonville, Oregon: South Umpqua Historical Society, Inc., 1993.

Roberts, Francis M. *100 Years of History of the Christian Church (Disciples of Christ) in Marion County, Iowa, 1846-1946.* By the author, 1946.

Rumer, Thomas A. *The Wagon Trains of '44: A Comparative View of the Individual Caravans in the Emigration of 1844 to Oregon.* Spokane, Washington: The Arthur H. Clark Company, 1990.

Russell, O. J. *The Church in Oregon – A Colorful History.* Desoto, Texas: O. J. Russell, 1969.

Schafer, Joseph. "William Lysander Adams." Dictionary of American Biography. Vol. l.

________. *Prince Lucien Campbell.* Eugene: University of Oregon Press, 1926.

Sherman, Wes., ed. *Polk County Centennial.* Dallas, Oregon: Polk County Itemizer-Observer, 1947

Smith, Benjamin Lyon. *Alexander Campbell.* St. Louis: The Bethany Press, 1930.

Smith, John E. *Bethel, Polk County, Oregon*. By the author, 1941.

________. *Christian College*. By the author, 1953.

Stebbins, Ellis A. *The OCE Story*. Monmouth, Oregon: Oregon College of Education, 1973.

Steeves, Sarah Hunt. *Book of Remembrance of Marion County, Oregon, Pioneers, 1840-1860*. Portland: The Berncliff Press, 1927.

Stewart, George R. *The California Trail*. Lincoln: University of Nebraska Press, 1962.

Stoller, Ruth, compiler. *Yamhill County Cemetery Records*. Volumes I, II, III. Lafayette, Oregon: Yamhill County Historical Society, 1980-1986.

________. *Schools of Old Yamhill*. Lafayette, Oregon: Yamhill County Historical Society, 1982.

________. *Old Yamhill: The Early History of its Towns and Cities*. Portland: Binfords & Mort Publishing, 1989.

Swander, C. F. *Making Disciples in Oregon*. By the author, 1928.

The Centennial Story of Monmouth, Oregon, 1856-1956: "The Growth of an Idea." Salem: Johnson and Siewert, n.d.

Udell, John. *Incidents of Travel to California, across the Great Plains; Together with the Return Trips through Central America and Jamaica; to which are Added Sketches of the Author's Life*. Jefferson, Ohio: Printed for the Author, at the Sentinel Office, 1856.

Unruh, John D. Jr. *The Plains Across: The Overland Emigrants and the Trans-Mississippi West*. Urbana: University of Illinois Press, 1979.

Velasco, Dorothy. *Lane County: An Illustrated History of the Emerald Empire*. Northridge, California: Windsor Publications, 1985.

Wallace, John H. *The Riggs Family Genealogy*, Vol. I. New York, by the author, 1901.

Walling, A. G. *History of Southern Oregon*. By the author, 1884.

_______. *Illustrated History of Lane County, Oregon*. By the author, 1884.

Wardin, Albert W. Jr. *Baptists in Oregon*. Portland: Judson Baptist College, 1969.

Webber, Bert. *Over the Applegate Trail to Oregon in 1846*. Medford, Oregon: Webb Research Group Publishers, 1996.

Wheeler, L. M., ed. *History of Linn County*. Portland: Boyce Wheeler Publishers, 1982.

White, Chris and Mary-Catherine Cuthill. *Overland Passages: A Guide to Overland Documents in the Oregon Historical Society*. Portland: Oregon Historical Society Press, 1993.

White, Richard. *"It's Your Misfortune and None of My Own" – A New History of the American West.* Norman: University of Oklahoma Press, 1991.

Wojcik, Donna M. *The Brazen Overlanders of 1845.* Portland: by the author, 1976.

Woodward, Walter Carleton. *The Rise and Early History of Political Parties in Oregon, 1843-1868.* Portland: J. K. Gill Company, 1913.

Yarnes, Thomas D. *A History of Oregon Methodism.* (Harvey E. Tobie, ed.) Portland: The Parthenon Press, 1957.

III. THESES AND DISSERTATIONS

Dornhecker, Douglas P. "A History of Annual Meetings of Disciples of Christ in Oregon to 1877." Johnson City, Tennessee: unpublished M. Div. thesis, Emmanuel School of Religion, 1979.

Goldston, Nimmo. "The Beginnings of the Disciples of Christ in East Texas." Fort Worth: unpublished B. D. thesis at Texas Christian University, Brite Divinity School, 1948.

Hargis, Mina Davis. *"The History of the Disciples of Christ in Iowa before the Civil War."* Iowa City: unpublished M. A. thesis, State University of Iowa, 1937.

Hoven, Victor Emanuel. *"The Beginnings and Growth of the Church of Christ in Oregon."* Unpublished master's thesis, University of Oregon, 1918.

Jones, Helen Butler. "The Contribution of Certain Leaders to the Development of the Oregon Normal School, 1850 to 1930." Eugene: unpublished Master's thesis, University of Oregon, 1947.

Major, James Brooks. "The Role of Periodicals in the Development of the Disciples of Christ, 1850-1910." Nashville: unpublished Ph.D. dissertation, Vanderbilt University, 1966.

Rushford, Jerry Bryant. "Political Disciple: The Relationship Between James A. Garfield and the Disciples of Christ." Santa Barbara: unpublished Ph. D. dissertation, University of California, 1977.

IV. OTHER UNPUBLISHED MATERIALS

Applegate, Lillian. "Biography of Maria Elder Watson." Mss #1089/Dye Coll. Box 1 in the Oregon History Center., Portland, Oregon.

Buffum, William Gilbert. "Reminiscences." Transactions of the Oregon Pioneer Association, 1889.

Hill, Abner. "An Autobiography of Abner Hill, Pioneer Preacher of Tennessee, Alabama and Texas." Unpublished manuscript in possession of R. L. Roberts, Abilene, Texas.

Hunsaker, A. J. "The Early History of McMinnville College." Unpublished document, 1912.

McBride, John Rogers. "Overland 1846." Mss #458 in the McBride Family Papers in the Oregon History Center, Portland, Oregon.

McKeel, John G. "Oregon: A Short History of the Churches of Christ." Bound typed manuscript, Cascade College, Portland, Oregon.

Miller, Bonnie. "Restoration Pioneer in Oregon: William Lysander Adams." Unpublished manuscript, Pepperdine University, Malibu, California, 1993.

Moxley, W. A. "Southern Route to Western Oregon—The First Wagon Trains to Travel This Route in 1846." Mss #855 in the Oregon History Center, Portland, Oregon.

Parker, Inez Eugenia Adams. "Early Recollections of Oregon Pioneer Life." Transactions of the Oregon Pioneer Association, 1889.

Porter, William. "Chronicles of Mill Creek Church, Aumsville, Oregon." Typescript by Mary Kowitz, July 1996.

Roddy, Vernon. "Mulkey Meeting House: A Tenntucky Experience." Unpublished manuscript, Center for Restoration Studies, Abilene Christian University, Abilene, Texas, 1972.

Index of Names

A

B

C

D

E

F

G

H

I

J

K

L

M

N

O

P

Q

R

S

T

U

V

W

"O OREGON!"

O Oregon!
Every Douglas fir tree
a cathedral spire.
Every flower-filled meadow
a sanctuary.
Every sparkling river
a center aisle.
Every rushing waterfall
a pulpit.
Every placid lake
a baptismal pool.
Every cheery songbird
a member of the choir.
Every apple blossom
a scent of grace.
Every formation of geese in flight
a band of angels.
Every ocean sunset
a stained-glass window.
Every purple mountain range
the Glory of God.
Every snow-capped mountain
the Head of Christ.
Every soaring eagle
the Spirit of God.
Every fallen timber
the Cross.
Every crushed violet
the Blood of Christ.
Every grazing sheep
a lost sinner.
Every bent fern
a broken life.
Every drop of rain
a tear from Heaven.
O Oregon!
Lift up your head,
open your eyes,
and lift up your hands
to the God who made this beautiful land!
– Victor Knowles